# Sutton Common
# The excavation of an Iron Age 'marsh-fort'

# Sutton Common
# The excavation of an Iron Age 'marsh-fort'

by Robert Van de Noort, Henry Chapman, and John Collis

*with contributions by*

*Gianna Ayala, Bruce Bradley, Christopher Bronk Ramsey, Ian Carstairs,
James Cheetham, Gordon Cook, Chris Cumberpatch, William Fletcher,
Benjamin Gearey, Allan Hall, Derek Hamilton, Julian Henderson,
JD Hill, Harry Kenward, David Knight, Christopher Knüsel,
Peter Marshall, Jacqueline McKinley, Keith Miller, Nigel Nayling,
Alan Outram, Ian Panter, Colin Patrick, Andrew Payne, Gavin Thomas,
Tina Tuohy, Alan Vince and Sue Watts*

*Drawings by Michael Rouillard*

CBA Research Report 154
Council for British Archaeology
2007

First published in 2007 by the Council for British Archaeology
St Mary's House, 66 Bootham, York, YO30 7BZ

Copyright © 2007 Authors and the Council for British Archaeology

ISBN: 978-1-902771-70-0

**British Library Cataloguing in Publication Data**
A catalogue record for this book is available from the British Library

Cover designed by BP Design, York
Designed and printed by The Alden Press, Oxfordshire

The publisher acknowledges with gratitude a grant from English Heritage towards the cost of publication

*Cover illustrations*
*Front cover:* (top) Aerial photograph of the site during the 2003 excavations of the larger enclosure, with the smaller enclosure in the background (© Neil Mitchell, APS UK below)
A bird's-eye view of Sutton Common *c* 350 BC. Artistic impression by Michael Rouillard, University of Exeter
*Back cover:* Excavating the posts of the box rampart in 2002

# Contents

List of figures ................................................................................................................................................. x
List of tables .................................................................................................................................................. xiv
Abbreviations ................................................................................................................................................ xv
Dating conventions as used in this report .................................................................................................. xv
List of contributors ....................................................................................................................................... xvi
Acknowledgements ...................................................................................................................................... xvii
Summaries ..................................................................................................................................................... xviii

## Chapter 1  Introduction
1.1 Background to the project  *by R Van de Noort and K Miller* ............................................................... 1
    1.1.1 Introduction ...................................................................................................................................... 1
    1.1.2 The terms 'marsh-fort' and 'mortuary rings' ................................................................................. 1
    1.1.3 About this book ................................................................................................................................ 3
1.2 Previous research at Sutton Common  *by H Chapman* ........................................................................ 4
    1.2.1 Enclosure, mapping, and early descriptions .................................................................................. 4
    1.2.2 Earliest excavations .......................................................................................................................... 4
    1.2.3 The work by C E Whiting ................................................................................................................ 4
    1.2.4 Damage and rescue: excavations in the 1980s and early 1990s .................................................. 6
    1.2.5 Humber Wetlands Project ................................................................................................................ 7
    1.2.6 The micro-topographical survey in 1997 ....................................................................................... 8
1.3 Research contexts and aims  *by R Van de Noort* .................................................................................. 9
    1.3.1 Research contexts ............................................................................................................................ 9
        1.3.1.1 Research contexts for the Iron Age ................................................................................ 10
        1.3.1.2 Research contexts for wetland archaeology ................................................................. 12
        1.3.1.3 Regional research contexts ............................................................................................. 12
    1.3.2 Overarching research aim ............................................................................................................. 13
    1.3.3 Research objectives ....................................................................................................................... 13
        1.3.3.1 Defining the character, morphology, and spatial patterning of the site ................... 13
        1.3.3.2 Dating and phasing the site ........................................................................................... 14
        1.3.3.3 Defining the social construction of the site and its place
                in the wider landscape .................................................................................................... 14
        1.3.3.4 Defining the interaction with the environment .......................................................... 15
        1.3.3.5 Describing the Late Iron Age mortuary rites ............................................................... 15
        1.3.3.6 Understanding material culture, symbolism, and cosmology .................................. 15
        1.3.3.7 Describing the Iron Age woodworking technology and woodland
                management ..................................................................................................................... 15
1.4 Project Design and organisation of the project  *by R Van de Noort and H Chapman* .................... 15
    1.4.1 Project Design ................................................................................................................................ 15
    1.4.2 Organisation of the work .............................................................................................................. 17

## Chapter 2  Setting the scene: the 'Sutton Common Project'
2.1 Introduction  *by R Van de Noort, I Carstairs, K Miller and H Chapman* ........................................ 20
    2.1.1 Background ..................................................................................................................................... 20
    2.1.2 Aims and objectives ....................................................................................................................... 20
2.2 Wetland management  *by R Van de Noort* .......................................................................................... 21
    2.2.1 The drainage and rewetting of Sutton Common ......................................................................... 21
        2.2.1.1 Drainage ........................................................................................................................... 21
        2.2.1.2 Rewetting ......................................................................................................................... 21
    2.2.2 English Heritage Strategy for Wetlands ....................................................................................... 23
    2.2.3 Sutton Common as a beacon site ................................................................................................. 25
2.3 Hydrological studies and monitoring  *by J Cheetham* ....................................................................... 25
    2.3.1 Introduction .................................................................................................................................... 25
    2.3.2 Hydrological monitoring ............................................................................................................... 26
        2.3.2.1 Water level monitoring ................................................................................................... 26
        2.3.2.2 The Sutton Common water budget model ................................................................... 27
        2.3.2.3 Archaeological wood model ........................................................................................... 28
    2.3.3 Soil redox monitoring .................................................................................................................... 28
    2.3.4 Microbiological assessment .......................................................................................................... 30
    2.3.5 Conclusions ..................................................................................................................................... 31

2.4 Rubbish and Archaeology  *by I Panter and R Van de Noort* ............................................................. 32
2.5 Conclusions: The past and present of Sutton Common  *by I Carstairs and R Van de Noort* ......... 33

**Chapter 3   Methodologies**
3.1 Introduction: excavations and research 1997 – 2003 ................................................................... 35
3.2 Fieldwork ........................................................................................................................................ 35
    3.2.1 Formation processes  *by R Van de Noort and H Chapman* ................................................ 35
    3.2.2 Excavation  *by H Chapman and R Van de Noort* ................................................................ 36
    3.2.3 Recording  *by H Chapman and R Van de Noort* ................................................................. 38
    3.2.4 Sampling ................................................................................................................................. 40
        3.2.4.1 Archaeological features  *by H Chapman* ................................................................... 40
        3.2.4.2 Insects and plant macrofossils  *by A Hall and H Kenward* ..................................... 41
    3.2.5 Geophysical survey  *by A Payne* ........................................................................................ 41
3.3 Analyses .......................................................................................................................................... 42
    3.3.1 Archaeological features  *by H Chapman* ............................................................................ 42
    3.3.2 Archaeological wood  *by G Thomas* ................................................................................... 42
    3.3.3 Dating ...................................................................................................................................... 44
        3.3.3.1 Radiocarbon Dating  *by D Hamilton, B Gearey, R Van de Noort,
            G Cook, C Bronk Ramsey and P Marshall* ............................................................... 44
        3.3.3.2 Dendrochronology  *by N Nayling* ............................................................................. 48
    3.3.4 Finds analysis ......................................................................................................................... 49
        3.3.4.1 Pottery  *by C Cumberpatch* ....................................................................................... 49
        3.3.4.2 Glass  *by J Henderson* ................................................................................................ 49
        3.3.4.3 Gold  *by J D Hill* ......................................................................................................... 49
    3.3.5 Bone remains .......................................................................................................................... 49
        3.3.5.1 Human bone – cremated  *by J McKinley* ................................................................. 49
        3.3.5.2 Human bone – not cremated  *by C Knüsel* .............................................................. 49
        3.3.5.3 Animal bone  *by A Outram* ....................................................................................... 49
    3.3.6 Palaeoenvironmental remains ............................................................................................... 50
        3.3.6.1 Pollen  *by B Gearey* .................................................................................................... 50
        3.3.6.2 Plant macrofossils and insects  *by A Hall and H Kenward* .................................... 50
        3.3.6.3 Geoarchaeology  *by G Ayala* ..................................................................................... 51
        3.3.6.4 Geology  *by C Patrick* ................................................................................................ 51

**Chapter 4   The landscape context**
4.1 Introduction  *by R Van de Noort* ................................................................................................. 53
4.2 Geology, physical landscape, and early human activity .............................................................. 53
    4.2.1 Geology  *by R Van de Noort and H Chapman* .................................................................... 53
    4.2.2 Landscape context  *by R Van de Noort and H Chapman* .................................................. 53
    4.2.3 Early human activity  *by R Van de Noort and H Chapman* ............................................... 54
    4.2.4 Bronze Age funerary remains at Sutton Common ............................................................... 56
        4.2.4.1 Introduction  *by R Van de Noort* .............................................................................. 56
        4.2.4.2 The human remains  *by J McKinley* ......................................................................... 56
        4.2.4.3 Cremation dating  *by D Hamilton, G Cook and C Bronk Ramsey* ......................... 57
        4.2.4.4 Discussion  *by R Van de Noort* ................................................................................. 57
4.3 Palaeoenvironment ......................................................................................................................... 58
    4.3.1 Introduction  *by B Gearey* ................................................................................................... 58
    4.3.2 Radiocarbon dating  *by D Hamilton, B Gearey, G Cook, C Bronk Ramsey
        and P Marshall* ....................................................................................................................... 60
    4.3.3 Early sediment accumulation in the Hampole Beck  *by B Gearey* .................................... 61
    4.3.4 The composition of the early Holocene vegetation at Sutton Common  *by B Gearey* ......... 62
    4.3.5 Evidence for human impact: the Neolithic and Bronze Age  *by B Gearey* ....................... 62
    4.3.6 The Iron Age  *by B Gearey* .................................................................................................. 64
4.4 Flaked stone artefacts from Sutton Common  *by B Bradley* ..................................................... 64
    4.4.1 Assemblage ............................................................................................................................. 64
    4.4.2 Results ..................................................................................................................................... 65
    4.4.3 Discussion ............................................................................................................................... 66
4.5 Conclusions  *by R Van de Noort* .................................................................................................. 66

**Chapter 5   The marsh-fort: the defences**
5.1 Introduction  *by R Van de Noort and H Chapman* ..................................................................... 68
5.2 The geophysical survey  *by A Payne* ........................................................................................... 68
    5.2.1 Introduction ............................................................................................................................ 68

|  |  |  | Contents vii |
|---|---|---|---|

|     |       | 5.2.2 Results .................................................................................................................................. 68 |
| --- | ----- | --- |
|     |       | 5.2.3 Conclusions ........................................................................................................................... 70 |
| 5.3 | Description of features  *by H Chapman and W Fletcher* ............................................................... 71 |
|     | 5.3.1 | Introduction ............................................................................................................................ 71 |
|     | 5.3.2 | The smaller enclosure............................................................................................................. 72 |
|     | 5.3.3 | The causeway ......................................................................................................................... 74 |
|     | 5.3.4 | The western entrance and approach including pavement .................................................... 76 |
|     | 5.3.5 | The defences – background ................................................................................................... 77 |
|     | 5.3.6 | The defences – the far outer bank ........................................................................................ 78 |
|     | 5.3.7 | The defences – the outer ditch .............................................................................................. 78 |
|     | 5.3.8 | The defences – the palisade bank ......................................................................................... 78 |
|     | 5.3.9 | The defences – the inner ditch .............................................................................................. 83 |
|     | 5.3.10 | The defences – the inner bank/box rampart......................................................................... 83 |
|     | 5.3.11 | The defences – summary ....................................................................................................... 85 |
|     | 5.3.12 | The eastern entrance including approach ............................................................................ 85 |
| 5.4 | Phasing and dating ............................................................................................................................. 91 |
|     | 5.4.1 | Stratigraphy  *by R Van de Noort* ........................................................................................ 91 |
|     | 5.4.2 | Dendrochronology  *by Nigel Nayling* .................................................................................. 91 |
|     | 5.4.3 | Radiocarbon dating  *by P Marshall and D Hamilton* ...................................................... 93 |
|     | 5.4.4 | Conclusion  *by R Van de Noort* .......................................................................................... 94 |
| 5.5 | Wood technology  *by G Thomas* ...................................................................................................... 95 |
|     | 5.5.1 | The western entranceway ...................................................................................................... 95 |
|     | 5.5.2 | The palisade bank .................................................................................................................. 97 |
|     | 5.5.3 | The box rampart ..................................................................................................................... 99 |
|     | 5.5.4 | The eastern gateway .............................................................................................................. 99 |
| 5.6 | Palaeoenvironmental sequences ....................................................................................................... 101 |
|     | 5.6.1 | Palynology  *by B Gearey* ..................................................................................................... 101 |
|     | 5.6.2 | Insects and plant macrofossils  *by A Hall and H Kenward* ............................................ 104 |
|     |       | 5.6.2.1 Introduction .............................................................................................................. 104 |
|     |       | 5.6.2.2 Assemblages associated with the stone walling .................................................... 104 |
|     |       | 5.6.2.3 Assemblages from the inner ditch fill to the north of the eastern gateway ........ 106 |
|     |       | 5.6.2.4 Assemblages from the inner ditch fill to the south of the eastern gateway ........ 107 |
|     |       | 5.6.2.5 Assemblages from the outer ditch fill to the north of the eastern gateway......... 107 |
|     |       | 5.6.2.6 Assemblages from the inner ditch fill in Trench 4 ................................................ 107 |
|     |       | 5.6.2.7 Discussion ................................................................................................................. 108 |
|     | 5.6.3 | Geoarchaeology  *by G Ayala* .............................................................................................. 109 |
| 5.7 | Conclusions  *by R Van de Noort and H Chapman* ...................................................................... 109 |

**Chapter 6  The marsh-fort – the interior structures**
| 6.1 | Introduction  *by H Chapman, W Fletcher and R Van de Noort* ................................................. 114 |
| --- | --- |
| 6.2 | Description of features  *by H Chapman, W Fletcher and R Van de Noort* ................................ 114 |
|     | 6.2.1 | General overview ................................................................................................................... 114 |
|     | 6.2.2 | Four-post structures .............................................................................................................. 114 |
|     | 6.2.3 | The 'well' ................................................................................................................................ 117 |
|     | 6.2.4 | Other features ........................................................................................................................ 119 |
|     | 6.2.5 | General plan ........................................................................................................................... 120 |
| 6.3 | Dating: dendrochronology  *by N Nayling* ..................................................................................... 123 |
| 6.4 | Wood technology  *by G Thomas* ..................................................................................................... 123 |
|     | 6.4.1 | Internal structures ................................................................................................................ 123 |
|     | 6.4.2 | The well .................................................................................................................................. 124 |
| 6.5 | Palaeoenvironmental studies ............................................................................................................ 126 |
|     | 6.5.1 | Plant macrofossils and insects  *by A Hall and H Kenward* ............................................ 126 |
|     |       | 6.5.1.1 Postholes of four-post structures ............................................................................ 126 |
|     |       | 6.5.1.2 Other posthole fills ................................................................................................... 129 |
|     |       | 6.5.1.3 Pit fills ...................................................................................................................... 129 |
|     |       | 6.5.1.4 The well .................................................................................................................... 130 |
|     | 6.5.2 | Geoarchaeology  *by G Ayala* .............................................................................................. 130 |
| 6.6 | Conclusions  *by R Van de Noort* ................................................................................................... 131 |

**Chapter 7  The marsh-fort – the finds**
| 7.1 | Introduction  *by R Van de Noort* ................................................................................................... 136 |
| --- | --- |
| 7.2 | The concept of 'structured deposition'  *by C Cumberpatch and R Van de Noort* ...................... 136 |
| 7.3 | Human remains  *by C Knüsel* ........................................................................................................ 137 |

|    | 7.3.1 | Introduction | 137 |
|---|---|---|---|
|    | 7.3.2 | Number of individuals represented and skeletal element representation | 137 |
|    | 7.3.3 | Age determination | 137 |
|    | 7.3.4 | Sex assessment | 139 |
|    | 7.3.5 | Conclusion | 139 |
|    | 7.3.6 | Non-human remains | 139 |
| 7.4 | Animal bone *by A Outram* | | 139 |
|    | 7.4.1 | Introduction | 139 |
|    | 7.4.2 | Species and Element Abundance | 139 |
|    | 7.4.3 | Age structures | 141 |
|    | 7.4.4 | Bone fracture and taphonomic history | 142 |
|    | 7.4.5 | Co-mingled human remains | 142 |
| 7.5 | Pottery *by C G Cumberpatch, Alan Vince and David Knight* | | 142 |
|    | 7.5.1 | Introduction and description | 142 |
|    | 7.5.2 | Discussion | 143 |
| 7.6 | Querns *by S Watts* | | 145 |
|    | 7.6.1 | Introduction and description | 145 |
|    | 7.6.2 | Discussion | 145 |
| 7.7 | Antler weaving comb *by Tina Tuohy* | | 147 |
| 7.8 | Yew wood fragments *by G Thomas* | | 147 |
| 7.9 | Conclusion *by R Van de Noort* | | 147 |

**Chapter 8  The mortuary rings**

| 8.1 | Introduction *by R Van de Noort* | 151 |
|---|---|---|
| 8.2 | Description of features *by H Chapman and W Fletcher* | 151 |
|    | 8.2.1 Introduction | 151 |
|    | 8.2.2 The mortuary rings | 151 |
|    | 8.2.3 Other features | 155 |
|    | 8.2.4 Summary | 156 |
| 8.3 | Dating *by D Hamilton, G Cook, and C Bronk Ramsey* | 156 |
| 8.4. | Cremated and burnt bone | 156 |
|    | 8.4.1 The human bone *by J McKinley* | 156 |
|    |     8.4.1.1 Introduction | 156 |
|    |     8.4.1.2 Results | 156 |
|    | 8.4.2 The animal bone *by A Outram* | 157 |
|    | 8.4.3 Geoarchaeology *by G Ayala* | 157 |
| 8.5 | Finds from the second phase | 157 |
|    | 8.5.1 Glass beads *by J Henderson* | 157 |
|    |     8.5.1.1 Introduction | 157 |
|    |     8.5.1.2 Description of the glass objects | 158 |
|    |     8.5.1.3 Scientific analysis | 158 |
|    |     8.5.1.4 The glass technology | 158 |
|    |     8.5.1.5 Dating | 160 |
|    |     8.5.1.6 Conclusions | 160 |
|    | 8.5.2 A gold bracelet or ingot fragment *by J D Hill* | 160 |
|    |     8.5.1.1 Introduction | 160 |
|    |     8.5.1.2 Description | 160 |
|    |     8.5.1.3 Discussion | 161 |
| 8.6 | Conclusions *by R Van de Noort* | 161 |

**Chapter 9  The marsh-fort's contexts**

| 9.1 | Introduction *by H Chapman and W Fletcher* | 166 |
|---|---|---|
| 9.2 | Local and regional contexts: overview of the Iron Age in the broader region *by H Chapman* | 166 |
|    | 9.2.1 Local context – site and landscape setting | 166 |
|    | 9.2.2 Regional context | 168 |
|    | 9.2.3 Conclusions | 170 |
| 9.3 | National context: Enclosed sites and marsh-forts in the lowlands of Birtain *by W Fletcher* | 170 |
|    | 9.3.1 Introduction | 170 |
|    | 9.3.2 Lincolnshire and East Anglia | 170 |
|    | 9.3.3 Shropshire and North Wales | 172 |
|    | 9.3.4 Other possible sites | 173 |
|    | 9.3.5 Conclusions | 174 |

**Chapter 10 Conclusions**
10.1  The Sutton Common enigma resolved?  *by R Van de Noort* .................................................................... 175
10.2  Sutton Common and Iron Age chronology  *by R Van de Noort* ................................................................ 177
10.3  The contribution to the 'enclosed settlement' debate: function and development
      *by R Van de Noort and J Collis* ........................................................................................................................ 179
10.4  Burial rituals in the middle Iron Age  *by R Van de Noort and J Collis* .................................................. 182
10.5  Sutton Common – taking the past into the future  *by I Carstairs* ............................................................ 184

**Appendix 1  Details of macrofossil remains** ................................................................................................. 186
**Appendix 2  Characterisation studies of pottery** ........................................................................................ 211

**Bibliography** ............................................................................................................................................................. 215

**Index** ........................................................................................................................................................................... 229

# List of figures

*Chapter 1*

1.1 The location of Sutton Common and the double enclosures ........................................................................ 2
1.2 Aerial photograph of Sutton Common looking north, taken in 1997; the Hampole Beck palaeochannel stands out clearly in the arable fields as a dark sinuous feature .................... 3
1.3 Extract from Ordnance Survey 1st edition 6" 1854 County Series map ............................................. 5
1.4 Plan of the site by Mr W T Bennett and Mr S Hill, with the smaller enclosure on the left, and the larger enclosure on the right; north arrows added ............................................................. 6
1.5 Excavation of Trench E in 1993 by the University of Sheffield, looking east .................................. 8
1.6 Digital Elevation Model (DEM) of Sutton Common based on the micro-topographical survey of 1997 ................................................................................................................................. 9
1.7 'False light' DEM of the enclosures based on the micro-topographical survey of 1997 ................ 10
1.8 Aerial photograph of Sutton Common in 2000, looking north ........................................................ 12
1.9 Artist's impression of Sutton Common in the image of Danebury hillfort, for Doncaster Museum ................................................................................................................................. 14
1.10 Overview of the excavation of the west-facing entrance in 1999, with the smaller enclosure in the background ................................................................................................................. 16
1.11 The location of the excavation trenches with the 30 × 30m grid superimposed .......................... 17
1.12 Aerial photograph of the excavations in 2002, looking south ........................................................ 18

*Chapter 2*

2.1 The Common before the bulldozing of the enclosures (Crown copyright. NMR, Riley collection) ............................................................................................ 22
2.2 The Common after the bulldozing of the enclosures (Crown copyright. NMR, Riley collection) ............................................................................................ 22
2.3 Map of the Common with the locations of the underfield drainage system ................................. 22
2.4 Monitoring locations for Sutton Common shown on a Digital Elevation Model (DEM) ................ 26
2.5 Hydrological model derived from monitoring results obtained on 1 March 2002 ....................... 27
2.6 The height range of the water table relative to that for archaeological wood identified through excavation. Graph A shows the situation before and Graph B following the instigation of drainage mitigation on Sutton Common ............................................. 28
2.7 Integrated piezometer level and soil redox values, adjusted to pH 7, obtained from within the Hampole Beck palaeochannel on Sutton Common ......................................................... 29
2.8 Rubbish and Archaeology: experimental material culture with (left) rush basketry before burial and (right) the baskets on excavation ........................................................................... 32
2.9 Rubbish and Archaeology: analysis of the retrieved artefacts in Campsmount School, Askern ........................................................................................................................................ 33

*Chapter 3*

3.1 Posthole [3531] in Trench 3 ........................................................................................................... 36
3.2 Reconstruction of the formation processes of posts and postholes. Structural posts were placed in carefully cut postholes, with little or no room for postfills. The bottom of posts survived; voids represent recent wood desiccation beneath the ploughsoil ................. 36
3.3 Removal of the topsoil using 360° excavators ............................................................................... 37
3.4 Cleaning the surface by shovel ...................................................................................................... 38
3.5 Using dGPS for recording and creation of internal 5 × 5m grid .................................................... 38
3.6 Excavation of three posts forming part of the box rampart in Trench 4 in box section ................ 39
3.7 Planning the inner ditch in Trench 1 .............................................................................................. 39
3.8 Low-level aerial photography using a helicopter ............................................................................ 40
3.9 Sampling for plant and insect macrofossils in the outer ditch next to the eastern gateway ........ 41
3.10 Excavation plan 1998–2003: all features ........................................................................................ 43

*Chapter 4*

4.1 Underlying geology, after Catt (1990) and Gaunt (1994). 1: Carboniferous Coal Measures; 2: Permian Upper Magnesian Limestone and Upper Permian Marl; 3: Triassic Sherwood Sandstone; 4: Triassic Mercia Mudstone; 5: Jurassic marls, limestones, sandstones and clays; 6: Cretaceous chalk ................................................. 53

4.2 Aerial photograph of the Common in 2002, looking north towards Wentbridge
and Eggborough power station .................................................................................................................. 54
4.3 Excavation plan 1998–2003: all features predating the marsh-fort and cemetery:
undated ditch [3108] – [3144] near the eastern entranceway; early Bronze Age
mortuary enclosure [7061] – [7100]; pit [7177] containing pyre debris .......................................... 55
4.4 Probability distributions of dates from cremation [7426] and [7074]. The replicate
measurements were combined prior to calibration (Ward & Wilson 1978).
Each distribution represents the relative probability that an event occurred at a
particular time. These distributions are the result of simple radiocarbon calibration
(Stuiver & Reimer 1993)............................................................................................................................ 57
4.5 Location of the boreholes transects set in 2002 on Rushy Moor and Sutton Common .................. 58
4.6 Pollen diagram of the analysis of the Hampole Beck core ................................................................. 59
4.7 Probability distributions of dates from Hampole Beck palaeochannel. Each distribution
represents the relative probability that an event occurred at a particular time. These
distributions are the result of simple radiocarbon calibration (Stuiver & Reimer 1993)............... 61
4.8 Examples of the flaked stone tools and debitage from the Common: cores: a – d;
microblades: e – g; microblade debitage: h; microliths: i – k; burins: l; unifacial retouch
flakes, blades, biface flakes, burin spalls: m; blades: n – o; retouched flakes, microblades
and blades, scrapers: p – s; core tablets: t; drills: u; *pieces esquillées* (wedges): v – w;
arrowheads: x – y; arrowhead performs: z – aa; flaked axes: bb – cc ............................................... 65
4.9 Flaked stone density distributions by 30 × 30m grid, showing concentration along the
Hampole Beck ............................................................................................................................................ 66

*Chapter 5*

5.1 Greyscale plot of magnetometer data after median filtering to remove anomalies;
note the ditch arrangements around the entrance of the smaller enclosure................................ 69
5.2 Interpretation of fluxgate magnetometer survey ................................................................................ 70
5.3 Excavation plan 1998–2003: all Iron Age features .............................................................................. 71
5.4 Aerial photograph of Sutton Common in November 1987, looking south. The photo
shows the backfilled trenches A/C and B in the smaller enclosure. (Crown copyright.
NMR, Riley collection)............................................................................................................................... 73
5.5 The oak 'wheel' as found by Whiting in the 1930s .............................................................................. 73
5.6 Plan of the causeway, showing the excavated posts and the out-turned ditches of the
smaller enclosure as identified by the geophysical survey in 2003; the sand deposit directly
overlying a woody peat or brushwood was identified in the trench excavated in 1998 ................ 74
5.7 Aerial photograph of the excavations in 1999, including open-area excavation of
the western gateway and adjacent part of the causeway ................................................................... 75
5.8 Photo of the western gateway under excavation in 1999, looking east. The deposit of
limestone is thought to have been 'dumped' in the entranceway..................................................... 76
5.9 Sections of the large posts of the western gateway [4963] and [41011] in context ......................... 77
5.10 Excavation plan 1998–2003: the outer ditch (excavated parts in black)......................................... 79
5.11 Section of the outer ditch, exposed in Trench 4.................................................................................... 80
5.12 Excavation plan 1998–2003: the palisade bank (excavated posts in the bank in black) ............. 81
5.13 Section of a row of stakes in the palisaded bank in Trench 3; no wood survived in [3144] .......... 82
5.14 Excavation plan 1998–2003: the inner ditch (excavated parts in black) ........................................ 82
5.15 West – east section of the inner ditch in Trench 3 ............................................................................... 83
5.16 Excavation plan 1998–2003: the box rampart (excavated posts of the box rampart
in black) ....................................................................................................................................................... 84
5.17 Section of three postholes of the box rampart in Trench 4; wood fragments survive in
[4729] only ................................................................................................................................................... 85
5.18 Excavation plan 1998–2003: the eastern entrance (detail) ............................................................... 86
5.19 Aerial photograph of the eastern entrance during excavation in 2003 ............................................ 87
5.20 Section of the avenue of stakes outside the eastern entranceway ..................................................... 87
5.21 Aerial photograph of the eastern entranceway, showing the ditch terminals and
shallow pits [3408], [3412], and [3497] in the avenue ......................................................................... 88
5.22 Photograph of the stake avenues outside the eastern entranceway and shallow pits
[3408], [3412], and [3497], looking west................................................................................................ 89
5.23 Section of 'double-cut' postholes of timbers [3560] and [3561] ........................................................ 90
5.24 Bar diagrams showing absolute dates of tree-ring series. A: TREE_1; B: TREE_2;
C: SCOM_T6 ............................................................................................................................................... 94
5.25 a) Probability distributions of dates from Sutton Common defences: each distribution
represents the relative probability that an event occurs at a particular time. For each of
the radiocarbon dates two distributions have been plotted, one in outline, which is
the result of simple radiocarbon calibration, and a solid one, which is based on the

xii *Sutton Common*

chronological model used. The other distributions correspond to aspects of the model. For example, the distribution '*Event ditch*' is the estimated date for the digging of the smaller enclosure ditch. The large square brackets down the left-hand side along with the OxCal keywords define the model exactly. ................................................................................95

b) Probability distributions for the dates of construction of the Sutton Common defences pre-dating 350 BC. These distributions are derived from the model shown in a) ........................95

5.26 a) [4985], split 500 × 110mm plank fragment, worn and probably broken and cut at one end and cut at the other, perhaps just before it was redeposited. The surviving half of a mortise hole halfway along its length provides the best evidence for more complex wooden structures and joinery on the site..................................................................................96

b) detail of [4998], a radially split plank of 110mm width (max), but with 146 rings....................97

c) detail of [1298], a 'pencil point' stake showing jam curves; the cutting edge of the blade used was very slightly curved......................................................................................98

5.27 a) [3561], one of the main posts forming the eastern entranceway............................................100

b) detail of [3561], showing axe facets and signatures on the base of the post..........................101

c) detail of [3560], showing chamfer and base ..........................................................................102

d) detail of [3561], showing the tow bar ....................................................................................102

5.28 a) [3703, 3705, 3707 – 12, 3740 – 1, 3743 – 4], off-cut fragments from below post [3560].............103

b) [3743], one of these off-cuts from beneath post [3560], resembling a wedge .........................103

5.29 Pollen diagram from ditch deposits south of the eastern entranceway.....................................105

5.30 Geoarchaeology: sampled profile, Trench 3 ...........................................................................110

5.31 Reconstruction of a cross-section of the defences on the east side of the larger enclosure .........111

5.32 Reconstruction of the eastern gateway ...................................................................................112

*Chapter 6*

6.1 Excavation plan 1998 – 2003: the four-post structures and variants .........................................115

6.2 Examples of two four-poster structures: plan of granary Z: [7246], [7264], [7265], and [7269], and photograph of section [7269]; plan of granary AA: [7340], [7341], [7342], [7343]; photograph of section [7246] ..............................................................................116

6.3 Excavation plan 1998 – 2003: the well in plan .........................................................................118

6.4 The well during excavation in 2002 ........................................................................................119

6.5 Excavation plan 1998 – 2003: unassigned posts and other internal structures
a) Posts and postholes in alignments with four-post structures: [7283] and [7388];
b) Posts and postholes in alignments with four-post structures: [31235], [31233], and [31163]; c) A hut or other temporary dwelling formed by eleven small stakeholes: [5243] – [5248], and [5250] – [5254].........................................................................121

6.6 Excavation plan 1998 – 2003: location of pit and photograph of section of [7171/7187]...............122

6.7 A Scots pine roundwood timber [31243], showing advanced desiccation..................................124

6.8 Excavation plan 1998 – 2003: location of timbers of Scots pine and reconstructed four-post structures: [31189] and [31190], [31243] and [31252] ..................................................125

6.9 Geoarchaeology: sampled postholes in Trench 3, F13..............................................................131

6.10 Geoarchaeology: a) sample 119: micrograph of clay infilling (CPL at 2.5 magnification)
b) sample 119: micrograph of clay infilling (PPL at 2.5 magnification)....................................132

6.11 Geoarchaeology: a) sample 120: micrograph of fabric microstructure (PPL)
b) sample 120: micrograph of oriented fabric (CPL) ................................................................132

6.12 Contrasting hypotheses explaining the presence of charred grain in postholes of granaries. The reconstruction on the left represents the long-held understanding that catastrophic fires caused the presence of charred grains in postholes; the reconstruction on the right represents the interpretation of the Sutton Common material, with a handful of charred grain ritually deposited in postholes at some stage in the building process...............133

*Chapter 7*

7.1 Excavation plan 1998 – 2003: the location of the human heads and photographs of the heads during excavation.........................................................................................................138

7.2 Animal bones: species and element abundance, a) Number of Identifiable Specimens;
b) Minimum Number of Elements ..........................................................................................140

7.3 Animal bones: Minimum Number of Elements data for a) cattle; b) sheep...............................140

7.4 Animal bones: fusion stages of sheep......................................................................................142

7.5 Pottery: small hand-made rim sherd .......................................................................................143

7.6 Excavation plan 1998 – 2003: location of quern stones, and plan of possible four-post structure with postholes [4301] and [4305] containing quern stone fragments..........................146

7.7 Antler weaving comb..............................................................................................................147

*Chapter 8*

8.1 Excavation plan 1998–2003: the mortuary rings, and contexts containing calcined or charred bone: human remains: [5123/5033], cattle remains: [5012] and [7246]; animal indet. remains: [4410], [5140], [5175], [5182], [5218], [5260], [5261], [5298], [5431], [5437], [5473], and [7244]......................................................................................................................................... 152
8.2 Plans of the mortuary rings from Sutton Common ................................................................. 153
8.3 Photograph of: a) mortuary ring 4 (looking south); b) mortuary ring 6 (looking north) .............. 154
8.4 Aerial photograph of mortuary rings 11 and 12 (looking north) ................................................ 155
8.5 Geoarchaeology: micrograph of bone material from [7246]/sample 53 (PPL) ............................. 157
8.6 The gold bracelet or ingot............................................................................................................ 161
8.7 Reconstruction of the suggested mortuary rituals at Sutton Common: pyre debris is scattered within one of the mortuary rings................................................................................. 163

*Chapter 9*

9.1 Sutton Common in its regional context, showing the principal sites mentioned in the text........ 167
9.2 Plans of Iron Age marsh-forts in Yorkshire, Lincolnshire, and East Anglia:
a) Sutton Common; b) Skipwith; c) Tattershall Thorpe; d) Borough Fen; e) Arbury Camp;
f) Wardy Hill; g) Stonea Camp; h) Narborough Camp; i) Wharham; j) Holkham; k) Burgh;
l) Clare Camp ............................................................................................................................... 171
9.3 Plans of Iron Age marsh-forts in Shropshire and North Wales: a) Wall Fort; b) The Berth;
c) Dinas Dinlle ............................................................................................................................. 173

*Chapter 10*

10.1 A bird's-eye view of Sutton Common c 350 BC (Artist's impression by Michael Rouillard)......... 178
10.2 Distribution of prehistoric and Roman period granaries (after Gent 1983, 246)......................... 181

*Appendix 2*

2.1 Chemical analysis of pottery: plot of two factors (F2 and F3) calculated in a factor analysis. CALC = calcite-tempered waves; ERRA = pottery from erratic basic igneous rocks from the Trent valley; IA = Iron Age pottery from Sutton Common................................. 213
2.2 Chemical analysis of pottery: Li and Sm in Sutton Common fragments plotted against comparative group. CALC = calcite-tempered wares; ERRA = pottery from erratic basic igneous rocks from the Trent Valley; IA = Iron Age pottery from Sutton Common..................... 213

Unless otherwise stated in the caption, the copyright for all aerial photographs belongs to Neil Mitchell, APS UK, and the copyright for all other illustrations belongs to the Sutton Common Project, the Universities of Exeter and Hull.

# List of tables

*Chapter 3*

3.1　Radiocarbon determinations from Sutton Common ................................................................... 46

*Chapter 4*

4.1　Human calcined bone: summary of results ................................................................................. 57
4.2　Description of Local Pollen Zones, based on core from the Hampole Beck ............................... 60

*Chapter 5*

5.1　Dendrochronology samples .......................................................................................................... 92
5.2　Description of Local Pollen Zones, based on samples from the enclosure ditch ...................... 104
5.3　Geoarchaeology: field description of Trench 3 profile (palisaded bank) .................................. 109
5.4　Summary chart of major micromorphological features of soil profile in Trench 3 ................. 110

*Chapter 6*

6.1　Summary description of the charred plant remains from four-poster structures;
　　 see Appendix 1 for detailed information ................................................................................. 127
6.2　Summary chart of major micromorphological features of posthole features in Trench 3 ....... 131

*Chapter 7*

7.1　NISP and MNE counts for cattle and sheep by element, secure contexts only ........................ 141
7.2　Associations of finds in the ditch terminals near the eastern gateway ................................... 149

*Chapter 8*

8.1　Human calcined bone: summary of results ............................................................................... 156
8.2　Summary chart of major micromorphological features of the cremation burials of Trench 7 ...... 158
8.3　Electron probe microanalyses of glass fragments ..................................................................... 159
8.4　Electron probe microanalyses of the gold bracelet or ingot ...................................................... 162

*Appendices*

1.1　Complete list of all plant and invertebrate taxa ....................................................................... 186
1.2　Data concerning assemblages of charred plant remains .......................................................... 194
2.1　Chemical analysis of pottery: major elements as percent oxides ............................................. 212
2.2　Chemical analysis of pottery: minor elements as parts per million ........................................ 212

# Abbreviations

| | |
|---|---|
| ARCUS | Archaeological Research and Consultancy at the University of Sheffield |
| ALSF | Aggregates Levy Sustainability Fund |
| CCT | Carstairs Countryside Trust |
| DEM | Digital Elevation Model |
| GIS | Geographic Information System |
| GPS | Global Positioning System |
| HER | Historic Environment Record |
| lpaz | local pollen assemblage zones |
| MNE | Minimum Number of Elements |
| NISP | Number of Identifiable Specimens |
| OD | Ordnance Datum |
| SMR | Sites and Monuments Record |
| SSSI | Site of Special Scientific Interest |
| SYAS | South Yorkshire Archaeology Service |
| TLP | Total Land Pollen |
| WYAS | West Yorkshire Archaeology Service |

## Dating conventions as used in this report

| Years cal BC | Common name as used in text | Needham's (1996) periods | Metalwork assemblage |
|---|---|---|---|
| 1500 – 1150 | middle Bronze Age | 5 | Acton 2 Taunton Penard |
| 1150 – 950 | late Bronze Age | 6 | Wilburton Blackmoor |
| 950 – 750 | | 7 | Ewart Park |
| 750 – 450 | early Iron Age | 8 | Llyn Fawr |
| 450 – 100 | middle Iron Age | | |
| 100 cal BC – AD 70[1] | late Iron Age | | |
| AD 70 – 410[1] | Roman period | | |

[1] denotes conventional 'historical' dates

# List of contributors

**Gianna Ayala** Department of Archaeology, University of Sheffield, Northgate House, West Street, Sheffield, S1 4ET

**Bruce Bradley** Department of Archaeology, University of Exeter, Exeter EX4 4QE

**Christopher Bronk Ramsey** Radiocarbon Accelerator Unit, Research Laboratory for Archaeology and the History of Art, Oxford University, 6 Keble Road, Oxford OX1 3QJ

**Ian Carstairs** Carstairs Countryside Trust, Apple Tree Cottage, The Common, Harleston IP20 9JT

**Henry P Chapman** Department of Archaeology and Antiquity, University of Birmingham, Arts Building, University of Birmingham, Edgbaston, Birmingham B15 2TT

**James Cheetham** Wessex Archaeology, Portway House, Old Sarum Park, Salisbury SP4 6EB

**John R Collis** Department of Archaeology, University of Sheffield, Northgate House, West Street, Sheffield S1 4ET

**Gordon Cook** SUERC, Rankine Avenue, Scottish Enterprise Technology Park, East Kilbride G75 0QF

**Chris Cumberpatch** 22 Tennyson Road, Lower Walkley, Sheffield S6 2WE

**William Fletcher** Suffolk County Council Archaeological Service, Shire Hall, Bury St Edmunds, Suffolk IP33 2AR

**Benjamin Gearey** Department of Archaeology and Antiquity, University of Birmingham, Arts Building, University of Birmingham, Edgbaston, Birmingham B15 2TT

**Allan Hall** Department of Archaeology, University of York, The King's Manor, York YO1 7EP

**Julian Henderson** Department of Archaeology, University of Nottingham, University Park, Nottingham NG7 2RD

**J D Hill** Department of Prehistory and Europe, The British Museum, London WC1B 3DG

**Harry Kenward** Department of Archaeology, University of York, The King's Manor, York YO1 7EP

**David Knight** Trent and Peak Archaeological Unit, Department of Archaeology, University of Nottingham, Nottingham NG7 2RD

**Christopher Knüsel** Department of Archaeological Sciences, University of Bradford, Bradford BD7 1DP

**Peter Marshall** ARCUS, University of Sheffield, West Court, Mappin Street, Sheffield S1 4ET

**Jacqueline McKinley** Wessex Archaeology, Portway House, Old Sarum Park, Salisbury SP4 6EB

**Keith Miller** English Heritage, Yorkshire Region, 37 Tanner Row, York YO1 6WP

**Nigel Nayling** Lampeter Dendrochronology Laboratory, Department of Archaeology and Anthropology, University of Wales Lampeter, Lampeter, Ceredigion SA48 7ED

**Alan Outram** Department of Archaeology, University of Exeter, Exeter EX4 4QE

**Ian Panter** York Archaeological Trust, 47 Aldwark, York YO1 7BX

**Gavin Thomas** c/o The RSPB, Westleigh Mews, Wakefield Road, Denby Dale, Huddersfield HD8 8QD

**Tina Tuohy** 39 Woodville Close, North Prospect, Plymouth PL2 2JX

**Alan Vince** 25 West Parade, Lincoln LN1 1NW

**Robert Van de Noort** Department of Archaeology, University of Exeter, Exeter EX4 4QE

**Sue Watts** c/o Department of Archaeology, University of Exeter, Exeter EX4 4QE

# Acknowledgements

The excavations at Sutton Common between 1998 and 2003, and the post-excavation analysis which was completed in 2006, were made possible by the encouragement, support and endeavour by numerous individuals and organisations – those who contributed directly to the final report are all mentioned by name in this publication. Most importantly of all, we wish to acknowledge the unwavering support of English Heritage for financial, specialist, and logistic support, and the role of Chief Archaeologist David Miles, Inspectors of Ancient Monuments Jon Etté and Keith Miller, and Project Officer Helen Keeley. The advice from Alex Bayliss, Matthew Canti, Gill Campbell, Andrew David, Jonathan Last and many others was much appreciated. Likewise, the Carstairs Countryside Trust and its trustees, in particular Ian Carstairs and Jan Knowles, played a pivotal role in making the excavations possible and a success. The organisations and individuals who were part of the wider Sutton Common Project are all acknowledged in the text (see section 2.5). We would also like to thank Peter Robinson of Doncaster Museum, Lisa Voden-Decker of the British Museum, Jens Andersen at the Camborne School of Mines, University of Exeter, and Frances and Michael Issett.

In addition, Bruce Bradly acknowledges the work undertaken by Patrick Lai (University of Exeter), who diligently undertook to separate and catalogue all of the flaked stone specimens, Chris Cumberpatch thanks Adrian Chadwick (University of Wales, Newport), Peter Robinson (Doncaster Museum), and Colin Merrony (University of Sheffield) for assistance in the preparation of this report, and Nigel Nayling acknowledges the support from Alex Bayliss (English Heritage) and Cathy Groves (University of Sheffield).

# Summary

Sutton Common, situated near the town of Askern some 13 km (8 miles) north of Doncaster in the county of South Yorkshire, is one of the best-known Iron Age multivallate sites in lowland Britain, famed for the wet-preservation of organic remains including one of Britain's oldest ladders. It has been studied throughout the twentieth century through small-scale excavations and geophysical survey, but a recent summary of the research on this site concluded that Sutton Common could justifiably be described as an enigma, in the sense that its function was largely unknown, its dating and phasing insecure, its significance in the wider landscape indefinite, and its future as a wetland site in doubt.

This volume describes the results of the very large-scale excavations (totalling $c$ 20,600m$^2$), undertaken here between 1998 and 2003, which have provided unparalleled insights into the function and meaning of this Iron Age 'marsh-fort'. The excavations exposed nearly the complete interior of the site (a first for British prehistoric research in fort-type sites), and uncovered a greater part of the extensive ditch and bank defences then all the previous research combined. The scale of this research, probably one of the largest in extent on any British Iron Age site, has enabled greater confidence in the interpretation of the morphology, function, and significance of the site. The excavations were part of a broader project that included land purchases to ensure the sympathetic management of the site, an extensive programme of high-resolution hydrological monitoring of the water table and its effect on the archaeological burial environment, educational activities for local school children, and extended engagement with a range of other stakeholders, in particular the local community.

An earlier phase of activity was uncovered in 2003, comprising a small mortuary enclosure on the main dune or island in this wetland landscape. A single burial of pyre debris was dated to the early Bronze Age.

The main part of the fort comprised a D-shaped enclosure measuring $c$ 200 × 100m occupying the whole of the main island, surrounded by a box rampart, inner ditch, palisaded bank, outer ditch, and further elaborations of the defences. Two gatehouses, one facing east, the other west, provided the only access to the site. The western gateway could be reached only by an 80m long causeway across the wetlands of a dried-up river channel. A cross-bank and additional bank-and-ditch arrangements controlled access to the causeway. The integrated dendrochronological and integrated radiocarbon analysis, undertaken to a much higher precision than has been achieved previously for any Iron Age fort-type site in Britain, dated the onset of construction of the defences to 372 BC, with the additional ditches and palisaded embankment completed by 350 BC.

The limited material culture associated with the marsh-fort, including a few pieces of fragmentary pottery, a quern fragment, and a worn antler weaving comb, were all recovered from the ditch terminals of the east-facing entrance. These were accompanied by animal bones, two human crania (one skull was found with accompanying vertebrae, indicating that on deposition this had been a fleshed head), and the only examples of yew wood found on the site. These are interpreted as forming part of structured deposition at the symbolic entrance to the site in line with many other examples from the British Iron Age.

The interior of the marsh-fort was dominated by four-post structures. Some 150 granaries, ordered in rows of up to eight structures, occupied and indeed dominated the site. In 25 instances, charred grain (mostly spelt and emmer) was found in one or two of the postholes of these structures. On the basis of detailed analysis of the possible deposition processes involved, this is interpreted as evidence of structured deposition of a 'handful' of charred grain during the construction of the granaries, rather than the consequence of catastrophic fires or other unintentional events. No other structures were identified and no houses were uncovered. The palaeoenvironmental studies of pollen, insect, and plant macrofossils, indicate that the site was never inhabited, and that by the time the first sediments accumulated in the bottom of the ditches (which must have been soon after the ditches had been dug), the landscape was used for grazing only.

A second phase of activity within the interior of the mash-fort was identified and dated somewhat provisionally to the 4th to 2nd century BC. This phase comprises twelve enclosures of basic geometric shape measuring between 3m and 6m across defined by narrow, steep ditches. On the basis of the excavations, and supported by micro-geoarchaeological analysis, it is suggested that these small enclosures acted as 'temenos' or sacred places where the ashes or pyre debris was scattered as the final part in the mortuary rituals. This interpretation offers an evidence-based explanation for the archaeological near-invisibility of middle Iron Age cemetery remains in Britain and western Europe.

Interpreting the evidence, Sutton Common could be understood as a place where the social identity of the local community was reinforced through the construction of the physical representation of the idea(l) of community, or a 'dwelling place', even though the logistics of everyday life dictated a 'taskscape' comprising villages dispersed in the region and isolated farmsteads. The social memory of the early Bronze Age mortuary enclosure, and a sense of sacredness of this wetland-encircled dune, possibly survived into the 4th century BC. The use of a bank-and-ditch arrangement that resembled defences used elsewhere for enclosed sites shows an interconnectivity of autonomous regional groups within broader zones. This interconnectivity is also illustrated by the adoption of widespread cosmological principles in dealing with the concept of enclosure (eg the east-facing gateway) and material culture (eg the structured deposition in ditch terminals). There is no reason, and indeed no archaeological evidence, to assume the guiding hand of a permanent elite in the construction of the marsh-fort, rather this was a communal effort, perhaps steered by a transitory leader or peripatetic 'architect'. Multivallation re-emphasized the symbolic nature of enclosure, which is also clearly shown by the deposition of artefacts and human remains at the liminal entrances, possibly during processions. At least one, and possibly both, human heads were still fleshed when deposited; these may have functioned as 'trophy heads' in specific rituals.

The importance of the granaries should be understood within the context of the significant shift from the ritualisation of warriors and weapons in the early and middle Bronze Age, to the ritualisation of agriculture/growing and storage of food in the late Bronze Age and Iron Age. The deposition of a handful of charred grains in one or two postholes of some granaries emphasises the ritual aspect of grain storage, and these structures became powerful symbols at a time that crop husbandry was in a period of transition.

The short-lived nature of the site is explained by its symbolic role – its construction was an event or a theatrical performance using well-established and well-understood rituals and forms. After the event, the entrances of the marsh-fort may have been damaged to signal the end of its life, but the site remained important within the landscape and as part of the social memory of the community that had built it. The reuse of the site as a final resting place for the deceased in the following centuries is no coincidence. It links the transition and destruction of the body after death directly to the locale chosen by the ancestors for their rituals.

# Résumé

Sutton Common, qui se trouve près de la ville d'Askern, à environ 13 km (8 miles) au nord de Doncaster, dans la comté du South Yorkshire, est l'un des sites à multiples défenses concentriques de l'âge du fer les mieux connus des basses terres de la Grande-Bretagne, et il est réputé pour la préservation en milieu humide de vestiges organiques, y compris l'une des plus anciennes échelles de toute la Grande-Bretagne. Ce site a été étudié pendant tout le vingtième siècle par le biais de fouilles à petite échelle et de relevés géophysiques, mais un récent résumé des recherches sur ce site a conclu que l'on pouvait à juste titre décrire Sutton Common comme une énigme, dans le sens où sa fonction était largement inconnue, sa datation et sa séquence de phases peu sures, sa signification dans un plus large paysage non définie, et son avenir en tant que site de terres humides en doute.

Le présent volume décrit les résultats de fouilles à très grande échelle (sur environ 20,600m$^2$), entreprises ici entre 1998 et 2003, lesquelles ont donné des aperçus sans parallèle de la fonction et de la signification de ce 'fort des marécages' de l'âge du fer. Les fouilles ont exposé l'intérieur presque complet du site (pour la première fois sur un site de type fort par des recherches préhistoriques en Grande-Bretagne), et ont révélé une plus grande partie des défenses étendues composées de fossés et de remblais que toutes les recherches précédentes combinées. L'échelle de cette recherche, probablement, de par sa superficie, l'une des plus importantes de tous les sites britanniques de l'âge du fer, a permis une interprétation plus sure de la morphologie, de la fonction, et de la signification du site. Les fouilles faisaient partie d'un projet de plus grande envergure, qui englobait des achats de terrains pour assurer une gestion favorable du site, un programme étendu de surveillance hydrologique à haute résolution de la nappe phréatique ainsi que de son effet sur l'environnement archéologique des sépultures, des activités éducatives pour les élèves des écoles de la région, et une participation de plus longue durée d'autres participants, tout particulièrement la communauté locale.

Une phase d'activité antérieure avait été découverte en 2003, et comprenait un petit enclos mortuaire sur la dune ou l'île principale de ce paysage de terres humides. Une sépulture unique de débris de bûcher funéraire a été datée au début de l'âge du bronze.

La partie principale du fort était composée d'un enclos en forme de D qui mesurait environ 200 × 100 mètres et qui occupait la totalité de l'île principale, entouré d'un rempart revêtu de bois, d'un fossé intérieur, d'un remblai couronné de palissades, d'un fossé extérieur, et d'autres élaborations des ouvrages défensifs. Deux portails, l'un faisant face à l'est, l'autre à l'ouest, donnaient les seuls accès au site. Le portail occidental ne pouvait être atteint que par une chaussée de 80 mètres de long, qui traversait les terres humides d'un bras de rivière asséché. Un remblai transversal et des agencements supplémentaires de fossés et de remblais contrôlaient l'accès à la chaussée. L'analyse intégrante au radiocarbone et l'analyse intégrante par la dendrochronologie, entreprises avec un bien plus haut niveau de précision que ce qui avait été réalisé auparavant pour tout autre site de type fortifié de l'âge du fer en Grande-Bretagne, ont daté le commencement de la construction des défenses à 372 avant J.C., et la complétion des fossés supplémentaires et du remblai couronné de palissades à 350 avant J.C. au plus tard.

La culture matérielle limitée associée au fort des marécages, y compris quelques morceaux de céramique fragmentaire, un fragment de meule, et un peigne à tisser en corne usé, ont tous été retrouvés dans les bornes des fossés de l'entrée qui faisait face à l'est. Ces objets étaient accompagnés d'os d'animaux, de deux crânes humains (un crâne a été découvert avec ses vertèbres, ce qui indiquait qu'il s'agissait d'une tête recouverte de chair lors de son dépôt, et des seuls exemples de bois d'if découverts sur le site. Leur interprétation est qu'ils faisaient partie des dépôts structurés à l'entrée symbolique du site, en ligne avec de nombreux autres exemples de l'âge du fer britannique.

L'intérieur du fort des marécages était dominé par des structures à quatre poteaux. Environ 150 greniers, agencés en rangs de huit structures au plus, occupaient et en fait dominaient le site. Dans 25 cas, du grain carbonisé (pour la plupart de l'épeautre et du froment) a été découvert dans un ou deux des trous de poteau de ces structures.

Sur la base d'une analyse détaillée des processus possibles de dépôt que cela suppose, ceci est interprété comme un indice d'un dépôt structuré d'une 'poignée' de grain carbonisé lors de la construction des greniers, plutôt que comme la conséquence d'incendies catastrophiques ou d'autres événements non intentionnels. Aucune autre structure n'a été identifiée et aucune maison n'a été découverte. Les études paléoenvironnementales du pollen, des insectes et des macrofossiles végétaux indiquent que le site n'avait jamais été habité et que, à l'époque où les premiers sédiments ont commencé à s'accumuler au fond des fossés (ce qui a dû se produire peu de temps après le creusement des fossés), le paysage était utilisé uniquement pour le pâturage.

Une deuxième phase d'activité à l'intérieur du fort des marécages a été identifiée et a été datée à titre quelque peu provisoire à la période entre le 4$^{\text{ème}}$ et le 2$^{\text{ème}}$ siècle avant J.-C. Cette phase comprend douze enclos de forme géométrique basique mesurant entre 3 mètres et 6 mètres de largeur et définis par des fossés étroits à pente raide. Sur la base des fouilles, appuyées par une analyse microgéoarchéologique, il a été suggéré que ces petits enclos servaient de 'temenos' ou lieux sacrés où les cendres ou débris des bûchers funéraires étaient éparpillés à la fin des rites funéraires. Cette interprétation offre une explication de la presque invisibilité archéologique des vestiges de cimetières du milieu de l'âge du fer en Grande-Bretagne et en Europe occidentale, explication qui est basée sur des indices.

L'interprétation des indices permet de supposer que Sutton Common aurait pu être un lieu où l'identité sociale de la communauté locale avait été renforcée par le biais de la construction de la représentation matérielle de l'idée (idéal) d'une communauté, ou d'un 'lieu d'habitation', même quand la logistique de la vie quotidienne imposait un 'taskscape' [perception du paysage à travers la pratique d'activités répétitives] composé de villages dispersés dans la région et de fermes isolées. La mémoire sociale de l'enclos funéraire du début de l'âge du bronze, et un sens du caractère sacré de cette dune entourée de terres humides, ont peut-être continué pendant le 4$^{\text{ème}}$ siècle avant J.-C. L'emploi d'un agencement de remblais et de fossés qui ressemblait aux défenses employées ailleurs pour les sites entourés d'une enceinte indique qu'il existait une interconnexion de groupes régionaux autonomes au sein de zones plus larges. Cette interconnexion est également illustrée par l'adoption de principes cosmologiques très répandus dans le traitement du concept de l'enclos (par exemple le portail faisant face à l'est) et dans la culture matérielle (par exemple le dépôt structuré dans les bornes du fossé). Il n'y a pas lieu de supposer, et il n'y a en fait aucun indice archéologique à l'appui, que la construction du fort des marécages avait été inspirée par une élite permanente, mais plutôt que c'était le résultat d'un effort en commun, peut-être dirigé par un chef temporaire ou par un 'architecte' péripatétique. Le système de multiples défenses concentriques à fossés et remblais mettait une fois de plus en valeur la nature symbolique de l'enclos, laquelle est également clairement indiquée par le dépôt des objets fabriqués et des restes humains aux entrées liminales, peut-être lors de processions. Au moins l'une des têtes humaines, et peut-être les deux, était encore couverte de chair lorsqu'elle a été déposée; ces têtes avaient peut-être servi de 'têtes trophées' au cours de rites précis.

On devrait comprendre l'importance des greniers dans le contexte du passage significatif de la ritualisation des guerriers et des armes au début et au milieu de l'âge du bronze, à la ritualisation de l'agriculture / de la culture et du stockage des aliments à la fin de l'âge du bronze et pendant l'âge du fer. Le dépôt d'une poignée de graines carbonisées dans un ou deux des trous de poteaux de certains greniers souligne l'aspect rituel du stockage du grain, et ces structures étaient devenues de puissants symboles à une époque où l'agriculture se trouvait dans une période de transition.

La brévité de l'utilisation du site s'explique par son rôle symbolique – sa construction avait été un événement ou une représentation théâtrale qui avait employé des formes et des rites bien compris. Après cet événement, les entrées du fort des marécages avaient peut-être été endommagées pour signaler la fin de sa vie utile, mais le site est resté d'importance au sein du paysage, et parce qu'il faisait partie de la mémoire sociale de la communauté qui l'avait construit. La réutilisation du site en tant que dernière demeure des morts pendant les siècles qui ont suivi n'est pas une coïncidence. Elle relie directement la transition et la destruction du corps après la mort à la localité choisie par les ancêtres pour leurs rites.

# Zusammenfassung

Sutton Common befindet sich in der Nähe der Stadt Askern, 13 km nördlich von Doncaster in der Grafschaft South Yorkshire. Es ist einer der berühmtesten gestaffelten Befestigungsanlagen aus der Eisenzeit in den Niederungen von Großbritannien, und ist vor allem durch die im Feuchtgebiet gut erhaltenen pflanzlichen Überreste bekannt, unter anderem eine der ältesten hölzernen Leitern aus Großbritannien. Während des 20. Jahrhunderts wurden regelmäßig kleine Sondiergrabungen und geophysische Untersuchungen durchgeführt, aber dennoch wird diese Anlage in einer jüngsten Zusammenfassung der Forschungsarbeit immer noch mit gutem Recht als ein Enigma beschrieben, weil dessen Funktion größtenteils unbekannt geblieben ist, die Datierung und Bestimmung der zeitlichen Phasen unsicher, die Bedeutung der Anlage innerhalb der Landschaft undefiniert war, und die Zukunft als Feuchtgebiet in Frage gestellt.

Dieser Band beschreibt die Ergebnisse von großflächigen Ausgrabungen (über eine Gesamtfläche von 20,600m$^2$), die während der Zeit von 1998 und 2003 durchgeführt wurden und unvergleichliche Einblicke in die Funktion und Bedeutung dieser 'Marschfestung' aus der Eisenzeit eröffneten. Die Ausgrabungen legten fast das gesamte Innere der Festung frei (einzigartig in der britischen Erforschung von festungsähnlichen Anlagen), und deckte einen größeren Teil der weitläufigen Gräben und Schutzwällen auf, als in allen früheren Ausgrabungen zusammengenommen. Das Ausmaß dieser Forschung, flächenmäßig wahrscheinlich die größte Britische Ausgrabung aus der Eisenzeit, hat es ermöglicht die Form, Funktion und Bedeutung dieser Stätte mit größerer Sicherheit zu interpretieren. Die Ausgrabungen waren Teil eines Großprojekts, bei dem unter anderem Land erworben wurde, um sicher zu stellen, daß die folgenden Ziele erreicht werden können: ein verständnisvolles Management dieser Anlage zu ermöglichen, ein umfassendes Programm von detaillierten hydrologischen Messungen des Grundwasserstands durchzuführen, um dessen Einwirkung auf die archäologischen Ausgrabungsbedingungen zu untersuchen, pädagogische Tätigkeiten für die einheimischen Schulkinder zu organisieren und Verbindungen mit einer Reihe anderer Interessenvertreter zu knüpfen, vor allem in den angrenzenden Gemeinden.

Eine frühe Siedlungsphase wurde 2003 entdeckt und besteht aus einem kleinen Friedhof der sich auf dem größten Sandhügel oder Insel in diesem Feuchtgebiet befindet. Die Reste einer Einäscherung wurden auf die frühe Bronzezeit datiert.

Der Hauptteil der Anlage bestand aus einer 200 × 100m großen, D-förmigen Einfriedung, die sich über die gesamte Insel erstreckte und einem gestaffelten Verteidigungskomplex umgeben war, der aus einem Blockwerkbau, einem inneren Graben, einem Palisadenwall, äußerem Graben und weiteren Ausarbeitungen der Verteidigungsanlagen bestand. Zwei Eingangstore, eins nach Osten, das andere nach Westen ausgerichtet, waren der einzige Zugang zu diesem Ort. Das Westtor konnte nur von einem 80m langen, erhöhten Fußweg über dem Feuchtgebiet erreicht werden, der an einem ausgetrocknetem Flußbett entlang verlief. Ein Querwall und ein zusätzliches Graben- und Wallsystem kontrollierten den Zugang zu dem Fußweg. Dendrochronologische Datierungen, eng integriert mit Radiocarbondatierung wurden mit einer viel größeren Präzision durchgeführt, als es bisher bei anderen Verteidigungsanlagen aus der Eisenzeit gelungen war. Damit wurde der Erbauungsbeginn der Verteidigungsanlagen auf 372 v. Chr. datiert, weitere Gräben und Palisadenwälle wurden bis 350 v. Chr. fertiggestellt.

Die spärlichen Kulturfunde aus der Marschfestung bestanden aus ein paar vereinzelten Keramikscherben, ein Bruchstück einer Querne, ein abgenutzter Webkamm aus Geweih, die aus den beiden Grabenenden neben dem Osteingang geborgen wurden. Weitere Begleitfunde bestanden aus Tierknochen, zwei Menschenschädeln (einer dieser Schädel wurde mit dem dazugehörenden Wirbelknochen gefunden, was darauf hinweist, daß es sich um einen noch befleischten Kopf handelte), und die einzigen Stücke von Eibenholz, die an dieser Stätte gefunden wurden. Es wird vermutet, daß diese Funde Teil einer strukturierten Beilegung an einem symbolischen Eingang waren, ähnlich wie sie aus anderen Beispielen aus der Britischen Eisenzeit bekannt sind.

Der Innenbereich der Marschfestung wurde von einer viereckigen Pfahlstruktur beherrscht. 150 Kornkammern waren in Reihen aus bis zu acht Strukturen angelegt und machten den Hauptteil der Anlage aus. An 25 dieser Kammern wurden verkohlte Körner (meist aus Emmer und Spelz) aus ein oder zwei Pfostenlöchern geborgen. Aufgrund detaillierter Analyse der Ablagerungsprozesse, wird dies als Beweis dafür interpretiert, daß eine Handvoll verkohltes Getreide bewußt während dem Bau dieser Strukturen dort deponiert wurde, und nicht das Resultat katastrophaler Brände oder anderen unvorhergesehenen Ereignissen war. Es wurden keine anderen Strukturen oder Häuser identifiziert. Die Umweltanalyse von Pollen, Insekten und pflanzlichen Überresten bezeugt, daß die Anlage nie bewohnt war, und daß zu dem Zeitpunkt, als die Verschlammung der Gräben ansetzte, das Umland ausschließlich als Weidefläche genutzt wurde.

Es wurde eine zweite Aktivitätsphase im Inneren der Marschfestung identifiziert, und provisorisch auf ungefähr das 2. bis 4. Jahrhundert v. Chr. datiert. Diese Phase bestand aus 12 geometrisch angelegten, 3–6m breiten Abgrenzungen, die durch schmale, tiefe Gräben definiert wurden. Aufgrund der Ergebnisse der Ausgrabungen und unterstützt durch micro-geoarchäologische Analyse wird vorgeschlagen, daß diese kleinen Abgrenzungen 'temenos', oder heilige Stätten sein könnten, in denen Einäscherungen als Teil der letzten Begräbnisriten verstreut wurden. Diese Interpretation gibt eine bewesliche Erklärung für die Tatsache, daß Begräbnisstätten aus der mittleren Eisenzeit in Großbritannien und Westeuropa nahezu archäologisch unsichtbar sind.

In Anbetracht der Beweise kann Sutton Common als eine Stätte verstanden werden, wo die soziale Identität der einheimischen Kommune durch die Erschaffung einer physischen Verkörperung der Idee/des Ideals einer Gemeinschaft in Form einer Art 'Wohnhauses' gestärkt werden sollte. Die Logistik des Alltags wurde allerdings eher von einer funktionalen Landschaft ('taskscape') geprägt, die aus verstreuten Dörfern und einzelnen Gehöften bestand. Es mag sein, daß eine sagenhafte Erinnerung an den Friedhof aus der frühen Bronzezeit innerhalb der Kommune bis ins 4. Jahrhundert v. Chr. andauerte, und ein Gefühl bestand, daß dieser, von einem Feuchtgebiet umschlossener Sandhügel eine heilige Stätte war. Die Konstruktion von einer Wall- und Grabenanlage, die andere Einfriedungen und Verteidigungsanlagen erinnert, demonstriert die soziale Verbindung von autonomen regionalen Volksgruppen über ein großes Gebiet hinweg. Diese Verbindung wird bezeugt durch die Übernahme von weitverbreiteten kosmologischen Prinzipien, wie zum Beispiel das Konzept der Einfriedung (z.B. das nach Osten gerichtete Eingangstor) und Kulturgüter (z.B. die rituelle Beisetzung an den Grabenenden). Es gibt keinen Grund, und in der Tat keine archäologischen Beweise, der darauf hinweist, daß die Erbauung der Marschfestung von einer Oberschicht geleitet wurde, es scheint eher eine kommunale Bemühung zu sein, vielleicht von einem vorübergehenden Führer oder peripatetischen 'Architekt' gelenkt. Das gestaffelte Wallsystem hat die symbolische Bedeutung der Einfriedung wiederbetont, die durch die Beisetzung von Gütern und menschlichen Überresten, eventuell bei Prozessionen, an den Eingangsschwellen erwiesen ist. Mindestens einer, aber vielleicht beide Menschenschädel hatten noch ihre Weichteile intakt, als sie beigesetzt wurden, die könnten als 'Kopftrophäen' bei bestimmten Ritualen gedient haben.

Die Bedeutung der Kornkammern sollte im Zusammenhang mit der Verlagerung von einer Ritualisation von Kriegern und Waffen im frühen und mittleren Bronzezeit zu der Ritualisation von Landwirtschaft und dem Anbau und der Erhaltung von Nahrung in der späten Bronzezeit und der Eisenzeit, gesehen werden. Die Beilegung von einer Handvoll verkohlten Körnern in ein oder zwei Pfostenlöchern in einigen der Kornkammern untermalt den rituellen Aspekt der Getreidelagerung, und diese Strukturen wurden somit mächtige Symbole zu einer Zeit, als sich der Ackerbau in einer Umschwungsphase befand.

Der kurzlebige Charakter dieser Stätte wird durch ihre symbolische Rolle erklärt – ihr Erbau war ein Ereignis oder eine theatralische Vorführung die sich herkömmlichen und geläufigen Ritualen und Formen bediente. Nach diesem Ereignis sind die Eingangstore zu dieser Marschfestung vermutlich zerstört worden, um dessen Ende zu signalisieren, aber die Stätte behielt ihre Bedeutung innerhalb der Landschaft als Teil einer sagenhaften Erinnerung innerhalb der Kommune, die sie erbaut hatte. Der erneute Gebrauch dieser Stätte in den folgenden Jahrhunderten als letzte Ruhestätte für die Toten ist kein Zufall. Er verbindet die Wandlung und die Zerstörung des Körpers nach dem Tod direkt an einen Ort, an dem die Vorfahren ihre Rituale vollzogen.

# 1 Introduction

## 1.1 Background to the project
*by R Van de Noort and K Miller*

### 1.1.1 Introduction

This monograph presents the results of the research excavations at the enigmatic double enclosure of Sutton Common, in South Yorkshire (centred on SE56251205 and SE56471214), undertaken between 1998 and 2003 (Fig 1.1). This site is situated on two slightly elevated dunes or 'islands' of sands and clays, intersected by the Hampole Beck palaeochannel at the edge of the Humber Wetlands (Fig 1.2). Alongside a complete overhaul of our understanding of this well-known site and a significant reappraisal of the socio-political character of this region, these excavations and post-excavation analyses offer answers to some long-standing debates in the Iron Age archaeology of Great Britain and continental Europe.

Whilst this monograph represents the end of the research at Sutton Common, identifying its beginning is somewhat harder – there are several moments in the last three decades which could be considered to represent the start of this project – but the year 1997 is the most appropriate. In that year, Michael Parker Pearson and Robert Sydes published the results of various smaller-scale works undertaken on the Common in the 1980s and 1990s, and provided the first modern reappraisal of the earthworks at Sutton Common (Parker Pearson and Sydes 1997). That year also saw the transfer of the ownership of the Common to the Carstairs Countryside Trust (CCT), which offered protection to the site from the damaging effects of annual ploughing, and opportunities to undertake fieldwork unhindered by farming constraints. Furthermore, the development of what was to become known as 'The Sutton Common Project', which included the excavations but also incorporated the management of the Common as a wetland landscape and the collaborative work with the local community, English Heritage and other national bodies, also commenced in 1997 (Olivier and Van de Noort 2002; see chapter 2).

The excavations were designed with current research debates in Iron Age archaeology manifestly in mind (see section 1.3), and the excavation and post-excavation strategies were revised during the project to progress aspects of these debates, taking advantage of the publication of the research framework *Understanding the British Iron Age: an agenda for action* (Haselgrove *et al* 2001). The realisation of our academic ambitions was made possible through a combination of financial support for the large-scale excavations from English Heritage, a supportive landowner in CCT, the character of the site and its location in northern England outside the core area of much of the Iron Age research undertaken to date, and the preservation of palaeoenvironmental materials such as pollen, insects, and plant macrofossils, including archaeological wood for dendrochronological dating, in this former waterlogged environment on the edge of the Humber Wetlands (cf Van de Noort 2004a). The research of the Iron Age period site at Sutton Common was of a multi-disciplinary nature, reflecting the preservation of a range of palaeoenvironmental source materials alongside the archaeological remains. The work presented in this volume represents the work of 31 specialists and collaborators, and is based on the fieldwork of some 100 staff and students from the Universities of Exeter and Hull, with assistance from volunteers from the Askern Ward, the archaeological societies of Doncaster and the East Riding, and additional support from English Heritage specialists (see chapter 3).

### 1.1.2 The terms 'marsh-fort' and 'mortuary rings'

Sutton Common is described in this monograph as a 'marsh-fort', and a second phase as comprising 'mortuary rings'. Neither term is incontrovertible.

The unconventional character of the site in its principal manifestation requires the use of a term that is not available in any thesaurus of archaeological site types, but the term 'marsh-fort' appears the most appropriate here. The excavations of the larger enclosure, on the east bank of the Hampole Beck palaeochannel, revealed ramparts, ditch-and-bank alignments and entranceways of 4th-century BC date that could all have been copied from hillforts elsewhere in Britain, but instead of a hill, local wetlands or marshy areas were utilised to create spatial separation. In line with *Understanding the British Iron Age* (Haselgrove *et al* 2001), the term marsh-fort is used as shorthand for a large enclosed Iron Age site, in this case situated within a wetland context. To paraphrase the Oxford English Dictionary, the word 'fort' should be understood in this context as 'a fortified place; a position fortified for defensive or protective purposes, usually surrounded with a ditch and rampart', but this does not mean that the site functioned as a defended settlement, or was garrisoned with troops.

In previous published work, the site has been described as camps, double-enclosures or simply as earthworks, with the eastern part of the site

2 *Sutton Common*

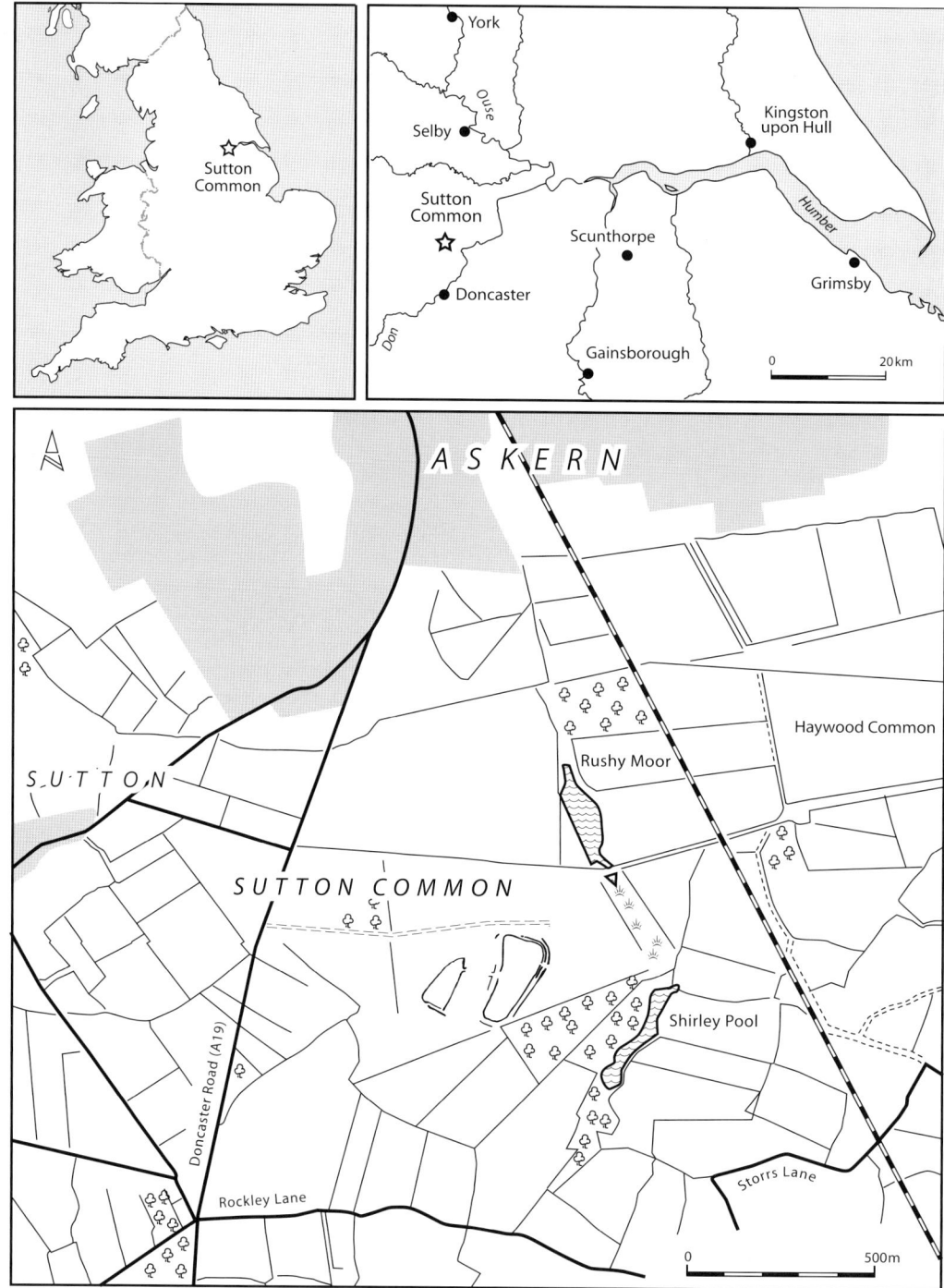

*Figure 1.1  The location of Sutton Common and the double enclosures*

labelled 'Enclosure A' or the 'larger enclosure', and the western part 'Enclosure B' or the 'smaller enclosure' (Whiting 1936; Parker Pearson and Sydes 1997). The terms 'larger enclosure' and 'smaller enclosure' have been used consistently throughout this book for the reader's convenience, but it should be noted that the latter may never have been an enclosure, rather we reinterpret it as an initial cross-bank with the addition of a triangular-shaped bank and ditch earthwork (see section 5.3.2).

A second phase of activity within the confines of the marsh-fort, dated to the 4th to 2nd centuries BC inclusive, included twelve small ephemeral enclosures of basic geometric shapes. Although the evidence is certainly not irrefutable, it is our interpretation that these small enclosures may have been used for the scattering of pyre debris and have been named 'mortuary rings' (see section 8.1). With this phase of activity comes the oldest evidence for glass manufacture in northern England, and a rare example of an Iron Age gold

*Figure 1.2  Aerial photograph of Sutton Common looking north, taken in 1997; the Hampole Beck palaeochannel stands out clearly in the arable fields as a dark sinuous feature*

object in the form of what are understood to have been grave goods.

### 1.1.3  About this book

In the production of this monograph, the editors have taken on board recent concerns that the orthodox archaeological monograph, where specialists reports are presented separately rather than integrated in the text, and where 'data' have been separated from interpretation, produces unreadable and sometimes incomprehensible narratives. These concerns are both generic to archaeological fieldwork (Jones et al 2003) and specific to the Iron Age archaeology of Britain (Haselgrove et al 2001, 10). Consequently, this monograph was designed to integrate and contextualise discussions of assemblages and reduce compartmentalisation into specialist categories and detailed presentation of archaeological facts. This has meant that many specialists' reports have been summarised, with only the information relevant to the academic questions presented here in full. In order to preserve standards of detailed reporting, a digital resource was submitted to the Archaeological Data Service in York, and the complete specialists' reports were included in the excavation archive, submitted to Doncaster Museum and the National Monuments Record in Swindon. This will allow detailed scrutiny of the primary record without adding numerous pages of text and tables to the monograph. Furthermore, where detailed discussions were considered more appropriate for specialist audiences, separate papers have been produced rather than included in the current research monograph.

The remainder of this chapter outlines the academic facets of the work at Sutton Common. It summarises previous research at Sutton Common, from the mid-19th century through to 1997, provides the research contexts within which the reasons for the excavations and post-excavation analyses were defined, and presents the aims and objectives of the project. This chapter concludes with a short overview of the project designs and organisation of the project between 1997 and 2006.

Chapter 2 considers the non-archaeological components of the work at Sutton Common. We feel strongly that the success of the academic work was embedded in the broader 'Sutton Common Project', and that due attention must be given to the wider programme of archaeological and environmental conservation and community partnership.

The various methodologies employed at the excavation and post-excavation stages are detailed in chapter 3. Chapter 4 provides the landscape context, and chapters 5, 6, and 7 offer the data and interpretations of the marsh-fort, whilst chapter 8 is concerned with the second phase of activity at Sutton Common. This information has been integrated as much as possible, and thus both the description of archaeological features and specialists' contributions are presented where most relevant for the understanding of the site.

Chapter 9 considers a number of geographical contexts in which the Sutton Common site can be understood. Chapter 10 offers the conclusions.

## 1.2 Previous research at Sutton Common *by H Chapman*

### 1.2.1 *Enclosure, mapping, and early descriptions*

The OS 6" 1st edition 1854 County Series map of the area depicts the earthworks on Sutton Common, labelling them as 'Crook Hills' (Fig 1.3). In 1858 the landscape of Sutton Common was enclosed. The first archaeological investigation took place shortly after this and involved the mapping, description, and interpretation of features by the Rev Scott F Surtees (Surtees 1868), who interpreted the site as the remains of a Roman military camp. His plan of the site included three wooden stumps aligned between the two enclosures that may have related to a causeway joining them. Forty years later, the interpretation of the site as a Roman military camp was challenged by Mr A Hadrian Allcroft who described the features on Sutton Common within his gazetteer of earthworks in England (Allcroft 1908, 246–7). Reflecting on the swampy context of the site, he believed that dwellings lay on top of the inner bank of the larger enclosure, and interpreted the site as a settlement that must have been a refuge for fugitives, driven from the more habitable dry areas to the west. Allcroft also noted that a line of wooden stakes ran between the western entrance of the larger enclosure and the eastern entrance of the smaller enclosure, each of the entrances being defined by breaks in the bank and ditch.

### 1.2.2 *Earliest excavations*

The earliest recorded excavation of the features on Sutton Common took place in 1909/1910 under the direction of a Dr Corbett from Doncaster, who discovered pottery and other finds. The records of these excavations were subsequently lost, although the work was referenced in a later paper by C E Whiting (1936). Between 1910 and 1914 further excavations were undertaken, this time by Major Crathorne Anne and Mr G V Charlton who dug trenches in three positions across the western side of the larger enclosure, examining many of the circular or oval depressions on top of the bank that had been interpreted by Allcroft as dwellings. In these areas, large quantities of material construed as decayed wood and thatch were identified, in addition to lithic artefacts including arrowheads and remains of human bone. At one of the 'gates' (the exact one not being recorded) a pathway of brown pebbles was also discovered. Again, no contemporary record of these excavations exists and the finds were lost (Whiting 1936).

In 1926, a Mr Day from Doncaster Grammar School undertook further excavations with a party of students. They excavated trenches across all three ramparts on the northern side of the larger enclosure, and across the entrance to what was interpreted as the north gate. In the latter area a number of human bones were recovered, in addition to fallen stakes discovered in the inner ditch, and the skull of a cow (*Bos longifrons*). Midway between the two enclosures a stake was also found *in situ*, perhaps part of the same alignment recorded by Surtees and Allcroft.

### 1.2.3 *The work by C E Whiting*

In 1933, the lack of records from the previous investigations on Sutton Common prompted C E Whiting to undertake further excavations. This work was directed and recorded by Whiting, with fieldwork taking place in 1933, 1934, and 1935, totalling approximately six weeks of excavation. In addition to the excavation, a plan of the site was made by W T Bennett and S Hill, both of whom had previously worked on the site under the direction of Mr Day in 1926 (Fig 1.4). On morphological grounds, Whiting classified the earthworks on Sutton Common as belonging to 'a type known as contour camps', but noted that they were unusual examples (Whiting 1936, 57). He also noted the local landscape context, with the earthworks surrounding natural sandy islands within the wetland.

Whiting excavated numerous trenches across both of the enclosures and between them. His work was largely restricted to sectioning the main earthworks and investigating features visible on the tops of the banks, as with previous excavators, and so most trenches either followed their alignment or were excavated at right-angles to them. Two of the perpendicular trenches were extended further away from the earthworks into

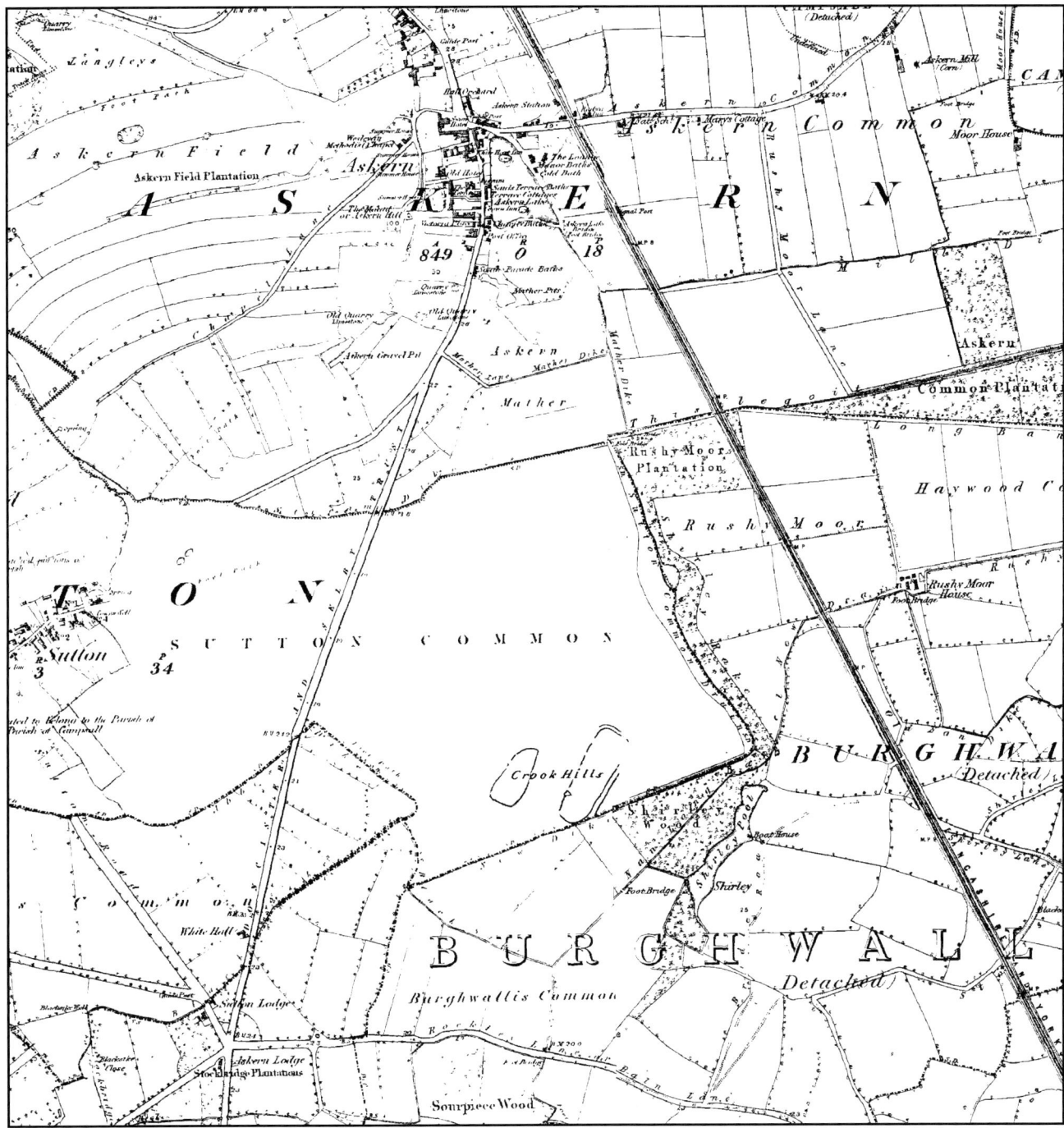

*Figure 1.3   Extract from Ordnance Survey 1st edition 6" 1854 County Series map*

the interior and exterior. Trench I cut across the centre of the smaller enclosure on the eastern side and was extended half-way across the interior of the enclosure and the same distance into the palaeochannel. Trench IIc was excavated further to the north and was extended from the bank approximately 40m into the channel. Finds from Whiting's work included charred wheat, a baked clay ball (interpreted as a possible net sinker), Romano-British pottery, an oak plank, a circular oak slab (interpreted as a wheel), a possible dug-out vessel, several lithic implements and waste, and a number of bones, including human, ox, sheep, and goat, in addition to cattle horns.

Whiting concluded that there were at least two phases of activity represented at the site. The first phase was represented by a wooden palisade or stockade found surrounding the northern section of the larger enclosure and visible in sections elsewhere, including under the bank at the northern end of the smaller enclosure. The second phase was at 'probably a much later date' (Whiting 1936, 79) when the two sandy islands were occupied by the people who erected the ramparts. These were faced with a stone revetment of poor-quality

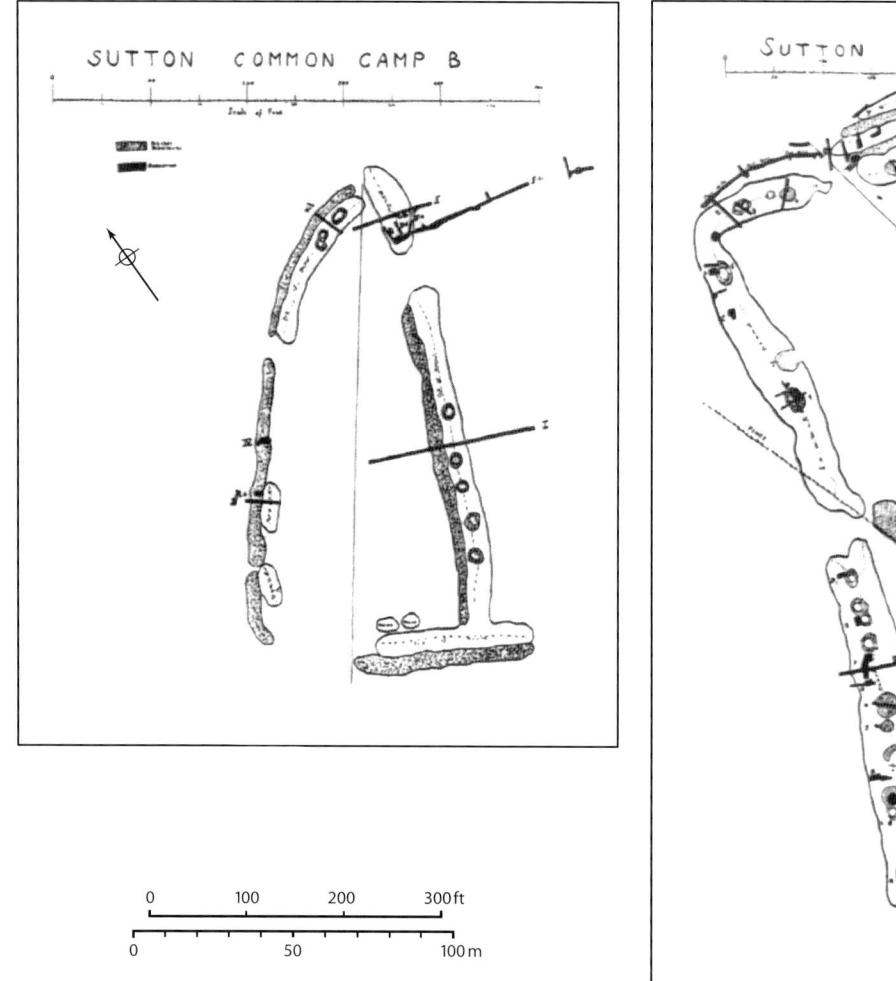
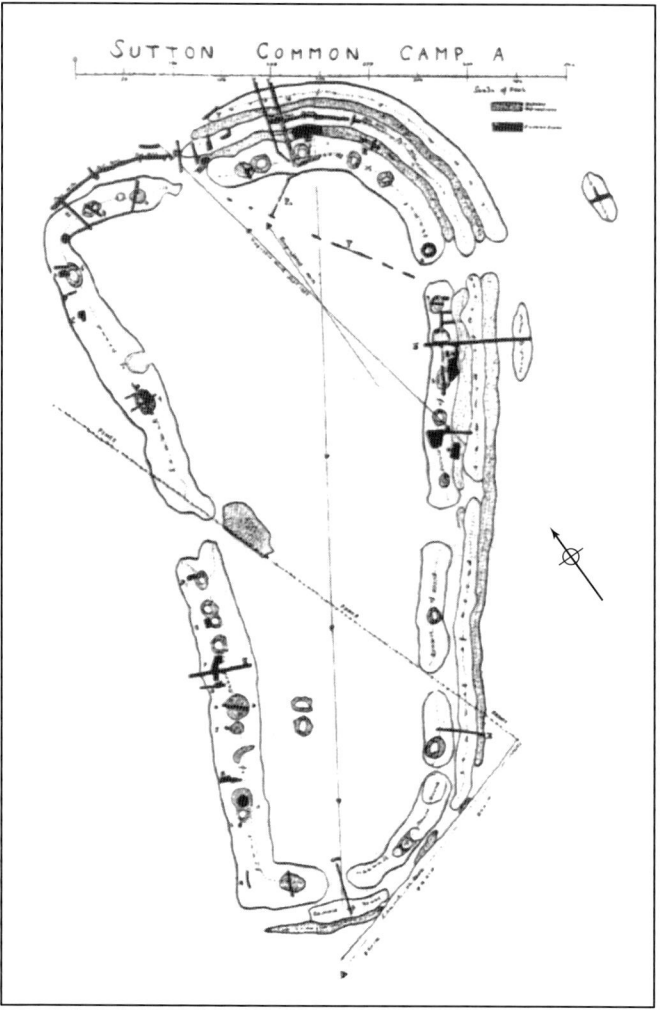

*Figure 1.4  Plan of the site by Mr W T Bennett and Mr S Hill, with the smaller enclosure on the left, and the larger enclosure on the right; north arrows added*

construction including pieces of wood. Whiting was certain that these occupants were generally unaffected by Roman culture and therefore suggested that the site was prehistoric. This conclusion was supported by the fact that the Romano-British pottery had been discovered high up within the ditch on the western side of the smaller enclosure. Furthermore, Whiting recognised the unusual nature of the site. It was not a lake village because there were no piles to suggest that any part of the site stood over water. He also noted that it was unusual within the classification of contour camps. He did not consider it to be a fortress either, due to the relatively low ramparts (although their height was not recorded), and therefore suggested that the site was a refuge, perhaps with the banks constructed to keep out the water on all sides. He interpreted the small number of finds as indicating that occupation had been short-lived. Whiting suggested that the first phase, characterised by the palisade, dated to the Bronze Age. The earthworks were considered to have been constructed at a later date by a poor, primitive people before the end of the 2nd century AD, and perhaps even before the Roman period. On the basis of Whiting's work, in 1937 the site was afforded protection in the form of scheduling (SAM 291).

### 1.2.4  Damage and rescue: excavations in the 1980s and early 1990s

Following the work of Whiting, the site received little archaeological attention until, in the spring of 1980, the larger of the two enclosures was bulldozed by the tenant farmer to expand arable cultivation. The bulldozing of the smaller enclosure was halted after being witnessed by Stuart Eastwood and Malcolm Dolby of Doncaster Museum, but only after it had already destroyed the south-east corner, where originally a bank of the southern earthwork extended towards the Hampole Beck palaeochannel. 'Before and after' aerial photographs were taken by Derrick Riley (1982, 20; see section 2.2.1) which demonstrate the amount of damage that was done to the site, particularly evident in the soil marks which show the dragged ditch deposits. At the time of bulldozing, large quantities of wood and stone walling were seen on the ground and a few fragments of quernstone were noted (Sydes and Symonds 1987). In addition to the direct physical damage to the site from bulldozing and ploughing, in 1982, the Ministry for Agriculture initiated a scheme of drainage whose deep dikes dropped local water levels on the Common by approximately 2m (Parker Pearson and Sydes 1997, 223).

The combined actual and potential impact from agriculture and drainage on the site prompted concerns over the preservation of the site, particularly as earlier investigations had demonstrated the high level of organic archaeological survival. As a consequence, in the late 1980s, English Heritage funded three separate research assessment projects that were undertaken by the South Yorkshire Archaeology Unit.

The first of these took place in 1987 (Sydes and Symonds 1987). The strategy involved firstly the re-excavation of one of Whiting's trenches, Trench II, at the northern end of the smaller enclosure, with a new trench, Trench A, in order to compare the level of organic preservation and deterioration since the 1930s. A second trench, Trench B, was positioned across the southern earthworks of the smaller enclosure within an undisturbed area to obtain material for radiocarbon dating. A third trench, Trench C, was excavated adjacent to Trench A to cut back the exposed bank material to observe stratigraphic relationships. In addition, a magnetometer survey was carried out over the smaller enclosure and an auger transect was located between the two enclosures to inspect peat depth, underlying stratigraphy, and depth of water table. A wider landscape examination at this time also identified other 'islands' and sites in the area. SUT1, to the north-west of the smaller enclosure, revealed large quantities of struck flint, as did SUT2, an 'island' to the north of SUT1. SUT3, an 'island' to the north of the larger enclosure, now occupied by a pylon, revealed no flint. SUT4, the area of a field drain between the islands of SUT1 and SUT2, revealed twelve roundwood stakes grouped in pairs approximately 0.1m apart, positioned at the base of the peat, in addition to a split log. SUT5 was the location of a possible circular mound within the area of Shirley Wood to the east of the site.

The results from the archaeological work in 1987 included the sampling of material for radiocarbon dating and the discovery of numerous wooden items and structures, including part of a possible bowl and a section of possible hurdling. In addition, a feature interpreted as a 'framework' or raft was discovered in the base of the inner ditch within Trench C and another in the outer ditch of Trench B. It was concluded that the archaeology probably related to the prehistoric period, confirming Whiting's suggestions, and that the preservation of the wood was good although prone to deteriorate given the instigation of additional drainage in 1982.

Following the work in 1987 (Sydes and Symonds 1987), a second assessment was carried out in 1988, with the excavation of two additional trenches, Trench D and Trench E, within the larger enclosure, aimed at assessing the preservation of organic material within the ditches (Adams *et al* 1988).

In 1992, a comparative study was carried out through the reopening of the 1987 Trench A/C (Sydes 1992). The conclusions of this work were that the deterioration of organic material indicated that it had reached a 'critical stage' (Sydes 1992, 6). It was argued that *in situ* preservation was no longer a possibility, and that the site should now be considered as a non-wetland site with locally exceptional organic preservation in the context of archaeological research. This conclusion was based on the archaeology in conjunction with the results of an assessment of the modified drainage system in the area, commissioned by English Heritage (Geomorphological Services Ltd 1990).

A further study was carried out in 1993 by Sheffield University Department of Archaeology and Prehistory, South Yorkshire Archaeology Service, and Doncaster Museum (Parker Pearson and Merrony 1993). The aims of this study were again focused on the assessment of preservation on the site, and this was addressed through the reopening of earlier trenches in addition to the excavation of a new trench, Trench F, on the eastern side of the smaller enclosure. This work also evaluated the huts originally identified by Whiting and concluded that the lack of beam slots and other diagnostic features could suggest no more than ambiguous post-built structures. However, on the top of one of the banks, within Trench E, a four-post structure was found which was considered by the excavators to be part of a granary rather than reflecting a box rampart (Fig 1.5). However, this conclusion could not be substantiated due to the narrow widths of the trenches. The results of this and additional work, including the integration of palaeoenvironmental assessments by Buckland and Hale (both included in Sydes and Symonds 1987), were integrated in the synthesis of work at Sutton Common published by Michael Parker Pearson and Robert Sydes (1997). This included the production of a contour plot of the wider Sutton Common landscape.

### 1.2.5 Humber Wetlands Project

In 1996, the site and its landscape were investigated by the Humber Wetlands Project based within the University of Hull (Van de Noort and Ellis 1997). Work consisted of field walking (Head *et al* 1997), aerial photographic analysis (Chapman 1997), and palaeoenvironmental assessment (Lillie 1997). Previously identified

*Figure 1.5 Excavation of Trench E in 1993 by the University of Sheffield, looking east*

scatters of lithics (Sydes and Symonds 1987) were again identified (SUT1 and SUT2), and the area of SUT3 again revealed no material. SUT2 (during the Humber Wetlands Project referred to as HWP Askern–7) produced 122 pieces of flint ranging in date from the later Mesolithic to the early Bronze Age (Head *et al* 1997, 233, 236–8), indicating that the palaeochannel was flowing during this earlier period (Lillie 1997, 73), and also demonstrated the longevity of landscape use.

### 1.2.6 The micro-topographical survey in 1997

Following the purchase of Sutton Common by CCT in 1997, a survey of the site and its immediate landscape was undertaken in order to create a baseline of data to facilitate the site's future management. It was decided that the most appropriate approach was to create a Digital Elevation Model of the site. The survey at Sutton Common was undertaken between 28 October and 5 November 1997, following the final cropping of the fields after the transfer of land ownership. The field conditions were therefore predominantly stubble, with grass at the eastern end running up to Shirley Wood. A total of 5290 positions were surveyed using a Spectra Precision Geotracer System 2000 L1 RTK differential Global Positioning System (GPS) in real time to a maximum accuracy deviation range of 0.56m horizontally and 0.029m vertically. A varying surface resolution was recorded, following the recommendations of Fletcher and Spicer (1988), of between 8m and 3m. In terms of density, this provided a mean of 184 points per hectare. Higher resolution was afforded to areas of major topographic variability such as around the surviving earthworks of the smaller enclosure. The data collected through this survey were processed and modelled within ArcInfo Geographic Information System (GIS) software on a UNIX platform. Various interpolation methods were used to generate a Digital Elevation Model (DEM) of the site to check for variations between them. The most appropriate method was found to be through the construction of a triangulated irregular network (TIN) surface, converted to a grid using quintic smoothing (Chapman 2000; Chapman and Van de Noort 2001).

The DEM showed the natural topography of the landscape, with both the 'islands' occupied by the enclosures and those surrounding the site, the position of the Hampole Beck palaeochannel, and the land dropping away towards Shirley Wood (Fig 1.6). The form of the landscape, with the approach from the nearby dry land to the west, reinforced Parker Pearson's suggestion that the smaller enclosure might have acted as an annex to the larger enclosure (Parker Pearson and Sydes 1997).

Through the application of surface modelling techniques within the GIS, additional features could be seen. Light shading of the DEM highlighted the extant earthworks of the smaller enclosure (Fig 1.7), and this provided a plan that was more complete than the one obtained by Whiting (1936). Additional earthworks survived in the micro-relief that had not been observed in the earlier survey, perhaps due to vegetation cover at that time. Primarily, the north-west side of the enclosure was continuous and cohesive, rather than interrupted as earlier plans suggested. In addition, a tongue of higher land extended into the palaeochannel from the eastern entrance of the smaller enclosure, indicating the possible use of natural topography in the choice of where to site a causeway if, indeed, one had been constructed. The DEM showed also that the shape of the larger enclosure did not wholly conform to the shape of the sandy island.

This enabled a comparison to be made with the earlier survey of the site and displayed some potential errors in the metrics of the earlier work (Chapman 2001). The topographic position of the larger enclosure also indicated an explanation for its architecture as revealed through earlier aerial photographs and the earlier survey. There was a

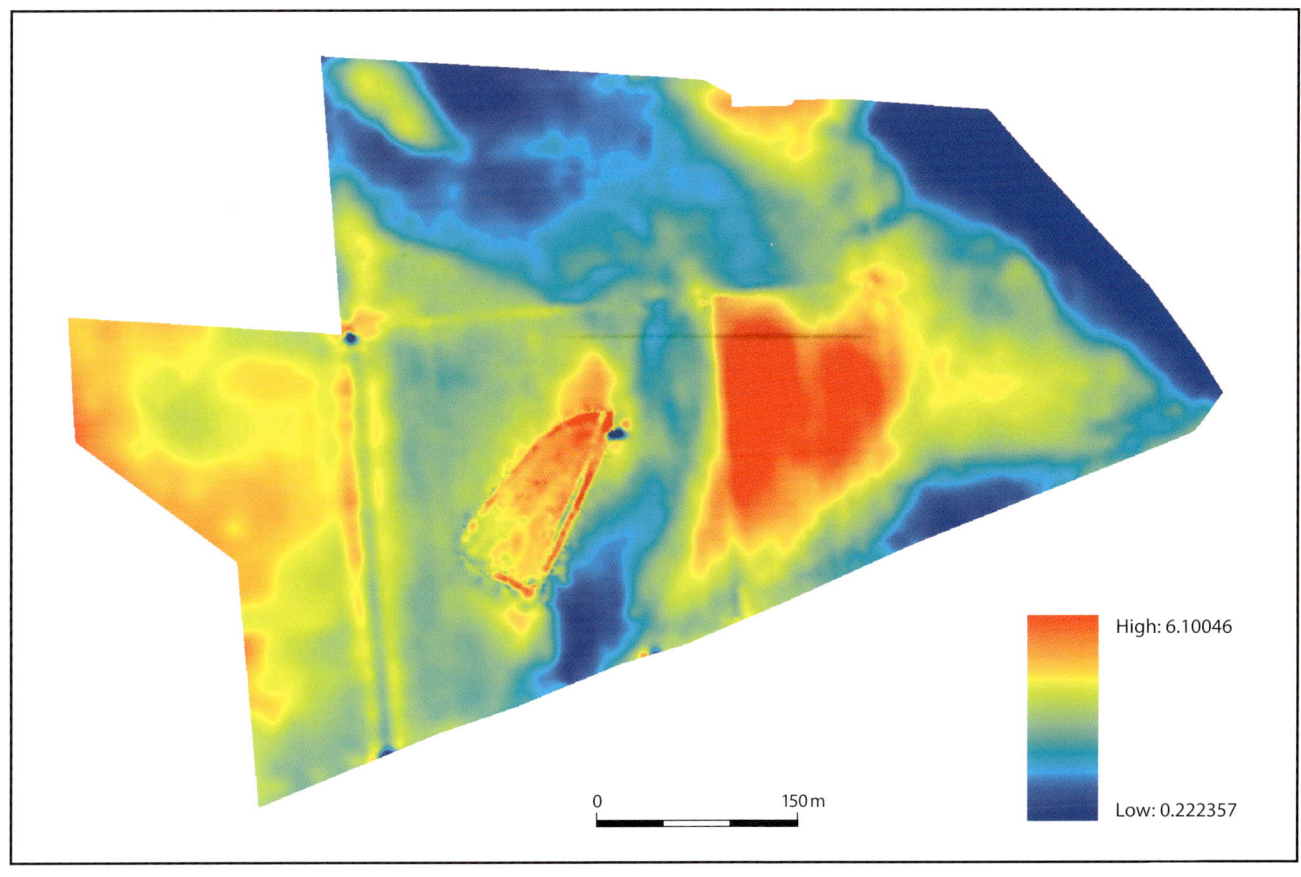

*Figure 1.6 Digital Elevation Model (DEM) of Sutton Common based on the micro-topographical survey of 1997*

correlation between greater numbers of ramparts and drier, or higher, positions, in contrast with the single bank on its western side adjacent to the lower, wetter areas.

Perhaps most surprisingly, and significant with regards to the preservation of the larger enclosure, the GIS modelling revealed evidence of a ditch running along the western edge of the larger enclosure. The presence of this ditch within the DEM provided evidence of differential desiccation of deposits over an eighteen-month period since the site was last ploughed. The biogenic sediments in the ditch fills had dried in this period leading to greater shrinkage compared with that of the surrounding minerogenic sediments. This shrinkage of ditch material had led to the dropping of the land surface overlying the ditch, making it identifiable on the DEM (Chapman and Van de Noort 2001). The broader significance of this was one of preservation potential. The fact that biogenic sediments do not significantly expand when rewetted indicated that desiccation had occurred over this eighteen-month period. Thus organic material was present within the ditch which, although drying out, held the potential for providing wet-preserved archaeological information.

## 1.3 Research contexts and aims
*by R Van de Noort*

### 1.3.1 Research contexts

In 1997, at the beginning of the current project, the Sutton Common site could justifiably be described as an enigma, in the sense that its function was largely unknown, its dating and phasing were insecure, its significance in the wider landscape indefinite, and its future as a wetland site in doubt (Parker Pearson and Sydes 1997). Any research undertaken here was to focus on these main issues. If not addressed successfully, then Sutton Common would remain something of an unknown entity, and its potential contribution to the study and understanding of the archaeology of Iron Age Britain and continental Europe would not be realised. Similarly, this potential would not be realised without a clear appreciation of current research contexts which can, for the sake of convenience, be split in three. The first concerns the study of the Iron Age in Britain within its European context; the second concerns the study of wetlands; and the third, the regional landscape.

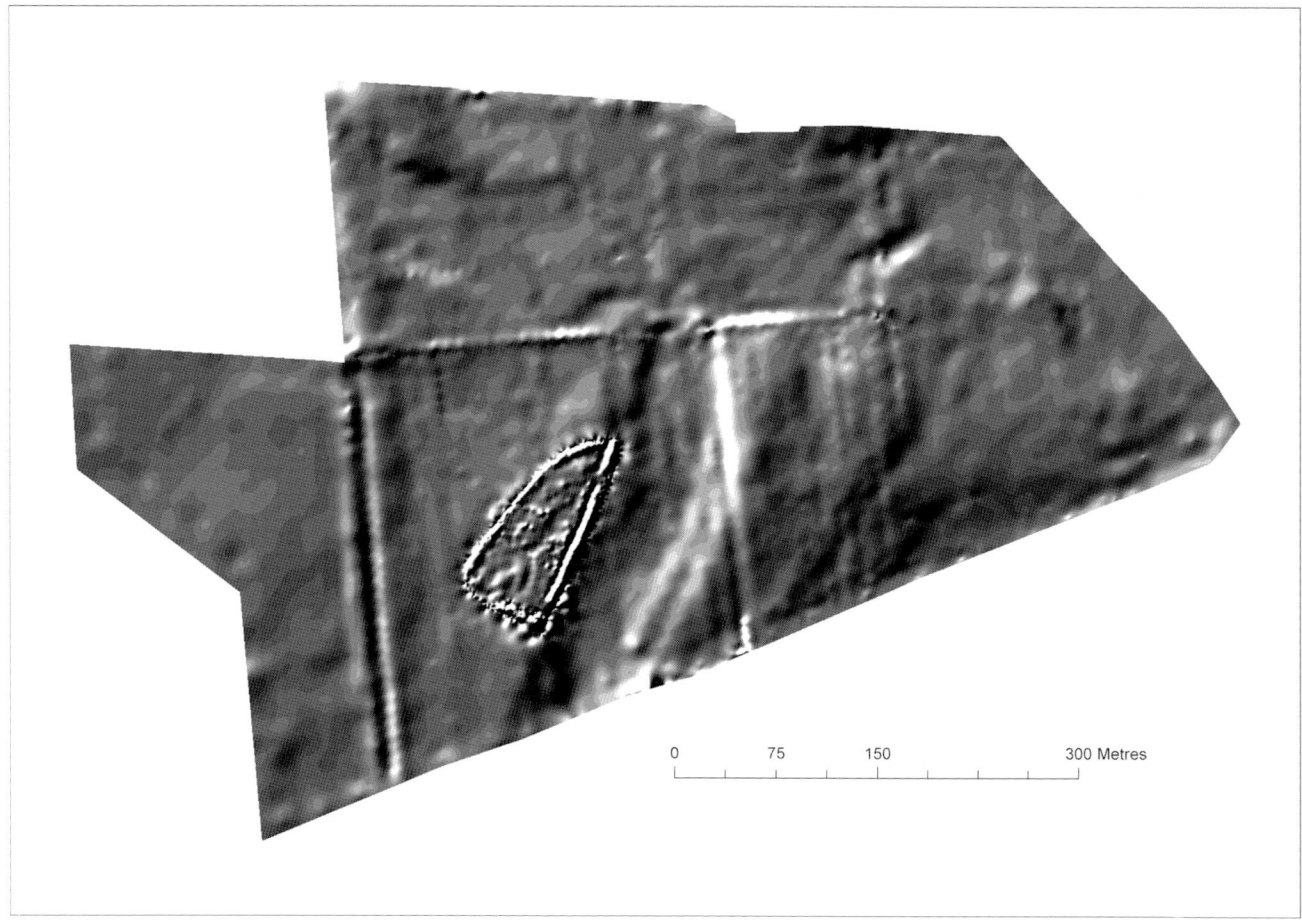

*Figure 1.7 'False light' DEM of the enclosures based on the micro-topographical survey of 1997*

### 1.3.1.1 Research contexts for the Iron Age

Our view of the Iron Age is changing. Visions of a Celtic society with its chiefs or kings living in hillforts no longer appear valid. The functions of hillforts as early urban centres, from where the surrounding countryside was governed, and which were the centres of early industrial specialisation and the redistribution of craft and agricultural produce, are being reconsidered. Even the analyses of mundane material culture from ditches and 'rubbish pits' as a source of information on the Iron Age economy are being challenged. This new thinking reflects three fundamental debates in Iron Age archaeology.

The first debate centres on the concepts of 'Celts' and 'Celtic'. Aspects of the debate regarding the significance of these terms for Iron Age Europe go back several decades (eg Champion 1987; Hill 1989; 1995a; Fitzpatrick 1991; 1997a; Webster 1995; Collis 1997), and the conviction that Iron Age societies across Europe were all similar because they were Celtic is now roundly rejected. This debate has important implications for how we interpret the Iron Age, since making use of written sources on the Celts is no longer acceptable. Thus, neither the description of the druids by Pliny (eg Cunliffe 2005, 573), nor the Irish Annals once believed to describe Celtic societies, bear any direct information on the British Iron Age. Neither should we attempt to 'fit' Iron Age archaeology in this specific, quasi-historical framework. Instead, we should consider the British Iron Age as an indigenous society, for which the archaeological record is the only primary source of information. This debate has direct relevance to Sutton Common in terms of the discussion on the significance and function of hillforts and, by inference, of other large enclosed sites. For example, it questions the defensiveness of the ramparts and ditches, it expresses the first doubts that all hillforts were the same and performed analogous functions, it develops alternative explanations for their construction, and suggests that hillforts could be communal rather than elite sites, or indeed ritual monuments. Furthermore, this debate also recognises that the large enclosed sites in low-lying parts of the landscape do not fit the standard model of what hillforts were.

Specifically for the population of Britain and Ireland in later prehistory, it is evident that none of the Classical authors who mentioned the Celts, from Hecataeus in the late 6th century BC to Isidore of Seville in the 6th century AD, ever suggested that Celts lived anywhere in the British Isles, and indeed many Classical authors, such as Strabo in his early 1st-century AD *Geographica*, describe the inhabitants of Britain as Britons, not Celts (Collis 2003, 16–25). The idea of Celts living in the British Isles and Ireland in prehistory developed in the 18th century as a result of the mistaken belief that the Celtic language survived in modern Breton, and could thus be associated with the ancient Britons. This idea gained wider acceptance with the concept of 'Celtic Art', which was first defined only in the 19th century, and was again mistakenly applied to Britain and Ireland in later prehistory (eg James 1999; Collis 2003; Morse 2005).

The second of these debates concerns the bias of archaeological research into the Iron Age to date. The major research projects in Iron Age archaeology have been concentrated in the regions of Wessex, the Thames Valley and south-east England, and these projects have contributed disproportionately to our understanding of the British Iron Age as shown in the available benchmarks, most notably Barry Cunliffe's *Iron Age Communities in Britain* (1974; 1978; 1991; 2005). The inappropriateness of using models of Iron Age society developed for southern English regions for explaining Iron Age society elsewhere in Britain has been made particularly strongly for northern England (eg Haselgrove 1999; Harding 2004), but is equally valid for Wales, Scotland, and south-west England (eg Gwilt and Haselgrove 1997b). The 'old' model, of Iron Age society being run by redistributing chiefs and kings from 'their' hillforts, which attain central-place functions, is no longer broadly accepted. In its place has come a realisation that the Iron Age in Britain accommodated a number of distinct regions with diverse socio-political characteristics, and that sites should be interpreted within their regional context, rather than attempting to 'fit' explanations into a Wessex-derived model.

This problem of biased research has been augmented by the long-standing research interest in hillforts in Britain and continental Europe to the detriment of other types of sites. This is a major factor in the creation of a perception of Iron Age society being almost synonymous with one that was lived in, and organised from, hillforts. The recognition of this research bias and the development of commercial archaeology in Britain have resulted in the excavation of many non-hillfort-type sites and settlements, shedding new light on the greater diversity of Iron Age society (Haselgrove *et al* 2001), although too little of this work has been fully incorporated into existing academic models. With the concept of hillforts as central places no longer considered valid in all cases, hillforts are increasingly understood as having had diverse functions, ranging from settlement, refuge, symbolic, and storage of food to monuments in the landscape, with the hillforts themselves forming part of wider landscapes that include a broad range of other type settlements and sites (Collis 1981; 1997).

The third of these debates is linked to the development of interpretative archaeologies or the post-processual critique of the established archaeology of the 1970s and 1980s (eg Trigger 1990; Johnson 1999). This debate includes a range of arguments and re-evaluations of what the Iron Age is really about, and incorporates to some extent aspects of the two debates presented above (eg see the many papers in volumes edited by Hill and Cumberpatch 1995; Champion and Collis 1996; Gwilt and Haselgrove 1997a; Bevan 1999; Humphrey 2003). Furthermore, this debate includes a greater interest in the non-economic aspects of society, as is shown in a large number of papers focusing on cosmology, ritual and religion, social identity and material culture, agency and the individual in the Iron Age, and a growing realisation that all these activities were part of people's everyday lives (eg Bradley 2005). It also includes an increased awareness of the importance of understanding regional diversity over grand narratives, abstracted models, and theories, albeit the loss of a certain level of abstraction is already bemoaned (eg Gwilt and Haselgrove 1997b; Gosden 1997), and we should not lose sight of the fact that certain cosmological concepts appeared to have been shared across the British Isles and much of continental Europe. The role of material culture, and its reappraisal from a reflective to an active part of social behaviour, has possibly caused the most significant changes in our approach to the archaeology of the Iron Age period. What was previously considered as 'rubbish' reflecting daily production and consumption is now frequently interpreted as social action, or structured deposition, adhering to cosmological frameworks, as a means of reproducing material conditions and social relations (eg Fitzpatrick 1994; Parker Pearson and Richards 1994; Hill 1995a). Within this debate, the critique of the cultural evolutionary processes previously imposed on the people of the Iron Age, as a chiefdom society inevitably on its way to state-formation under the Romans, has found broad support, and the need to develop interpretative frameworks that explain the Iron Age within more appropriate contexts provides a new challenge to archaeology (Webster 1999). Finally, and specifically relevant for understanding Sutton Common, is the discussion surrounding the symbolic rather than physical importance of boundaries and 'defences', especially those of hillforts, and the associated symbolic importance of crossing these boundaries (eg Bowden and McOmish 1989; Hingley 1990; Evans 1997; Robbins 1999).

### 1.3.1.2 Research contexts for wetland archaeology

An additional and quite distinct research context that must be considered here is that of wetland archaeology. The Sutton Common Project developed effectively as a continuation of the Humber Wetlands Project, which had undertaken extensive surveys and some small-scale excavations in the lowlands of the Humber basin. The remit of this project was the study of how people had lived in and off the wetlands over the last 10,000 years, and how their perception of it changed through time (Van de Noort 2004a).The study of wet-preserved remains, where anoxic environments enable the survival of organic artefactual and ecofactual remains, was a key aspect of the Humber Wetlands Project. The group that undertook this project was to form the core of the excavation team at Sutton Common, which lies just within the Humber Wetlands and is also characterised by wet-preservation of archaeological remains (Fig 1.8).

Proponents of wetland archaeology have claimed for several decades that the higher levels of preservation in wetlands have made it possible for wetland studies to enlighten aspects of the past that remain invisible in 'dryland' archaeology (eg Coles and Coles 1996; Coles 2001). The study of organic artefacts, and our understanding of the inter-relationship between people and the landscape, have benefited greatly from this. The higher-resolution dating made possible through radiocarbon and dendrochronological assay has also been seen as a significant contribution of wetland studies over its dryland equivalents.

Our view of wetlands archaeology is, however, also changing. Following criticism of a number of edited books on wetland archaeology (eg Scarre 1989; Evans 1990), or of the work of wetland research projects (Haselgrove *et al* 2001), wetland archaeology is increasingly developing a contextualised approach. Within this approach, it has become accepted that few, if any, wetlands can be studied without a geographical context that includes surrounding areas of higher and drier grounds from where, for example, flint and metals were obtained. The contextualised approach is also aiming at becoming more relevant to the theoretical debates in mainstream archaeology, and it has recently been proposed that wetland archaeology is particularly well placed to advance the study of the perceptions of landscapes, social identities, and material culture biographies (Van de Noort and O'Sullivan 2006).

### 1.3.1.3 Regional research contexts

The national debate on the function of hillforts and large enclosed sites, with all the socio-political implications springing from this, is of

*Figure 1.8 Aerial photograph of Sutton Common in 2000, looking north*

particular relevance for northern England. Barry Cunliffe (2005, fig 4.3) depicts the area (of 'northern and western' England) as one where 'villages and open settlement' dominate in the 2nd century BC, with no identified settlement pattern for the preceding centuries. Sutton Common, hillforts such as Grimthorpe on the Yorkshire Wolds, and multiple-enclosed sites such as nearby Little Smeaton (Stead 1968; Riley 1980; Manby 1988) sit uncomfortably in such a description, and in essence, the fundamental basis of Iron Age society or societies in this part of Britain remains poorly understood (Haselgrove 1999; Harding 2004).

Within the regional context, a number of recent contributions to Iron Age archaeology which touch on this and other relevant debates should be mentioned here. Dennis Harding's (2004) *The Iron Age of Northern Britain* offers a wide-ranging, albeit rather traditional view of the period. The recent publication of *The Archaeology of Yorkshire. An Assessment at the beginning of the 21st Century* (Manby *et al* 2003) disappoints somewhat in its treatment of the Iron Age outside East Yorkshire, but this exemplifies the paucity of well-dated sites that can make a significant contribution to our understanding of this period. It also is characterised by a rather conventional understanding of the Iron Age. Naomi Field and Mike Parker Pearson's (2003) book on the Iron Age timber trackway at Fiskerton, Lincolnshire, fully engages with the current debates in Iron Age archaeology discussed above, and must be recognised as a significant innovative approach to Iron Age studies. The publication of the excavations preceding the construction of the M1–A1 Link Road (Roberts *et al* 2001) is especially welcome for the diversity of (non-hilltop) sites it offers. Sites such as the large D-shaped enclosure from Swillington Common (*ibid*, 49), thought to be of middle Iron Age date, are as yet without parallel in this part of Britain. The recent write-up of many decades of research in the Trent Valley (Knight and Howard 2004) is also to be welcomed as a comparative study of a nearby lowland landscape. Finally, several of the edited volumes rethinking the British Iron Age (Hill and Cumberpatch 1995; Champion and Collis 1996; Gwilt and Haselgrove 1997a; Bevan 1999; Humphrey 2003) include papers considering the Iron Age of northern Britain, several of which are recognised as having made a significant contribution to the regional research context that is of direct relevance to the work at Sutton Common, most notably those by Chadwick (1999) and Robbins (1999).

We should not be seduced, to paraphrase Barry Cunliffe, by 'transient fashions and spurious political correctness' (1995, xi). However, we must also not be seduced by simply trying to make the evidence from Sutton Common 'fit' established ideas of the Iron Age. The recent publication of the research framework for the Iron Age (Haselgrove *et al* 2001) provides us, as excavators and authors of this report, with a contemporary structure for addressing issues that are pertinent to advancing our understanding of the British Iron Age, and has a clear resonance in the broader archaeological community. Time-honoured themes are neither forgotten nor ignored, and the archaeological evidence from Sutton Common has forced some long-standing research issues, as well as several novel ones, to be addressed.

### 1.3.2 *Overarching research aim*

The academic research design was built around the need to understand the character, morphology, development, spatial patterning, and environmental context of the Iron Age enclosures within local, regional, national, and international research contexts – the overarching research aim throughout the period of work presented here. The explicitly formulated aims and objectives of the project, however, developed significantly between 1998 and 2004. What started as an assessment of the state of preservation of the organic waterlogged archaeological and palaeoenvironmental remains in 1998, became an assessment in preparation for a management plan and a wetland conservation project in 1999, developing into the large-scale research excavations in 2002 and 2003 set within broader research contexts. Not until 2004, when the updated project design was written following the completion of the assessment of the excavation and formulation of the statement of potential, were the research objectives finalised.

Throughout this period, the importance of the management of the wetlands and the waterlogged remains was fully recognised, as was the role of Sutton Common as a 'beacon site' in the development of the strategy for the archaeological management of wetlands in England (Olivier and Van de Noort 2002). This aspect of the work is described in detail in chapter 2. This section is concerned principally with the research objectives related to the excavations.

### 1.3.3 *Research objectives*

Guiding the excavation and post-excavation analysis, seven research objectives were defined.

#### 1.3.3.1 Defining the character, morphology, and spatial patterning of the site

Defining the character, morphology, and spatial patterning of the site and features inside the larger enclosure was the first defined objective. Achieving this was seen as a potentially significant contribution to the study of enclosed settlements, including hillforts, elsewhere in Britain and further afield. The fact that Sutton Common is the only large enclosed site of Iron Age date for which the interior has been almost completely excavated, provides an unrivalled opportunity to understand the character of the site. When combined with the high-precision dating and palaeoenvironmental and material culture studies, the value of this understanding was to be much enhanced. Following the existing proposition that the smaller enclosure was effectively an elaborate entranceway leading to the large enclosure (Parker Pearson and Sydes 1997), full-scale excavations were not required here to attain this research objective.

### 1.3.3.2 Dating and phasing the site

The broad date ranges obtained from radiocarbon dates for the Iron Age period in England have resulted in an imprecise understanding of temporality and the dynamics of processes of change (Haselgrove *et al* 2001, 2–7, 25–31). Sutton Common, where dendrochronology provides absolute dates for the main activities such as the construction of the defences, gateways, and four-post structures, will be the first such site in England in terms of its potential to study the dynamics of the processes observed.

### 1.3.3.3 Defining the social construction of the site and its place in the wider landscape

The social construction of society in the Iron Age is one of the main themes of current debate (Haselgrove *et al* 2001, 22). The concept of hillforts or multivallate sites as residences of elite groups with redistributive functions continues to be understood by some Iron Age archaeologists as the best-fit model (Fig 1.9; Cunliffe 2005). In the last few decades, alternative models, for example that of hillforts as groups of enclosed farmsteads without evidence for social differentiation and redistribution, has gained considerable support (eg Hill 1995a; 1995b). Much of this debate is based on the evidence from Wessex and southern England (see section 1.3.1.1), and the excavations at Sutton Common will provide an important 'northern' perspective on the issue. 'All regions are important to reconstructing the complex social mosaic of the period, and need to be understood in their own right' (Haselgrove *et al* 2001, 23). The full analysis of the archaeological features and their dating will provide an important contribution to this debate.

On a local and regional level which comprises a landscape with undated or poorly dated sites and field systems, a clearer understanding of the temporal development of the site would provide the

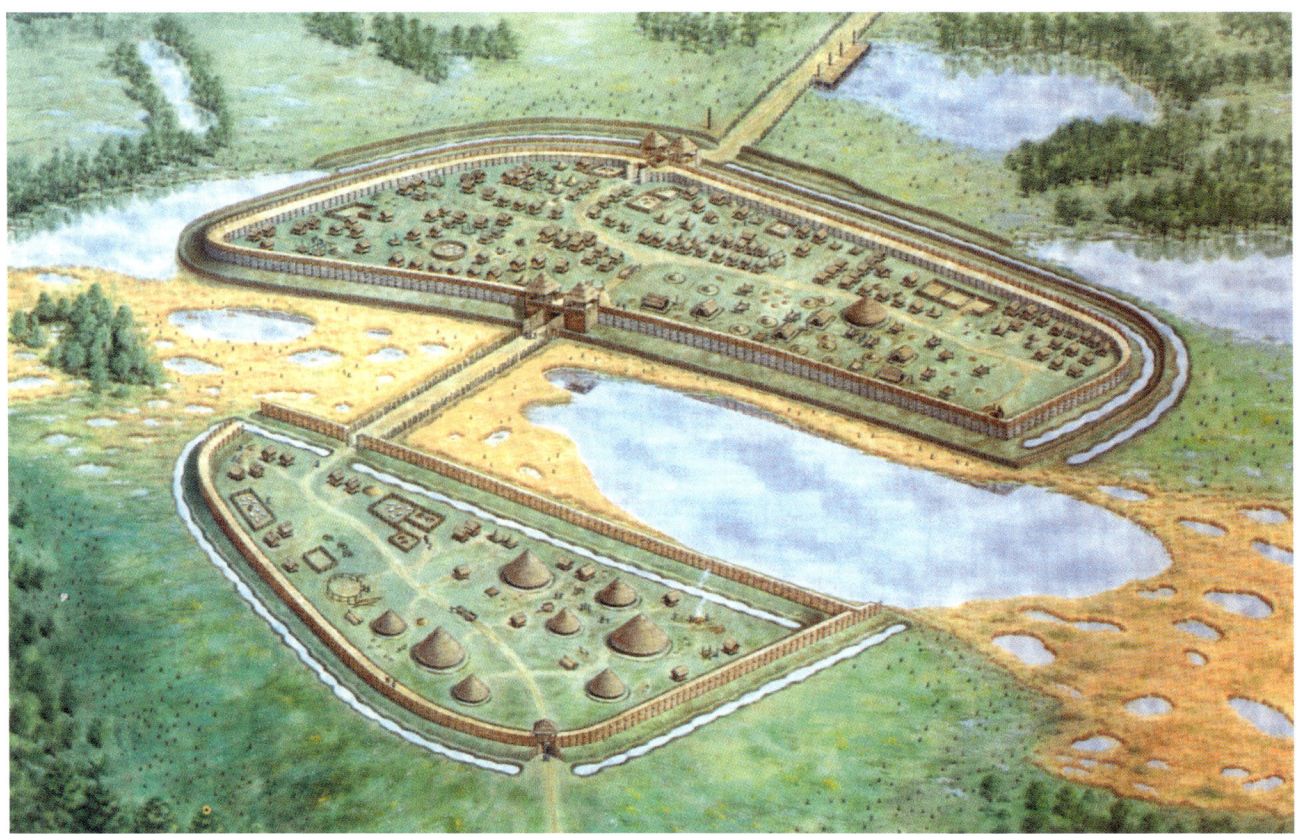

*Figure 1.9 Artist's impression of Sutton Common in the image of Danebury hillfort, for Doncaster Museum*

first step towards building a 'genuine Iron Age' (cf Haselgrove 1999). The excavations at Sutton Common can provide a significant advance in our understanding of the social system in the region – regionality lies, after all, at the heart of much debate on the British Iron Age (*ibid*, 22).

#### 1.3.3.4 Defining the interaction with the environment

As a former wetland, Sutton Common has the potential to provide a more detailed understanding of the interaction of enclosed sites with the environment than has ever been possible for hillforts, a theme identified as of importance in Iron Age archaeology (*ibid*, 14). The impact of the construction of the site on woodland in the region, through detailed study of the archaeological wood, and aspects of agriculture, through the analysis of plant macrofossils and animal bones, will greatly enhance our understanding of this aspect.

#### 1.3.3.5 Describing Iron Age mortuary rites

Outside the East Yorkshire 'Arras culture' burials, the mortuary archaeology of the Iron Age remains very poorly understood. Haselgrove *et al* (2001, 12–14) understandably highlight the need for detailed study of Iron Age burials wherever these are encountered. The integrated detailed study of the archaeological features, human remains, and associated small finds (glass bead and golden bracelet or ingot) from Sutton Common provides an important contribution to our understanding of Iron Age funerary behaviour. The Sutton Common mortuary activity connects with three current debates in mortuary archaeology: the use of the past in the past (eg Bradley 2002); the concept of personhood (Ingold 2000; Fowler 2004); and the concept of ephemerality of funerary monuments (eg Williams 2003).

#### 1.3.3.6 Understanding material culture, symbolism and cosmology

Recent discussions on the Iron Age have highlighted the concept of 'structured deposition', whereby material is deposited using guiding cosmological principles which may have been used to actively construct social identities and are thus agents of social reproduction (Haselgrove *et al* 2001, 19–20). The material from Sutton Common that is considered to represent structured deposits, excluding the material associated with the mortuary rings, includes:

- the two human heads and the pieces of yew found on the site in the outer ditch terminal to the north of the entrance;
- the bone weaving comb and the only substantial piece of pottery from the site, from the inner ditch terminal to the north of the eastern entrance;
- the majority of the animal bones from the two terminals to the south of the eastern entrance, intermingled with some human bone fragments and teeth;
- the charred grains of spelt and emmer found in specific postholes, especially those interpreted as being part of four-post structures;
- the fourteen quern stone fragments, from several diverse contexts.

The structurally deposited artefacts and bones from the ditch terminals were found within a matrix of well-preserved deposits containing palaeoenvironmental information. Through the integration of all this material, new insights into the phenomenon may be obtained.

#### 1.3.3.7 Describing the Iron Age woodworking technology and woodland management

The archaeological wood collection from Sutton Common is biased towards the architectural side, with no portable artefacts present, but nevertheless is unrivalled for the early Iron Age. The construction techniques used, with flat-bottomed posts set into very tight post pits, may not be typical for Britain but are better known from the Low Countries, where people adapted to building in relatively soft sediments in similar fashion. The study of the archaeological wood, combined with dendrochronological studies, may also provide an unmatched insight into the woodland management of the Iron Age.

## 1.4 Project Design and organisation of the project  *by R Van de Noort and H Chapman*

### 1.4.1 Project Design

Working within the *Managing Archaeological Projects* 2, or MAP2 (English Heritage 1999) structure, several project designs and reports were produced during the decade of research that has resulted in this report – Project Designs in 1998, 1999 (which included an assessment of the 1998 excavations) and 2001, which set out the large-scale excavations undertaken in 2002 and 2003 (Van de Noort and Chapman 2001), and an Updated Project Design including the statements of potential in advance of the post-excavation analysis (Van de Noort 2004b).

The 1998 excavations were small in scale, and aimed principally at determining the state of preservation of both wet-preserved and other archaeological remains in both enclosures. They included a trench in the Hampole Beck palaeochannel, where the causeway linking the two enclosures was expected to have been. Five small trenches were excavated that year, ascertaining that the site still contained significant wet-preserved remains, but that these were drying out in all but a few places.

Recognising that all previous research had been located against previous trenches or the eroding corners of the monument itself, a new 30×30m grid system was developed for Sutton Common in advance of the excavations in 1999. The new grid was fixed to the Ordnance Survey National Grid Reference System using differential GPS (see section 1.2.6), and all work from 1999 onwards has taken place utilising this grid system.

In 1999, an assessment of the state of preservation of the larger enclosure was undertaken. This included the excavation of the west-facing entrance (in an area of 30×30m) and ten trenches across the site, each measuring 30×3m (Figs 1.10 and 1.11). This work showed that enough of the archaeological features survived within the interior of the larger enclosure to allow for the reconstruction of a complete ground plan. This work also showed that any wet-preserved wood, and thus the ability to date the phases of the features through high-precision dendrochronology, was under imminent threat. It was estimated that within ten years the continued desiccation of the archaeological wood here would have rendered dendrochronology unsuccessful, and any further work should therefore commence without further delay. The subsequent large-scale excavations in 2002 and 2003 were to vindicate this assessment fully.

In 2002 and 2003, after a delay of just over a year during an outbreak of Foot and Mouth Disease in Britain, the larger enclosure was excavated. Using the grid system, eight west–east orientated trenches were planned, with the even-numbered trenches excavated in 2002, and the odd-numbered trenches in 2003 (Fig 1.11). The merits of this approach, as opposed to excavating the larger enclosure in one large-scale excavation or two halves, included the minimisation of machine movements on the site, which was to remain a scheduled ancient monument, and the creation of an excavation strategy that allowed for any lessons learnt during the work in 2002 to be applied in 2003 (Fig 1.12). This was the case, for example, with the sampling strategy of postholes, which was changed for the 2003 campaign on the basis of the assessment of the samples taken in 2002.

In advance of the 2003 campaign, further amendments to the original excavation plan were introduced following the publication of the research framework for the British Iron Age (Haselgrove *et al* 2001). These included a series of ten trenches each 3m wide exploring the area to the north and east of the larger enclosure, the full

*Figure 1.10 Overview of the excavation of the west-facing entrance in 1999, with the smaller enclosure in the background*

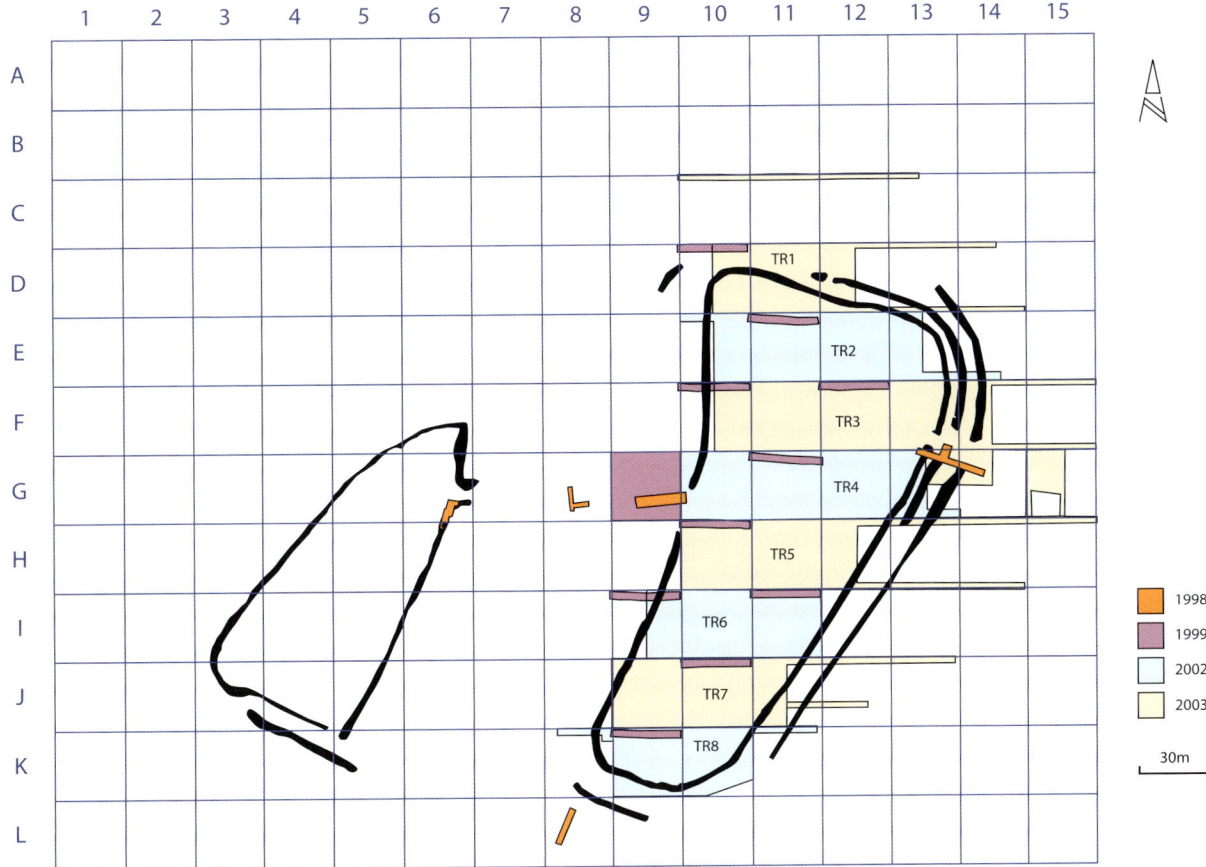

*Figure 1.11   The location of the excavation trenches with the 30×30m grid superimposed*

excavation of the principal ditch terminals of the east-facing entranceway of the larger enclosure, and an intensive programme of on-site wet sieving.

In advance of the 2003 excavation, English Heritage undertook a full geophysical survey of the site, including the Hampole Beck palaeochannel and the smaller enclosure. Although this did not reveal any additional internal features, it did produce fresh insights into the outline of the smaller enclosure (see section 5.2). From 1997 onwards, the Common was regularly photographed from the air, and these photographs were considered during the various stages of analysis. During the penultimate weeks of both the 2002 and 2003 campaign, low-level aerial photography of the site was achieved by using a helicopter.

Following the 2003 excavation, assessment of the material and formulation of the statements of potential resulted in defining the research objectives (see section 1.3.3). This work was undertaken in 2004 through to 2006, when the current report was completed.

### 1.4.2   Organisation of the work

The excavations in 1998 and 1999 were undertaken by the University of Hull, the 2002 and 2003 excavations by the Universities of Exeter and Hull. The archaeological research was directed by Robert Van de Noort and co-directed by Henry Chapman.

The fieldwork was organised in trenches. In 1998 and 1999, these were supervised by Henry Chapman. In 2002 and 2003, the trench supervisors were Helen Fenwick (Trenches 1 and 2), William Fletcher (Trenches 3 and 4), Gavin Thomas (Trenches 5 and 6) and James Cheetham (Trenches 7 and 8). Each trench supervisor was supported by two experienced excavators, and a variable number of students from the Universities of Exeter and Hull, and also local volunteers. Archivist Robert Smith ensured consistency of recording across the trenches, and Malcolm Lillie was the site's photographer.

Environmental specialists met as a team before and after the excavations, and they visited the site during both campaigns. Sampling strategies were discussed and agreed on site with the site director. Environmental samples were kept in cold stores at Exeter and Hull, and the sediment processing for macrofossils was undertaken by Frances and Michael Issitt at Exeter. Neil Mitchell of APS UK was responsible for the aerial photography of the site before, during, and after the excavations.

*Figure 1.12 Aerial photograph of the excavations in 2002, looking south*

The post-excavation work was organised by Robert Van de Noort, and Henry Chapman undertook the digitisation of the excavation plans and the analysis of the features in ArcInfo GIS. The individual specialists involved in the post-excavation analysis are all included as named authors in this report. The editing of the reports was undertaken by Robert Van de Noort and Henry Chapman, and John Collis was invited on to the editorial team as the 'Iron Age specialist', ensuring that the report was fully integrated within the current archaeological research contexts for that period.

The archaeological investigations at Sutton Common between 1998 and 2003 were funded by English Heritage. The total cost for the project was approximately £470,000, with the excavations accounting for £290,000 and the post-excavation analysis and writing of this report for £180,000. These amounts exclude the cost of English Heritage staff time. The management of the project was, as required by MAP2, determined by the project manager (Robert Van de Noort), Dr Helen Keeley as the Project Officer for English Heritage, and Inspectors of Ancient Monuments Jon Etté (up to 2000) and Keith Miller (from 2000).

# 2 Setting the scene: the 'Sutton Common Project'

## 2.1 Introduction  *by R Van de Noort, I Carstairs, K Miller and H Chapman*

### 2.1.1 Background

The archaeological excavations and research at Sutton Common were, from 1997 onwards, part of a larger project. To the many individuals and organisations that were involved here, this project was known as the Sutton Common Project, but it was never designed as such; rather, it evolved and developed over the years from 1997.

In terms of achieving the research ambitions as set out in the previous chapter, it should be noted that the excavations as described in this book would never have taken place without the broader project. There are several reasons for this. Logistically, it would simply not have been possible to excavate on the scale of the 2002 and 2003 excavations during the summer (the only period when the water table was sufficiently low) without being constrained by the arable use of the land or, conversely, be required to pay significant sums of compensation to the farmer for loss of income. Close cooperation between the excavators and landowner, CCT, and the Trust's licensee farmer, Andrew Booth, is recognised as a key aspect to the success of the project, and this ranged from such simple things as access to running and clear water to rehydrate the exposed archaeological timbers and exhausted diggers and allow for on-site wet sieving, to complex matters of liability and third party insurance. Politically, without the Sutton Common Project, it is unlikely that English Heritage would have supported the excavations financially to the extent it did. Notwithstanding the merits of the academic aspects of the research, the fact that these were embedded in policies to create a sustainable environment for the site, alongside unparalleled joined-up action by a number of governmental organisations and the empowerment of the local community, undoubtedly convinced officers, advisors, and commissioners at English Heritage of the value and importance of the excavations of the Iron Age site at Sutton Common. Ethically, many archaeologists have come to realise that ownership of the archaeological remains is not simply theirs alone, but that we are, at best, the guardians of these relics from the past. The question 'Whose archaeology is it anyway?', is now frequently asked, and high-profile debates surrounding Stonehenge and 'Seahenge' have provided clear responses that we must recognise all interested parties and individuals as stakeholders. The broader Sutton Common Project, spearheaded by CCT, provided the vehicle for active and passive participation of local people interested in the archaeology and wildlife of the Common, which is exemplified in the publication of *The Marsh of Time. Saving Sutton Common* (Smith 2004), a popular book aimed at providing the local community with up-to-date and accessible information on their Common. The project also provided a framework for governmental and non-governmental organisations to take part in, and learn from, this rather special venture.

This chapter presents the diverse aspects of the Sutton Common Project. A vision for the future of the Common is included in the final chapter (see section 10.5).

### 2.1.2 Aims and objectives

The ultimate aim for the broader project was the development of a sustainable future for Sutton Common. This was rather an ambitious goal. Albeit a former wetland, it was evident that without immediate action the last remaining wet-preserved archaeological remains would desiccate and disappear in a matter of years. Two decades of intensive arable agriculture had significantly changed the soil chemistry, and it was unclear what irredeemable damage had been done to the archaeological and palaeoenvironmental remains below the surface. Alongside the concerns for the archaeology on the Common, the preservation or improvement of the nearby Shirley Pool SSSI had become a major objective. It was also recognised that sustainability was not just a matter of creating the right physical environment. The development of a sense of local involvement and ownership of Sutton Common was part of that sustainability strategy. The objectives set by the Sutton Common Project can be divided into four themes.

First, the need for practical actions to halt the loss of water was recognised as a principal objective. The purchase of the Common, and the extension of CCT's ownership northwards to include the Rushy Moor fields as far north as Stream Dike, made possible financially by English Heritage, the Heritage Lottery Fund, English Nature, the Countryside Agency, and WREN Environmental, provided opportunities to explore various schemes of retaining precipitation. However, despite the many decades of archaeological research in wetlands (eg Coles and Coles 1996), relatively little research had been done in the field of preserving wetland sites *in situ*. This is not to suggest that no work had been undertaken in this field, but the available publications (eg Coles 1995) simply did not provide a basis for the scale of the problems faced at Sutton Common. In particular, the return of formerly intensively farmed land into semi-natural wetland, and the recreation of a burial environment that reduced microbial activity in the soil, had never been undertaken on this scale. Thus, no scientific evidence or best-practice guidance was available, and much of the practical work on the Common was innovative. This aspect of this research, and its wider implications, are discussed further below (see section 2.2).

Second, recognising the paucity of research in large-scale and long-term rewetting projects, the need for continued research into a range of aspects of *in situ* preservation of wet-preserved archaeological and palaeoenvironmental remains at Sutton Common was identified as an issue. To address this, a hydrological monitoring study was set up to monitor the groundwater table on the Common, and to monitor changes in the soil chemistry and soil micro-organism activity (see section 2.3).

Third, the need for integrated management of the site, within the partnership forged with statutory and other organisations, became an important aspect of the Sutton Common Project in its own right. The need for multi-agency cooperation to achieve significant results in wetland protection is now broadly accepted (see section 2.2.2), but in 1997 this was not the case.

Fourth, the need to share the 'ownership' of the archaeological site and the Common with the local community and others with an interest was an important objective of the Sutton Common Project, and was recognised as a key aspect of sustainable management of the Common.

## 2.2 Wetland management
*by R Van de Noort*

### 2.2.1 The drainage and rewetting of Sutton Common

#### 2.2.1.1 Drainage

Sutton Common lies on the edge of the Humber Wetlands, in the Humberhead Levels region. This once extensive wetland in the low-lying lands of the Humber basin had been brought into cultivation in the Middle Ages. Large-scale arterial drainage projects were undertaken here in the 17th century, including those by Cornelius Vermuyden and his Participants in the 1620s just to the east of Sutton Common in Hatfield Chase (Van de Noort 2004a). The main changes in the water table, from the point of view of its impact on wet-preserved archaeological remains, did not occur however until the mid-19th century with the introduction of steam pumps into the region, and, again, in the 1970s when agricultural intensification associated with the Common Agriculture Policy was accompanied by a significant drop in the already artificially low water table (Van de Noort and Davies 1993).

Being located on the very margins of the Humberhead Levels, and with the Hampole Beck palaeochannel ceasing as an active part of the river system sometime in prehistory, no significant attempts had been made to drain the Common in the 17th or 18th centuries. The Common was enclosed in 1858, being by then the last sizeable Common in the Humberhead Levels (Miller 2004), and it seemed likely that with the privatisation the first attempts were made to improve the land by the digging of ditches and draining of the land. Thus, the first detailed recording of the enclosures on the Common by the Rev Scott F Surtees (1868; see section 1.2.1) included the observation of (presumably) Iron Age timber stumps in the ground belonging to the causeway linking the smaller and larger enclosures, a clear sign that the peat was desiccating and shrinking.

Matters came to a head in the 1980s. The larger enclosure was bulldozed in 1980, with the upstanding earthworks being dumped into the ditches, and field drains were installed across the Common in 1982, avoiding only the smaller enclosure (Figs 2.1, 2.2). The local drainage had two important negative impacts on the archaeology. First, it increased the rapidity of precipitation run-off further, lowering the water table in the process and bringing much of the archaeology within the zone of aeration. Second, the land became suitable for arable use, thus introducing a new regime that included ploughing and high levels of fertilisation, damaging all near-surface remains and changing the soil chemistry. The various small-scale excavations in the 1980s and early 1990s recorded the effect of these changes on the archaeology at Sutton Common (see section 1.2.4).

#### 2.2.1.2 Rewetting

The transfer of the Common to CCT in 1997 was intended to halt the harmful effects of arable farming in the short term, and to minimise the impact of the changes of the water table in the medium term, whilst providing the opportunity for large-scale excavations to take place without delay or limitations. Although the move from arable to pasture landuse was not without its problems (for example, the uncontrolled growth of thistles in the nutrient-rich soil increased the evapotranspiration), the main focus of this work involved attempts to raise the groundwater table to a level where primary archaeological material could be preserved in a saturated environment.

22  Sutton Common

*Figure 2.1   The Common before the bulldozing of the enclosures (Crown copyright. NMR, Riley collection)*

*Figure 2.2   The Common after the bulldozing of the enclosures (Crown copyright. NMR, Riley collection)*

The modelling of the land (see section 1.2.6) had already shown that the Common could not be fully returned to a wetland. Raising the groundwater table to a level where it would saturate all soil that contained organic archaeological remains would have required either damming the Common or flooding large tracts of land, recreating something the size of the Late-glacial Lake Humber (see section 4.2.1); neither option was considered sustainable. Thus a minimum target was set, at 4.1m OD, whereby the ditch deposits thought to be associated with the construction and use/occupation of the site and the peats of the Hampole Beck palaeochannel would be waterlogged year-round (eg Van de Noort *et al* 2001a; 2001b). Raising the groundwater table on the Common would impact directly on Shirley Pool SSSI, the lowest part of the catchment, but English Nature welcomed more water here, in what is one of the last remaining ancient fenland areas in the Humber Wetlands (Kohler 2004).

Two sets of action were taken in 1999 and 2000. First, the ditches surrounding the Common were dammed, with the tops of the dams designed to contribute to retaining all water up to the 4.1.m OD level. Second, the permeable underfield drains (Fig 2.3) were connected first to an impermeable pipe, several metres back from their original outfall, and then to an upturned pipe within a concrete chamber, with the upturned pipe again set at a height whereby groundwater below 4.1m OD would not be discharged. The removal of the field drains would have caused considerable damage to the Iron Age enclosures, and the re-engineering of the underfield drainage system would enable future management of the groundwater table of the Common by varying the outfall height of the upturned pipe (Carstairs 2004).

These actions have undoubtedly helped to raise the groundwater of the Common (see section 2.3), but the impact has been insufficient to achieve the set target of a year-round minimum water table at 4.1m OD. During the winter months, the water budget is positive, but during the summer months the water budget is a negative one, with precipitation insufficient to balance the evaporation and evapotranspiration. Further actions are being considered, including the possibility for a reservoir of oxygen-deficient rainwater which would permeate the ground during the summer months.

### 2.2.2 English Heritage Strategy for Wetlands

On World Wetlands Day 2002, English Heritage published its *Strategy for Wetlands* (Olivier and Van de Noort 2002). It considers the future of the wetland resource from an archaeological point of view and it is the first such statement for a whole nation (Olivier 2004). The work at Sutton

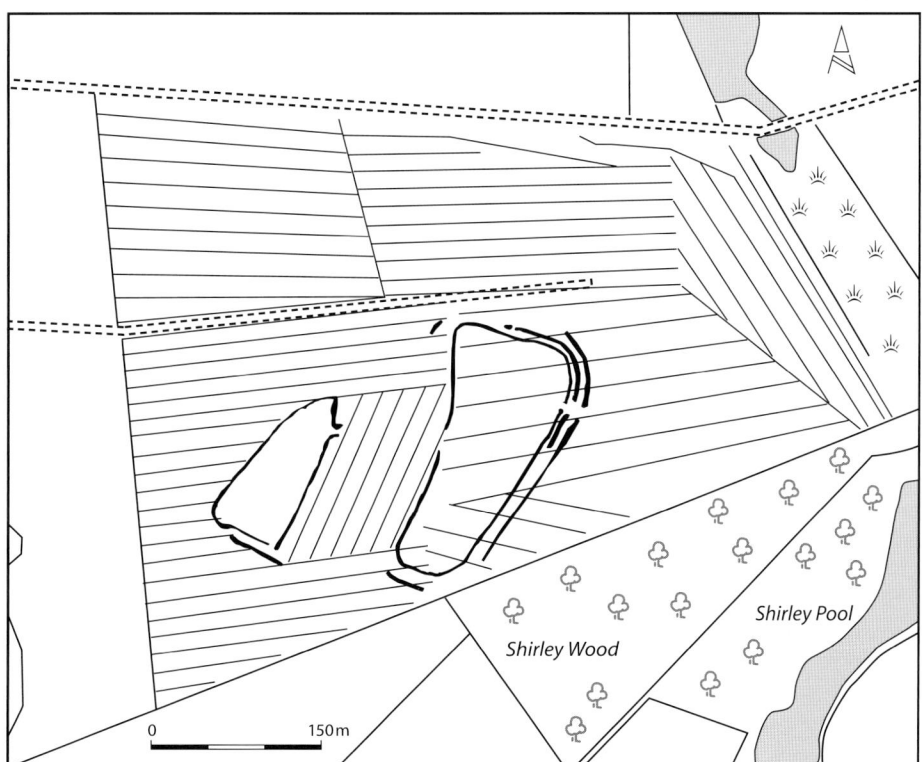

*Figure 2.3 Map of the Common with the locations of the underfield drainage system*

Common can be considered as having acted as a catalyst or test case for many of the ideas that have been included in the *Strategy*.

The *Strategy* defined its objectives under four headings. These were:

- Policy and procedure: promote the cultural heritage interests of wetlands in the work of local authorities, national, international, and intergovernmental agencies;
- Management strategies: promote practical mechanisms to integrate cultural and nature conservation interests in wetland management;
- Education and outreach: raise awareness of the value of wetland archaeology by promoting and disseminating understanding and appreciation of wetland heritage;
- Research and understanding: develop a coherent research strategy to enhance the understanding of monuments at risk in England's wetlands and the various pressures on them.

The promotion of the cultural heritage interests of wetlands in the work of local authorities, and national, international, and intergovernmental agencies is an important task. Research had found that the overwhelming majority of local authorities had no policy in place on the identification, assessment, preservation or management of wetland archaeology, which results in the ongoing damage and destruction of waterlogged remains (Van de Noort *et al* 2002). This issue has been addressed through the enhancement of existing HER and SMR data and the inclusion of this in the Wetland Vision GIS being developed by Natural England and the Royal Society for the Protection of Birds. On a national level, a mid- to long-term aim is to amend the national legislation so that palaeoenvironmental archives can be included in the definition of an archaeological monument, and to consider changes that allow control of the hydrology of wetlands that are important as archaeological sites and landscapes. On an international level, the inclusion of the cultural values into conventions of wetlands, notable in the definition of Ramsar sites, would encourage further cooperation between archaeological and nature conservation organisations, and also promote the holistic protection of wetlands.

The promotion of practical mechanisms to integrate cultural and natural conservation interests forms the core of the *Strategy*. Waterlogged sites can only be sustainably preserved *in situ* by controlling their associated hydrology. Thus, we must protect whole wetlands rather than 'monument islands' (cf Darvill and Fulton 1998) and, in order to protect whole wetlands, archaeologists must develop practical cooperation with non-archaeological bodies that have an interest in wetlands. Importantly, such cooperation enables the conservation of evidence for human activity that falls short of the definition of 'monument' in the Ancient Monuments Act 1979, including palaeoenvironmental archives. In cases where wetlands are designated as National Nature Reserves, Special Protection Areas, Sites of Special Scientific Interest, or Ramsar sites, these archives will benefit from statutory protection, if and when cooperating organisations are willing to consider the needs of the archaeological resource. In fact, such cooperation is at present the *only* way in which we can achieve protection of this component, short of purchasing the whole wetland for the purpose of protecting the archaeological and palaeoenvironmental resource. Therefore, a prime objective of the *Strategy* was to ensure that nature conservation agencies take on board the needs of the archaeological resource in their own management process. In order to achieve this, the archaeological community will need to develop accessible best-practice guidelines for other stakeholders, and produce management guidelines for the most important wetland archaeological sites and landscapes. One of the implementation projects commissioned by English Heritage since the publication of the *Strategy* is designed to address these issues, and involves the creation of an inventory of the most important wetland sites, the production of management plans for these, the creation of generic management plans for different wetland landscapes, and training for archaeologists and the other stakeholders.

The need to continue to raise awareness of the value of wetland archaeology forms one of the most challenging tasks. Wetland archaeology is mostly invisible, buried by peat or alluvium, and every opportunity must be taken to provide public access to excavations of wetland sites, be it during Open Days, public participation in fieldwork, or community involvement at all stages of research. The 'Preservation Hall' at Flag Fen is currently the only place in England where practical wetland archaeology is accessible year-round. A number of reconstructions are visible, notably at the Peat Moors Centre in the Somerset Levels, but reconstructions are at best a good alternative to the real thing. The publication of non-specialist books and use of other media must also be promoted. The special wetland issue of *Current Archaeology* (no. 172, February 2001) is a good example of how exposure of wetland archaeology can be achieved, and (in this case) distributed to a readership of over 20,000 people.

Lastly, the development of a coherent research strategy to enhance the understanding of monuments at risk and the various pressures on them is required. In doing this, wetland archaeology would follow a wider trend in English archaeology, where the production of regional, periodical, and thematic research frameworks has been promoted (Olivier 1996; eg Williams and Brown 1999; Haselgrove *et al* 2001). Such a prioritisation of research would build upon the inventory of the most important wetland sites in England, and would include both academic objectives and the development of a coherent approach to the monitoring of wetland sites, taking into account the growing body of scientific work undertaken internationally (eg Van Heeringen and Theunissen 2002).

### 2.2.3 Sutton Common as a beacon site

The Sutton Common Project has played a significant role in the development of many of the ideas presented in the *English Heritage Strategy for Wetlands*, and several of the key players involved with the research underpinning the *Strategy*, and developing the *Strategy* itself, were involved at various levels of the work at Sutton Common. For example, the team that drafted the *Monuments at Risk in England's Wetlands* report was drawn from the various participants of the Sutton Common Project (Van de Noort *et al* 2002). Recognising its potential role for disseminating good practice in wetland management, Sutton Common has been made one of the national beacon sites.

The wetland beacon sites are to offer platforms for practical cooperation between different governmental and non-governmental agencies involved with wetland management, conservation, and restoration, a keystone in the *Strategy*. It is foreseen that this will not only result in the long-term and sustainable management of these sites within their wider landscape context, but also in the forging of contacts between inspectors and managers across the cultural heritage – natural environment conservation spectrum. As part of this development, management plans have been produced for all beacon sites in England in close cooperation with the local stakeholders and the relevant regional Archaeological Science Advisors and Inspectors of Ancient Monuments. The structure of management plans adheres to that in general use within the Ramsar framework (*New Guidelines for management planning for Ramsar sites and other wetlands*), and as used by most nature conservation organisations including English Nature, the Royal Society for the Protection of Birds, and the National Trust (available at www.ex.ac.uk/hmew).

As a beacon site, Sutton Common has forged links between various agencies and individuals involved in wetland management in the Yorkshire and Humber Region, and was presented to the directors of the Heritage Lottery Fund as a best-practice example by English Heritage Chief Archaeologist David Miles. It also featured, significantly, as a key component in the Value in Wetness Initiative. This project, undertaken by the Countryside Agency, pursued sustainable land and water management, using the Humberhead Levels as its study area and Sutton Common as the principal site for testing and demonstrating its ideas. The initiative aimed to show that alternative management of water could bring economic, social, and environmental benefits and that draining the low-lying lands in the winter as quickly as possible, followed by droughts in the summer was not sustainable, and contradicts the European Union Water Framework Directive (Pasley and Cheetham 2004).

## 2.3 Hydrological studies and monitoring *by J Cheetham*

### 2.3.1 Introduction

Shortly after the transfer of landownership to CCT in 1997, recommendations were made that any rewetting should be accompanied by a programme of monitoring and this began in 1998. The broad aims of this research encompassed two areas:

- to research and develop techniques and standard practices for monitoring sites containing organic archaeological remains, with the aim of securing the future successful *in situ* preservation of such sites;
- to characterise the burial conditions of the archaeological resource on Sutton Common and identify the impacts of the mitigation strategy that had been carried out.

The successful management of archaeological sites containing organic remains must include an element of monitoring. Without this, there is no mechanism by which the quality of waterlogged archaeological sites can be assessed. Developing standard practices, methodologies, and equipment for this purpose should encourage more widespread monitoring and therefore identify where successful preservation *in situ* can take place.

Three key variables have been the subject of study on Sutton Common:

- soil hydrology relating to the dynamics of the water table (see section 2.3.2);
- soil chemistry (see section 2.3.3);
- microbiological activity through the soil profile (see section 2.3.4).

This multidisciplinary approach was chosen to provide the most accurate assessment of conditions within the burial environment within the financial and temporal constraints of the project. By utilising varied methods, the data acquired were considered to have the potential to provide supporting evidence for any observed chronological trends, which is considered crucial when measuring a complex burial system.

### 2.3.2 Hydrological monitoring

Hydrological monitoring was undertaken on Sutton Common in order to gain an understanding of the form and the dynamics of the water table and how these varied throughout the yearly cycle. The data have also been used to attempt to identify the impact of the drainage mitigation. It is vital to account for the degree of saturation within the burial environment when studying organic archaeological remains, as it is the primary factor in determining the level and extent of preservation. Previous studies into preservation *in situ* have recognised this (eg Björdal and Nilsson 2002; Brunning *et al* 2000; Powell *et al* 2001). Without this, the impact of significant factors such as seasonal variation cannot be assessed accurately and therefore no meaningful insight into preservation potential or characterisation can be made.

#### 2.3.2.1 Water level monitoring

The water table was monitored through a network of 50 piezometers in a 50 × 50m grid stretching across the main features of the site. The equipment was installed in the second half of 1998 as part of a short-term assessment (Van de Noort and Chapman 1999), and formed the core of the research monitoring programme following on from this. The location of all monitoring points used during the research carried out on Sutton Common can be seen in Figure 2.4. A piezometer is a simple field device for measuring hydraulic head (that is the sum of the gravitational energy and the groundwater pressure energy). It consists of a pipe, open to the flow of water at its base and open to the atmosphere at its top. At Sutton Common, it is the near-surface, unconfined aquifer that has been the subject of monitoring as its water table has contributed to the wet-preservation of the archaeological remains. Monitoring was undertaken on a two-week basis, with depths of water within the piezometers being obtained via an acoustic sounder. Monitoring took place between October 1998 and March 2002. Depth readings were recorded against OD and were used to model the form of the water table by using ESRI ArcGIS and a tension spline interpolation method.

This modelling showed a number of significant features, including the presence of a dome-shaped groundwater table beneath the topographically higher area which includes the larger enclosure (Enclosure A). The size and extent of this groundwater dome varied significantly across the seasons, being at its largest during times of greater saturation in the winter months. A second, much smaller, groundwater dome was shown to exist in

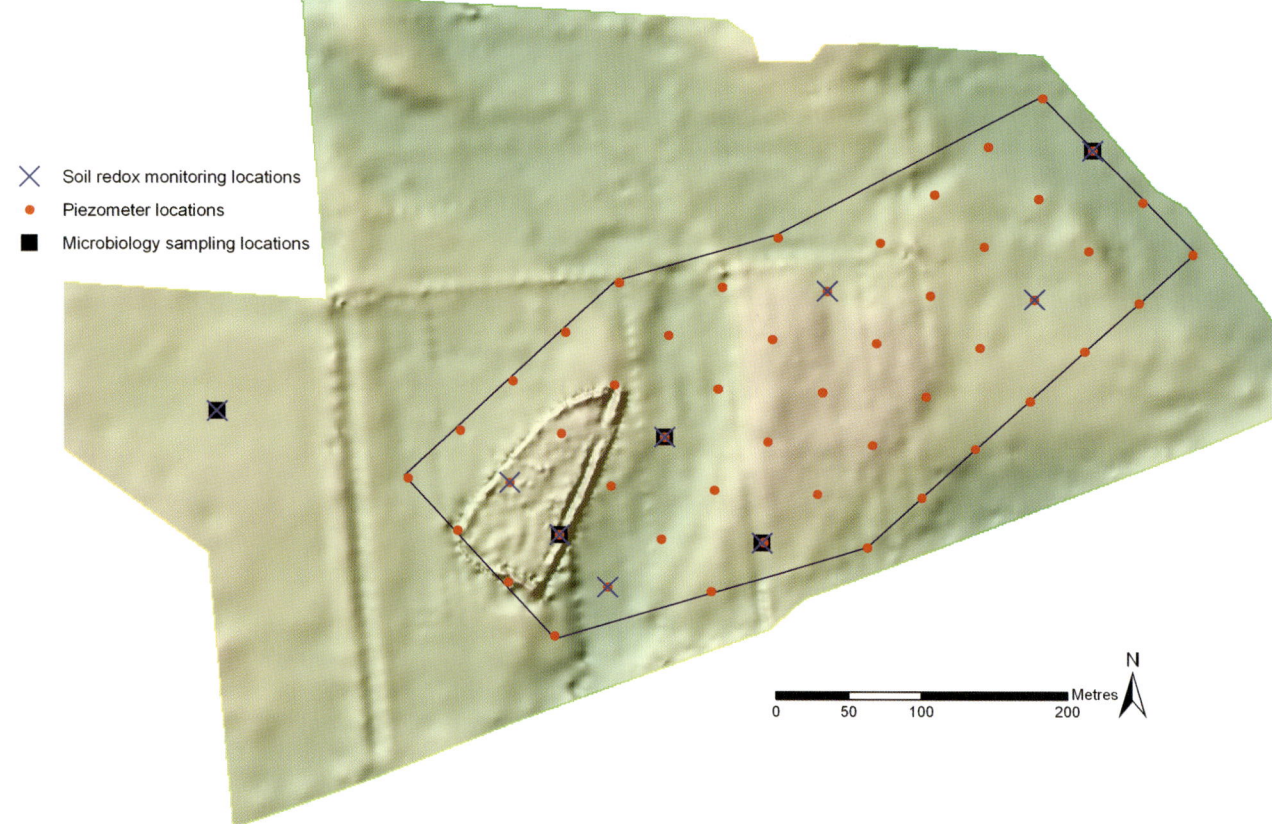

*Figure 2.4  Monitoring locations for Sutton Common shown on a Digital Elevation Model (DEM)*

the area of the smaller enclosure (Enclosure B), but only during the wetter winter months. Figure 2.5 illustrates this doming of the water table, including that occurring beneath Enclosure B, using data obtained during March 2002. The seasonal fluctuation in the height of the groundwater table in some areas was almost 2m, and was consistent throughout the monitoring period. These changes relate to increased rates of precipitation during the winter months and to a reduction in the loss of groundwater through evapotranspiration. The period of maximum water table height can be considered to occur between approximately December and June. The change in conditions from high to low water levels happened rapidly, over a matter of a few weeks. Whereas winter water levels were more or less constant, summer levels invariably continued to fall until the return of winter conditions in December.

The hydrological models also showed that the water table responded to single precipitation events but that this is, to some extent, controlled by existing soil conditions and the time of year: where saturated conditions are prevalent during winter months, the water table can be seen to react rapidly to precipitation events; however, during the summer months this is not necessarily the case as precipitation, even from quite large events, may not actually reach the groundwater reservoir but instead is intercepted by surface vegetation and absorbed by the soil itself.

### 2.3.2.2 The Sutton Common water budget model

The rainfall received on Sutton Common during 2000 was in excess of 700mm, much of this falling in the final quarter of the year, against an average annual rainfall of c 600mm (Ellis 1997). As a result, extensive flooding was experienced in the region at this time. During this period, the drainage pumps on the Thistle Goit drain were turned off, resulting in the backing up of water onto Sutton Common. This provided an opportunity to study the potential consequences of such an event.

Although the flood waters were allowed to stand for only a few days, an elevated water table continued to be recorded in the following months. The flooding occurred in November 2000 and elevated levels were maintained on the site until the following summer, with levels only dropping in June/July 2001. This showed, on the one hand, that the drainage mitigation (see section 2.2.1.2) had been effective at preventing drainage of the site but, on the other, it also demonstrated that water loss from the site was occurring by other means. In order to identify this loss, a water budget model was created identifying inputs and outputs to the groundwater reservoir for the area

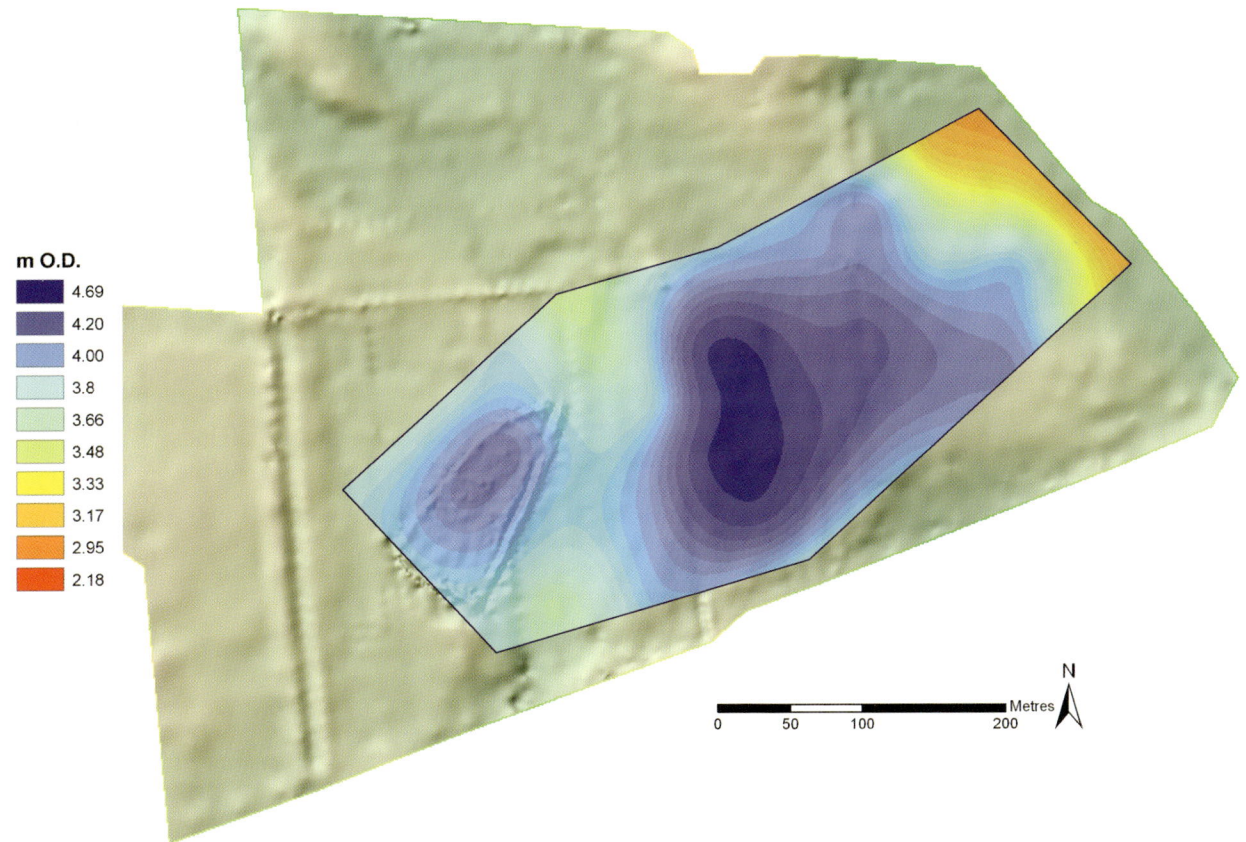

*Figure 2.5 Hydrological model derived from monitoring results obtained on 1 March 2002*

within the monitoring grid. Through the use of GIS it was possible to calculate the volume of water held within the groundwater reservoir and how this changed over time.

The hypothesis was proposed that the Sutton Common site is hydrologically isolated as a result of the drainage mitigation and underlying impermeable clays and that water storage was determined by inputs from precipitation and losses from evapotranspiration only. Testing this hypothesis established that there was a significant correlation between changes in effective precipitation (total precipitation minus evapotranspiration), and changes in the water storage component. This indicated that precipitation arriving direct on the site was the predominant source of water at Sutton Common, rather than any introduced by the drainage infrastructure or as groundwater flow. This conclusion is further supported by comparison with changes within the water levels of deep boreholes recorded by the British Geological Survey in the area. Although seasonal variation could be identified in one of these, there was significant lag between changes observed on Sutton Common and those in the borehole records, suggesting that Sutton Common is not significantly influenced by changes in the water levels of the underlying deep aquifer.

#### 2.3.2.3 Archaeological wood model

Comparing the location of individual pieces of archaeological wood with the recorded levels of the water table made it possible to link preservation with saturation, and allowed for predictions to be made for the future preservation *in situ* of the remaining archaeological resource. Three zones of saturation were identified which provide an insight into the potential for continued preservation (Chapman and Cheetham 2002). These are:

- Zone 1: permanently dry, which are generally surface soils only subject to periodic saturation from individual precipitation events;
- Zone 2: intermittently saturated zone, which occurs where the water table rises and falls on a seasonal basis;
- Zone 3: the permanently saturated zone existing below the lowest level of the annual water table.

Utilising ArcGIS to generate average water level models representing the water table at Sutton Common before and after the rewetting work had taken place, Figure 2.6 presents data showing the depth of archaeological wood relative to the height range of the water table prior to, and following, drainage mitigation. The results of this exercise suggest that the drainage mitigation has had a positive effect. This is indicated by higher minimum water levels indicating an increase in the extent of Zone 3 conditions of permanent saturation. However, whether this is as a direct result of reduced drainage or a decrease in evapotranspiration resulting from more controlled management of on-site vegetation remains undecided.

### 2.3.3 Soil redox monitoring

Previous studies have identified that sites exhibiting well-preserved organic material consistently

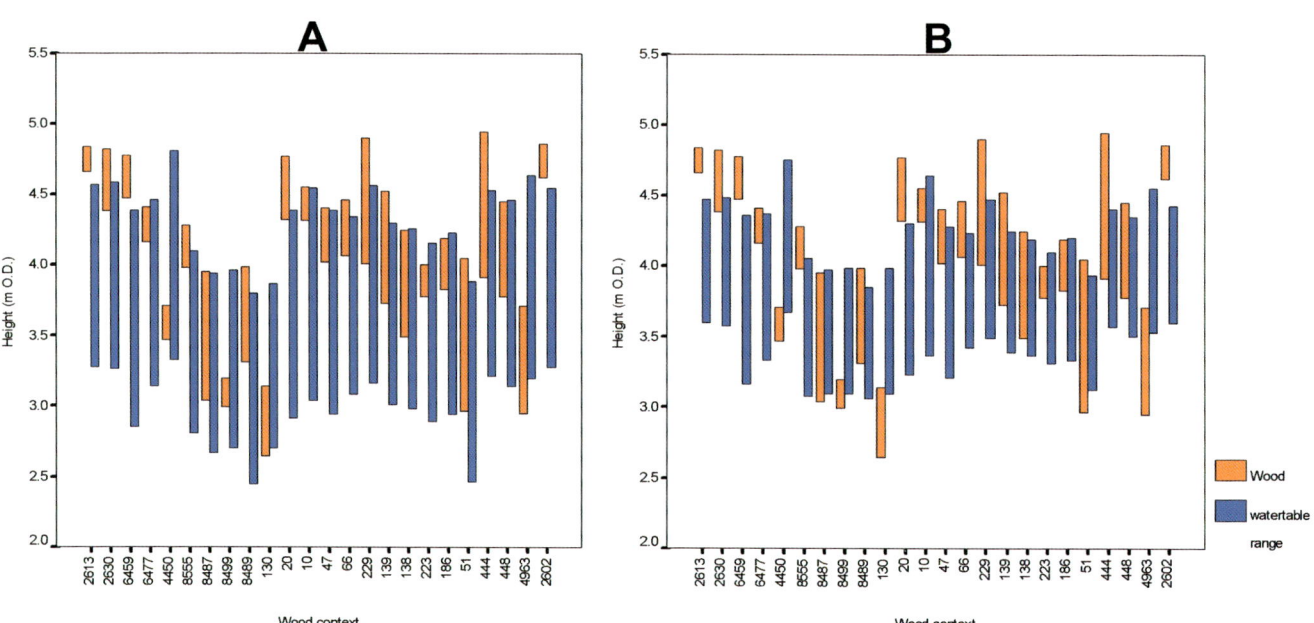

*Figure 2.6 The height range of the water table relative to that for archaeological wood identified through excavation. Graph A shows the situation before and Graph B following the instigation of drainage mitigation on Sutton Common*

demonstrate reduced conditions within the burial environment (Caple 1996; Caple and Dungworth 1997; 1998). The use of soil redox (reduction-oxidation potential) monitoring has been successfully applied to the monitoring of burial environments containing organic archaeological remains (Brunning *et al* 2000; Hogan *et al* 2002) and was therefore seen as an essential element of the work being carried out on Sutton Common. Monitoring took place at nine locations between January 2000 and March 2002. Readings were obtained at approximately monthly intervals from clusters of sixteen platinum-tipped copper electrodes, following the design of Faulkner *et al* (1989), installed at four depths, ranging from just beneath to 1.9m below the surface.

The monitoring showed that there was a definite trend towards reduced conditions with an increase in depth. The extent of this stratification was determined by the local site conditions, specifically the behaviour of the water table, and was also influenced by the presence of organic matter, which aids reduction. The effects of significant vertical fluctuations in the water table were revealed in the redox readings throughout the soil profile, showing the existence of generally oxidised conditions. This was particularly observed in the topographically higher parts of the site. Where the water table remained high throughout the year, soil redox readings by and large indicated reduced conditions.

The most significant stratification of redox readings was observed within the Hampole Beck palaeochannel where the water table was maintained at a relatively shallow depth. Figure 2.7 shows the adjusted redox results from this location. It shows several processes and interactions between the soil and the fluctuating water table. Initially, redox stratification was quite extreme, with measured values showing that the sediment was highly oxidised at the surface and severely reduced at depth, reflecting the relatively stable water table in this location. A falling water table through the summer of 2000 resulted in rising redox values at depth, most likely the result of increased aeration and bioturbation of the burial environment. A significant change occurred throughout the soil profile between October and November of that year, when redox values at all depths indicated very similar conditions. The corresponding, and significant, rise in the water table was the result of flooding. During this period, surface redox values were suppressed, whereas those at depth were elevated. Once the trapped water was removed in the spring of 2001, surface values rapidly increased to their former levels and a return to significantly stratified conditions was observed. The hatched lines in Figure 2.7 represent the period when readings could not be obtained from the site due to damaged equipment caused by the cattle that grazed the Common.

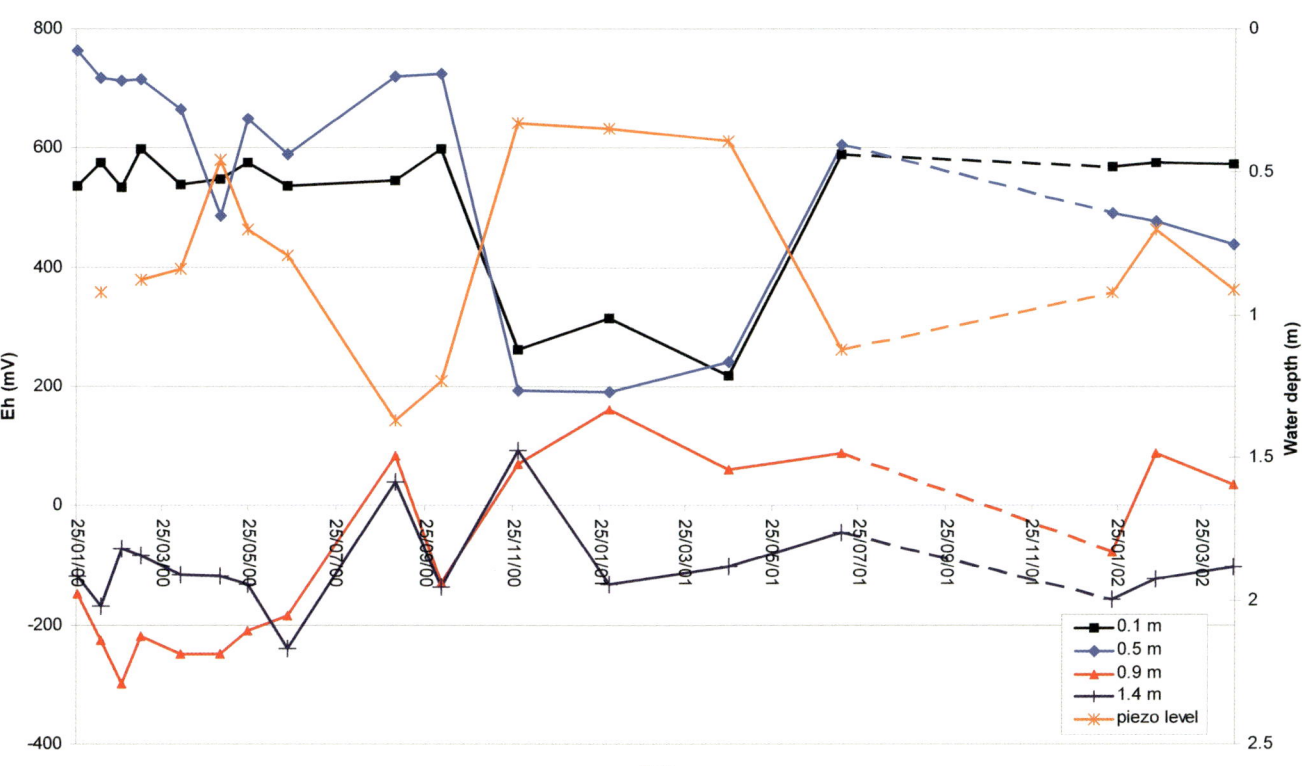

*Figure 2.7 Integrated piezometer level and soil redox values, adjusted to pH 7, obtained from within the Hampole Beck palaeochannel on Sutton Common*

Longer-term changes resulting from the flooding were identified within the burial environment which persisted after the return to previous hydrological conditions. Ponnamperuma (1972) describes the effects of submergence on soils as increasing the pH of acidic soils and depressing it for alkaline ones. This process has been identified in the monitoring at Sutton Common with an average shift upwards in pH of 0.5 units being observed nine months after the flooding took place.

The soil redox readings from Sutton Common have revealed significant patterns within the burial environment. A general trend of less-oxidising conditions with depth has been observed but the degree to which this occurred was dependent upon the characteristics of the individual monitoring locations and the environmental changes that they experienced. The occurrence of a flood event has provided evidence of the reaction of the burial environment to a rapid influx of large volumes of water and, as a result, has provided insight into the potential effects of future management strategies. The flooding event has been shown to affect the entire soil profile, causing longer-term changes to the soil chemistry that are capable of disturbing the delicate stability of anoxic deposits, and that a period of several months is required for the original conditions to be re-established.

### 2.3.4 Microbiological assessment

Microbiological activity within the soil is the major agent of decay of organic archaeological materials, and it should be measured to some degree when assessing the potential of preservation *in situ*. To date, research in this field has been targeted almost entirely on the microbial impact upon wooden materials (eg Powell *et al* 2001), and not on characterising the microbial activity itself. The work undertaken on Sutton Common has given baseline information using easily available and established techniques that are able to provide a holistic overview of microbial dynamics within the soil profile. The use of three approaches covering the assessment of microbial biomass, extracellular enzyme activity, and microbial metabolic activity, can account for the inherent complexities in soil microbial dynamics. Such methods have been used extensively in investigations into the marine environment (Ainsworth and Goulder 2000a; 2000b; Mayer 1989; Poremba 1995) and have recently been applied to the study of composting environments and waste management (Tiquia *et al* 2001; Tiquia 2002).

Five locations were chosen for sampling and each location was sampled twice, at an interval of approximately twelve months. This exercise has been considered as an assessment rather than a monitoring programme, to provide a framework by which further studies can take place and identify the most effective means by which monitoring can take place. General patterns identified through the analysis of soil samples obtained from Sutton Common include decreasing enzymatic and metabolic activities and biomass with depth, although the relative variation between these factors is more complex. For example, there is a significantly stronger association between enzyme activity and organic matter content than between enzyme activity and depth. This has two potential causes: first, enzymatic complexing with organic matter may result in the accumulation of extracellular enzymes within the burial environment; second, organic matter acts as a substrate and therefore is associated with concentrated microbial activity.

Metabolic activity, identified through the measurement of assimilation rates of radio-labelled leucine, is concentrated at the ground surface, indicating that the greatest amount of microbial turnover takes place where aerated conditions exist. In contrast to this, bacterial biomass was identified through the entire soil profile, suggesting that microbial activity, although present at depth, may have a lower turnover and may also be metabolising anoxically. To test such an assertion, the leucine assimilation method was further developed so that collection, transport, preparation, and incubation of soil samples could be undertaken under anoxic conditions. This exercise was successful in identifying anaerobic activity within archaeological contexts and proved that such field measurements can be implemented in future studies.

Across the wider site, little variation was identified between the samples obtained in consecutive years, apart from at a single control site located outside the monitoring grid, which saw a significant increase in bacterial biomass and microbial metabolic activity. These changes can be attributed to the influence of changing management practices upon Sutton Common, such as the introduction of cattle and a more intensive grass-cutting regime, which are essential to the future land management of the site.

No clear effect of the flooding event has been identified within the microbiological results. Although there are indications of changes in soil redox potentials and pH that could be attributable to microbial activity, no significant evidence for similar changes in microbial dynamics were found. However, initial soil samples were only obtained from the site following the flood event and therefore if changes occurred rapidly, then they would not have been identified. Although the second round of sampling occurred twelve months later, when hydrological conditions had reverted to those prior to the flooding, no significant changes attributable to the flood could be identified. Reasons for this may be that any changes that occurred as a result of the flooding persisted during the entire period of sampling. Alternatively, it is possible that the opposite is true and that the flood event had little impact and that the microbial conditions observed approximate those prior to it occurring.

### 2.3.5 Conclusions

The range of techniques used during this research has produced significant results relating to the effectiveness of the monitoring approach itself and also on the consequence of drainage mitigation on Sutton Common. These have provided a new insight into the dynamics of the burial environment of buried organic archaeological remains, specifically on Sutton Common, but also applicable to many other sites containing wet-preserved archaeological remains.

It appears that the impact of the drainage mitigation has been negligible. This is because the effects of field drainage are not the direct cause of the lowered water table; field drainage purely increases the rate at which water is removed from the soil profile. The real cause for the lowering of the water table from the height that existed in the past, which ensured the preservation of organic archaeological remains on the site, was the significant improvement in *regional* drainage instigated during the late 1970s and early 1980s. This involved the excavation and deepening of new and existing drainage ditches across the site and may have resulted in a net drop in the water table of at least 1m, possibly more, across a wider area than Sutton Common alone (Geomorphological Services Ltd 1990). Therefore, during periods of soil moisture deficit prior to the implementation of this scheme, the water table remained near to the surface due to a large reservoir of groundwater. Restricting drainage on Sutton Common, although effective at keeping excess water on the site, as identified with the maintenance of high water table conditions following the flood event of 2000/01, ultimately fails to prevent water being removed via evapotranspiration during phases of high vegetation growth.

This situation was effectively demonstrated by the creation of the archaeological wood model. By integrating water table data with the spatial locations of pieces of excavated archaeological wood, it has been possible to identify the changing saturation conditions throughout an annual cycle and to compare the situation both prior to and following the implementation of the rewetting activities. This, along with analysis of piezometer data, showed that although there is some evidence of a slight rise in the water table, it is not nearly great enough to alter the burial conditions significantly. Most of the archaeological material identified does not exist within the desired Zone 3, the zone of permanent saturation, and therefore the outlook in terms of the continued preservation of the bulk of the organic archaeological remains on Sutton Common is poor. However, to qualify this statement, there are 'hotspots', such as the deep archaeological ditches associated with the smaller enclosure and within the palaeochannel, where conditions may remain suitable for good-quality preservation.

Few of the redox monitoring locations exhibited readings that were indicative of stable anoxic conditions and these were restricted, in general, either to the greatest depths or the wettest locations. These observations support the findings of the hydrological monitoring programme in indicating that only in a very few locations, and at depth, do the required conditions for the continued preservation of organic archaeological remains exist. Also, the impact of the re-engineering of the field drainage on the site cannot be identified within the results, suggesting that this has had little impact upon the burial environment.

Intense microbiological metabolic activity has been identified at the ground surface across the site, particularly where there is a high organic content within the soil. This activity decreases significantly with depth, although the potential for aerobic and anaerobic activity, and therefore degradation, still remains as bacterial cells and enzyme activity have been identified throughout the soil profile.

The data generated during site flooding, and the subsequent twelve months, demonstrated that flooding an archaeological site may in fact be destructive where it perhaps is assumed to be beneficial. This is highly significant for the future management of Sutton Common and also for other sites of high archaeological potential that may be subject to flooding. Soil redox potential data were particularly effective at identifying the action of flushing within the burial environment, whereby the redox conditions throughout the soil profile matched those of the flood water itself. This shows that, at least within a relatively dry soil profile, the burial environment is significantly influenced by the flooding event. However, in a number of locations there was evidence that, even below the level of the water table, there was an upward shift in redox conditions. Regular flooding could therefore have a long-term, detrimental impact upon the potential for *in situ* preservation of organic archaeological remains.

The implementation of an effective monitoring package resulting in the understanding of the burial environment, and the changes within it, has enabled an accurate assessment to be made regarding the impact of the re-engineering of the site drainage. There was evidence that there had been an overall positive response to the work that had been carried out and that the work was effective at retaining water on-site. However, this was small and demonstrably not sufficient to affect the preservation potential of the archaeological materials identified on the site.

## 2.4 Rubbish and Archaeology
*by I Panter and R Van de Noort*

Within the context of the Sutton Common Project's aim to develop education and outreach programmes, the Rubbish and Archaeology Project was intended to provide a way to integrate local school children with the work on the Common. This was considered to be a particularly challenging part of the project.

However, the basic concept was a simple one. About 150 youngsters from Askern Junior School, Norton Junior School, and Campsmount School were asked to select one item from their lunchbox, analyse and record these items, bury them for six months or so, retrieve them, and then record what had happened to the lunchbox items. The selection of the objects was left to the schoolchildren, and ranged from cheese sandwiches and fresh fruit to foil-wrapped sausages and canned drinks. In the process, the children would learn something about Sutton Common and its archaeology, undertake a number of archaeology-inspired scientific tests, and possibly also get some insight about the issue of waste disposal – what deteriorated naturally and what would remain unchanged in the environment if thrown away.

The project also had a more experimental side. Despite the enhanced preservation of organic archaeological remains in waterlogged, anoxic environments, not all raw materials are recovered from wetland sites. The assumption was that some raw materials, such as non-woody plants used for weaving and basketry, did not survive the first six or twelve months of burial before a preservational near-equilibrium was achieved. Furthermore, we were interested in the possibility of testing post-depositional processes in the months immediately after burial in a field situation. Therefore, a range of experimental archaeological objects were buried side-by-side with the lunchbox items (Fig 2.8). The items included organic materials (rush baskets, linen bags, uncharred wheat grains, wooden stakes, and joints of lamb) and inorganic objects ('Iron Age' replica pots, copper buckles, and coins). A total of four test pits were dug for the burial experiment, two in the drier part of the site which was not permanently waterlogged, and two in the wetter, permanently waterlogged, area.

The artefacts were buried in September 2000, but the retrieval of the objects had to be delayed for a considerable time as an outbreak of Foot and Mouth Disease intervened. The second part of the experiment was therefore delayed until 2002, when all the youngsters had progressed to Campsmount School (Fig 2.9). The impact of the burial on the various lunchbox items was largely unsurprising, but served to illustrate the principles of preservation and decay well. All plastics and foils survived virtually unscathed, metal cans were variously corroded, but the majority of food materials had all but fully decayed. The survival of the skin of an apple but not the flesh was attributed to higher (natural or artificial) preservative toxins, and both animal and fish bones were retrieved without any meat.

From the point of view of experimental archaeology, the project was also a success. The linen bags, the uncharred wheat grains, the wooden stakes, and lamb bones were all retrieved in

*Figure 2.8   Rubbish and Archaeology: experimental material culture with (left) rush basketry before burial and (right) the baskets on excavation*

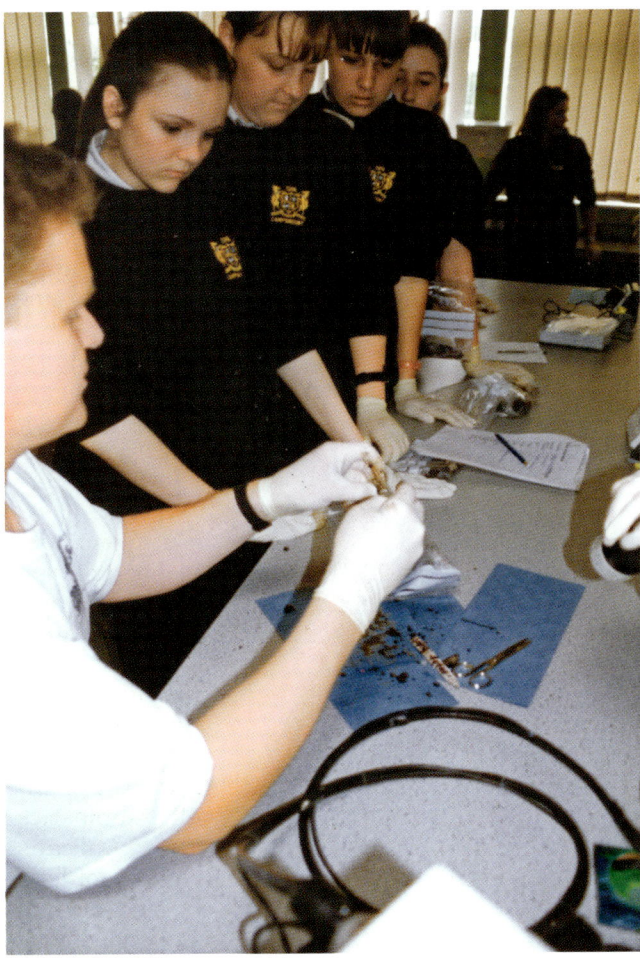

*Figure 2.9 Rubbish and Archaeology: analysis of the retrieved artefacts in Campsmount School, Askern*

various states of preservation, but very little survived of the rush baskets. This is, we assume, due to the near-absence of lignified tissue and the structure of rush which, even when crushed and flattened, retains sufficient air including oxygen to feed the microbes required to break the raw material down. However, further work, in controlled environments, is required to establish the exact cause of the non-survival of this type of material. The success of the project, including the retrieval of nearly all objects for analysis, shows how an experimental wetland project might one day complement the Experimental Earthwork Project (eg Bell *et al* 1996).

## 2.5 Conclusions: The past and present of Sutton Common  *by I Carstairs and R Van de Noort*

Reflecting on the four objectives of the Sutton Common Project outlined above (see section 2.1), a number of achievements can be recognised, but also the need for further action in the future. This section considers the current situation of the Common.

Reverting Sutton Common to a wetland or, to be more precise, to a managed landscape with a high groundwater table to preserve archaeological remains below 4.1m OD, and with a thriving wetland ecology in Shirley Pool SSSI and the lowest parts of the Common, was one of the most ambitious aims set by the project. In terms of rewetting, the actions identified in 1998 as required to achieve this aim have all been implemented, but as the hydrological monitoring has shown, the outcome of these actions was disappointing (see section 2.3). The reasons for this are the unbalanced water budget, and the significantly altered soil chemistry.

From the onset, the participants of the Sutton Common Project accepted that reverting the arable lands of the Common into a wetland landscape was an unparalleled venture which might not succeed. It was also accepted that research in landscape management did not provide the necessary information or guidance on how to succeed. Therefore, research into the effects of the rewetting on the archaeological burial environment became another aim of the project. The research itself has already been presented (see section 2.3), and the results have been disseminated in a number of publications (eg Van de Noort *et al* 2001a; 2001b; Chapman and Cheetham 2002).

In terms of building inter-agency cooperation with all the stakeholders involved with Sutton Common, this is recognised as one of the outstanding successes of the project. It is reflected in the range of sponsors for purchasing the land, with the Heritage Lottery Fund and English Heritage making the initial purchase possible, and English Nature, WREN Environmental, and the Countryside Agency all supporting the purchase of Rushy Moor. It is also reflected in the larger number of organisations who joined the project in other ways. By 2004, the list of organisations who had actively taken part in the Sutton Common Project included CCT, North Doncaster Rural Trust, English Heritage, Heritage Lottery Fund, English Nature, Countryside Agency, WREN Environmental, DEFRA, the Pilgrim Trust, E Sheard Family Trust, APS UK, Dun Drainage Commissioners, Grantham, Brundell and Farran, Doncaster Naturalists' Society, Doncaster Community Arts, Doncaster Museum, Norton Parish Council, Askern Town Council, Askern Miners' Welfare, The Starr Inn at Moss, The Doncaster and District Scout Association, Askern Junior School, Norton Junior School, Campsmount School, and the Universities of Exeter and Hull, alongside a large number of individuals, including Andrew Booth (farmer), Neil Mitchell (air photographer), Neville Turton (land management advice), Richard Watson (solicitor), Mike Husdon (accountant), Bev Wiegel, Stan Longley, and many more local volunteers.

The education and outreach programmes fully achieved their objectives. The Rubbish and Archaeology Project, involving over 150 schoolchildren from the Askern Ward, has already been described (see section 2.4). Education and outreach were even more extensive. Thus, local volunteers were invited to take part in the excavations. The 'Open Days' during the 1999, 2002, and 2003 excavation campaigns received more than 1500, mostly local, visitors. The conference, *Time Present and Time Past* in 2003 was held in the Askern Miners' Welfare, rather than a distant university. The publication of the popular book, *The Marsh of Time: Saving Sutton Common*, edited by Roly Smith (2004), and written by the key participants, again principally aimed at the local market, was a priority. The project's broad support also facilitated the education of staff of other governmental and non-governmental agencies, by raising awareness of the value of wetland archaeology amongst others involved with wetland management, and by promoting and disseminating understanding and appreciation of wetland heritage. Certain aspects of this work, especially inter-agency cooperation, are becoming more widely adopted.

# 3 Methodologies

## 3.1 Introduction: excavations and research 1997 – 2003

This chapter presents the methodological statements. The excavation methodology at Sutton Common is, for a British excavation, somewhat unorthodox, but was tailored to the formation processes on the site. These processes will, therefore, be presented in advance of the discussion of the excavation methodology.

## 3.2 Fieldwork

### 3.2.1 Formation processes   by R Van de Noort and H Chapman

Sutton Common in the 4th century BC was a relatively dry site bordered by the wetlands of the Hampole Beck and the Shirley Pool complex. This is clearly shown by the complete dearth of waterlain sediments in even the deepest postholes on the islands on either side of the Hampole Beck. Analysis and interpretation of plant macrofossil evidence preserved beneath the limited remains of the surviving bank which delineated the larger enclosure on its western side (see section 5.6.2) suggests that the vegetation had been burned off or cleared with the aid of fire, and that turves were cut to form the body of the ramparts, thus leaving little of the pre-marsh-fort surface for analysis. The postholes for the defences and the internal structures (described in chapters 5 and 6), were then cut into the finely layered sands and silts derived from the reworking by wind of Lake Humber deposits. Undisturbed, these sediments provide a reasonable firm setting for posts but, once disturbed, they become soft and yield easily to any pressure and are quite unsuitable for post settings which bear significant superstructures.

Thus the largest postholes, used for posts for the gateways and the four-post structures, were carefully 'carved' into the sands and silts, forming a space wherein individual posts were carefully sunk and fitted tightly; stone rather than Lake Humber sands and silts were used as post packing if required. These postholes had flat bottoms, and there is evidence in a few cases that the floor of the posthole had been levelled with stone or wood fragments. The tight fit, and the fact that the archaeological wood survived in many cases, prevented the formation of any secondary 'postfills' (Fig 3.1). This is an important observation for understanding the significance of material found in postholes at Sutton Common (see sections 6.5.1 and 6.6). Smaller posts, such as those forming part of the box rampart or those along the causeway, had been tapered to a point like a sharpened pencil and were driven directly into the Lake Humber sands and silts or the peats of the Hampole Beck palaeochannel.

Following deposition, it is unclear what happened to the upstanding structures in antiquity. There is some evidence for limited destruction of the ramparts at or near the various entranceways (see section 5.3.4 and 5.3.11), and for the reuse of some postholes, with the limestone post-packing still *in situ*, for the secondary deposition of pyre debris (see section 8.2.2), but considering the longevity of the survival of the ramparts into the 20th century, it must be assumed that the site was left to the elements. Soon after the marsh-fort was constructed, however, the area appears to have become wetter, contributing to the wet-preservation of the archaeological wood. This increased wetness was probably the consequence of one or more changes in the local or regional catchment in terms of water run-off and drainage, rather than climate change. Possibly, the construction of the causeway linking the smaller and larger enclosures across the Hampole Beck palaeochannel impeded the natural drainage (see section 5.3.3). Alternatively, pollen analysis suggests increased clearances in the hinterland of the Common in the Iron Age, presumably on the limestone edge to the west of the site, resulted in the increased run-off of rainwater from these free-draining soils into the low-lying Common (see section 4.3.5).

The soil on the Common remained waterlogged until its enclosure c 1850, and was still too wet to cultivate arable crops effectively until the 1980s, when the new underfield drainage system was installed causing the lowering of the groundwater table (see section 2.2.1.1). Around this time, the upstanding earthworks of the larger enclosure were pushed into the ditches, or what remained of these, and into the Hampole Beck palaeochannel. The subsequent use of the site for arable agriculture meant that the whole of the larger enclosure and the Hampole Beck palaeochannel have been ploughed on approximately twenty occasions.

These post-depositional processes affected the archaeology in a number of ways. First, whilst any upstanding remains were comprehensively destroyed, the bottoms of the ditch-fills were effectively preserved. Second, the Iron Age living surface was destroyed, and no floors were found at any time during the excavations, with the exception of fragments of a cobbled path inside the western entranceway of the larger enclosure (see section 5.3.4). Third, the lowering of the groundwater table resulted in the onset of rapid desiccation of the archaeological remains,

*Figure 3.1   Posthole [3531] in Trench 3*

especially the wood. On excavation, voids were frequently found between the ploughsoil and the surviving fragments of wood, and the largest posts, all of oak, were deteriorating inside-out, with often little more than a shell of desiccated wood left (Fig 3.2). The lower water table also contributed to the rapid decay of the peat in the Hampole Beck palaeochannel.

### 3.2.2 Excavation   by H Chapman and R Van de Noort

The excavation strategy for the large-scale campaigns in 2002 and 2003 had been informed by our understanding of the state of the archaeology and preservation of the larger enclosure gained during the excavations of 1998 and 1999. The need for rapid action was evident – in 1999 the period for retrieval of wood suitable for dendrochronology was estimated at five to ten years. The need for large-scale excavations was determined by the research contexts, in particular the realisation that no large enclosed Iron Age site, including hillforts, had been fully excavated in Britain, and that this had become a main obstacle in understanding this phenomenon and its significance to Iron Age society.

The location of the trenches excavated after 1998 all used the 30 × 30m grid system (see section 1.4.1). In 1999, one square was fully excavated and ten trenches each measuring

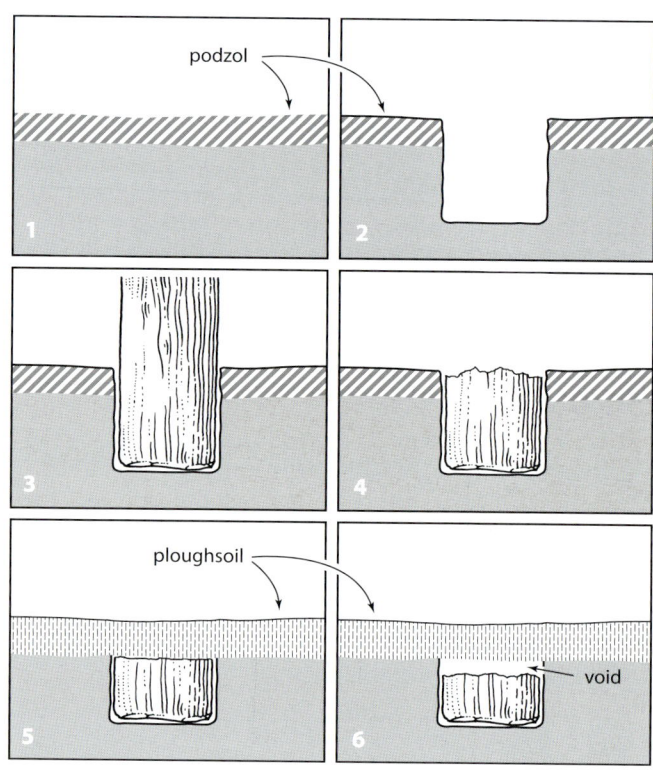

*Figure 3.2   Reconstruction of the formation processes of posts and postholes. Structural posts were placed in carefully cut postholes, with little or no room for postfills. The bottom of posts survived; voids represent recent wood desiccation beneath the ploughsoil*

30 × 3m were dug as an evaluation exercise. In 2002 and 2003, a total of eight trenches were excavated, adhering to the grid, all measuring 30m wide and varying in length from 60m to 120m, together covering over 95% of the interior of the larger enclosure. Additional extension trenches were used to explore the defences on all sides of the enclosure and, in 2003, also of the area to the north and east of the larger enclosure. In 1998 and 1999, a JCB Sitemaster had been used to remove the ploughsoil, and in 2002 and 2003, two 360° excavators on caterpillars were employed, all with toothless buckets (Fig 3.3). Very few archaeological artefacts and no features had survived the two decades of ploughing, and we were confident that the use of mechanised excavators was fully justified; no topsoil was dug by hand or sieved.

Trenches were marked out using differential GPS. The removal of the topsoil by mechanical excavator was supervised by the relevant trench supervisor who ensured the correct depth of topsoil that needed removing. The spoil was accumulated along one long side, allowing for easy access during the excavations and the Open Days. Subsequently, the surface was cleaned manually by shovel (Fig 3.4). An internal 5 × 5m grid was then created, again using differential GPS (Fig 3.5), and planned (see section 3.2.3). Subsequently, c 10% of all the features were excavated using box-cuts.

The decision to excavate only 10% of all the features was based on discussions with English Heritage and their desire to retain the scheduled status of the monument. From a research point of view, it seemed probable that this approach would not undermine the principal aims and objectives. The 1999 evaluation had already shown that the diversity of features was limited, and that no additional information or insights were obtained by digging all parts of the larger features, such as the palisade and the box-ramparts. Box-cuts, rather than sections of the features themselves, were employed to avoid damaging the wood remains. As discussed earlier (see section 3.2.1), much of the archaeological wood survived, albeit frequently in an advanced state of decay, and only by using box-cuts could the wood or its outline be established (Fig 3.6). In 2002 and 2003, the trenches were systematically surveyed using a metal detector by Ian Stead of the Doncaster Archaeological Society.

*Figure 3.3 Removal of the topsoil using 360° excavators*

*Figure 3.4   Cleaning the surface by shovel*

*Figure 3.5   Using dGPS for recording and creation of internal 5 × 5m grid*

### 3.2.3   *Recording*   by H Chapman and R Van de Noort

Following the investigations in 1998, it was realised that the various types of trench numbering and recording by different archaeologists had become complicated. In order to remedy this problem, the 30 × 30m alphanumeric grid was established for the site and located using GPS. This meant that a coding would immediately define a 30 × 30m area of the site. This grid also determined the positioning of trenches in a systematic way for the work in 1999, 2001, and 2002.

The excavated areas were sub-gridded at 5m intervals using GPS, forming the basis of all planning. Within the trenches, cleaned areas were planned at a scale of 1:20 in blocks of 10 × 15m to fit on A3 drawing film sheets, including levelling information. Ordnance Survey National Grid co-ordinates for the 5m nails were added to the plans to assist with post-excavation digitising (Fig 3.7). Photographs were also taken of each cleaned 10 × 15m planning area. Areas of additional excavation were marked on the plans, or overlays. Features were sectioned to provide additional information, and to obtain material for further analysis. Sectioned features were recorded at a scale of 1:10.

Each trench was considered as a separate site, set out along the alphanumeric 30m grid, and thus each trench was 30m wide. A single context

*Figure 3.6    Excavation of three posts forming part of the box rampart in Trench 4 in box section*

*Figure 3.7    Planning the inner ditch in Trench 1*

recording system, derived from the English Heritage Centre for Archaeology's system, was used for all features. Context Sheets included information relating to alphanumeric grid square, with context numbers in most cases being four figures, starting with the trench number. For example, contexts in Trench 5 were numbered from [5001] to [5999]. In the one case where there were in excess of 1000 contexts, numbering extended to five figures (eg [3001] to [3999] and then [31001] onwards).

Context Sheets facilitated the full recording of deposit and cut features. In addition to these forms, specialist wood context forms were created for recording wooden features, including information regarding any modifications and preservation indicators. Where wood was recorded, a Wood Recording Form in place of a Context Sheet was used. A Context Index Form kept record of all allocated contexts. In addition to the context recording, drawings were numbered sequentially by trench, with the unique number for each drawing added to the Drawing Index Form for each trench. A similar process was used for recording the appropriate context numbers of features that were photographed. Each camera film was given a unique number from a Film Index Form, and a Photo Index Form was used to note the context numbers of features in each photograph. This system was designed to ensure that features in photographs were identifiable, with the Film Index Form providing space for recording the stage of photographic production.

During the 1998 and 1999 excavations, a movable hydraulic platform was used for photography, but in view of the size of the trenches in subsequent years, an alternative strategy was required. Thus, in the penultimate week of excavation during the 2002 and 2003 campaigns, low-level near-vertical aerial photographs were taken of all the trenches from a helicopter by Neil Mitchell of APS UK (Fig 3.8). It also gave all staff and students the opportunity to see their work in a wider context.

Finds, small finds, and samples were recorded using a similar system of numbering, with a trench number prefix and unique sequential numbering, or with the context number. All finds were recorded on the Finds Index Form, with specific finds being recorded in more detail on the Small Finds Index Form, with a three-dimensional GPS position and more detailed description. Samples were recorded using the same system, and catalogued on a Sample Index Form.

### 3.2.4 Sampling

#### 3.2.4.1 Archaeological features *by H Chapman*

In order to comply with the scheduled status of the site, a sample of not more than 10% of features could be excavated. As a result, features were

*Figure 3.8 Low-level aerial photography using a helicopter*

excavated in order to address questions relating to the original project design. Fundamentally, this was carried out to obtain samples for specialist analyses. Bulk samples were taken from posthole and pit fills for macrofossil analyses. Sectioned ditches were sampled by monolith for palynological analysis. Bulk samples were obtained at the same time as monolith samples for plant macrofossil and beetle analyses, providing direct comparison between the different approaches. Wood was sampled from all sectioned postholes and stakeholes for species analysis, dating, and for the examination of tool marks.

Specialists from all fields visited the site during the two years of excavation to examine the most appropriate places for sampling to tackle the questions outlined in the original project design, and to identify other questions that could potentially be addressed. In many cases, including pedological sampling, samples were extracted by specialists themselves, and their location recorded by the excavation team. In other cases, such as the posthole fills, samples were systematically bagged during excavation following advice from the appropriate specialists. Geological samples were selected by the specialist in 2002 only.

The location of each sample was recorded on the site plans and section drawings, with the sample being given a unique sample number, recorded using the Sample Index Form. Samples were stored in appropriate wet or cold-store conditions before being passed to specialists.

### 3.2.4.2 Insects and plant macrofossils
*by A Hall and H Kenward*

Samples for the study of plant and insect macrofossils were taken from all trenches opened during the excavations of 2002 and 2003; in all, 165 samples or subsamples from 137 contexts were examined during the assessment and/or analysis stages of this project, material from some deposits being investigated by means of separate subsamples at these two stages, and that from others being examined only during analysis (but on the basis of assessment of samples of similar lithology or context type). Two stages of assessment established that assemblages dominated by well-preserved wet-preserved remains were present in many of the ditch fills (Fig 3.9), and occasionally in feature fills, with assemblages of charred cereal grains and associated chaff and weed seeds occurring in many of the posthole and other fills. Samples selected for examination of plant and invertebrate macrofossils during the analysis phase of this project were from two groups of deposits: firstly, from the fills of postholes (and some pits and a feature interpreted as a well), all within the Iron Age enclosure; and secondly from the fills of the inner and outer enclosure ditches. As discovered during assessment, preservation of plant material was largely by charring, both throughout the feature fills from within the enclosure, but also in many of the ditch fills; plant and insect remains preserved by anoxic waterlogging were present in some quantity in the ditch fills and in some of the 'well' fills and also, much more rarely, in other deposits. In a number of instances, these uncharred remains were regarded as recent contaminants in deposits which lay not far beneath the modern topsoil and certainly within the zone of modern root and earthworm penetration.

### 3.2.5 Geophysical survey *by A Payne*

The conditions for magnetic detection in the semi-waterlogged environment of Sutton Common

*Figure 3.9  Sampling for plant and insect macrofossils in the outer ditch next to the eastern gateway*

were considered to be poor, especially given the insubstantial nature of the features already recorded by excavation in the larger enclosure in 2002. Approximately 95% of the internal features comprised posts and stakes with a diameter of 0.4m or less. Previous geophysical survey carried out over the smaller enclosure by the University of Sheffield in 1993, using a Geoscan RM4 resistivity meter and FM18 Fluxgate gradiometer, had suggested that the fluxgate gradiometry was largely ineffective (Parker Pearson and Merrony 1993). Resistivity had succeeded in mapping the boundary ditches and banks of the enclosure earthwork and the course of the adjacent palaeochannel, but little else of note.

On this basis, it was proposed that a magnetometer survey of the interior of the larger enclosure would be carried out with Bartington Grad601–2 dual fluxgate gradiometer systems, with a 1m vertical separation between the fluxgate sensors. These instruments have the advantage of being able to operate effectively over steep and uneven terrain and are therefore well suited for surveying over upstanding earthworks such as those of the smaller enclosure. Instrument readings were recorded at 0.25m intervals along successive 30m parallel traverses spaced 1m apart on the grid. The data was recorded using the 200 nanotesla per metre (nT/m) range setting of the magnetometer (recording the data to the nearest 0.1 nT/m).z

## 3.3 Analyses

### 3.3.1 Archaeological features
by H Chapman

The analysis of the archaeological features within the excavated area was undertaken digitally using GIS software. The decision to approach the analysis, and archiving, of the site in this way lay in the software's ability to manage large quantities of data from different sources together, facilitating visualisation at a variety of scales and interrogation of the database at all phases of the analysis process, and enabling the creation of new layers of interpreted data. Furthermore, the on-site positioning using the GPS enabled the excavated data to be compared and analysed in relation to the previously generated layers already in the GIS, including the surface Digital Elevation Model (DEM) and water table data.

The GIS database was generated in ESRI ArcGIS 9.0 software. As noted above (section 3.2.3), as part of the recording process, the positions of nails set at 5m intervals across the excavated area were marked on the plans in relation to absolute Ordnance Survey National Grid coordinates. All of the A3 sheets that formed the site plan archive were scanned and added to the GIS.

These were geo-referenced using the National Grid coordinates, providing a high level of spatial accuracy in relation to all other datasets collected during the duration of the project. The scanned plans were thus positioned accurately within the GIS. From these, each of the archaeological deposit features was digitised on-screen (Fig 3.10).

All deposit features were digitised in polygon format. In contrast to polyline-based formats, polygons relate to an area and were thus more appropriate for the recording of archaeological features which could be linked with context databases. Each archaeological context was digitised from the plans, with each resulting polygon given an attribute relating to its context number. At its simplest level, this enabled a user to click on any polygon to be provided with its context number. Furthermore, it enabled fast measurement of features on-screen to assess dimensions. Using a GIS viewer it was possible to export the digital site archive during its production to other members of the team so that they could perform their own analyses using the digital data. Each trench was digitised as a separate file, creating eight principal context databases, which could be joined within the GIS software as required.

Separate textual databases were generated linking the context numbers to additional fields representing context descriptions and, where appropriate, context interpretations. By joining these textual databases to the spatial databases within the GIS, it became possible to interrogate the archive to display all features of a certain type together. This enabled various interpretations of the site to be considered rapidly and contrasted against one another. During the phase of site interpretation, the GIS archive formed the basis for creating new interpretative layers of different feature types, enabling a rapid visualisation of different possible interpretations.

One value of digital archiving using GIS is that multiple copies may be generated for those working on the project. It also enables the archive to be more freely available than paper records. Following the completion of the archiving and analysis, the digital archive was submitted to the appropriate record offices, and made publicly available through the Archaeology Data Service (ADS), as part of the Arts and Humanities Data Service (AHDS – cf Gillings and Wise 1999). (http://ads.ahds.ac.uk/catalogue/resources.html?suttoncommon_eh_2007)

### 3.3.2 Archaeological wood  by G Thomas

Some 235 samples of archaeological wood were recovered from the 2002–2003 excavations at Sutton Common. All were stored in wet-tank facilities at the Universities of Hull and Exeter. The largest entranceway timbers, which could

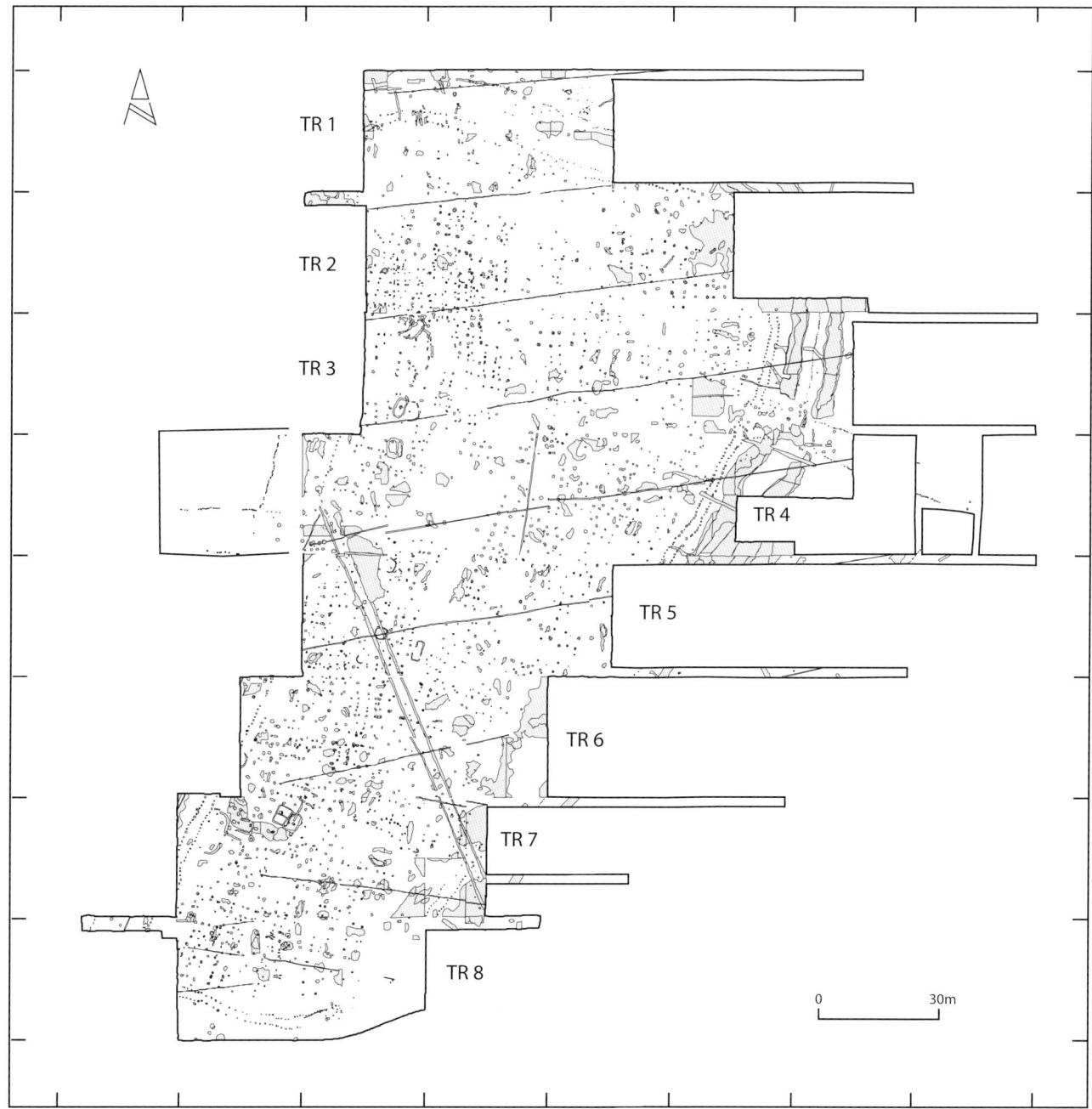

*Figure 3.10   Excavation plan 1998 – 2003: all features*

only be moved by pallet truck, were wrapped in thick black plastic pond lining, padded with sponge foam, kept wet and stored on pallets. Smaller samples that had suffered greatly from desiccation were wrapped in plastic bags and stored in the cold store of Exeter University.

All samples had been allocated a wood context number on site. After being cleaned, data on the wood sample dimensions, morphology, and condition were recorded. A great deal of information on woodworking technology could be recorded from samples where tool marks were clear. The manner of wood conversion, whether the sample be whole or radially split for example, the number, dimensions, and concavity of axe facets, jam curves, signatures, minimum cutting angles, and point types on stakes were all recorded. Further details on the thin sectioning methodology used and recording of tool marks can be found in Fletcher and Thomas (2001).

The vast majority of structural wood from Sutton Common is oak and could be identified with the naked eye. All non-oak wood was sampled for microscopic analysis by thin sectioning. Some samples could not be identified due to severe decay and loss of structural integrity, the sample simply turning to powder when attempting to mount a frozen thin section on a microscope slide. At this stage, growth ring counts and patterns were recorded where possible. The majority of samples were record photographed and several in more detail from various angles to record distinctive features, tool marks or extremes of desiccation.

### 3.3.3 Dating

#### 3.3.3.1 Radiocarbon Dating  by D Hamilton, B Gearey, R Van de Noort, G Cook, C Bronk Ramsey and P Marshall

*Introduction*

Twenty radiocarbon determinations have been obtained on material from Sutton Common. Fourteen measurements were acquired from the current research programme undertaken between 1998 and 2003 and six from excavations in 1987 and 1998.

*Methods*

Twelve samples (ten fragments of waterlogged wood and two bulk peat samples) from a core taken from the Hampole Beck palaeochannel (SC1) were submitted for Accelerator Mass Spectrometry (AMS) radiocarbon dating to the Scottish Universities Environmental Research Centre (SUERC), East Kilbride in 2005. Details of sample preparation and dating are provided by Slota *et al* (1987) and Xu *et al* (2004).

Four samples of cremated bone, two each from two cremations, were submitted for radiocarbon dating by Accelerator Mass Spectrometry (AMS) to SUERC and the Oxford Radiocarbon Accelerator Unit (ORAU) in 2005. These samples were prepared following the procedures outlined in Lanting *et al* (2001), with measurement at SUERC following the procedures described in Xu *et al* (2004), and at ORAU as described in Bronk Ramsey *et al* (2004).

One sample of peat, two samples of wood, and one sample of charred spelt and emmer seeds were dated by the radiocarbon laboratory at AERE Harwell in 1988. These samples were prepared as described by Otlet and Warchal (1978) and combusted to carbon dioxide and synthesised to benzene (using a method similar to that initially described by Tamers 1965) and a vanadium-based catalyst (Otlet 1977). The radiocarbon content was measured using Liquid Scintillation Counting as described by Otlet (1979).

Two radiocarbon age determinations were obtained on samples of wood in 1995. These were processed by the Scottish Universities Research and Reactor Centre at East Kilbride, and were prepared using the methods outlined in Stenhouse and Baxter (1983) and measured using liquid scintillation spectrometry (Noakes *et al* 1965).

All the laboratories maintain continual programmes of quality assurance procedures, in addition to participation in international inter-comparisons (Rozanski *et al* 1992; Scott 2003; Scott *et al* 1998). These tests indicate no laboratory offsets and demonstrate the validity of the precision quoted.

*Results*

The results are given in Table 3.1, and are quoted in accordance with the international standard known as the Trondheim convention (Stuiver and Kra 1986). They are conventional radiocarbon ages (Stuiver and Polach 1977).

*Calibration*

The calibration of the results, relating the radiocarbon measurements directly to calendar dates, are given in Table 3.1 and in Figs 4.4, 4.7, and 5.25. All have been calculated using the calibration curve of Reimer *et al* (2004) and the computer program OxCal (v3.10) (Bronk Ramsey 1995; 1998; 2001). The calibrated date ranges cited in the text are those for 95% confidence. They are quoted in the form recommended by Mook (1986), with the end points rounded outwards to ten years if the error term is greater than or equal to 25 radiocarbon years or to five years if it is less. The ranges quoted in italics are *posterior density estimates* derived from mathematical modelling of archaeological problems (see below). The ranges in plain type in Table 3.1 and throughout the text have been calculated according to the maximum intercept method (Stuiver and Reimer 1986). All other ranges are derived from the probability method (Stuiver and Reimer 1993).

*Methodological approach*

A Bayesian approach (Buck *et al* 1996) has been adopted for the interpretation of the chronology of the samples submitted from the defences (see section 5.4.3). Although the simple calibrated dates are accurate estimates of the dates of the samples, this is usually not what archaeologists really wish to know. It is the dates of the archaeological events which are represented by those samples which are of interest. In the case of Sutton Common, it is the chronology of the use of the defences and the date of the ditch and palisade that is under consideration, not the dates of individual samples. The dates of this activity can be estimated not only using the absolute dating information from the radiocarbon measurements on the samples, but also by using the stratigraphic relationships between samples.

Fortunately, methodology is now available which allows the combination of these different types of information explicitly, to produce realistic estimates of the dates of archaeological interest. It should be emphasised that the *posterior density estimates* produced by this modelling are not absolute. They are interpretative *estimates*, which can and will change as further data become available and as other researchers choose to model the existing data from different perspectives.

The technique used is a form of Markov Chain Monte Carlo sampling, and has been applied using the program OxCal v3.10 (http://www.rla-ha.ox.ac.uk/), which uses a mixture of the Metropolis-Hastings algorithm and the more specific Gibbs sampler (Gilks *et al* 1996; Gelfand and Smith 1990). Details of the algorithms employed by this program are available from the on-line manual or in Bronk Ramsey (1995; 1998; 2001). The algorithm used in the models described below can be derived from the structures shown in Fig 5.25.

*Palaeoenvironmental sample selection*

There is a diverse range of materials that can be used to provide radiocarbon measurements from contexts (in this case sediments within a palaeochannel) used in palaeoenvironmental reconstruction, for example terrestrial seeds and plant material, fossil wood, and bulk sediment samples (eg peat). All these sample types are affected by physical processes (including reburial or redeposition) and/or chemical alteration that is dependent on the context from which they were recovered and the mechanism by which they were transported into that context (Lowe and Walker 2000).

*Plant remains*

Since the early 1990s there has been a tendency for radiocarbon measurements on samples from palaeoenvironmental cores to be obtained by accelerator mass spectrometry of plant macrofossils/fossil wood. This is due to two main factors:

- Sample size: improvements in the size of sample that can be measured (2mg of organic carbon), thus increasing the degree of stratigraphic resolution;
- Taphonomic: the belief that plant macrofossils are more reliable than 'bulk' samples of sediment matrix as the source of carbon in the former is known and they are not made up of heterogeneous material that could be of dierent ages (Walker *et al* 2001; Lowe and Walker 2000).

Although plant macrofossils and fossil wood can easily be identified as short-lived, care must be taken when they come from aqueous environments (eg fluvial, alluvial, estuarine, etc). In these environments there is some possibility that such material was in-washed. While in-washing is more likely to bring in material that is of an older, rather than younger, date, wet-dry cycles and invasive reeds, such as *Phragmites*, present the possibility of younger material being brought down through the sediment column. These potential problems demand that the radiocarbon programme employed is one with consistency as its foremost aim.

Consistency can be demonstrated in two ways. The first is through good overall agreement between the radiocarbon measurements and the core sequence (see Blockley *et al* 2004). The second is through the replication of results from a specific level in the core. The replication of results is why it is preferred to have two macrofossils submitted from any given level; it is also part of the reasoning behind dating multiple fractions of peats, soils, and sediment (see below). If the resultant measurements are statistically consistent (Ward and Wilson 1978) then it is probable that the two dates correctly date that level. When the two measurements are not statistically consistent, the data need to be re-evaluated.

*Peat and sediments*

When macrofossils were not available from horizons down the core that corresponded with both litho- and bio-stratigraphic changes, and therefore environmental changes, bulk sediment samples were submitted. The dating of peat and the reliability of the resultant measurements from various fractions (eg humins, humic acids, etc) has been a topic of contention in the literature (see Blaauw *et al* 2004; Kilian *et al* 1995; 2000; Shore *et al* 1995). The two most commonly dated fractions from peat samples are the humins (ie alkali and acid insoluble organic detritus) and the humic acids (ie alkali soluble and acid insoluble matter). If there is not enough available material to date the separate fractions then the bulk sediment can be dated (ie humin and humic fractions combined).

As the humin fraction is composed of the actual organic detritus, the resultant date from measuring this fraction may have been affected by many of the same processes that affect the dating of macrofossils. Firstly, organic material that forms all or part of the humin fraction could be in-washed, which would result in a date that is too old for its context. Contamination of this material by geological age carbon (eg coal, hard-water error) would have the same effect. The humin fraction can also be too young, if for example the environment is prone to wet-dry episodes or bioturbation, allowing intrusive material to work its way down the sediment column. Therefore, the humin fraction is not necessarily homogenous, and so it might be best to avoid dating this fraction by AMS as the

Table 3.1 Radiocarbon determinations from Sutton Common

| Laboratory Number | Sample reference | Material | $\delta^{13}C$ (‰) | Radiocarbon Age (BP) | Weighted Mean (BP) | Calibrated Date (95% confidence) | Posterior Density Estimate (95% probability) |
|---|---|---|---|---|---|---|---|
| **Hampole Beck Core SC1** | | | | | | | |
| SUERC-8168 | SC1 0.0 – 0.02m | bulk sediment; humic acid | −29.2 | 1730±35 | | cal AD 230 – 410 | |
| SUERC-8169 | SC1 0.0 – 0.02m | bulk sediment; humin fraction | −29.9 | 2265±35 | | 400 – 200 cal BC | |
| SUERC-7608 | SC1 0.14m | bark, unidentified | −26.3 | 2465±35 | | 770 – 400 cal BC | |
| SUERC-5697 | SC1 0.5m | *Alnus glutinosa*, roundwood | −27.6 | 3310±40 | | 1690 – 1490 cal BC | |
| SUERC-5698 | SC1 0.54m | *Alnus glutinosa*, roundwood | −27.8 | 3520±35 | | 1950 – 1740 cal BC | |
| SUERC-7612 | SC1 0.58m | *Alnus glutinosa*, roundwood | −28.0 | 2495±35 | | 790 – 410 cal BC | |
| SUERC-7615 | SC1 0.7m | cf *Alnus*, roundwood | −25.6 | 3880±35 | | 2470 – 2200 cal BC | |
| SUERC-7614 | SC1 1.12m | *Corylus avellana*, roundwood | −28.1 | 4480±35 | | 3360 – 3020 cal BC | |
| SUERC-7613 | SC1 1.3m | bark, unidentified | −29.3 | 5140±35 | | 4040 – 3800 cal BC | |
| SUERC-7616 | SC1 1.56m | *Betula sp*, roundwood | −27.6 | 7985±35 | | 7060 – 6700 cal BC | |
| SUERC-7617 | SC1 1.8m | *Alnus glutinosa*, roundwood | −29.2 | 5370±35 | | 4330 – 4050 cal BC | |
| SUERC-8018 | SC1 2.63m | bulk sediment; humic acid | −29.8 | 8920±60 | 8879±33 (T'= 0.7; v = 1; T'(5%) = 3.8) (Ward and Wilson 1978) | 8230 – 7840 cal BC | |
| SUERC-7622 | SC1 2.63m | bulk sediment; humin fraction | −30.1 | 8860±40 | | | |
| SUERC-7618 | SC1 3.34m | *Corylus avellana*, roundwood | −31.0 | 8935±35 | | 8260 – 7960 cal BC | |
| **Cremations** | | | | | | | |
| OxA-14608 | 7074A | cremated human bone | −19.9 | 3445±31 | 3467±23 (T'= 1.1; v = 1; T'(5%) = 3.8) | 1885 – 1690 cal BC | |
| SUERC-6143 | 7074B | cremated human bone | −19.9 | 3495±35 | | | |

| Lab code | Sample | δ13C | BP | cal BC | cal BC |
|---|---|---|---|---|---|
| OxA-14609 | cremated animal bone | −17.8 | 2229±27 | 390–200 cal BC | |
| SUERC-6147 | cremated animal bone | −22.9 | 2245±35 | | |
| | | | 2235±21 (T′=0.1; v=1; T′(5%)=3.8) | | |
| **Defences** | | | | | |
| HAR-8916 | SC022C02 | Peat; from the upper peat layer [022] directly beneath bank of the smaller enclosure | −30.7 | 2240±90 | 490–40 cal BC | 540–350 cal BC |
| GU-5524 | 051 | Debarked & roughly trimmed stake used in the palisade. *Quercus* sp < 30 years old (J Hillam, 1995) | −25.8 | 2370±50 | 740–380 cal BC | 510–360 cal BC |
| GU-5525 | 055 | Debarked & roughly trimmed stake used in the palisade. *Quercus* sp < 30 years old (J Hillam, 1995) | −24.4 | 2360±50 | 730–370 cal BC | 500–360 cal BC |
| HAR-8915 | SC059C01 | Roundwood from the primary fill [059] of the ditch in the smaller enclosure. Sub-sample *Alnus* (R Gale, 1999) | −29.5 | 2260±70 | 410–160 cal BC | 490–270 cal BC |
| HAR-8914 | SC108C03 | Roundwood, from a timber 'framework' within the fill of the ditch [108] in the smaller enclosure. Sub-sample possibly *Quercus* sp (R Gale, 1999) | −32.1 | 2320±70 | 730–200 cal BC | 480–340 cal BC (85%) or 320–230 cal BC (10%) |
| HAR-8917 | SC057C04 | Carbonised seeds; spelt, some emmer (G Jones, 1987) from ditch fill [057] | −23.2 | 2340±70 | 750–200 cal BC | 430–200 cal BC |

smallest contamination would greatly affect the resultant measurement. Humins may be dated better through conventional radiocarbon dating techniques, as it is unlikely that a sufficient volume of such contamination would be present to bias the results significantly.

The second peat fraction that is often dated is the humic acids, which are the *in situ* products of plant decay. Although they are produced *in situ* and imply a stability to the ground surface, it has been shown that they can be mobile in groundwater, both vertically and horizontally (Shore *et al* 1995), but that their mobility is probably limited. Therefore, humic acids cannot be relied upon to always correctly date the level from which they were collected either. However, unlike the humin fraction, humic acids are homogenous, as they are alkali soluble, and therefore are better suited to AMS dating than the humin fraction.

In some cases, when there is not enough material for dating of separate fractions, the humic acid and humin fractions can be bulked together to provide an average date for all the organic material in that level. As stated above, however, it is preferable to have the dates on the two fractions as this provides the data necessary for using replication as a measure of consistency. When the dates on two fractions are obtained, if they are statistically consistent, a weighted average can be taken before calibration as described in Ward and Wilson (1978). If the two results are statistically inconsistent then the data need to be reevaluated, in an attempt to determine which sample more reliably relates to the date of peat formation at the level under consideration.

It is important to stress once more that, because of the various scientific opinions regarding the fractions of peat that can be reliably dated and site-specific factors, consistency is sought within the radiocarbon dating programme.

In Table 3.1, where more than one fraction has been dated and the fractions are statistically consistent, a weighted mean and error has been calculated (Ward and Wilson 1978). This combined result has then been used for all subsequent analyses as it is the best representation for the date of the level from which it came.

### 3.3.3.2 Dendrochronology *by N Nayling*

Methods employed at the Lampeter Dendrochronology Laboratory in general follow those described by English Heritage (1998). The selection of samples for analysis was carried out through desk-based assessment of descriptions of timbers held in store, followed by visual examination of these timbers during a visit to the University of Exeter. Samples were taken from all oak timbers which had sufficient rings (ie >50) for analysis. Each sample was labelled with its timber code to ensure linkage between the samples and the site record. This was not possible in two instances where the timbers retained no label. These samples have been given temporary codes ANON and ANON2. Samples were either cleaned with a razor blade, or frozen for 48 hours and then cleaned with a 'Surform' plane before final cleaning with a razor blade to expose the complete ring sequence of each piece.

The complete sequences of growth rings in the samples that were selected for dating purposes were measured to an accuracy of 0.01mm using a micro-computer-based travelling stage (Tyers 1999). The ring sequences were plotted onto semi-log graph paper to enable visual comparisons to be made between sequences. In addition cross-correlation algorithms (Baillie and Pilcher 1973; Munro 1984) were employed to search for positions where the ring sequences were highly correlated. These positions were checked visually using the graphs and, where these were satisfactory, new mean sequences were constructed from the synchronised sequences. The *t*-values were derived from the original CROS algorithm (Baillie and Pilcher 1973). A *t*-value of 3.5 or over is usually indicative of a good match, although this is with the proviso that high *t*-values at the same relative or absolute position must be obtained from a range of independent sequences, and that satisfactory visual matching supports these positions. Timbers from the same tree generally have *t*-values greater than 10.0. Lower values from timbers from the same tree, for example on morphological grounds, are, however, quite common. It is the visual similarity in medium-term growth trends of the samples that is the critical factor in determining 'same tree' origin.

All the measured sequences from this assemblage were compared with each other and any found to cross-match were combined to form a site master curve. These and any remaining unmatched ring sequences were tested against a range of reference chronologies, using the same matching criteria of high *t*-values, replicated values against a range of chronologies at the same position, and satisfactory visual matching. Where such positions are found these provide calendar dates for the ring-sequence.

The tree-ring dates produced by this process initially only date the rings present in the timber. The interpretation of these dates relies upon the nature of the final rings in the sequence. If the sample ends in the heartwood of the original tree, a *terminus post quem (tpq)* for the felling of the tree is indicated by the date of the last ring plus the addition of the minimum expected number of sapwood rings which are missing. This *tpq* may be many decades prior to the real felling date. Where some of the outer sapwood or the heartwood/sapwood boundary survives on the sample, a felling date range can be calculated using the maximum and minimum number of sapwood rings likely to have been present. The sapwood estimates applied throughout this report are a minimum of ten and maximum of 46 annual rings, where these figures indicate the 95% confidence limits of the range. These figures are applicable to oaks from the British Isles (Tyers 1998). Alternatively, if bark-edge survives, then a felling date can be directly utilised from the date of the outermost ring.

### 3.3.4 Finds analysis

Artefacts were examined by the specialists and classified using appropriate typological systems, unless otherwise indicated. In addition, the composition of small finds of pottery, glass, and gold was analysed using a range of technologies.

#### 3.3.4.1 Pottery *by C Cumberpatch*

The pottery was examined with a ×10 hand lens and selected samples were submitted to Dr A Vince for petrological and chemical analysis. These were thin-sectioned at the Department of Earth Sciences, University of Manchester, and stained using Dickson's Method (Dickson 1965).

#### 3.3.4.2 Glass *by J Henderson*

Microsamples of each object were removed, mounted in epoxy resin and chemically analysed using electron probe microanalysis. The full conditions of analysis are described in Henderson (1988).

#### 3.3.4.3 Gold *by J D Hill*

The gold ingot was analysed using a JEOL JXA–8200 electron probe microanalyser, undertaken by Jens Anderson at the Camborne School of Mines, University of Exeter. Ten readings were taken along the length of the ingot.

### 3.3.5 Bone remains

#### 3.3.5.1 Human bone – cremated *by J McKinley*

Recording and analysis of the cremated bone followed the writer's standard procedures (McKinley 1994a, 5–21; 2004). Age was assessed from the stage of skeletal and tooth development (Van Beek 1983; Scheuer and Black 2000), and the patterns and degree of age-related changes to the bone and teeth (Brothwell 1972; Buikstra and Ubelaker 1994). Sex was ascertained from the sexually dimorphic traits of the skeleton (Bass 1987; Buikstra and Ubelaker 1994).

#### 3.3.5.2 Human bone – not cremated *by C Knüsel*

Due to the incompleteness and fragmentary condition of the remains, standard recording procedures could not be employed. Fragments were separated into axial and appendicular components and then sorted into skeletal elements such that a conjoining exercise could be performed within and between the two assemblages. At this stage, any non-human remains were separated from those of human origin. This procedure permitted the determination of the minimum number of individuals (MNI) who contributed to the assemblage. In the absence of substantial infra-cranial remains, sex determinations were made on the basis of skeletal development (fusion of sutures and secondary growth centres), robusticity, and non-metric features of the remains (see Bass 1987; Buikstra and Ubelakker 1994). Age-at-death determinations were based on tooth wear, in the absence of other indicators provided by the infra-cranial skeleton, following Brothwell (1981).

#### 3.3.5.3 Animal bone *by A Outram*

The identification of the animal bones was carried out by comparison with modern reference material at the Department of Archaeology, University of Exeter. Distinction between sheep and goat was only attempted on those elements that are particularly diagnostic. Where distinction was attempted, it followed the criteria laid down by Boessneck (1969) for the appendicular skeleton and Payne (1985) for teeth.

All elements of the skeleton were included in the analysis, but the following points should be borne in mind. The skull was represented in the counts by the maxilla, horn cores, and occipital condyles. Vertebrae were only counted if the centrum was present. Ribs were only counted if the articular end was present and identification to species was not undertaken. Instead, ribs were separated into large mammals (cattle/horse size), medium mammals (sheep/goat/pig size), and small mammals. The countable zone on the pelvis was the acetabulum and the scapula was only counted if the glenoid cavity or collum was present. The assemblage was quantified in terms of a simple Number of Identifiable Specimens (NISP) count and a Minimum Number of Elements (MNE) count (Klein and Cruz-Uribe 1984). For both the NISP and MNE, the proximal and distal ends of long bones (humerus, radius, metacarpal, femur, tibia, and metatarsal) were counted as separate elements. The NISP included all identified, countable specimens, including loose teeth. In calculating MNEs, specimens were only discounted if, during analysis, it was clear that two fragments from the same context might derive from the same bone. The MNE count also excluded loose teeth.

The ageing of sheep mandibles followed the system of allocating mandibular tooth rows to wear stages devised by Payne (1973). Cattle mandibular tooth rows were aged in a similar way following an adaptation by Halstead (1985) of Payne's (1973) methodology for sheep, using wear patterns observed by Grant (1982). Pig mandible ages were based on tooth eruption data given by Silver (1969). Epiphyseal fusion ages were taken from Silver (1969). Neonatal specimens were identified by virtue of their size, external, and internal (where visible) texture, general morphology, and by comparison with reference material. The sexing of pig mandibles was based on the morphology of the canine as given by Schmid (1972) or, in the absence of the canine, on the nature of the canine socket (P Halstead pers comm). A selection of useful measurements was taken on each element, as defined by von den Driesch (1976).

Bone fracture analysis was undertaken to identify bone marrow exploitation and help to understand the taphonomic history of the assemblage (see Outram 2005). The identification of fracture types and dynamic impact scars follows criteria laid down by Morlan (1984), Johnson (1985), and Outram (2002). All shaft fragments were analysed for fracture type, whether identified to species and element or not (see Outram 2001). Only those fragments which were too small or too eroded for analysis were discounted. For each fragment, the presence or absence of a particular fracture type or dynamic impact scar was noted. More than one type of fracture can be present on any given specimen. The fracture types were defined as follows: 'helical' (bones broken peri-mortem, whilst still very fresh), 'dry' (bones broken sometime after deposition that display a mixture of fresh and unfresh fracture features), 'mineralised' (fractures occurring long after deposition, when organic content has been almost totally lost and all features of fresh fracture have gone), and 'new' (recent fractures resulting from damage during excavation or storage). Surface features such as gnawing and evidence of butchery were also recorded. The identification of such marks was aided by low-incidence lighting and low-power magnification.

Co-mingled human bone fragments and teeth were identified using reference material at the Department of Archaeology, University of Exeter, and with reference to Schwarz (1995) and White (1991).

### 3.3.6 *Palaeoenvironmental remains*

#### 3.3.6.1 **Pollen** *by B Gearey*

The Hampole Beck deposits were sampled using a standard pattern Russian corer. A pit *c* 0.17m deep was excavated through the topsoil and all sample depths are from the base of this pit. Cores were extruded into plastic tube and wrapped in polythene. Open sections across the ditches were available and these sequences were therefore sampled using monolith tins. All samples were stored in the dark at 4°C prior to analysis. Sub-samples were initially extracted at 0.08m intervals but this interval was reduced to 0.04m and 0.02m in places of especial interest. Pollen preparation was carried out using standard techniques including acetolysis and HF treatment (Moore *et al* 1991). *Lycopodium* spores were added to enable calculation of pollen concentrations (Stockmarr 1971). Counting was carried out on a Leica DMLB microscope at a magnification of ×400 and ×1000 oil immersion for critical identifications. Identification used standard keys (Moore *et al* 1991) and the type-slide collection in the Department of Geography at the University of Hull. Pollen nomenclature follows the recommendations suggested by Bennett *et al* (1994). A pollen sum of at least 300TLP (Total Land Pollen) was employed, increasing to 500TLP in places. Pollen preservation and concentration was found to be particularly variable and in some segments of the core, a sum of 300TLP was not always attained despite the counting of multiple slides. Some samples were found to contain extremely low concentrations of pollen and certain others were entirely bereft of palynomorphs or had clearly been affected by differential preservation. This was found to be a particular problem for the sequence from Trench 3. Further analyses indicated that preservation of pollen in these deposits was very poor. For this reason, full analyses were not carried out and this sequence will not be discussed further here.

The results of the analyses of the Hampole Beck sequence (Fig 4.5) and the Trench 4 sequence (Fig 5.29) are presented as pollen diagrams produced using the programme TILIA and TILIA*GRAPH (Grimm 1991). All percentages values are of TLP unless otherwise specified. Each diagram has been divided into local pollen assemblage zones (lpaz) to aid interpretation, with the prefix HBSC for the Hampole Beck sequence and T4SC for the Trench 4 diagram.

#### 3.3.6.2 **Plant macrofossils and insects**
*by A Hall and H Kenward*

Samples, which were usually 3 kg in size, were prepared by disaggregation and sieving following the methods of Kenward *et al* (1980), using sieves with a mesh size of 300μm, with paraffin flotation (*ibid*) being used where it was judged that invertebrate remains were present. In other cases, a 'washover' was sometimes used to separate lighter (charred plant) material from the denser fraction, but under the particular circumstances at this site this was not usually very effective: it was very characteristic of most of the deposits, as noted by Boardman and Charles (in Parker Pearson and Sydes 1997), that there was at least some impregnation of the charred plant material by iron salts which made this component unusually dense. At its strongest, this impregnation resulted in plant macrofossils (here essentially wood charcoal and charred cereal grains) being so far replaced or coated by iron oxide that they appeared orange in colour. In other cases, grains and charcoal fragments had sand grains cemented to their surfaces to some degree. The grains were entirely coated and sometimes the presence of a grain inside the shell of cemented sand could only be deduced from the size and shape of the object (or by breaking it open!). Clearly material with this kind of iron impregnation and/or surface-cemented sand would not respond to normal washover techniques for separation. The residues were therefore usually simply dried and sieved and each sieve fraction examined. In those cases where the 2–4mm fraction was rich in cereal grains, a proportion of the fraction by weight was subsampled at random and this was used to estimate the numbers of grains and large chaff fragments used in the analysis, with full counts of grain, chaff, and charred weed seeds being made for the other fractions. The abundances of all other plant remains in the samples, along with other components such as sand, charcoal, and bone, were estimated using a four-point scale from 1 (up to 5 individuals per kg, or one or a few fragments or 'traces') to 4 (abundant specimens or a major component of the sample, representing more than 50% of the original volume of sediment).

Any invertebrates in the residues from paraffin flotation (reviewed by AH during the botanical analysis) were passed to HK. Following an initial assessment of the flots, detailed analysis for invertebrate remains was made where appropriate: only four contained more than a trace of invertebrate remains and only three yielded sufficient fossils for interpretation. Identifications were made in the flot (for familiar taxa) or placed on damp filter paper for more careful inspection where necessary. The remains of adult beetles and bugs from three subsamples were 'detail' recorded, and one small group 'scan' recorded, in the terminology of Kenward (1992). A record of preservational condition was made using the scales presented by Kenward and Large (1998). Fossils were identified by comparison with modern reference material and using the standard works. Adult beetles and bugs, other than aphids and scale insects, were recorded fully quantitatively and a minimum number of individuals estimated on the basis of the fragments present. Other invertebrate macrofossils were usually recorded semi-quantitatively using the scale described by Kenward *et al* (1986) and Kenward (1992), again using estimates for extremely abundant taxa. Data pertaining to invertebrate remains were recorded directly or transferred from a paper record to a computer database (using *Paradox* software) for analysis and long-term storage.

The interpretative methods employed for invertebrates were essentially the same as those used in work on a variety of sites by Hall, Kenward and co-workers (see Kenward 1978, with modifications outlined by, for example, Kenward 1982; 1988; Hall and Kenward 1990; and Kenward and Hall 1995; 1997).

### 3.3.6.3 Geoarchaeology *by G Ayala*

In August 2003 a site visit was undertaken by the author and Matt Canti of the Environmental Studies branch of English Heritage. The geoarchaeological investigation of the site focused on both the identification of remnants of the Iron Age land surface that was compromised during the earth works of the 1980s, as well as other questions which arose during excavation. Oriented soil samples were taken with a series of overlapping kubiena tins as well as bulk samples from profiles and sectioned features for further laboratory analysis. The oriented samples were impregnated with resin and thin sections were prepared at the McBurney Laboratory for Geoarchaeology at Cambridge. The micromorphological analysis was undertaken with a polarising petrological microscope and description followed the standardised methods and terminology of Bullock *et al* (1985).

### 3.3.6.4 Geology *by C Patrick*

Magnesian Limestone from the marsh-fort, used within the revetment wall on the west side of the larger enclosure, was sampled and compared with samples from local quarries and outcrops. It was hoped that the stone from the Iron Age site could be provenanced and thus provide an understanding of the 'hinterland' of the marsh-fort in terms of materials used in its construction.

Samples were taken from seven Upper Magnesian Limestone quarries and outcrops, and from one Lower Magnesian Limestone quarry, all located within 5km from Sutton Common. The assessment was based on three characteristics: lithology and overall appearance, stone size, and stone thickness. Colour and surface crusting were ignored as possible diagnostic features because of the diverging weathering histories of samples from the site and newly exposed stone faces in the quarries. Similarly, lamination, fossils, and cavities were omitted from the analysis as these did not offer objective criteria for comparison.

The result of matching the lithologies of stone samples from the excavations with the quarries and outcrops did not produce a clear result concerning the provenance of the stone used in the construction of the marsh-fort. Nevertheless, the most probable source of this limestone was found to be Askern/Askern Hill area, with North Park Quarry, Owston, and Suttonfield Quarry, Campsall, identified as somewhat less likely sources. Further analysis of the stone was considered to be unlikely to pinpoint the source of the material used in the construction of the marsh-fort, and this line of enquiry was therefore discontinued.

# 4 The landscape context

## 4.1 Introduction  *by R Van de Noort*

This chapter is concerned with the landscape context of Sutton Common. It considers the geology, physical landscape, and evidence for pre-Iron Age activity in the broader landscape, including the evidence for an early Bronze Age mortuary enclosure on the Common excavated during 2003. It presents the results of the palynological work undertaken as part of the current project on a deep core taken from the Hampole Beck palaeochannel between the two enclosures. These results incorporate indications for the various phases of woodland clearances and intensification of a mixed agricultural use of the surrounding land, presumably concentrated on the limestone immediately to the west of the Common. This section also presents the analysis of the flaked stone artefacts from the Common, related to human presence on the Common of Mesolithic, Neolithic, and early Bronze Age date, found during the excavations between 1998 and 2003.

## 4.2 Geology, physical landscape, and early human activity

### 4.2.1 *Geology*  by R Van de Noort and H Chapman

Sutton Common lies immediately to the east of the dipslope of the Magnesian Limestone where it encounters the Triassic Sherwood Sandstone (Gaunt 1994). The geological strata in this region dip generally eastwards, giving the appearance of a series of north–south aligned strips of scarp slopes, ridges, and valley lowlands. Thus, from west to east, the Carboniferous Coal Measures are overlain by Magnesian Limestone and Magnesian Marl, which in turn are replaced as the uppermost geological strata by Triassic Sherwood Sandstone and, at the Isle of Axholme and the in Trent valley, by Triassic Mercia Mudstone (Fig 4.1).

The Magnesian Limestone landscape is one of low, rolling hills, smoothed by the actions of ice during the Quaternary, and with some incising stream valleys. The land is free-draining, and is today given overwhelmingly to arable agriculture.

The Triassic Sherwood Sandstone landscape, including Sutton Common itself, is characterised by drift deposits overlying the Sandstone. These sands, silts, and clays are largely derived from Lake Humber, the name commonly used to describe the lake or lakes that formed around the Devensian ice sheet in the Humberhead Levels and the Vale of York (eg Van de Noort 2004a, fig 11). Lake Humber ceased to exist not later than

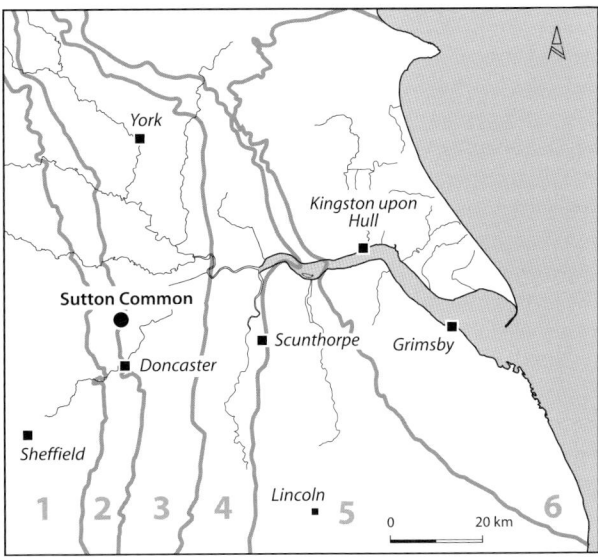

*Figure 4.1  Underlying geology, after Catt (1990) and Gaunt (1994). 1: Carboniferous Coal Measures; 2: Permian Upper Magnesian Limestone and Upper Permian Marl; 3: Triassic Sherwood Sandstone; 4: Triassic Mercia Mudstone; 5: Jurassic marls, limestones, sandstones and clays; 6: Cretaceous chalk*

*c* 11,000 cal BC (*c* 11,100 BP), when the ice sheet blocking the Humber Gap between the Yorkshire Wolds and the Lincolnshire Wolds retreated, or possibly somewhat earlier through silting of the lake itself (Bateman *et al* 2000). The Lake Humber deposits were subject to aeolian reworking during the Loch Lomond Stadial of the Devensian, *c* 11,500–10,500 cal BC (*c* 11,700–10,500 BP), and this reworking resulted in the formation of dunes or 'islands', including those at Sutton Common. These flatlands extend eastwards towards the raised mires of Thorne and Hatfield Moors and the River Trent and, before the large-scale drainage projects in the early modern period, the land was used for pasture or survived as extensive wetlands (see section 2.2.1.1).

### 4.2.2 *Landscape context*  by R Van de Noort and H Chapman

Within the immediate landscape of Sutton Common, the fluvial and aeolian reworking of Lake Humber deposits resulted in the formation of five dunes or 'islands' of relatively higher ground. Cutting through the centre of Sutton Common is an infilled palaeochannel of the Hampole Beck which separates the two largest islands, these

## 54 Sutton Common

*Figure 4.2 Aerial photograph of the Common in 2002, looking north towards Wentbridge and Eggborough power station*

being occupied by the Iron Age marsh-fort features (Fig 4.2). At the time of the construction of the marsh-fort, this palaeochannel would have been largely infilled, being defined by a locally wetter peaty hollow with associated vegetation coverage; originally this Late-glacial meltwater stream flowed north towards the proto-river Went at Wentbridge. The eastern edge of Sutton Common is defined by deeper peats that follow a fault line in the bedrock, now occupied by Shirley Wood, Shirley Pool, and Rushy Moor. The area of Sutton Common lies between 2.38m OD and 5.77m OD, with a mean height of 4.30m OD. Four of the five raised 'islands' have produced lithics dating to the Mesolithic, Neolithic, and /or Bronze Age periods, discovered during field walking (Parker Pearson and Sydes 1997; Head *et al* 1997; see also section 4.4).

### 4.2.3 Early human activity
*by R Van de Noort and H Chapman*

Archaeological evidence for human activity predating the Iron Age comes principally in the form of flaked stone artefacts. Mesolithic period finds have been made from the island of the larger enclosure (see section 4.4), and from the smaller island to the north of the smaller enclosure, where early Neolithic material was also found (Parker Pearson and Sydes 1997, 234). The larger enclosure also produced some evidence for human presence in the Bronze Age, presumably the result of a short-lived hunting expedition. The distribution of Mesolithic, Neolithic, and Bronze Age artefacts reflects that observed for the Humberhead Levels and other regions of the Humber Wetlands, with the exception of the Vale of York. The prevalence of riverside locations, especially in the Mesolithic period, hints at the use of logboats and possibly hideboats as the principal way of travelling through the landscape, allowing for the easy identification of the watering places of the larger mammals being hunted (Van de Noort 2004a, 91). The pollen evidence from the Hampole Beck palaeochannel shows clear evidence for woodland clearances in the Neolithic and later periods (see section 4.3.4). The discovery of a small Neolithic period axe on the edge of the Common can be linked temporally to this, although lack of exact provenance prevents any further inferences being drawn from this find.

The presence of six bronze objects of middle Bronze Age date in the area around Sutton Common, including a flanged axe from the Common itself, has been highlighted by Parker

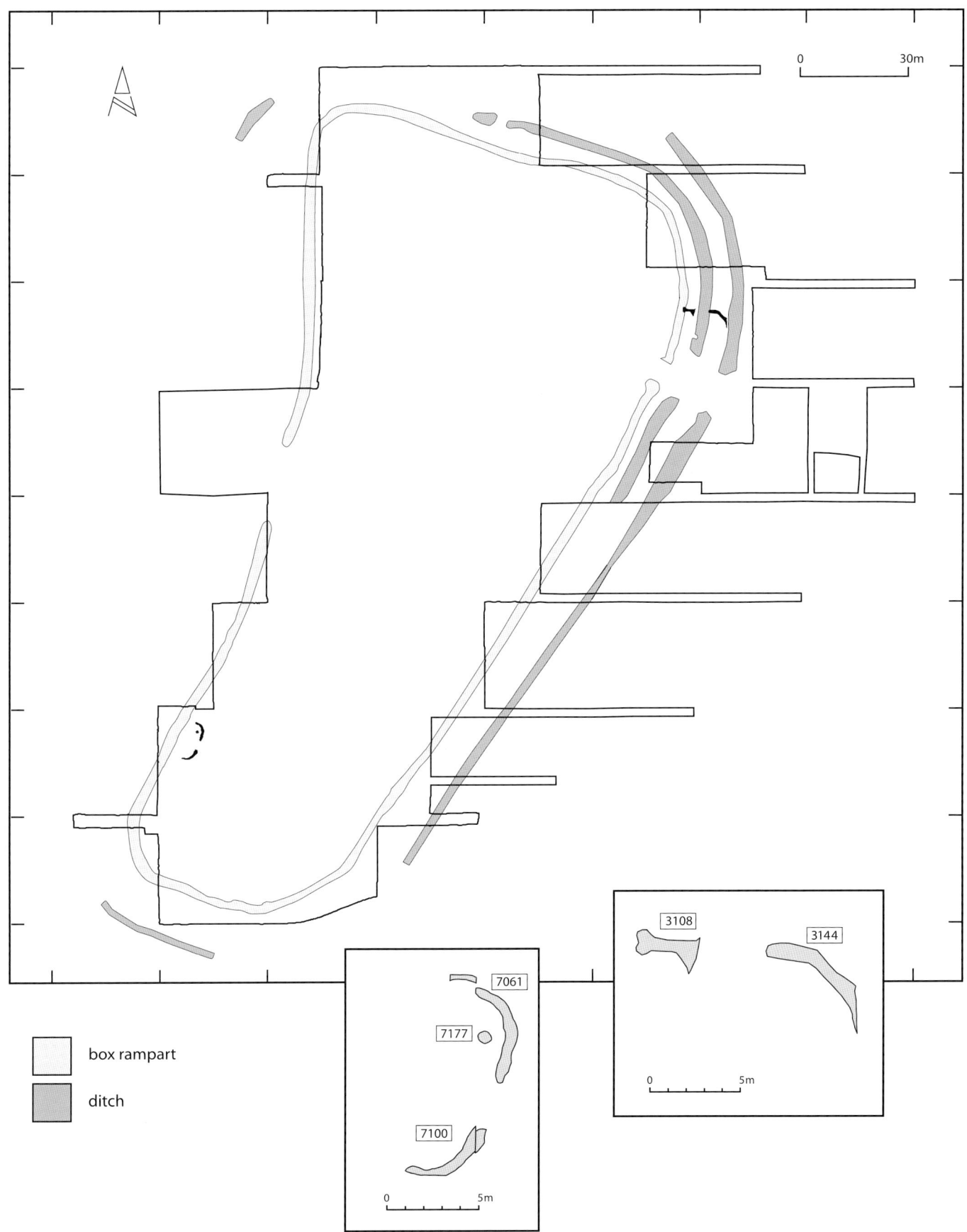

*Figure 4.3   Excavation plan 1998–2003: all features predating the marsh-fort and cemetery: undated ditch [3108]–[3144] near the eastern entranceway; early Bronze Age mortuary enclosure [7061]–[7100]; pit [7177] containing pyre debris*

Pearson and Sydes (1997, 234). They have suggested, partly on the basis of this relative density of bronze artefacts in the wider landscape, that 'Sutton Common may have sat on a broad political/cultural boundary', represented by Wallington-style metalwork to the north and Wilburton styles to the south (*ibid*, 245). This inference can not be upheld, however, in the light of the redating of the marsh-fort itself. As will be shown below, the palisade previously thought to be of late Bronze Age/early Iron Age date is, in fact, an integrated element of the defences dated to the 4th century BC. Nevertheless, the distribution is significant, and may be associated with the increased anthropogenic activity in the middle Bronze Age landscape as shown in the pollen analysis (see section 4.3.4), and with votive depositions of bronze artefacts in the Humber wetlands and elsewhere in Britain and western Europe (Bradley 1990; Van de Noort 2004a).

There is no doubt that by the 4th century BC, when the marsh-fort was built, the higher and drier part of the landscape to the west of the Common was inhabited, and the extensive woodland clearances indicate that both this area of habitation and the practice of mixed farming were extensive, even though the archaeological evidence for this is rather limited.

### 4.2.4 Bronze Age funerary remains at Sutton Common

#### 4.2.4.1 Introduction *by R Van de Noort*

During the 1998–2003 excavations, a limited number of features were noted that were considered to predate the 4th-century BC marsh-fort (Fig 4.3). Most prominent amongst these was the semicircular feature comprising ditch segments [3108] and [3144], located in Trench 3 some 15m to the north of the larger enclosure's eastern entranceway. Stratigraphically, these ditch segments were cut by the inner and outer ditches of the marsh-fort's defences, and must therefore predate the marsh-fort, but no additional information on the significance of this feature was forthcoming (see also section 5.4.4, for additional discussion of the dating of the defences). Nevertheless, during the excavations it had been remarked that the ditch segments resembled the ditch of a Bronze Age mortuary enclosure, but this was not proved in any way.

The other significant features found to predate the construction of the marsh-fort were segments [7100] and [7061] in Trench 7, forming part of a semicircular or oval enclosure measuring 10.4 × 5.8m, aligned north-northeast by south-southwest, following the alignment of the western box rampart. The western third of this mortuary ring was missing, although an interpolation of the complete shape would have underlain the rampart. The feature was 0.5m wide and only 0.08m deep. A real break in the enclosure in the eastern side could not be confirmed given the shallow nature of the surviving ditches. Within this enclosure, a shallow grave (cut: [7631] fill: [7074]) included cremated remains of a single individual, possibly a mature/older male.

#### 4.2.4.2 The human remains *by J McKinley*

The form of the deposit in grave [7631] is slightly enigmatic. A layer of fired clay appeared to 'line' the cut (0.20m diameter, 0.10m deep); the burning was not *in situ*. The material may be the remains of a pyre base constructed of clay and represent pyre debris deliberately laid as a primary deposit within the grave fill; this has been observed with other forms of pyre debris (mostly fuel-ash; eg McKinley 1997b, 138; 2000, 41). Generally, the bone within a formal unurned burial is made as a separate deposit within the grave fill, which may also include other cremation-related deposits such as pyre debris. Deposits of pyre debris – formal or incidental – are represented by a mix of archaeological components, predominantly fuel-ash with small amounts of bone, sometimes burnt flint and fired clay (McKinley 1997a, 56–7). The distribution of bone within the fill of cut [7631] is unclear; although the excavator recorded it as a mix of bone and fine fraction fuel-ash, it is difficult to distinguish visually bone distribution in these types of deposit.

The bone from grave [7631] is visually in good condition, but the assemblage contains only a few small fragments of trabecular bone. Although [7631] is likely to represent an unurned burial with a secondary deposit of pyre debris, this cannot be stated conclusively since the whole fill was processed as a single sample, and consequently the bone distribution remains uncertain. The slightly better preservation of the bone may be related to the burnt clay 'lining', which sealed off the burial remains from the surrounding natural sediments, and the fuel-ash-rich fill having an ameliorating effect on the acidity of the burial environment. The poor condition of the bone from the fuel-ash-rich environment within posthole [5033] (see below, section 8.4.1) may indicate either the effectiveness of the burnt clay 'lining' within [7631] or that the bone was in a more exposed burial environment prior to its final deposition. The bone was visible at surface level and it is probable that some will have been lost from the deposit as a result of disturbance. The surviving bone was white in colour, indicative of full oxidation (Holden *et al* 1995a and b). The weight of bone in the burial was relatively low, representing *c* 22% of the total weight of bone expected from an adult cremation (McKinley 1993), though the significance which may be attached to this observation is limited by the probable loss of at least

## Table 4.1  Human calcined bone: summary of results

| context | cut | deposit type | bone weight | age/sex | pathology summary |
|---|---|---|---|---|---|
| 7074 | 7631 | ?un burial + rpd | 348.8 g | adult >30 yr ??male | osteophytes – atlas |

KEY: rpd – redeposited pyre debris, un – unurned

some bone from the deposit due to disturbance and possibly also poor preservation. The weight is similar to that recorded from some prehistoric cemeteries, the undisturbed unurned burials from Westhampnett, West Sussex, containing an average of 301.1g (McKinley 1997a), though other sites in central England have recorded much higher bone weights of up to *c* 2200g (*ibid*, 68; 1990; Havis and Brooks 2004).

The largest recorded bone fragment was 40mm and about half of the bone was recovered from the 5mm sieve fraction. A number of factors may affect the size of cremated bone fragments and most of these are exclusive of any deliberate human action other than that of cremation itself (McKinley 1994b). In this instance, the relatively small fragment size is probably largely due to the acidic soil conditions and truncation of this feature, resulting in increased breakage along dehydration fissures formed during cremation. The burial contained some identifiable elements from all areas of the skeleton; the low percentage of identifiable axial skeletal fragments (1.5% of identifiable bone) probably reflects the largely trabecular nature of most of this bone (see above) and the relatively high percentage of identifiable skull (59%), its distinctive morphology visible even as small fragments (McKinley 2004, 11).

A minimum of one individual was identified, a mature/older adult, possibly male (Table 4.1). Slight osteophytes (new bone on joint surface margins) were observed on the anterior facet of the atlas vertebra. Seen alone, these lesions are largely age-related and in this case may have resulted in a slight feeling of stiffness in the joint (Rogers and Waldron 1995).

### 4.2.4.3 Cremation dating  *by D Hamilton, G Cook and C Bronk Ramsey*

The two measurements on cremated human bone from [7074] are statistically consistent, and so a weighted mean has been taken before calibration (T' = 1.1; ν = 1; T'(5%) = 3.8; Ward and Wilson 1978). The resultant mean is 3467±23 BP and gives a calibrated date range for the human cremation of 1885–1690 cal BC or the early Bronze Age (Fig 4.4; Needham 1996, Period 3).

### 4.2.4.4 Discussion  *by R Van de Noort*

Initially, it was thought that this oval-shaped feature comprising [7100] and [7061] and discovered during the 2003 excavations in Trench 7 was one of the 'mortuary rings' of Iron Age date (see section 8.2), even though it was at least four times the size of any of the other mortuary rings. It was also considered exceptional, as it contained the only 'formal' burial or redeposition of pyre debris, ie grave [7631]. The radiocarbon dating of the cremated remains proves beyond doubt that this feature predates the construction of the marsh-fort by 1300 years, and that it does not belong to the second phase activity of on the Common.

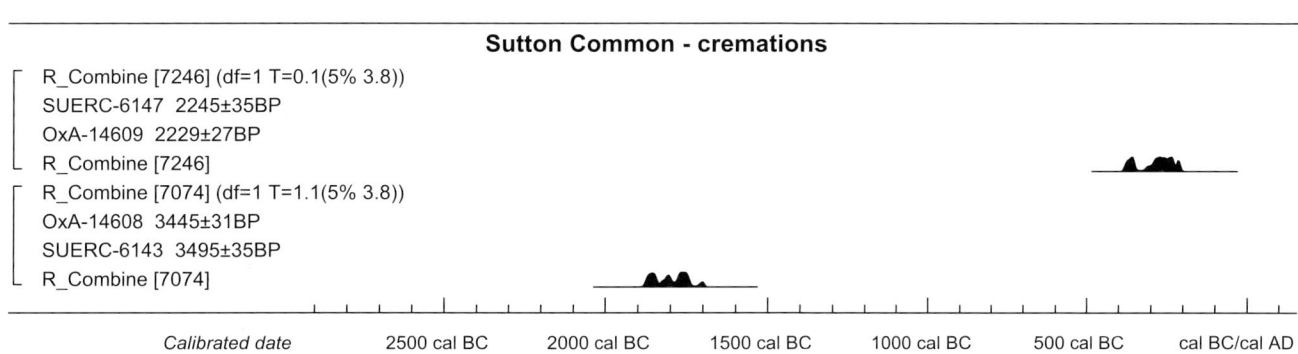

*Figure 4.4   Probability distributions of dates from cremation [7426] and [7074]. The replicate measurements were combined prior to calibration (Ward & Wilson 1978). Each distribution represents the relative probability that an event occurred at a particular time. These distributions are the result of simple radiocarbon calibration (Stuiver & Reimer 1993)*

In the context of the early Bronze Age of Yorkshire, cremation (as a funerary rite) and mortuary enclosures are not commonly known. Instead, our understanding of the mortuary rituals in this period remains dominated by inhumations beneath barrows, often accompanied by late-style Beakers and Beaker sherd scatters or Food Vessels (Manby *et al* 2003a: 61–4), a perception that undoubtedly reflects in part long-standing fieldwork and research biases. However, whilst cremation was a 'minority rite' of Food Vessel associations, it appears more common when accompanying Collared Urns and, interestingly, in upland areas such as the North York Moors and the southern Pennines, new monuments such as ring-banked or cairned enclosures were constructed to accommodate burials at this time (*ibid*, 63). The reappraisal of the circular site at Catfoss in Holderness, albeit of middle Bronze Age date, shows that mortuary enclosures were also constructed and used for the redeposition of pyre debris in lowland contexts (McInnes 1968).

The semicircular feature at Sutton Common containing the early Bronze Age cremation burial may be explained within this broader perspective of the construction of less monumental, but nevertheless formalised, circular and semicircular spaces where the remnants of pyre were deposited. It seems likely that the deposit at Sutton Common was enclosed, but possibly with an east-facing entrance. The construction of the marshfort's defences appears to have included the removal of topsoil (see section 5.6.2.2) and its probable reuse within the box rampart structure. This may have destroyed the western half of the enclosure's shallow ditches. The bulldozing of the banks, including the remnants of the box rampart, may have eroded these features further.

## 4.3 Palaeoenvironment

### 4.3.1 Introduction  by B Gearey

The sediments preserved in the Hampole Beck palaeochannel had previously been identified as having potential for providing a long record of vegetation change (eg Parker Pearson and Sydes 1997, 230; Lillie 1997, 67–73), and to this end, a systematic stratigraphic survey of the channel was carried out. This consisted of the excavation of 65 cores in seven locations across the Hampole Beck in the near vicinity of the site (Fig 4.5; Lillie and Schofield 2002). As part of this exercise, samples for pollen analysis were collected from organic deposits, with the aim of assessing the temporal framework of palaeochannel evolution and to identify a location suitable for the recovery of a sediment sequence for detailed pollen analysis. The main requirement for this was that the sequence recorded as much of the later prehistoric period as possible. However, the uppermost sediments in the Hampole Beck have clearly been badly affected by peat wastage and ploughing since the 1980s. It was also evident that sediment accumulation in the Hampole Beck had begun early in the Holocene with the majority of pollen samples recovered from these deposits (1–3.00m depth) characterised by pollen spectra indicative of this timeframe. Evidence for later Holocene contexts were identified in only four of the samples analysed and only one of these samples contained a pollen spectrum suggesting a 'cultural' landscape, which was tentatively suggestive of a later prehistoric date.

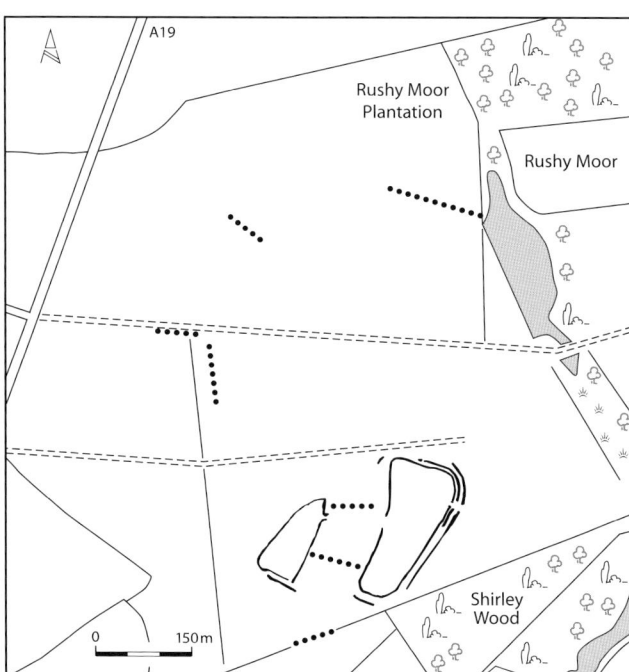

*Figure 4.5  Location of the boreholes transects set in 2002 on Rushy Moor and Sutton Common*

This location, immediately to the south of the causeway linking the smaller and larger enclosures, was therefore selected as the sampling site for the recovery of a long sequence for more detailed pollen analysis (henceforth referred to as the Palaeochannel core). Although the sequence provides details of various aspects of vegetation change at Sutton Common, the following discussion will concentrate on the evidence for human activity in the pollen record. Sample recovery, pollen preparation, and analyses followed the methods described in section 3.3.6.1. The results from the pollen analysis are shown in Figure 4.6 in the form of a percentage pollen diagram. The diagram has been divided into five local pollen assemblage zones based on changes in the taxa; these zones are summarised in Table 4.2. The chronology was derived from radiocarbon dating of critical horizons in the sequence.

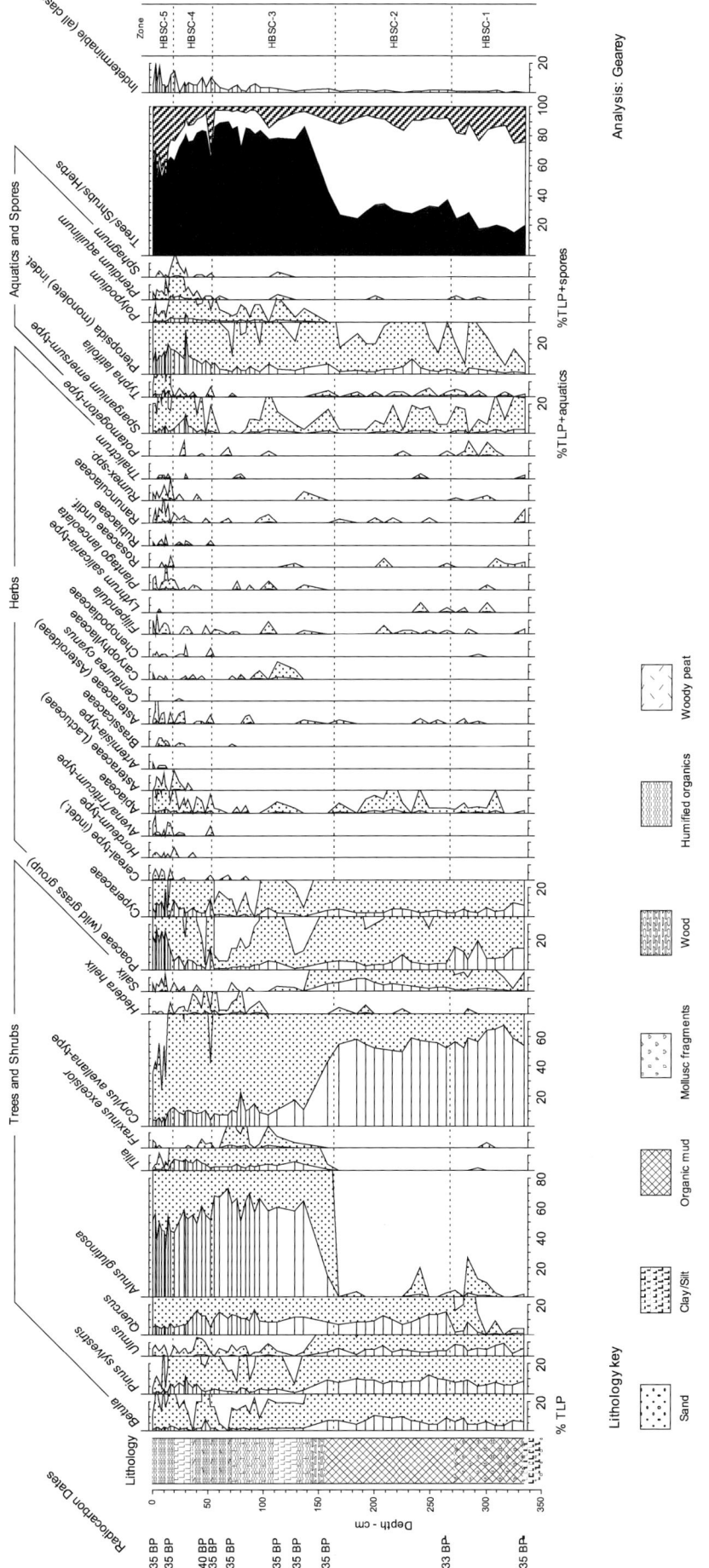

*Figure 4.6 Pollen diagram of the analysis of the Hampole Beck core*

**Table 4.2  Description of Local Pollen Zones, based on core from the Hampole Beck. LPAZ = local pollen assemblage zone. Percentages are of total land pollen (tlp) unless otherwise stated**

| LPAZ | Depth (m) | Main Taxa |
|---|---|---|

**Short description**

*HBSC-1*          3.34–2.68          *Corylus avellana*-type–*Ulmus*–*Betula*–*Pinus*–Poaceae

This zone is dominated by tree and shrub pollen at over 80%. *Corylus* accounts for over 50% of this, with *Betula* and *Pinus* both recorded at up to 10%, but *Quercus* and *Salix* are present at trace values (<1%) only, although the former displays a small peak towards the top of the diagram. Poaceae is fairly well represented at up to 20%, with Cyperaceae slightly lower at 5–10%. Other herbs are rare, with occasional grains of *Filipendula*, *Lythrum salicaria*, and *Rumex*. Aquatics are evident in the form of low but consistent values for *Sparganium emersum*-type and traces of *Potamogeton*-type and *Typha latifolia*

*HBSC-2*          2.68–1.63          *Corylus avellana*-type–*Quercus*–*Betula*–*Pinus*–*Salix*

Tree and shrub pollen continue to dominate this zone at up to 90% tlp. *Quercus* increases at the base of the zone to peak at 20%, before steadying at $c$ 15%. *Salix* also rises to $c$ 10% by the top of the zone. *Betula* and *Pinus* are recorded at similar values to the previous lpaz. Herbs remain sporadic and Poaceae is reduced to 5–10%. Aquatics continue to be represented by *Sparganium emersum*-type and occasional grains of *Typha latifolia*. There is a slight increase in Pteropsida (monolete) indet

*HBSC-3*          1.63–0.54          *Alnus glutinosa*–*Quercus*–*Corylus avellana*-type–*Tilia*

The most pronounced feature of this zone is the marked rise in *Alnus*, which replaces *Corylus* as the dominant arboreal taxa at up to 70%. *Tilia* also increases up to 10%. *Betula*, *Pinus*, and *Ulmus* are all reduced, whilst *Salix* almost disappears from the spectra. Both Poaceae and Cyperaceae are aected, dropping to trace levels by the top of the zone. Other herbs recorded at trace values include Caryophyllaceae, *Filipendula*, and sporadic records of *Plantago lanceolata*. The trace values of *Sparganium emersum*-type are initially maintained, but this taxon becomes increasingly rare towards the close of the lpaz. An increase in Pteropsida (monolete) indet is apparent at the base of the zone to over 20% tlp+spores, after which percentages fall to $c$ 5%tlp+spores

*HBSC-4*          0.54–0.18          *Alnus*–*Tilia*–*Corylus avellana*–type–Poaceae–Cyperaceae

This zone sees a slight reduction in *Alnus*, although it remains the dominant species at $c$ 50%. *Tilia* increases slightly whilst *Corylus* remains steady at $c$ 10–15%. *Quercus* shows an initial rise to 15% before declining steadily towards the close of the zone. *Pinus* drops at the base of the zone before increasing to $c$ 15%. Abrupt peaks in both Poaceae and Cyperaceae are evident at the opening of the zone, after which these taxa are reduced but rise steadily again to $c$ 10% and 15% respectively. Other herbs are restricted to low and sporadic occurrences. After its reduction in the previous zone, *Sparganium emersum*-type percentages increase to a peak of $c$ 15% tlp+aquatics. Pteropsida (monolete) indet values also rise to a peak of $c$ 30%tlp+spores and other spores including *Polypodium* and *Pteridium* are recorded at low but consistent values

*HBSC-5*          0.18–0.0          *Alnus*–Poaceae–Cyperaceae

This zone is distinguished by a sharp reduction in *Tilia* to trace values. Reductions in other arboreal taxa including *Corylus* and *Pinus* are apparent, although *Alnus* and *Quercus* are less aected and are recorded at similar percentages to the previous zone. Poaceae increases to its highest values for the diagram reaching $c$ 25%. Cyperaceae also increases to $c$ 10%. A wider suite of herbs is recorded compared to HBSC-4, although none of these attains values above 1–2%. These include *P. lanceolata*, Asteraceae (Lactuceae and Asteroideae), *Rumex* spp, Ranunculaceae, Caryophyllaceae, and Chenopodiaceae. Grains of cereal-type including *Avena*/*Triticum* are also present. *Sparganium emersum*-type is reduced relative to the previous zone, but Pteropsida (monolete) indet is well represented at $c$ 15% tlp+spores

### 4.3.2 Radiocarbon dating  by D Hamilton, B Gearey, G Cook, C Bronk Ramsey and P Marshall

Twelve samples were submitted from SC1, a core taken from the sediments preserved in the Hampole Beck palaeochannel, resulting in fourteen measurements. Two samples, SC1 0.0–0.02m and SC1 2.63m, were bulk sediment samples, while the other samples were short-lived macrofossils recovered from the core.

Figure 4.7 shows the calibrated radiocarbon dates. Most of the dates are in good agreement with the stratigraphy, but there are discrepancies in three places down the core and specifically with the results from SC1 0.0–0.02m (SUERC–8168 and –8169), SC1 0.58m (SUERC–7612), and SC1 1.56m (SUERC–7616) and SC1 1.8m (SUERC–7617).

Measurements on the humic acid (SUERC–8168) and humin (SUERC–8169) fractions from the top of the core (SC1 0.0–0.02m) are not statistically consistent (T' = 116.6; ν = 1; T'(5%) = 3.8; Ward and Wilson 1978) and suggest the presence of either residual or intrusive material in one of the fractions. Erroneous dates through humic

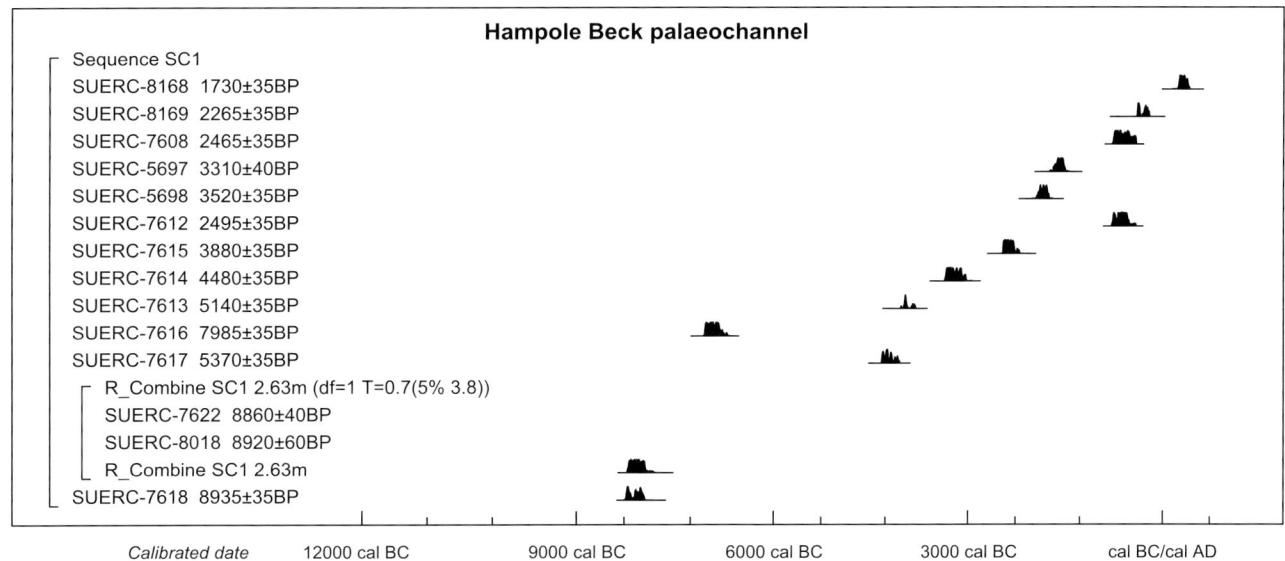

*Figure 4.7 Probability distributions of dates from Hampole Beck palaeochannel. Each distribution represents the relative probability that an event occurred at a particular time. These distributions are the result of simple radiocarbon calibration (Stuiver & Reimer 1993)*

acid mobility are primarily the product of downward and lateral migration of younger humic acids. Furthermore, the fact that sediment is by definition redeposited material and not formed *in situ* means the humin fraction (ie, the actual organic detritus) is likely to be composed of older material that has provided an erroneous date on the bulk AMS sample. Therefore we believe that the humic acid fraction provides the more reliable date for this level.

Sample SC1 0.58m (SUERC–7612) appears to be too young for its statigraphic position. While the material was identified as *Alnus* sp roundwood, it was also noted that it might possibly be root wood (Rowena Gale, pers comm). The disagreement between the date and the stratigraphic position of this sample would suggest that it is root wood and it is therefore intrusive. As such, it does not provide a date for this level.

The third and final location down the core where there is a discrepancy between the radiocarbon results and stratigraphy is between samples SC1 1.56m (SUERC–7616) and SC1 1.8m (SUERC–7617). Figure 4.7 clearly shows that either SC1 1.56m is too old in the sequence, or SC1 1.8m is too young. This reversal is difficult to explain solely on the physical material or its chemical characteristics. However, the accuracy of these measurements to date the horizons from which they came may be assessed in part by comparison with the corresponding pollen spectra. SUERC–7616 dates the rise in alder and lime at Sutton Common, and whilst the alder rise tends to be erratic in time and space, with dates of between 5000 and 7000 cal BC (Bennett and Birks 1990) it has been dated in this region to 6650–6450 cal BC (OxA–8260; 7720±50 BP) at Askham Bog, Vale of York (Gearey and Lillie 1999) and to 5470–5050 cal BC (Beta–7527; 6290±70 BP) at Bole Ings, Nottinghamshire (Brayshay and Dinnin 1999). This implies that SUERC–7616 is likely to provide a more accurate date. If SUERC–7617 is accepted as accurate on the other hand, this would mean that both the alder and lime rise at Sutton Common post-dated 4330–4050 cal BC, which would appear strongly anomalous in comparison to the dates available for these events elsewhere in the region.

However, if SUERC–7616 is accepted, this indicates either an extremely low sediment accumulation rate between 1.56m and 1.30m, where SUERC–7613 provides a date of 4040–3800 cal BC, or suggests that there is a hiatus in the sequence. The latter seems probable, possibly connected to the presence of a large chunk of subfossil wood in the stratigraphy between 1.44m and 1.56m. The sediment above this point is a silty peat indicating increased input of minerogenic material into the palaeochannel and possibly some sediment erosion and/or reworking.

### 4.3.3 Early sediment accumulation in the Hampole Beck  by B Gearey

The lowermost deposits in the palaeochannel are non-polleniferous and consist of laminated sands and clays, which were probably deposited and/or reworked during the Late glacial period (*c* 13,400–9900 cal BC; *c* 13,000–10,200 BP). Channel incision in the Hampole Beck had ceased by the beginning of organic accumulation and the opening of the pollen diagram at 8260–7960 cal BC (8935±35BP, SUERC–7618). Aggradation thus began relatively early in the Holocene, a feature of many other river channels in the Humberhead Levels, where a very rapid phase of channel incision appears to have been followed shortly afterwards by aggradation (Dinnin 1997; Lillie 1997). The sediments in the Palaeochannel core and also in the other deposits recovered during the course of the stratigraphic survey (Lillie and Schofield 2002), consist of intercalated peats and silty peats, indicating a relatively low energy flow regime. There is evidence of phases of increased flow as the sediments continued to aggrade in the form of discrete sand and clay-silt lenses, which suggest occasional episodes of higher energy fluvial events and the inwash of minerogenic material. Radiocarbon dating of the palaeochannel core indicates that such processes may have resulted in a hiatus in the pollen sequence around 1.50–1.60m (see below).

### 4.3.4 The composition of the early Holocene vegetation at Sutton Common  by B Gearey

The woodland represented in HBSC–1 between 8260–7960 cal BC (SUERC–7618; 8935±35BP) and 8230–7840 cal BC (mean of SUERC–7622 and 8018; 8879±33 BP) appears to be typical of that seen at other sites in the Humber lowlands during the early Holocene (eg Tweddle 2001; Gearey and Lillie 1999; Lillie and Gearey 2000; Brayshay and Dinnin 1999), with hazel and elm dominant but with birch and Scots pine probably also present on poorer soils. Pollen data from the River Hull floodplain has been interpreted as showing that soils formed on sand and gravel contexts might have been characterised by more open birch/pine-dominated vegetation during the mid to late Holocene (Gearey and Lillie 2000) and it is possible that similar communities were present on the 'islands' at Sutton Common (see above section 4.2.2).

Aside from grasses and sedges, which probably derived from channel edge or bankside communities, records for other herbs are few and sporadic in this zone and probably also reflect vegetation on the damper soils proximal to the palaeochannel. The wider environment thus seems to have been densely wooded, but it is possible that more open conditions existed in some parts of the landscape. The picture of the lowland forests in this region as a whole tends to be one of closed-canopy conditions, except in certain wetland or perhaps geomorphologically unstable areas (see eg Tweddle 2001). A single grain of ribwort plantain at 3.00m may suggest openings in the dryland woodland canopy, although the size and location of such clearings are unclear and cannot have been extensive locally.

The establishment of oak as a significant component of the local woodland occurs at the opening of HBSC–2, c 8230–7840 cal BC. The spread of oak appears to have been partly at the expense of elm, perhaps on base-rich soils such as on the Magnesian Limestone ridge to the west. The spread of willow carr, most likely at the channel margins, is the other major feature of this zone. Following this, there is little obvious change in the composition of the vegetation until the alder rise at the opening of HBSC–3, at a date of 7060–6700 cal BC (SUERC–7616; 7985±35 BP). The expansion of this tree reflects the growth of alder fen carr at the expense of willow within and around the palaeochannel itself as a result of the development of suitable ecological conditions locally (cf Chambers and Elliot 1989; Bennett and Birks 1990). The *Tilia* (lime) rise is recorded shortly after that of alder; *Tilia* produces only low quantities of pollen (Andersen 1973) which is poorly dispersed (Grieg 1982) and pollen evidence thus suggests that this tree appears to have become been a dominant component of the lowland woodlands in eastern England, possibly on a range of different soils (Tweddle 2001; Kirby and Gearey 2001, 55).

### 4.3.5 Evidence for human impact: the Neolithic and Bronze Age  by B Gearey

The radiocarbon dates suggest that there is almost certainly a hiatus at the opening of HBSC–3, between 1.30m and 1.56m (see section 4.3.2). The abrupt decline in *Ulmus* (elm) c 1.30m dates to just before 4040–3800 cal BC (SUERC–7613; 5140±35 BP), suggesting that this event reflects the Elm Decline, which occurred broadly synchronously across Britain c 3700 cal BC and is believed to have been caused by a combination of pathogenic attack (Dutch Elm Disease, Girling 1988) and anthropogenic woodland clearance (Parker et al 2002). Generally, the first unequivocal evidence for anthropogenic impact on the vegetation in the Humber lowlands is recorded from the time of the Elm Decline onwards (Tweddle 2001), indicating low levels of Neolithic activity in the area. A layer of organic clay with charcoal fragments is evident in the Palaeochannel stratigraphy, between 1.10m and 1.30m, suggesting some form of disturbance within the catchment that resulted in the in-wash of minerogenic material onto the sampling site between the dates of 4040–3800 cal BC (SUERC–7613; 5140±35 BP) and 3360–3020 cal BC (SUERC–7614; 4480±35 BP). Interpretation is hindered by only low concentrations of poorly preserved pollen in the samples from 1.44m and 1.20m, which are thus not plotted on the diagram, but there is no clear evidence in the pollen record either in the form of marked reductions in tree/shrub pollen or increases in 'anthropogenic indicators' (*sensu* Behre 1981) that might have resulted from human activity. Erosion of soils resulting from disturbance to woodland further up the drainage network cannot be ruled out entirely. The beginning of a low curve for ash around this time may represent the spread of this light-demanding species onto soils where elm had previously been growing.

Less equivocal evidence for human disturbance to the vegetation at Sutton Common is observed in the middle section of HBSC–3. Low and sporadic records of ribwort plantain from 1.04m can be regarded as reflecting the presence of small and/or distant clearings in the woodland, although there are no clear fluctuations in the arboreal taxa that could reflect impacts upon specific tree populations. There is an increase in grasses towards the middle of the zone, but as discussed above, this probably includes a local component from wetland grasses as well as pollen from any open grassy areas within the dryland woodland and disentangling the signal of the two source areas is problematic. The implications of the high representation of local pollen sources and the physical 'screening' effect of the on-site alder carr woodland as is evident in this zone must be considered here. Recent work has begun to quantify the representation of 'on site' and 'off site' vegetation in alder carr sampling sites (Bunting et al 2005; Waller et al 2005; Binney et al 2005). This work has demonstrated that the palynological signal within alder fen carr is heavily biased towards local vegetation with a limited pollen source area of up to c 130m. Species growing adjacent to the fen carr edge tend to be better represented than those further away, even if the species are those that are thought to generally produce large quantities of well-dispersed pollen such as Scots pine. The position of the sampling site relative to the edge of the fen carr is also significant in controlling the representation of these 'dryland' taxa.

On the basis of such studies, it is probable that the Palaeochannel pollen diagram reflects localised vegetation changes, and the interpretation of the pollen record with respect to possible anthropogenic disturbance to dryland vegetation communities must therefore take account of this. Human activity was possibly taking place in the pollen catchment and hence in close proximity to the sampling site. This may perhaps have been in the form of low-intensity pastoral activity within small woodland clearings or a form of forest farming sensu Göransson (1986). Ribwort plantain disappears from the record towards the top of this zone, at which point percentages of grasses are also reduced whilst the representation of oak and alder increases across the same levels and low but consistent rises in ash and ivy are also recorded. Taken collectively, this might be interpreted as reflecting a curtailment of the low-intensity human activity near to the sampling site, which led to an expansion in oak and alder with ash established at the edges of abandoned clearings and ivy also characteristic of secondary rather than primary woodland (Rackham 1980). A date of 1950–1740 cal BC (SUERC–5698; 3520±35BP) is available for the close of HBSC–3, suggesting that the previous phase of sporadic activity dates to the later Neolithic, with the cessation or reduction in human activity in the earlier part of the Bronze Age.

Increased wetness on the sampling site is apparent during HBSC–4, leading to a spread of sedges and bur-reeds and also reflected in a stratigraphic transition from a wood-rich peat to organic clay silt at c 0.36m. This may also explain the increased representation of the extra-local 'dryland' vegetation of lime, oak, hazel, and pine concomitant with the increase in grasses and sedges and a steady fall in alder. Increased representation of extra-local vegetation would be anticipated as a result of an expansion in pollen source area subsequent to some thinning out of the local alder cover.

However, there is also evidence for actual changes in the composition of the extra-local canopy during this zone being at least partly a result of anthropogenic activity. A marked peak in grasses at 0.52m is concomitant with falls in hazel and oak and a single record of Avena-Triticum type. This points to an expansion in grassland and cereal cultivation following some clearance of the hazel-oak woodland. This event is bracketed by the radiocarbon dates of 1690–1490 cal BC (SUERC–5697; 3310±50BP) from 0.50m and 1940–1740 cal BC (SUERC–5698; 3520±35 BP) from 0.54m, the early Bronze Age. Any phase of farming must have been reasonably brief, as the subsequent sample sees a pronounced peak in birch pointing to the reinvasion of the cleared land by this tree prior to the re-establishment of oak and hazel. However, the precise nature of human activity at this time is difficult to establish since no other herbs present in this sample are unequivocally associated with cultivation or ruderal habitats. Likewise, it is not clear whether the deposition of the clay layer in this zone is associated in any way with anthropogenic disturbance to local soils.

This period is followed by evidence for a subsequent re-intensification of human activity across this zone, with a steady rise in grasses paralleled by the appearance of other possible indicators of disturbed, pastoral habitats such as ribwort plantain, dandelions, docks, and bracken towards the top of the zone. Clearance seems to have concentrated on oak-dominated woodland, with a steady reduction in this taxon but other arboreal components apparently less affected. Grains of oats and wheat and a record of cornflower at 0.24m are very good evidence of arable plots within the landscape mosaic. The impression is thus of anthropogenic clearance of oak woodland for mixed farming. If the above hypothesis that oak partly replaced elm on base-rich soils during HBSC–2 is correct, then it can also be hypothesised that this clearance activity was taking place predominantly on the limestone ridge to the west of the site. The reduction in oak woodland also corresponds closely to the deposition of the clay-silt layer between 0.36m and 0.19m and might indicate that the deposition of this minerogenic sediment was a direct consequence of the destabilisation of soil through woodland clearance on the upland areas and accelerated run-off into local watercourses, such as the Hampole Beck.

### 4.3.6 The Iron Age *by B Gearey*

The final zone, HBSC–5, opens at a date of 770–400 cal BC (SUERC–7608; 2465±35 BP), suggesting an early Iron Age timeframe. This zone is characterised by a marked expansion in grassland at the expense predominantly of lime and pine, although hazel was also affected. Lime was probably the dominant tree in the woodland beyond the fen carr, and the sudden drop in this taxon must reflect a large-scale and apparently abrupt clearance of trees by human communities. Alder populations fall gradually across the zone, but the wetland area of the Hampole Beck itself does not appear to have been especially targeted for clearance at this time.

However, although the wider environment must have been significantly more open, the response from herbs other than grasses is somewhat subdued. The range and percentage value of herbs is much the same as in the previous zone. After grasses and sedges, the most pronounced increase in herbaceous taxa is in the carrot family, a large family including many tall herbs. The poor representation of ruderal communities during this zone may be due to taphonomic factors such as those discussed above, with the pollen record remaining heavily biased towards the on-site alder fen carr. However, this explanation may not be entirely satisfactory. Although the pollen record suggests that relatively dense alder carr remained present on and around the sampling site at this time, some opening up of this canopy, perhaps at the dryland edge of the fen carr, seems likely on the basis of the fluctuations in the alder curve. This might be expected to result in enhanced representation of dryland herbs, even if no actual real increase in these communities had taken place. In other words, the pollen data implies that the removal of much of the extra-local woodland cover resulted primarily in an expansion in grassland but not arable land or other disturbed ruderal vegetation communities. By the close of the diagram at cal AD 230–410 (SUERC–8168; 1730±35 BP), or the Roman period, the impression is of alder carr persisting in and near to the palaeochannel, with areas of shallow water with reedmace and other wetland plants indicated. Some oak and hazel woodland was growing, but the wider landscape must have been generally open, with some arable plots but grassland clearly dominant nearby. The precise character of the extra-local and regional vegetation and the extent and character of human activity remains somewhat elusive.

## 4.4 Flaked stone artefacts from Sutton Common *by B Bradley*

### 4.4.1 Assemblage

During the excavations at Sutton Common between 1999 and 2003, a total of 1202 flaked stone artefacts were examined and recorded as part of the Sutton Common post-excavation analysis, adding to the 796 worked lithics found during earlier research (Parker Pearson and Sydes 1997, 234). These artefacts were, without significant exception, recovered from secondary contexts, either within the ploughsoil or from the Lake Humber deposits, the finds in the latter context being the result of downward translocation of the artefacts within the soil. The primary aims of the flaked stone tool analyses were the determination of the periods and activities they represent.

Two basic groups were identified: debitage and cores (flaking waste), and tools (items intentionally shaped into a tool form, utilised or resulting from use). Debitage and cores inform about the flaking technologies that were practised and the presence and/or absence of expected products and by-products. Although generalised flake production may have occurred at any period, there are certain technologies that are diagnostic of particular periods. Microblade production was the main flaking technology used during the Mesolithic and this was distinguished in the assemblage through the presence of microblades, microblade rejects, core tablets (platform rejuvenation flakes), and microblade cores. Large blades may be associated with the end of the Upper Palaeolithic, the Neolithic, or the Bronze Age. Minor variations in core preparation and production sequence may help distinguish between these different blade technologies, but this sample is too small to be useful in this area. Debitage categories include: miscellaneous flakes and fragments, microblade debitage (eg corner microblades Fig 4.8: h), unifacial retouch flakes, blades, biface flakes, burin spalls (Fig 4.8: m), core tablets (Fig 4.8: t), and cores (Fig 4.8: a–d).

Tool forms do not automatically inform on the intended or actual use of a given tool, but in this analysis basic functional tool classes were used in the assumption that the general activities exhibited in the assemblage could be identified. For example, axe forms are assumed to represent wood-working activities and arrowheads are assumed to indicate hunting. Identified tools

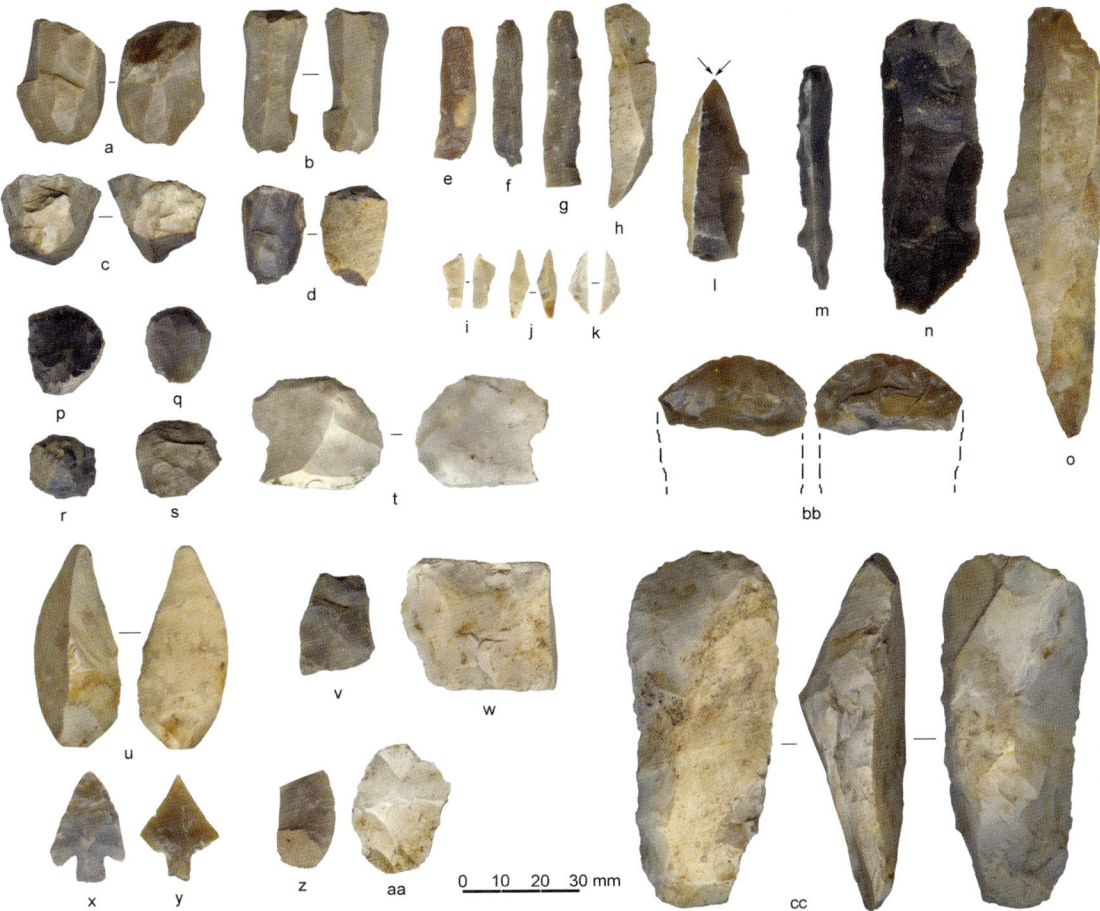

*Figure 4.8 Examples of the flaked stone tools and debitage from the Common: cores: a–d; microblades: e–g; microblade debitage: h; microliths: i–k; burins: l; unifacial retouch flakes, blades, biface flakes, burin spalls: m; blades: n–o; retouched flakes, microblades and blades, scrapers: p–s; core tablets: t; drills: u; pieces esquillées (wedges): v–w; arrowheads: x–y; arrowhead performs: z–aa; flaked axes: bb–cc*

included microblades (Fig 4.8: e–f), utilised flakes, microblades (Fig 4.8: g–h), and blades (Fig 4.8: n–o), microliths (Fig 4.8: i–k), flaked axes (Fig 4.8: bb–cc), *pieces esquillées* [wedges] (Fig 4.8: v–w), retouched flakes, microblades and blades, scrapers (Fig 4.8: p–s), burins (Fig 4.8: l), drills (Fig 4.8: u), arrowhead preforms (Fig 4.8: z–aa), and arrowheads Fig 4.8: x–y).

### 4.4.2 Results

Debitage analysis indicates that there were only three basic production technologies represented in the assemblage: percussion microblade, generalised flake, and blade. The presence of unifacial retouch flakes and a small number of biface flakes indicates that unifacial tools, such as scrapers, were being produced or re-sharpened in the site area, and perhaps the same was true for flake axe re-sharpening. The presence of two arrowpoint preforms (both abandoned during manufacture) also indicates that arrowheads were being made, albeit to a limited scale.

Microblade production was commonly represented, but the number of cores far exceeds what would be expected for the quantity of microblade debitage. With the exception of a couple of microblade cores that were abandoned early in their production, all of the cores were exhausted.

Blades were recovered in small numbers and although some could be oversized microblades, others were clearly intended to be large. No blade cores were recovered, probably indicating that the blades were introduced into the area and not made there.

Tools types represented the kinds of activities one would expect in a highly mobile lifestyle. The majority were utilised flakes, microblades, and blades, probably resulting from multiple small-scale cutting activities. The small number of microliths could have come from a single compound tool such as a point or knife. Since they were recovered from adjacent squares this seems likely. Scrapers are small and do not seem to have been heavily used, probably just for preliminary hide cleaning and or light woodworking. The single burin and drill (unmodified

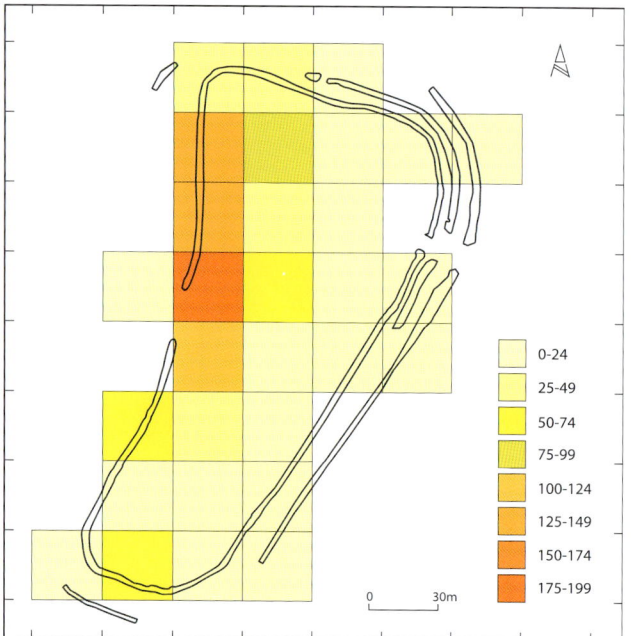

*Figure 4.9 Flaked stone density distributions by 30×30m grid, showing concentration along the Hampole Beck*

flake but heavily worn) represent grooving and perforating activities, again on a small scale. Although of different styles, the two barb and tang points could easily represent a single hunting episode. They too were recovered from adjacent units. The single complete flaked axe exhibits little if any use damage, while the bit fragment clearly resulted from breakage on impact, probably while cutting a tree.

In terms of the distribution of flaked stone collected in the 30 × 30m grid system, a general scatter of flaked stone artefacts was found in the 2002 and 2003 excavations (Fig 4.9). A single area of concentration was located on the west side of the large enclosure nearest the Hampole Beck palaeochannel.

### 4.4.3 Discussion

Only two cultural periods are clearly represented in the flaked stone assemblage: Mesolithic and early Bronze Age. There is no direct evidence of exploitation of the area of the larger enclosure during the intervening Neolithic, although such evidence was recorded for the small dune or 'island' c 300m north of the smaller enclosure (Parker Pearson and Sydes 1997, 234). Riverside concentrations of flaked stone artefacts and debitage of Mesolithic and Neolithic date have been found along the Hampole Beck north of modern Askern, at the confluence of the Hampole Beck with the River Went at Wentbridge (Head *et al* 1997, 233–7), elsewhere in the Humberhead Levels, and generally throughout the Humber Wetlands (Van de Noort 2004a, 35–40). These have been interpreted as riverside camps of mobile hunter-gatherers possibly using logboats to travel through the landscape, utilising the location of watering places frequented by larger animals as ideal places for hunting (*ibid*, 91). There is enough evidence of flaking, use, and discard of Mesolithic items at Sutton Common to indicate widespread exploitation of the area, at least for expedient hunting and gathering activities and possibly including temporary camps.

The Bronze Age activities seem to be more limited in type and intensity. The arrowheads and few utilised blades could all easily have been the result of only a small number of hunting forays into the area. The only indication of even short-term camps is the presence of two unfinished arrowpoints, possibly the result of attempted rearming at an overnight hunting camp. There is no evidence of Bronze Age blade manufacture in the site.

## 4.5 Conclusions  *by R Van de Noort*

When viewing the landscape context of Sutton Common at the beginning of the 4th century BC, several observations can be made of direct relevance to subsequent developments. These may be summarised as follows.

Ample evidence exists for the use of the Common as a hunting ground during the Mesolithic, Neolithic, and early Bronze Age, and as a place for the deposition of pyre debris in the early Bronze Age within a mortuary enclosure. The reasons for selecting this dune or island for the early Bronze Age mortuary enclosure probably incorporated concepts such as separateness and the symbolic or practical isolation offered by this wetland-surrounded island in the broader landscape. Such concepts may also have been important for the marsh-fort builders, but the relationship between the mortuary enclosure and the marsh-fort may have gone further. Even though the archaeological evidence from Sutton Common does not appear to indicate the physical survival of the mortuary enclosure into the 4th century BC, or its recognition by the marsh-fort builders, people in the early Iron Age may have shared a social memory of the earlier use and symbolic significance of that place. The perception of wetlands as different and possibly sacred places persisted in the Humber Wetlands throughout later prehistory (*cf* Van de Noort 2004a, 93–106). The middle Bronze Age depositions of bronze weapons in the wetlands around Sutton Common may be understood to illustrate just that.

In the broader landscape, the palynological study shows that clearances of woodland on the Magnesian Limestone, immediately to the west of the Common, and agricultural activities, commenced during the Neolithic c 4000 cal BC (c 5200 BP), with additional evidence of woodland clearances during the Bronze Age and Iron Age. The existence of agricultural communities on the Magnesian Limestone in late prehistory is undoubted, but relatively little is known about the nature of these communities, and the origin of the pre-Roman 'nuclear' field systems, as originally observed by Derrick Riley (1980), remains essentially undated (see section 9.2). The pollen analysis has also shown that the alder carr within the palaeochannel of the Hampole Beck remained largely unaffected, but the higher and drier islands of the Common were cleared of the lime woodland around the time the construction of the marsh-fort commenced.

# 5 The marsh-fort: the defences

## 5.1 Introduction  *by R Van de Noort and H Chapman*

This chapter presents the results of the excavations and allied research relating directly to the marsh-fort's defences. The description of the features is presented from west to east, commencing with the smaller enclosure, followed by the causeway linking the smaller with the larger enclosure across the Hampole Beck palaeochannel, entering the larger enclosure through the western gateway and continuing through the eastern gateway. The description of the features is followed by a section on the dating of the construction of the defences, a description of the wood technology used, and information on the palaeoenvironmental sequences that are based on the detailed analysis of the ditch fills around the eastern gateway.

The use of the term 'defences' is not without controversy, but has been used here for want of a better alternative. As argued earlier (see section 1.3.1.1), the physical importance of the ditch-and-bank arrangements enclosing many Iron Age sites in terms of defensive efficacy has fallen under increasingly critical scrutiny. Many commentators consider the symbolic significance of these boundaries of far greater importance, and this appears also to be the case for Sutton Common. Nevertheless, we recognise that the architecture employed at Sutton Common was, at the very least, based on principles of defensiveness as perceived by those who determined its layout, even though in execution, and presumably in use, the marsh-fort's defences never functioned to repel attackers.

Concomitant with this symbolic function of (multiple) boundaries is the significance of crossing these boundaries. At Sutton Common, this can be clearly observed at the eastern gateway, where the ditch terminals included a range of artefacts, raw materials, and human and animal bones which have been interpreted as structured deposition (see chapter 7), and in this context were used to reinforce the symbolic significance of going over the threshold into the larger enclosure.

## 5.2 The geophysical survey  *by A Payne*

### 5.2.1 Introduction

A magnetometer survey of the two enclosures and the intervening palaeochannel was carried out by the English Heritage, Centre for Archaeology, prior to the excavations in 2003. Geophysical survey had not been used on the larger enclosure previously, and it was believed that the opportunity to test the magnetic response of the site in advance of excavation should not be missed: the site would provide a valuable opportunity to assess the effectiveness of geophysical survey over a wetland site containing waterlogged organic remains against the information subsequently recovered by excavation. Images of the combined magnetometer data are presented on Figures 5.1 and 5.2.

### 5.2.2 Results

The palaeochannel is visible as a wide band of pronounced magnetic disturbance. A second marshy area of peaty deposits has been detected in the far south-eastern extremity of the survey, and represents surface peat of the Shirley Pool SSSI wetland.

The majority of internal anomalies of the larger enclosure relate to modern field-drains and responses to small ferrous objects in the areas already excavated. The excavation trenches of 2002 stand out as distinctly noisier areas in the data compared to the adjacent, unexcavated, 30m strips. Larger ferrous anomalies evenly distributed across the survey area relate to vehicle tyres placed on the ground to mark the position of groundwater monitoring borehole stations (see section 2.3.2).

The ditches of the larger enclosure are only partially defined in the magnetic data. The definition of the enclosure circuit is clear, albeit variable, along the east and north-east sides. Anomalies from the north-eastern segments of the enclosure ditches are particularly pronounced suggesting the incorporation of magnetic material in the ditch fills in 1980. The innermost ditch on the north-east side is only partially and weakly resolved compared to the outer ditches, which produced the much stronger response described above, but this reflects the 'causewayed' nature of the inner ditch here (see section 5.3.9). There is good agreement between the position of the cropmarks of the ditches visible on aerial photographs on the east and north-east sides of the larger enclosure and the magnetic data.

Unfortunately, where the cropmarks become fainter or disappear on the aerial photographs around the southern, northern, and western circuit of the larger enclosure, the magnetometer survey is similarly uninformative. Nevertheless, a series of linear positive magnetic anomalies at A (on Fig 5.2) suggests that an outer ditch existed

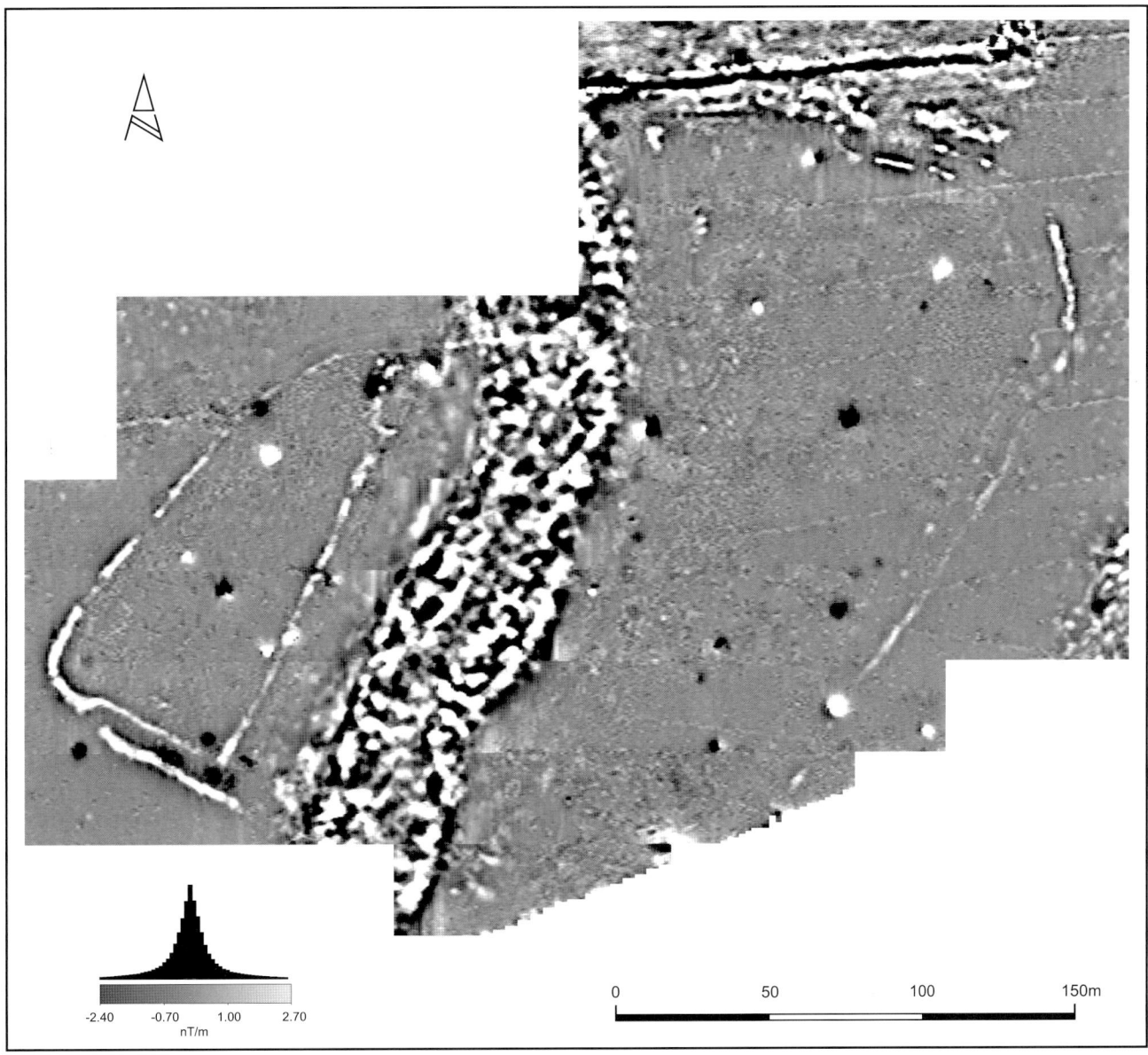

*Figure 5.1 Greyscale plot of magnetometer data after median filtering to remove anomalies; note the ditch arrangements around the entrance of the smaller enclosure*

to the south of the previously known bank and ditch. Its southern side possibly lined up with the double-ditched alignment forming the south side of the smaller enclosure across the palaeo-channel (B). Anomalies at C suggest that the larger enclosure also included an additional ditch on its north-east side. The earthworks bounding the enclosure on the west along the edge of the palaeochannel are therefore possibly wider than previously thought. A spread of anomalies just outside the eastern entranceway (D) probably results from natural variation in the soils of the Common. A considerable amount of magnetic disturbance immediately north of the larger enclosure is associated with vehicle access to the site from the A19 to the west, and the dumping and spreading of modern road-surfacing material.

The circuit of the smaller enclosure is well preserved, and its boundary ditch is more clearly resolved. The ditch deposits were excavated at three points around the circuit of the smaller enclosure (Trenches A/C, B and F; Parker Pearson and Sydes 1997), visible as intense magnetic disturbance (respectively E, F, and G on Fig 5.2). The eastern gateway of the smaller enclosure, giving access to the timber-lined causeway, is clearly visible in the magnetic data (H) and the ditches either side of the entrance appear somewhat out-turned.

The entrance into the smaller enclosure from the west is somewhat offset from the south-east corner of the smaller enclosure (I). Once through the entrance, the way in is defined by a ditch-lined path (J) leading to the south-west corner before entering the smaller enclosure. Few if any

70  *Sutton Common*

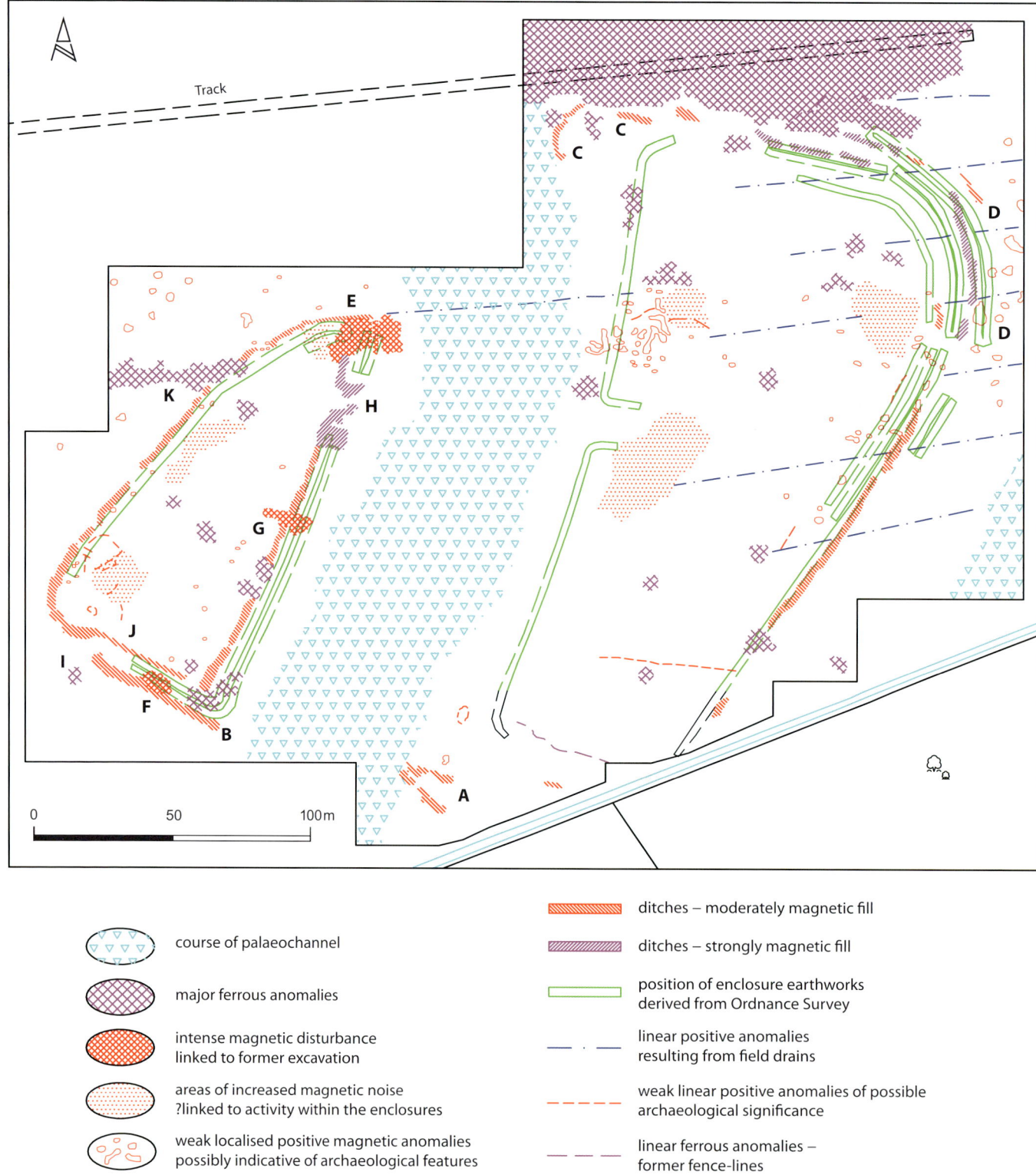

*Figure 5.2   Interpretation of fluxgate magnetometer survey*

significant anomalies are visible within the smaller enclosure, suggesting a low level or even absence of internal occupation activity. A former field boundary visible as a narrow line of stronger magnetic disturbance (K) has been detected running up to the north-west side of the smaller enclosure.

### 5.2.3  Conclusions

The magnetometer survey has successfully defined the entrance to the smaller enclosure from the nearby dryland to the west, and thus to the complex as a whole (but note the reinterpretation of the nature of the smaller enclosure in section 5.3.2). It has also shown the extent of multivallation of the larger enclosure beyond what was previously recorded. The relative dearth of internal features is corroborated by the excavations, which identified very few features other than individual posts and postholes.

In terms of advancing the methodological aspects of geophysical survey on wetland sites, magnetometry can be used for the identification of large, linear anomalies such as ditches, but survey with a more sensitive instrument, for example a Caesium-vapour magnetometer, is required for the identification of smaller features. Such a survey may yet radically transform our existing understanding of the internal character and function of the smaller enclosure.

## 5.3 Description of features
*by H Chapman and W Fletcher*

### 5.3.1 Introduction

This section provides the integrated results of the excavations undertaken between 1998 and 2003, and considers earlier research (Fig 5.3). The first part of the presentation (sections 5.3.2 to 5.3.4) follows the way in which people in the past would

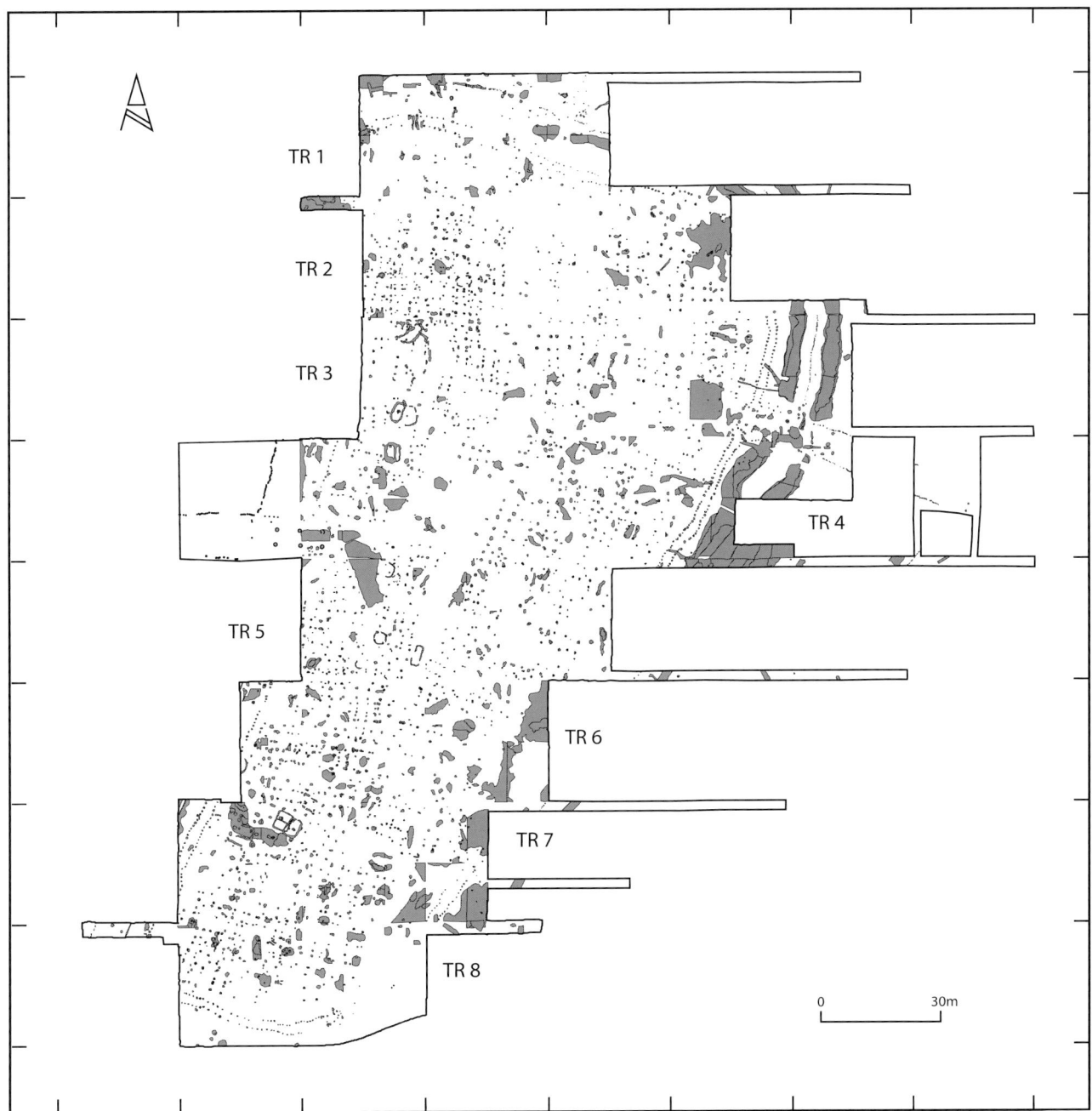

*Figure 5.3   Excavation plan 1998 – 2003: all Iron Age features*

have entered the site, that is through the smaller enclosure, across the causeway, and entering the larger enclosure through the western gateway. The second part (section 5.3.5 to 5.3.11) describes the defensive features of the marsh-fort starting from the far outer bank moving towards the interior. The third part (section 5.3.12) considers the eastern entranceway.

### 5.3.2 The smaller enclosure

The smaller enclosure is roughly triangular in shape, broadly following the natural topography and formed from a single bank and ditch. An extension of the earthwork forming its southern side originally ran to the edge of the palaeochannel, although this was bulldozed at the same time as other parts of the site and thus no remains of it survive on the surface. When the site was investigated in the 1930s, the gap in the earthworks in the south-west corner was amorphous, and it was suggested on this basis that the earthworks were never actually completed (Whiting 1936, 70). Instead, Whiting suggested that the western entrance to the enclosure lay about a third of the way from the northern section of the enclosure in a break in the mapped earthworks. More recent survey work (see sections 1.2.6 and 5.2.2) has demonstrated that there is a slight bank in this area suggesting that this was not one of the entrances. A second break in the earthworks is present in the northern section of its eastern bank from which the larger enclosure was accessed. The location of the entrance into the smaller enclosure was finally established in 2003 through geophysical survey (see section 5.2.2).

A striking feature of the 'smaller enclosure' is the arrangement of its banks and ditches. Recorded in part by Bennett and Hill (Whiting 1936) and in later work (eg Parker Pearson and Sydes 1997), the ditches on the western and southern sides of the enclosure are external, whereas the ditch on its eastern side is internal. The arrangement of ditches, coupled with the likely access from the west, indicates that this enclosure formed something of an annex to the larger enclosure, or an elaborate entranceway. On approach, the arrangement of the breaks in the earthworks dictates a dog-legged avenue within an elaborate entrance structure leading to the edge of the palaeochannel and the main entrance to the larger enclosure. Considering that 'defensive' bank and ditch arrangements will normally have the ditch on the outside, the earthworks forming the smaller enclosure are perhaps most appropriately considered as two conjoined banks with external ditches, perhaps representing a two-phase structure. Thus, the eastern bank could represent the earlier phase, with a ditch to the west, a sort of cross-bank, though unusually backing on to the palaeochannel. To this was then added the bank with external ditch which now forms the western and southern sides of the triangular enclosure. A similar and perhaps relatively contemporary arrangement, the 'barbican', can be seen in the west entrance of Maiden Castle (Wheeler 1943, 34, fig 5; 128, fig 24, Phase II) and which he compared with Blackbury Camp in Devon (Wheeler 1943, 35, fig 6).

There have been a number of archaeological investigations into the smaller enclosure, with differing objectives (Whiting 1936; Parker Pearson and Sydes 1997). Whiting referred to the smaller enclosure (or outworks) as 'Camp B'. Whiting's excavations are the only recorded investigations into the western earthworks of this feature, where he dug four trenches: III, IIIa, IV, and V (see Fig 1.4). These trenches revealed the variable depth of the ditch, which, in places, was very shallow, although he gives no quantification. In Trenches III, IIIa, and IV, he recorded bone, including a total of four sheep skulls, in addition to willow branches and sticks. Trenches III and V were excavated across the bank. A layer of humic material, interpreted as the palaeo-land surface, defined the base of the bank in each case. Interestingly, in Trench V at the northern end of the bank, a turf layer was recorded within the bank material. It was not possible to say whether this layer indicated a second phase of bank construction or whether the turf was part of the structural material of the bank, but recent plant macrofossil analysis from the bank of the larger enclosure has suggested the use of turves in its construction, and it appears likely that this was the case for the smaller enclosure or annex as well.

The South Yorkshire Archaeology Unit investigated the earthworks that form the southern edge of the smaller enclosure in 1987 (Fig 5.4; Sydes and Symonds 1987). A single trench, Trench B, was excavated across the bank and ditch, primarily to obtain samples from an undisturbed part of the site for radiocarbon dating. The trench was 2m wide and 15m long, extending 4.2m into the interior of the enclosure. Here the bank was recorded as 0.8m high and 5.8m wide at its base. Within the ditch, pieces of timber were identified which were supposedly interlocking and interpreted as a 'raft'. One timber, 2.20m long, had a series of notches cut into it between 0.20m and 0.26m apart. More recently, this latter timber has been interpreted as a 'ladder' (Parker Pearson and Sydes 1997, 233–4), and is on display in Doncaster Museum.

The earthworks forming the eastern side of the enclosure have been investigated on a number of occasions. The earliest recorded investigations were undertaken by Whiting, who excavated six trenches: I, II, IIa, IIb, IIc, IId, and IIe. Trench I was excavated approximately half way along the bank, south of the eastern entrance. The trench identified both the ditch and the bank and extended both inside and outside the enclosure. It demonstrated that there was no outer ditch, and identified the humic layer or palaeo-land surface beneath the bank. Trenches II and IIe were all

*Figure 5.4 Aerial photograph of Sutton Common in November 1987, looking south. The photo shows the backfilled trenches A/C and B in the smaller enclosure. (Crown copyright. NMR, Riley collection)*

excavated in the area to the north of the eastern entrance to the smaller enclosure. Trench II cut across the bank and ditch, extending outside and inside the enclosure, with IIe forming a widening of Trench II on top of the bank. Trench IIc was cut eastwards from the top of the bank, tracing a line towards the larger enclosure, well outside of the smaller enclosure. Trenches IIa, IIb, and IId extended perpendicularly from IIc towards the north, with IIa joining the eastern end of Trench II. Trench IIa, on the outer edge of the bank, revealed worked oak that was interpreted as part of a wheel (Fig 5.5). The extension of Trench IIc to the east revealed a line of stakes over a distance more than half of the way towards the larger enclosure.

In 1998, an additional trench was excavated as part of the current project across the south side of the eastern entrance, focusing on the ditch of this structure. The results from this work proved the ditch to be up to 2.53m deep, with the basal unit [1998–016] providing approximately 0.5m depth of wet conditions and good organic preservation. Surviving partly within this layer was the tip of oak stake [1998–063]. The conclusions from the excavation of this trench disagreed with the interpretation of previously excavated trenches to both the north and south, and considerable reworking of deposits was postulated.

*Figure 5.5 The oak 'wheel' as found by Whiting in the 1930s*

### 5.3.3 The causeway

Whiting's Trench IIc extended from the eastern bank of the smaller enclosure over half way across the palaeochannel towards the larger enclosure. At the point where trenches IIe and IId met, a line of 25 posts and postholes was discovered, 'beginning under the rampart and crossing the space between the two camps' (Whiting 1936, 71), perhaps those stakes identified previously by Allcroft (1908). One of the largest stakes was 17″ (c 0.43m) long and 12″ (c 0.30m) in diameter, with a worked point that was 6″ (c 0.15m) long. An additional line of posts was also discovered at the northern end of the larger enclosure which was interpreted as part of the same structure, although it is perhaps more likely that these stakes form part of the outer palisade.

In 1997, the GPS survey and GIS modelling of the site identified a tongue of higher land extending eastwards from the eastern entrance of the smaller enclosure, running into the area of the palaeochannel (Chapman and Van de Noort 2001), indicating the possibility of a causeway structure connecting the two enclosures. This possibility was investigated in 1998 through the excavation of a trench 10.5m (north – south) × 1.9m (1998 Trench 2) across its projected alignment, with an extension eastwards along the southern edge of the causeway measuring 6.6 × 2m. This trench verified the presence of a causeway constructed of sand directly overlying a woody peat (Fig 5.6). Examination of the peat, [1998 – 003], indicated a brushwood layer, although it seems most likely that much of this unit was natural. The sandy layer, [1998 – 004], was approximately 9.5m wide (though the main concentration, [1998 – 002], was c 6m wide) and up to 0.25m deep, but the top had been truncated by ploughing. The material was light-grey fine sand with very few inclusions other

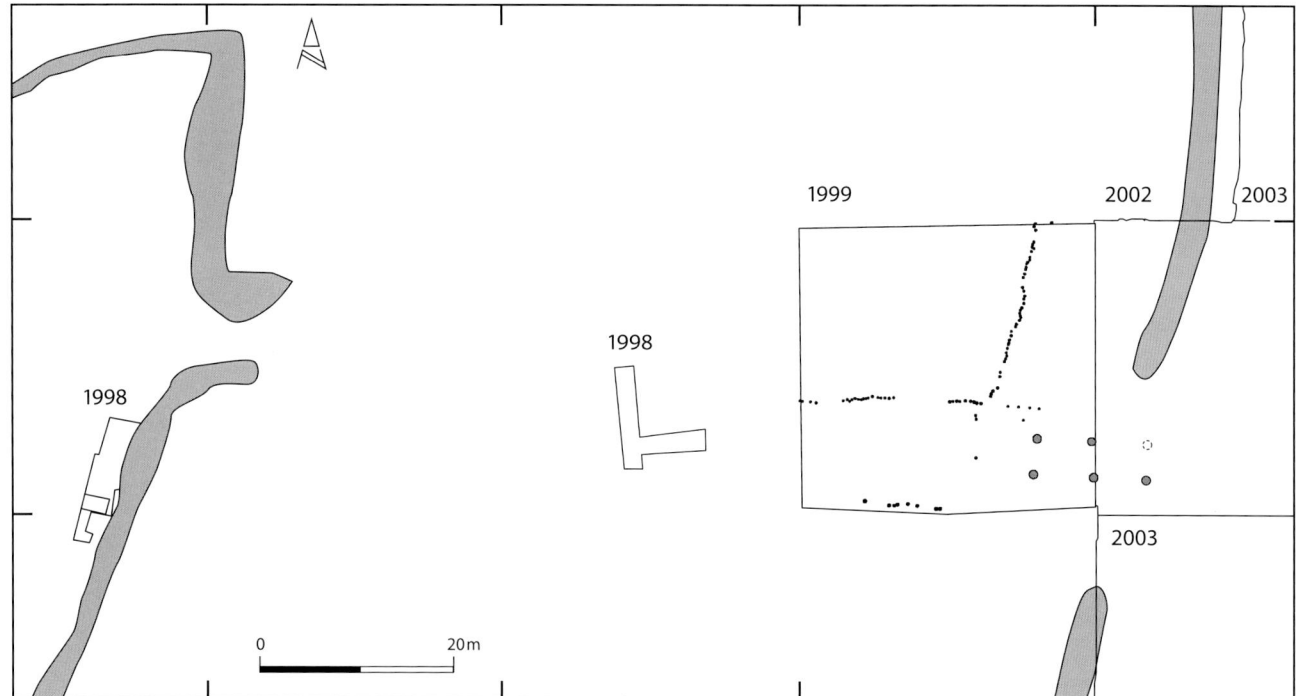

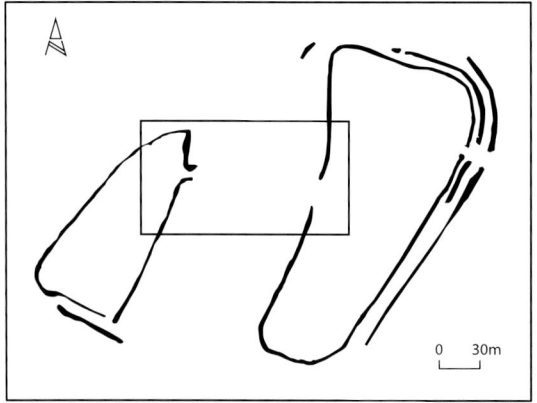

*Figure 5.6 Plan of the causeway, showing the excavated posts and the out-turned ditches of the smaller enclosure as identified by the geophysical survey in 2003; the sand deposit directly overlying a woody peat or brushwood was identified in the trench excavated in 1998*

than occasional limestone blocks, up to 0.20m in size. It is possible that these blocks represented the remains of an upper construction layer of the road, but this could not be confirmed due to the truncation. On the south side of the causeway, within an extension of the trench, were two oak stakes, *c* 6m apart. The trench was not widened sufficiently to check for additional stakes on this side or on the north side of the causeway, although it was postulated that these features, in conjunction with Whiting's line of stakes on the north side of the causeway, might represent an avenue bounding the edges of the route.

Additional excavation of the causeway was undertaken within Trench G9 in 1999, as the western half of the trench extended into the palaeochannel (Fig 5.7). In the western half of the trench, the sandy material with occasional fragments of limestone that represented the causeway was revealed, though less well preserved with the rise in elevation, and presumably truncated by ploughing. Beneath this sandy layer there was no evidence of a brushwood structure, indicating that there had been no prior levelling of the ground before the construction of the causeway. Marking either side of the causeway was a line of stakes, irregularly spaced but with the two alignments *c* 9m apart, indicating its maximum width. The alignment on the north side was in two sections with a gap between them. The westernmost section consisted of 25 stakes or stake pipes, nineteen of which contained upright stakes. At the eastern end of this section, three additional stakes were found, although these were relatively shallow, with a maximum length of only 0.2m. The second section of stakes on the north side of the

*Figure 5.7  Aerial photograph of the excavations in 1999, including open-area excavation of the western gateway and adjacent part of the causeway*

enclosure was separated from the first by *c* 7m, and offset slightly to the south, thus narrowing the causeway as the entrance to the larger enclosure was approached. Nearing the entrance, the sandy causeway was not identifiable, although the ground level rose, perhaps indicating either that it had been truncated by ploughing, or that the sand was not used on higher, drier areas. Twelve stakes and one stake pipe were revealed, including some in the 1998 excavation.

The southern stake alignment ran along the southern edge of Trench G9, and consisted of nine upright stakes and ten possible stake pipes. Sectioning revealed a maximum length of 0.36m for the stakes. As with the northern alignment, an extension of this alignment continued eastwards towards the entrance to the larger enclosure, but slightly offset, narrowing the causeway.

The Sutton Common causeway has few, if any, close parallels. In comparison with Fiskerton, Lincolnshire, the only other excavated Iron Age causeway in eastern England, the Sutton Common causeway lacks the sophisticated construction or, indeed, any evidence of structured deposition in the wetlands of the Hampole Beck (Field and Parker Pearson 2003). Unlike the Fiskerton parallel, which crossed the River Whitham, the Sutton Common causeway did not cross a flowing river, and there was evidently no need for a raised wooden path. The timbers aligning the causeway seem to have been constructed for symbolic rather than functional purposes.

### 5.3.4 The western entrance and approach including pavement

The western entrance to the larger enclosure was excavated in part in 1998, and more comprehensively in 1999, with the last two of the entrance posts seen in Trench 4 during the 2002 season (Figs 5.7, 5.8).

The narrowing of the causeway, identified from the alignments of stakes (and mentioned above) ran up to the western entrance of the larger enclosure, defined on Whiting's plan as a break in the earthworks. With the rise in ground level, the sandy surface of the causeway disappeared, and the stakes marking its boundary extended to the sides of the main entranceway. Four large, flat-bottomed posts in two pairs defined this entranceway, each up to 0.7m in diameter (Fig 5.9). The northern pair was connected by a slot with a U-shaped profile, perhaps indicative of a 'beam slot', which might have held the foundations of a wooden wall structure between the larger posts. A similar, though more fragmentary beam slot also connected the two southern posts, indicating

*Figure 5.8 Photo of the western gateway under excavation in 1999, looking east. The deposit of limestone is thought to have been 'dumped' in the entranceway*

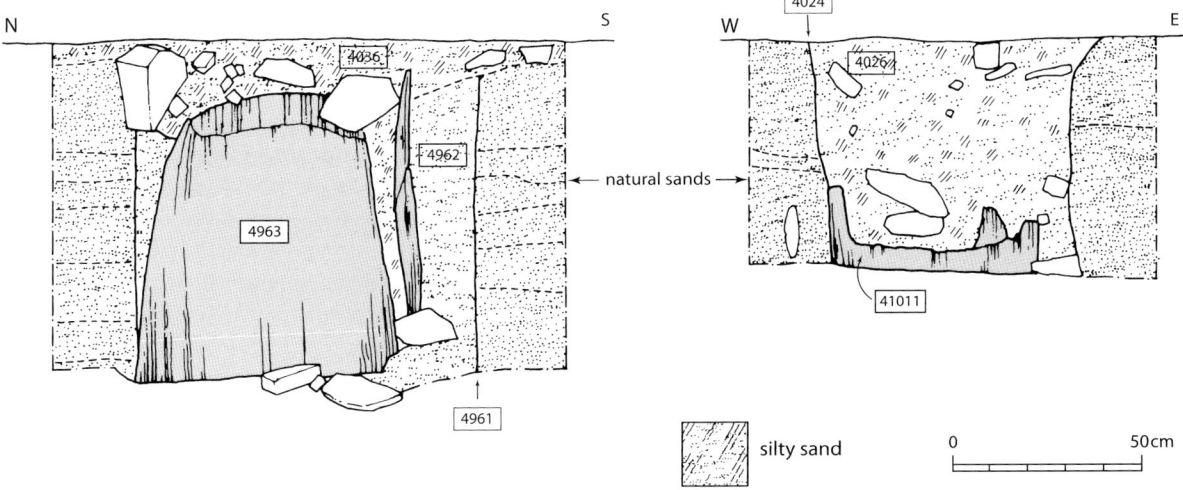

*Figure 5.9  Sections of the large posts of the western gateway [4963] and [41011] in context*

that there might have been a partly enclosed wooden-walled entrance. These linear features indicate that the entrance between these pairs of posts would have been walled or fenced, with the size of the posts indicating that they could have carried a gate, although there is no direct evidence for one. Further inside the enclosure, a second pair of large posts, [4963] and [4025], was discovered. Thus the entrance structure was created from six large timbers arranged in pairs to create an opening 3.5m wide and 11.5m long. On the southern side of this structure, an arrangement of eight further posts indicated some further structural complexity, perhaps similar to the arrangement discovered around the eastern entranceway (see below).

The excavation of one of the posts [4963] revealed a 0.7m wide flat-bottomed post within a vertical-sided cut [4961]. Here the cut was considerably wider than the post and had been filled with post packing material. This packing included numerous limestone blocks placed both beneath and around the post, and a number of reused timbers, including the end of a plank and a mortise joint. The post survived to a length of 0.75m, although the upper section was hollow due to decay. A second post [41011] was less well-preserved, surviving to a maximum length of 0.2m.

Immediately outside the entrance structure, overlying a palaeosol, was a spread of limestone chunks, filling the width of the entrance and *c* 2.5m deep. Additional smaller spreads were recorded to the west and south-west. Effectively this spread was blocking the entrance to the larger enclosure. The feature was irregular and did not appear to be structural. A section through the stones failed to reveal any significant hollow that this material might have been infilling. Rather, it has been interpreted here that construction appears to have been placed to block access to the entrance of the larger enclosure some time in antiquity, perhaps following the abandonment of the site.

### 5.3.5  The defences — background

There is no record of the height of the original earthworks that formed the larger enclosure, although Whiting excavated numerous trenches through them and recorded the overall plan of the site. On his plan, a single bank defined the western edge, and no ditch was shown to be present. Trenches excavated by Whiting along its full length revealed varying levels of drystone walling in limestone, of up to eight courses, and up to 2′ 6″ (*c* 0.76m) thick. Frequently, this structure was found to be backed by turf, and contained degraded wood indicative of some type of timber framework. In the centre of the western earthworks was a break, although Whiting suggested that this might have been caused by more recent land drainage. The stone wall did not continue around the south side of the site and the break in the earthworks was interpreted as a natural depression. The eastern side of the site, south of the eastern entrance, was characterised by a double bank and ditch. It was noted by Whiting that the nature of both ditches was extremely variable in terms of depth. Textual descriptions of sections excavated across the ditches by Whiting suggested that the outer ditch was deep and the inner ditch was slight in some areas, and in others the converse was the case. In 2003, Trench 3 inadvertently followed one of Whiting's old trenches, and it was noted that he had not fully bottomed the ditch at that point. Near the entrance, an outer, third bank was recorded in plan and sectioned by Trench III, although little was mentioned about it in Whiting's text. In this area, up to eight courses of revetment walling were identified facing the outside of the inner bank, similar to the walling along the west side of the enclosure. However, there were insufficient excavations along the east side of the enclosure to examine whether this phenomenon was consistent. North of the eastern entrance, three banks were recorded with two ditches between them. It is not clear whether the wall continued along the outside of the inner bank in this area. The inner ditch was found to have various 'crossings', and was likened by Whiting to the plan of Neolithic causewayed enclosures. The middle bank was underlain by a row of stakes along its centre line. This row of stakes continued round the north side, although east of Whiting's postulated northern entrance they survived alone, without any indication of associated earthworks. The hypothesised northern entrance was investigated in part, with the discovery of pit-like features in Trenches VIII and XII, containing bones and part of an oak plank.

Whiting's excavations provide an indication of the nature of the upstanding earthworks that form what may be termed the 'defences'. The recent work has, however, provided a much clearer indication of the overall plan of the site, although its full interpretation is partly dependent upon a consideration of the earlier work.

### 5.3.6 The defences — the far outer bank

The outermost line of defences, identified by Whiting, was the earthwork that surrounded the north-east corner of the site, also visible on early aerial photographs (see Fig 2.1). This feature was not encountered during the recent excavations, although most of it would have lain outside of the excavated area. However, within the extension to the east of Trench 3, a line of stakes was discovered within a narrow trench, extending for 2.4m, with additional stakes nearly 15m to the north-east that may have been a continuation of this feature. The alignment of these stakes was parallel to the other lines of defences, positioned over 35m from the outer edge of the outer ditch. It seems possible that this line of stakes might have been a palisade, which could have been associated with a bank, as observed with the middle bank described below. Given its distance from the main lines of defences, however, it is possible that this feature might have been associated with the outworks to the east that were marked on Whiting's plan of the site. Where these were investigated, Whiting dismissed this feature as a heap of yellow sandy loam lying on the peat, although it has more recently been argued that this could not have been a natural feature (Sydes and Symonds 1987).

### 5.3.7 The defences — the outer ditch

Moving inwards, the next line of defences defining the larger enclosure was characterised by a ditch (Fig 5.10). This ditch was identified surrounding the north-east, east and part of the south side of the site, but was not identified on the west side in either Whiting's excavations or in 2002–03. However, within the ditch on the east side of the enclosure, Whiting noted variability in the depth of this feature in his Trenches III and X, also recording cattle bones from within the ditch fill.

During the 2002 and 2003 excavations, the outer ditch was encountered in Trenches 1 and 3, and within the extensions of Trenches 2, 4, 5, 6, 7, and 8. Full sections were excavated at the eastern entrance and in the area to the south. Trench 4 revealed the ditch to have a maximum depth of 1.5m below present land surface (1.1m below the base of plough soil at 3.44m OD), and a width of $c$ 3.5m (Fig 5.11). The ditch was cut into the natural reworked Lake Humber deposits [5100]. The primary fill of the ditch [5668] was dark-grey sandy silt, overlain by a grey clay-silt [5667]. The upper fill of the ditch comprised a peaty deposit [5666], initiating at a depth of 0.95m below land surface (3.96m OD). Above the peaty layer were mixed deposits including charcoal lenses, probably relating to surface fires on the Common prior to the bulldozing of the banks. It seems most likely that the lower fills of the ditch resulted from initial silting following construction and subsequent abandonment of the site, derived from a combination of slumping and natural infill. The upper peaty layer is most likely to relate to the wet ditch conditions following the growth of vegetation across the site and the stabilisation of the land surface. This peaty layer is likely to be derived from vegetation that was growing within the wet ditch.

### 5.3.8 The defences — the palisade bank

Moving inward from the outer ditch, the next line of 'defences' consisted of a bank with a central row of stakes (Fig 5.12). This feature has been characterised as a 'palisade' in previous work, and was originally considered to represent an earlier phase of the site, in parallel with other hillforts and enclosed settlements, and possibly dated to the early Iron Age (Parker Pearson and Sydes 1997, 254). It is now demonstrated to belong to the overall single-phase construction, but the term palisade remains the most useful description. The palisade was identified as a row of stakes, each up to 0.13m in diameter and positioned at intervals of up to 0.3m in a sinuous line. On the north side of the western entrance, the 1999 excavations exposed an 18.5m length of this feature, with additional sections along the western edge of the enclosure identified in Trench I9 during the same year of excavations, and in the western extension of Trench 8 during 2002. To the north, excavation in D10 in 1999 exposed a row of palisade stakes and, in Trench 1 in 2003, Whiting's back-filled trenches were identified containing *in situ*

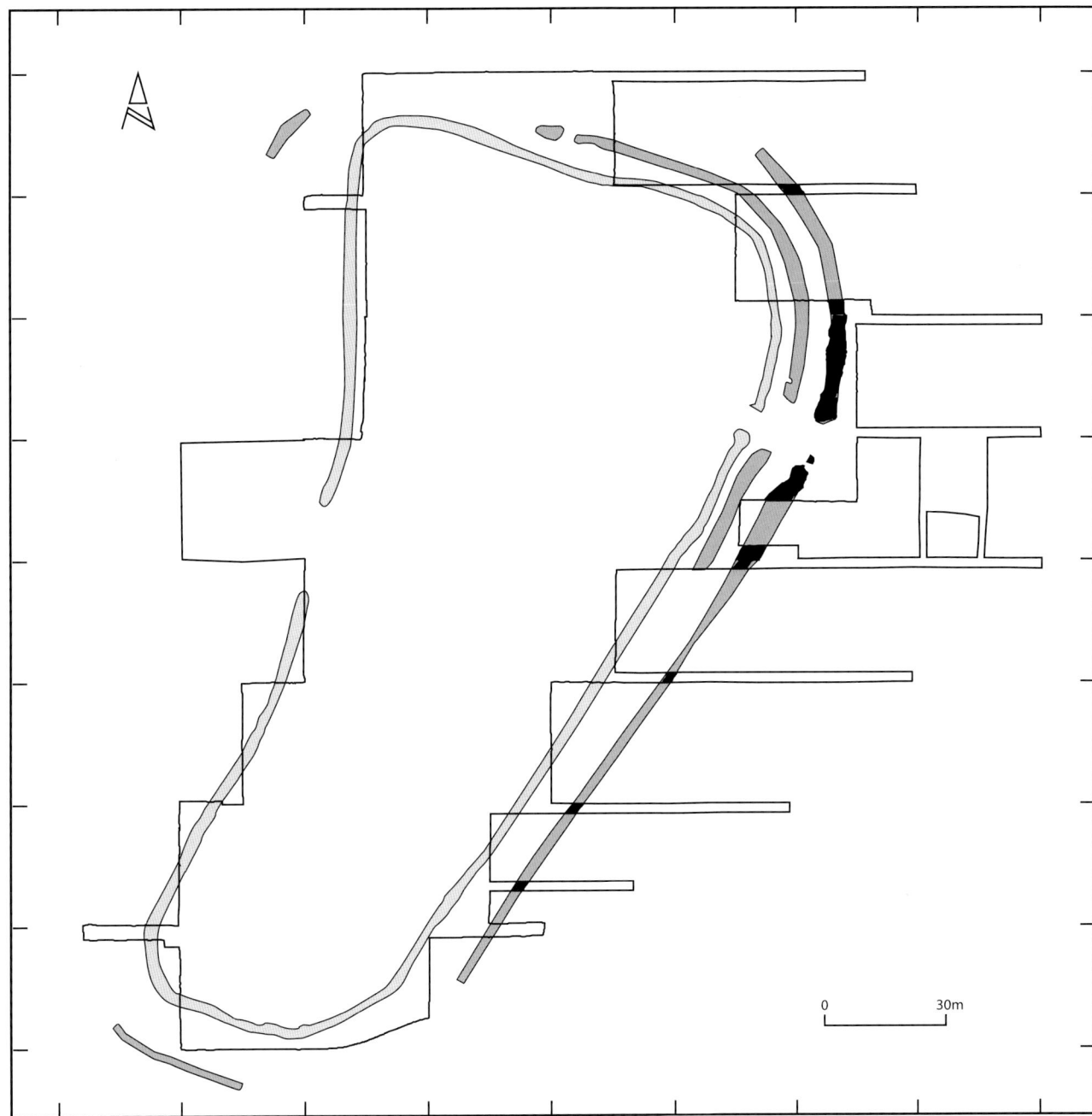

*Figure 5.10   Excavation plan 1998 – 2003: the outer ditch (excavated parts in black)*

stakes. Within the north-east section of Trench 1, the palisade stakes were not identified, perhaps because they had not survived, although Whiting recorded stakes within the centre of the middle bank. Around the eastern entrance, nearly 25m of the palisade structure was exposed on the north side of the entranceway. To the south of the eastern entrance, the palisade was not identified during the 2003 excavations, although a section of it was exposed during 1998.

The relationship between the earthworks, revealed in Trench 3 in 2003 and mapped by Whiting, and the position of the palisade stakes is inconsistent across the site. On the west and north-west side, there is no evidence to suggest that it was associated with a bank, although on the north-east side Whiting recorded evidence for the palisade under the bank, perhaps leading to his interpretation of two phases of defences. In Trenches 3 (excavated in 2003), and 4 (in 2002), to the south of the eastern entrance, the bank was shown to survive above the palisade stakes to a thickness of 0.2m, but with no trace visible on the surface; however, to the north of the same entrance traces were visible within the bank matrix at a higher level (Fig 5.13, but note also the results of the geoarchaeological analysis in section 5.6.3). It seems most likely that the stakes were placed at the centre of the bank, but whether they formed the part of the construction, such as a marking-out

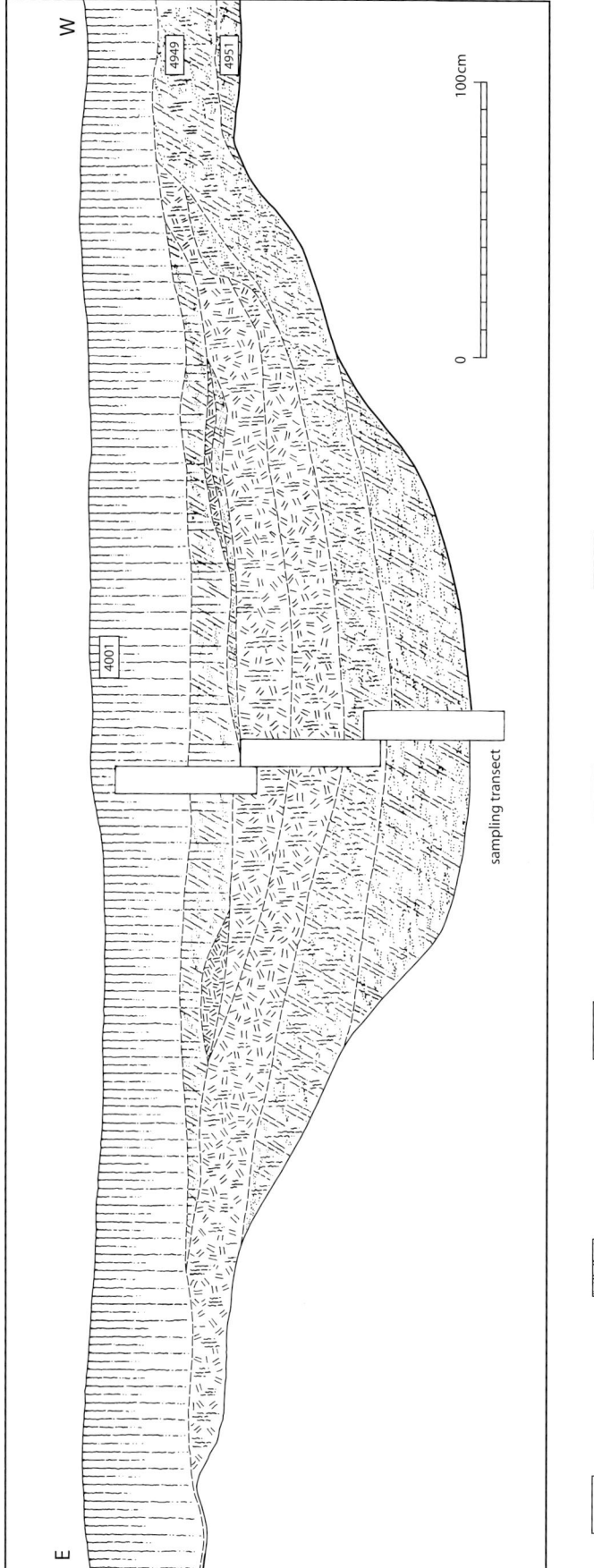

*Figure 5.11 Section of the outer ditch, exposed in Trench 4*

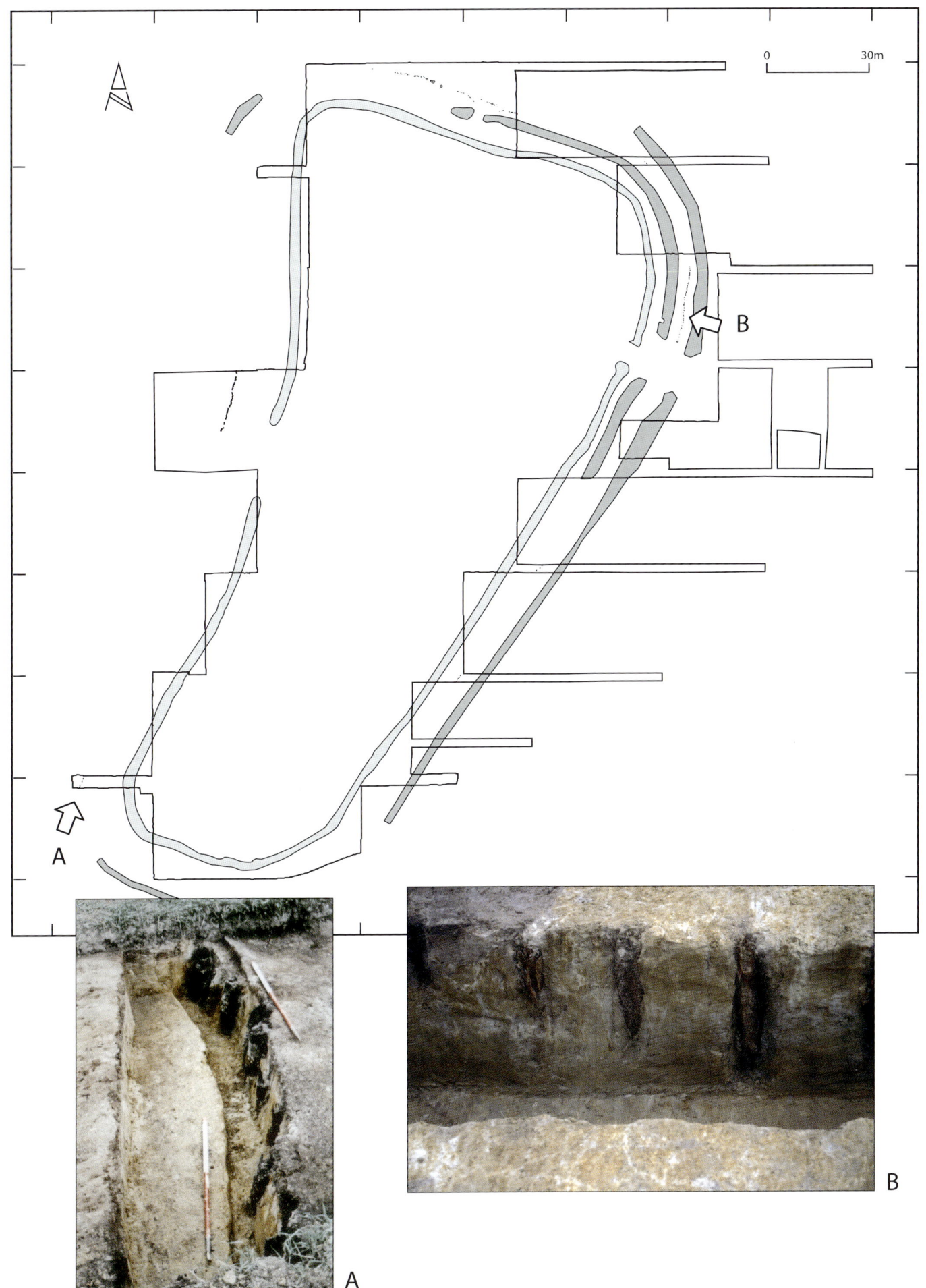

*Figure 5.12   Excavation plan 1998 – 2003: the palisade bank (excavated posts in the bank in black)*

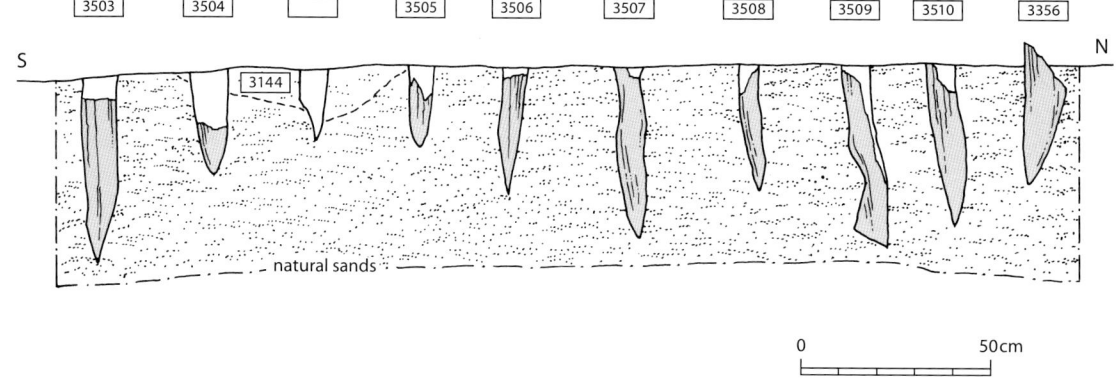

*Figure 5.13 Section of a row of stakes in the palisaded bank in Trench 3; no wood survived in [3144]*

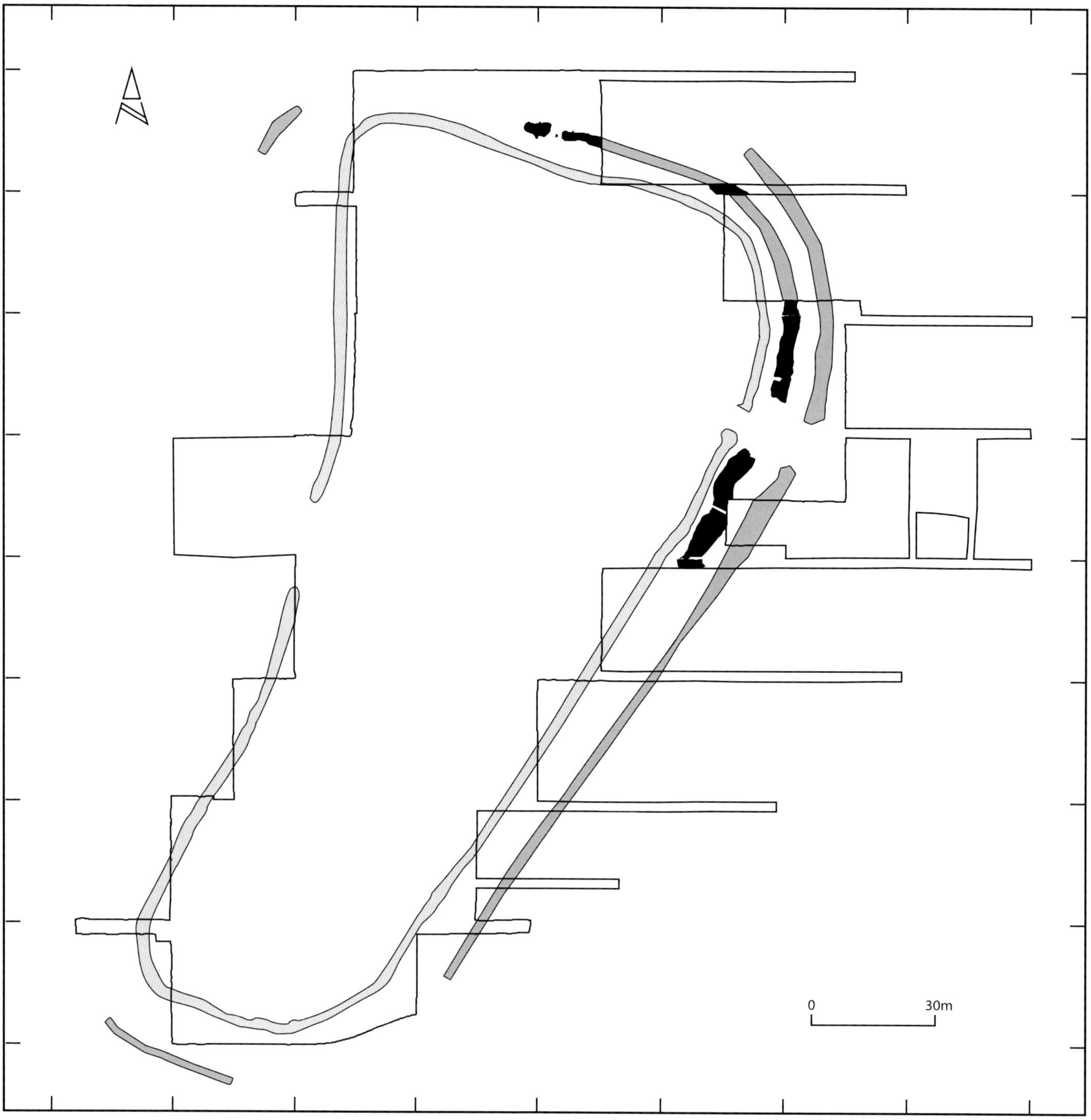

*Figure 5.14 Excavation plan 1998–2003: the inner ditch (excavated parts in black)*

process, or were hammered into the bank after its construction could not be determined. On the east side of the enclosure, some of the palisade stakes were very narrow (less than 0.1m in diameter), indicating that they might have been too weak to be hammered through the bank, even allowing for desiccation shrinkage. As with the outer ditch, the nature of the palisade was found to be variable across the site, in places more of a palisade than in others, although it seems that in its various forms this structure probably encircled the whole of the larger enclosure; the stakes of the palisade may have been sharpened at the top.

### 5.3.9 The defences — the inner ditch

As with the outer ditch, Whiting noted that the inner ditch varied considerably in depth in different areas (Fig 5.14). Furthermore, he noted the presence of a number of 'crossings', most notably in his Trench VI, in the north-eastern section of the site. He likened these to the gaps in Neolithic causewayed enclosures. This phenomenon was also identified during the excavations in 2002 and 2003. In Trench 1, for example, the ditch seen in the eastern half of the trench was in two segments, the end section being just 6m long and $c$ 3.5m wide, with the causeway between the segments being 3.1m across (Fig 5.15). The primary fills of the ditch segments in Trench 1 were inorganic, though with occasional fragments of wood within their matrix (eg [1476] and [1475]). The upper fill of the ditches was more organic and peaty (eg [1288]), perhaps indicating a slower infill process. The segmentation of this inner ditch was also identified in Trench 3 (see section 5.3.12) and Trench 4.

### 5.3.10 The defences — the inner bank/box rampart

The inner bank appears to have been the most complex structure on the site (Fig 5.16). This feature, exposed in Trenches 1, 2, 3, 4, 6, 7, and 8 as a double line of posts, each $c$ 0.3 – 0.5m in diameter. Within each line, the posts were arranged at intervals of between 0.5m and 2m, with the two lines being positioned up to 3m apart. These were most clearly seen across Trench 1, within the eastern ends of Trenches 3 and 4, within the western sections of Trenches 2, 6, and 7, and across Trench 8. Additional sections of this feature were identified in F10, excavated in 1999.

It seems most likely that this structure represents the remains of a type of box rampart, effectively a timber framework filled with turves and earth, held together by internal timber lacings, providing a raised platform that could be walked upon. This box rampart formed the innermost earthwork surrounding the larger enclosure. Along the east side of this feature, Whiting recorded up to eight courses of drystone wall on its outer face, although this was not identified in the recent excavations, presumably either because the bulldozing demolished it, or the wall was never continuous. On the west side of the enclosure, however, an area of stone walling was identified in Trenches 2, 6, and 8. In these cases, the walling was positioned over 2m outside of the box rampart. Whiting recorded this walling along the west side of the enclosure as up to eight courses high, and up to 0.75m wide at its base. The maximum width of the *in situ* walling, in Trench 8, was nearly 0.9m. Whiting also recorded a turf construction behind this walling, and it seems perhaps most likely that

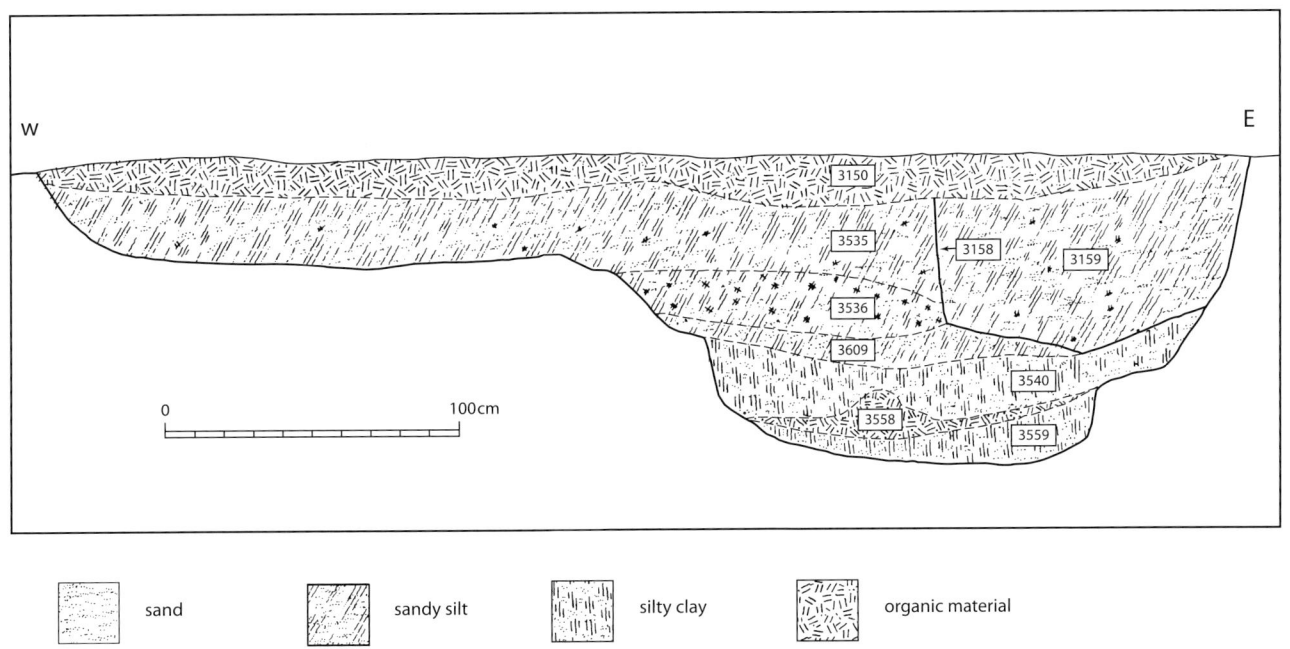

*Figure 5.15  West – east section of the inner ditch in Trench 3*

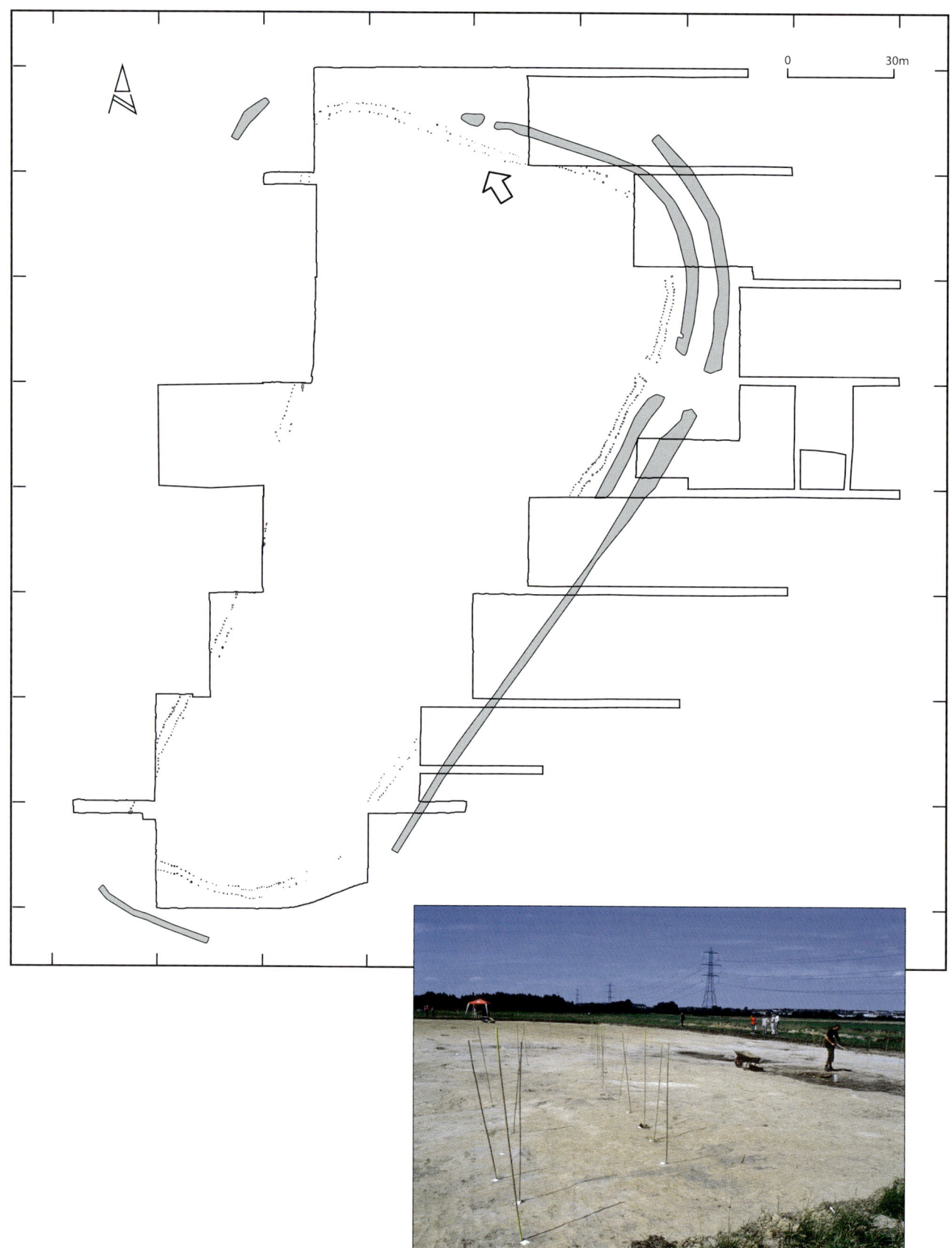

*Figure 5.16 Excavation plan 1998 – 2003: the box rampart (excavated posts of the box rampart in black)*

this formed an outer revetment to the box rampart, faced with a considerable wall of white limestone, effectively widening the bank in these areas to *c* 5m. The sections excavated through the box rampart in Trench 1 may suggest something of its construction, with an apparent trace of organic material seen between the inner and outer rows, suggesting they may have been joined by wood at some point (Fig 5.17). An alternative interpretation would see this as a two-phase construction, with the earlier box rampart later faced with a stone-revetted turf bank perhaps with internal timber lacing.

### 5.3.11 The defences — summary

In summary, the defences are more complicated than was considered by previous archaeologists, and also variable in their style in different areas of the site. The outermost defences, for example, were only excavated and recorded by Whiting as a short section of bank around the north-east corner, although this is validated from aerial photography. Inside this is the outer ditch, which varies in depth, and again may not surround the entire enclosure, as it appears to recede to the north of Trench 1 (seen in 2003) and south of Trench 8 (seen in 2002). Inside this ditch on the western side there is good evidence for a palisade, but on the east, this line of defence is characterised by a large earthwork bank with a central line of stakes, at its most impressive around the eastern entrance. Inside the outer bank is a further inner ditch, also variable in depth, but constructed in sections, leaving partial 'causeways' between them. In Trench 1 this inner ditch appeared to terminate, but perhaps it was literally just the hollow between the two banks prior to the bulldozing episode. The innermost feature is the box rampart which appears consistently around the enclosure. Variation in this feature is most marked by some areas displaying limestone walling, although gaps in this might just be a result of the recent damage to the site through bulldozing and ploughing. The ditches appear to have infilled rapidly, mostly through ditch-side slumping, although the high water table on the Common has preserved organic material within this unit. The upper unit of the ditches, up to *c* 0.4m thick, appears to have infilled more slowly with an organic, peaty material. This presumably reflects a stabilisation of the surface of the partly in-filled/slumped ditch, and the growth of vegetation within the wet hollows.

### 5.3.12 The eastern entrance including approach

The eastern entrance was excavated in 2003 and provides a comprehensive picture of the nature of the entrances to the larger enclosure. At the end of the machine stripping in 2003 it remained outside the excavation area. The project design and the excavation strategy was modified to accommodate this, and an additional 45 × 30m extension was made to the area of Trench 3, with a series of long, thin extension trenches stretching east, out to the wetland edge (Figs 5.18, 5.19). The eastern entrance presents something of a paradox in term of its interpretation. The structure is impressive, with all lines of defences represented, including additional details within the earthworks. However, the approach to the enclosure from this eastern side would have been impractical, with the deep wetlands of the Shirley Pool complex forming an effective barrier.

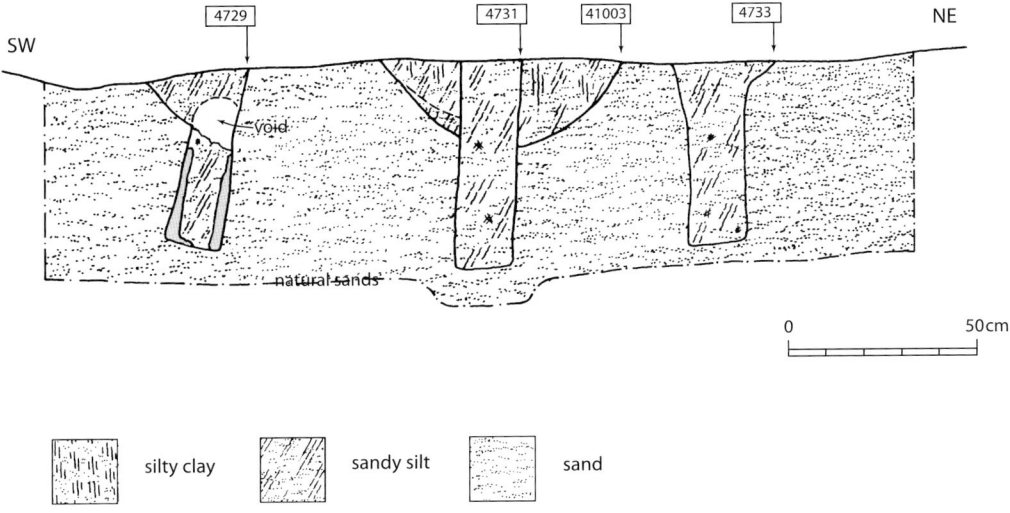

*Figure 5.17  Section of three postholes of the box rampart in Trench 4; wood fragments survive in [4729] only*

*Figure 5.18   Excavation plan 1998 – 2003: the eastern entrance (detail)*

Entering the marsh-fort through the eastern entrance, the first feature encountered would have been an avenue of tightly spaced stakes, similar to those outside of the western entrance. The two lines of stakes were positioned c 8.3m apart, with individual timbers positioned between 0.2m and 0.6m apart. Nearer the entrance, the avenue becomes narrower, funnelling to 7.4m between the two lines of stakes, leading to a narrower gateway structure, again reflecting the sequence on the west side of the enclosure. The preservation of the avenue timbers was variable, with a maximum timber length of 0.7m [3439]. The stakes, which were up to 0.2m in diameter, with pencil points, were hammered into the ground; neither postholes nor outer cuts accompany these pointed stakes (Fig 5.20).

Within the area bounded by the avenue timbers, 7m outside of the entrance structure, were three large pits [3408], [3412], and [3497], between 0.6m and 0.9m in diameter, arranged across the avenue, c 2m apart and with the largest pit in the centre (Fig 5.21). A fourth posthole [3410] was positioned to the east of these within the southern half of the avenue. Excavation of these features provided depths of between 0.2m and 0.4m, although they might have been deeper prior to truncation by ploughing or bulldozing. Initially, it was felt that these pits might have originally held a structure, which would have blocked or restricted access to the eastern entranceway, although their shallowness may preclude this interpretation, and no trace of timber residue was recovered within the homogenous brown sandy fills. Beyond this line of pits, the avenue continued to funnel down on either side of the entrance to the main timber structure. The density of the timbers forming the avenue becomes increasingly sparse, with gaps of up to 1.2m, providing enhanced visibility of the various lines of earthwork and timber defences to anyone approaching (Fig 5.22).

Near the eastern entrance, the outer ditch was c 4.2m wide on either side of the entranceway, with the ditch terminals widening to a maximum of 5.5m. The ditch on the south side of the entrance revealed a series of upright stakes, which had been driven into the nose of the terminal. These

*Figure 5.19  Aerial photograph of the eastern entrance during excavation in 2003*

stakes not only distorted the size and shape of the ditch, but might also have performed some structural entrance function on this side. Both ditch terminals were excavated in quarters, and an additional profile of the ditch was obtained against both baulks in Trench 3. The outer ditch was broad and shallow with rounded, sloping sides, with a maximum depth of 0.8m (bottom at 3.92m OD). The profile of the ditch revealed that the primary clay-silt deposits (contexts [3590]

and [3589]) were overlain by a charcoal-rich layer (context [3582]) with a peaty upper deposit (context [3492]). The uppermost layer comprised heterogeneous clay deposits, which appear to have been bulldozed bank material. Within the peaty layers, particularly near the terminals, the peat matrix contained a jumble of large straight oak timbers, presumably redeposited structural timbers from elsewhere on site (wood contexts [3541] to [3552] inclusive within fills [3574] and

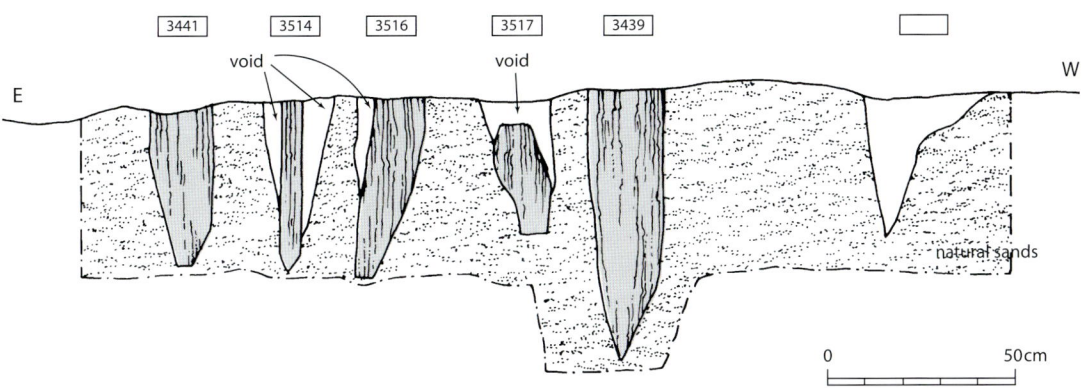

*Figure 5.20  Section of the avenue of stakes outside the eastern entranceway*

*Figure 5.21 Aerial photograph of the eastern entranceway, showing the ditch terminals and shallow pits [3408], [3412], and [3497] in the avenue*

[3537]). Within the terminal on the north side of the entranceway, human remains were recovered from the primary peat deposit (context [3574]; see section 7.3.1) at a depth of 0.7m below the excavated surface (c 3.9m OD). The bodies had been placed or dumped on their side, amongst the wood, and appear to be contemporaneous with this primary ditch fill. The wet preservation of these deposits indicates that the water table has been high in this area since at least the Iron Age. Furthermore, encountering a high water table would have precluded the need for a deeper ditch, and might explain the relative shallowness of the ditch in this area.

Moving inwards, the next line of earthworks is the outer bank. This feature was recorded by Whiting, although bulldozing had destroyed most of the structure, leaving only a small deposit, 0.2m thick, of yellow silty clay. The space between the outer and inner ditches that bound the outer bank indicates that it could have been up to 5m wide. Running along the central point between the two ditches, presumably at the centre of the original bank, was a line of stakes up to 0.5m in diameter, though most commonly less than 0.2m, and spaced at intervals of between 0.1m and 0.4m along the line (eg contexts [3351] to [3380]). As at the western entrance and in other parts of the site, this alignment of stakes was sinuous and in places fragmentary. It seems most unlikely that the stakes were driven through the bank following its construction, and may instead be a precursor to the bank construction.

The position where the stake-lined avenue and the outer bank meet forms the beginning of the main entrance structure. The primary feature forming the entrance is a series of twelve flat-bottomed posts, up to 1m in diameter, arranged symmetrically in pairs across the entrance route. On the southern side of the entranceway, it is unclear where the avenue meets the outer bank because the latter is missing. However, the avenue stakes finish just inside the outer ditch, and it seems most likely that this feature originally terminated at the nose of the bank. On the north side of the avenue, the structure is more complicated. The avenue timbers finish at a T-junction with a slot trench (context [3333]), arranged perpendicularly to the avenue. The slot was 2.8m long, of which 2m extended into the centre of the avenue, thus narrowing the access route into the site. The slot was steep sided and

*Figure 5.22 Photograph of the stake avenues outside the eastern entranceway and shallow pits [3408], [3412], and [3497], looking west*

filled with an organic-rich sandy deposit, containing the remains of a number of wooden posts (context [3591]); unusually, they were chocked in place by large limestone blocks. The slot trench appears to form the east side of a structure built into the terminal of the northern outer bank, defined elsewhere by posts (contexts [3598], [3267], and [3538]), creating a niche measuring 3.5 × 2m, with its longer side aligned with the entranceway. Thus, this feature forms the end of the outer bank. Elsewhere, similar structures have been referred to as 'guard chambers' when they are set within entrances such as this.

The innermost, south-western timber forming the 'guard chamber' structure also formed the northern post of the first pair of large timbers, its southern counterpart being 3.5m away, excavated in 1998 and 0.8m in diameter (context 1998[444]). A second pair of flat-bottomed posts, [3181] and [3187], was arranged 2.8m apart, and set 3.5m to the west of the first pair, moving in towards the enclosure. The alignment of, and distance between, the inside edge of the 'guard chamber' and the latter pair of posts is reflected by the next line of defences, defined by the inner ditch discussed below.

The third pair, [3183] and [3189], was characterised by a double-cut posthole on each side of the entranceway. In these double holes were a larger and a smaller timber. The larger structural timber on both sides was up to 0.7m in diameter, with the pairs set 2m apart, further narrowing the entranceway. This position represents the narrowest point of the entrance, marked by double timbers and aligned with the outer edge of the inner box rampart bank. It is considered to be the most indicative position for any gate or formal entrance structure to the enclosure (Fig 5.23).

Moving inside, the entranceway widens to 3.5m, with another pair of timbers (contexts [3185] and [3193]) positioned 1.5m inside of the paired ones. Interestingly, the widening of the approach only affects the northern side, with the timbers on the southern side following a constant alignment from the outside all the way in to the enclosure. To the north, however, the narrowing has resulted in something of a dog-leg. The final pair of timbers (contexts [3123] and [3209]) is positioned c 1.5m inside of the previous pair, maintaining a similar width and abutting the edges of the box rampart. Intriguingly, on the southern side of the entrance,

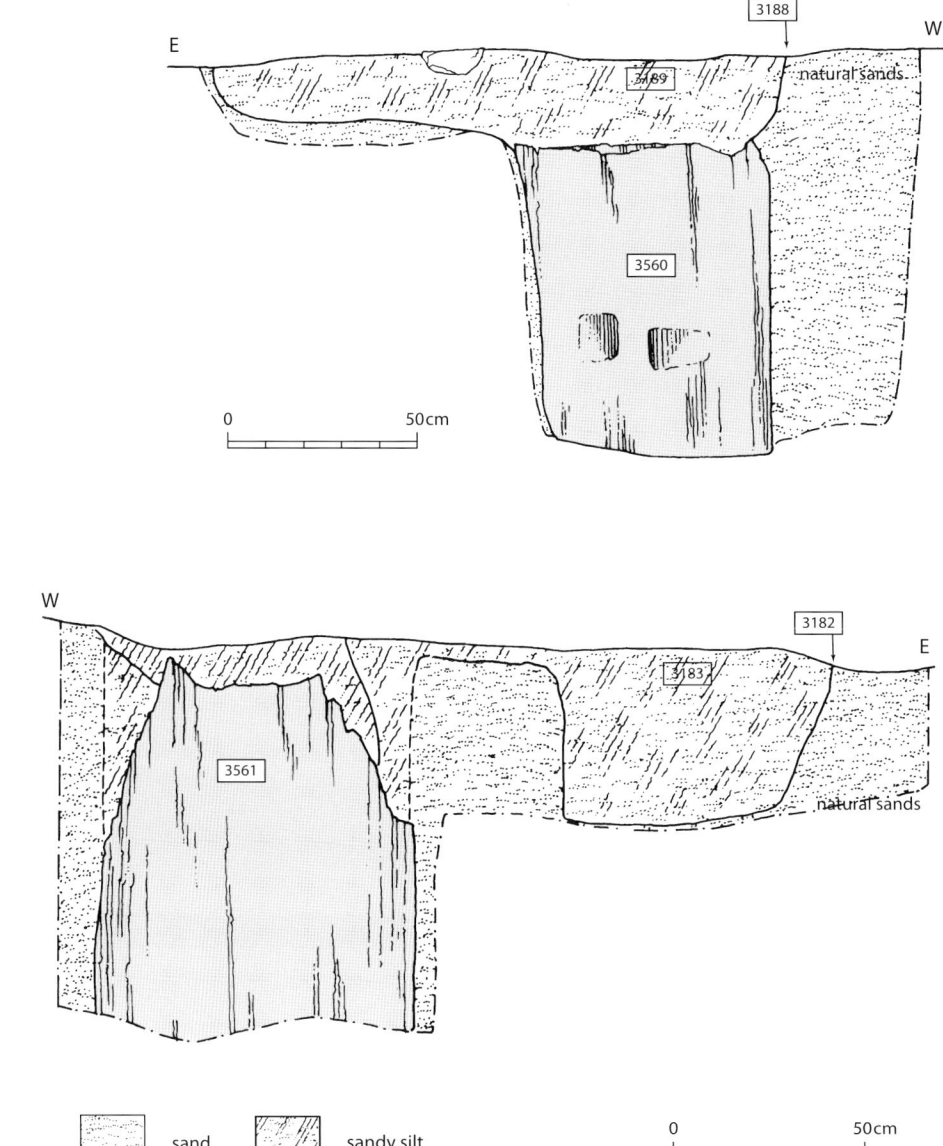

*Figure 5.23 Section of 'double-cut' postholes of timbers [3560] and [3561]*

an additional line of posts (contexts [3201], [3199], [3197], and [3195]) at the end of the box rampart indicates a more complex structure on this side. Perhaps this indicates the existence of an inner chamber under, or cut into, the southern terminal of the box rampart. Additional postholes were found, however, in abundance to both north and south of the entrance way in a space created between the inner ditch terminal, the entranceway, the bank, and the box rampart.

The large entranceway timbers were placed within snugly cut postholes, with straight, near-vertical sides and a flat-level base. Post packing was evident in a number of cases across the site but, unlike the variation of material used in the western entrance, here only wooden offcuts were used under posts (eg context [3566]), although they were from a very different source to the majority of the posts, in some cases suggesting reuse and reworking of material. A number of large posts also displayed notches cut into their sides, perhaps for tying rope to them for transporting them to site (eg contexts [3561], [3560], and [3530]).

The terminals of the inner ditch were recessed c 5m behind the entrance passage. The southern terminal had a classic profile, c 2.5m wide by 0.6m deep, with only two distinct fills. An upper organic soil comprising heavily degraded peat formed an upper fill, which covered a thick charcoal-rich deposit in a mixed clayey sandy matrix, over a thin, naturally derived basal soil. The amount of charcoal and the size of the pieces is very unusual and the sections through the inner ditch differ widely from those through the outer one. The northern terminal was also unusual: it had a near-vertical concave profile to the front, which dropped to 1.2m deep. The rear profile was different, with a stepped appearance. It levelled out at 0.4m deep to create a shallow platform or ledge in the back of the ditch. In plan, the terminal also appeared to be segmented, but only partly so, with a small tongue of natural creating a 4 – 4.5m segment. The stratigraphy in the northern terminal was similar to that of the south, but more complex, not least in that it was cut by an old excavation trench, presumably one of Whiting's trenches from the 1930s. The centre of the excavated segmented ditches reached depths of up to 0.7m below the plough soil (c 1.1m below the modern land surface – 4.03m OD). Within the northern terminal of this ditch, just north of the eastern entrance, a bone comb and quernstone were recovered.

The box rampart forms the innermost line of defence and is intimately associated with the structures forming the entranceway. As described above, the rampart is represented by two closely spaced rows of timbers set c 1.9m apart. The stakes were probably paired and evidence from Trench 1 shows organic staining across the middle, between the rows, possibly representing conjoined timbers. A number of sections were cut through the box rampart timbers on both side of the entrance in Trenches 1, 3, and 4. These sections (see Fig 5.17) show that the features extended to c 0.8m below the cleaned surface, with wood surviving in many of them. The wood had been sharpened to a pencil point (eg context [3526]). At the entrance, the rampart on both sides splays and rounds off, with the appearance of a 'knobbed terminal'. At the northern terminal, this structure adjoins closely the back of the entranceway timbers, and the southern terminal is similar, although set c 1.4 – 1.6m back; this leaves another recess (see above). It, too, bends outwards lining the edge of the entranceway, at least as far as the end of the inner ditch.

Overall, the entranceway measures between 2m and 3.5m wide, and is 11.7m long. Within its centre, a deposit of degraded limestone [3329], between 0.2m and 0.3m thick, was encountered. This deposit was similar to one found within the centre of the western entranceway [1999 – 130]. It differs in that it is widely spread throughout the outer part of entrance, in a thin but highly compacted layer mixed with clay, animal bone, and charcoal, which respects the features around it.

## 5.4 Phasing and dating

### 5.4.1 *Stratigraphy*  by R Van de Noort

Occasions where features of the marsh-fort's defences were cut by other features were very rare. For example, none of the c 350 posts and postholes of the box rampart construction had been replaced or the postholes recut. It may therefore be assumed that the defences were constructed in a relatively short period of time, possibly in one or several years, and were never repaired, though there is evidence, especially in the western entrance, that there may have been two phases of construction which occurred within a short period of one another. Had the ramparts been built or used over any great length of time, then regular repairs would have undoubtedly been required, with the relatively soft Lake Humber-derived sands, silts, and clays giving way rather easily to pressure (see section 3.2.1).

### 5.4.2 *Dendrochronology*  by Nigel Nayling

A total of 34 samples were taken for dendrochronology (Table 5.1). During the process of cross-matching samples, it became clear that a group of samples from fourteen timbers closely correlated with each other. The $t$-values for the synchronised samples assigned to this group, designated Tree 1, where very high. A 226-year mean sequence was calculated for this group (TREE_1; Fig 5.24: A). A further three samples were cross-matched with similarly high $t$-values and assigned to Tree 2, for which a 154-year mean sequence was calculated (TREE_2, Fig 5.24: B). The sequence TREE_1 was found to cross-match with five other tree-ring sequences from individual timbers and a combined 236-year mean sequence (SCOM_T6, Fig 5.24: C), was calculated. These mean sequences and the sequences from unmatched, individual timber measurements were then compared with dated reference chronologies from throughout the British Isles and northern Europe, as well as with sequences from previously analysed samples from the site (Nayling 2001). The 236-year mean sequence (SCOM_T6) exhibited significant correlations with dated series at the dating position identified as 597 – 362 BC.

On the basis of high $t$-values and closely matching absolute ring-widths, fourteen timbers are interpreted as having been derived from the same parent tree. These comprise one of the inner two entranceway posts [3530], one of the outer two entranceway posts [3560], and radially cut timbers from within the fill of the latter's posthole [3703], [3705], [3707 – 12] inclusive, [3740 – 1], [3743 – 4]. On the basis of the presence of complete sapwood on the sample from timber [3740], the felling of this tree is dated to 372 BC. At the time of its death, the tree was between 226 and 236 years old, given that the innermost rings were close to the pith in the sample from timber [3530], and therefore represent the earliest growth of the tree.

The felling date of one other sample, from timber SCANON2, is resolved to the season, with the parent tree having been felled in the winter of 362 BC. Dated timbers with identified felling dates ranges based on the probable

**Table 5.1 Dendrochronology samples**

| Sample No | Context/ Comment | Cross-section of tree | Total rings | Sapwood rings | ARW mm / year | Date of sequence | Felling period |
|---|---|---|---|---|---|---|---|
| [1208] | posthole cut 1246 | Half | 87 | +?HS | 1.20 | Undated | |
| [31449] | within fill 31037, cut 31450 | Radial | 261 | | 0.91 | 699 – 439 BC | after 429 BC |
| [3439] | part of (northern) post alignment running towards entranceway (outside enclosure) | Radial | 67 | +?HS | 2.14 | Undated | |
| [3530] | massive entranceway post, one of inner two inside enclosure, lies at end of box rampart. Lies below fill 3209, cut 3208. Part of 'Tree 1' | Whole | 203 | +?HS | 1.28 | 597 – 395 BC | 385 – 49 BC? |
| [3560] | massive entranceway post, one of outer two inside enclosure, lies at end of box rampart. Fill of 3189, cut 3188. Part of 'Tree 1' | Whole | 192 | +?HS | 1.43 | 581 – 390 BC | 380 – 44 BC? |
| [3561] | massive entranceway post, one of outer two inside enclosure, lies at end of box rampart. Fill of 3183, cut 3182 | Whole | 107 | +?HS | 2.90 | 495 – 389 BC | 379 – 43 BC? |
| [3566] | Lies just E of massive post 3561 in line with north inner ditch terminus at entranceway. Below fill 3181 | Whole | 132 | +?HS | 1.19 | 527 – 396 BC | 386 – 50 BC? |
| SC3586 | Trench 3, cell G14, within cut 3443. Timber within posthole 3443 next to south terminal of outer ditch in entranceway | Half | 94 | +?HS | 1.54 | Undated | |
| [3593] | within cut 3336. Within entranceway between ditch termini | Whole | 55 | – | 3.14 | Undated | |
| [3700] | within cut 3180. Below/ packing for post 3566 | Half | 62 | +?HS | 2.78 | Undated | |
| [3703] | fill of 3188. Below massive entranceway post 3560. Part of 'Tree 1' | Radial | 152 | – | 0.92 | 565 – 414 BC | after 404 BC |
| [3705] | As above | Radial | 89 | – | 0.94 | 588 – 500 BC | after 490 BC |
| [3707] | As above | Radial | 123 | – | 1.14 | 518 – 396 BC | after 386 BC |
| [3708] | As above | Radial | 52 | 14 | 1.84 | 426 – 375 BC | 375 – 43 BC |
| [3709] | As above | Radial | 110 | – | 0.87 | 589 – 480 BC | after 470 BC |
| [3710] | As above | Radial | 94 | 2 | 1.51 | 478 – 385 BC | 377 – 41 BC |
| [3711] | As above | Radial | 92 | – | 0.93 | 588 – 497 BC | after 487 BC |
| [3712] | As above | Radial | 111 | – | 0.90 | 589 – 479 BC | after 469 BC |
| [3717] | within cut 3457. Post on edge of southern terminal of outer ditch | Half | 97 | – | 1.38 | Undated | |

(continued)

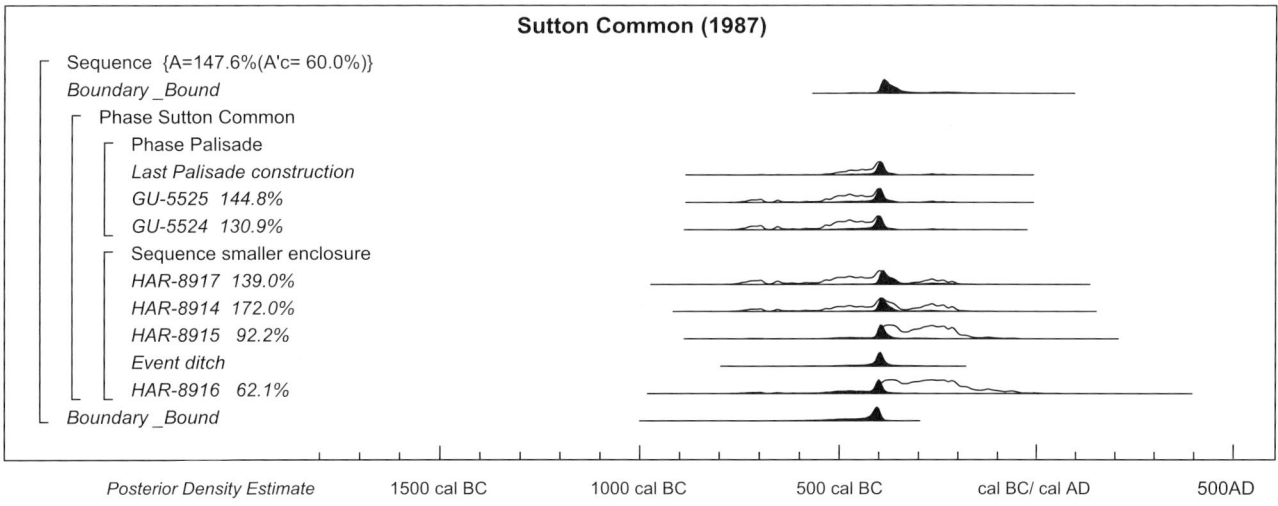

*Figure 5.25a  Probability distributions of dates from Sutton Common defences: each distribution represents the relative probability that an event occurs at a particular time. For each of the radiocarbon dates two distributions have been plotted, one in outline, which is the result of simple radiocarbon calibration, and a solid one, which is based on the chronological model used. The other distributions correspond to aspects of the model. For example, the distribution 'Event ditch' is the estimated date for the digging of the smaller enclosure ditch. The large square brackets down the left-hand side along with the OxCal keywords define the model exactly*

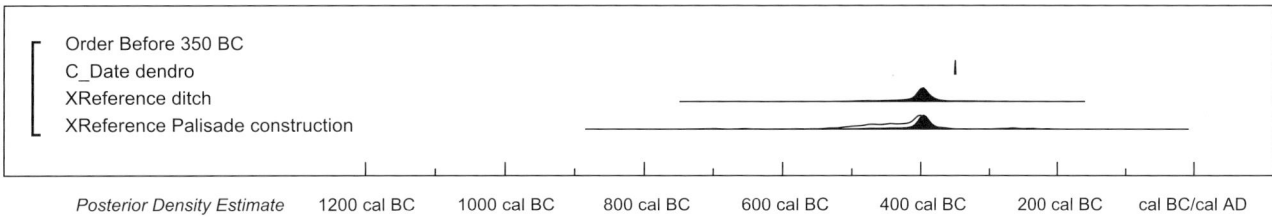

*Figure 5.25b  Probability distributions for the dates of construction of the Sutton Common defences pre-dating 350 BC. These distributions are derived from the model shown in (a)*

were sufficiently green to be (re-) worked and adjusted on site, whilst the construction was ongoing. On the basis of the inference that the defences of the marsh-fort had been planned in advance and constructed in a relatively short period of time, it seems probable that the rest of the eastern gateway, the western gateway, and the box rampart were all constructed in that same phase. It seems highly likely that the inner ditch was dug at the same time as the box rampart, providing the turves and soil to create a solid defensive structure.

It is probable that the defences were elaborated by constructing additional features outside the box rampart and the inner ditch, as has been suggested for other Iron Age multivallate enclosed sites. Thus, the palisade bank, the outer ditch, the far outer bank, and any additional alignments of stakes beyond the far outer bank (see sections 5.3.6–12) are likely to postdate the construction of the eastern entranceway in, or shortly after, 372 BC. No additional dendrochronological dates are available for the construction of these extensions or elaborations. However, when combined with all the available radiocarbon dates, the probability that the digging of the ditches dates to before 350 BC is 93.3% and that construction of the palisade bank dates to before 350 BC is 97.9% (see Fig 5.25b), although it is accepted that hardwood, rather than bark, was dated, and thus the dates of these timbers predate the felling of the parent trees (Parker Pearson and Sydes 1997, 227). On the basis of the radiocarbon and dendrochronological results it is most probable that all the defences of the marsh-fort were constructed between 372 and 350 BC, or the second quarter of the 4th century cal BC.

## 5.5  Wood technology  *by G Thomas*

### 5.5.1  *The western entranceway*

Post [4963] was the largest excavated, with a maximum diameter of 640mm and surviving to a height of 660mm. It is the most informative sample on the construction of the western entranceway. This gateway post is a full segment of oak trunk wood but appears to have been squared off in cross section, although there is no clear tool-mark evidence for this due to severe desiccation along its length. Despite its size the post shows only 95 growth rings with an average annual ring width of 3.14mm and is therefore a relatively fast-grown tree. This post is typical of the large flat-based posts from Sutton Common in terms of the chosen species and conversion (several examples appear to have been split, with box-quartered conversions and sections of radial cleft also noted in the assemblage). It retains numerous facets, some with clear signatures, across parts of its base which has been worked by a single axe to produce a flat base to the post. All the axe marks are orientated in the same general direction. There was no chamfering on the base of this post. Maximum facet dimensions are 47mm long by 58mm wide and have been produced by a flat axe with a gently curved cutting edge. Two notches have been cut into one side of the post near the base but these are very worn and desiccated with no surviving facets. Particular attributes of this post are discussed later alongside its counterparts in the eastern entranceway.

Fourteen pieces of wood were analysed from the basal fill of the posthole for [4963], ranging in character from woodchips and off-cuts to plank fragments. These are some of the best-preserved wood finds from the site. They appear to have been used to firm up the base of the posthole. Sandy iron concretions adhere to a number of these but otherwise their condition is very good, especially where tool marks have been cut across the tougher heartwood. Ten of these samples are of oak and one of hazel, whilst three remain unidentified. The ring patterns are variable, some appearing fast grown, others very slow grown, and 80+ rings are present on some. Sample [4998], a radially split plank no more than 110mm in width but with 146 rings, must have come from a large slow-grown oak.

The type of wood conversion of these samples varies widely, with whole roundwood, box-quartered, tangential, and radial splits, radial cleft, tangentially faced cuts and offsets thereof all represented. It is clear that sophisticated splitting of timber is evidenced here. Sample [4985] is one such example (Fig 5.26a). This is a 500 × 110mm plank fragment, worn and probably broken and cut at one end, and cut at the other, probably just before it was redeposited. This worked face is in excellent condition compared to the sample as a whole. [4985] also retains half of a mortise hole halfway along its length, providing the best evidence for more complex wooden structures and joinery on the site. The mortise has been cut using a much smaller tool with a straight cutting edge and provides evidence of a wide range of tools and technologies employed on site.

Several other plank-like timbers, off-cuts, and woodchips were recovered from fill [4962] in variable states of preservation. The maximum dimensions of the tool mark facets present on these samples were 70mm in length and 65mm in width. Cutting angles were as shallow as 5° and again, large, flat, very efficient axes were used to produce these tool marks. A variation in tools used on site is illustrated by sample [4998]. This plank fragment does not show tool marks as described for the earlier samples. It appears not to have been modified before being employed as post packing – both ends appear broken rather than worked and the faces of the plank show nothing other than natural wear and have presumably been split rather than cut. However, one small

*Figure 5.26a [4985], split 500 × 110mm plank fragment, worn and probably broken and cut at one end and cut at the other, perhaps just before it was redeposited. The surviving half of a mortise hole halfway along its length provides the best evidence for more complex wooden structures and joinery on the site*

*Figure 5.26b  detail of [4998], a radially split plank of 110mm width (max), but with 146 rings*

facet at the thinner end of the plank on the flat worked face may be evidence of hewing. It is only 9mm in length (truncated by the broken end of the plank) and 32mm in width with a deeply curved narrow jam curve (ridges in the wood where the edge of an axe blade became embedded) (Fig 5.26b). The full profile of the blade end appears to be present where the tool has become embedded in the plank. It is the only example of its kind from the site's wood assemblage.

Woodworking debris was not a major component of the wood assemblage from Sutton Common, thus it appears that much of the production of timber for construction of the site was done elsewhere. The 'post packing' samples provide the exception. It is likely that old timbers were reused for this function, being cut up prior to erection of the massive gateway timbers and used to level out and/or firm up the posthole bases. The excellent condition of the tool marks on these off-cuts would support this, as they would have spent very little time exposed to the elements before being buried.

A similar picture comes from Fiskerton, where only ten pieces of wood were categorised as general debris or woodchips (Taylor 2003). All this suggests that timbers were fashioned before their transportation to site. If they were worked on site, one would expect a large amount of woodworking debris to be present; however the site is very 'clean' with no such material recovered.

### 5.5.2  The palisade bank

The so-called palisade is likely to be part of a coherent design forming the spine of the defences within a low earthen bank. Post pipes, or voids formerly occupied by sharpened stakes, were found within the bank remains in 1999 and 2003, particularly on the east side of the site. Some stakes, although extremely desiccated, were found surviving *in situ*. In all 37 samples were recovered. Eight were in such poor condition that their species could not be determined; all others were identified as oak apart from six samples of Scots pine.

The palisade stakes survive to a maximum length of 785mm and range up to 180mm in diameter. Their condition varied widely across the site but in general the best-preserved examples were the ones that had been driven deepest into the ground. All were severely desiccated towards their tops but decay was advanced in all, with large desiccation cracks and fragmentary remains commonly encountered. No bark or sapwood was present on any of the samples and all were very straight-grained. There was no evidence for any side branches apart from the tough resinous branch nodes retained on most of the pine stakes. Evidence for trimming of branches was forthcoming from stake [3509] which retained axe facets towards its upper end where four branches had clearly been removed prior to the stake's insertion into the ground.

The method of conversion of these stakes shows a range of styles. It appears that whole roundwood was not exclusively used for stakes but that larger timbers were fashioned for employment as stakes too. For example, [1293] is an irregular conversion having been cut into a stake from a very large slow-grown oak timber. Over 40 rings with no curvature were identified in this sample, a pattern indicative of a large parent timber. The manner of conversion was not discernable in nine samples due to their fragmentary nature or general poor condition. Only fifteen samples were whole and most were irregular conversions. Of those identifiable, halved, quartered, radial splits and portions thereof had all been fashioned to produce stakes. Sample [1297] was a box-quartered conversion, the parent tree having been split into four then one quarter trimmed on all sides to produce the stake (Fig 5.26c). Of the 6 pine stakes, 3 were whole whilst the other 3 were irregular conversions.

Many stakes retained tool marks at their worked points and three were in such good condition that signatures also survived on the individual facets. Sands (1997) states that such marks are typically the first attributes of a tool mark which are lost to decay, hence the burial environment of these examples must represent some of the best wet-preservation conditions on site. Of the other stakes with surviving tool marks, their dimensions were very similar: 50–70mm in length and 43–50mm wide. As evidenced across the site as a whole, the axes used in the woodworking on these stakes were very flat with flat or very slightly concave facets. Due to the generally immaculate nature of the woodworking technique in producing the pencil points on the stakes, very few jam curves survive. Traces were present on stakes [1295] and [1298] and these show that the cutting edges of the blades used were straight and slightly curved, respectively. The efficiency of the blades used is evidenced in the very shallow cutting angles on the worked points, as shallow as 3° on stake [1294]. Stake [1295] was particularly well worked with very long (up to 85mm) thin facets down the length of the stake, far longer than all others in this group. It is possible that this represents removal of bark and sapwood from the original piece of roundwood, evidence which is elusive from the site as a whole due to advanced desiccation.

On stakes where clear facets survive and a point was recognisable, all appeared to be pencil points with the wood worked from all directions. However, stake [1229] was worked on two sides only and split down a third. Stake [1297] was worked only on three sides. Also of interest was stake [1224] as its extreme tip had been axed off to produce a small flat tip rather than a sharp point. Most were concentric pencil points, thus utilising the toughest heartwood to form the extreme point of the stake tip for maximum durability. Three

Figure 5.26c  detail of [1298], a 'pencil point' stake showing jam curves; the cutting edge of the blade used was very slightly curved

were non-concentric with the stake tips offset from the centre of the piece of wood. Signatures were present on only three stakes [1224, 1293, and 1298], with possible traces present on one other, stake [1294].

Due to the poor condition of particularly the upper portions of the stakes, it was difficult to study ring patterns without damaging the well-preserved points. On the stakes where patterns were discernible, a range of conditions are evidenced but slow-grown trees predominate with narrow rings more frequent. Up to 40+ rings were present in several of the converted oak stakes with a number of these cut from large mature trees, [1298] in particular probably cut from a large, slow-grown oak. The six pine stakes all showed very similar ring patterns with regular growth and ring widths all between 1–2mm. It is possible that at least three of these stakes were fashioned from the same tree. Timber [3507], however, appears to be from a different parent tree, with 50+ rings present.

### 5.5.3 The box rampart

The small stakes of the box rampart included some of the most desiccated found on site. Six wood samples were recovered. No clear similarities were drawn from these samples, with flat-based posts as well as stakes utilised in its construction. All were in poor condition and fragmentary – one had almost completely disintegrated. As such, no reliable information was forthcoming on the conversion of these samples. All were oak except sample [3356], which was Scots pine. The best-preserved of these samples, [3525], retained some tool marks and was clearly a flat-based post. The facets were again very flat but the junctions were noticeably stepped. Conversely, sample [3526] had been worked to a pencil point and was not too dissimilar to the palisade stakes. The facets however seemed generally smaller and the minimum cutting angle was 15°, as opposed to the much shallower angles on the palisade stakes, perhaps an indication of a less-efficient axe being used here.

### 5.5.4 The eastern gateway

Numerous structures with large surviving timbers were identified outside this gateway and parallel with the outer ramparts. The structures either side of the gateway, which have been identified as 'guard chambers' elsewhere, comprised of a number of large flat-based posts and large stakes. During the 2003 excavations, four massive gateway posts, [3530], [3531], [3560], and [3561], were removed from the site for post-excavation analysis. The largest (latter two) posts forming the outer part of the eastern gateway, up to 0.82m in diameter and 1.05m tall, had to be lifted from the site by machine and were subsequently only moveable by pallet truck due to their sheer size and weight.

Post [3561] represents the largest timber recovered from the site (Fig 5.27a). It has been fashioned from a large whole oak trunk from a relatively fast-grown tree; 107 growth rings were counted with an average ring width of 2.9mm. It survived to a height of 1.05m and was 0.70m in diameter at its base. Desiccation cracks were present along the length of the post making identification of tool marks and evidence for any bark or sapwood removal very difficult to gather. It had a chamfered base, however, and here tool marks remained in very good condition although there were heavy sandy concretions obscuring many of the several hundred surviving axe facets. The adjacent gateway post [3560] showed clear signatures: ridges or striations traceable across many of the axe facets on the post's base (Fig 5.27b). These show that it had been worked by the same axe. Such evidence on the base of [3561] was less clear but it was shown that a different axe had been used to cut the base of this post. Deliberate cutting of the sides of the base of these two gateway posts to produce a chamfered edge was also clearly evident (Fig 5.27c), perhaps to ease their entry into the postholes. The axe used was large and flat, as evidenced by the 50 × 70mm flat facets. Its cutting edge was slightly curved, as displayed by the many jam curves left on the base of this post.

Of particular note was the presence of an apparent 'tow bar' near the base of the post (Fig 5.27d). This represents some of the more delicate woodworking from the site. Two of these 'tow bars' are present near the bottom of oak gate post [3560], which is even broader than [3561], being 0.82m at its worked base. These tow bars are present on the same side of the oak trunk rather than on opposite sides, are desiccated, and retain no clear axe facets. Short linear indentations however are probably jam curves from the tool used to cut them. These appear to have been cut with a small narrow-bladed axe, two small holes being cut into the trunk towards each other until they have met and thus retaining the outer wood of the trunk in between to form the tow bar. There is no evidence to suggest a gouge has been used although any such marks would have been lost through desiccation and decay. One of the notches which accommodates one of the tow bars on post [3560] has been cut into the post to a depth of 80mm and is 360 × 180mm in area. Other shallower notches, with no apparent tow-bar feature having ever been present, were also evident. On [3530] for example these notches were cut into opposite sides and may well have been used to help manoeuvre this massive post into position with poles. Parallels of such tow bars and holes come from timbers found at Fiskerton (Taylor 2003) and the tree from the centre of the timber circle from Holme (Brennand and Taylor 2003.). On the Trent floodplain, oak logs have been found, in association with a log boat, with notches cut through them by an axe or adze as well as having transversely flat cut ends (Guilbert and Garton 2001). These are generally similar to the gateway posts at Sutton Common and the notch features have been interpreted as tow holes to allow the trees to be transported from the felling site. But in the case of Sutton Common it is also possible that they were used to allow the massive gateway posts to be manoeuvred into their postholes. These notches could have acted as propping points where the post could be supported by wedging poles

*Figure 5.27a [3561], one of the main posts forming the eastern entranceway*

into the notches whilst these massive gateway posts were lowered into position. The possibility that they are mortises where the tow bar has been lost to decay can be discounted as they had not been cut any deeper into the side of the post and survived just above a surviving tow hole complete with tow bar on the same gateway post.

Eighteen fragments of oak [3700–12 and 3740–44] were analysed from the basal fill of the posthole for gateway post [3560]. These paralleled those found below gateway post [4963], being plank off-cuts and large woodchips apparently used to firm up or level out the base of the posthole (Fig 5.28a). The condition of these samples was largely excellent and clear tool marks survive despite sandy iron concretions adhering to them. No signatures survived on the facets but a large flat axe with a wide, curved cutting edge had been used to cut them – the largest facets being 60 × 57mm in size. Although radial splits, which would offer greatest strength using the grain of the wood, represented the commonest wood conversions, they are varied and complex, showing that cutting against the grain of these oak timbers was undertaken with ease. These fragments have originally come from large, slow-grown oak(s) with up to 152 rings present on some.

*Figure 5.27b  detail of [3561], showing axe facets and signatures on the base of the post*

One of these off-cuts, [3743], resembled a wedge, an artefact which has been reported from sites elsewhere and likely to be a common artefact on large woodworking sites (Fig 5.28b). For example, Cunliffe (1995) states that at Danebury, splitting of tree trunks utilised iron or hardwood wood wedges. The size of iron cleats and bolts were used to infer that planks 20 – 60mm in diameter were in use here, similar to the width of the Sutton Common off-cuts. It is possible that [3743] was used for the purpose of splitting timbers, but the quality of the tool marks, and the lack of wear or signs of hammering or burring on its broad, flat end suggest its wedge-like form is more likely to be just coincidence.

## 5.6  Palaeoenvironmental sequences

### 5.6.1  *Palynology*  by B Gearey

The ditches around the large enclosure were identified as having high potential for providing a record of environmental change, although clearly this would only be for the period following the excavation of these features. Since the pollen source areas for such deposits may be regarded as predominantly local (*sensu* Jacobson and Bradshaw 1981), the palynological record from these deposits should be dominated by vegetation growing in, and in the close vicinity of the ditches. Following assessment of samples collected during the first season of excavation, two sequences were selected for more detailed analyses. These were from the ditch deposits revealed in Trench 3 and Trench 4. These deposits appeared to provide both the deepest and potentially the best-preserved records.

The pollen are described in Table 5.2 and depicted in Figure 5.29.

The lack of pollen from the basal clays in the ditch probably indicates a fairly rapid phase of inwash following the construction of this feature, which is believed to have been dug at the same time of the construction of the box rampart and gateways. As such, the basal pollen samples in T4SC – 1 most probably date to the 4th century BC. However, the lack of suitable organic remains for radiocarbon dating means that an absolute chronology for this pollen sequence could not be established. The data nevertheless provide evidence regarding the environment of Sutton Common in the later Holocene period.

The environment around the ditch during T4SC – 1 was probably largely open, almost certainly as a result of human activity and woodland clearance in the period prior to and/or at the time of site construction. Some alder must have been present on the wetter soils, although it is unclear whether the spectra represent more extensive areas of carr on the Hampole Beck and perhaps Shirley Pool, or whether more scattered alder was growing nearer to the sampling site. The grains of cereal pollen from the base of the zone suggest that cereals were being cultivated or processed in the near vicinity of the site, whilst the presence of herbs such as ribwort plantain indicates that the open aspect was maintained by farming activity and quite possibly by the grazing of animals.

The regeneration of alder in T4SC – 2 is associated with the deposition of silty peat, probably reflecting the infilling of the ditch with sediment and the subsequent development of suitable habitats for alder locally, rather than a cessation of human activity leading to woodland regeneration. Indeed, the remaining 'dryland' trees seem to have been largely cleared by the end of the zone. The ribwort plantain curve is maintained, implying that pastoral activity was continuing on the dryland areas around the sampling site and a steadily increasing pressure on the land resource, rather than specific episodes of clearance, was probably responsible for the final demise of the woodland. Evidence for anthropogenic activity increases in the final two zones, with the range of herbs indicating the presence of arable plots nearby, but the overwhelming impression is of grassland typical of that created and maintained by pastoral activity.

102  Sutton Common

Figure 5.27d  detail of [3561], showing the tow bar

Figure 5.27c  detail of [3560], showing chamfer and base

*Figure 5.28a   [3703, 3705, 3707 – 12, 3740 – 1, 3743 – 4], off-cut fragments from below post [3560]*

*Figure 5.28b   [3743], one of these off-cuts from beneath post [3560], resembling a wedge*

**Table 5.2** Description of Local Pollen Zones, based on samples from the enclosure ditch. LPAZ = local pollen assemblage zone. Percentages are of total land pollen (tlp) unless otherwise stated

| LPAZ | Depth (m) | Taxa | |
|---|---|---|---|
| **Short description** | | | |
| *T4SC-1* | *1.14–0.73* | *Alnus*–Poaceae–*Corylus*–*Quercus* | [4953], [4952] |

Moderate percentages of *Alnus glutinosa* (40%) are recorded, falling slightly to *c* 20% by the close of the zone. Both *Quercus* and *Corylus* are present at *c* 10%, whilst lower values for *Tilia* and *Pinus* (<5%) decline across the zone. Other trees are present at trace values only. Poaceae drops slightly before recovering to 30%, whilst Cyperaceae is steady at *c* 10%. A range of other herbs at lower percentages are recorded, including Apiaceae, Asterceae, Caryophyllaceae, Chenopodiaceae, Ranunculaceae, *Rumex* spp, and *Plantago lanceolata*, with the latter reaching *c* 5% by the top of the zone. *Triticum/Avena* type is present at trace values, whilst a peak in *Hordeum*-type is observed mid zone. *Sparganium emersum*-type increases to *c* 20%TLP+aquatics. Pteropsida (monolete) indet is consistent at *c* 10%. Indeterminable grains reach 20% mid zone

| *T4SC-2* | *0.73–0.60* | *Alnus*–Cyperaceae–Poaceae | [4951] |
|---|---|---|---|

*Alnus* increases abruptly to *c* 60% before steadying at *c* 50%. Both *Quercus* and *Corylus* drop to trace values. Cyperaceae increases to 20%, whilst Poaceae is reduced slightly to 10–15%. The range of other herbs present is similar to the previous zone, although *P. lanceolata* percentages are consistently higher. *Sparganium emersum*-type is much reduced, whilst Pteropsida (monolete) indet and indeterminable grains drop to trace values

| *T4SC-3* | *0.60–50* | Poaceae–Cyperaceae–*Alnus* | [4950] |
|---|---|---|---|

*Alnus* declines steadily across this zone to *c* 10%. *Corylus* shows a slight recovery to *c* 5% with *Salix* also increasing to a low peak. Other trees and shrubs are poorly represented. Poaceae rises to 40%, but Cyperaceae is reduced to 10%. The range and percentage values of other herbs are similar to the previous zone, although small increases in Asteraceae (Asteroideae and Lactuceae) are seen at the top of the zone and other herbs such as *Centaurea nigra* and *C cyanus* appears albeit at low levels. *Sparganium emersum*-type is reduced, but *Myriphyllum alterniflorum* increases to *c* 20%TLP+aquatics. Both Pteropsida (monolete) indet and indeterminable grains rise to *c* 15%

| *T4SC-4* | *0.50–0.42* | Poaceae | [4949] |
|---|---|---|---|

Poaceae dominates this zone, rising to over 90%. Other herbs including Asteraceae (Asteroideae and Lactuceae) continue to be recorded, although some including *Thalictrum*-type and *Cirsium*-type disappear from the record. There is a low peak in *Triticum/Avena* type at the opening of the zone, with a single grain of *Agrostemma githago* recorded at the same level. All tree and shrub taxa are reduced to trace values, with aquatics and spores also falling to low values

## 5.6.2 Insects and plant macrofossils
*by A Hall and H Kenward*

### 5.6.2.1 Introduction

This section concerns the macrofossil remains from the inner and outer ditches near the eastern gateway of the larger enclosure, and the results from the analyses of samples associated with the collapsed limestone wall on the west side of the larger enclosure. The results of the macrofossil studies from contexts from the interior of the marshfort are discussed in sections 6.5.1 and 2. In Appendix 1, Table App 1.1 lists all the plant and invertebrate taxa recorded from these deposits, with details of the charred plant assemblages in Tables App 1.2a and App 1.2b. For additional detail, the technical report submitted as part of the excavation archive to Doncaster Museum should be consulted.

### 5.6.2.2 Assemblages associated with the stone walling

Deposits associated with the wall [6021]: three contexts were investigated from the area in Trench 6 where some collapsed stone walling had been recorded during excavation at the front of the rampart on the west side of the larger enclosure. These comprised context [6022], a layer in front of wall [6021], [6023], a layer of build-up behind the wall, and [6025], a spread outside and considered to predate the construction of the wall. The first two produced no remains of interpretive significance, but the assemblage from [6025] was characterised by the presence of some charred remains thought very likely to have originated in burnt turves. Alongside abundant oak charcoal, there were moderate numbers of nutlets of sedges (*Carex*) and seeds of blinks (*Montia fontana* ssp *chondrosperma*), with traces of bugle (*Ajuga reptans*), bristle scirpus (*Scirpus setaceus*), and sclerotia of *Cenococcum*. One other very probable diagnostic indication of turf was the presence of charred root/rhizome fragments. This group together has been noted from many sites (Hall 2003). The association of these remains with coarse oak charcoal (the largest fragments here were 80mm in maximum dimension) will be considered further below, in connection with some of the ditch fills near the eastern entranceway.

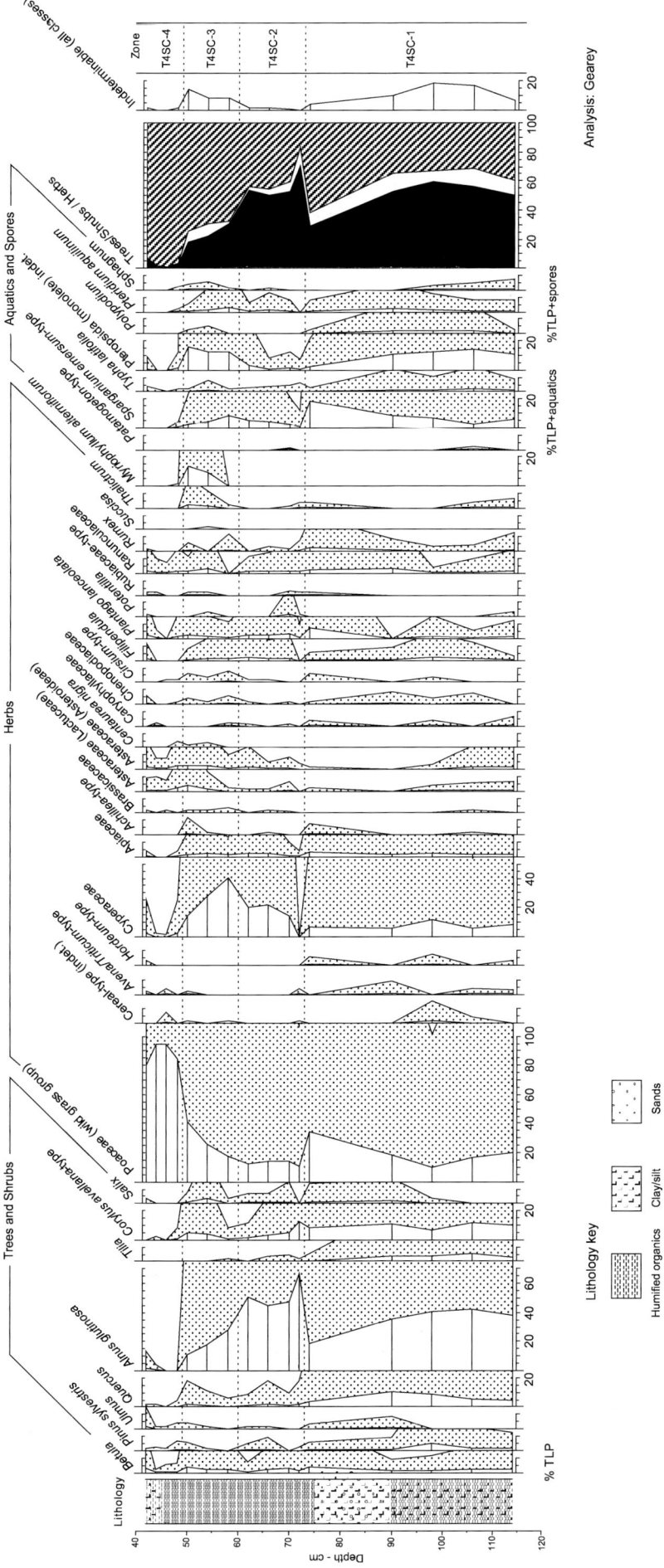

*Figure 5.29 Pollen diagram from ditch deposits south of the eastern entranceway*

### 5.6.2.3 Assemblages from the inner ditch fill to the north of the eastern gateway

A full sequence from the inner ditch fill to the north of the eastern gateway was excavated, comprising contexts (from bottom to top): [3559], [3558], [3540], [3609], [3536], [3535], and [3150]. The lowermost layer investigated was [3559], which was the first fill and was described during excavation as a silt. For the most part, the plant remains were uncharred and indicative of vegetation in the ditch, with a small woody component (including traces of blackthorn thorns and thorny twig fragments). A single charred glume-wheat glume-base was recorded and a small component of possibly burnt turves taxa in the form of modest numbers of *Cenococcum* sclerotia was present. Insect remains from this sample showed variable and often rather poor preservation; some fossils of 'peatland' species were especially decayed, suggesting the possibility that there might be a redeposited component from imported peat. A quite large assemblage of adult beetles and bugs was recovered, and their diversity was very high, inspection of the species list suggesting ecological mixture. There were immense numbers of *Daphnia* (water flea resting eggs), some chironomid midge larvae, and traces of other aquatics, together suggesting fairly clean still or sluggish water. Damp ground or waterside fauna was rather well represented, and included a range of species found on waterside or emergent plants, on waterside mud, and in moist plant litter. Taxa coded as decomposers (ie associated with decaying matter of some kind) were rare by comparison with occupation site deposits in general, and most might be found (together with numerous uncoded taxa) in natural plant litter. Species from trees or dead wood were rare. There were clear indications of (probably herbivore) dung from various scarabaeid dung beetles and a range of others may also have originated in dung. There may therefore have been grazing quite nearby. Some other elements probably originated from this kind of vegetation, too. There was no evidence of human occupation in the sense of dwellings or byres: a very small part of the fauna was contributed by synanthropes (here defined as species favoured by human occupation sites), and of these two-thirds were facultative forms probably originating (at this site) in natural litter.

Above this, [3558], a deposit containing small amounts of what is thought to be uncharred peat, was examined (the field description was 'silty peat', but the peat clasts here seem more likely to be an inclusion rather than merely undisaggregated sediment). The assemblage was also characterised by a small group of mosses – perhaps eleven taxa, all present in very small amounts. Some are likely to have arrived on tree bark (or perhaps through deliberate collection of brushwood), one or two to have been growing in or close to the ditch. Some of these mosses were the same taxa recorded at two levels in the sequence from [413] (at 1.30 – 1.40m and 1.40 – 1.50m), and giving much the same interpretive evidence (see below).

There was a moderately large assemblage of insects in the sample from [3558] examined, their preservation, as for [3559], being somewhat variable. The fauna was very diverse, and fairly mixed ecologically. Among the beetles and bugs, a third of the individuals were aquatics (indeed, the four most abundant beetles fell in this category), and these were complemented by numerous *Daphnia* ephippia and various others. There thus can be little doubt that the deposit formed in water, the fauna suggesting still to sluggish conditions, with no more than slight pollution. There was a single riffle beetle, which requires clean flowing water, but this may have arrived in flight or flood. Damp ground and waterside taxa contributed a modest number of individuals, but many of the terrestrial species recorded, including most of the decomposers, could have exploited plants or natural plant litter by water.

There was limited evidence for conditions further away, with a hint of live trees and clearer indications of dead wood. Modest numbers of scarabaeid dung beetles hint at the presence of herbivore faeces not too far away, and some of the other beetles may also have exploited dung. There were only weak hints of grazing land vegetation in the immediate vicinity. Synanthropic insects were rare, and mostly facultative or 'typical' forms which would have been found in local natural habitats ('typical' synanthropes are mostly found in association with humans but are able to live in nature). There is thus no evidence for human occupation contemporaneous with deposition.

Next in sequence was [3540], from which some wetland plant taxa were noted, including yellow water-lily (*Nuphar lutea*), indicative of a body of standing water, unless it arrived with imported peat. Material thought to be *charred* peat was also present, though there were only traces, up to 5mm in size. That some scrub may have been growing locally is perhaps suggested by the presence of traces of thorny hawthorn twig fragments to 40mm.

Immediately above [3540] was [3609], in which there was abundant charcoal (including oak to 70mm), a small component of charred cereal grains, and some burnt soil and perhaps other material from burnt turves. Uncharred remains were sparse and suggested damp ditch conditions with some standing water. The next context in sequence was [3536], from which much the same kinds of remains were recorded. Above this was [3535], investigated through two samples. Again, there was abundant oak charcoal (to 70mm), some wetland taxa, modest numbers of charred spelt grains in one of the samples, and some evidence for turves, more abundant in this sample than in the other, suggesting a degree of heterogeneity of the ditch fills – perhaps not surprising if the charred component was tipped or collapsed wholesale into it rather than accumulating slowly. The abundant charcoal and consistent evidence for what may have been burnt turves (and in some cases peat) in these outer ditch fills presumably relates to the destruction and collapse of a superstructure on the bank above the ditch.

#### 5.6.2.4 Assemblages from the inner ditch fill to the south of the eastern gateway

The full sequence from the inner ditch to the south of the eastern gateway comprised [3590], [3589], [3582], and [3492]. Samples from this sequence gave much the best evidence from the site for charred remains from burnt peat or turves. The sample from [3590] appeared to be iron-rich masses of fused charcoal mixed with a little waterlogged material. The less dense material consisted mainly of uncharred fruits and seeds of wetland plants with a small component of bark and herbaceous detritus, but with a 'background' of charred herbaceous material which seemed to be a mixture of stems and rhizomes and some amorphous peat-like material; some of the charred herbaceous detritus gave the appearance of being 'soot-coated' rather than charred in a conventional sense – one explanation of this is that it is material from within a roof (and perhaps indicating, therefore, that much or all of the charred material here is peat, turf or wetland vegetation used in roofing). The charred plant remains also included cone-axes of alder, together with some rhizome fragments that sometimes seemed somewhat 'collapsed'; both of these are perhaps more likely to represent fen peat than grass turves. There was also a single, rather worn ?spelt grain. The small beetle assemblage from assessment included some synanthropic forms, among them spider beetles (*Ptinus* sp).

Above [3590] was [3589], in which much the same kinds of material were encountered though with no evidence of cereal remains, and with a single poppy seed thought to be opium poppy (*Papaver somniferum*), perhaps simply from a plant growing as an escape from earlier cultivation. Oak charcoal was present, but much less abundant. Above this again, context [3582] contained some of the same 'burnt turf' indicators, though in smaller amounts; oak charcoal was quite well represented. The uppermost context in this sequence was [3492], with only small amounts of oak charcoal and a few charred remains likely to have originated in burnt turves (the charcoal was frequent enough in the whole sediment to be recorded, along with yellow clay lumps, as an inclusion in a dark grey/brown loamy sand matrix – perhaps further evidence for the presence of burnt structural material). This sequence rather clearly suggests the diminution upwards of the charcoal/turves component, presumably related either to gradual lessening of the input from the levels above, or a large initial input followed by gradual sedimenting out of charred material. Context [3150], from the uppermost part of the sequence, was sampled close to the terminal at the entranceway. It was rich in oak charcoal (to 50mm) with a trace of ?spelt grain and some hints of the presence of material from burnt turves. Other remains were uncharred fruits and seeds from wetland taxa.

#### 5.6.2.5 Assemblages from the outer ditch fill to the north of the eastern gateway

From the outer ditch to the north of the eastern gateway, the following samples were investigated: [3597], [3347], and [3600]. The lowermost, [3597], yielded a small assemblage of uncharred plant remains of wetland taxa, rather frequent wood fragments, and some bark, only stinging nettle achenes being abundant amongst the fruits and seeds. There was a small group of beetles which included some synanthropes, notably spider beetles (*Ptinus* sp). From [3347], which directly overlay [3597], there were further remains of wetland plants but with some indications of woody vegetation. There were modest numbers of wetland and waterside insects, together with a few hinting at grazing land. Also noted were traces of burnt soil and burnt ?peat up to 10mm. Immediately above this, in [3600] (at the middle of the sequence), the few uncharred wetland plant remains and a trace of barley grains were accompanied by further material, in modest amounts, which may have been mor humus or peat – both in charred and uncharred states. The presence of a trace of small (<5mm) fragments of charred herbaceous detritus might also indicate that material originating in burnt turves was present.

The shallow terminal of the outer ditch to the south of the eastern gateway provided two samples, from contexts [3454] and [3537]. Most of the remains of [3454] were uncharred wetland taxa, but there was a very small component of glume-wheat chaff and barley grain and one or two other charred remains which might have originated in burnt turves. Two samples from [3537], roughly in the middle of the vertical sequence, yielded for the most part uncharred plant remains similar to those described for the sequence from [413], but with traces of ?spelt grains in both samples.

#### 5.6.2.6 Assemblages from the inner ditch fill in Trench 4

Finally, a set of twelve samples were collected from the fill of the inner ditch, some 40m to the south of the eastern gateway in Trench 4, comprising, from bottom to top [4953], [4952], [4951], [4950], and [4949] (all fills of [413]). There was abundant evidence from the sequence of samples for the natural flora and inverterbrate fauna of a ditch containing standing water for much of the period during which it infilled. Typical plant remains were water-plantain (*Alisma*), water crowfoot (*Ranunculus* Subgenus *Batrachium*), hemp agrimony (*Eupatorium cannabinum*), ?fine-leaved water-dropwort (*Oenanthe* cf *aquatica*), and bur-reed (*Sparganium*). Weeds were limited to a few taxa that are as likely to have been living in or by the ditch as to have arrived with occupation material or from disturbed ground further off — apart, that is, for long prickly-headed poppy (*Papaver argemone*), for which there were two records from deposits in the middle of the sequence. With regard to other possible indicators of human activity during the time the deposits formed, traces of uncharred hazel (*Corylus avellana*) nutshell were present in two ditch fills, whilst single charred sloe (*Prunus spinosa*) fruitstones were recorded from four of them. In three cases, the sloe stones had been 'holed', presumably by a small rodent, prior to charring, suggesting a rather complex taphonomic pathway from plant to buried remains. Wood charcoal was present in all but four of the samples, but always in very small amounts and usually in small fragments. No other charred material was recorded apart from a little bark and twig and a single tentatively identified and rather shrunken barley grain; all of these might represent debris blowing or washing in from within the enclosure.

### 5.6.2.7 Discussion

Regarding charred remains from the ditch deposits, wood charcoal was often rather abundant here. There were fragments of amorphous material which seemed to be burnt peat, mor humus, or even simply burnt mineral soil. This component was most prominent in some of the ditch fills near the eastern gateway, where coarse oak charcoal was also abundant, and these together may therefore represent incidental tumble or deliberate disposal of burnt structural material into the ditch when wooden structures within the enclosure, perhaps mainly those close to the ditch, were destroyed. Several samples included a very small component of glume-wheat chaff and barley grain, which is interpreted here as being contemporaneous with the much larger amounts of charred grain from samples taken from the interior of the marsh-fort (see section 6.5.1.1), in addition to one or two other charred remains which might have originated in burnt turves.

Uncharred plant macrofossils were abundant in some of the ditch fills, particularly the sequence investigated from Trench 4, some 40m to the south of the eastern gateway. The waterlogged remains accepted as being ancient largely represented plants growing in damp places, from wet meadows to the standing water of a ditch, with some weed taxa indicative of disturbed soils (though not especially of cultivation) and sometimes woody plants which may have originated in carr woodland or scrub.

The invertebrate assemblages were mathematically diverse ($\alpha$, the index of diversity of Fisher *et al* 1943 = 111–154, with standard errors from 15 to 22), though ecologically rather less so. This suggests a rich natural environment, with the impact of human occupation limited. Aquatics were abundant in each of the assemblages recorded in detail (% NW in the range 16–33% of the adult beetles and bugs); the diversity of this component was not very high ($\alpha = 8-13$, SE 2–7), at first sight suggesting a restricted range of habitats (although the values to be expected in death assemblages in undisturbed modern wetland habitats of various kinds are not known). There were moderate proportions of damp ground forms (% ND = 7–15) and plant feeders (% NP = 11–13). A few species associated with trees and dead wood were present, especially in 'well' fill [8460] (13 individuals, 7% of the fauna). Beetles and bugs coded as associated with decomposer habitats were present in restricted numbers by comparison with occupation site faunas (% NRT = 26–29), and within this group there were few species typical of drier accumulations of decaying matter (% NRD = 1–3). An appreciable number of the uncoded taxa ('u') probably lived in plant litter, however. Foul-matter associates (RF), especially dung beetles, were consistently present, and occurred in significant quantities in ditch fill [3559] (15%).

Synanthropes as a whole were strikingly uncommon (% NSA in the range 5–11; compare with the much higher values given by Kenward 1997 for occupation sites). Within this component, facultative forms (SF) were very well represented (half or more of the synanthropes falling in this category), while 'typical' synanthropes were relatively rare and strong (effectively obligate) synanthropes absent. Although many of the taxa recorded at Sutton Common occur in occupation site assemblages, they did not form obvious synanthropic communities, and there was thus no evidence of human occupation of the site at the time the deposits with good preservation of insect remains formed.

In short, the macrofossil analysis from deposits associated with the defences indicates the use of turves in the construction of the marsh-fort. These turves had either been cut from a burnt surface or formed part of the defensive structures which had burnt before entering the ditches. The frequent occurrence of large lumps of oak charcoal higher up in the various sequences from the ditches, especially those near the eastern gateway, suggest either a burning event of the oak structures, or the 'structured deposition' of this material (see chapter 7). The samples from the ditch fills indicate that soon after construction, the ditches had filled partly with water, and that the anthropogenic impact on the fauna and flora in the period after construction was limited to the point of being barely detectable. The presence of dung beetles points to the presence of herbivores on the Common. The inclusion of charred grains is thought to be associated with the more extensive deposition of this material in the interior of the marsh-fort, and is discussed in detail below (see sections 6.5.1.1 and 6.6), and the formation of the deposits in the ditches was contemporaneous with this activity.

### 5.6.3 Geoarchaeology *by G Ayala*

The outer and inner ditches were exposed in the north section of Trench 3, showing the area between the ditches. The excavators believed that the space between the two enclosing ditches could have comprised the palisaded bank that had subsequently been truncated in the 1980s. The identification of this feature as a bank instead of a natural soil profile has significant implications for the overall interpretation of the site. If it is a bank, it represents a buried soil horizon associated with the period of the construction of the enclosure rather than a modern soil sequence.

The micromorphological analysis of the three thin sections taken from this profile spanning context [3000] and what was described by the excavators as the natural subsoil (Table 5.3) confirmed the field interpretation of this profile as representing a podzol soil sequence (Table 5.4) (Avery 1990). The effects of the bulldozing in the 1980s can be seen in the abrupt lower boundary and further characteristics present in layer I (context [3000]) (Fig 5.30). The fact that layer I is organically enhanced with inclusions of fragments of limestone (which are not present in the lower horizons of the profile) would suggest that this Ap layer (plough zone) was formed not only through the act of ploughing but more importantly through the introduction of new soil material (seen in the mineral component) from further away. This could have happened after the upper horizons had been bulldozed off, effectively truncating the sequence.

Unfortunately, there is no way to establish the age of this soil. The development of the distinct horizons would seem to indicate a quite mature profile, but there is no clear indication from the micromorphological evidence to support claims that this is Iron Age bank material.

## 5.7 Conclusions *by R Van de Noort and H Chapman*

The defences of the Sutton Common marsh-fort may be concisely described as follows: the core of the site was the eastern, larger enclosure; the western, smaller enclosure was essentially an elaborate entrance of the larger enclosure, and not an enclosure in its own right. Here, we concur with the interpretation of previous researchers (Parker Pearson and Sydes 1997, 255), and

Table 5.3  Geoarchaeology: field description of Trench 3 profile (palisaded bank)

| layer # | depth (cm) | Description | interpretation |
|---|---|---|---|
|  | 0 |  |  |
| I |  | Greyish-brown silty clay loam (2.5Y5/2 (dry); 2.5Y4/2 (wet)), with common fine CaCO$_3$ nodules and exhibiting discontinuous iron mottling | Ap |
|  | 21 | abrupt boundary |  |
| II |  | light brownish-grey silty clay loam (2.5Y6/2 (dry); 2.5Y4/2 (wet)) | A/E |
|  | 24 | gradual boundary |  |
| III |  | white very fine sand (2.5Y8/1(dry); 2.5Y7/1(wet)) with some iron mottling | Ea |
|  | 28 | gradual boundary |  |
| IV |  | pale-yellow very fine sand (2.5Y7/4(dry); 2.5Y6/4 (wet)) with common orange streaks of iron mottling | E/B |
|  | 40 | gradual boundary |  |
| V |  | light yellowish-brown clay (10YR6/4 (dry); 10YR5/4 (wet)) with streaks of organic material | Bt |
|  | 53+ |  |  |

Table 5.4 Summary chart of major micromorphological features of soil profile in Trench 3

| Sample | Fabric type (Horizon) | Microstructure & porosity | C/F Ratio & related distribution | Coarse fraction description | Micromass description (CPL) | Major pedofeatures |
|---|---|---|---|---|---|---|
| 105 | Bt | Sub-angular blocky, vughs and channels | 45/55; close porphyric | predominately quartz and plagioclase with rare mica and microcline | gloden limpid clay with porostriated b-fabric | frequent limpid clay coatings and fe mottling with common typic and aggregate fe nodules |
| 106 | Ea | Weakly developed platy, vughs & packing voids | 50/50; close porphyric | predominately quartz with common plagioclase and trace mica | dusty yellow clay with stipple speckled b-fabric | predominantly mottling with few aggregate fe nodules |
| 107 | Ap | crumb; vughs, packing voids & channels | 55/45; single spaced porphyric | predominately quartz and plagioclase, with rare mica and limestone | dusty amber clay; mosaic to slightly stipple speckled b-fabric | predominately silty clay coatings, typic and aggregate fe nodules, common organic material |

Figure 5.30 Geoarchaeology: sampled profile, Trench 3

interpret the results from the geophysical survey as reinforcing their conclusion. After completion of the marsh-fort, visitors to the site in the Iron Age would have followed a clearly defined route, which took them from the limestone edge to the south-west corner of the smaller enclosure, then along its southern and eastern earthworks before crossing the alder carr within the Hampole Beck palaeochannel by means of the constructed and delimited causeway.

From the causeway, one would have entered the marsh-fort through the western gateway. The larger enclosure had only two entrances, rather than four (*contra* Whiting 1936; see Parker Pearson and Sydes 1997, 224), and both had been much elaborated, with the eastern gateway proving the more impressive of the two. The gateways and the box rampart formed an integrated structure which surrounded the complete circuit of the larger enclosure, some 600m in length, possibly constructed in a single phase. The inner ('causewayed') ditch may have been excavated originally to provide the material for the core of the rampart, but the palisaded bank, outer ditch, far outer bank, and further minor lines of stakes on the east side of the larger enclosure were elaborations of the system of defences. The existence of a palisade, noted in previous excavations (*ibid*), was confirmed, but this has been shown to form part of these elaborations rather than an earlier phase of enclosure. The low limestone wall on the west side of the larger enclosure functioned presumably as a barrier between the box rampart and standing water in the Hampole Beck palaeochannel (Figs 5.31 and 5.32).

In terms of the defences constructed at Sutton Common, it parallels a number of other large enclosed Iron Age sites. Within the area of Yorkshire, Lincolnshire, and Nottinghamshire, uni- and multi-vallation of large sites is known from throughout the 1st millennium cal BC, ranging from the early 1st millennium BC circular fortified hilltop enclosure at Thwing on the Yorkshire Wolds through to the late Iron Age 'oppidum' of Stanwick (Manby 2003a; 2003b). Within Yorkshire, only the enclosure at Skipwith Common, some 30km north-east of Sutton Common in the Vale of York, lies in a lowland location. The Skipwith Common site was destroyed in 1941 during the construction of the military airfield runway, but antiquarian reports describe it as measuring $c$ 160 × 130m, and formed by bank and ditch arrangements involving one, two or three sets of defences (Stead 1961; outline recently illustrated in Cunliffe 2005, 545). The site has not been dated independently, but is thought to be associated with the early and middle Iron Age square-ditched barrows on the Common. Tattershall Thorpe, somewhat further afield in Lincolnshire, the enigmatic multivallate enclosure complex at Aslockton in Nottinghamshire, and the univallate curvilinear enclosure at Swarkestone Lowes in Derbyshire, provide additional examples of large enclosed lowland sites of the 1st millennium BC (Chowne *et al* 1986; Knight and Howard 2004, 94–6). None of these sites has been extensively excavated.

The majority of large fortified or enclosed sites in the region are situated on hilltops, such as those at Almondbury, South Kirby, Barwick-in-Elmet, Castleheads, Ingleborough, and Downholme in Pennine Yorkshire, Staple How, Devil's Hill, and Grimthorpe on the northern margins of the Yorkshire Wolds, and Wincobank on the Coal Measures outside Sheffield (Challis and Harding 1975, 130–8; Manby 2003b; Harding 2004, 23–6). Few of these have been the subject of large-scale archaeological research, but the Grimthorpe hillfort was partly excavated. It has a box rampart which, in its dimensions, closely resembles the box rampart at Sutton Common, but without further elaborations of added ditches and 'palisades' (Stead 1968). The density of large sites with uni- and multi-vallation in this region is, nevertheless, much lower than from other regions in Britain, and Cunliffe (2005, 74) depicts the zone as one characterised by open settlement.

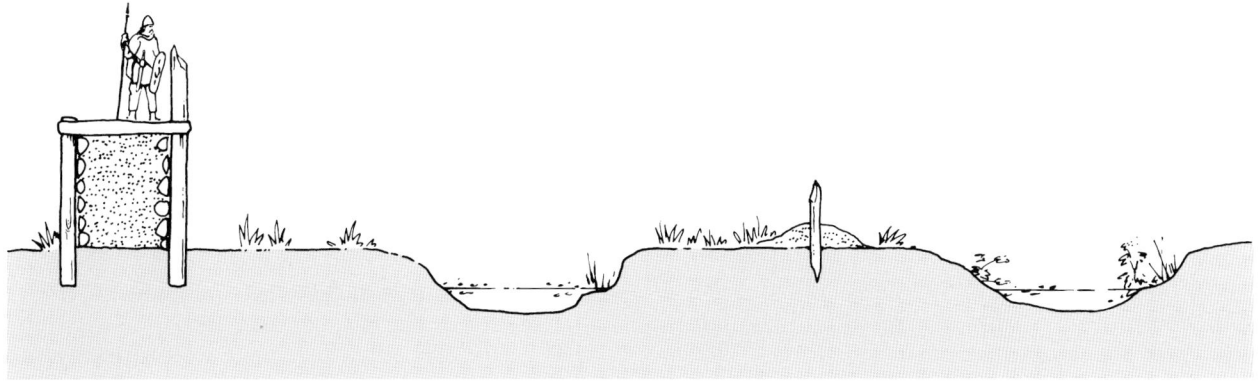

*Figure 5.31  Reconstruction of a cross-section of the defences on the east side of the larger enclosure*

*Figure 5.32   Reconstruction of the eastern gateway*

In the introduction to this chapter and earlier (see section 1.3.1.1), we referred to the use of the term 'defences' as somewhat controversial, and suggested that the symbolic value rather than the physicality of the ditches and banks may have been considered the most important reason for their construction. In this, we follow others who have recently questioned the function of hillforts and other enclosed sites in terms of defence and warfare (eg Stopford 1987; Haselgrove 1992; Hill 1995b), and through this, the significance of enclosed settlements to understanding the Iron Age societies under study. The enclosing of settlements and other foci of human activity with ditches and banks and the construction of linear boundaries and pit alignments appear as interrelated trends for many regions in Britain, broadly dated to the 1st millennium BC (eg Thomas 1997). Whereas increased pressure on resources as a consequence of population growth is often quoted as the driving force behind these developments, resulting in the need to (re)state one's ownership or tenure of the land, in cases such as Sutton Common the symbolic significance of enclosing sites must be considered alongside such functional explanations. A number of features of the larger enclosure at Sutton Common undermine any suggestion of martially defined objectives.

The elaboration of the entrances and the gateways provide a pertinent illustration. These elaborations demonstrate considerable effort on behalf of the builders, including the procurement and transportation of suitable timber and limestone, in addition to the on-site efforts of construction. From a point of view of defensiveness, reinforcing entranceways is prudent, especially in the wetland setting at Sutton Common which restricts the potential points of access. We can assume that the Hampole Beck palaeochannel, a peatland with dense alder carr throughout the Iron Age, was impassable and that the causeway which linked the two enclosures was effectively the only way into the larger enclosure. However, its width, of $c$ 9m, seems to challenge any urgency to make the core of the site easily defendable. Rather, the impression is left of an imposing or ceremonial crossing of the wetlands of the former Hampole Beck as part of the way in which people entered the site.

Similarly, the 'causewayed' inner ditch is intriguing. As argued earlier (see section 5.3.9), the inner ditch in fact comprises a series of aligned elongated pits. Whilst these might have provided the quarry material for the box-rampart core, it is most likely that the 'causeways' were a deliberate feature of the construction process, given the completeness of the site otherwise, again undermining the protective capability of the ditch. Furthermore, these 'defences' tail off in scale considerably as one moves away from the entrances, and thus from the viewpoint of visitors to the site in the 4th century BC.

The eastern entrance itself was unlikely to be used as the principal approach to the larger enclosure, as it leads to only a small area of wetland-surrounded land, but it offers the most imposing and sophisticated way into the larger enclosure (Fig 5.32). Access from the Magnesian Limestone, where the free-draining soils would have offered a suitable environment for arable agriculture and which is the likely setting for the arable fields and houses, must have been through the smaller enclosure, across the causeway over the Hampole Beck palaeochannel and into the larger enclosure through the western gateway. The existence of the eastern entranceway at Sutton Common can not, therefore, be explained as a defence against attackers from the east. Instead, it can be understood to have functioned as the 'proper' way into the enclosure in terms of cosmology and perception, and that the orientation to the east was the required orientation for the crossing of the threshold into the marsh-fort. Similar arguments have been made for hillforts and enclosed settlements in central southern England (Hill 1994; 1995b), and for houses throughout Britain (eg Fitzpatrick 1994; Parker Pearson 1996; Oswald 1997; Parker Pearson and Richards 1994). At Sutton Common, as at many other places, we recognise the structured deposition of a range of artefacts, raw materials, food waste, and human remains in the terminals of the eastern entrance (but not in the western gateway), reinforcing the symbolic significance of this threshold. These are discussed and interpreted in more detail below (see chapter 7).

Nevertheless, we accept that the architecture used at Sutton Common was, at the very least, based on principles of defensiveness as perceived by the people of the Iron Age. This is unsurprising as the architecture of warfare, regardless its efficacy, would have been embedded in the perception of what constituted formal boundaries which could not be crossed, and thus formed part of a cosmology as much as what constituted the 'proper' way of entering an enclosed site. This explains why the defences at Sutton Common are paralleled across the country and why the plan for the Sutton Common bank and ditch arrangements may have been copied from other enclosed sites such as hillforts. Thus the use of the term 'fort' for describing the site seems justified, although this should be understood as a morphological, rather than a functional idiom.

The evidence allows for greater accuracy and precision in the dating of the site than has been possible for any other large enclosed site in Britain. The dendrochronological evidence from the eastern gateway shows that, where bark survives, timbers were felled from 372 to 362 BC, and that all the samples investigated could fall in this period. Assuming that the gateways and connected box rampart were built first, and subsequently elaborated by the series of banks and ditches, then the period of construction of the defences at Sutton Common falls probably between 372 BC and 350 cal BC.

The palaeoenvironmental evidence shows unambiguously that the area around the marsh-fort's defences did not see any intensive or prolonged anthropogenic activity after its construction. The ditches filled up with water soon after they had been dug, and the pollen, insect, and plant macrofossil evidence indicates the use of the Common as a grazing ground for herbivores with a flourishing alder woodland within the Hampole Beck palaeochannel, but with only very minor signs of humans living and working here.

# 6 The marsh-fort – the interior structures

## 6.1 Introduction *by H Chapman, W Fletcher and R Van de Noort*

This chapter presents the evidence available for the structures and finds of the interior of the marsh-fort. The near-complete excavation of the interior of the large enclosure of the Sutton Common site, coupled with the limited period of its use and integrated palaeoenvironmental work, allows for a relatively clear-cut view of the structures in the interior of the marsh-fort, and thus, we believe, a clearer understanding of the function of the site in the 4th century BC.

Following the description of the archaeological features, the limited evidence for the dating of the site is presented. This is followed by a presentation of the wood technology utilised for the structures in the interior of the marsh-fort, and the palaeoenvironmental data, and a concluding section.

## 6.2 Description of features
*by H Chapman, W Fletcher and R Van de Noort*

### 6.2.1 General overview

A general overview of the site (see Fig 5.3) has only been available since the end of the 2003 season. The interior of the larger enclosure displays one phase of activity, which is considered to be contemporaneous with the defences. The overall picture of activities within the enclosure in the 4th century BC indicates a planned layout dominated almost entirely by four-post structures, multiplied by the hundred across the whole site. These features begin on the outside and are aligned against the nearest section of box rampart, providing concentrations to the north and south of the entrances and a dense cluster in the southern half of the enclosure. The overall impression is of a 'V' shape, with a lesser density of features in the centre and to the north. The structures were positioned in rows along these alignments. Within the interior, no contemporaneous or later evidence of domestic structures was identified, indicating that the site was not inhabited for any length of time during the Iron Age. The lack of evidence for the recutting of ditches, intercepting features or secondary phases of activity, and the absence of evidence for any structural repairs to the four-post structures, indicate that the human activity at Sutton Common site was short-lived. This view is reinforced by the palaeoenvironmental analysis of the fills from the ditches, which failed to detect evidence of on-going activity in the marsh-fort (see section 5.6.2).

Other types of features were notable by their absence, but there were a number of small pits, and a timber-lined feature, probably a well. Taking the site as an entity it is also the empty space or voids that are important, and the absence of features in certain areas may also be important, functioning as internal paths and spatial divisions of the site. Nevertheless, a significant number of postholes could not be attributed to identifiable structures, and we recognise the possibility for structures such as hay-drying racks or temporary shelters to have remained concealed in the jumble of features.

### 6.2.2 Four-post structures

The most prevalent feature within the interior of the site was the posthole. Over 2000 such features were identified altogether within the interior of the site, a significant number of these arranged in groups of four, hence the term 'four-post' structure, but occasionally appearing in groups of six (see below). In reconstructing structures from the excavation plan, interiors of other Iron Age enclosed sites were used as examples, notably the detailed and explicitly formulated spatial analysis from Danebury hillfort (eg Brown in Cunliffe 1995, 137–92), but the analysis was anything but a sophisticated procedure (Fig 6.1). The excavation strategy, which included the sectioning of only a sample of features (see section 3.2.2), is recognised as a limiting factor in the analysis of the interior of the marsh-fort, although we submit that the overall understanding of the site would not have been significantly different if all features had been excavated.

The palaeoenvironmental potential of the postholes of the four-post structures was only demonstrated during the assessment after the 2002 excavation, and in 2003 posts were excavated and sampled in groups of four whenever their association was apparent, such as was the case in the four-post structure made up by [7246], [7264], [7265], and [7269], and the structure combining [7340], [7341], [7342], and [7343] (Fig 6.2).

However, during the excavations not all four-post structures were readily identified and some structures only became identifiable during the analysis of the plans. Even after the post-excavation analysis, the pattern of features was not always clear. On more than one occasion, a fourth post hole was found by intensive cleaning in a group which appeared at first to only have

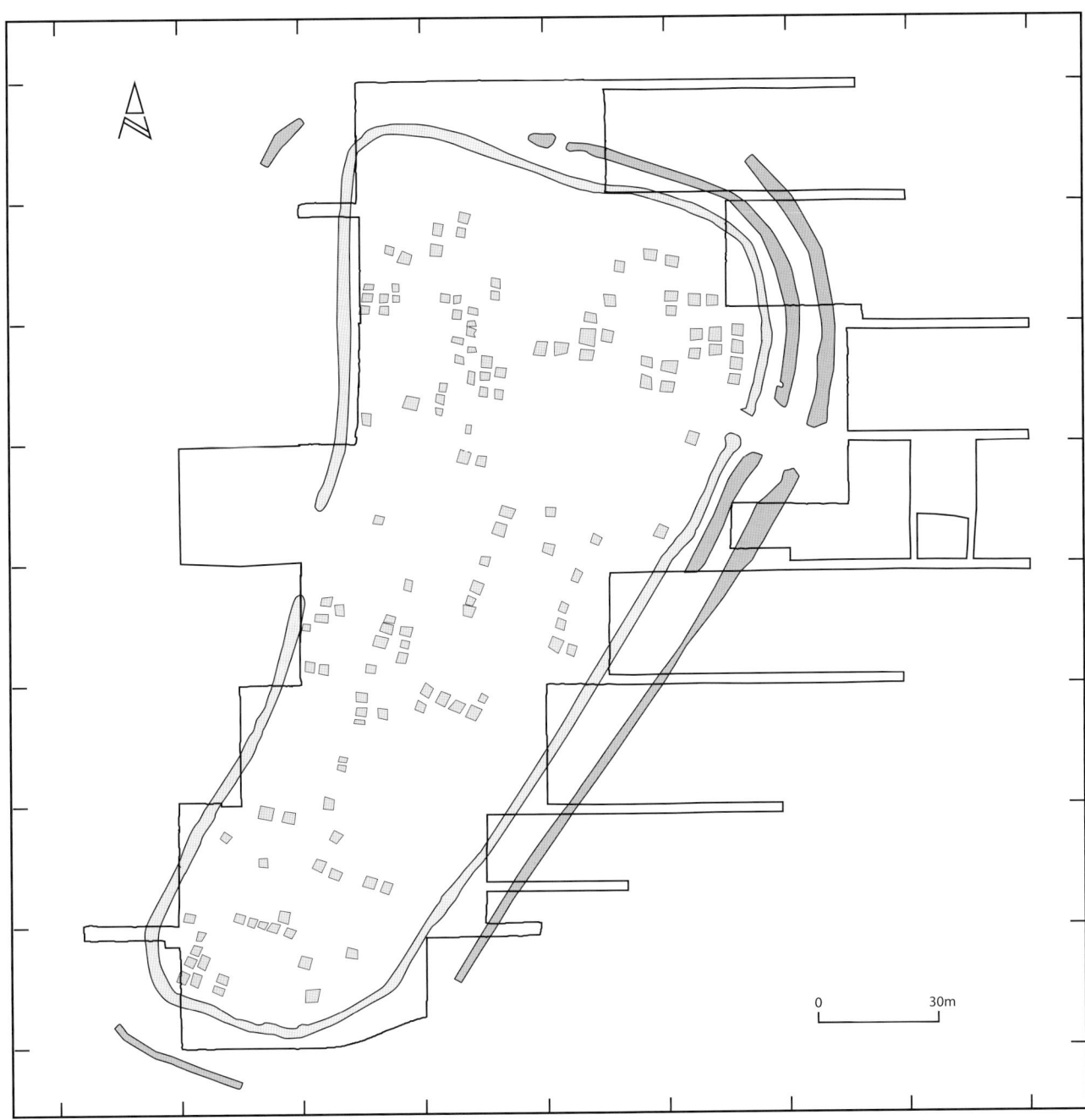

Figure 6.1  Excavation plan 1998 – 2003: the four-post structures and variants

three visible posts. Another common occurrence was complete translocation of the top of a post or posthole through recent sub-soiling or ploughing. In section, the upper 0.10m of the posthole which had been visible on the surface was found 'decapitated' from its lower part that often including the remains of the timber post. Finding and recording instances of this nature does have an implication for the rest of the interior, suggesting some four-post structures could possibly appear incomplete or distorted in plan. Where posts or preserved organic remains were not visible, the sandy soil caused problems for feature identification, particularly with organic material leaching through the section, leaving only vague determinations of post positions and odd distorted posthole shapes.

In all, some 115 four-post structures could be identified with confidence, and an additional 30 to 40 four-post structures are thought to have existed in the marsh-fort's interior, but not all four posts survived or were recorded. Where these structures appear in isolation, their identification is unquestionable. For example postholes [1093], [1096], [1098], and [1100] appear as a perfect square of 2.4 × 2.4m, surrounded by few other features. More frequently, however, these structures appear in aligned rows, with up to six buildings in a single row. The distance between them is in most instances less than 1.5m, but often little

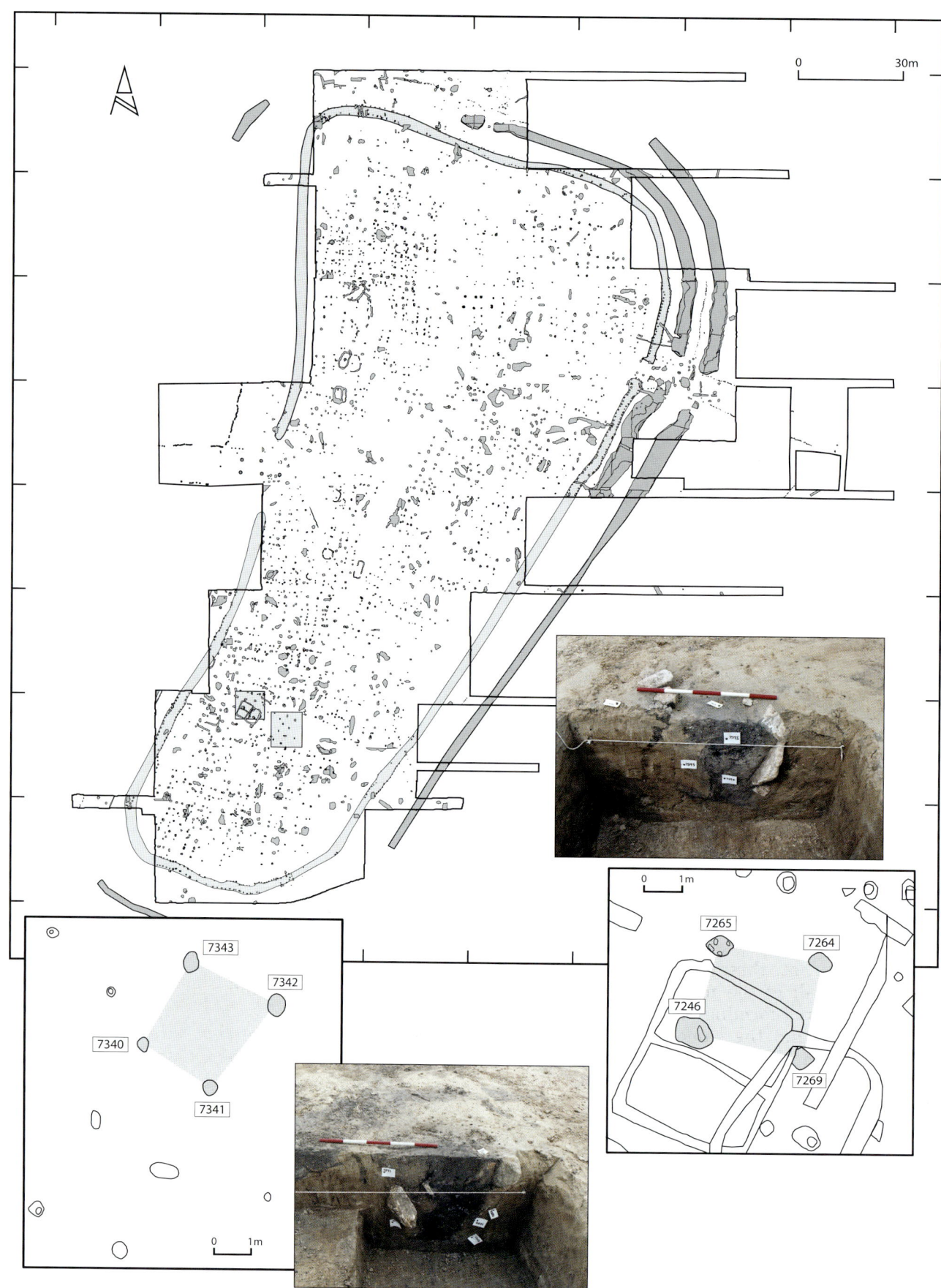

*Figure 6.2  Examples of two four-poster structures: plan of granary Z: [7246], [7264], [7265], and [7269], and photograph of section [7269]; plan of granary AA: [7340], [7341], [7342], [7343]; photograph of section [7246]*

more than 0.75m. This creates a distinctive, and therefore easily identifiable, pattern comprising two parallel lines of postholes between 2.5m and 2.9m apart, with the posts or postholes in each line emerging in pairs (with the postholes of each pair 0.75–1.5m apart), and with a distance between the pairs of 2.5–3.0m. However, each pair of postholes represents the corners of two adjacent four-post structures. There are many clear examples of this from the marsh-fort's interior, for example the row of two such buildings in Trench 4 comprising [4313], [4315], [4335], [4336], [4341], [4343], [4345], and [4347]. All the posts found to be part of four-post structures were flat bottomed. The postholes themselves were again a tight fit, and up to 0.55m deep (eg [31190] and [31189]).

Alongside the four-post structures appear several six-post structures, and rectangular structures incorporating even more posts or postholes. For example, the near-perfect (2.3 × 2.6m) rectangle formed by contexts [5304], [5307], [5309], and [5312] includes posts [5306] and [5311] at opposite ends along the long side of the rectangle. In Trench 6, a rectangle (2.3 × 3.0m) includes eight posts or postholes: [6130], [6179], [6181], and [6185] on the west side and [6210], [6213], [6231], and [6233] on the east side. It is not impossible that these more-than-four-post structures served different functions from the four-posters, but their incorporation in the rows of four-post structures and the consistency of the dimensions suggest a common or similar function. It is noteworthy that analyses of other Iron Age enclosed sites, such as Danebury, has found comparable variations on the four-posters (Cunliffe and Poole 1991).

Within the interior, the rows of rectangular structures appear as broadly aligned on the defences of the marsh-fort and, in most cases, the alignments of the rows follow that of the nearest line of defences. In fact, on the basis of the orientation of the individual four-posters and the alignment of the rows, we note three groups. Four-posters in the western half of the marsh-fort are aligned on the structures forming the west side of the enclosed area, and the same structures on the eastern half on the eastern structures, but to the north and south of the eastern gateway the structures and rows are aligned slightly differently, suggesting that their construction was undertaken in three phases, or by three different groups of people.

Four-post structures have, as a rule, been interpreted as granaries or raised platforms, although a range of alternative functions has been proposed (eg Ellison and Drewett 1971; Challis and Harding 1975, 149–52; see also Gent 1983, 245–7). If the four-posters at Sutton Common were indeed granaries, then an occasional fifth posthole, lying just outside the rectangle, could conceivably be interpreted as the stand of a ladder providing access to a raised platform (eg posthole [4339] next to the four-poster structure [4336], [4341], [4345], and [4347]). The wooden notched ladder (of poplar or willow) discovered in 1988 in Trench B in the smaller enclosure, could have functioned in this way (Parker Pearson and Sydes 1997, 233–4).

The principal reason for building raised grain storages was to encourage air circulation to avoid overheating and fire, and prevent rising damp and vermin from damaging the stored grain. Considering the relatively high groundwater table at Sutton Common, it is unsurprising that no storage pits were found within the marsh-fort, and raised storage would have been the only method available. The problem of vermin must, however, have been significant. One way of stopping vermin such as mice from entering the grain store was the use of discs which were placed on the uprights. It may be the case that the oak 'wheel' discovered by Whiting in the 1930s in the smaller enclosure (1936; see section 1.2.3), was in fact such a disc.

Overall, the four-posters measured between 2.5m and 3m square, providing a potential raised floor area for the storage of grain and other foodstuffs of between $6.25m^2$ and $9m^2$. We may assume that these elevated grain stores included an enclosed structure, for example of the same kind as those shown in the reconstructions of the middle Iron Age four-post granaries from Danebury (Cunliffe 1993, fig 50). This allowed for produce to be piled up for a metre or more. Thus, each raised store would have been able to hold something between $6m^3$ and $10m^3$ of provisions or seed corn. With some 150 four-post structures identified at Sutton Common, the total storage capacity can be determined at between $900m^3$ and $1500m^3$.

### 6.2.3 The 'well'

Within the south-west corner of the larger enclosure, a feature interpreted as a well was excavated during 1999 and 2002 (Fig 6.3). It was originally identified as a dark, sub-circular feature, sectioned to reveal that it was a pit. The base of the pit, 1.5m below the cleaned surface (2.87m OD), produced a line of eleven stakes following an east–west alignment adjacent to the northern edge of the base of the pit. Between the stakes a number of pieces of brushwood and mossy detritus were also found, perhaps indicating a horizontal structure running between the upright stakes in the manner of a hurdle. The base of the pit was lined with brushwood and other woody fragments. An exploration of this area revealed at least four wooden rails aligned east–west, each with a diameter of c 0.15m (eg context [1999–142]). Beneath these rails, and cut into by the stakes, was a deposit of blue-grey medium coarse sand indicative of the natural, high-energy alluvium.

118 *Sutton Common*

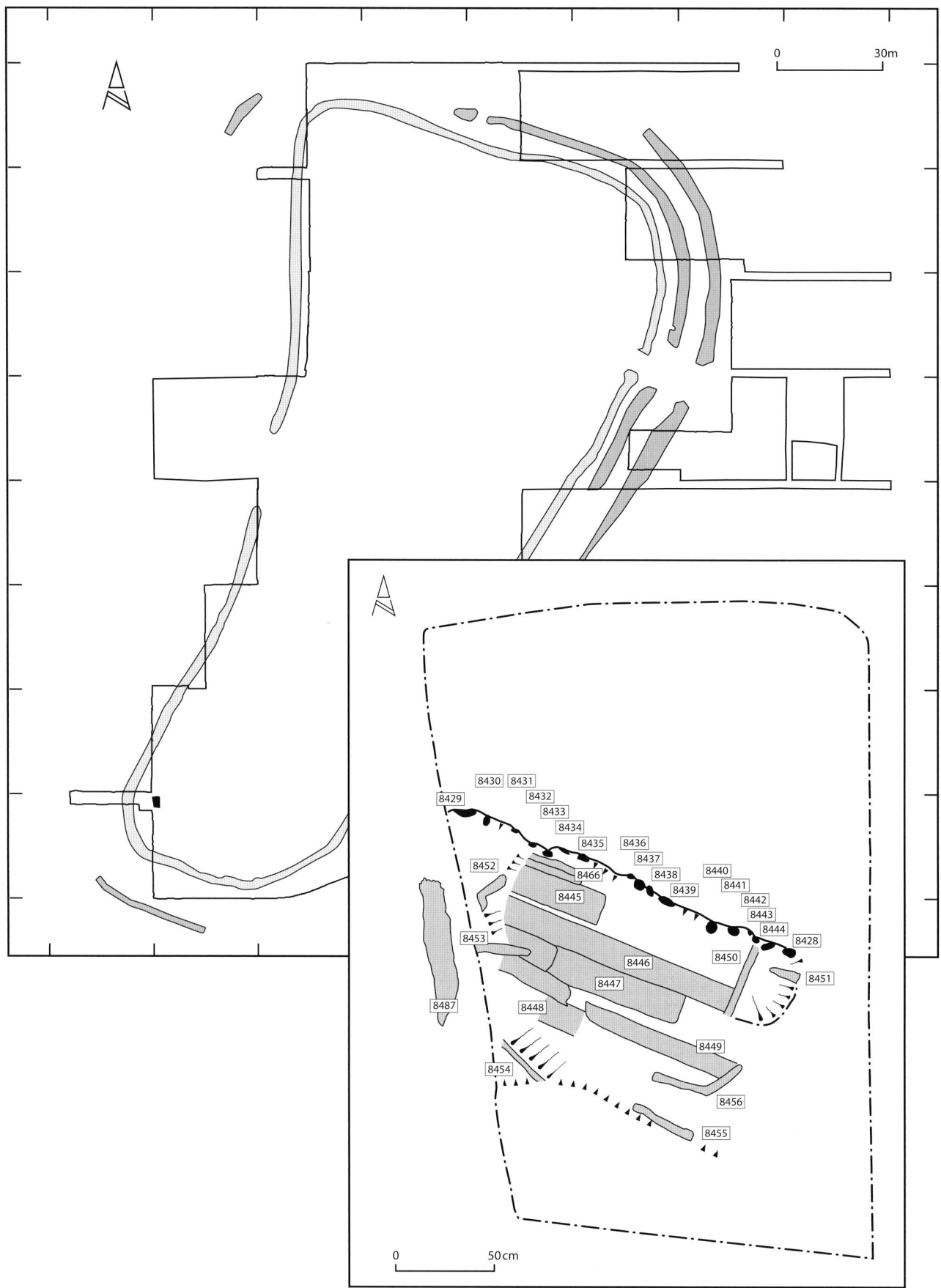

*Figure 6.3   Excavation plan 1998 – 2003: the well in plan*

Above the base of the pit, the profile was V-shaped, with ill-defined edges indicating that the sides of the pit had slumped considerably following its construction. The lower layers were largely inorganic, reflecting the fast infilling of the pit, although the upper layers [1999–109] and [1999–106] were more peaty, indicating a slower infilling, suggesting that the hollow generated by the slumped pit was more stable. Within the upper peaty unit [1999–106] a fragment of a bronze bangle was recovered. This was typologically similar to one found previously (Parker Pearson and Sydes 1997, 236–7), and was dated to the Roman period. Apart from these two fragments, no other Roman period material has been found on the Common in the last three decades.

The great depth of the pit cut into the 'running sands' of the wet base, which presumably made the sides of the structure very unstable. The stakes lining the edge of the base of the pit might have been intended for restricting this slumping activity by creating some type of revetment (Fig 6.4). The wooden rails in the base of the pit appear to have been placed to generate some type of basal stability. In terms of interpretation, the depth of this unstable feature and the revetting of the sides indicated that it might have served as some type of well feature. The rails at the base would have assisted in this by maintaining a solid footing so that the sediment would have been less strongly mixed into the water when it was drawn. The slumping, however, had destroyed much of the edge of the feature, and it had also been obscured on the surface by the post-occupation slumping of the box rampart against which it was dug. Hence the precise shape of the original profile of the feature will remain unknown. The presence of Roman material towards the top of the feature reinforces the interpretation of a rapid backfilling of the feature through slumping such that its destruction as a functional area would have coincided with the end of occupation at the site.

### 6.2.4 Other features

Within the defences of the larger enclosure, some 500 postholes have been, with reasonable confidence, attributed to the four-post structures, but this leaves some 1500 features unaccounted for.

*Figure 6.4 The well during excavation in 2002*

Most probably, some of these belong to four-post structures, or possibly six-post granaries, but these were not identified as such during the analysis of the plans. A considerable number of posts and postholes can be seen to continue along the line of the rows of granaries, but without opposite features that could complete the rectangles indicating granaries. An example is formed by [7283], [7383] and [7388], located within a row of four granaries and in line with the northern side of the granaries (Fig 6.5a). It is unclear what such a link between granaries or an extension of the row of granaries signifies.

Throughout the interior, a significant number of features appear in lines of between four and twelve posts and postholes. An example of such a single alignment is formed by the east–west line of posts and postholes [31108], [31141], [31143], [31163], [31235], and [31665] (Fig 6.5b). Without being able to determine functions or purposes for these lines of posts, establishing the orientation of such lines is rather fraught with subjectivity, but it should be noted that these lines appear to reflect the orientation of the granaries. In fact, the non-allocated features also give the impression that an overall division of the interior of the marsh-fort in to three zones existed, as argued above.

One other structure was identified within the interior of the marsh-fort. A group of eleven small stakeholes ([5243] – [5248] and [5250] – [5254]) measuring 0.1m in diameter in a rough oval of 1.6 long and 1.3m wide was identified in Trench 5, and may have been associated with postholes [5228] and [5255] (Fig 6.5c). This may have been a temporary, stake-built structure such as a hut or other temporary dwelling, with the two larger posts forming the door posts. We note, however, that this structure was located directly beside one of the mortuary rings, and was thought to be associated with the second phase of activity, giving rise to the speculation that a small hut had been built alongside (see section 8.2.2). In the absence of any stratigraphic relationship, and without independent dating of the stake-built structure, this must remain speculation.

A number of shallow pits were exposed during the excavations. For example, pit [4293] was 1m in diameter and 0.4m deep. A range of similar pits was encountered within Trenches 6, 7, and 8, although no artefactual remains were recovered. In Trench 7, a deeper pit [7171/7187] was uncovered that was 0.8m in diameter and 0.9m deep displaying a fill of inorganic material, with a more organic upper fill (Fig 6.6). Inside the western entrance, and depicted as a hollow by Whiting (1936), a large 16m by 5.5m sub-oval feature [5162] was exposed during excavation. This feature was very shallow, being just 0.05m to 0.30m deep, with an irregular base.

### 6.2.5 General plan

The overall layout of the site appears to have been determined initially by topography. The shape of the defences broadly echoes that of the sandy dune or 'island', except for a tongue of higher land to the east, beyond the eastern entranceway. It has been noted previously that the variation in the defences on different sides of the enclosure, and particularly the single bank on the western side as depicted by Whiting might reflect the use of water and natural barriers and hence a reduced need for human-made structures (Chapman 2000). Whilst the recent excavation has demonstrated an overall standardisation of lines of defence surrounding the site, it seems that the variability in the details of these structures in different areas might still have been a response to differing environmental conditions on different sides of the site. Particularly, the outer palisade structure reveals evidence of a bank on the eastern side of the enclosure, but no bank on the western side where it was naturally wetter.

The dominating four-post structures that nearly fill the interior appear to follow the architectural alignments created by the construction of the defences. In most cases, the alignments of the rows of these features follow that of the nearest line of defences, and particularly the eastern and western defences that provide the overall axis for the site. The laying out of these features in rows indicates that the construction was aimed at maximising space within the enclosure, with particular areas devoted to high-density storage.

The arrangement of the limited number of other features identified through excavation also reveals spatial trends. Primarily, the distribution of pit features is much higher within the southern part of the site than the northern part, and included the shallow pits and deeper pit and 'well' features.

Open areas within the site are few, although there are some parts with a notably lower density of archaeological features. In particular, the area inside of the western entrance, towards the centre of the enclosure and directly to the north, is devoid of four-post structures. Similarly, the area inside the eastern entrance and south of it is relatively clear of features. The joining of these two areas indicates that the main area of open space within the enclosure connected the two entranceways, with higher densities of features elsewhere. There appears to have been no clear 'road pattern' within the interior of the enclosure as has been argued at sites such as Danebury. Rather, the site appears to display a regular, planned interior enabling movement within it, but with the only clear space linking the two entrances.

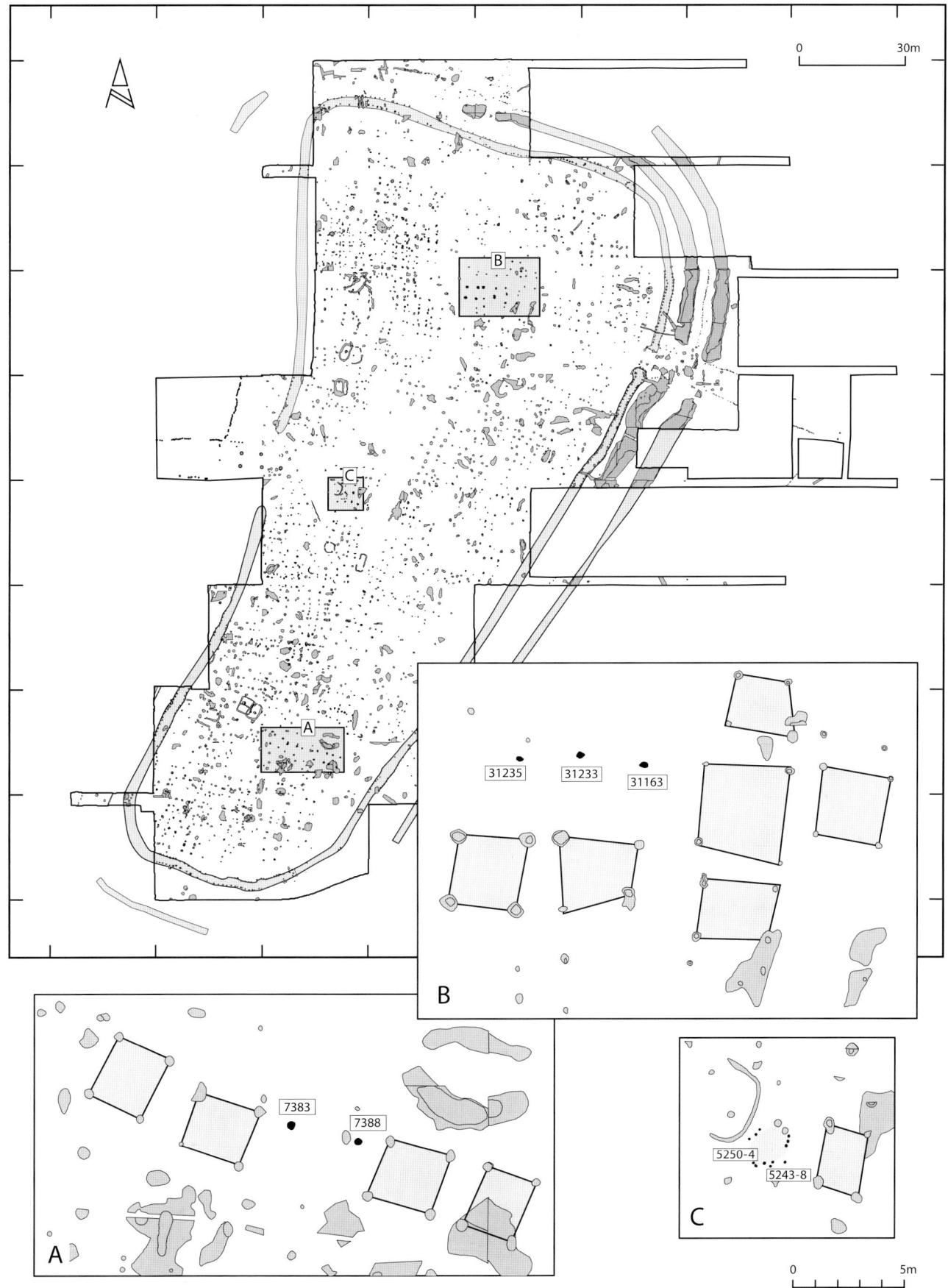

*Figure 6.5 Excavation plan 1998–2003: unassigned posts and other internal structures
a) Posts and postholes in alignments with four-post structures: [7283] and [7388]; b) Posts and postholes in alignments with four-post structures: [31235], [31233], and [31163]; c) A hut or other temporary dwelling formed by eleven small stakeholes: [5243]–[5248], and [5250]–[5254]*

122 *Sutton Common*

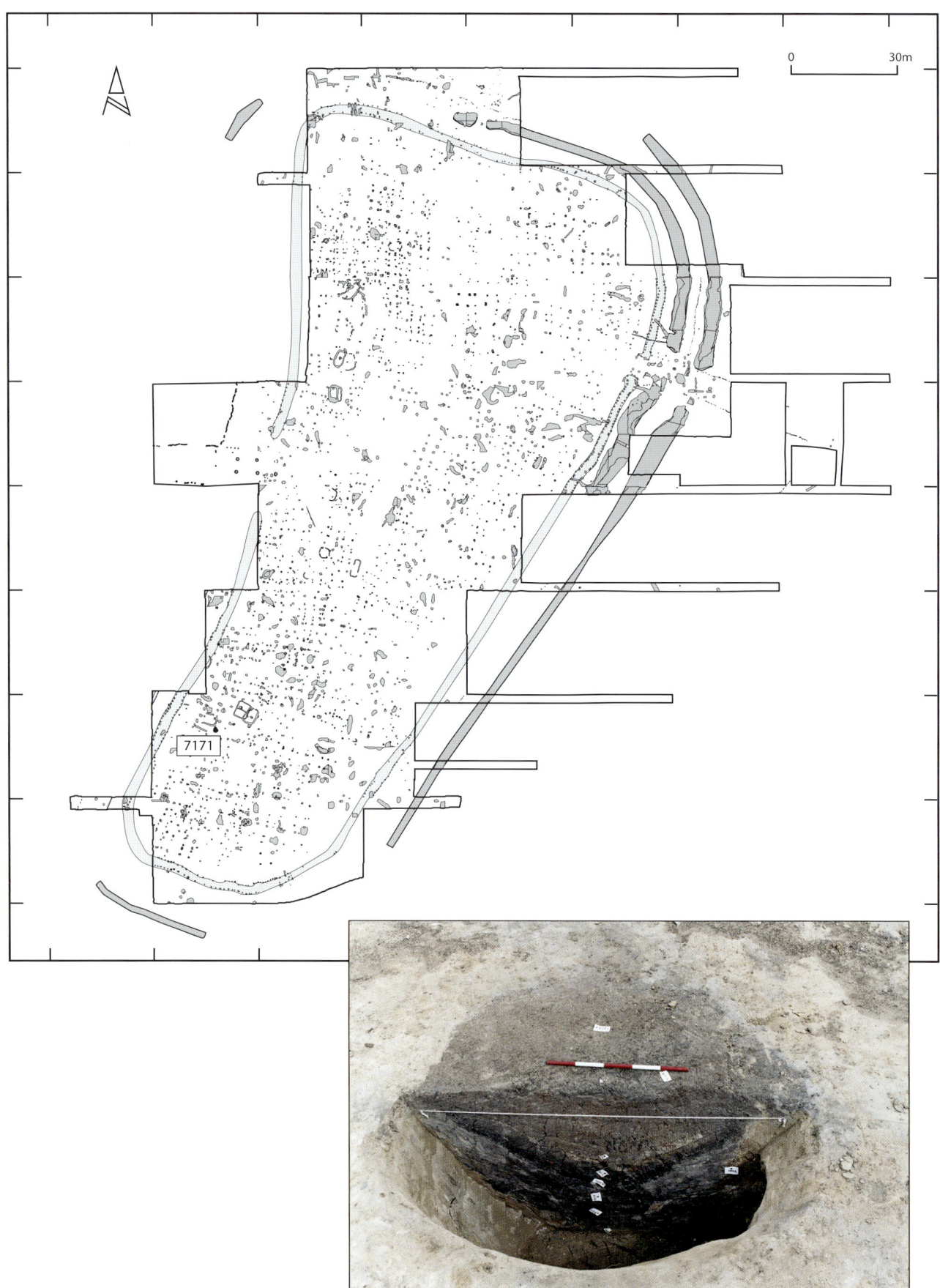

*Figure 6.6 Excavation plan 1998 – 2003: location of pit and photograph of section of [7171/7187]*

## 6.3 Dating: dendrochronology
*by N Nayling*

Very few timbers from the interior of the marsh-fort survived in a state of preservation that made them suitable for dendrochronological analysis. This is, at least in part, linked to the height of the water table on the Common following the drainage in the 19th and 20th centuries. Whereas much of the system of defences follows the dune's or island's perimeter, the interior of the marsh-fort occupies the highest part, where the fluctuations of the water table were found to be most pronounced (see section 2.3.2). Translocation of clay particles down the soil horizon, leaving the more permeable sands near the surface, was also evident. Furthermore, the structures within the interior of the marsh-fort were not as formidable as those used for the gateways and only two timbers from the interior contained sufficient year rings for potential dating through dendrochronological analysis.

Timber [1208], a half section of an oak tree missing sapwood, contained 87 year rings, but these could not be matched against fixed chronologies. On the basis of its location, it is conceivable that this timber formed part of the inner alignment of posts belonging to the box rampart. Its half section, however, would be at odds with the wood technology used elsewhere on the site for this structure, and it is thus more likely that it formed part of an internal feature. Timber [31449] was a radial section of oak and contained 261 year rings. The date of this sequence was established from 699 to 439 BC, but in the absence of a heartwood-sapwood boundary, the *terminus post quem* of the felling date can only be determined as after 429 BC.

## 6.4 Wood technology  *by G Thomas*

### 6.4.1 Internal structures

Of all the hundreds of internal posthole features excavated in the larger enclosure, only a fraction contained any wooden remains at all. Some 25 samples were recovered from the excavations for laboratory analysis. Most were fragmentary, in many cases due to complete rotting of the heartwood or from large cracks down the length of the timbers. All had suffered from severe desiccation and no bark or sapwood was present, although this may have been removed prior to their use, as appears to have been the case with some of the larger well-preserved timbers on site. Despite the poor condition of these posts, their bases were often the best preserved and it was clear that most if not all had been worked to produce flat bases. On several, this could be confirmed by the presence of tool marks. There was no clear pattern to the conversion of the wood used for these internal posts. Ten samples were whole with no conversion of the full roundwood. One was a half section whilst the remaining posts were either irregular conversions (as revealed by the ring patterns relative to the size of the associated posts or postholes) or were fragmentary having suffered severe decay and/or breakage. Clarifying whether much of the wood had been lost to decay or had been converted was difficult to establish due to the poor condition and lack of tool marks on the majority of these samples. Only seven samples displayed clear evidence of woodworking. Oak [2630] retained three or four axe facets which were flat and short but up to 50mm wide, giving some indication of the minimum width of the axe. The facet junctions were stepped but survival of jam curves was poor. Oak [41011] retained a similar number of facets which were very similar in form but up to 58mm wide and bearing the impression of a slightly curved axe in the jam curve. Oak [5454] had been cut at an angle of 50° to the vertical despite no axe facets surviving. Oak [5634] had been worked on both ends and one side but again facets were in very poor condition. Nonetheless, these facets were flat with a minimum cutting angle of 5°, suggesting a fine, flat-bladed axe had been used to cut the base of this post to a chisel point, at a 35° angle to the vertical. The flat base of oak [5638] also retained some facets but these were too small and the wood too decayed for accurate tool mark measurements. Several of the facet junctions were stepped and one or two partial jam curves were still present, showing a gently curved cutting edge to the axe.

Of the 25 samples, 19 were oak and 6 were Scots pine. The pattern of rot on these samples included almost complete heart rot to the point were the sample recovered was nothing more than a hollow cylinder of wood. This was not dependent on the type of species but affected oak and pine equally, with samples [5460], [31190], and [31243] graphically displaying this type of decay. The surviving lengths of these samples ranged from 122mm to 560mm, with diameters ranging from 61mm to 310mm in diameter. The wood for these structures does not appear to be as straight grained as for the entranceway timbers, with knots, root, and branch nodes and twisted wood quite common in this assemblage. The samples of pine in particular displayed prominent branch nodes on often otherwise straight pieces of roundwood. These nodes also survive inside the hollow cylinder of wood, giving the impression of spokes within a wheel (Fig 6.7). It is thought that the tough, resinous nature of these pine samples, in particular the branch nodes, is the reason for this distinctive pattern of decay. There is no evidence for trimming of these on any of the surviving samples and it is possible that these would not have been projecting from the posts at the time of their use once bark and soft outer wood had been removed.

*Figure 6.7  A Scots pine roundwood timber [31243], showing advanced desiccation*

Despite the poor condition of the samples, some information was attainable from the visible ring patterns providing an idea of the size and age of the trees utilised. Of the oaks, between 25 and 40 rings were generally present on the surviving samples and of the pine posts, between 40 and 50 rings survived. Oak posts [8511] and [8526], however, clearly had been cut from much larger trees, with 122 and 142 rings respectively. The pattern of growth was very regular, with growth rings all between 1mm and 1.5mm in width. The apparent favourable growth conditions may suggest that the pine trees at least must have come from further afield, as the wetness of the immediate area of the marsh-fort is not suitable for growth of the species, which prefers light, free-draining sandy soils. The similar dimensions of these posts, coupled with the near-identical narrow, regular-width growth ring patterns, suggests that they have probably come from the same tree. They were also utilised in the construction of two adjacent four-post structures, with [31189] and [31190], and [31243] and [31252] forming pairs of posts (Fig. 6.8). It is a matter for conjecture as to whether the use of pine in these particular four-post structures was purely coincidental or whether it was intended and had a particular significance.

Flat-based posts have not been widely reported from waterlogged contexts in England and parallels are not available for comparison in the literature. In the case of Sutton Common, their use may have been forced by the fort's construction in soft sediments and marshy conditions; indeed flat-based posts are more commonly encountered on waterlogged sites in the Low Countries.

### 6.4.2  The well

A number of well-preserved wood finds included 21 branchwood rod fragments [8460a–u] recovered from within fill [8460] of the 'well' feature on site. Many retained bark and displayed some valuable growth-ring data. Critically, no worked points were recovered to provide a rough date for the assemblage. Species analysis revealed 10 fragments of ash, 7 hazel, 1 of oak, 1 of alder, and 2 alder/hazel which could not be specifically identified. The diameters of these rods were quite consistent, with all but three falling between 22–41mm. The growth pattern in the rings is quite variable, but slow-grown examples seem to predominate. All the ash rods displayed a distinctive pattern of becoming progressively slower grown, particularly in the last few years of growth. Felling of many of these rods appears to have taken place in either the late spring or early summer. The age ranges of between 10 and 27 years of growth is not particularly convincing for coppicing evidence. Furthermore, several of the samples had branch nodes present and were quite knotty, certainly not typical of long, straight coppiced rods. The presence of four different species within this small sample is also atypical for coppice. The practice of draw felling would be more acceptable to explain the origins of this wood assemblage.

A stake alignment present at the base of the well running north-west to south-east was part sampled. Six roundwoods [8430] – [8433], [8438], and [8441] were analysed. These were all of similar dimensions, between 50–75mm in diameter, 4 whole and 2 modified, with one being quartered, the other box quartered. All were in good condition but worn, especially at the tops, and retained no bark. Unfortunately, no worked points were recovered. Of the 6 stakes, 3 were ash, 1 hazel, and 2 remain unidentified. Some 19 or 20 fast-grown rings were present on each, with outer rings indicating a probable felling season of late spring or early summer.

Several larger timbers lining the well base were also sampled. The largest were aligned north-west to south-east and were in very good condition save for a lack of bark and very worn surfaces. The largest horizontal [8446] was at least 1.2m in length and 140mm in width. All appeared to be whole samples showing no evidence of conversion. Most if not all were waterlogged, several showed fungal decay under the microscope, and sample [8449] displayed compression wood. Of the 8 horizontals, 1 was ash, 3 hazel, and 1 or 2 alder; the remainder were not identified. Growth ring analysis was possible on five of the samples. Much variation was apparent with ring counts ranging from 5 to 60+, felling seasons of late spring or summer, and autumn, and growth rates being fast and slow. At least one of the samples showed a pattern of very slow growth in the years just prior to felling – a pattern which is particularly prevalent in samples, especially ash, on the site as a whole.

*Figure 6.8 Excavation plan 1998–2003: location of timbers of Scots pine and reconstructed four-post structures: [31189] and [31190], [31243] and [31252]*

## 6.5 Palaeoenvironmental studies

### 6.5.1 Plant macrofossils and insects
*by A Hall and H Kenward*

#### 6.5.1.1 Postholes of four-post structures

Posthole fills were by far the largest group of deposits examined for plant and invertebrate remains at this site: nearly 65% of all contexts selected for assessment or subsequent analysis were of this type. On the basis of the results of the two assessments, it was clear that these were sometimes very productive of charred plant remains, especially grain. Uncharred remains of either plants or insects considered to be ancient rather than recent intrusions were (with the exception of modern roots) usually absent or very sparse. The results of these analyses have been summarised in Table 6.1.

It is difficult to see any very clear pattern in the assemblages of charred plant remains in relation to the spatial distribution of the posthole fills. The richest assemblages of grain were from postholes scattered across the area excavated. In relation to the deposition of material in domestic settings, certain cosmological rules can be observed (eg Parker Pearson 1996), and the question should be asked whether this is also the case for the granaries. Within the context of the constraints of reconstructing four-post structures from the profusion of postholes, some 55 samples could, with reasonable confidence, be assigned to a known corner of the four-post structures (see Table 6.1; the samples from four-post structure AA were ignored). South-west corner posts contained 4 rich assemblages, 4 moderately rich assemblages, 2 assemblages with a few grains, and 2 samples produced no grain. South-east corner postholes produced 2 rich and 3 moderately rich assemblages, 8 samples contained a few grains and 1 produced none. North-west postholes produced 1 rich and 4 moderately rich assemblages of charred grain, with 5 samples producing only a few grains and 3 samples none at all. Finally, the north-east posts produced 1 rich and 6 moderately rich assemblages alongside 7 samples with a few grains and 2 with none. Unfortunately, there were rather few cases where all four corners of a quartet were sampled and examined, and it should also be borne in mind that the groupings of postholes into fours is open to a number of interpretations and that some of those used here might easily be reclassified. Nevertheless, it appears that the south-west corner postholes were favoured over others, with rich and moderately rich assemblages representing 67% of all south-west corner postholes samples, compared to 44% for north-east, 38% of north-west, and 36% of south-east corner posts.

With regard to the proportion of grains of wheat and barley in these assemblages, it having been noted that this varied widely, though with wheat usually predominating, there was some tendency for the larger assemblages overall to be mainly wheat, though with exceptions in the form of material from [3004] and [3008], both from four-poster F, where the moderately large grain counts showed barley to be in the majority. It should be remembered, however, that many grains in most of the samples could not be identified beyond 'cereal' and that an assumption, which may be unwarranted, has been made that the 'indet' category contains proportions of wheat and barley grains similar to those amongst the grains identified more closely.

The proportion of grains to chaff, where numbers are high enough to make a valid calculation, also seems to follow no particular pattern. It may be noted, with some comfort, given the disparity in results between some parallel samples from certain contexts, that three samples from [7246] gave almost identical grain:chaff ratios (although a fourth, which had a rather small overall content of grain, did not fit this pattern). Given the variation in grain:chaff ratios, it has not been felt justifiable to attempt to calculate numbers of whole spikelets represented, nor is there a basis for an extended discussion of crop-processing regimes, other than to note four relevant points. First, the charred remains, which are all grain-rich, almost certainly represent the remains of burnt product rather than any of the by-products of crop processing. Second, the crop was well cleaned, as there were rarely more than a very few weed seeds present in the grain-rich assemblages and those weed taxa present offer no particular evidence for where the crop may have been grown. Third, the remains also suggest that the charred wheat grain was burnt as spikelets, as some of the wheat grain still had fragments of chaff adhering to it. The general lack of chaff in the assemblages may partly be a reflection of differential preservation (Boardman and Jones 1990). Finally, it is also interesting that some assemblages consist largely of wheat grain (with only a little barley) while in those with more barley than wheat, there is always a similar proportion of wheat. This might suggest that wheat is being burnt (and therefore stored) in a largely pure form (presumably for human consumption, grown as a monocrop), whereas the barley/wheat mixtures might represent mixed crops or maslins, perhaps intended for animal consumption (Jones and Halstead 1995).

One last phenomenon which requires some brief discussion is the evidence for shrivelled grains in some of the samples, noted especially during the second assessment exercise. Grains of this kind were seen in samples from Structures A (Trench 1), B and D (Trench 2), Q (Trench 5) and Z (Trench 7), ie spread across the site with no particular spatial 'clumping', and in one context from the last of these ([7246], sampled as a cremation)

Table 6.1  Summary description of the charred plant remains from four-poster structures; see Appendix 1 for detailed information

| Structure | Contexts | Sampled | Comments on results of analysis of samples |
|---|---|---|---|
| A | [1093] [1097] [1099] [1069] | [1093] = SE [1099] = NE | rich assemblages of grain dominated by ?spelt (indeed, no barley was detected in the sample from 1093) and there was rather a lot of glume-wheat chaff and a modest-sized (for this site, at any rate!) group of weed seeds. Both samples showed some evidence of shrivelled grains |
| | | [1097] = NW | no plant remains other than a little oak charcoal |
| B | [2552] [2553] [2555] [2561] | [2552] = NE | grain was moderately common, but not quantified (assessment only); the assemblage was unusual in containing what may have been rare grains of bread wheat, oats and even rye, though these identifications have not been checked subsequently. There were a few chaff fragments and weed seeds and some of the wheat grains were noted as being 'dimpled', as if partly shrunken before being charred. Such shrinkage might have occurred because the grain was not fully ripe when harvested or because it had begun to germinate or decay to some extent during storage. The absence of any indications of sprouting, however, allows us to discount the later stages of germination through poor storage or as part of a malting process |
| C | [2496] [2498] [2512] [2517] | [2512] = SE | examined during the assessment stage only, it mainly yielded charcoal with moderate amounts of grain, mostly well-preserved, and mainly wheat, with some (hulled) barley, but no chaff; there were also traces of weed seeds. Traces of oats were noted |
| D | [2435] [2458] [2488] [2490] | [2458] = NE | a moderate amount of charred cereal grain and chaff present with what seemed to be both emmer and spelt represented amongst the latter. Amongst the grains, some were small and others shrunken |
| E | [2452] [2461]; two remaining posts possibly not uncovered if beneath [2438] | [2452] = NE | a moderately large assemblage of charred grain with some chaff and a few weed seeds, examined only during the assessment. It was notable for having rather abundant barley grains (some of which were hulled) and for including what may have been emmer wheat, rather than spelt, amongst the chaff, together with a trace of barley rachis. Many of the cereal grains were noted as being distinctly shrunken (perhaps as a result of having started to germinate or decay, or having been unripe, prior to charring) and many of the barley grains seemed very small, even allowing for shrinkage |
| F | [3002] [3004] [3008] [3010] | [3004] = NW [3008] = SW | rather rich assemblages characterised by very low wheat:barley ratios (ie there was more barley than wheat) and there were modest amounts of chaff and a few weed seeds |
| | | [3010] = SE | very few grains and almost no other remains |
| | | [3002] = NE | |
| G | [3012] [3016] [3022] [3026] | [3016] = SW | a modest-sized assemblage of grain, predominantly wheat, with a very little chaff, and a single weed seed |
| | | [3012] = NW [3022] = SE | assemblages were much smaller, and produced almost nothing but grain and charcoal |
| H | [3018] [3020] [3032] [3030] | [3032] = SW | yielded 50 grains per kg; nearly twice as much wheat as barley, with a few chaff fragments and traces of weed seeds |
| | | [3018] = NW | fewer than 50 grains per kg |
| | | [3020] = NE | fewer than 50 grains per kg; rather more barley than wheat, though the numbers of grains are probably too small for the ratio statistic to be treated with much confidence |
| I | [3036] [3034] [3249] ?[3239] | [3036] = NE | no remains other than charcoal |

*(continued)*

Table 6.1 Continued

| Structure | Contexts | Sampled | Comments on results of analysis of samples |
|---|---|---|---|
| J | [31317] [31434] [31435] | [31434] = NW | yielded a modest-sized assemblage of grain, mainly ?spelt wheat, with a little wheat chaff |
| | | [31317] = NE | produced nothing more than a little charcoal |
| | | [31435] = SW | gave a single ?spelt grain |
| K | [31375] [31379/80] [31381/2] [31376] [31383] | [31375] = SW [31381/2] = fifth posthole on E-side | moderately large assemblage of ?spelt, with some barley and a few fragments of chaff and a few weed seeds |
| | | [31379/80] = SE | very few charred remains |
| L | [31270] [31274] [31351] [31366] | [31270] = SE [31351] = SW | moderate-sized or large assemblages of grain with modest amounts of chaff but almost no weed seeds |
| M | [31086] [31088] [31090] [31092] | [31088] = NE | gave modest amounts of grain and traces of chaff and weed seeds |
| N | [5051] [5052] [5101] [5110] | [5052] = NW | no charred material other than a trace of charcoal |
| O | [5220] [5222] [5276] [5278] | [5220] = SW | a small grain assemblage (mainly ?spelt, with some barley) with a little chaff |
| | | [5277] = NE | only examined during the assessment; it yielded a few poorly preserved ?spelt grains and some even more eroded barley, as well as some burnt bone |
| P | [5212] [5282] [5283] [5357] | [5282] = NE | small numbers of charred grains in a sample examined during one of the assessments |
| Q | [5430] [5431] [5433] [5351] | [5433] = SE [5431] = SW | rather large assemblages of grain though with only very little chaff and a few weeds seeds. 5431 yielded some wheat grains that were noted as having a somewhat shrivelled appearance |
| | | [5430] = NW | about 20 grains, all probably spelt, but no other remains |
| R | [5231] [5234] [5237] ?[5288] | [5234] = SE | rare ?spelt grains were recorded |
| S | [5260] [5262] [?] [?] | [5260] = ? | was the fill of a posthole whose relation to any others is uncertain. The sample from it produced a single tentatively identified cereal grain |
| T | [5003] [5013] [5073] [5081] | [5013] = NW | gave traces of ?spelt grains |
| U | [5365] [5368] [5371] [5398] | [5393] = NW | examined during an assessment only, the sample produced some wheat grain but with rather more frequent spelt glume-bases and perhaps also emmer spikelet-forks |
| V | [5190] [5195] [6283] [?] | none | |
| W | [5024] [5029] [5039] [5040] | [5024] = SW | a single barley grain and one unidentified cereal grain |
| | | [5029] = SE | barren but for a trace of charcoal |
| X | [5365] [5368] [5371] [5373] | [5373] = SE | produced only a little wheat grain and ?spelt chaff |
| Y | [7143] [7145] [7243] [7244] | [7244] = SE | low concentration of charred grains with a little chaff and no weed seeds; this posthole also included calcined animal bone |
| | | [7243] = NE | very few grains |
| | | [7143] = SW | almost barren |
| | | [7145] = NW | |

(continued)

**Table 6.1 Continued**

| Structure | Contexts | Sampled | Comments on results of analysis of samples |
|---|---|---|---|
| Z | [7246] [7264] [7265] [7269] | [7246] = SW | moderately large concentrations of grain, with nearly twice as much barley as wheat. This context also included calcined animal bone, thought to be redeposited pyre debris |
| | | [7264] = NE | moderately large concentrations of grain |
| | | [7265] = NW | moderately large concentrations of grain, predominantly ?spelt, with a rather a large component of chaff and weed seeds |
| | | [7269] = SE | moderately concentrations of grain with a little chaff and traces of weeds |
| AA | [7340] [7341] [7342] [7343] | [7340] = W [7341] = S | charred remains other than wood charcoal were almost completely absent |
| | | [7342] = E | charred remains other than wood charcoal were almost completely absent. A single tentatively identified onion couch 'tuber' recorded |
| BB | [7315] [7344] [7345] [7347] | [7345] = NE | a moderate amount of grain (examined only during the assessment) in which both spelt and emmer, as well as barley, are thought to have been present, with traces of weed seeds but no chaff |
| CC | [7429] [7430] [7431] [7471] | [7429] = NE | a small assemblage of grain with a little chaff and traces of weed seeds |
| DD | [7428] [7433] [7486] [7488] | [7433] = SW | modest amounts of grain with rather more barley than wheat, along with a single chaff fragment |
| | | [7486] = NE | traces of grain |
| | | [7488] = SE | |
| EE | [7043] [7045] [7050] [7053] | [7050] = SE | yielded a little barley, and even less wheat (one grain!) |
| FF | [7204] [7207] [7209] ?[7376] | [7204] = NW | the merest traces of grains and no other remains |

some barley grains showing evidence of germination were noted in three of the four samples examined. In the case of the Danebury hillfort, Martin Jones (in Cunliffe 1984, 493, following Peter Reynolds' experiments at Little Butser) suggested that this germination enabled storage of fresh grain in storage pits, with the germination of an outer skin of grain creating an anoxic environment within the pit that conserved the bulk of the grain. However, such an explanation is not applicable for Sutton Common, where no storage pits have been found. It is perhaps just a matter of chance that some barley had begun to sprout (in a wet season, or under poor storage conditions?) before being charred and deposited in this posthole. Were the germination of some significance to the inhabitants of the enclosure, one might expect it to be repeated in other cases. Similarly, the shrivelled grains (mainly wheat), in which signs of germination were not noted, were not so widespread, taking the evidence as a whole, as to suggest that the shrivelling had some interpretive significance.

#### 6.5.1.2 Other posthole fills

A number of posthole fills (from nine holes) associated with the box rampart, or which were isolated and not thought to be part of any four-post structure (a further four) were examined. It is perhaps of some significance that, with the exception of one of two subsamples from [5635], none produced more than traces of charred material other than charcoal, and many yielded neither grain nor chaff. The grain-rich subsample from [5635] (the third highest concentration for the site as a whole) may therefore be from a cut from an unidentified four-post quartet, although it should also be remembered that many of the postholes from four-post groupings were barren. This one assemblage was relatively rich in wheat grain and with very little chaff.

#### 6.5.1.3 Pit fills

Nine samples came from 8 contexts in 7 features interpreted as pit fills. Charred plant remains other than charcoal were sparse, indeed, five samples failed to yield any grain or chaff. Of the remainder, two contexts in Pit [7260] gave some positive results. In the case of [7255] and [7256], the middle to upper fills respectively, these were restricted to some moderately well-preserved charred cereal grains, recorded only during the assessment; they were mainly barley (and, of these, some specimens showed a degree of shrivelling, a phenomenon noted in some postholes fills associated with four-post structures, as mentioned above), plus a few wheat grains. The layer below, [7257], gave a sample in which grain was much more abundant, an example where barley was more abundant than wheat and where chaff was restricted to a trace of material of barley, with no glume-wheat chaff at all. There were also a few weed seeds, typical of the site as a whole.

### 6.5.1.4 The well

Across the two assessments and subsequent main analysis, eight contexts from the enigmatic 'well' feature were investigated. Most yielded at least a few 'waterlogged' plant remains but charred material was restricted to moderate numbers of charred hulled barley grains and a spikelet of two fused cereal grains, probably spelt, from (perhaps not surprisingly) the uppermost fill investigated [8537].

The lowermost deposits examined were from [8460] and [8492], associated with planks and other wood in the lowest levels excavated. Altogether, 5 separate subsamples were examined for plant remains (2 and 3 from these two contexts, respectively), and they gave broadly similar results, with small numbers of fossils from a limited range of taxa perhaps indicating an origin in wet scrub or woodland. Whilst remains of woody taxa such as elder, blackberry, and raspberry could always be explained as the result of natural dispersal from birds perching above the feature, were it to have had any kind of superstructure, the presence of remains including seeds of dog's mercury (in 2 samples from [8492]) and stinging nettle (from these 2, plus 1 from [8460]) or of ?ground ivy (in [8460]), are much more difficult to explain in this way, as is also the case for the trace of ?holly leaf in [8492] and fruiting bodies of the fungus *Rosellinia* cf *mammiformis* (which grows on the bark of various hardwood species) in both contexts; surely these must either have arrived with brushwood or some similar material collected from nearby woodland, or have been part of a developing scrub vegetation on the abandoned site?

Many insect remains from [8640] were very difficult or impossible to identify because they were so decayed; some of the fossils were very 'floppy', and some were crumpled. Adult beetles and bugs were abundant, and mathematically (and to an extent ecologically) diverse. Aquatics were sufficiently abundant to indicate deposition in water, the more abundant species suggesting fairly clean conditions, with mud and some vegetation. Much of the terrestrial fauna would have been at home on waterside plants, or in the litter below them, or on mud. While decomposers (defined in 5.6.2.3) were not abundant, this assemblage was notable for an appreciable component of scarabaeid dung beetles, together with other elements which may have originated in dung (but also from other kinds of decaying matter). The presence of grazing land was also suggested by two species of chafer beetles. There were indications of decaying wood, some at least bearing bark (indicated by a range of species including six bark beetles *Dryocoetinus villosus*, mostly associated with oak). Presumably, many of the insects were exploiting decaying structural timbers. In contrast to these elements, the bark beetle *Hylesinus oleiperda* indicated the local presence of ash trees (*Fraxinus*). Synanthropes (defined in 5.6.2.3) were very uncommon in this assemblage and, in combination with the evidence for timber in advanced decay, it seems likely that the part of the site from which these insects came was abandoned by this stage.

None of the rest of the sequence (in ascending stratigraphic order: [8548], [8542], [8540], [8539], and [8538]) yielded more than a few seeds of woody taxa such as elder and blackberry, which may reflect differential preservation in the probably rather freely draining sandy fills of this feature, and sheds no more light on its history of infilling.

### 6.5.2 *Geoarchaeology*  by G Ayala

Almost all the postholes in Trench 3, and throughout the site in general, were 'haloed' by light-grey soil material. The excavators were not sure of the nature of this light-grey material. There were two possibilities: either it was Iron Age soil material that had infilled the postholes as they dried out, or microbiological activity had bleached the surrounding subsoil.

As the Iron Age soil horizon has been effectively destroyed, it was impossible to make a direct comparison. Therefore, monolith samples were taken radiating out from two different postholes to compare the grey bleached material with the background subsoil (see Fig. 6.9). These samples were compared with the profiles sampled in both Trenches 3 and 5.

Three oriented samples were taken from two postholes in cell F13. This proved to be a lucky sampling strategy for they had very different characteristics. In thin section, samples 118 and 119 did not show any signs of soil material that had been introduced around the post as it dried out (see Table 6.2). The microstructure and

*Figure 6.9  Geoarchaeology: sampled postholes in Trench 3, F13*

mineral composition appeared the same between the two layers, the light-grey fabric [3524] and the Bt horizon (referred to as 'the natural'). The colour difference between the two is due to the leaching of clay and iron oxides from the fabric of [3524] through water percolation and microbiological activity and its subsequent accumulation in the micromass in the surrounding soil material. This process could have been advanced through the funnelling of water along the contact between the post and the surrounding soil material during cycles of wetting and drying after the area was drained. This is seen in thin section with the iron mottling and clay coatings that are present in this matrix of the layer surrounding [3524] (Fig 6.10a – b).

In sample 120, however, there is an indication that the bleached material [3524] is foreign soil material (see Table 6.2). The [3524] fabric, in this instance, has a very distinct structure and texture representing a fine sandy loam with the surrounding material a silty clay loam. Moreover, in section, the [3524] fabric appears to have its coarse fraction and b-fabric oriented around the post (Fig 6.11a – b). It is also possible to see that some of the oriented fabric has undergone subsequent shrinking and swelling due to the dewatering of the site; this has induced cracking against the orientation of the fabric (Fig 6.11b). Neither of these characteristics appeared in the other postholes and could suggest a scenario in which, at the time of erecting the post, sandy soil material was packed around it under stress for support. This scenario would appear more convincing than the original interpretation that soil material fell into the crevice as the post shrank upon drying out. If this had been the case, the soil material would not have been moulded to the post or changed in any way.

## 6.6 Conclusions  *by R Van de Noort*

The debate on the reconstruction and function of four-post structures and their variants goes back, at least, to Pitt-Rivers' publication of a four-poster on Cranborne Chase in 1888 (Pitt-Rivers 1888, 57), and was further promoted by Gerhard Bersu in 1940 as part of the analysis of the excavations at Little Woodbury, and by Geoffrey Wainwright (1979) for Gussage All Saints. This hypothesis has certainly not been left unchallenged, and alternative propositions for the late prehistoric four-post structures include rectangular buildings such as watch towers or platforms, or fighting platforms (eg Ellison and Drewett 1971, 186), and rows of aligned four-post structures have been interpreted as rectangular houses or dwellings (eg Stead 1968; Stanford 1971; Wainwright 1968; Challis and Harding 1975, 149 – 52; Bradley 1978, 43, 121; Grant 1983, 245; Dixon 1994).

Table 6.2.  Summary chart of major micromorphological features of posthole features in Trench 3

| Sample | Fabric Type (Context) | Microstructure & porosity | C/F Ratio & related distribution | Coarsefraction description | Micromass description (CPL) | Major pedofeatures |
|---|---|---|---|---|---|---|
| 118 | [3524] | crumb, vughs, packing voids & channels | 60/40; close porphyric | predominately quartz with common plagioclase and trace mica | dusty yellow clay with porostriated b-fabric | predominantly mottling with few typic iron nodules, common charcoal and few organic punctuations |
| 119 | natural (Bt) | vughy, vughs & channels and packing voids | 45/55; close porphyric | predominately quartz with common plagioclase and trace mica | golden limpid clay with porostriated b-fabric | few typic iron nodules, abundant excrement with associated organic material |
| 120 | [3524] | lenticular; vughs & channels | 45/55; close porphyric | predominately quartz with common plagioclase and trace mica | dusty pale yellow clay with unistrial b-fabric | predominately silty clay coatings with frequent typic fe nodules, and charcoal |

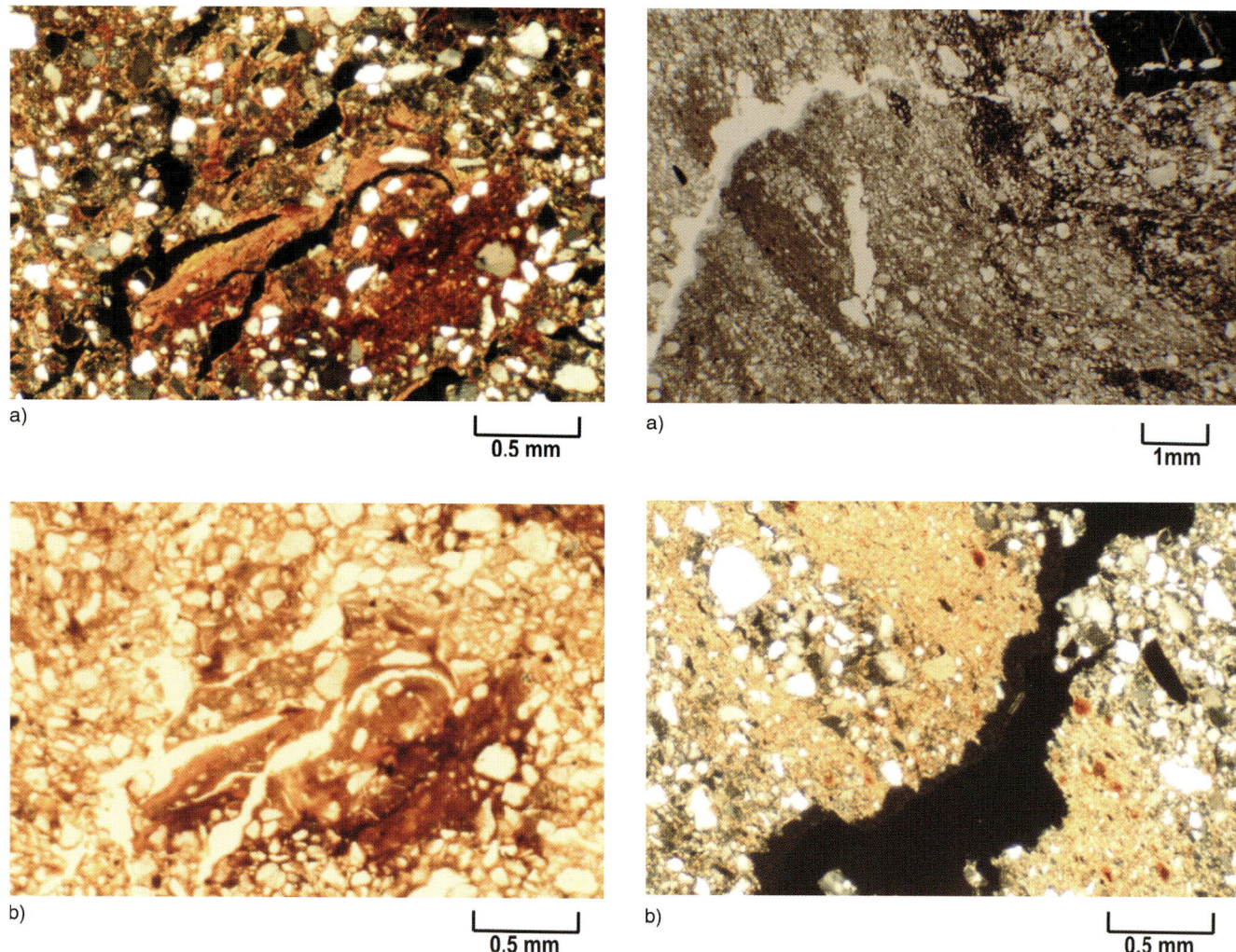

*Figure 6.10 Geoarchaeology: a) sample 119: micrograph of clay infilling (CPL at 2.5 magnification); b) sample 119: micrograph of clay infilling (PPL at 2.5 magnification)*

*Figure 6.11 Geoarchaeology: a) sample 120: micrograph of fabric microstructure (PPL); b) sample 120: micrograph of oriented fabric (CPL)*

Nevertheless, to date, most archaeologists tend to interpret four-posters and their variants as raised stores or granaries, but always with the proviso that conclusive evidence for this interpretation has, as yet, not been forthcoming (eg Jones 1999, 35; Cunliffe 2005, 411; see also Hill 1995a, 22–4 for a recent reappraisal).

The principal reason for this uncertainty lies in the supposed taphonomic processes that have been invoked to explain the creation of the deposits of charred grain, which frequently contain chaff, in one or more of the postholes of a raised platform or store. It has been suggested (eg Gent 1983, 249–50; Dark 2000, 36) that such a taphonomic process could conceivably be the result of a fire, which charred the stored grain and burnt the granary, including its uprights, and resulted in the charred grain finding its way into the posthole or postpipe of the burnt upright. Stanford (1974, 81–2, 106–8; 1981, 109) argued for this scenario to have been responsible for the creation of the charred grain deposits in several granaries at Croft Ambrey and Midsummer Hill. Other processes, such as the preservation of uncharred grain in a waterlogged environment, are only possible in wetland conditions, and have been suggested for the Glastonbury and Meare lake villages in the Somerset Levels (Gent 1983, 247–9).

The Sutton Common evidence advocates an alternative explanation for the deposits of charred grain in postholes of four-post structures, principally on the basis of taphonomy. As demonstrated above (see section 3.2.1), the soft Lake Humber-derived sediments did not provide a solid base once postholes were overcut, and across the site structural timbers such as the uprights of the four-poster structures were placed in carefully carved tight postholes. Where so required, limestone blocks were used for post packing. The opportunity for grain, after burning, to enter in moderate to large amounts into these tight postholes, is difficult to conceive. The partial survival of three, uncharred, uprights of four-post structures alongside deposits of charred grain (wood in contexts [3032], [3018], and [7429]), supports the concept that fire did not play a role in the post-depositional processes of the granaries. On the basis of this evidence, we propose the alternative hypothesis that the deposits of charred grain in one or two postholes of granaries were the result of deliberate actions (Fig 6.12). It must be emphasised here, however, that our excavations did not identify layers of charred grain *in situ*, nor was the sampling sufficiently selective to be able to state here with confidence that the charred grain came from below the original upright timbers; the recent desiccation of the Common and the collapse of ancient wood prevented such a sampling approach.

If our hypothesis on the inclusion of a handful of charred grain in one or two postholes of a granary during the building process is correct, then this should be understood within the concept of structured deposition and should be seen as a 'special deposit' (see also chapter 7). The practice of structured deposition has been related to the concepts of transformation and regeneration which have been observed frequently in the middle and late Bronze Age and Iron Age of Britain (see Hill 1995a; 22 – 4, 109 – 10; Brück 1999; 2001), and relates to these concepts both if the grain was to be used as seed corn or was meant for consumption, providing nourishment and life. The charring of wheat and barley grains, as opposed to the deposition of uncharred grains, may have had a specific purpose in this respect, in that the firing of the grains would have a stabilising (or fossilising) effect on the grain, and thus the impact and importance of the deposition act was to promote the length of existence of the granary. The significance of this structural deposition seems to be reinforced by the use of fragments of quern stone in postholes of four-post granaries, being symbolic of the specific transformation and regeneration of grain, or fertility in general (see section 7.6).

The context of structured deposition may also be extended to the deposition of charred grain in pits. It seems highly probable that charred grain and quern stones deposited in pits were not simply the result of some food-processing or cooking disaster. Rather, having hypothesised the significance of charred grain in the construction of four-post granaries, its deposition elsewhere may reflect similar intent. In this context, we should also consider the significance of the charred plant remains from the ditch of the smaller enclosure, excavated in 1987 (Trench A/C, context 068; Parker Pearson and Sydes 1997, 229, 248). This 'dump' of charred spelt, which also contained some emmer grains and weeds, was dated to 800 – 200 cal BC (HAR – 8917). In line with interpretations from other Iron Age sites, the charring of the grain from the ditch of the smaller enclosure has been interpreted as part of the processing of the grain, for example parching of the harvest to assist the husking, but a catastrophic fire was not ruled out (*ibid*, 248 – 50). In view of the reinterpretation of the significance and meaning of the deposition of charred grains in selected postholes, it may also be necessary to review the deposits of charred remains in the ditches of enclosed settlements. Rather than being interpreted as the dumping of grain accidentally burnt during processing or through combustion of a grain store, the presence of charred grain in ditches could equally be

*Figure 6.12 Contrasting hypotheses explaining the presence of charred grain in postholes of granaries. The reconstruction on the left represents the long-held understanding that catastrophic fires caused the presence of charred grains in postholes; the reconstruction on the right represents the interpretation of the Sutton Common material, with a handful of charred grain ritually deposited in postholes at some stage in the building process*

interpreted in the context of structured deposition. Here, however, the purpose of the deposition in ditches surrounding enclosed sites was to cover the whole site, rather than a single granary. The difference in scale, it could be argued, is reflected in the different sizes of the depositions.

Charred grain has been found in many other Iron Age contexts in Britain. For example, such deposits have been found in the postholes of four-post structures at Rotherley Group III (Pitt-Rivers 1888, 55), Little Woodbury (Bersu 1940), Tollard Royal A and B (Wainwright 1968, 112), Tallington 37 (Simpson 1966, 19), and at Croft Ambrey and Midsummer Hill (Stanford 1974; 1981). Charred grain deposits have also been uncovered from pits, often interpreted as (grain) storage pits, at Danebury hillfort, Hampshire (eg Cunliffe 1995, 260–1), Asheldam Camp hillfort, Essex (Bedwin 1991), the Wardy Hill enclosed lowland site, Cambridgeshire (Evans 2003), Concerto Camp hillfort, Worcestershire (Monckton 1999), and Ham Hill hillfort, Somerset (Smith 1991). It is also a not infrequent find from ditches and ditch terminals of enclosed settlements such as Thorpe Thewles, Cleveland (Van der Veen 1992, 39–42). These sites represent a timespan from the late Bronze Age/early Iron Age, through to the early Roman period. The contexts of deposits of charred grain dated to the 1st millennium BC from elsewhere in the British Isles are similar to the contexts observed at Sutton Common. It is our submission that our alternative hypothesis may also be valid for other significant charred grain deposits in the postholes of four-post granaries, pits (including storage pits), and ditches and ditch terminals of enclosed sites across Britain, and that these may also be understood as the result of deliberate and cosmologically structured acts.

Thus, the interior of the Sutton Common marsh-fort was dominated by granaries, mostly four-post structures, but occasionally six- or more post structures, aligned in rows of between two and possibly ten granaries. Over 115 rectangular post-settings were identified at the analysis stage, but the total number of granaries is likely to be nearer to 150, if possible and partial structures are included in the calculations. We recognise three broad zones of granaries on the basis of the alignment of granaries and granary rows: the western half of the marsh-fort, the north-eastern quarter, and the south-eastern quarter. Importantly, no granaries appear to have been either repaired or replaced. The granaries were constructed from flat-bottomed oak timbers, but the selection of pine in the case of one granary next to the eastern gateway is considered to be significant, and the selected use of pine instead of oak has been observed elsewhere, for example at Ferrybridge, West Yorkshire, where pine charcoal and charred grains were found in one of the postholes of a four-post structure (Denise Druce, pers comm). There is little doubt that temporally the granaries are closely linked to the construction of the defences of the site; the alignment of the granaries on the defences, the parallels in construction technique using flat-bottomed posts, and the palaeoenvironmental evidence all support such a reading.

A limited number of pits were found, concentrated in the southern half of the interior, along with one well, and one possible stake-built structure, but neither circular post-settings nor ring-ditch gullies typical of Iron Age houses were identified. Thus, there is no archaeological evidence which indicates that habitation of the site occurred for any length of time. The palaeoenvironmental evidence from the ditches near the eastern gateway reinforces this interpretation – the pollen, plant macrofossil, and insect analyses all indicate the existence of an immediate environment and broader landscape without occupation by people. Rather, the area was probably used as grazing grounds. Clear paths within the interior were not identified, although it is possible to move between the two gateways relatively unimpeded by granaries. It is also possible to envisage a road from the north to the south of the marsh-fort, in between the western zone of granaries and the two eastern zones. In terms of the interior, the Sutton Common marsh-fort reflects a number of other enclosed sites, both in northern Britain and further afield (cf Challis and Harding 1975, 149–52). Most striking is the correspondence with the interior of the Yorkshire Wolds' hillfort at Grimthorpe. Although only partially excavated, no roundhouses or other evidence signalling long-term occupation within the interior of this enclosed site were found, and the only structures identified were eight four-post structures, found in a row or alignment parallel to the box rampart (Stead 1986).

It has been argued (eg Dark 2000, 36) that granaries were the northern and western British alternative to the southern British storage pits, but we note a number of other sites throughout Britain, both enclosed and open, where rows of granaries were present. These include, for example, Moel-y-Gaer hillfort, Credenhill hillfort, Croft Ambrey hillfort, and Midsummer Hill Camp in the Welsh Marches. The distribution of the granaries in these sites was described as 'grid-iron' patterns (Stanford 1971, 47–8). Granaries in rows or alignments are also recorded at the enclosed sites of Ivinghoe Beacon, Buckinghamshire (Cotton and Frere 1968), Maiden Castle, Dorset (Wheeler 1943; Sharples 1991), Rainsborough (Avery *et al* 1967), Balksbury, Hampshire (Wainwright 1969), the 'Late Phase' of Danebury, Hampshire (Cunliffe 1984; Cunliffe and Poole 1991), and at Crickley Hill, Gloucestershire (Dixon 1994). The existence of morphological parallels over broad geographical distances should not be used uncritically to assume widespread socio-political analogies, but attention should be drawn to the observation that several sites in the later part of the early Iron Age appear to share the characteristic of including rows of granaries, and that roundhouses were introduced in later phases only (see Guilbert 1975; Bond 1991). The apparent dominance of large enclosed sites in the examples given here should be understood in the context of the bias in research, especially in terms of hillfort research (see section 1.3.1.1), and many open sites are known to have had granaries. Nevertheless, from the late Bronze Age onwards, a marked increase in the construction of granaries has been noted (eg Gent 1983, 245), and in the early Iron Age these frequently appear in orderly rows.

What does this mean for our understanding of Sutton Common? The Sutton Common marsh-fort appears to have been constructed as a place for granaries in a period of expanding crop husbandry. The palaeoenvironmental evidence from the Common and the wider region indicates increasingly extensive woodland clearances during the Iron Age, with evidence for cereal production which grew throughout the Iron Age, and with spelt replacing emmer (Jones 1999; Van der Veen 1992). The *c* 150 granaries would have been able to hold an enormous amount of grain: the total storage capacity has been estimated at between $900m^3$ and $1500m^3$. However, the alternative hypothesis from Sutton Common presents an important paradox: the reinterpretation of the charred grains in the postholes of four-post structures, and the taphonomic processes that led to their inclusion, means that there can be no doubt that the structures were *intended* as granaries but that, at the same time, no *actual* evidence exists for grain ever being stored here. It is conceivable that, as was the case with the defences of the marsh-fort itself (see section 5.7), the construction of the granaries served symbolic objectives alongside practical use. Whether the granaries at Sutton Common were ever used to their full capacity during the very short period of its existence seems unlikely.

# 7 The marsh-fort – the finds

## 7.1 Introduction *by R Van de Noort*

Previous excavations were more productive in terms of finds than those described here (see sections 1.2.2 and 1.2.3). Flint artefacts were noted from the first excavations in the early 20th century. Human and animal remains were similarly identified during these early explorations, especially associated with the main gateways, but also elsewhere, including the north side of the larger enclosure. Whiting's work in the 1930s added a baked clay ball or net sinker, Romano-British pottery, the oak 'wheel', and a possible dug-out vessel, to the array of finds.

The finds from the excavations undertaken between 1987 and 1993 have all been published (Parker Pearson and Sydes 1997), and only need summarising here. The wooden notched ladder, found in 1988, has already been mentioned (see section 6.2.2). Nine quern fragments were found during the excavations, all from unstratified contexts (*ibid*, 234). In 1988, a small fragment of a bronze Wallington complex dirk blade was found on the Common, and is dated on the basis of the metalwork assemblage to the Penard phase of the middle Bronze Age. Various other Bronze Age finds are known from the 10km$^2$ around Sutton Common (*ibid*, 234–7). Other finds of importance include the unstratified find of a globular bead and an amorphous lump of translucent cobalt blue glass, an unstratified globular amber bead, and a small globular shale bead from the outer ditch of the larger enclosure.

The finds from the excavations between 1998 and 2003 were sparse. Discounting the flint artefacts and debitage (discussed above, section 4.4) and artefacts thought to be associated to the second phase of activity at the Sutton Common site (discussed below, section 8.5), finds included human and animal bone, some very small fragments of pottery, several fragments of quern stone, a single antler weaving comb, and two fragments of yew wood which appear not to form part of any structure. This chapter explores these finds. In line with recent discussions on late prehistoric deposition of 'rubbish', it approaches the discarded material as structured deposition.

## 7.2 The concept of 'structured deposition' *by C Cumberpatch and R Van de Noort*

As mentioned earlier (see section 1.3.1.1), Iron Age material culture studies, following reappraisals of Neolithic material culture research in the 1980s, no longer consider the deposition of artefacts and food waste as simply reflecting people's economic lives, rather material culture is now understood within the conceptual framework of structuration theory as a process of social reproduction, whereby the production, use, and discard of raw materials, artefacts, and food waste by human beings can often be structured according to sets of culturally specific rules and principles which establish and reinforce social identities and relationships. These rules, which in their nature and complexity are sometimes time and space specific, but otherwise alike across long periods of time and large areas, are themselves structured by perceptions regarding the nature of artefacts, their social and/or economic status, the classification of what constitutes 'dirt', 'rubbish', and 'contamination', and by ideas regarding space and its proper use.

Whilst it may be relatively straightforward to identify structured depositions, for example in the case of an articulated burial of a part of a human or 'non-human person'[1] in a pit, it is more difficult to determine whether specific deposits are ritual deposits, or what aspects of a deposit were intended as identifiable aspects of religious activity. Ritual has to be understood as a specific form of social practice related to everyday life, but the finds from later prehistoric settlements can be just as structured as those from obvious 'ritual' contexts such as hoards or burials (Hill 1995a, 125). Religion can not be isolated from broader social practices, and the concept of cosmology, in the sense of the world view of a group which encompasses their understanding of the universe, origins, existence, and nature, is therefore often preferred over a notion of separated, and identifiable, ritual practices. It can be argued that, all over the world and at all times, human communities act in ways which result in the formation of archaeological deposits which, to a greater or lesser extent, incorporate regular associations of artefact and ecofact classes which are in some sense structured and from which data pertaining to this structure can be recovered through the application of archaeological techniques. The principles which inform the creation of such deposits may be based upon culturally specific perceptions of, and beliefs regarding, the wider world and the human place within it. Structured deposition should not therefore be equated to ritual activity, but contemporary cosmologies determine much of this practice and certain actions were undoubtedly undertaken wholly or partly with religious intent.

Hill's (1995a) insight regarding the Wessex Iron Age was to identify certain specific characteristics within the structures of deposition on the sites that he studied and to document and interpret these in terms of the practices that may have led to their creation. The wider question arising from his work is the precise character of the deposition and the definition of the kinds of structures which can be discerned. As Hill demonstrated in his published case study (*ibid*), the characterisation of structured deposition requires the integration of data from across the traditional categories employed by archaeologists to structure their analyses and discussions of material culture.

The excavations at Sutton Common integrated the recovery of artefacts and palaeoenvironmental information with the aim of achieving such a characterisation, and structured deposition was noted both in the interior of the marsh-fort and in the terminal ditches at the eastern entranceway against a background of a scarcity of man-made objects. In fact, with the possible exception of five very small fragments of pottery, discovered in a modern plough scar and therefore without a primary context (see section 7.5.1), all such objects appear purposefully placed in specific locales within the site, and can therefore considered to be structured deposits. These finds are presented below and the associations are discussed and interpreted in the conclusions.

## 7.3 Human remains *by C Knüsel*

### 7.3.1 Introduction

Human remains were revealed in the outer ditch terminal to the north of the eastern entranceway [3347] in 2003 (Fig 7.1). They were found on two separate days and each deposit, within its soil matrix, was recovered, boxed, and at a subsequent date excavated in laboratory conditions. The two boxes containing the remains were designated 'A' and 'B', and those remains from Box A were marked with a letter 'A' (in ink) to permit a refitting exercise to help determine the number of individuals contributing to the assemblage, as well as to determine if there are any conjoined fragments that demonstrate that the bones in one relate to fragments in the other.

Although the remains are heavily fragmented, the majority are still identifiable to anatomical unit (eg viscerocranium, neurocranium, vertebral column, pectoral girdle, etc), and many can be identified to skeletal element. The bone is friable and the quality of the cortical bone is fragile due to delamination of cortical bone surfaces. There are a number of recent bone breaks and rounding of fracture margins, the presence of which suggests that the bones may have been more complete at the time of deposition than they are at present. The bone is a deep brown colour, which contrasts with bone found on well-drained sites (usually a yellow or white colour).

### 7.3.2 Number of individuals represented and skeletal element representation

Based on the apparent absence of skeletal element duplication and the presence of two relatively complete right and left temporal bones of similar morphology, Box A would appear to contain the remains of one individual. By similar criteria, Box B also seems to contain a single individual. The skeletal part representation of B is more diverse than that of A. The presence of a large dens from an axis vertebra indicates that the second cervical vertebra was present in the deposit from which B derives. It is curious, though, that no fragments of the more superiorly placed atlas or more inferior cervical vertebral elements are present. This may suggest either that the upper-most cervical vertebrae were once present and did not preserve or that the axis vertebra alone was included in the deposit, only a small fragment of which was recovered. There are no cutmarks present on any of the remains. The absence of mandibular fragments – with not even more resilient teeth represented – may suggest localised and differential destruction or recovery of these anatomical areas. The presence of two sets of left maxillary teeth, namely 26, 27, and 28, suggest that A and B are discrete individuals. No conjoined fragments or elements were identified that would link the remains in the two boxes.

The remains of B are more heavily fragmented than those of A. The breakages of these bones suggest that the majority relate to post-mortem breakage. A few fragments have fracture surface colouration and the appearance of what may be dry fractures (Outram 2002; Knüsel 2005). This possibility is especially apposite for the occipital fragments from Box B. The internal occipital protuberance has a 'torn' appearance that may suggest that this is a dry fracture that occurred in the past when some collagen was still retained in the bone; it does not appear, however, to be perimortem trauma. The presence of this fracture thus suggests that some fragmentation occurred in the ground in the distant past.

### 7.3.3 Age determination

Due to the incompleteness of the individuals in this assemblage and their fragmentary state, age determination assessments were based more on morphological appearance, dental development, and dental wear, rather than the standard techniques that rely upon complete or nearly complete infra-cranial elements. The tooth wear of the nearly complete maxilla of B suggests that

138  *Sutton Common*

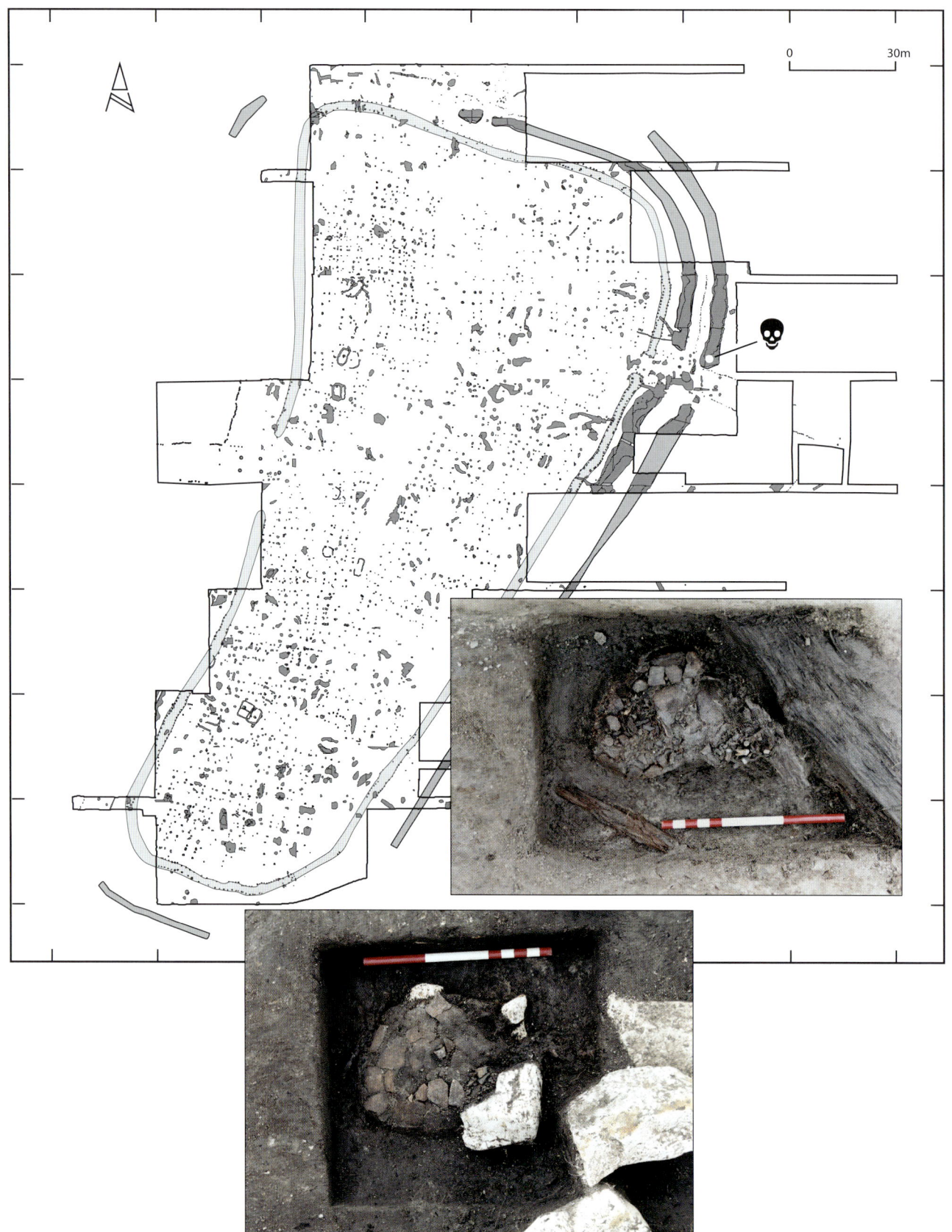

*Figure 7.1   Excavation plan 1998 – 2003: the location of the human heads and photographs of the heads during excavation*

this individual was an adult who was aged 25–35 years at death, based on Brothwell's (1981) age determination from dental wear method and applied to the left maxillary dentition. This assessment is consistent with the development of cranial thickness of the neurocranial fragments and with the morphology of the cranial base remains. The same age range is indicated by the teeth from A.

### 7.3.4 Sex assessment

Sex assessment was based more on morphological robusticity, rather than the standard techniques that rely upon complete or nearly complete infra-cranial elements. The large right mastoid process found amongst the remains in Box B, coupled with the absence of duplication of the fragments suggests that a single male is most likely represented. The male assessment is supported by the size of the dens and odontoid process present (large), as well as the rugosity and thickness of the occipital reconstructed from fragments, and the size of the malars and mastoid process. The size of the mastoid processes found in Box A also suggests a male assessment for these remains, although this male does not appear to have been as robust as B.

### 7.3.5 Conclusion

The human remains recovered from Sutton Common include a minimum of two individuals, represented, mainly, by cranial remains. Both individuals appear to have been males, one more robust than the other, in the age range 25–35 years at death. Individual B is represented by fragments of the infra-cranial skeleton, but with no mandibular fragments present, while A includes mainly cranial fragments with some fragments deriving from the mandible, including isolated mandibular teeth. Both individuals were highly fragmented. The individual in Box B is represented by cranial remains and a fragment of the second cervical vertebra (the axis) that suggest that a head and neck were included in the deposit. The assumption here is that they entered the ditch as fleshed remains. The close proximity of the remains supports this assumption. The individual in Box A is represented only by cranial and mandibular remains that may suggest that only a head was deposited.

### 7.3.6 Non-human remains

There are two cheek teeth from a canid present, the right maxillary second and third molars. There is also a very abraded fragment of what may be a proximal ulna fragment from the trochlear notch of a canid. It is possible that the canid remains belong to the same individual in that there are no duplicated elements within and between the two boxes, but the incompleteness of the remains does not permit a more forceful statement to be made with regard to a count of minimum number of individuals. On present evidence, therefore, the minimum number of non-human individuals represented is one in each box and by NISP (number of identifiable specimens), two and possibly three animals. These remains derive from adult animals.

## 7.4 Animal bone *by A Outram*

### 7.4.1 Introduction

The total number of identified bones or bone fragments from the Sutton Common assemblage was 418. Of these, 33 came from unstratified contexts or topsoil, leaving 385 from sealed Iron Age contexts. Of these, 289 bone and bone fragments came from the ditch terminals around the eastern entranceway, and will be considered further in the discussion on associations of structured depositions (see section 7.9.2). The calcined material associated with human cremations is discussed in the chapter on the mortuary rings (see chapter 8).

Only the material from sealed contexts will be considered in detail in this section. The assemblage is a relatively small one: too small to carry out intra-site contextual comparison with any statistical significance. As a result, and because the whole site was used only for a relatively short period, all the Iron Age material will be considered as a single sample.

The general condition of the bones was poor. Most had lost their cortical bone surface and were cracked and fragile. Almost certainly as a result of poor surface preservation, no surface features such as butchery or gnawing marks could be observed. A number of bones could be measured, but an insufficient quantity to warrant metrical analyses. These data are available in the archive database.

### 7.4.2 Species and Element Abundance

Figures 7.2 a–b are pie charts displaying the relative abundances of species based upon NISP and MNE counts, respectively. NISP counts were as follows: cattle 155 (34.9%), ovicaprids 274 (61.7%), pigs 8 (1.8%), horse 4 (1.0%), roe deer 2 (0.5%), red deer 1 (0.2%). MNEs were: cattle 114 (34.1%), ovicaprids 214 (64.1%), pigs 2 (0.6%), horse 1 (0.3%), roe deer 2 (0.6%), red deer 1 (0.3%). Amongst the ovicaprid bones there was no evidence for goats. Fourteen specimens (mainly metapodials and young jaws) could be assigned

140 *Sutton Common*

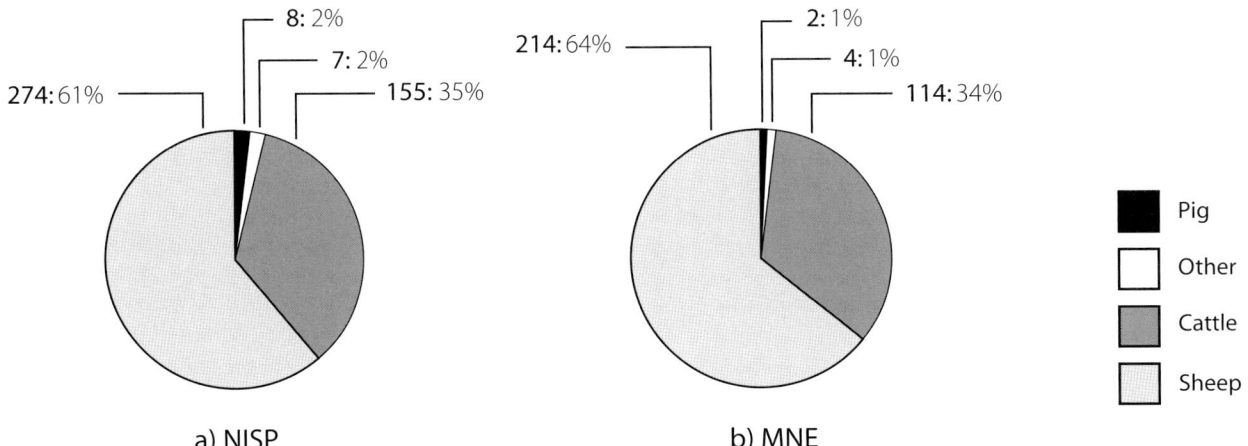

*Figure 7.2 Animal bones: species and element abundance, a) Number of Identifiable Specimens; b) Minimum Number of Elements*

definitively to sheep and it is highly likely that sheep are being dealt with throughout. The roe deer remains included a naturally shed antler burr, which, in itself proves little about human exploitation of that species, but there was also a humerus shaft that might indicate that deer formed part of the diet. The one specimen of red deer was also a humerus shaft (rather tentatively identified). Horse was represented by loose teeth and a fragment of metapodial. Pig was represented by two mandibles and some loose teeth (there was also a pig tibia in the topsoil).

Hambledon's (1999) comparative study of faunal assemblages from the British Iron Age revealed that most Iron Age sites are strongly dominated by cattle and sheep in differing proportions, with relatively few pigs. Pigs are, in particular, consistently poorly represented in Northern and Scottish sites, ranging from 0 to 20% of Iron Age assemblages (*ibid*, 47). Romano-British and continental

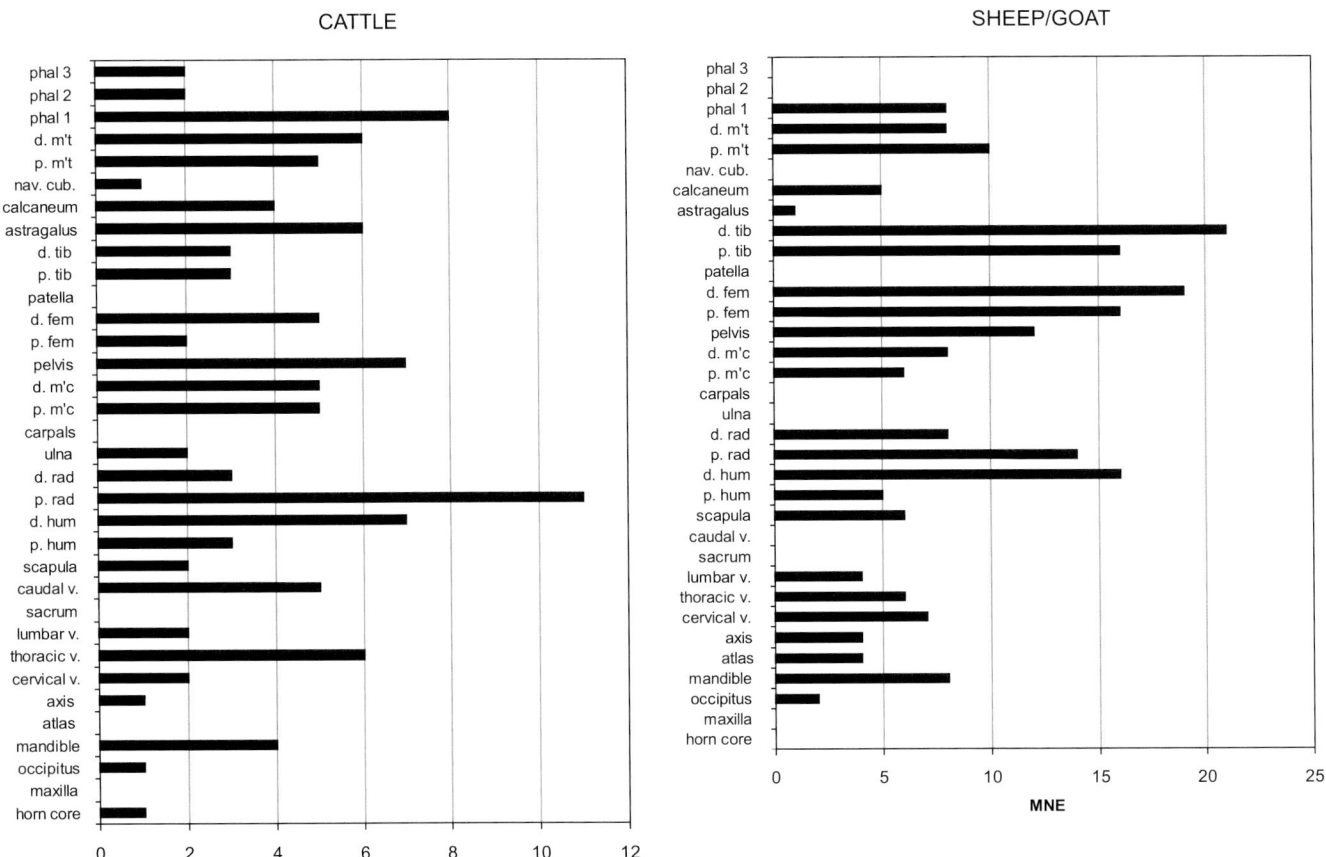

*Figure 7.3 Animal bones: Minimum Number of Elements data for a) cattle; b) sheep*

Iron Age sites contain a vastly higher proportion of pigs (*ibid*, 44). Sutton Common is consistent with this in the extremely low proportion of pigs. Northern sites vary in whether cattle or sheep dominated (*ibid*, 47) and Sutton Common is clearly one of the latter.

Table 7.1 provides a breakdown of the NISP and MNE counts of cattle and sheep by element. To this element representation one should add 5 rib articulations from large mammals (cattle-sized) and 2 of medium mammals (sheep-sized). Figures 7.3 a–b display graphically the MNE data for cattle and sheep respectively. It is clear that, for both species, all areas of the body are present; there is no obviously selective patterning. Those elements that are particularly well represented, such as the proximal radius, distal humerus, pelvis acetabulum, and distal tibia, generally tend to survive well due to their robustness. The assemblage does not, therefore, provide any evidence for any particular practices, whether functional or ritual, that would produce a bias in element representation. The presence of almost all parts of the skeleton suggests that either carcasses were brought to the site whole, or, more likely, the animals were killed on or near the site.

### 7.4.3 Age Structures

Very few mandibles were recovered, so it was not possible to examine age structure through that line of evidence. However, a small amount can be gleaned from bone fusion data. The sample for bone fusion in cattle was rather small to carry out a detailed study by fusion stage. However, 37 of the 43 epiphyses where fusion state could be ascertained were fused, some 86% of the total. Four of the six unfused specimens belonged to the last fusion stage (36–48 months). The cattle assemblage appears to have contained mainly adult animals, with a few animals having been killed at prime meat age. Cattle mortality patterns are quite diverse in the Iron Age, but it is not unusual to see cattle kept until they are slightly older than prime meat culling age (Hambledon 1999, 78). This may well be in keeping with the use of cattle for traction as part of a mixed stock breeding and arable economy. Alternatively, we may only be seeing a selection of the herd at Sutton Common, such as the adult cows from a milk herd. Unfortunately, there is insufficient evidence regarding sex ratios to differentiate between the two possibilities.

Fusion state could be ascertained on 81 sheep epiphyses, allowing for a more detailed look at mortality patterns in the first four years of life. Figure 7.4 shows the percentage fused, meaning the percentage that survived beyond that stage, for the fusion stages of sheep. There is no evidence for culling in the first year and a half, but almost half appear to have been culled at around 18 months to 2 years old. This is consistent with slaughter for meat and is not out of step with the range of patterns seen in Iron Age Britain (Hambledon 1999). Whilst the Sutton Common

Table 7.1 NISP and MNE counts for cattle and sheep by element, secure contexts only

| Elements | Cattle NISP | Cattle MNE | Sheep NISP | Sheep MNE |
|---|---|---|---|---|
| loose teeth (max) | 16 | – | 31 | – |
| loose teeth (man) | 16 | – | 7 | – |
| horn core | 1 | 1 | 0 | 0 |
| maxilla | 0 | 0 | 0 | 0 |
| occipitus | 1 | 1 | 2 | 2 |
| mandible | 5 | 4 | 12 | 8 |
| atlas | 0 | 0 | 4 | 4 |
| axis | 1 | 1 | 4 | 4 |
| cervical v. | 2 | 2 | 7 | 7 |
| thoracic v. | 6 | 6 | 6 | 6 |
| lumbar v. | 2 | 2 | 4 | 4 |
| sacrum | 0 | 0 | 0 | 0 |
| caudal v. | 5 | 5 | 0 | 0 |
| scapula | 2 | 2 | 8 | 6 |
| p. humerus | 5 | 3 | 6 | 5 |
| d. humerus | 10 | 7 | 18 | 16 |
| p. radius | 11 | 11 | 15 | 14 |
| d. radius | 4 | 3 | 9 | 8 |
| ulna | 2 | 2 | 0 | 0 |
| carpals | 0 | 0 | 0 | 0 |
| p. metacarpal | 5 | 5 | 6 | 6 |
| d. metacarpal | 5 | 5 | 8 | 8 |
| pelvis | 7 | 7 | 14 | 12 |
| p. femur | 2 | 2 | 17 | 16 |
| d. femur | 5 | 5 | 22 | 19 |
| patella | 0 | 0 | 0 | 0 |
| p. tibia | 4 | 3 | 18 | 16 |
| d. tibia | 4 | 3 | 22 | 21 |
| astragalus | 6 | 6 | 1 | 1 |
| calcaneum | 4 | 4 | 5 | 5 |
| navicular cuboid | 1 | 1 | 0 | 0 |
| p. metatarsal | 5 | 5 | 11 | 10 |
| d. metatarsal | 6 | 6 | 9 | 8 |
| 1st phalange | 8 | 8 | 8 | 8 |
| 2nd phalange | 2 | 2 | 0 | 0 |
| 3rd phalange | 2 | 2 | 0 | 0 |
| **TOTAL** | **155** | **114** | **274** | **214** |

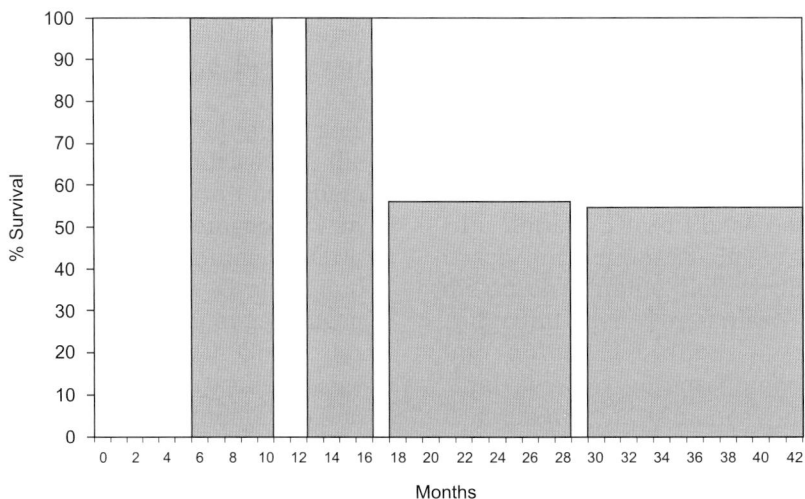

*Figure 7.4  Animal bones: fusion stages of sheep*

assemblage fits best with the supply of sheep for meat, one must bear in mind that not all of the livestock necessarily ended up on this site.

### 7.4.4  Bone fracture and taphonomic history

The study of the fracture patterns of bones from the site reveals something about the deposition and taphonomic history of the assemblage. Fracture types could be discerned on 290 identified or unidentified shaft specimens. The vast majority (91.7%) of fractured specimens displayed a relatively recent fracture. These 'mineralised' and 'new' breaks appear to have occurred largely during the recovery of the bones. This is not surprising, given the weakened and cracked state of the bones. Many would have fallen apart along existing cracks upon lifting, whilst others would easily succumb to the slightest knock from an excavation implement. Of the evidence, 13.1% showed helical fracture, and three of these specimens had clear dynamic impact scars that probably indicate deliberate breakage of fresh bones. Only 4.8% appear to have been broken in a 'dry' state, when they still showed some features of fresh bone fracture, but the bone was beginning to lose organic content and develop micro-cracks. Despite poor bone condition, and the problems of keeping the fragile bones in one piece during excavation and subsequent storage, the assemblage was actually not highly fragmented. About 10% of identified specimens were entirely whole and undamaged, which is a fairly high proportion.

The presence of helical fractures and dynamic impact scars may well indicate a small amount of marrow extraction from long bone shafts; this is entirely expected. The very low prevalence of 'dry' fracture and the relatively high proportion of whole bones seem to indicate that the bones were not subjected to trampling or surface weathering for a long period of time before they were deposited and covered in the ditches (where most of the assemblage comes from). There is also no evidence for gnawing, though poor surface preservation may have obscured some. It is also rather unlikely that the ditches were recut during the Iron Age, after the bones were deposited, as this would also have produced more dry breaks or obviously old mineralised breaks.

### 7.4.5  Co-mingled human remains

Mixed in with the animal bone assemblage were 9 specimens of human bones and teeth. Context [3347] produced 2 incisors, a canine and 2 molars from the upper jaw, which may be associated with the heads described above (see section 7.3). These were all permanent adult teeth. Context [3535], from the terminal of the inner ditch to the north of the eastern gateway, contained a shaft fragment from the proximal radius on the left side. Context [5454] produced, in three refitted pieces, most of the shaft of a left humerus. Both these arm bones were of adult size.

## 7.5  Pottery  *by C G Cumberpatch, Alan Vince and David Knight*

### 7.5.1  Introduction and description

Five fragments of pottery and one piece of an unidentified burnt material were recovered from the interior of the marsh-fort. These were retrieved from a modern plough scar in grid square G12 in Trench 4 in 2003, and have been treated as unstratified finds. They were assigned small find numbers [1] to [6] to distinguish them, and these numbers have been used to structure the catalogue.

1 Two small body sherds, one weighing 2 grams and the other less than 1 gram. Both appeared to be hand-made and were predominantly black throughout, although the larger sherd had a dull orange internal margin and the smaller had a light-coloured silty deposit on one side (the internal and external faces of the smaller sherd were not distinguishable). The uniformly black colour of the fabric and the small size of the sherds made the identification of inclusions difficult, but the larger sherd appeared to contain angular non-crystalline rock fragments while the smaller contained voids lined with a reddish deposit.
2 An irregularly shaped, hand-made body sherd weighing 6 grams, black throughout with a pale-grey silty deposit on the external surfaces and covering part of the broken edge. The fabric was dense with a 'blocky' fracture and contained occasional angular black rock fragments up to 2mm in length and, immediately below the surfaces, voids with reddish internal margins. Beneath the silty deposits the sherd had a cracked surface which suggested that some form of conservation should be considered to prevent its break-up. A sample from this sherd was submitted for petrological and chemical analysis. For this purpose it was allotted the code number V2373 and is described in the characterisation report, below.
3 Four small body sherds which were probably originally part of the same sherd, together weighing *c* 1 gram. The sherds were of a dark-grey, homogenous fabric with occasional irregular voids with reddish internal margins. The small size of the sherds precluded a more detailed description.
4 One small, irregular body sherd weighing less than 1 gram. The sherd was black throughout with thin dull orange margins internally and externally. The size of the sherd and the thin coating of silt made observation of the fabric difficult, but it appeared to be similar in all respects to sherds 2 and 3.
5 One irregularly shaped body sherd weighing 4 grams. The sherd had a similar black homogenous fabric to that seen in the other sherds and had dull orange margins and occasional soft reddish inclusions and voids. A sample from this sherd was submitted for petrological and chemical analysis. For this purpose it was allotted the code number V2372 and is described in the characterisation report, below.
6 Although initially identified as a sherd of pottery, item number 6 appeared to be a fragment of burnt material and was far too light in weight (less than 1 gram) to be a sherd of pottery. Its precise composition was not determinable.

None of these fragments was diagnostic.

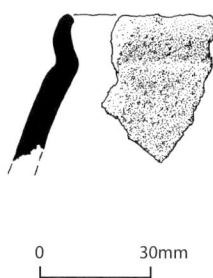

*Figure 7.5  Pottery: small hand-made rim sherd*

A small hand-made rim sherd weighing 8 grams, with a distinctive rim profile (Fig 7.5), was recovered from the inner ditch terminal on the north side of the eastern entrance in the larger enclosure (context [3150]). The sherd appeared to be from a small, thin-walled ovoid jar with a sharply everted neck and a tapered rim. The fabric is moderately hard and dense with voids in the broken surfaces apparently resulting from sub-rounded inclusions falling out after breakage. Without breaking the sherd to expose a fresh edge, it was not possible to identify these inclusions. The surfaces of the sherd were black and had an irregular texture, without the surface cracking which was visible on the sherds from the unstratified contexts. The irregular top of the rim made it difficult to determine the precise orientation of the rim, but it appeared to have been carefully and deliberately made so as to give a slightly dished or channelled shape rather than being simply vertical. A sample from this sherd was submitted for petrological and chemical analysis. For this purpose it was allotted the code number V2371 and is described in the characterisation report, below.

No specific parallels have been located for the sherd although two Iron Age vessels with channelled rims have been reported from Fiskerton, Lincolnshire (Knight 2002, fig 12.3:19; Elsdon and Knight 2003) in a context post-dating 375/4 BC. These vessels were significantly larger than the Sutton Common vessel and had distinctive wide flared rims. They appear to have been made from raw materials obtained from within 5 km of the Fiskerton site. A date for this sherd can probably only be obtained from associated material, although an earlier Iron Age date appears to be the most probable. It is not entirely beyond the bounds of possibility that the sherd represents an attempt to copy by hand a later Iron Age wheel-thrown vessel (Knight pers comm).

### 7.5.2  *Discussion*

The quantities of the Sutton Common pottery were too low and the forms insufficiently diagnostic to allow the pottery to be dated on the basis of its own characteristics or to be used as a means of dating the contexts in which it occurred.

Nevertheless, on the basis of the context it seems probable that it was deposited sometime in the 4th century BC. This material represents the earliest Iron Age pottery yet found in South Yorkshire. The majority of other ceramic finds from the county have been recovered from sites which form part of the cropmark landscape and appear to date to the latter part of the later prehistoric period, while some may actually date to the period after the Roman Conquest, being wares manufactured within an Iron Age tradition during the early years of the occupation.

The sherd of pottery from [3150] was the only fragment of any recognisable or identifiable form, the remainder being undiagnostic body sherds. Earlier finds of pottery from the site were similarly undiagnostic and fragmentary (Parker Pearson and Sydes 1997, 237). The largely aceramic nature of the later prehistoric period in South Yorkshire has been discussed on a number of occasions (Cumberpatch and Chadwick 1995; Bevan 2000; Chadwick 1997, 1999, 2004). While recent excavations have revealed more pottery than was known hitherto (Cumberpatch, in prep; Cumberpatch *et al*, in prep) the fact is that, in comparison with areas such as Lincolnshire, Nottinghamshire, and the central midlands, South Yorkshire remains distinguished by a generally low prevalence of ceramic finds from later prehistoric sites. In this it is similar to areas to the west, notably Derbyshire and the Cheshire Plain (Matthews 1997, 1999). Analysis of the pottery from Mellor, near Stockport, on the western edge of the Peak District suggested that at least one of the small number of vessels from this site was manufactured from clay sources within the immediate region, although most probably not on the site itself (Ixer in Cumberpatch *et al* 2003). The scarcity of pottery on sites across the region suggests that it was made in small quantities and this might also suggest that it was not intended for utilitarian purposes.

As outlined in Appendix 2, the lack of clay samples from the immediate vicinity of Sutton Common precluded a positive identification of the sources of the clay used to make the pottery but a local source seems to be most probable. Whether the apparent similarity in these aspects of the character of the pottery in the cases of Sutton Common and Mellor can be said to be a significant indicator of some basic similarity in the organisation of production is difficult to determine, but it would seem to suggest that in these cases at least, the vessels were not imported from further south or east, as appears to be the case with vessels from the very late prehistoric or early Roman period sites such as Red House Farm (Cumberpatch, in prep 1) or Pickburn Leys (Sydes 1993).

As noted above, other finds of later prehistoric pottery from South Yorkshire appear to be somewhat later than those from Sutton Common. They have generally been from the kind of small-scale excavation compelled by the dictates of the development industry and nurtured under a regime of preservation *in situ* which combine to restrict and limit the possibilities for innovative research leading to the development of informative interpretations of the archaeological record.

Questions of the distribution of finds within settlements do not appear to have been addressed in the case of the sites at Topham Farm, Sykehouse (Roberts 2003) or Moss Carr, Methley (Roberts and Richardson 2002). This is particularly unfortunate in the case of Moss Carr, in that the earlier phase of the site may be broadly contemporaneous with Sutton Common.

In her discussion of the results of work on sites on the M1–A1 link road in West Yorkshire, Burgess (2001, 263–9) has cited examples of deposits that might be considered to be in some way deliberately placed or structured but has not drawn the evidence together or attempted to draw out examples of regular associations between artefact categories that might be interpreted in the light of Hill's work in the south. Amongst the examples referred to by Burgess, the one with perhaps the best chronological relationship to Sutton Common is Swillington Common, which, amongst other features, produced a middle to late Iron Age pot from a heavily truncated pit which contained a fragment of charcoal with a radiocarbon date range of 410–200 cal BC (AA–32013; 2275±50 BP). The character of the deposit led the excavator to describe it as 'ritual' in nature (Howell 2001, 63) and no other Iron Age pottery was recovered from the site.

More generally, looking at evidence from later prehistoric sites across South and West Yorkshire and north Nottinghamshire there are some indications that, amongst the sites excavated which have produced pottery, a number exhibit signs that the creation of deposits was, to some extent, deliberate. At present much of the data is in a largely anecdotal form (some remains unpublished but much has been drawn together by Chadwick 2004), with examples of the deposition of pottery, quernstones, and burnt material in ditches (particularly in ditch terminals and ditch junctions), the apparently deliberate deposition of animal carcases and part-carcases in pits and ditches, and some evidence of the deposition of parts of human bodies alongside those of animals. What are lacking at present are formal and detailed comparisons which draw together the evidence in a manner which will allow the identification of possible regular associations between the location of deposition and the different types and classes of material on an intra- and inter-site basis and will also take into account the chronological issues which, in spite of an increasing amount of data, have yet to be fully resolved. Only when these tasks are complete will it be possible to move beyond simple assertions that the deposition appears to be structured in possibly significant ways.

See also Appendix 2, Characterisation studies of pottery by Alan Vince.

## 7.6 Querns *by Sue Watts*

### 7.6.1 *Introduction and description*

Excavations at Sutton Common in 2002 and 2003 recovered nineteen fragments of quern stone (Fig 7.6). A number of the fragments join, however, and, in addition, other non-joining fragments found within the same context may also have derived from the same stone(s). The number of saddle quern stones represented, therefore, is lower. The fragments are described below, ordered by context.

From context [4301]:

1 Four joining fragments. Fine-grained sandstone. Part of nicely finished saddle quern with rounded sides showing evidence of having been pecked to shape. Appears to have had a smooth flat base. Flat grinding surface, particularly worn around the periphery. L385/W125/T123mm. [4301] 1–4
2 Fragment. Fine-grained sandstone. From top edge of saddle quern, showing evidence of having been worked to shape. Possibly from same stone as 4301/1–4. L129/W91/T51mm. [4301] 5
3 Fragment. Fine-grained sandstone. Retains a small area of probable grinding surface. Possibly from same stone as 4301/1–4. L72/W35/T85mm. [4301] 6
4 Fragment. Fine-grained sandstone. No features. L44/W43/T13mm. [4301] 7
5 Fragment. Fine-grained sandstone. Flat, worn grinding surface with glazed high spots. L245/W113/T113mm. [4301] 8
6 Two joining fragments. Fine-grained sandstone. Slightly concave grinding surface. Worn with glazed high spots. L183/W175/T111mm. [4301] 9–10
7 Fragment. Fine-grained sandstone. Flat grinding surface with worn high spots. L243/W219/T157 mm. [4301] 11
8 Fragment. Sandstone. From edge of stone with neatly finished side. Worn grinding surface with glazed high spots. L154/W71/T108 mm. [4301] 12
9 Fragment. Sandstone. Worn grinding surface. Other side roughly flat. L141/W108/T71mm. [4301] 13
10 Fragment. Sandstone. Flat grinding surface. No evidence of wear. L143/W118/T62mm. [4301] 14

From context [4305]:

11 Fragment. Sandstone. Possible remains of grinding surface. L112/W99/T67mm. [4305] 1
12 Two joining fragments. Very fine-grained, silty sandstone. From edge of stone. Slightly convex grinding surface, particularly worn around periphery. Other side fairly smooth but uneven. Possibly remains of a rubbing stone. L161/W100/T54mm. [4305] 2–3
13 Fragment. Very fine-grained, silty sandstone. From edge of stone with remains of very worn grinding surface. Possibly from same stone as 4305/2–3. L54/W42/T57mm. [4305] 4

From context [3535]:

14 Fragment. Coarse-grained sandstone. Sub-triangular-shaped piece with slightly concave grinding surface. Worn with glazed high spots. Other side roughly flat. L208/W201/T67mm. [3535] 1

The fragments are predominantly of fine-grained sandstone although there are also fragments of coarser-grained sandstone and a very fine, silty sandstone. All may have been obtained from local drift deposits, as may the nine fragments found during earlier excavations (Parker Pearson and Sydes 1997, 234). The earlier fragments all came from unstratified contexts, but it should be noted that six fragments came from the smaller enclosure, and three from the larger.

### 7.6.2 *Discussion*

Since the stones are fragmentary it is difficult to determine their original size and shape, although the majority appear to derive from the lower stones of saddle querns. No 12, however, comprising two joining fragments of very fine sandstone with a very worn, slightly convex grinding surface, is small enough to have been an upper or rubbing stone. The surviving grinding surfaces are flat, slightly concave or slightly convex and generally appear worn through use. No 1, four joining fragments of fine sandstone, seems to have been a neatly made lower stone. It is sub-rectangular with rounded sides that show evidence of having been pecked to shape and has an even base and a flat grinding surface that is particularly worn around the periphery. No 14 is from a thinner stone of coarse-grained sandstone. The surviving piece is sub-triangular in shape, with a slightly convex grinding surface, which is worn with glazed high spots.

Fourteen of the fragments, from at least two saddle querns, were found together in the same posthole [4301]. There was no space for the post itself and it is presumed that the pieces were inserted when it was removed. Three additional fragments of quern or rubbing stones were found in posthole [4305]. Saddle querns do not break easily and this, together with the fact that although the extant grinding surfaces generally

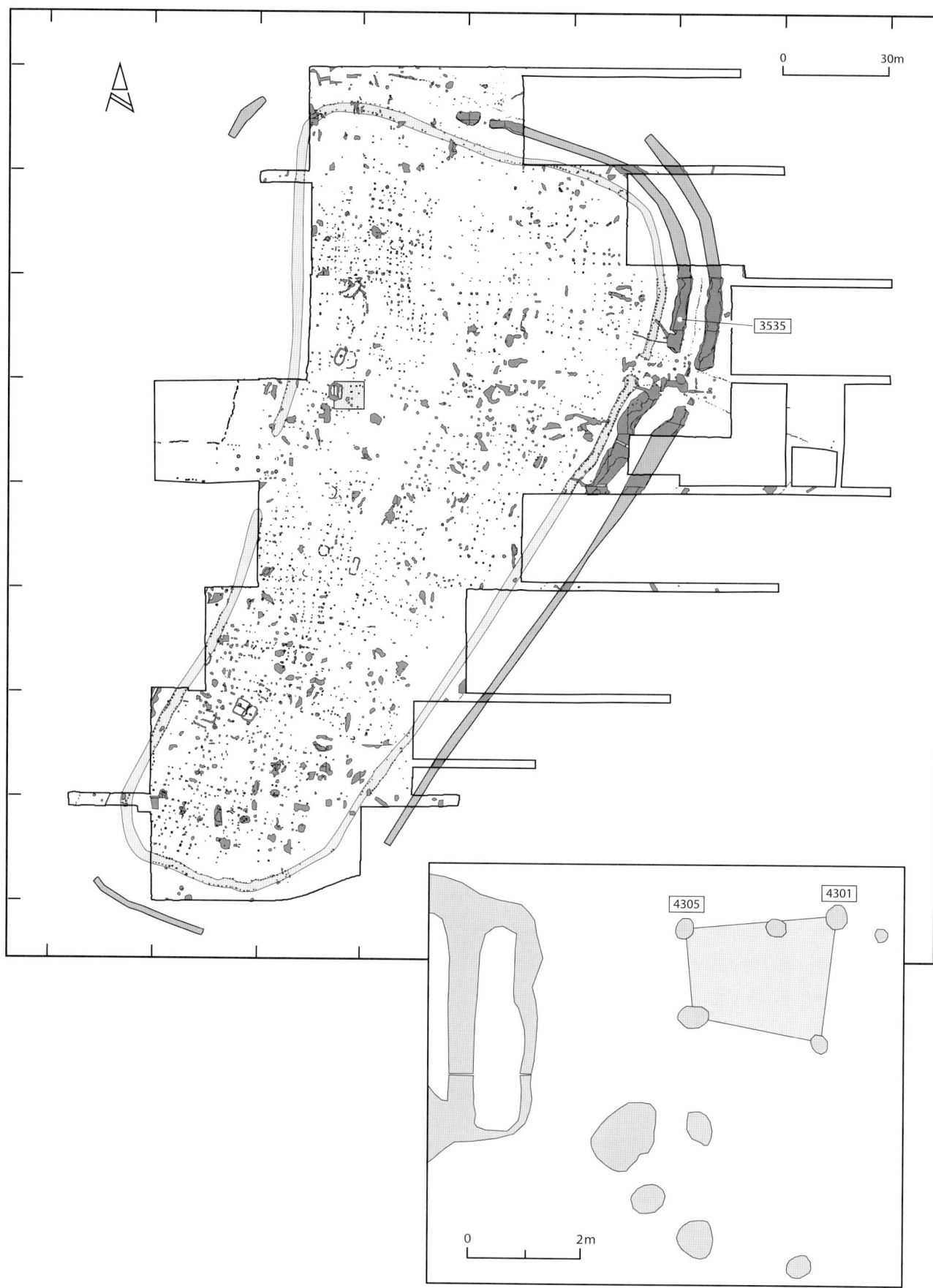

*Figure 7.6 Excavation plan 1998–2003: location of quern stones, and plan of possible four-post structure with postholes [4301] and [4305] containing quern stone fragments*

show evidence of use, most do not appear to have been worn out, suggests that their presence in the posthole is not the result of random reuse of discarded material but that the querns were deliberately broken and pieces chosen for burial. Fragmentary querns have been found at other sites such as Carshalton, Surrey, where pieces from five saddle querns were found in a late Bronze Age/early Iron Age pit. It was suggested that the breaking of such objects may have been an important part of the ritual associated with their deposition (Proctor 2002). The use of quern stone (fragments) in structured deposition has been noted elsewhere (eg Hill 1995a; Gwilt and Haselgrove 1997b). Saddle querns were predominantly used for grinding grain and they may have been perceived, therefore, as symbolic of grain and fertility. Postholes [4301] and [4305], together with [4295] and [4297], possibly form a four-post structure, although this example, if the inference is correct, is not as clear as other such structures on the site.

## 7.7 Antler weaving comb  *by Tina Tuohy*

One comb of red deer (*Cervus elaphus*) antler was recovered from the inner ditch terminal on the north side of the east entrance [3150] of the larger enclosure. The comb is in two pieces, which clearly fit together and have been treated as such. It is well preserved and has a circular butt above a narrow neck, which broadens towards the toothed end. There are 20 teeth remaining, all broken. These would have been fine and set close together when complete. The comb is undecorated and appears to have been polished when in use (Fig 7.7).

Length 102.5mm; width below butt 20mm; width above teeth 40.5mm. Antler varies in thickness from 7mm at the centre of the comb to 3.5mm above the teeth. Weight: 42g.

The comb is made from a portion of the beam of red deer antler, cut longitudinally to make maximum use of the outer bony layer of this material for the teeth and to minimise the problem of cancellous tissue. This tissue has been removed from behind the teeth prior to cutting to give a concave effect. It is noticeable on examination that the two outer teeth were worn down during wear. The inner teeth have been broken off at the base. This could have happened after deposition as one would normally expect some but not all of the teeth to be broken when the comb was discarded. Owing to lack of decoration it is not possible to estimate the length of the comb or to determine whether the teeth were recut. The surface still bears some evidence of the rough outer layer of antler but most has been smoothed to give a polished surface, now somewhat cracked through weathering.

The butt end of the comb is circular in shape. There is no perforation for suspension. Cut marks on either side of the butt at the neck of the comb are just visible but there are no corresponding marks on the front, so it is likely that these are the result of manufacture rather than wear.

Combs with circular butts are most common at the Somerset sites of Glastonbury and Meare and in Wessex, but it is recognised that relatively few antler combs are known from outside this area, which reflects the research biases (see section 1.3.1.1). A few come from East Anglia, one from Iron Age deposits at Harborough Cave, near Brassington in Derbyshire (Armstrong and Jackson 1923; cf Challis and Harding 1975, fig 5), but none from Yorkshire, where the butt shape is normally square and often decorated (Tuohy 1999, I:83 – 5; II: 42 – 3).

*Figure 7.7   Antler weaving comb*

## 7.8 Yew wood fragments  *by G Thomas*

The outer ditch terminal to the north of the eastern gateway yielded the only example of yew wood from the site. The wood finds from this ditch terminal were in poor condition in the loose ditch fill, being very desiccated and fragmentary, although during the excavation they appeared to form a grid-like arrangement of small planks or rods laid across and on top of each other. One of these wood samples was the piece of yew wood, a fairly knotty, short section of plank, 1015mm in length, 120mm in width and *c* 40mm thick but due to its condition it alas produced little further evidence from analysis.

## 7.9 Conclusions  *by R Van de Noort*

Earlier in this chapter (see section 7.2), the need to integrate data from across the traditional categories employed by archaeologists to structure their analyses and discussions of material culture was emphasised. This conclusion sets out to provide such an integrated approach to the finds from Sutton Common. Although all depositions were part of something like a coherent cosmology, these can be introduced here in two parts: the deposition of charred grain and quern fragments in a range of contexts, and the deposition of selected artefacts and human and animal bones at the entrances to the larger enclosure.

In chapter 6, we have argued that the construction of granaries at Sutton Common included the deposition of a small amount (a handful?) of charred grain in one or two of the postholes before the uprights were placed in the holes. The inclusion of a handful of charred grain into one or two postholes of granaries was explained in terms of structured deposition. Much has been written in the last decade about the meaning and significance of structured deposition. Joanna Brück (following Hill 1995a) has probably expressed the general denotation of this practice most clearly, describing these deposition practices as appearing to focus increasingly on concepts involving the idioms of transformation and regeneration, which were 'central cultural metaphors through which people conceptualised the passage of time, the production of food and other categories of material culture, and the creation of social agents' (Brück 2001, 158; see also Bradley *et al* 1994; Brück 1995; 1999). Studies of iron and iron working (eg Hingley 1997), human remains such as bog bodies (eg Van der Sanden 1996), and especially depositions in and around the house (eg Fitzpatrick 1994; Parker Parson and Richards 1994) and (enclosed) settlements (eg Hill 1995a), have reached similar conclusions. At Sutton Common, the deposition of charred grain in the postholes of granaries could be explained effortlessly using these idioms.

The depositions of quern stones, representing the 'opposite end' of the transformation and regeneration metaphors, seem to underpin this scenario. Postholes [4301] and [4305], which both produced fragments of quern stones, together with [4295] and [4297], could possibly have been the four corner-posts of a four-post structure. Alternatively, the quern stones could signify the use of the relevant granary for storing grain for consumption, rather than for sowing, and thus linking the storage of the grain with future consumption *via* the transformation process of the grinding of the grains. Unfortunately, no samples for plant macrofossil analysis were taken from these postholes (the four posts not having been identified as forming a four-post structure during the excavations), thus we are not able to exclude the co-occurrence of fragments of quern stone with charred grain in the said postholes. Few parallels have been found from Iron Age contexts which could demonstrate how widespread the structured deposition of quern stones was, but the excavations of the Breiddin hillfort in Shropshire produced a fragment of a heavy oval lower stone of a saddle quern used as packing in a posthole belonging to a conjectured Iron Age four-post structure (Musson 1991, 151).

The context of structured deposition may also be extended to the deposits of charred grain in pits and the ditches of the Sutton Common larger enclosure itself. Examples of the deposition of charred grain in these three types of contexts have been observed at many other sites in Britain (see section 6.6), and although the exact understanding of the significance of this practice may have varied from site to site, and from region to region, a common belief system or cosmology must have underpinned this practice.

The consideration of the deposition of selected material culture in enclosure ditches, and especially in ditch terminals near entrances, revisits the essence of late prehistoric enclosure itself. As argued earlier (see section 5.7), from the middle of the 2nd millennium BC phenomena including the surrounding of settlements and other foci of human activity with ditches and banks, the introduction of field systems, and the construction of linear boundaries and pit alignments, are considered to be interrelated. These activities have been linked to increased population pressure, and the need to express, physically and symbolically, land ownership or tenure. The ditch terminals around the eastern gateway were excavated with the specific objective of investigating the material culture that was anticipated to be found here (cf Haselgrove *et al* 2001, 10). This material could be taken as expressing the way in which people defined the transition from the internal '*cosmos*' to the external '*chaos*', or vice versa, with this ceremonial rather than practical gateway (see section 5.7), which acted as threshold or liminal space, and thus could be considered to elucidate aspects of their perception of the meaning and purpose of enclosure.

The sediments within the ditch terminals near the eastern gateway were intensively wet-sieved on site, and sampled for palaeoenvironmental analysis, thus providing integrated information on deposition, association, and context (for the palaeoenvironmental description, see section 5.6).The finds are listed in Table 7.2. Unfortunately, we do not have independent dating for the ditch sequences or the individual finds from them, as no material for dendrochronological dating was identified, and radiocarbon dating was considered unlikely to provide dates of sufficient resolution to improve the dating framework for this aspect of the work (see section 5.4.3). The detailed palaeoenvironmental studies of the shallow sequences in the ditch terminals show that these represent the natural succession sequences of wet ditches, with the developments commencing

**Table 7.2  Associations of finds in the ditch terminals near the eastern gateway**

| Description | Contexts/source | Material culture |
| --- | --- | --- |
| Inner ditch terminal to the south of the eastern gateway | [3493] [3492] [3319] | • piece of saddle quern<br>• 9 animal bone fragments<br>• trace of ?spelt grain<br>• oak charcoal |
| Inner ditch terminal, north of gateway | [3146] [3150] [3259] | • rim sherd of pottery |
|  | [3535] [3536] [3540] | • antler weaving comb |
|  | [3558] [3559] [3609] | • shaft fragment from human proximal radius on the left side<br>• charred cereal grains |
| Outer ditch terminal, south of eastern gateway | [3452] [3454] [3537] | None |
| Outer ditch terminal, north of eastern gateway | [3339] [3347] [3349] | • remains of two humans, including crania, mandibular fragments, an axis fragment and scapula fragment |
|  | [3588] [3597] [3600] | • 5 additional human fragments: 2 human incisors, a human canine and 2 human molars from the upper jaw, possible directly from the skulls?<br>• yew wood<br>• >200 animal bones and bone fragments |

immediately after the ditches had been constructed and had, naturally, filled with water. These developments represent decades rather than centuries. Furthermore, the presence of charred spelt and emmer in some of the uppermost layers of the short sequences implies an association with the deposition of charred grain elsewhere on the site. We can, therefore, assume reasonably safely that the human and animal bones, artefacts, and yew wood came from contexts that are contemporaneous with the use of the marsh-fort, and can be dated to the middle part of the 4th century BC.

The context of the finds is of some importance. None of the finds listed in Table 7.2 were found on the bottoms of the ditches, and therefore cannot be associated with the construction of the inner or outer ditches. As shown by the palaeoenvironmental analysis, soon after the digging of the ditches at Sutton Common, the ditch bottoms would have filled with ground water, and the unstable nature of the Lake Humber-derived sediments on the Common caused some bank erosion and silting of the ditches. Both the plant and insect macrofossil remains from the sediments originated in standing water, and wetland communities must have been present. The deposition of finds was made in these wet, half-overgrown ditches. This implies that these finds were either placed on one or more occasions marking the entering or leaving of the larger enclosure through this gateway by individuals or by processing groups, or it represents a closing deposit, signalling the end of the use of the site.

The depositions appear to some extent to follow the cosmological rules of depositions in the entrances of domestic dwellings (Fitzpatrick 1994) and the presence of the human remains to the north of the entrance in particular seems to be mirrored at many other enclosed sites of Iron Age date (Hill 1995b). However, the dipolar characterisation of the domestic house cannot easily be translated to the marsh-fort itself and, although different zones have been identified within its interior, divided by an imaginary line linking the two entrances, the use of the northern part of the marsh-fort appears to mirror that of the southern half. The 5 other human fragments from this terminal (2 human incisors, a human canine, and 2 human molars from the upper jaw) were probably directly derived from the crania in this deposit. The only other human bone came from the inner ditch terminal to the north of the eastern gateway, but the left humerus may not have been recognised for what it was at the moment of deposition. The animal bones from the same terminal present a 'normal' consumption pattern for Iron Age sites, and considering the absence of evidence of other occupation activity on the site, we could speculate that these bones are the result of an event such as a feast, or the introduction of the remains of such an event from outside the Common.

The finds of the (well-worn) antler weaving comb and the pottery rim from the inner ditch to the north of the eastern entranceway, and that of the piece of saddle quern in the inner ditch terminal opposite, are intriguing. These could indicate that the cosmological rules of depositions in the entrances extended to include a sharp conceptual *chaos-cosmos* divide, with the external ditches representing the former, and the inner ditches the latter. Admittedly, the number of artefacts supporting this statement is rather slight, and the observation is not universally mirrored on British enclosed sites of Iron Age date. The presence of charred cereal grains in both inner ditch terminals, and their absence in the outer ditches, could be understood to underpin this fundamental divide between the enclosed and encultured space and the exterior where nature reigned.

In addition to the structured depositions at the threshold of the marsh-fort and the deposition of charred grains and quern stones in its interior, we also recognise the deposition of artefacts into burials as a form of structured deposition. The second phase of activity at Sutton Common, described in detail below (see chapter 8), has produced only two examples that are believed to be grave or pyre goods: some glass beads and a gold ingot or part of a bracelet. In both cases, it is possible to interpret these specific grave goods in terms of transformation and regeneration.

# Notes

1 In the concept of non-human person, person refers to 'any entity, human or otherwise, which may be conceptualised and treated as a person' (Fowler 2004, 7). Thus animals with names and attributed traits such as loyalty or stubbornness, are non-human persons.

# 8 The mortuary rings

## 8.1 Introduction *by R Van de Noort*

This chapter presents the evidence from a second phase of activity, provisionally dated to the 4th to 2nd centuries BC, and comprising principally a series of small enclosures of simple geometrical shape from within the interior of the marsh-fort. These are believed to have played a role in mortuary rituals, but the evidence is anything but conclusive. We acknowledge that in earlier research, including our own excavations prior to 2003, excavation and sampling strategies were not sufficiently focused on the recovery of fragmentary cremated bone to fully realise the potential of this part of the research.

Much debate has been dedicated to the appellation of the small enclosures. Alternative suggestions to the concept that these features had a role in mortuary rituals were not found credible, even though their precise role remains somewhat elusive. For example, it is not impossible that the material from the narrow ditches was redeposited over burials placed on the surface, thus creating small but distinctive barrows, and the name 'barrowlet' has been suggested by one colleague (Powlesland 2005 and pers comm). However, such a term implies that burial preceded the digging of the small enclosure and construction of a mound. No stratigraphic or other archaeological evidence exists for this suggestion at Sutton Common, as any upstanding remains had been destroyed in the events since 1980 (see section 1.2.4). Furthermore, several ditches intersect each other in Trench 7, indicating that the structures were intended to be ephemeral and temporary rather than monumental and eternal. Thus we have opted for the term 'mortuary rings', adopting the element 'rings' from established work in late Iron Age funerary archaeology (eg Hill *et al* 1999) and using the element 'mortuary' to signal that the activities that took place within the rings were possibly related to remains of deceased (human and/or animal) persons but may, or may not, have involved any form of burial or formal deposition of such remains.

This chapter commences with the description of the archaeological features. This is followed by sections on dating, the cremated and burnt bone, and a description and discussion of the limited finds from the second phase activity at Sutton Common, the glass beads and the fragment of a gold bracelet or ingot, and closes with a discussion and conclusion.

## 8.2 Description of features *by H Chapman and W Fletcher*

### 8.2.1 Introduction

This second phase activity is characterised by at least twelve small circular, oval and square ditch-defined mortuary rings (Figs 8.1, 8.2). The precise function and intended three-dimensional form of these small mortuary rings is unclear, but the creation of an enclosed space through the digging of ditches may have formed an integral part of the funeral and burial ritual. The distribution of the mortuary rings is focused along the western edge of the larger enclosure, alongside the Hampole Beck palaeochannel. Stratigraphically these features post-date the four-post structures and other internal features within the marsh-fort.

### 8.2.2 The mortuary rings

The northernmost feature in this group (mortuary ring 1, comprising [2335] and [2336]) was a small oval enclosure measuring 3.9 × 2.5m and found during the 2002 excavations in Trench 2. What makes this shape unusual is that only four corner-segments had been created (or survived), leaving gaps down either side of 1.5m and at either end of 0.6m. No associated features were excavated although the eastern corners both clipped the edges of postholes belonging to a four-post structure. Sections excavated through this feature showed that the profile of each gully was reasonably similar: shallow at less than 0.2m, straight-sided, and with a level base.

Trench 3 revealed three related features. Within the north-western part of the trench, an amorphous feature (mortuary ring 2, [31529]) was identified within a patch of very soft sand and had been so heavily destroyed by animal activity that its shape could not be ascertained, although its overall dimensions were c 6 × 6m. The second feature (mortuary ring 3, [31453] and [31421]) was located within the south-western corner of the trench and consisted of a well-defined sub-rectangular, almost oval, ditch-like gully measuring 5.1 × 2.8m (4.3 × 1.9m internally), aligned north-northeast by south-southwest, and with ditches 0.3–0.5m wide. Adjoining the eastern side of this feature was another ditch forming a sub-circular enclosure which was apparently part of the same feature. This part had narrower ditches (0.2m wide) with overall dimensions of 5.0 × 3.7m. No stratigraphic relationship between

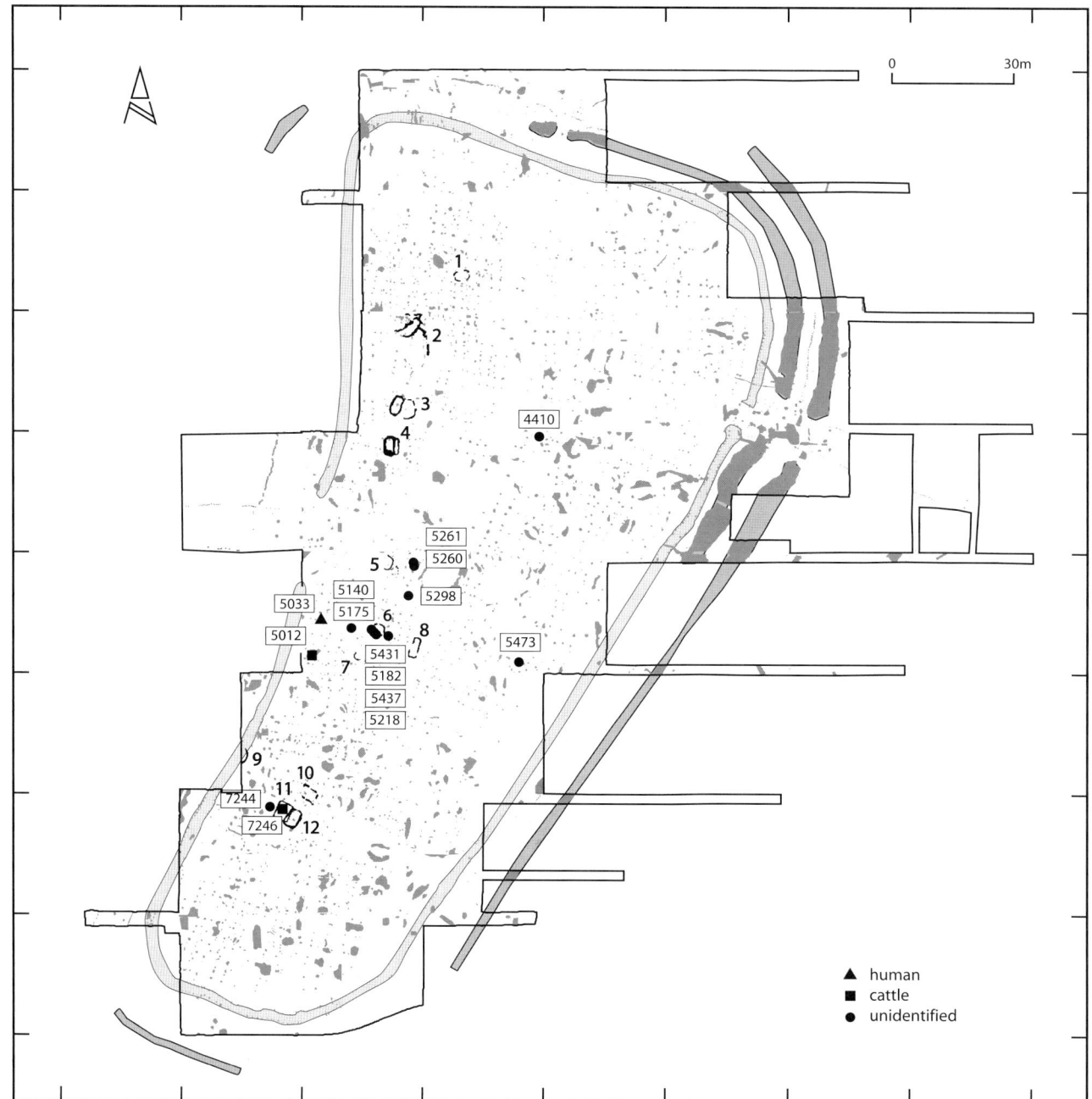

*Figure 8.1 Excavation plan 1998 – 2003: the mortuary rings, and contexts containing calcined or charred bone: human remains: [5123/5033], cattle remains: [5012] and [7246]; animal indet. remains: [4410], [5140], [5175], [5182], [5218], [5260], [5261], [5298], [5431], [5437], [5473], and [7244]*

the two sections of the enclosure could be ascertained. The profile of the ditch of the western feature was a broad, shallow 'U' shape, up to 0.1m deep. The eastern enclosure was not as clearly defined and in three sections the ditches had been destroyed. The internal dimensions measured 4.7 × 3.5m, and the ditch was more rounded here, with a possible terminal to the south. The ditches were very shallow and had a maximum width of a little over 0.3m.

Just 5m to the south in Trench 4, another similarly shaped sub-rectangular enclosure was excavated (mortuary ring 4, [4309]; Fig 8.3a). The interior measured 3.1 × 1.7m across but a pit or former posthole, which was found in the southern end, distorted this shape to the south. The ditches were better established, with broad U-shaped profiles and a width that varied from 0.4m to 0.6m. This feature also had an ephemeral extension on the eastern side, a narrow version of its neighbour with an interior measuring 3.5m long by 0.6–0.8m wide. The ditches here were very shallow, barely 0.2m at their deepest and between 0.4m and 0.1m across. The fills varied

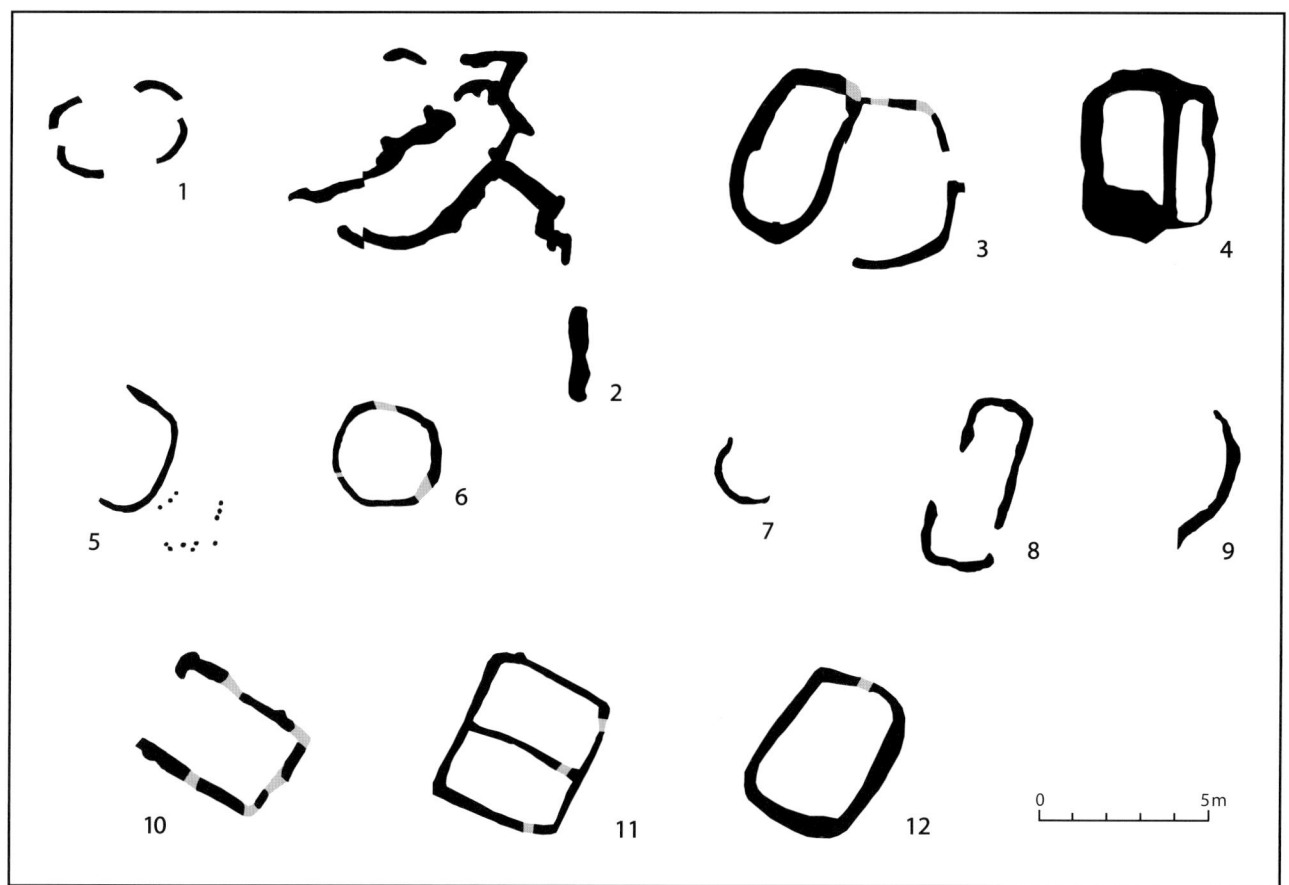

Figure 8.2  Plans of the mortuary rings from Sutton Common

and there was a hint from the variation in colours that one was earlier than the other, but the section evidence proved inconclusive.

Trench 5 contained four examples of the mortuary rings, displaying variation in morphology over a local area, including two semicircular ditches, a full circle, and a sub-rectangular structure. The northernmost feature (mortuary ring 5, [5223]) appeared to be part of a sub-rectangular structure, although the western portion was missing. This internal arch measured 3.0m long by 1.5m at its widest part, with a small shallow gully less than 0.2m deep. Immediately to the south-west of this ring was a stake-built structure such as a hut or temporary dwelling (see section 6.2.4), which was considered to be associated with the mortuary ring. However, no evidence other than proximity exists to confirm this association.

To the south a circular enclosure was identified (mortuary ring 6, [5182]; Fig 8.3b) with an average internal diameter of 2.75m. This feature was badly damaged and had been cut by the line of a modern fence (seen on the 1976 AP) which had two shallow ditches on either side traversing the site from north-west to south-east. A deep field drain had also been cut through it, some time in the last 30 years. The ditch of the mortuary ring was up to 0.3m wide and 0.15m deep, cutting one of the four postholes defining an earlier four-post structure, demonstrating its relatively later date. Within the fill of this structure, several glass beads were recovered (see section 8.5.1). The fill also contained calcined bone, which was considered to be of animal origin but could not be determined to species or element; additional indeterminable calcined bone was recovered from fill [5431] of posthole [5432], which was cut by [5182] (see section 8.4.2).

A very ephemeral, small half-circular feature (mortuary ring 7, [5133]) to the south-west of mortuary ring 6 measured 1.6m long and 0.8m at it widest part, with a single shallow ditch measuring less than 0.2m wide and deep. A sub-rectangular enclosure to the east (mortuary ring 8, [5284]), was formed from two 'fish hook'-shaped segments of ditch. The ditches ran around the ends of the feature and partly down either side, leaving an offset segment unexcavated. Once again the ditches were very narrow and shallow, being 0.3m wide and 0.05m deep.

Within Trench 6 was a semicircular section of a ditch (mortuary ring 9, [6003]) measuring 3.5 × 1.5m. This feature would presumably have originally been larger, as part of it remained unexcavated, outside of the trench. The western

*Figure 8.3 Photograph of: a) mortuary ring 4 (looking south); b) mortuary ring 6 (looking north)*

section of this enclosure would have originally run into the edge of the bank of the box rampart. Its lack of survival on this side might mean that the bank had collapsed by the time of the mortuary ring's construction, with the western edge of the mortuary ring either being constructed over the slumped bank and thus destroyed by bulldozing, or running up to it.

Straddling Trenches 6 and 7 was a rectangular ditch (mortuary ring 10, comprising [6120], [6119], [7323], [7320], and [7277]). Internally, it measured 3.9m (north-west by south-east) by 2.5m (south-west by north-east), with ditches up to 0.4m wide. To the south of mortuary ring 10 was a pair of mortuary rings, numbers 11 and 12, that overlapped one another, providing evidence of stratigraphy (Fig 8.4). Mortuary ring 11, the earlier of the two, was rectangular in plan measuring 4.7 × 3.8m ([7245] and [7262]) with the ditch between 0.3m and 0.4m wide. A further ditch cut the feature in near-equal halves, forming two symmetrical rectangular enclosures, each 3.4 × 2.0m internally. This dividing ditch cut through post [7269] that formed the south-east corner of a four-post structure ([7246], [7264], [7265], and [7269]), demonstrating a direct stratigraphic relationship whereby the mortuary ring postdated the four-post structure. In posthole [7246], the original post-packing of limestone chunks effectively surrounded the calcined bone and charcoal and was interpreted, during the excavations in 2003, as representing the *in situ* packing of the post of a four-post structure. This would suggest that the lower part of the post of this four-post structure had survived into the second phase of activity (in itself unsurprising on this site where much wood survived into the 21st century), and had been removed in order to reuse the posthole for the burial of the calcined bone and charcoal. The calcined bone that could be identified was a cattle radius (see section 8.4.2). Additional geoarchaeological analysis of thin sections from [7246] and [7269] showed that these contained ample burnt bone and charred plant remains (see section 8.4.3).

The later mortuary ring (mortuary ring 12, [7262]) was more oval in shape, measuring 4.6 × 3.5m, overlapping the eastern edge of ring 11. The ditch here was up to 0.5m wide. The overlapping of the ditches indicates that the first mortuary ring was not in use when the second was dug, and perhaps that it was not visible on the ground, reinforcing the interpretation of these features as ephemeral or temporary.

### 8.2.3 Other features

In addition to the twelve enclosures described here, at least ten other features were identified across the site that might also fall into the category of mortuary rings. These features were identified as paired spreads of a fill deposit arranged in broadly symmetrical patterns. For example, one feature ([4453] and [4454]) covered an area of 4.1 × 3.2m. It was formed from two

*Figure 8.4   Aerial photograph of mortuary rings 11 and 12 (looking north)*

deposits with opposing breaks, giving an oval shape in plan. The maximum width of the fills was 0.8m. Excavation of these features demonstrated them to be extremely shallow and insubstantial, without clear evidence of a cut. Lack of artefactual material makes it difficult to determine whether these features were related to the features believed to represent aspects of mortuary behaviour found elsewhere on the site. Alternatively, they might have been related to other grain-processing activities on site such as straw stacks, although at least two examples were demonstrated to overlap with the four-post structures, indicating that the two were not contemporaneous. The distribution of these features was across the whole area of excavation within the larger enclosure, in contrast to the mortuary enclosures which dominated its western edge.

### 8.2.4 Summary

The principal twelve identified mortuary rings displayed a range of styles and morphologies, including subdivided features and a range of geometric shapes and alignments. All of them had ditches in the region of 0.3–0.5m wide, with numerous breaks, although these are perhaps likely to be due to their fragmentary survival. The distribution of these features was between Trenches 2 and 7, inside the larger enclosure, and in each case on the western side of the sandy 'island'. This area is the highest part of the 'island', forming a slight ridge along the western bank of the enclosure. It seems likely that the choice of location for these features was both topographic (choosing the higher areas of the site) and respectful of the earlier marsh-fort site, with all enclosures located within the centre of the site, away from the northern or southern boundaries. The features were extremely ephemeral, perhaps even before they were truncated by more recent agricultural activity. This is also demonstrated by the over-cutting of mortuary rings 11 and 12, indicating that the earlier enclosure was not strongly visible on the ground when the second was constructed. Therefore, it seems likely that the enclosures had a short-lived function, providing perhaps a sacred area, or *temenos*, within which ceremonial funerary activities took place. Individually, the features did not act as memorials that could be visited at later times, but perhaps collectively, they altered the function of the site to create a large sacred area.

### 8.3 Dating *by D Hamilton, G Cook and C Bronk Ramsey*

Only cremation [7246] in mortuary ring 11 provided identifiable material suitable for radiocarbon analysis (two fragments of a cattle radius; see section 8.4.2). The two measurements (OxA–14609; 2229±27 BP and SUERC–6147; 2245±35 BP) are statistically consistent, and so a weighted mean has been taken before calibration (T' = 0.1; ν = 1; T'(5%) = 3.8; Ward and Wilson 1978). The resultant mean of 2235±21 BP gives a calibrated date range for the cremated animal remains of 390–200 cal BC (Fig 4.4). Stratigraphically, the bone deposit found in [7246] appears to represent the reuse of a posthole of a four-poster granary, and thus postdates the construction of this granary, which is thought to have taken place in the second quarter of the 4th century BC (see section 6.3).

## 8.4. Cremated and burnt bone

### 8.4.1 The human bone *by J McKinley*

#### 8.4.1.1 Introduction

Cremated bone from a single context was received for analysis, representing redeposited pyre debris from the fill of a posthole. Material from a further seventeen contexts believed to be cremation-related deposits had previously been subjected to assessment by the writer. All were found to comprise burnt, and occasionally unburnt, animal bone and were not related to human cremation or, at least, not directly so. A summary of the results is presented in Table 8.1. Full details of identifications are held in the archive.

The surviving depth of cut [5123], containing [5033], was 0.15m with clear truncation due to ploughing (see Fig 8.1).

#### 8.4.1.2 Results

The bone from posthole [5123] (fill: [5033]) was eroded with a chalky appearance and includes no trabecular bone. It has been demonstrated that

Table 8.1 Human calcined bone: summary of results

| context | cut | deposit type | bone weight | age/sex | pathology summary |
|---|---|---|---|---|---|
| 5033 | 5123 | rpd | 4g | subadult/adult >13 yr | |

KEY: rpd – redeposited pyre debris.

trabecular bone (eg articular surfaces and most of the axial skeleton) is the first to be lost in soil conditions adverse to bone survival (McKinley 1997a, 245; Nielsen-Marsh *et al* 2000). The former acidic nature of the Humber Lake-derived sediments on the Common will have had a detrimental effect on the bone where the matrix was in contact with it, and it is probable that some bone will have been lost as a result of the soil conditions. Posthole [5123] is located some 12m west of mortuary ring 6, and within 20m of mortuary rings 5 and 7.

### 8.4.2 The animal bone  by A Outram

Fourteen contexts containing charcoal with small fragments of cremated or charred bones were analysed, and two of these could be identified as of animal origin. The vast majority of these tiny calcined fragments could not be identified to species and element. The exceptions were two fragments from the proximal shaft of a cattle radius and a fragment of cattle molar. These identifiable fragments came from [5012] and [7246]. The unidentifiable fragments were from contexts [4410], [5140], [5175], [5182], [5218], [5260], [5261], [5298], [5431], [5437], [5473], and [7244] (see Fig 8.1).

Fill [5012] of small pit [5011] contained some limestone and charcoal and the calcined bone of a fragment of a cattle molar.

Context [7246] is a posthole of a four-post structure (the other three postholes being [7264], [7265], and [7269]) which lies within mortuary ring 11. The fill [7247] contained two identifiable fragments of a cattle radius, dated by radiocarbon assay to 390–200 cal BC (see section 8.3), as well as much limestone and charred grains (see section 6.5.1 and Table 6.1). This fill also contained ample charcoal and could possibly be interpreted as redeposited pyre debris within a posthole of a former four-post structure, even though no human remains were identified. The limestone from this posthole was thought to represent the *in situ* post packing (see section 8.2.2)

Of the other contexts containing fragments of calcined bone, all but one were broadly distributed in the area of the mortuary rings. The exception is fill [4410] of oval feature [4414], which contained ample charcoal and a calcined bone fragment which was too small to determine species or element, but was definitely not human. The feature, *c* 35m east of mortuary ring 4, is somewhat isolated from the distribution of mortuary rings and other features containing cremated or calcined material. Of the other features, [5182] is the fill of the ditch of mortuary ring 6, and [5431] is the fill of posthole [5432], which is located within mortuary ring 6. Contexts [5431] and [7244] also included charred grains (see section 6.5.1 and Table 6.1).

*Figure 8.5   Geoarchaeology: micrograph of bone material from [7246]/sample 53 (PPL)*

### 8.4.3 Geoarchaeology  by G Ayala

Two of the postholes attributed to the four-post structure within mortuary ring 11 were sampled ([7246]/sample 53 and [7269]/sample 52) in order to ascertain if both contained cremations. Micromorphological analysis of both features has revealed that the deposits contained high concentrations of charred bone material and charcoal (Fig 8.5), confirming the field interpretations of the presence of cremations (Table 8.2).

## 8.5   Finds from the second phase

### 8.5.1   Glass beads  by J Henderson

#### 8.5.1.1   Introduction

Glass was an exotic material used in quite specific ways in the complex society of Iron Age Europe. Glass beads and armlets were used to adorn the living and the dead. During the earlier part of the Iron Age in Britain much of the glass was imported from the Continent in the form of beads. However, an exceptional site for glass production in a European context is the Meare Lake Village in Somerset dating to the 4th to 2nd century BC, where glass beads were made using moulds and by winding glass filaments around metal rods. During the later part of the Iron Age, especially during the 1st century BC, glass was not only imported as beads but also as raw chunks of furnace glass. Thus, although we have evidence for secondary glass production (glass working) in both the earlier and later parts of the Iron Age, the evidence for fusing glass from primary raw materials (primary glass production) is lacking. This does not mean that it did not take place. For example, there is no clear evidence for the primary production of Hellenistic glass which occurred on

Table 8.2 Summary chart of major micromorphological features of the cremation burials of Trench 7

| Sample | Fabric type (context) | Micro structure & porosity | C/F Ratio & related distribution | Coarse fraction description | Micromass description (CPL) | Major pedofeatures |
|---|---|---|---|---|---|---|
| 7246–53 | 7246–53 | spongy, vughs, packing voids & channels | 75/25; geufuric | predominately quartz and plagioclase with rare mica | dusty amber clay with non-striated b-fabric | abundant bone and organic material, abundant charcoal with few typic fe nodules |
| 7269–52 | 7269–52 | spongy, vughs, packing voids & channels | 75/25; geufuric | predominately quartz and plagioclase with rare mica | dusty amber clay with non-striated b-fabric | abundant bone and organic material, abundant charcoal with few typic fe nodules |

a much larger scale than in contemporary Iron Age Europe. It is possible that evidence will eventually be found in Iron Age Europe, even if raw glass was also imported from the classical world to be worked in northern Europe.

The largest concentration of Iron Age glass in northern England has been found at Wetwang Slack (Dent 1982), but up to now, no evidence has been found for glass-working and bead production in the region. The evidence that has been found at Sutton Common, although on a very small scale, is important since it constitutes the first evidence for glass-working in the northern British Iron Age. It must be the tip of the iceberg: the production location, which is yet to be found, must have a much larger quantity of evidence. All the glass fragments from Sutton Common came from [5182], the fill of the ditch of mortuary ring 6.

#### 8.5.1.2 Description of the glass objects

Five objects of translucent cobalt blue glass were found:

Sample 1: an unperforated elongated bead;
Sample 2: an unperforated, unfinished elongated bead with a projecting glass filament;
Sample 3: half of an annular bead;
Sample 4: a globular 'sphere' which is probably an unfinished bead. It has one facet with an 'eye' created from annular opaque white glass. Opaque white glass is also visible in a second location and is presumably the remains of an 'eye'. There are two other possible locations for such eyes. According to Guido (1978), the bead types with eyes are either the earlier Iron Age Arras types I and II (class 1; *ibid*, 45–8) or the later Iron Age South Harting type (class 3; *ibid*, 49–50). Both bead classes have been found in northern England but the South Harting type is of the wrong size and shape. The Sutton Common bead comes closest to the Arras type I beads. However, even here, the match is not perfect;
Samples 5 and 6: two small fragments of glass.

#### 8.5.1.3 Scientific analysis

The chemical analyses, expressed in weight percent oxide, are given in Table 8.3.

#### 8.5.1.4 The glass technology

Chemical analysis of the glass was used to investigate its technology and especially the raw materials used to make it. The five chemical analyses indicate that all of the glass falls into the same compositional family. The glasses are all of a soda-lime-silica composition and all are coloured blue with a cobalt-rich mineral colorant. The raw material which is likely to have been used as a source of the alkali (soda) is natron, a mineral source which is associated with low magnesia, potassium oxide, phosphorus pentoxide, and chlorine impurities. Judging from the alumina content of the glasses (between 1.17% and 2.28%), the silica source was sand with mineral impurities such as feldspar that would have introduced the alumina. The lime (CaO) content was probably introduced as shell fragments in the sand. Therefore a two-part recipe is likely to have been used to make the glass: sand and natron.

This composition and the suggested raw materials are typical of Iron Age European glass. It has been tacitly assumed that glass was not manufactured from raw materials in Iron Age Europe but that raw glass, of which there are several examples from secure archaeological contexts, was imported and worked on individual sites to manufacture beads and armlets. In this case, presumably, chunks of raw blue glass would

## Table 8.3 Electron probe microanalyses of glass fragments

| Sample | Na2O | SiO2 | MgO | As2O3 | K2O | P2O5 | Al2O3 | Cl |
|---|---|---|---|---|---|---|---|---|
| 1 | 17.66 | 68.58 | 0.52 | ND | 0.81 | 0.08 | 2.28 | 0.81 |
| 2 | 19.42 | 65.21 | 0.55 | ND | 0.5 | 0.15 | 1.17 | 0.79 |
| 3 | 17.86 | 69.51 | 0.55 | ND | 0.49 | 0.1 | 2.22 | 0.77 |
| 4 | 16.27 | 67.12 | 0.7 | ND | 0.72 | 0.33 | 1.53 | 0.63 |
| 5 | 16.18 | 68.68 | 0.79 | ND | 0.79 | 0.13 | 1.98 | 0.62 |

| Sample | SO3 | PbO | CaO | TiO2 | SnO | BaO | Sb2O5 | Cr2O3 |
|---|---|---|---|---|---|---|---|---|
| 1 | 0.3 | ND | 6.72 | 0.03 | ND | 0.04 | 0.02 | ND |
| 2 | 0.43 | 0.64 | 7.78 | 0.15 | 0.04 | ND | 1.18 | ND |
| 3 | 0.29 | 0.15 | 6.72 | 0.07 | 0.02 | 0.05 | 0.09 | ND |
| 4 | 0.39 | 1.66 | 8.57 | 0.03 | ND | ND | 0.06 | ND |
| 5 | 0.23 | 1.06 | 6.97 | 0.05 | ND | ND | 0.03 | ND |

| Sample | MnO2 | Fe2O3 | CoO | NiO | CuO | ZnO | Totals |
|---|---|---|---|---|---|---|---|
| 1 | 0.4 | 0.64 | 0.11 | 0.03 | 0.33 | ND | 99.34 |
| 2 | 0.06 | 1.58 | 0.12 | ND | 0.07 | 0.11 | 99.96 |
| 3 | 0.23 | 0.57 | 0.13 | ND | 0.12 | 0.03 | 99.98 |
| 4 | 0.04 | 0.9 | 0.18 | 0.04 | 0.26 | 0.1 | 99.51 |
| 5 | 0.06 | 1.12 | 0.21 | ND | 0.31 | ND | 99.21 |

ND = Not Detected.

have been imported to manufacture the beads. Since cobalt-coloured glass was the most popular for the manufacture of Iron Age beads and armlets in Europe, there would have been established sources for raw blue glass. The outstanding question is where precisely the glass was fused from raw materials. It is most likely that the raw glass was imported from the Hellenistic world to the south, although without definite evidence for the manufacture of Hellenistic glass from primary raw materials we cannot be sure where it was made. It has been assumed that one production area would be the Levant, and certainly Hellenistic glass vessels were frequently made from highly coloured (yellow, blue or purple) translucent glass, the colours used for the manufacture of beads and armlets in Iron Age Europe.

Having said this, however, there is a strand of evidence which could suggest that glass was actually fused from primary raw materials in prehistoric Europe. The impurities associated with cobalt-rich minerals which are found in the Black Forest in Germany appear to have been used to colour Iron Age glass; Hahn-Weinheimer (1955) was one of the first to note this. Since a trans-Alpine European source of cobalt was used for coloration it can be argued that it is likely that at least the colorant was added to a glass melt in Iron Age Europe, and possibly that the full batch was fused in trans-Alpine Europe.

The Sutton Common blue glasses have all been coloured with a cobalt-rich mineral. The impurities which are likely to be associated with the cobalt use are: lead (oxide), antimony (trioxide), manganese (oxide), iron (ferric oxide), nickel (oxide), copper (cupric oxide), and zinc (oxide). Two kinds of cobalt-rich minerals have been discussed in the literature: manganese-rich and arsenic-rich. A complicating factor here is that there are potentially other sources of iron and manganese: ferric oxide could also be introduced as an impurity in the sand, and manganese oxide was introduced as a glass decoloriser in the 2nd century BC. Many other glass colours tend to contain manganese oxide after this date because it was used to produce a base glass to which colorants were added. The presence of manganese oxide can therefore obscure the manganese impurity associated with cobalt-rich colorant sources. Elevated manganese oxide levels have been detected in the unperforated elongated bead and the globular 'sphere' (which is probably an unfinished bead). This potentially could show that a manganese-rich cobalt source was used in two samples. The three samples with lower manganese oxide levels contain significantly higher lead oxide levels and somewhat higher iron oxide levels, so these patterns need to be explained.

#### 8.5.1.5 Dating

If we compare the relative levels of iron and cobalt oxides in these blue glasses with the patterns based on chemical analyses of securely dated Iron Age blue glasses from England (Henderson 1991, figs 6–9), an interesting pattern emerges. Only the unperforated, unfinished elongated bead with a projecting glass filament can be seen as falling into the group which dates to the 5th to 2nd century BC; the remaining four fall within a positively correlated group which dates to between the 1st century BC and 1st century AD. Indeed these four samples adhere so closely to a correlation line that we can refer to this (geologically) as a 'solution line'. This suggests strongly that these glasses with a mixture of 'high' and 'low' manganese oxide levels have been coloured with mineral-rich colorants obtained from different locations on the same cobalt-rich mineral outcrop, leading to this solution line. It can therefore be suggested that the elevated manganese oxide levels in Samples 1 and 3 are the result of being added as a decoloriser in the base glass. What is even more significant is that the unperforated, unfinished elongated bead with a projecting glass filament which has relative levels of iron and cobalt indicating that it is of an 'earlier' Iron Age date, is also the only one which contains elevated antimony trioxide. This is significant because manganese oxide replaced antimony trioxide in the 2nd century BC, so the presence of this level of antimony trioxide is a second reason for suggesting that the glass was made before the 2nd century BC.

#### 8.5.1.6 Conclusions

The glass finds from Sutton Common provide putative evidence of glass-working at or near the site. It is the only evidence of this activity in northern England at this date. The most comprehensive evidence to date for glass-working in early Iron Age Europe was found at Meare Lake Village, Somerset (Henderson 1991, 123–6), with a further (later) site through which raw glass was imported being Hengistbury Head, Hampshire. Hengistbury is important from this point of view because of it shows its articulation with the European Iron Age glass industry (Henderson 1991, 134–135). Evidence for glass-working has been found at sites such as Manching, Germany (Kunkel 1961; Gebhard 1989), and Aulnat 'La Grande Borne' (Henderson 1982; 1991), and Clermont-Ferrand 'Pâtural' in central France (Deberge et al in press).

As noted elsewhere (Henderson 1991), Iron Age glass-working can certainly be regarded as a specialised industry. It is clear from the level of perfection that was sometimes achieved in the manufacture of the range of glass objects found in Iron Age Europe that specialists were at work. The sensitive use of colorants in glass to achieve exactly the right balance of components *may* have taken place in the Hellenistic and early Roman spheres, but, as discussed above, there is still a possibility that glass was made from raw materials in Iron Age Europe. Although only one of the Sutton Common glass objects is a diagnostic Iron Age artefact (Guido 1978; Haevernick 1960), the chemical compositions are sufficiently diagnostic to be able to show that glass of mixed production dates is involved. Only one sample has early (pre-2nd century BC) characteristics; the unfinished eye bead has a later Iron Age chemical composition, which helps us to reject the possible Arras type I classification, based on a comparison with chemical analyses of Arras type I beads from Wetwang Slack. We are able to do this by comparing the impurities associated with the cobalt colorant used in the beads (Henderson 2000, 30–2).

We are seeing the products of mixed technological traditions being used as part of a ritual deposit. Perhaps the relative rarity of Iron Age glass-working and the high degree of specialisation involved led to the deposition of such debris in a special sacred context.

### 8.5.2 *A gold bracelet or ingot fragment*
*by J D Hill*

#### 8.5.1.1 Introduction

The gold bracelet or ingot fragment was found by Ian Stead who undertook the systematic metal detector survey of the site (Fig 8.6). The find was made, according to established tradition, on the very last day of the final excavation campaign, in the spoil of Trench 5 after the trench had been reinstated by bulldozer. It is not possible to associate the find to a particular context, but the method of excavation and subsequent restoring of the trenches allows the pre-excavation location of this fragment to be determined as the westernmost part of Trench 5. The association of the gold bracelet or ingot fragment with the second phase activity at Sutton Common is therefore, at best, tentative.

#### 8.5.1.2 Description

A ribbon or thin bar of gold 73mm long, 9mm wide and 1.25mm thick, originally with a curved profile

*Figure 8.6 The gold bracelet or ingot*

on an arch of an approximate diameter of 80–90mm, but sharply bent 43mm from the squared-off end. The object appears to have been cut from a larger object. The squared-off end is probably the original end; the other is less regularly finished off. The object is relatively poorly finished compared with other prehistoric gold objects and has ample evidence for hammering and working across all surfaces. Analysis across the surface of the object suggests the object is made from a number of originally different pieces of gold worked into a single piece, rather than from a single melt, or possibly from a poorly mixed melt created from different small pieces of gold (Table 8.4). The profile of the ribbon or thin bar suggests it was part of a bracelet-shaped object, although the lack of a fine finish suggests either the original object was an unfinished bracelet or it was part of a bracelet-shaped ingot.

#### 8.5.1.3 Discussion

Gold objects, other than coins, are extremely rare from Iron Age Britain (Jope 2000; Stead 1985; 1991b). Apart from the well-known gold torcs from eastern England and the West Midlands, there are very few other Iron Age gold objects from Britain. The torcs, coins, and most other gold objects probably or definitely date to after *c* 250/150 BC. Most of the twisted multi-strand torcs, such as the finds from Snettisham, Ipswich, and Glascote, probably date to after 250/200 BC on stylistic grounds, although secure dating is lacking for all except the Snettisham Great Torc. Gold coinage began in southern England from 175/150 BC onwards. The small number of gold brooches (fewer than six), chains, bracelets, and ingots all probably or definitely date to after 250/150 BC.

Although not closely dated, this fragment from Sutton Common is probably older than 200/150 BC and so adds to the very small number of earlier dated Iron Age gold objects from Britain. These are extremely few in number. They include parts of gold torcs from Snettisham that can be suggested to be this early in manufacture on stylistic grounds, but were probably deposited much later. There is the gold openwork wire ring from Queen's Barrow, East Yorkshire (Stead 1979), and a small gold object found during recent investigations at Fiskerton, Lincolnshire (M Parker Pearson, pers comm). There is also some gold foil on the pin from Cart Burial 2 at Wetwang Slack (Dent 1985).

If this object is part of an ingot and not part of a finished object, it might be related to later deposits of broken objects ('scrap') and complete ingots or parts of ingots seen at a small number of sites such as Snettisham, the Winchester hoard, Essendon, Hertfordshire, and the East Leicestershire hoard (eg Stead 1991b). While sometimes seen as the deposition of wealth in a raw form, the presence of broken parts of gold objects and ingots might also be related to the deliberate deposition of a range of other material in Iron Age deposits that appear to be linked to the theme of the transformation of materials, the natural world, and people (Hill 1995a).

### 8.6 Conclusions *by R Van de Noort*

The nature of the second phase activity at Sutton Common is anything but clear. Even though the

Table 8.4 Electron probe microanalyses of the gold bracelet or ingot

| Analysis | Au | As | Cu | Ag | Fe | Sn | Pd | Pt | Pb | Total |
|---|---|---|---|---|---|---|---|---|---|---|
| 1 | 91.016 | 0.000 | 0.000 | 6.588 | 0.230 | 0.000 | 0.000 | 0.000 | 0.000 | 97.834 |
| 2 | 83.603 | 0.000 | 0.265 | 13.364 | 0.133 | 0.000 | 0.000 | 0.000 | 0.000 | 97.365 |
| 3 | 93.169 | 0.000 | 0.000 | 6.200 | 0.145 | 0.001 | 0.000 | 0.000 | 0.000 | 99.515 |
| 4 | 90.766 | 0.000 | 0.232 | 9.519 | 0.080 | 0.008 | 0.000 | 0.000 | 0.000 | 100.605 |
| 5 | 95.061 | 0.000 | 0.000 | 3.893 | 0.189 | 0.011 | 0.000 | 0.000 | 0.000 | 99.154 |
| 6 | 79.781 | 0.000 | 0.966 | 16.835 | 0.105 | 0.000 | 0.000 | 0.000 | 0.000 | 97.687 |
| 7 | 90.141 | 0.000 | 0.389 | 9.461 | 0.050 | 0.000 | 0.000 | 0.000 | 0.000 | 100.041 |
| 8 | 93.721 | 0.000 | 0.000 | 6.298 | 0.133 | 0.000 | 0.000 | 0.000 | 0.000 | 100.152 |
| 9 | 82.621 | 0.000 | 0.000 | 14.197 | 0.230 | 0.005 | 0.000 | 0.000 | 0.000 | 97.053 |
| 10 | 88.252 | 0.000 | 0.000 | 9.042 | 0.076 | 0.000 | 0.000 | 0.000 | 0.000 | 97.370 |
| 11 | 93.923 | 0.000 | 0.000 | 6.030 | 0.051 | 0.038 | 0.000 | 0.000 | 0.000 | 100.042 |
| Average | 89.278 | 0.000 | 0.168 | 9.221 | 0.129 | 0.006 | 0.000 | 0.000 | 0.000 | 98.802 |

use of the term 'mortuary rings' was considered justified in this context, the lack of spatial correlation between these features and identifiable human remains has left many questions unanswered. However, rather than leaving these features unexplained, this conclusion sets out to explore the hypothesis that the fragmentary and unidentifiable charred bone remains were the result of mortuary rituals, and that the glass beads from [5182], the fill of the ditch of mortuary ring 6, were some sort of pyre goods.

The poor spatial correlation between the mortuary rings and identifiable human remains may be a result of recent processes. For example, it is possible that some of the most ephemeral ditches of the mortuary rings may have been obliterated during two decades of ploughing, thus leaving apparently isolated deposits of redeposited pyre debris in deeper postholes (eg posthole [5123]), but this is not demonstrable. It is certainly the case that the limited sampling of features (see section 3.2.4) and the late recognition of the ditches as possible mortuary features are factors which would have contributed to the lack of such associations. In effect, none of the mortuary rings contained identifiable human remains, but reused posthole [7246], located within ring 11, included calcined, possibly cremated, cattle bones. We must, however, also consider the possibility that this poor spatial correlation may in fact reflect local burial practices in the middle Iron Age. Numerous tiny fragments of calcined bone were seen in several of the ditches of the mortuary rings, and the fill of mortuary ring 6 [5182] included calcined animal bone material. If the mortuary rings had been dug prior to the deposition of pyre material, and this was simply placed or scattered within the enclosed space without the subsequent construction of a barrow or mound, then the transport of the smallest calcined bone fragments into the ditches through the action of water and wind is straightforwardly explained. Dominic Powlesland (2005, 38) provides an alternative suggestion for the similar structures at Heslerton in the Vale of Pickering, namely that the cremation remains could have been incorporated in a small mound that occupied the centre of the mortuary ring.

In other words, the hypothetical burial practice at Sutton Common could have involved the cremation of (selected) deceased person(s) on a pyre elsewhere in the landscape. We are reasonably confident that these included human and 'non-human persons', but in terms of bone remains, only the latter can be proven. The pyre debris would have been collected and taken to the marsh-fort. Here, an area was defined through the digging of a narrow, steep-sided ditch forming a basic geometric shape such as a circle, rectangle or oval, in what we have named a mortuary ring. This may have served as a sacred area or *temenos*. The pyre debris was subsequently redeposited within the enclosed area. In certain instances this may have involved the reuse of existing postholes after the remains of the post had been removed, but on other occasions, the pyre debris may have been simply placed or scattered within the area enclosed by the mortuary ring. Rain and wind would have dispersed the pyre debris, resulting in the inclusion of calcined bone fragments in the surrounding ditch fills. It is pertinent to recall that the only 'grave goods' (or pyre goods) found in context, that is the five glass objects and fragments (see section 8.5.1), all came from [5182], the fill of the ditch of mortuary ring 6, and may have found their way into the ditch as part of the deposition or scattering of pyre debris. Cremated remains may have been deposited elsewhere within the larger enclosure without the construction of mortuary rings (eg [5123]), but possibly utilising elements of the former marsh-fort to create distinct and separated spaces. No evidence exists for the burial of the pyre debris under mounds, and if these ever existed, they went unnoticed in the archaeological excavations preceding 1980 (Fig 8.7). As stated previously, the archaeological evidence is not robust enough to present this as anything more than a hypothesis.

The nearest parallel to the mortuary rings at Sutton Common are the so-called 'barrowlets' found near Heslerton in the Vale of Pickering (Powlesland 2005). These features have been dated to the late Iron Age and Roman period on the basis of pottery from the ditches. Geophysical survey and excavations have shown many similarities, with the (mostly circular) examples from Heslerton being of comparable size and with the narrow, steep-sided ditches including fragments of charred bone and charcoal. As was the case at Sutton Common, the rings sometimes had openings to one side, and the frequent intersections indicate the short-lived or ephemeral function of the features. The discovery of post settings in the base of one of the barrowlets could indicate the use of timber shuttering or vertical planking to emphasise the separateness of the area thus enclosed (*ibid*, 38).

The use of ditches in Iron Age cemeteries has been observed in many other places. In nearly all cases, ditches are linked to mounds which were constructed over the burial. Iron Age barrows did not compare, in terms of size or monumentality, with their Neolithic and early Bronze Age precursors and the mounds are invariably slight. For example, the 'Arras'-type square-ditched burials from East Yorkshire were covered by low mounds flattened over many centuries by ploughing, with some evidence suggesting that this had already happened in the Roman period (Stead 1991a, 6). The mounds at the cemeteries on Skipwith Common, at just over 30km the nearest Iron Age cemetery to Sutton Common, survive in the local woodlands, but are difficult to spot unless one knows where to look (Stead 1961; Finney 1994). The five Iron Age barrows at Kirkby la Thorpe in Lincolnshire were equally small (Bonnor and Allen 2000), and the reconstructed mound profiles of the Hinxton Rings in the Cam valley in Cambridgeshire are only 0.6m high (Hill *et al* 1999, 249). When considering the ring-ditches and mounds of Iron Age burials, we should not explain these in terms usually used for Neolithic and Bronze Age monuments. Rather, we should reflect on the ephemerality of much of the middle Iron Age mortuary rituals (see section 10.4).

Where, in previous research, ring-ditches have been proposed without mounds, the ditches include causeways, or narrow openings, such as is the case with the two circular ditches at the Arras-type cemetery of Kirkburn on the Yorkshire Wolds and the cremation cemetery at Westhampnett, West Sussex (Stead 1991a, 25; Fitzpatrick 1997b). These causeways could be interpreted as entrances, implying the use of ditches as a means of creating a separated space for the burial or other rituals, and would have probably been excavated in advance of these rituals taking place. Any grave-covering mound would have been an addition at a later point in time. Several mortuary rings from Sutton Common display interruptions that could be interpreted as causeways. Bearing in mind the survival of the mortuary rings, it can nevertheless be shown that ring 1, the appendage of ring 3, and ring 10, all have four interruptions each, and ring 8 has two interruptions, but that rings 6, 10, and 11 all had closed ditches. Whatever significance is attributed to the causeways, it is obvious that their inclusion did not constitute a uniform practice at Sutton Common.

Hill *et al* (1999, 265) wonder if the significance of ring-enclosed Iron Age burials can be found in their interrelationship with circular domestic architecture. On the basis of the Sutton Common cemetery, it could be suggested that not too much significance should be placed on the shape of the mortuary rings in local burial custom. At Sutton Common the ditches vary in shape and similar variability has been noted elsewhere, even at several classic Arras-type cemeteries, despite the predominance of the square-ditched burials. For example, the cemeteries of Rudston, Garton Station, and Kirkburn included some circular ring-ditches among the square-ditched burials (Stead 1991a, 5–28). The Kirkby la Thorpe

*Figure 8.7 Reconstruction of the suggested mortuary rituals at Sutton Common: pyre debris is scattered within one of the mortuary rings*

cemetery in Lincolnshire similarly included two round and up to three square barrows (Bonner and Allen 2000), and the five circular rings making up the known extent of the Hinxton late Iron Age cemetery seem to form an exception rather than the rule (Hill *et al* 1999).

Within the context of the late Iron Age in northern and eastern England, the cremation of deceased persons and subsequent burial of pyre debris as seen at Sutton Common is not exceptional. For example, the square-ditched barrows at Skipwith Common were constructed over both inhumed bodies and redeposited pyre debris (Finney 1994). At some distance to the south, cremations are known both from the rich 'Welwyn'-type burials and cemeteries of the Northern Aylesford-Swarling group in Bedfordshire, Cambridgeshire, and Suffolk (Whimster 1981, 147–66; Hill *et al* 1999). Although the archetypal Arras-type cemeteries of East Yorkshire were used extensively for the burial of uncremated bodies (Stead 1991a), some exceptions exist from this area as well, for example Riggs Farm and Thorganby (Challis and Harding 1975, 167).

The two identifiable bone fragments from fills [5012] and [7247], interpreted as possible redeposited pyre debris, were both from cattle. This echoes, to some extent, the burial or disposal of human and animal carcasses in ditch terminals, pits, and wells in southern England, a practice which is interpreted as forming part of the rituals of feasting and sacrifice (Hill 1995a; 1996), but the treatment of selected animals within cremation rituals requires an alternative explanation. If our interpretation of these contexts is correct, then we may presume that these animals were perceived in the late Iron Age as 'non-human persons', that is they had an identity which made them worthy of a treatment after death that was also used for, presumably selected, human persons (Ingold 2000; Fowler 2004). In the case of an agrarian community, we could imagine that the cattle in question were used as plough animals, and had been attributed names and characters not unlike pets in the modern era. Sutton Common would not be the only cemetery where animals were treated as 'non-human persons', even if their cremation is unparalleled. For example, the excavations of the Arras site at Kirkburn (Site–2) on the Yorkshire Wolds included two horse inhumations (Stead 1991a, 27, 144–7). Intriguingly, these burials were surrounded by slight ring-ditches (*c* 3.5 × 4.5m and 4.5 × 5m), rather than square-ditched enclosures, which would reflect different practices in the local burial custom. At Garton Slack, on site VII, also on the Yorkshire Wolds, the skull and articulated limb bones of an ox were found in a square-ditch cemetery, albeit this example was discovered in a shallow pit within a semicircular enclosure, and on nearby site V, burials of an ox and a sheep were found within a ring of narrow deep pits (Challis and Harding 1975, 169). The inclusion of animal bones in cremation burials has been observed elsewhere (eg Fitzpatrick 1997b; Hill *et al* 1999, 249), but these cases relate to the inclusion of (uncharred) cuts of meat. It is, in this context, appropriate to note that the cuts of meat included as pyre goods in cremation and inhumation burials are invariably pork and mutton or lamb, but beef or horse are never represented as grave offerings (eg Legge in Stead 1991a, 140–4; Hill *et al* 1999, 252). This reinforces the suggestion that the calcined cattle bones from Sutton Common should not be interpreted as pyre goods, but were instead the focus of the burials.

It has, for some time, been recognised that many Iron Age sites seem to reuse older monuments (eg Hingley 1999; Bradley 2002). Previous literature has focused on examples where the time difference was great, and especially the reuse of Neolithic and early Bronze Age upstanding monuments in the Iron Age has been highlighted, such as the late Iron Age Uley shrine in Gloucestershire, constructed on top of a Neolithic long barrow or mortuary enclosure (Woodward and Leach 1993). The reuse of the marsh-fort as a cemetery at Sutton Common must be considered as an example of such reuse of an existing monument. At Grimthorpe on the Yorkshire Wolds, we note a similar reuse for late Iron Age burials in the (presumably) hillfort, where a richly furnished weapon burial was found in the bottom of the ditch of the hillfort (Stead 1968).

One final thought that should be considered here is whether or not we should seek a direct association of the cemetery with the granaries and the ritual of food storage, or with the whole marsh-fort as an ancestral monument. Richard Bradley (2005; see also below, section 10.3), has recently argued for the occurrence of a significant shift from the ritualisation of warriors and weapons in the early and middle Bronze Age, to the ritualisation of agriculture/growing and storage of food in the late Bronze Age and Iron Age. This may be reflected in the function of the Sutton Common marsh-fort, but is this also the case for the second phase activity? A number of mortuary rings definitely (rings 5, 10, 11, 12, and 13) or possibly (rings 4 and 6) occupy the area of former four-post granaries, whilst the remaining mortuary rings are all situated within a few metres of four-post structures. The reuse of a granary posthole [7246] for the reburial of charred animal bone and charcoal implies a direct association between the rituals surrounding food storage and mortuary behaviour. In this case, it seems that the (remains of) one of the granary's upright timbers had been removed carefully, leaving the limestone post-packing and charred grain deposit intact, before the charred remains were inserted.

Several aspects of the second phase at Sutton Common can also be found across the North Sea in the Low Countries. For example, the coexistence of circular, square, and rectangular ditches, with and without central cremation burials, are known from a large number of excavations (Hessing and Kooi 2005, 634–5) and in several instances these cemeteries were found adjacent to older burial monuments and occupying areas previously used for granaries, as noted in the cases of Someren-Waterdael and Lent-Laauwiksstraat. Evidence for the practice of scattering ashes, however, was not found here.

The scattering of pyre debris hypothesised for Sutton Common may have formed a part, and possibly only a small part, in the social and ritual practices that could have started even before death, and would have had the cremation of the deceased as probably the focal point of the funerary process (eg Parker Pearson 1999, 6–7; Williams 2003). The activities inside the mortuary rings were ephemeral and transitory in nature. This aspect of the ritual transformation and destruction of the body was not intended to create a monument in the landscape, rather the events were designed to contribute to social memory. This was probably greatly enhanced by the selection of the location, within the former marsh-fort, which strengthened any connotation with the ancestors and with the ritual of food production and storage.

# 9 The marsh-fort's contexts

## 9.1 Introduction  by H Chapman and W Fletcher

The Sutton Common marsh-fort, however one interprets its meaning and significance, can only be fully appreciated in a broader geographical context. This includes a regional context comprising parts of the current South and West Yorkshire. This region was the likely source of the timber and stone used in the construction of the site and, most probably, as the place where the people who built the marsh-fort lived. In this region, the principal advances in our understanding of Iron Age archaeology come from planning-related surveys, evaluations, and assessments (eg Chadwick 1999; Roberts *et al* 2001), alongside some smaller-scale research projects. The accumulated fragmentary evidence reveals a cultural landscape that was increasingly developed during the Iron Age (see section 9.2).

The 'grand narrative' in British Iron Age archaeology appears for most to be something of the past, and the importance of regional and multiple 'archaeologies' has been emphasised by many (see 1.3.1). However, at the same time as national and supra-national generalisations of the socio-political nature of Iron Age society have been rejected, the existence of cosmologies or belief systems that result in often striking parallels in the archaeological records of distant regions has become widely acknowledged (eg Parker Pearson and Richards 1994; Giles and Parker Pearson 1999). Widening our search for such parallels, and considering a national context for Sutton Common, it is obvious that the limits of the basic sets of belief and belief systems that we observe in the Iron Age extend in unexpected directions. The existence of marsh-forts elsewhere in the British Iron Age is a case in point (see section 9.3).

## 9.2 Local and regional contexts: overview of the Iron Age in the broader region  by H Chapman

### 9.2.1 Local context — site and landscape setting

The Iron Age cultural landscape within the vicinity of Sutton Common closely reflects the different geological units (see section 4.2.1). In part this may be due to the original choice of site location, with more sites located on the better-drained areas with lighter soils, although it is also likely to reflect themes of archaeological visibility. It is widely understood, particularly in terms of aerial reconnaissance and the development of cropmarks, that the visibility of archaeological remains relies on differential moisture retention between archaeological features and the surrounding soils. In the case of the well-drained geologies such as the sandstone and gravel areas, the development of cropmarks is optimal, whilst in contrast the high water tables of the Levels restrict the potential for crop marks to be generated (Jones and Evans 1975; Riley 1982; 1983). Furthermore, the accreting nature of some areas of the wetland landscape means that sites can become buried, restricting their visibility to both aerial and ground reconnaissance. However, at one possible site directly south of Sutton Common, adjacent to a drain named Black Sike on Ordnance Survey mapping, a small group of cropmarks indicative of a possible field system has been recorded from aerial photographs (Head *et al* 1997, 233). Here, a single linear ditch extends from east to west with at least two other ditches crossing it at right-angles demarcating possible fields. The date of this feature is unknown, and fieldwalking across the area has failed to produce any artefactual material, although morphologically it would not appear out of place in an Iron Age context.

Within the wetland landscape of the Humberhead Levels, evidence of Iron Age activity is extremely restricted. Until very recently, Sutton Common was the only Iron Age 'site' known from the area, or from the islands within the Humber wetlands more broadly (such as the Isle of Axholme; Fig 9.1), despite concentrated archaeological survey within the area (Van de Noort 2004a). It has been noted that this absence from the archaeological record might be a result of differences in recording cropmark features on morphological grounds, particularly in relation to the Isle of Axholme (Van de Noort and Davies 1993). However, the potential for new discoveries of Iron Age sites may have to be reconsidered; in 2006, Peter Robinson of Doncaster Museum (pers comm) identified the cropmarks of a large lowland enclosure of a size comparable to the larger enclosure of the Sutton Common marsh-fort on Potteric Carr, south of Doncaster, a landscape also on the very edge of the Humberhead Levels. This site appears to have two or three ditches, and includes a multivallated entranceway facing south-east. On the basis of its morphology and location, it could be another marsh-fort.

The most dramatic evidence for Iron Age or later prehistoric activity is in the form of the extensive field systems that focus on the areas of Triassic Sherwood Sandstone and glacial sands and gravels on the south-east side of the River

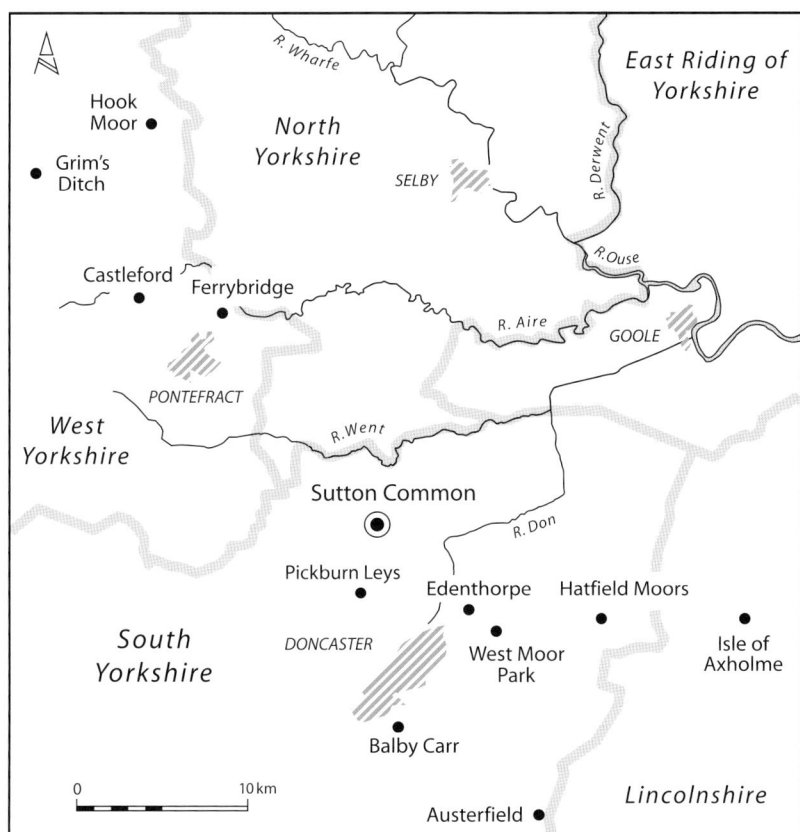

*Figure 9.1   Sutton Common in its regional context, showing the principal sites mentioned in the text*

Don, starting c 6km away from Sutton Common. These cropmark remains were first noticed during flying in 1971 and 1972, and were reported the following year (Riley 1973). They were again published, but in greater detail, in 1980 as part of a larger study of cropmarks in South Yorkshire and North Nottinghamshire (Riley 1980). These landscapes of prehistoric and Romano-British field systems have been gradually added to during the intervening years, through additional aerial survey, geophysical survey, and large-scale topsoil stripping in advance of development, most notably within areas where they have not been previously noted from aerial reconnaissance (Roberts in prep). Riley classified these field systems into three different types, with the most distinctive being the 'brickwork pattern' (Riley 1980), characterised as a coaxial, regular pattern of rectangular fields. The dating and interpretation of these field systems has always been a point of conjecture, particularly due to the low levels of Iron Age pottery normally encountered within South Yorkshire (Chadwick 1997). Thus, whilst ceramic remains shows continued use of the field systems in the Roman period, the earlier activity that can be identified stratigraphically remains largely undatable through the absence of pottery (eg Chadwick and Cumberpatch 1995). Despite this, Riley's original interpretation of these landscapes suggested that the brickwork pattern is likely to have been a later addition to a more open landscape characterised by sinuous routeways connecting nucleated settlements defined by clusters of enclosures (Riley 1980).

Where excavations have taken place within the areas of the field systems of Yorkshire and Nottinghamshire, most sites have revealed evidence of Romano-British period activity (eg Magilton 1978; Samuels and May 1980; Cumberpatch 1993; Atkinson 1994; Chadwick and Cumberpatch 1995; Roberts in prep), most commonly dating to between the 2nd and 4th century AD, although a carinated bowl probably dating to the earlier Romano-British period that was found at Edenthorpe, South Yorkshire, has a form derived from later Iron Age styles (Chadwick and Cumberpatch 1995). Evidence for late Iron Age activity was discovered from Pickburn Leys, near Doncaster (Cumberpatch 1993), but otherwise prehistoric material has remained rare. However, increasing numbers of excavations across these Romano-British sites are beginning to demonstrate a complex history of reworking and maintenance. This indicates a certain longevity which suggests these sites may have been in use from an even earlier date and that the field systems are more likely to have been destroyed by later activity (Chadwick and Cumberpatch 1995, see below). Similarly, this points to a degree of continuity of settlement and approach to the landscape throughout the later prehistoric and Roman periods. This has been identified at Austerfield, near Bawtry, where a Roman road cuts obliquely across the fields. The road is likely to date to the AD 70s (Margary 1957), providing a *terminus ante quem* for the original construction of the fields.

Other than questioning the dating of these field systems, past and current research has moved towards questioning the function of these sites. Three main types of field system have been identified on the basis of morphology: nucleated, irregular, and brickwork (Riley 1980). Of these, most interest has been focused on the brickwork patterns. These have been interpreted as being too large for ploughing (Riley 1980) and this, coupled with the limited amount of pottery from fieldwalking, has led to a conclusion that they represent pastoral activity (Branigan 1989), or at least a mixed farming practice (Roberts in prep). However, other reasons for the limitations in ceramic evidence have been outlined above. More recent research has been concerned with the theoretical interpretations of landscape which are based upon structuralist understandings and ways of thinking (eg Chadwick and Cumberpatch 1995; Chadwick 1997; Robbins 1999, cf Tilley 1994). In these cases, the traditional focus on the economic function of these field systems has been replaced with discussions of their social function, the role of boundaries, the control of access, perceived wealth, complex belief systems, and systems of renewal. It has been understood from fieldwork that these landscapes are more complex than they appear from the cropmark evidence alone, and that they would have altered over time. These changes may have reflected both economic and social changes. Finally, it has been stressed that these changes came about within a society which was otherwise preoccupied with their everyday practices, and so such changes may have held a greater social significance than is generally understood today (Robbins 1999).

### 9.2.2 *Regional context*

The regional landscape context for Sutton Common is provided in part by the palaeoenvironmental evidence. Within South Yorkshire, pollen records suggest that the area of Doncaster and the Humberhead Levels had been largely cleared by the Iron Age, with phases of forest clearance for mixed farming continuing through to the end of the Romano-British period (Buckland 1986; Dinnin 1997). The regional environmental picture has also been provided by recent work on Hatfield Moors (Gearey 2005) which has indicated that large-scale clearance occurred within the area from the 4th or 3rd century BC, broadly contemporaneous with the construction of the Sutton Common marsh-fort. After approximately 580 cal BC (*c* 2500 BP), the pollen record indicates an opening up of the landscape, with rises in *Plantago lanceolata*, *Pteridium*, and Poaceae, and with *Ulmus* leaving the record completely. This may indicate that elm-dominated woodlands might have been targeted specifically for clearance, with other tree species such as oak also declining, but at a more steady rate. After approximately 410–200 cal BC (2286±40 BP), woodland clearance was accelerated, with significant falls in the abundance of *Alnus*, *Quercus*, *Corylus*, *Pinus*, and *Betula* within the pollen record, and this also appears to be reflected by the pollen evidence from the lower ditch fills on site (see chapter 4). Thus, for a sustained period of the Iron Age, woodland was being cleared, even on the relatively marginal areas of wetter or poorer soils that support alder, birch, and pine. By this period, based on the Poaceae and *Plantago lanceolata* curves, the landscape around Hatfield Moors, 14km from Sutton Common but less than 4km from some of the more dramatic field systems identified from cropmarks, was dominated by open grassland rather than woodland. The evidence for cereal cultivation is also reflected by the regional pollen data, although at a low resolution. After *c* 170 cal BC – cal AD 80 (2012±45 BP), the pollen evidence indicates a phase of woodland regeneration, with increased alder, oak, and hazel within the region, around the later Iron Age and early Roman period, continuing until *c* 240–430 cal AD (1686±40 BP), or the later Roman period after which anthropogenic activity appears to have decreased. However, the failure of some species, including elm and lime, to return to the record and the generally low levels of oak and alder indicate that some level of management persisted. Similar drops in taxa indicative of ruderal habitats and an absence of cereal pollen indicate that many areas of arable and pastoral land that had previously been cleared may have reverted back to hazel-oak-alder woodland.

The palaeoenvironmental evidence for anthropogenic woodland clearance is reflected by the cultural record, predominantly provided by aerial reconnaissance. Building on the work of Riley (1980), a number of studies have provided a broader context for the landscape picture during the Iron Age. The National Mapping Programmes undertaken by English Heritage have covered large swathes of Nottinghamshire, Lincolnshire (Bewley 1998), the Yorkshire Wolds (Stoertz 1997), the Vale of York (Horne and Kershaw forthcoming), and large areas of West Yorkshire. In addition, the ongoing ALSF-funded study of the Magnesian Limestone is being undertaken by English Heritage and West Yorkshire Archaeology Service. In addition to these sources of data, additional information has been provided by a number of large-scale excavation projects, perhaps most notably in advance of the M1–A1 Link Road (Roberts *et al* 2001), but also in advance of other developments (Roberts in prep).

At the broadest level, the aerial photographic evidence indicates that the density of Iron Age settlement and land division is focused within the eastern areas of South and West Yorkshire, with less activity within the western areas of both counties (Roberts in prep). This density of activity extends around Sutton Common, to both the west and the south-east, running into the edge of the Humberhead Levels. It seems likely that the lack of features within this area is partly due to restricted formation of cropmarks in wetlands (cf Chapman 1997). Recent work at Balby Carr, Catesby, to the south-west of Doncaster, revealing brickwork pattern fields within an area of clay where cropmarks had not been visible (Jones 2002), indicates that the heavier soils might also have been divided up and enclosed.

The recent aerial photographic mapping within the area, and particularly that stemming from the Magnesian Limestone Project, has demonstrated that the brickwork-pattern fields cover a distinctive region surrounding Sutton Common. Extending from north Nottinghamshire, the eastern area of South Yorkshire, and along the Magnesian Limestone into West Yorkshire, the cropmark evidence is dominated by morphologically consistent brickwork-pattern fields. Beyond this region, the evidence for later prehistoric and Romano-British activity is less formal, with a combination of nucleated settlement, sinuous routeways, and ladder settlements with larger fields, as demonstrated on the Yorkshire Wolds (Stoertz 1997). Thus it appears that the wider landscape surrounding Sutton Common was regionally distinctive during the later prehistoric and Romano-British periods.

The date of the brickwork-pattern fields, and thus its relevance in relation to the site on Sutton Common, is difficult to ascertain, as is their function, as mentioned previously. Early work by South Yorkshire Archaeology Service and ARCUS produced limited quantities of pottery dating to the Romano-British period, with Iron Age pottery only represented at Pickburn Leys (Cumberpatch 1993). However, complex phasing of ditch recutting was interpreted as suggesting that these features might date back into the later prehistoric period. More recently, considerable excavation undertaken largely by WYAS has produced additional dating material. At West Moor Park, Armthorpe, for example, an open-area excavation revealed a complex of late Iron Age iron-working enclosures, accessed by trackways. The brickwork-pattern fields, aligned with the trackways and surrounding the enclosures, were interpreted as filling in the landscape surrounding the enclosures at a later date, somewhere between the 2nd and 4th century AD (Roberts in prep). At Ferrybridge, the transition from Iron Age to Romano-British fields has been examined through excavation. Here, the late Iron Age is represented by large fields, subdivided into smaller fields with integral field corner settlement enclosures. By the Roman period this was adapted to become a single large field without subdivisions but with a single central enclosure – a transition dated to the late 1st or 2nd century AD, arguably related to the Romanisation of the landscape with the building of the later fort and *vicus* at Castleford (Roberts in prep). From the excavated evidence, particularly incorporating the results from the M1–A1 Link Road project (Roberts *et al* 2001), it seems likely that the initial large-scale divisions of the landscape began at some time between 800 cal BC and 400 cal BC (*c* 2620 – 2350 BP). By *c* 400 – 200 BC (*c* 2350 – 2150 BP), additional boundaries, often based on the earlier ones, were constructed, with the addition of smaller enclosures and other subdivisions. The coaxial brickwork-pattern fields appear to have been constructed during the Romano-British period, between the 2nd and 4th century AD, creating large, regular rectangular fields, commonly filling in the spaces between and incorporating the earlier landscape features of trackways and other boundaries (Roberts *et al* 2001; Roberts in prep). Despite the dating evidence, recent research into the land division of this region has also demonstrated a degree of complexity. It appears that these field systems might not have been directly planned from the start, but rather developed organically. The complex at Edenthorpe displays evidence, for example, of alignment shifts on different sides of a trackway which might indicate at least two phases of construction (Chapman 1997).

Thus it seems that the evidence from the excavation of the numerous brickwork-pattern field sites remains far from complete, and its beginnings in Yorkshire and Nottinghamshire poorly dated. In the context of the environmental data, we should be expecting an intensification of clearance and agricultural activity from the 4th century through to the 1st century BC to be reflected in the archaeological record, followed by a decline, but the archaeological data is suggesting the opposite. Evidence from elsewhere, such as the Bronze Age field systems known from the Fens (Pryor 2001) or Dartmoor (Fleming 1988), cannot be used in support of an early date for the field systems in Yorkshire and Nottinghamshire, as these and many other Bronze Age field systems did not continue to function into the Iron Age.

Regardless of date, the interpretation of the function of these field systems has been a matter of some debate. It has been argued that the deep ditches, in places cut into bedrock, indicate an excessive expenditure of effort for arable functions and thus are more likely to relate to stock control (Roberts in prep). Similarly, Branigan (1989) has argued that the long fields associated with the brickwork patterns may reflect sheep farming on planned, intensified farms during the Roman period. However, the shape of the fields has also been argued to reflect processes such as strip ploughing (Riley 1980), indicative of arable functions, although other non-agricultural functions have also been identified in association with the fields, such as metalworking (Roberts in prep). The regional pollen signals from Hatfield Moors, South Yorkshire, although limited, indicate cereal cultivation during the Iron Age, but more restricted agriculture throughout the Roman period. Perhaps some level of mixed farming was taking place within these landscapes, possibly with a greater emphasis on stock rearing (Cunliffe 2005).

### 9.2.3 Conclusions

The construction of the earthworks at Sutton Common coincided broadly with a period of dramatic woodland clearance, but the construction of even the earliest phases of brickwork-pattern field systems as early as the first half of the 4th century BC is, in the absence of unequivocal dating evidence, not contended here. At the time of construction, the regional context of the marsh-fort was likely to have been a comparatively open, unenclosed landscape, with sporadic but very large land divisions such as Grim's Ditch, and possibly nucleated sites connected by sinuous routeways (Riley 1980). Although the evidence is anything but conclusive, one could image eastern England in the 4th century BC to comprise a number of relative independent or largely self-sufficient regions. Sites such as Sutton Common could be understood as their focal points, and the larger land divisions such as Grim's Ditch and major rivers as their boundaries. The newly discovered multivallate enclosure at Potteric Carr, just south of Doncaster, could represent the focal point of the region south of that which had Sutton Common as its focal point, with the River Don representing the boundary between the two regions. Field-based research on the Potteric Carr site is required first, though, to determine whether this site was contemporaneous with the Sutton Common marsh-fort.

In the absence of datable evidence for an early start of the construction of any of the 'Celtic Field' systems in Yorkshire and Nottinghamshire, it must be assumed that sometime during the middle or late Iron Age, possibly overlapping with the second phase of activity at Sutton Common, the early phases of the brickwork-pattern field systems were developed. These more regular fields were added to continuously throughout the Iron Age, effectively filling in the gaps of land that were not already enclosed. By the end of the Iron Age, woodland was regenerating and there is less palaeoenvironmental evidence for agricultural intensification, although finds within the bases of field ditches indicate that these fields were at least being maintained into the period from the 2nd to 4th century AD.

## 9.3 National context: enclosed sites and marsh-forts in the lowlands of Britain *by W Fletcher*

### 9.3.1 Introduction

The enclosures at Sutton Common have few parallels in the region and beyond, but the assumption that multivallation in the British Iron Age is, nearly always, restricted to hillforts, can no longer be sustained (see sections 1.3.1.1 and 5.7). Large, multivallated enclosed sites in lowland Britain have been documented since the 1940s, but more recent research in the lowlands and wetlands of Britain, and especially England, provide a hitherto unexpected richness of examples of such sites; several of these could be termed marsh-forts on the basis of morphology and location. This section provides a broader overview of the evidence of large, often multivallated, enclosed sites from lowland contexts in England.

### 9.3.2 Lincolnshire and East Anglia

The Witham Valley in Lincolnshire has within it a number of large enclosed sites, of which the one at Tattershall Thorpe has received most archaeological attention (Fig 9.2; Chowne *et al* 1986; Seager-Smith 1998). The site at Tattershall was excavated between 1979 and 1986, and is a double-ditched enclosure at *c* 9.2m OD, with dimensions of *c* 200m by 150m, enclosing 2.2ha. Dated material from the organic deposits gave a range of 780–200 cal BC, with a similar environmental context to that at Sutton Common. The pottery suggests a middle to late Iron Age date for the site, with some later Roman activity. Little of the interior has been excavated and of the defences, only the outer ditch of the south-east-facing entrance has been investigated. This appears to lack the complexity of the entrance posts that characterise Sutton Common, and is perhaps similar to a 'single-portal' entrance (Cunliffe 1991, 331). A combination of a bivallate entrance flanked by opposing terminals is repeated elsewhere in the region, and has been identified as a unifying theme for other late Bronze Age to Iron Age enclosures by Knight (1984). Other, but smaller, examples of enclosed sites from the Whitham Valley come from the Tattershall Thorpe airfield, which was lost to quarrying in the 1940s, and a D-shaped triple-ditched enclosure on the 5m contour at Kirkstead, known from aerial photography (Parker Pearson and Field 2003, 162).

A number of large Iron Age enclosures are known from the East Anglian Fens (eg Hall and Coles 1994: 94–101). Borough Fen earthwork near Peterborough, situated on the Bedford Levels, is a bivallate enclosure, at 3m above OD

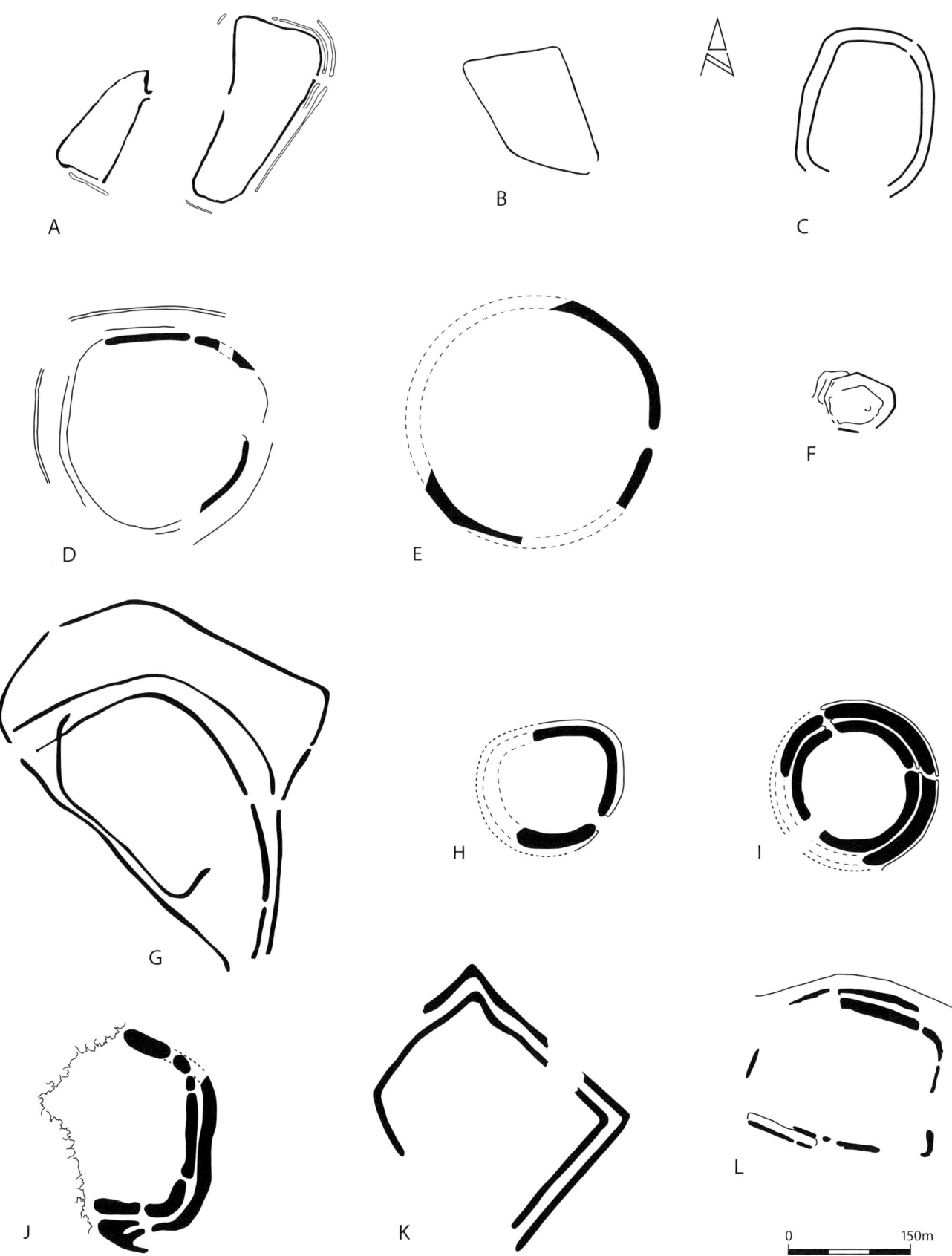

*Figure 9.2 Plans of Iron Age marsh-forts in Yorkshire, Lincolnshire, and East Anglia: a) Sutton Common; b) Skipwith; c) Tattershall Thorpe; d) Borough Fen; e) Arbury Camp; f) Wardy Hill; g) Stonea Camp; h) Narborough Camp; i) Warham; j) Holkham; k) Burgh; l) Clare Camp*

with an approximate internal area of 3.8ha, although the outer ditch is not continuous (Hall 1987). The site was first investigated between 1982 and 1986 (French and Pryor 1993) and again in 1992 (Malim and McKenna 1993), when drainage work on the fen bisected the entire enclosure. This work showed the remains of a 2.3m deep inner ditch with revetment on the internal bank, some smaller internal features, and the outer defence, which was smaller and shallower than the inner. In the late Iron Age the site was abandoned and ploughed up, and then activity ceased altogether in the Roman period, with the entire site buried beneath a thick layer of alluvium.

Arbury Camp, near Cambridge, is a univallate circular enclosure that was initially considered a stock enclosure (Evans 1992). The excavation of the ditch, 7.5m wide and 1.5m deep, produced no finds at all apart from leather, and a few artefacts from the northern terminal of the eastern entrance. No interior features were identified despite extensive test pitting throughout the c 5ha interior. The eastern entrance had a 20m gap between the terminals. A complex post-built entrance feature of two phases was uncovered, with the earlier phase identified as the most imposing. Evans (*ibid*) compares Arbury with an enclosure at Wandlebury, which is also univallate and has a similar size and shape, but sits on a low hill. Narrow trench excavations in the 1990s identified use in the 5th and 4th centuries BC, including grain storage pits and possibly larger structures (French 2004).

Wardy Hill, on a spur of higher clay jutting into the fen near Ely, emphasises the variety of enclosures in this area. Essentially it is a later Iron Age site, with a complex irregular and multi-ditched pattern, which has more in common with a Wessex-style enclosure (Evans 1992), apart from its wetland location. Because of its later date and its shape it would also seem to have less in common with Sutton Common; however, as a later site it may still have some commonalities which look back to earlier sites. In particular, the entrances were considered unusual. A much-used and much recut entrance in the south-east led to the dry land, but in the north-east an 'access-staggered' causewayed entrance, termed the 'water gate', led straight onto the fen (Evans 2000); it is not unlike the eastern gate at Sutton Common.

Stonea Camp at 2m OD is another fen edge site, but at 9ha (including ditches) is larger than most (Malim 1992; 2005). It also has an irregular shape which has been modelled distinctly on the microtopography of the small rise on which it was sited. Organic-rich deposits from the ditches have yielded finds of wood and human bone, which have been radiocarbon dated to the 1st century BC. However, despite several extensive excavations (Jackson and Potter 1996) little evidence of occupation or interior use has been found.

Six large Iron Age enclosures in Norfolk and Suffolk are known (Davies *et al* 1991; Green 1993), three of which have a low-lying aspect. Narborough fort, a univallate example, sits on the south bank of the river Nar overlooking the river crossing and the fen edge. Warham is a circular bivallate example on the river Stiffkey, overlooking the north Norfolk marshes. This site also has a smaller associated Iron Age enclosure adjacent to it. Both are on the 15m contour. Another fort, at Holkham to the west, at less than 5m OD has the most similarity with Sutton Common. At 375 × 255m, with an internal area of 2.5ha, it was constructed on the southern end of a natural sand spit, within a 1.5km wide coastal strip of marsh, dunes, and beach. Surrounded by tidal salt marsh on three sides until 1722 (Clarke 1940), it was accessed via the spit, which forms a natural causeway. It has an irregular shape with multiple but not complete banks and ditches on the south and east and a bank to the north. It only has the one enclosure, but comparable aspects are the causeway and irregular-shaped ditches. It has perhaps been overlooked archaeologically, being considered only as a late Bronze Age to early Iron Age stock enclosure. It is also thought to be the likely setting for the Roman defeat of the rebellious Iceni in AD 47, as described by Tacitus; the other candidate is Stonea Camp. Other East Anglian examples in low-lying settings are the Burgh enclosure (Martin 1988) at 25m OD, a multivallate site with evidence for both Iron Age and Roman activity, and a similar but undated site at Clare in Suffolk (Matin 1999). Though not wetlands as such, the clay lands of Suffolk in which these two sites are located are low-lying with naturally poor drainage. With no prominent hills, these sites are certainly outside the hillfort category.

### 9.3.3 *Shropshire and North Wales*

Two of the most unusual sites encountered in this area are Wall Camp and The Berth (Fig 9.3). The Welsh Marches are well known for the density of Iron Age sites (cf Jones and Mattingley 1990) but have largely been associated with traditional hillfort sites. Wall Camp is a multivallate enclosure which does have a set of very complex earthworks reminiscent of the highly developed hillfort models. It is, however, situated in the centre of a large, low-lying basin mire called the Weald Moors, within view of the more imposing hillfort on the Wrekin and within a few kilometres of the Roman town of Wroxeter. The Weald is thought to be a Late-glacial lake c 3km wide (Leah *et al* 1998), in which later deposits of organic soils developed. Two natural till islands dominate the centre of the moor, the larger one being home to the historic village of Kynnersley, while the other, smaller, 12ha island

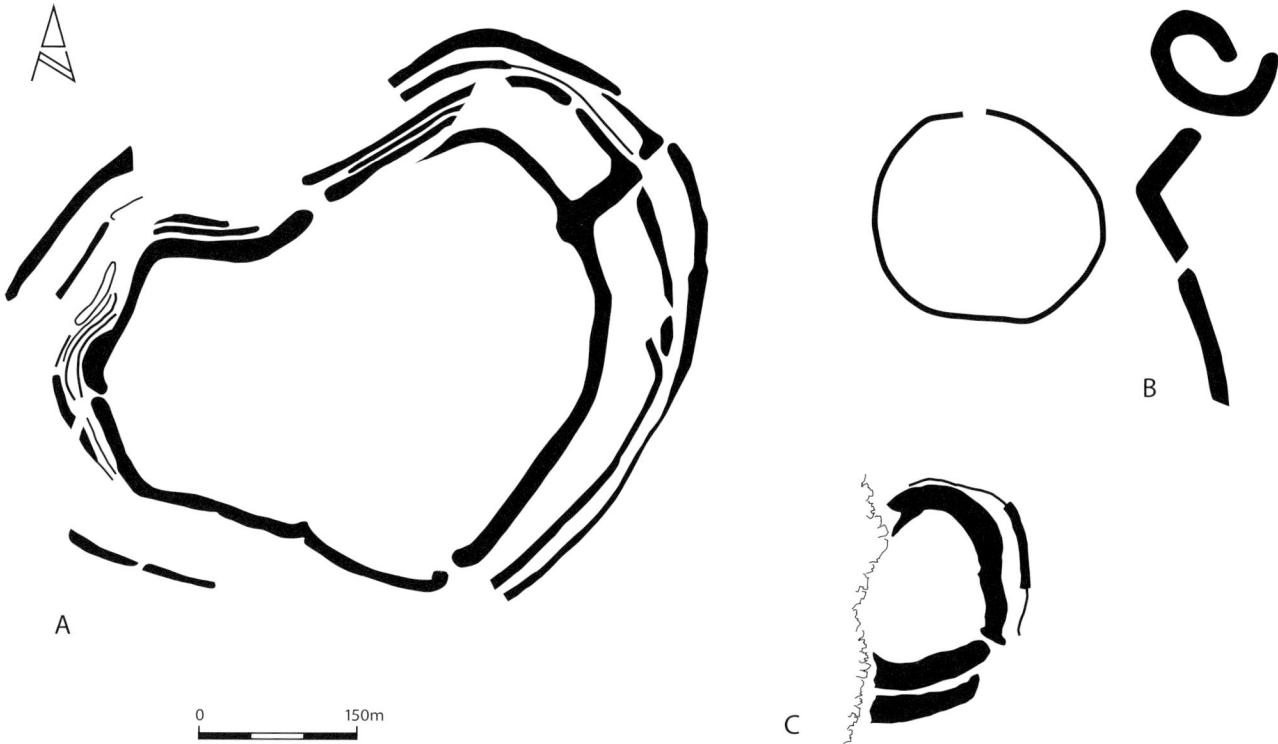

*Figure 9.3 Plans of Iron Age marsh-forts in Shropshire and North Wales: a) Wall Fort; b) The Berth; c) Dinas Dinlle*

to the east is entirely enclosed by Wall Camp. Earlier excavations on the defences by Padget (in Bond 1991) indicated two phases of activity, and a small trench by Bond (*ibid*) revealed small ditches and at least three four-post structures. Pottery indicated an early 3rd- century occupation, along with other later Iron Age activity (Morris 1991). An early phase could very well be contemporaneous with Sutton Common, but the site and its wet location have been overlooked academically in favour of the bigger sites in the area such as the Wrekin (eg Stanford 1984).

The evidence for The Berth summarised in Watson (2002), and Leah *et al* (1998), suggests the site is a 3ha Iron Age enclosure, with evidence for a single, stone-revetted gravel rampart. The site has been described as 'atypical' (Watson 2002) and is more interesting in the Sutton Common context, because it sits on a natural island in the middle of a former lake. Furthermore, there is a smaller, univallate enclosure on the south-east side and the two sites are linked to each other, and then to the mainland by a man-made stone and gravel causeway. Evidence from the trenching indicates multiple phases from the mid Iron Age to the Roman period, although environmental evidence indicated phases of activity from the Bronze Age through to the post-Roman period (*ibid*).

Dinas Dinlle, on the north Wales coast, is the most westerly example in this assessment. It is variously described as a cliff fort (Griffiths 1949), an early defensive enclosure (RCAHMW 1960), a hillfort (Smith 1993), and a defended hilltop enclosure (Davison 2002). The earliest written description from Pennant (1773 – 76) perhaps unwittingly gives a more accurate description, locating the site on a 'mount of sand and gravel on the verge of a great marsh'. This site is a large, multivallate site sculpted from a natural sand and gravel island rising from sea level to a height of 25m OD. The island is situated in an extensive coastal marsh, and, like Holkham, appears to have been joined to the mainland by a natural causeway. At the time of construction it is likely the marshes were much more expansive, and may have protected the site from the sea. Recently, however, erosion by the sea has been severe, and much of the western defences and some of the interior have been lost to the sea.

### 9.3.4 *Other possible sites*

During this assessment a number of other sites were considered for comparison. These were either low-lying enclosures or sites which have some evidence for Iron Age activity but perhaps not enough to be sure of their suitability. In particular Boney's Island, a bivallate enclosure on a spur of heath jutting out into the Beccles Marshes, on the Suffolk-Norfolk border, would appear to be a perfect candidate. There has, unfortunately, never been an excavation or any circumstantial finds to date the site. Equally of interest is the site of Athelney in Somerset. Again on a wetland island within the Somerset Levels, it was known to have been the site of a fort constructed by King Alfred in AD 878, which later became a monastery and an abbey. Recent excavations by Time Team have suggested that an Iron Age phase is also present, with earth banks and ditches. Although the evidence is sparse, the site location and aspect make it an excellent candidate for a Sutton Common-style enclosure.

### 9.3.5 Conclusions

The enclosed sites discussed here vary considerably, in age, size, and shape, and in details in their morphology. Each one, however, to a greater or lesser degree mirrors aspects of the Sutton Common site. The Berth, for example, not only has two enclosures, but these are linked together by an extensive man-made causeway. Many sites utilise natural islands (eg Holkham, The Berth, Wall Camp, Dinas Dinlle) or a promontory within a wetland context (eg Stonea or Borough Fen), often with a natural causeway and dry-land link. Wardy Camp, although two centuries later that Sutton Common, even has a so-called 'water gate', an entrance that only leads into the wetlands. Several sites appear early in date or have an early phase; the two Shropshire sites, for example. Wall Camp housed four-post structures during the earlier phase. Some sites appear never to have been used, or sparsely used with almost no evidence of material culture.

This summary of large enclosed sites from lowland contexts in England and Wales serves to demonstrate two important points related to the Sutton Common site. First, that Sutton Common as an Iron Age marsh-fort was not a unique site, but has a number of parallels, especially in eastern England but also in lowland and wetland landscapes elsewhere. Second, that very little research has been undertaken into the lowland enclosed sites, especially when compared to the research into hillforts, and that research into marsh-forts is in its infancy.

# 10 Conclusions

## 10.1 The Sutton Common enigma resolved? *by R Van de Noort*

At the start of our work at Sutton Common in 1997, the site was something of an enigma. In their summing up of function of the Sutton Common enclosures, Mike Parker Pearson and Robert Sydes (1997, 255) concluded somewhat hesitantly that the 'defensibility of the Sutton Common enclosures is questionable', and that 'people seem to have been living in the larger enclosure, but it may also have had important ceremonial and high status significance'. Our research has been able to elucidate this tentative and limited description of the double enclosures at Sutton Common, but, inevitably, new questions have been thrown up by the large-scale excavations.

Our research objectives for this site were set out at the beginning of this report (see section 1.3.3). These objectives largely have been met.

In terms of defining the character, morphology, and spatial patterning of the marsh-fort, the excavations have shown that the defences enclosing and defining the site resemble those of enclosed sites elsewhere in Britain in the early Iron Age (see chapter 5). As with many other enclosed sites, the larger enclosure had two entrances. The one facing west was for access to the Magnesian Limestone landscape via the smaller enclosure (or more probably the cross bank with triangular extension) and the causeway across the Hampole Beck (Parker Pearson and Sydes 1997, 225). The other, facing east, was more elaborate and although considered impractical in terms of access, it was symbolically the more important entrance to the marsh-fort. The box rampart which surrounded the site resembles defences already known from other enclosed sites, including hillforts, such as Grimthorpe (Stead 1968; see also section 10.3). The elaboration of ditches and banks and further stake alignments at Sutton Common has also been observed at many other enclosed sites. The interior of the marsh-fort was devoid of houses or other direct evidence for habitation on the site; instead up to 150 granaries were found, organised in rows in three zones. Few other features were found here, bar some pits, a well, and what may have been a small stake-built hut (see chapter 6).

The dating and phasing of the site shows that an early Bronze Age mortuary enclosure preceded the construction of the marsh-fort. Dendrochronological analysis of the well-preserved timbers of the eastern gateway has shown that this part of the marsh-fort was constructed from timbers felled between 372 and 362 BC, and that all construction activity could be placed with considerable confidence in the second quarter of the 4th century BC. The second phase of activity on the site, dominated by what we have called mortuary rings, was dated by radiocarbon assay of one sample of charred animal bone to the 4th and 3rd centuries BC, with the glass beads suggesting that this phase of activity may have continued into the 2nd century BC (see sections 8.3 and 8.5.1). Suggestions that a palisaded enclosure preceded the ditch and bank arrangement (Parker Pearson and Sydes 1997, 224), were refuted. Apart from some isolated finds, no evidence for late Iron Age or Roman period activity has come forth.

The objective of defining the social construction of the site and its place in the wider landscape was only partly met. The absence of any houses in the interior of the marsh-fort strongly suggests that we should not consider Sutton Common as the settlement of a local or regional élite, nor is there any archaeological evidence suggesting that Sutton Common was a place where specialised craft production was undertaken. The presence of the 150 or so granaries could indicate that Sutton Common was a central grain store, but this could equally be taken to mean that it represents communal, rather than élite-controlled storage of grain. Sutton Common has produced an alternative hypothesis, namely that the construction of the four-post structures was accompanied by ritual acts, and that granaries had symbolic meanings alongside their practical use (see section 6.6). It was initially hoped that the provenancing of the Magnesian Limestone utilised for the revetment wall on the west side of the marsh-fort could provide a glimpse of Sutton Common's 'hinterland', but this turned out to be unsuccessful. A glimpse of the social construction of Sutton Common in the wider landscape is, however, provided by the palaeoenvironmental analyses. Despite the cutting down of some 6000 oak trees for the construction of the box rampart and the granaries, the impact of this event on the environment is near-invisible in the analysis of the environment through pollen, insect, plant macrofossil, faunal remains, soil micromorphology, and charcoal analysis. It can thus be argued that the trees were felled either at some distance away from the Common or that the impact of the acquisition of the material used in the marsh-fort's construction was spread over a large area.

In terms of defining the interaction of Sutton Common with the environment, the project has been more successful, even though, paradoxically, the palynological and macrofossil evidence from the ditch fills and the pollen from the Hampole Beck palaeochannel all indicate that the site was not occupied by people over any great length of time. Indeed, even the analysis of the lowest deposits in the inner ditch shows that the local area was a relatively open landscape used for grazing.

The Iron Age mortuary rites remain somewhat poorly understood, which is at least in part the result of the excavation and sampling strategy and the belated recognition of what the ill-defined enclosures represented. Nevertheless, we have inferred that the second phase of activity included the construction of the mortuary rings, possibly distinct places created through the digging of narrow ditches where the ashes of deceased persons (or more correctly: the pyre debris, occasionally containing artefacts such as the glass beads) were placed or scattered, as a final stage in a longer funerary practice. The inclusion of charred cattle bones in the practice suggests that certain animals were treated as 'non-human persons', a phenomenon recognised in other Iron Age cemeteries in Britain and northern Europe.

Despite the very small numbers of artefacts retrieved from the site, the material culture studies undertaken on the pottery, antler weaving comb, glass beads, gold object and other items reveal that such artefacts were not simply discarded, but had been disposed of in a structured way, again with clear parallels with other Iron Age sites in Britain. Thus, we understand the material culture in terms of symbolism and cosmology, including the significance of the transformation and regeneration concepts in the cases of charred grain and saddle quern stones (see sections 6.6 and 7.9), and defining the liminal entranceways through depositions of used and broken artefacts and human and animal remains. Significantly, whereas the deposition of charred grain and querns precedes the construction of granaries, the deposition in the ditch terminals at the entrance forms part of the activities towards the end of the use the marsh-fort.

Describing the Iron Age woodworking technology and woodland management can also be considered as one of the project's achievement. The species assemblage from Sutton Common is dominated by oak. This species is well-regarded for its strength and durability so the enclosures were clearly built as structures that appeared to be long-lasting. Great effort was made to fashion high-quality stakes and massive flat-based posts. No bark and almost no sapwood survived on any of the site's major structural timbers and its deliberate removal implies major effort and the aim of longevity. In contrast, at the Iron Age site of Goldcliff on the Welsh Severn Estuary, for which seasonal occupation has been suggested, a range of wood species, including field maple and ash, were used for the buildings, and the wood used was often quite twisted and knotty, the stakes often retaining bark and sapwood (Brunning *et al* 2000). The use of oak at the alder-dominant environment of the Sutton Common enclosures adds weight to the idea that this was linked to the site's special status, and in this respect the site resembles the wooden causeway at Fiskerton (Taylor, in Field and Parker Pearson 2003). The selection of yew wood for a structure near the entrance, or deposition in a ditch terminal, is noteworthy. Yew wood can have ritual connotations, being associated both with life as an evergreen tree, and death because of the high toxicity of its leaves. The only place on the site where yew wood was found was the outer ditch terminal where elements of ritual or structured deposition are known.

That leaves us to answer the question: 'What was Sutton Common?' On the basis of the descriptions presented here, we offer three alternative and possibly complementary interpretations, based on different theoretical paradigms, of how the marsh-fort and the second phase activity may be understood.

From a functionalist perspective, Sutton Common could be interpreted as a defensible refuge, offering protection in times of conflict and combat. It functioned primarily as safe storage for grain, as shown by the granaries and charred grain deposits from a number of contexts within the site. It may also have accommodated livestock during turbulent times, for example within the smaller enclosure, thwarting cattle rustlers. The defensive nature of the bank and ditch arrangements attest to the need for protection against raids, which would have increased in periods of environmental pressure. The location of the marsh-fort was chosen for its defensiveness – in the absence of any suitable hills, the 'island' surrounded by wetlands offered the best option. Two alternative explanations could be put forward to explain the relatively short period of use of the marsh-fort. First, the underlying reasons for its construction, the increase in conflict and combat, may have disappeared once a new environmental equilibrium had been achieved. Second, the wetland environment of Sutton Common was simply too damp to store grain during the winter period, resulting in the premature germination of seed corn, as shown, perhaps, by the smaller than usual charred cereal grain from a number of contexts (see section 6.5.1). Thus, the marsh-fort did not fulfil its function, and was abandoned for a better alternative. The selection of the site of the (by then) former marsh-fort as a cemetery could be explained as avoiding the use of good agricultural land for funerary rituals.

From a processual perspective, Sutton Common could be interpreted as a specialised form of settlement, either 'representing the communal effort of a large sector of the social group working under the coercive power of the leadership' (Cunliffe 2005, 347) or representing forms of self-direction by communities. It did not have the central place functions that have been proposed (and contested) for the developed hillforts of southern Wessex (see 1.3.1.1). For example, there is no evidence for specialised manufacture, and the marsh-fort was not the residence of a leadership. Nevertheless, the concentrated storage of grain as exemplified in the c 150 granaries shows centralised control through the redistribution of this vital commodity. The importance of the role of the inter-regionally connected élite, in the organisation of labour and materials in the construction of the marsh-fort, is illustrated in the use of the military-style defences, which had been copied from hillforts elsewhere in the country. Multivallation, with an emphasis on building activity around the principal entrance(s), was explained previously as military reinforcement, but is now understood as representing acts reinforcing the symbolic nature of enclosure alongside their function in warfare (eg Cunliffe 2005, 576–8, following Hingley 1990, Hill 1995b and others). The location of the marsh-fort in the wetland landscape was chosen for its defensiveness. The short period of use of the marsh-fort could be attributed to the absence of political processes, for example core-periphery exchange, that sustained the position of the élite in the region. As such, the Sutton Common marsh-fort is something of an anomaly in the eastern zone of Britain, where villages and open settlements are the dominant settlement form.

From an interpretative perspective, Sutton Common could be understood as a place where the social identity of the local community was reinforced through the construction of the physical representation of the idea(l) of community, or a 'dwelling place', even though the logistics of everyday life dictated a taskscape[1] comprising villages dispersed in the region and isolated farmsteads (Fig 10.1). The social memory of the early Bronze Age mortuary enclosure, and a sense of the sacredness of this wetland-encircled dune, possibly survived into the 4th century BC. The use of a bank and ditch arrangement that resembled defences used elsewhere for enclosed sites shows an interconnectivity of autonomous regional groups within broader zones (see, for example, Field and Parker Pearson 2003, 191–3). This interconnectivity is also illustrated by the adoption of widespread cosmological principles in dealing with the concept of enclosure (eg the east-facing gateway) and material culture (eg the structured deposition in ditch terminals). There is no reason, and indeed no archaeological evidence, to assume the guiding hand of a permanent élite in the construction of the marsh-fort, rather this was a communal effort, perhaps steered by a transitory leader or peripatetic 'architect'.

Multivallation re-emphasised the symbolic nature of enclosure, defining and redefining the opposition between the internal cosmos and external chaos, which is also clearly shown by the deposition of artefacts and human remains at the liminal entrances, possibly during processions. At least one, and possibly both, human heads were still fleshed when deposited, and may have functioned as 'trophy heads' in specific rituals. The importance of the granaries should be understood within the context of the significant shift from the ritualisation of warriors and weapons in the early and middle Bronze Age, to the ritualisation of agriculture/growing and storage of food in the late Bronze Age and Iron Age (Bradley 2005). The deposition of a handful of charred grains in one or two postholes of granaries emphasises the ritual aspect of grain storage, and these structures became powerful symbols at a time that crop husbandry was in a period of transition. The short-lived nature of the site is explained by its symbolic role – its construction was an event or a theatrical performance using well-established rituals and forms. After the event, the entrances of the marsh-fort may have been damaged to signal the end of its life, but the site remained important as a feature within the landscape and as part of the social memory of the community that had built it. The reuse of the site as a final resting place for the deceased is no coincidence: it links the transition and destruction of the body after death directly to the locale chosen by the ancestors for their rituals.

Our intimate interaction with the archaeological remains during the excavation and the post-excavation analysis has led us increasingly to embrace interpretative perspectives which may represent the perceptions of the people who built the Sutton Common marsh-fort. It also allows us to explain the detailed findings from the excavations, without the need to impose modern functionalist common sense or models which have been essentially derived from research in other regions or are based on how classical authors understood the barbaric north. However, we expect readers to make up their own minds as to which of these perspectives is the most appropriate in their view, accepting that alternative discourses already exist, and others will undoubtedly be developed for Sutton Common in the future.

## 10.2 Sutton Common and the Iron Age chronology  *by R Van de Noort*

The ability, through dendrochronology and integrated radiocarbon analysis, to date the phases of activity at Sutton Common to a much higher precision than has been achieved previously for any Iron Age fort-type site in Britain reveals

178 Sutton Common

Figure 10.1  A bird's-eye view of Sutton Common c 350 BC (Artist's impression by Michael Rouillard)

something of the real-time dynamics of this site. Previously dated to 550–200 cal BC (Parker Pearson and Sydes 1997, 229), the various activities on the site can now be dated to between 372 BC and 350 cal BC (see section 5.4). Away from wetland contexts that may offer timbers for dendrochronological analysis and ample organic sediments for radiocarbon-dated sequences, the dating of phases of activity on Iron Age sites has relied principally on pottery typologies and, over the last four decades, radiocarbon dating of artefacts and bone remains. For the British Iron Age pre-dating the 1st century BC, the pottery assemblages are typically dated to two or three centuries. Thus, the Staple Howe group dates to the 8th to 6th centuries BC, and the Dane's Graves-Staxton style to the 3rd to 1st centuries BC, with coarse wares providing even longer date ranges (eg Cunliffe 2005, 611–51). Similarly, radiocarbon dating of artefacts has generally provided results with date ranges at 95% confidence that typically include several centuries, a product of what is now referred to as the '800–400 cal BC radiocarbon plateau' (Haselgrove et al 2001, 5; see section 5.4.3). Reliance on pottery associations or simple radiocarbon dating has led to activities that could, in reality, have taken little more than a few hours, days or weeks (such as the burning and charring of grain, the deposition of animal bones or the construction of a four-post granary), being given date ranges spanning several centuries.

Our understanding of the past has, to a significant extent, been based on the best available dating evidence, and for the Iron Age this evidence has been rather poor. Thus, Iron Age archaeology tends either to describe socio-political change through a broad-brush approach of phases each spanning hundreds of years (eg Manby 2003b; Harding 2004; Knight and Howard 2004; Cunliffe 2005), or presents daily life and aspects of cosmology that are virtually timeless within the Iron Age (eg Hill 1995a; 1995b; 1996; Parker Pearson 1996; Fitzpatrick 1997a). Notable exceptions to this come from wetland sites where dendrochronological dating has been successful, and where the social structures and agency have been fruitfully integrated, such as the Fiskerton timber causeway or the Glastonbury lake-settlement (Coles and Minnett 1995; Field and Parker Pearson 2003; see also Van de Noort and O'Sullivan 2006). Sutton Common offers a rare opportunity, and for Iron Age fort-type sites the first occasion, to connect these different time frames.

Extrapolating the well-dated evidence from Sutton Common to fort-type sites elsewhere in Britain which lack precise dating, we could argue that many of the 3300 or so known hillforts, hillslope enclosures, and large lowland enclosures could each have been constructed in time-spans lasting little more than one or maybe a few years in the case of univallate sites, and possibly up to a decade for multivallate enclosures (cf Collis 1981). Undoubtedly, a number of these sites were subsequently elaborated, and the essence of multivallation lies in the symbolic reinforcement of the concept of enclosure (see section 10.1). Nevertheless, the probably short-lived nature of the construction of many of these sites, and the absence of evidence for any form of long-term occupation from the overwhelming majority of these enclosures, requires the re-examination of the existence of a chiefdom-type structure of socio-political differentiation in this region (Hill 1995b). Even where great densities of pits and postholes have been found in enclosed sites, and where long-term occupation has been proposed, detailed analysis often shows the short-lived nature of these features. The one-off use of grain storage pits in the Danebury hillfort provides a good example of this practice (Cunliffe 1995, 85; see section 10.3). Thus, instead of signifying the essence of the Iron Age in Britain, with hillforts representing central places from where the hinterland was governed or controlled, the fort-type sites may represent relatively short-lived periods of exceptional socio-political or ritual activity. Invoking Braudel's (1949) concept of the different rhythms of time, it could be argued that the enclosed sites of the British Iron Age are not part of the *conjunctures* (social time), but should be seen as part of the *histoire événementielle* (individual time), and we should seek to explain these sites from the perspective of the people who actively constructed them at particular points in time, rather than as depersonalised social structures. Elsewhere in Europe, similar conclusions have been drawn on the short-term use of large settlements at sites where archaeological timbers have been available for dendrochronological dating. Their longer-term survival as landscape monuments, and appropriation for alternative uses, is of course not disputed, as is illustrated by the use of the Sutton Common marsh-fort as a possible burial ground in the second phase of activity.

## 10.3 The contribution to the 'enclosed settlement' debate: function and development  *by R Van de Noort and J Collis*

Alongside the significance of the dating of Sutton Common to the enclosed settlement debate, the morphology, spatial patterning, and inferred function of this site also provides important results for the study of Iron Age forts or large enclosed sites in the wider sense; the site is thus of direct relevance to our understanding of hillforts and other enclosed sites in Britain and elsewhere in western Europe. The near-complete excavation of the site's interior, and the integrated palaeoenvironmental research, leaves no doubt that this site was never a settlement or village, and indeed may never have been intended for habitation. Instead, the people who constructed the marsh-fort at Sutton Common were more likely to have lived their lives in unenclosed and enclosed farms on the limestone immediately to the west of the Common. The landscape analysis (see section 9.2) hints at a scene whereby Sutton Common is a key monument within a local and regional taskscape.

In the absence of the excavation of the interior of many hillforts and other enclosed sites, the defences, comprising palisades, various styles of ramparts, bank and ditch arrangements, and additions such as the *cheveaux-de-frise*, have invoked impressions of these sites as serving a role in Iron Age warfare and conflict. There is no doubt that people in the Iron Age took to war or raids (eg Cunliffe 2005, 533–42). It also seems likely that defended sites may have been attacked, and that the architecture of the defences was understood by people in the Iron Age in terms of warfare and protection. Nevertheless, the defences of Sutton Common include a number of elements, such as the 9m wide causeway across the Hampole Beck palaeochannel, the elaborate east-facing entrance, and the causewayed nature of the inner ditch, which suggest that protection from an hostile enemy was not foremost in the mind of the people who constructed the 'fort' (see chapter 5 and in particular section 5.7). Archaeologists have increasingly acknowledged the symbolic significance of enclosure (eg Hill 1995b), and whilst multivallation and elaborate entrances are now explained as symbolic enhancements, the Sutton Common evidence suggests that this is also true for the (causewayed) ditches surrounding the rampart, and probably also for the defences as a whole. This is not to suggest that enclosure had no relationship to warfare; rather, in the same way that the symbolic position of the Iron Age warrior was expressed with intricately decorated armour, so the symbolic significance of enclosure was expressed with an architecture that was recognised and understood in military terms.

While the excavation and study of the defences of Sutton Common contribute to a long-standing debate in Iron Age archaeology, the excavations of the interior have farther reaching consequences. To date, no multivallate enclosed site of early Iron Age date has been so comprehensively excavated as Sutton Common, and for this reason alone, the results are of significance to the wider debate on the function and meaning of enclosed settlements. The high-resolution dating and integrated palaeoenvironmental research adds further weight to the findings of Sutton Common. In chapter 6, the interior of the marsh-fort has been described in some detail, which can be summarised as comprising *c* 150 four-post structures or granaries, a small number of pits and post alignments, a single well and possibly one, very small, hut, but no houses or other evidence for people living here.

Similarly, the palaeoenvironmental analyses of the lowest ditch deposits from near the eastern entrance produced no evidence for people living in the immediate surroundings of the sample site, but evidence for grazing of the land was found (see section 6.5).

The debate on the reconstruction and function of four-post structures that has remained unresolved since 1888 has already been presented above (see section 6.6), and the evidence for Sutton Common provides a new dimension to this debate. The 24 granaries from Sutton Common with one or two postholes containing moderate or large amounts of charred grain show incontrovertibly that these structures were indeed intended to be understood as raised grain stores. When bearing in mind the post-depositional formation processes on the Common and the taphonomy of the charred grain (see sections 3.2.1 and 6.6), the possibility that this happened as the result of some sort of catastrophic event is most improbable; rather we have proposed that at Sutton Common charred grain was deposited into the postholes before or during the insertion and securing of the upright timbers, and the ritual aspect of this behaviour had not been recognised previously. Ritualised behaviour surrounding the storage of grain has also been suggested for the storage pits of the Danebury hillfort in Hampshire. It has been argued (Cunliffe 1995, 85) that the storage pits were used, for the most part, only once, and that the pits had their own 'biographies'. These commenced with construction in the month of August, after which the pit was filled with seed corn and sealed. This was followed by a six-month liminal period, with the seed lying dormant and 'protected by the chthonic deities'. In March, the pit was opened, the seed sown, and the first thanks offering was made. The pit was then left unused till harvesting, when a second thanks offering was made, and the pit was subsequently abandoned. Charred grain and (fragments of) quern stones are included in the special deposits interpreted as thanks offerings. Richard Bradley (2005) has suggested that ritualised aspects of behaviour connected to food production and food storage in later prehistory are recognisable in different aspects of material culture, ranging from unusable ards deposited in wetlands, granary-modelled ceramic urns, and certain metal deposits, to the late Iron Age rectangular shrines modelled on granaries. And although the prehistoric granary itself is not described by Bradley as ritual (*ibid*, 209), the evidence from Sutton Common has indicated that the construction of the granary was accompanied by ritual acts. The rituals that accompanied their construction, and possibly their use, imply the social significance of the storehouses (*ibid*, 209–10), but this significance is not linked to any élite warriors or warrior groups; rather it is linked to the activity of ordinary farmers going about their daily work.

The recognition of the possible ritualised aspects of grain or food storage is important for our understanding when explaining the concentrations of granaries at Sutton Common and other enclosed sites, both in Yorkshire such as Grimthorpe on the Yorkshire Wolds, and elsewhere in Britain including the early phase at Crickley Hill, Gloucestershire, Moel y Gaer, Clwyd, the late phase at Danebury, Hampshire, and possibly further afield as well, at sites such as the multivallate enclosures of middle Iron Age date Zeijen II in the northern Netherlands, a 2nd-century BC multivallate enclosure with granaries ('*spiekers*') but no houses, and six other similar sites from the Netherlands (Waterbolk 1977). Whilst we could interpret at least some of these structures as functioning granaries, the buildings may have been meant principally for display and symbolism, and thus the defences and the granaries performed similar functions. If this interpretation is correct, then the location of the granaries found outside the defences next to the entrance at the Castle Henllys hillfort could also be explained, as their display, rather than their protection, was of greater importance. To date, few excavations of enclosed sites have included the exterior (Haselgrove *et al* 2001, 10), and such research may show the widespread use of granaries in this way. This argument should not be taken to suggest that late prehistoric granaries did not function as store houses, quite the contrary: the symbolic significance of the four-post structure was intrinsically connected to its practical function.

The use of charred grains in rituals cannot be restricted to the construction of granaries. Ritualised behaviour has already been invoked to explain concentrations in storage pits (eg Cunliffe 1995, 85; see above), and this phenomenon has a distribution that includes much of Britain, northern Germany, the eastern part of the Benelux, and northern France (Fig 10.2). The presence of charred grain in pits has been noted at both enclosed and unenclosed sites. For example,

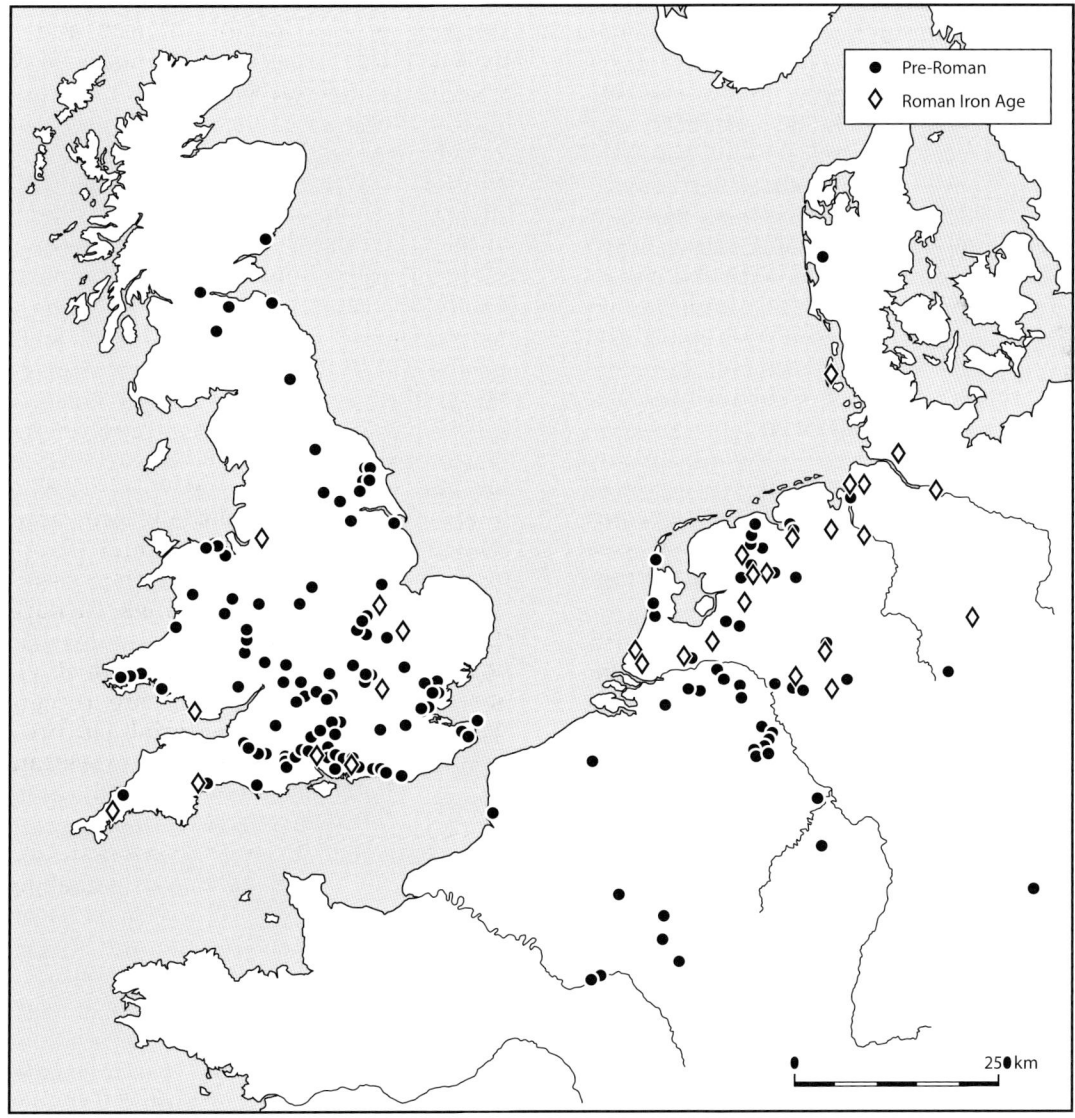

*Figure 10.2  Distribution of prehistoric and Roman period granaries (after Gent 1983, 246)*

at the enclosed site of Asheldam Camp, Essex, some pits and postholes dating to the middle Iron Age contained substantial deposits of charred grain, mostly spelt and emmer, plus fragments of a large pottery storage vessel and fragments from a small oak barrel (Bedwin 1991). At Concerto Camp, Worcestershire, and Ham Hill, Somerset, spelt and emmer were found in pits (Smith 1991; Monckton 1999), and the unenclosed site of Stanway in Essex, middle Iron Age pits included charred remains of emmer, spelt, and barley (Murphy 1992). Furthermore, the ritual significance of charred grain may be extended to the deposits in settlement ditches and ditch terminals, as argued for Sutton Common (see section 6.6), and such deposits from ditches are known from many Iron Age sites, such as the Wardy Hill ringfort, Ely, Cambridgeshire, where systematic sampling showed the greatest concentrations of charred grain to be found in the inner ditch of the ringfort (Murphy, in Evans 2003, 109–10).

Taking a wider perspective, the 4th and 3rd centuries in Britain and much of temperate Europe are notable for the lack of evidence of 'centralisation' of power (in the form of rich burials) or of population (in the form of large settlements, defended or open), and these centuries form a contrast with, say, the 6th and 5th centuries in eastern France and southern Germany, where one finds centralised settlements such as Mont Lassois or the Heuneburg dating to Hallstatt D, and the rich burials of Hallstatt D and La Tène A in the same areas, or with the oppida of the 2nd to 1st centuries, and the contemporary rich burials of northern France and south-east Britain (Collis 1995). Outside parts of Britain and Brittany, even small defended sites are rare. The only evidence of social groupings larger than small villages and farms tends to be in the appearance of ritual sites such as Gournay-sur-Aronde and Ribemont-sur-Ancre, where human remains and weapons were deposited on sites which were later to evolve into Roman sanctuaries (Brunaux 1988; 1991; Brunaux *et al* 1985). There is increasingly a recognition however that centralised storage is another feature of the period (Collis 2000). The best-documented cases are in Wessex, where sites such as Danebury and Maiden Castle have a combination of four-post structures and storage pits, though even in Wessex recent geophysical work has shown that this is unusual for hillforts. What has also been emerging is that in other parts of Britain there are undefended sites which show a similar concentration of storage pits, notably Gravelly Guy in Oxfordshire (Lambrick 1990), and around Kilham and Burton Agnes in Yorkshire (Stoertz 1997; Dent 1995, 60–2). This is also a phenomenon which has been recognised recently on the continent, for instance at Soupir in northern France (Gransar 2002).

The research at Sutton Common has also reinforced the idea that enclosed settlements were not restricted to hills and hilltops, and that the defensive architecture already known from hillforts was also used in other landscape settings. The overview of lowland enclosed sites in England (see section 9.3) indicates that the enclosed settlement phenomenon may have been more widespread than previously thought, and especially in the intensively farmed regions of eastern England, lowland forts may have been under-represented in the archaeological record. Although it is impossible to quantify, we should understand the traditional division of Britain into zones of different settlement forms (eg Cunliffe 2005, 74) in the light of this bias.

In past research, the enclosed settlements of Iron Age date, and in particular the multivallate enclosed sites such as many hillforts, have been taken to reflect the existence of social structures that included élite groups or leaders who resided within these places. These sites were understood as central places where political leadership, craft specialisation, and product redistribution was based. Sutton Common has been interpreted as a separate and distinctive place where the social identity of the local community was reinforced through the construction of the physical representation of the idea(l) of community, which included strong defences and protection of the storehouses within the enclosed site. The construction of this physical representation was a display, a theatrical performance, undertaken for reasons of social reproduction or the reinforcement of local social identities. There is no archaeological evidence implying a leadership, craft specialisation or redistribution of food or other goods, nor is there any evidence for habitation. We postulate that many other enclosed sites of early and middle Iron Age date, in Britain and continental Europe, were constructed for similar reasons, and that for most people the concept of enclosed settlement remained little more than an idea(l).

## 10.4 Burial rituals in the middle Iron Age *by R Van de Noort and J Collis*

The contributions of the hypothesised burial rituals at Sutton Common should also be noted, despite the limited nature of the archaeological evidence. Burial rituals in the early and middle Iron Age include two, somewhat distinct, set of practices. Both sets are present at Sutton Common.

On the one hand, human (and animal) remains are found in a range of contexts which, as a rule, would not be interpreted as burials but as structured depositions within a ritual context, which may have involved feastings and sacrifices (eg Hill 1995a; 1996). At Sutton Common, the two human remains from the outer ditch terminal to the north of the eastern entrance (see section 7.3) fall into this category, and these possibly represented the victims of sacrifice of sorts, or possibly the heads of enemies who had fallen during fighting or raids (eg Green 2001, 93–110). Human remains, especially skulls, have been found in many Iron Age contexts and at least one of the two examples from Sutton Common is thought to have been deposited as a fleshed head. Their occurrence on the north side of entrances (both of individual houses and of enclosed sites) clearly suggests the widespread embracement of cosmological principles as seen within the dipolar structure of the Iron Age house (Fitzpatrick 1994, 72; Parker Pearson 1996). Furthermore, the animal bone fragments deposited in the same ditch terminal could also be interpreted as falling into this group of ritual placement, rather than deposition of rubbish.

On the other hand, little is known about formal burial rituals, used in the widest sense of the term. Several explanations have been considered to explain the near-invisibility of early and middle Iron Age burial rites, including the practice of excarnation and secondary deposition in exposed places of deceased persons (Carr and Knüsel 1997). In his overview of the British Iron Age mortuary archaeology, Rowan Whimster (1981, 180) concluded that 'with the exception of a handful of scattered inhumations and cremations [which includes the kind of deposits discussed above]...the evidence for the methods of disposal used between c 1000 BC and 400 BC is almost non-existent and prohibits the definition of any distinctive, recurrent burial type'. Despite the research undertaken since this publication, several distinct regional exceptions such as the Arras-type burials of East Yorkshire, and claims that we now have a 'well-defined series of ritual [burial] practices' (eg Cunliffe 2005, 543), the essence of Whimster's statement still holds true, in that our understanding of early and middle Iron Age burial rituals pales into insignificance when compared with that for the preceding or subsequent archaeological periods. This is possibly, in part, a consequence of the lack of datable artefacts or structures from Iron Age graves, as suggested for the 4th and 3rd centuries BC unaccompanied burials at Yarnton, Oxfordshire (Hey *et al* 1999).

The problem of the 'disappearing dead' is not merely a phenomenon in Britain and Ireland in the last millennium BC, but of extensive areas of central and western France and northern Spain as well, and this becomes even more marked in the Late La Tène when it affects much of temperate Europe. Though there is evidence of rites such as excarnation, cremation becomes common, especially in the later phases of the La Tène period, and there are regions where the burials may be very ephemeral and only survive in exceptional circumstances, for instance where there has been accumulation on, rather than erosion of, contemporary surfaces, or where remains may survive fortuitously in ditches. In the latter category is Burial 69 from Owslebury in Hampshire, the cremation of a child accompanied by two fragmentary pots and a burnt bronze bracelet with a glass ring threaded on it (Collis 1994), which predates the establishment of a formal cemetery in the mid 1st century BC. A similar case is to be found in the late 1st century BC at Chauniat in the Auvergne where the heavily cremated pottery and metal objects from two very rich burials were shovelled into the ditch of a square enclosure (Guichard and Orengo 1999). The nearby cemetery of Pâtural at Clermont-Ferrand dates to the early Augustan period; here the cremated remains and grave goods were simply left on the surface (Gouzel 1996; Deberge *et al*, in press) and only survived due to continued deposition of alluvium on the site. Sutton Common can be added to the increasing numbers of these ephemeral burial rites.

The contribution of Sutton Common to this broader debate of Iron Age mortuary rituals can only be limited, as the evidence from the excavations of the second phase activity is anything but unequivocal (see chapter 8). Nevertheless, the recognition that the small enclosures potentially played a part in funerary rituals, probably as separate locales defined by narrow ditches, where pyre debris could have been scattered or placed as a final stage of the mortuary rituals at Sutton Common, is important in this context. The scattering of the pyre debris, rather than burial, could account for the archaeological near-invisibility of the deceased, and their absence as 'burials' from the small mortuary enclosures may have resulted in these not being recognised as playing a role in mortuary rituals. Since scattered ashes can only be identified through the application of specific techniques, such as soil micromorphology (see section 8.4.3), one wonders how many mortuary enclosures elsewhere in Britain have gone unrecognised. For example, Whimster (1981, 339–44) lists 52 locations where small square enclosures have been identified by aerial photography outside Yorkshire, mostly in eastern England and the West Midlands. Several of these appear to be accompanied by graves or buried pyre debris, such as the group of six aligned squares at Greatford, Lincolnshire (*ibid*, 342), but the majority of sites include no trace burial. The presence of several small (c 5 × 5m) square and rectangular enclosures with openings to one site, and a circular enclosure without opening, next to the cremation cemetery at Westhampnett, West Sussex (Fitzpatrick 1997b), suggests that, conceivably, these small square enclosures could have been used for the scattering of the deceased's ashes and pyre debris or could have played some role in mortuary rituals in the Iron Age. The observations concerning the scattering of ashes from Sutton Common are applicable to wider areas of the British Iron Age and offer, for the first time, a realistic and archaeologically corroborated explanation for the near-invisibility of funerary rites.

## 10.5 Sutton Common – taking the past into the future  *by I Carstairs*

It is now almost twelve years since Jon Etté, the then regional Ancient Monuments Inspector with English Heritage, explained to me the importance of Sutton Common and how it would be desirable to find a way to bring it into protective ownership. Undaunted, and ever game for a challenge, the trustees of CCT boldly asserted 'We'll have a go!' And the rest, as they say, is history. Looked at from today, this adventure into the unknown has yielded extraordinary results, forged many friendships, and hopefully advanced our confidence that it is possible to truly integrate environmental, social, and economic activity in the heritage management of land.

But, it was a long gaze into a crystal ball, bolstered by hope rather than expectation. Nevertheless, what followed proved that concerted effort and a genuine willingness by all to work as a team can deliver wonderful results. The land has been reverted from arable to grassland and the edges of the smaller enclosure are no longer ploughed each year; the field drains have been re-engineered to raise groundwater levels; extensive research has been carried out on water tables and monitoring of the buried environment; large-scale archaeological investigations and analysis have been undertaken; and we have helped lessen the drying-out of the adjacent Shirley Pool SSSI along the way. These outcomes have been well beyond anything we could have dreamed at the outset.

Major issues remain, however. Despite everyone's best efforts it has not been possible to retain sufficient wetness throughout the year to guarantee the degree of preservation *in situ* we sought. When deciding what should be excavated, a clear rationale was developed. Based on an assessment of the groundwater fluctuations, a judgement was made as to the status of buried archaeological deposits, categorising them as those which (a) would survive into the future; (b) would not survive our lifetimes; and (c) were marginal.

Unfortunately, there is simply not enough water held on the Common throughout the summer months. Thus, virtually the same issues face the trustees of CCT today as at the outset of the project, only now there is a much greater understanding of the site. With advice from English Heritage and the specialists who have worked on the project from Exeter, Hull, and Sheffield universities, the trustees will need to consider whether further excavations should be sought for any areas we still fear will not survive our lifetimes, especially of the wet fill of the ditches around the enclosures.

Based on the research undertaken over the last six years, judgement seems to hold that further excavation of the ditch infill of the large enclosure would, on balance, be unlikely to yield much new information and on a cost-benefit basis could not be justified. The small enclosure presents a different situation. It is one of the very few upstanding prehistoric remains in South Yorkshire and to disturb its shape and authenticity unless absolutely necessary would be undesirable. However, it is known from the excavations carried out by various teams over the years that the ditches of the small enclosure contain interesting artefacts, such as the Sutton Common ladder, the then earliest known ladder in this country. Thus, sample excavations of strategically significant sections of the ditches here might be an effective compromise option.

The question also has to be asked as to whether new engineering works might be undertaken to try to sustain the groundwater levels over the whole Common through construction of a reservoir from which to top-up the deficiency. Given that it is the impact of the drop in groundwater in the surrounding area, not just on the Common, it seems unlikely that such action could be considered without the availability of significant funds for major works. Even if it was possible to undertake a project to isolate the Common from its surroundings and hold the levels by, for example, sinking vertical membranes in key areas to halt lateral loss of water, the quantity of water which would be needed to compensate for loss through evapo-transpiration and unavoidable seepage would be colossal and constructing a reservoir of sufficient size might not be desirable. It would, in any event, be highly intrusive to introduce such an artificial feature into this flat and still slightly haunting place.

Alternatively, thought could be given to trying to protect the small enclosure, by isolating it as a unit within the larger area of Sutton Common, but again the scale of engineering works could not be contemplated without significant funds and very careful planning to avoid adverse effects on the character of the area. On a more modest scale, perhaps a membrane to directly impede the groundwater flow out of the palaeochannel would be of benefit. Of the options facing CCT at the present time, evaluation as to whether further excavation work should be encouraged in connection with the ditches of the small enclosure seems worthy of early consideration. There is, of course, always the choice to do nothing other than establish a regime to manage the site as it is, though in the face of the drier summers predicted as a result of climatic change and a commitment to a sustainable future for the site, such a choice, at this stage, is unthinkable.

It would have been gratifying to have been able to have say that we had succeeded in maintaining adequate groundwater levels; however, being unable to do this should not be seen as failure. The experiences gained throughout the project, the outputs from the research, and the advancement of research techniques, have contributed widely both to the understanding of the site and of the Iron Age in this country. And we shouldn't overlook the mysterious, almost spiritual aspects of our experiences. The work over the last ten years has forged links forever between the site and the people of Askern, many of whom have worked on, or enjoyed and learned from the project in one way or another, and between the archaeological world and the hundreds of members of the public who visited on open days. The results of all of our endeavours can further fuel the imaginations of people who will visit here in the future. They will be able to stand on the banks of the palaeochannel at the entrance where the causeway reaches the larger enclosure and know that this enigmatic place was once full of granaries, with huge gateways and yet inexplicably people never lived here.

The discoveries in the larger enclosure remind us that we should never accept anything we are told without question, particularly when we consider that prior to this project, received wisdom held that the enclosure was empty or everything that might have been there had been destroyed. From the preceding pages in this volume it can be seen that this demonstrably was not the case.

Perhaps, one day, demonstration reconstructions might be built of the ramparts, gateways, and grain stores which stood here, not over the ancient site, but where Rushy Moor reaches the town, acting as a gateway from our time through which we can pass to an extraordinary place rooted in the past. It is remarkable how much has been achieved from what, to the untutored eye, were little more than a few humps and bumps in a bare arable field. But this is not the end of the story!

## Notes

1 The anthropologist Tim Ingold (1993) coined the term 'taskscape', meaning a socially constructed space of everyday human activity. The taskscape is an array of related activities, just as the landscape is an array of related features.

# Appendix 1  Details of macrofossil remains

Table 1  Complete list of plant and invertebrate taxa recorded from deposits excavated at Sutton Common, South Yorkshire (site code SCOM02-3)

*The list of plants includes all those recorded from assessments of material in 2002 and 2003 as well as the samples analysed in more detail from the 2003 excavation. Nomenclature and taxonomic order follow Tutin et al (1964–80) for vascular plants, Smith (1978) for mosses, and Kloet and Hincks (1964–77) for insects. Except in the case of remains of cereals (where all material was charred), plant material was preserved by anoxic waterlogging unless explicitly indicated otherwise. For insects: where both secure and tentative identifications for a given taxon were recorded, only the former are listed here. Ecological codes: d – damp ground/waterside taxa; l – wood associated taxa; oa – 'certain' outdoor taxa; ob – 'probable' outdoor taxa; p – strongly plant-associated taxa; rd – 'dry' decomposer taxa; rf – 'foul' decomposer taxa; rt – decomposer taxa not included in rd and rf; sf – facultatively synanthropic taxa; st – typical synanthropic taxa; u – uncoded (for statistical purposes); w – aquatic taxa. * = not used in calculating assemblage statistics. The remains were of adults unless otherwise stated. 'Sp' indicates that record was probably an additional taxon, 'sp indet' that the material may have been of a taxon listed above it.*

| Taxon | Vernacular | Parts |
| --- | --- | --- |
| Filicales | fern | pinnule fragments |
| *Salix* sp(p) | willow | twig epidermis fragments |
| cf *Salix* sp(p) | ?willow | twig fragments |
| *Salix/Populus* sp(p) | willow/poplar/aspen | charcoal fragments |
| *Populus tremula* L. | aspen | catkin scales |
| *Betula* sp(p) | birch | fruits |
| *Alnus glutinosa* (L.) Gaertner | alder | buds and/or bud-scales, female cones/cone-axes, female cone scales, fruits, immature leaves, male catkin fragments, twig fragments, charred female cone axis/axes |
| *Betula/Corylus* | birch/hazel | charcoal fragments |
| *Corylus avellana* L. | hazel | charred and uncharred nuts and/or nutshell fragments |
| *Quercus* sp(p) | oak | buds and/or bud-scales, twig and wood fragments, charcoal fragments, charred cotyledons and immature cupules |
| *Urtica dioica* L. | stinging nettle | achenes |
| *Polygonum aviculare* agg | knotgrass | charred and uncharred fruits |
| *P. hydropiper* L. | water-pepper | charred and uncharred fruits |
| *P. persicaria* L. | persicaria/red shank | charred and uncharred fruits |
| *P. lapathifolium* L. | pale persicaria | charred and uncharred fruits |
| Polygonaceae | dock/knotweed family | charred fruits |
| *Bilderdykia convolvulus* (L.) Dumort | black bindweed | charred and uncharred fruits and charred fruit fragments |
| *Rumex acetosella* agg. | sheep's sorrel | fruits |
| *Rumex* sp(p) | docks | charred and uncharred fruits |

| Taxon | Vernacular | Parts |
|---|---|---|
| *Chenopodium ficifolium* Sm. | fig-leaved goosefoot | seeds |
| *C. album* L. | fat hen | charred and uncharred seeds |
| *Atriplex* sp(p) | oraches | charred and uncharred seeds |
| Chenopodiaceae | goosefoot family | charred and uncharred seeds |
| *Montia fontana* ssp *chondrosperma* (Fenzl) Walters | blinks | charred and uncharred seeds |
| *Moehringia trinervia* (L.) Clairv. | three-nerved sandwort | seeds |
| *Stellaria media* (L.) Vill. | chickweed | seeds |
| *S.* cf *neglecta* Weihe in Bluff & Fingerh. | ?greater chickweed | seeds |
| *S. palustris* Retz./*S. graminea* L. | marsh/lesser stitchwort | seeds |
| *Stellaria* sp(p) | stitchworts/chickweeds | seeds |
| *Cerastium* sp(p) | mouse-ear chickweeds | seeds |
| *Silene dioica* (L.) Clairv. | red campion | seeds |
| Caryophyllaceae | pink/campion family | seeds |
| *Nuphar lutea* (L.) Sibth. & Sm. | yellow water-lily | seeds |
| *Ranunculus* Section *Ranunculus* | meadow/creeping/bulbous buttercup | charred and uncharred achenes |
| *R. sceleratus* L. | celery-leaved crowfoot | achenes |
| *R. flammula* L. | lesser spearwort | charred and uncharred achenes |
| *R.* cf *lingua* L. | ?greater spearwort | achenes |
| *R.* Subgenus *Batrachium* | water crowfoots | achenes |
| *Papaver somniferum* L. | opium poppy | seeds |
| *P. argemone* L. | long prickly-headed poppy | seeds |
| *Nasturtium officinale* R. Br. in Aiton | watercress | seeds |
| *Brassica rapa* L. | 'turnip' | charred seeds |
| *Raphanus raphanistrum* L. | wild radish | charred pod segments and/or fragments |
| *Filipendula ulmaria* (L.) Maxim. | meadowsweet | achenes |
| *Rubus idaeus* L. | raspberry | seeds |
| *Rubus fruticosus* agg. | blackberry/bramble | seeds |
| *Rubus* sp(p) | blackberries, etc. | charred and uncharred seeds, uncharred prickles |
| *Rosa* sp(p) | roses | achenes |
| *Potentilla palustris* (L.) Scop. | marsh cinquefoil | achenes |
| *P. anserine* L. | silverweed | charred and uncharred achenes |
| *P.* cf *erecta* (L.) Räuschel | ?tormentil | charred and uncharred achenes |
| *Potentilla* cf | cinquefoils, etc. | achenes |
| cf *Aphanes microcarpa* (Boiss. & Reuter) Rothm. | ?slender parsley-piert | achenes |

*(continued)*

**Table 1 Continued**

| Taxon | Vernacular | Parts |
|---|---|---|
| *Crataegus monogyna* Jacq. | hawthorn | pyrenes |
| *Crataegus* sp(p) | hawthorns | twig fragments with thorns |
| cf *Crataegus* sp(p) | ?hawthorns | pyrenes |
| *Prunus spinosa* L. | sloe | charred and uncharred fruitstones, thorns, twig fragments with thorns |
| *Prunus* sp(p) | sloe/plum/cherry, etc. | twig fragments |
| *Vicia* cf *tetrasperma* (L.) Schreber | ?smooth tare | charred seeds |
| *Vicia* sp(p) | vetches, etc. | charred seeds |
| Leguminosae | pea family | charred cotyledons and seeds |
| *Oxalis acetosella* L. | wood-sorrel | seeds |
| *Mercurialis perennis* L. | dog's mercury | seeds |
| *Ilex aquifolium* L. | holly | seeds |
| cf *I. aquifolium* L. | ?holly | leaf epidermis fragments |
| *Viola* sp(p) | violets/pansies, etc. | seeds |
| *Lythrum salicaria* L. | purple loosestrife | seeds |
| *Epilobium* sp(p) | willow-herbs, etc. | seeds |
| Umbelliferae | carrot family | mericarps |
| *Hydrocotyle vulgaris* L. | marsh pennywort | mericarps |
| *Berula erecta* (Hudson) Coville | narrow-leaved water-parsnip | mericarps |
| *Oenanthe aquatica* (L.) Poiret in Lam. | fine-leaved water-dropwort | mericarps |
| *Oenanthe* sp(p) | water-dropworts | mericarps |
| *Aethusa cynapium* L. | fool's parsley | mericarps |
| *Fraxinus excelsior* L. | ash | wood fragments |
| *Galium aparine* L. | goosegrass, cleavers | charred and uncharred fruits, uncharred epicarp |
| *Galium* sp(p) | bedstraws, etc. | charred fruits |
| *Ajuga reptans* L. | bugle | charred and uncharred nutlets |
| cf *Marrubium vulgare* L. | ?white horehound | nutlets |
| *Galeopsis* Subgenus *Galeopsis* | hemp-nettles | nutlets |
| *Galeopsis* sp(p) | hemp-nettles | charred nutlets |
| *Lamium* Section *Lamiopsis* | annual dead-nettles | nutlets |
| *Stachys* sp(p) | woundworts | nutlets |
| cf *Glechoma hederacea* L. | ?ground-ivy | nutlets |
| *Prunella vulgaris* L. | selfheal | nutlets |
| *Lycopus europaeus* L. | gipsywort | nutlets |
| *Mentha* sp(p) | mints | nutlets |
| Labiatae | mint family | nutlets |
| *Hyoscyamus niger* L. | henbane | seeds |

| Taxon | Vernacular | Parts |
|---|---|---|
| *Solanum* cf *nigrum* L. | ?black nightshade | seeds |
| *S. dulcamara* L. | woody nightshade | seeds |
| *Rhinanthus* sp(p) | yellow rattles | charred seeds |
| *Plantago* cf *media* L. | ?hoary plantain | charred seeds |
| *Sambucus* cf *ebulus* L. | ?danewort | seeds |
| *S. nigra* L. | elder | seeds and seed fragments |
| cf *S. nigra* | ?elder | wood fragments |
| *Eupatorium cannabinum* L. | hemp agrimony | achenes |
| *Bidens* sp(p) | bur-marigolds | achenes |
| *Matricaria maritima* L./ *M. perforata* Mérat | sea/scentless mayweed | charred achenes |
| *Carduus/Cirsium* sp(p) | thistles | achenes |
| *Sonchus asper* (L.) Hill | prickly sow-thistle | achenes |
| *S.* cf *oleraceus* L. | ?sow-thistle | achenes |
| *Taraxacum* sp(p) | dandelions | achenes |
| *Lapsana communis* L. | nipplewort | charred achenes |
| *Alisma* sp(p) | water-plantains | carpels and/or seeds |
| *Potamogeton* sp(p) | pondweeds | pyrenes |
| *Zannichellia palustris* L. | horned pondweed | fruits |
| *Juncus inflexus* L./*J. effusus* L./ *J. conglomeratus* L. | hard/soft/compact rush | seeds |
| *J.* cf *compressus* Jacq. | ?round-fruited rush | seeds |
| *J. compressus/J. gerardi* Lois. | round-fruited/saltmarsh rush | seeds |
| *J. bufonius* L. | toad rush | seeds |
| *Juncus acutiflorus* Ehrh. ex Hoffm./ *J. articulatus* L. | sharp-flowered/jointed rush | seeds |
| *J.* cf *articulatus* L. | ?jointed rush | seeds |
| *Juncus* sp(p) | rushes | seeds |
| *Glyceria* sp(p) | sweet-grasses | caryopses |
| *Bromus* sp(p) | bromes, etc. | charred caryopses |
| cf *Arrhenatherum elatius* ssp *bulbosum* (Willd.) Schübler & Martens. | ?false oat-grass | charred rhizome fragments |
| *Alopecurus* sp(p) | foxtails | waterlogged caryopses |
| *Danthonia decumbens* (L.) DC. in Lam. & DC. | heath grass | charred and uncharred caryopses |
| Gramineae | grasses | charred and uncharred caryopses, charred culm nodes, charred spikelets/spikelet fragments |
| Gramineae/Cerealia | grasses/cereals | charred caryopses |
| *Triticum dicoccon* Schrank | emmer | charred spikelet forks |

*(continued)*

**Table 1 Continued**

| Taxon | Vernacular | Parts |
|---|---|---|
| *T.* cf *dicoccon* | ?emmer | charred caryopses, glume-bases, spikelet forks |
| *Triticum spelta* L. | spelt wheat | charred caryopses, glume-bases, spikelet forks, spikelets/spikelet fragments |
| *Triticum* cf *'aestivo-compactum'* | ?bread/club wheat | charred caryopses |
| *Triticum* sp(p) | wheats | charred caryopses, glumes, glume-bases, spikelet forks |
| *Hordeum* sp(p) | barley | charred caryopses, rachis fragments, rachis internodes |
| *Avena* cf *fatua* L. | ?wild oat | charred spikelets/spikelet fragments |
| *Avena* sp(p) | oats | charred caryopses |
| Cerealia indet | cereals | charred awns/awn fragments, caryopses, lemmas and/or glumes |
| cf Cerealia indet | ?cereals | charred culm-nodes |
| *Lemna* sp(p) | duckweeds | seeds |
| *Sparganium* sp(p) | bur-reeds | charred and uncharred fruits |
| *Typha* sp(p) | reedmaces | seeds |
| cf *Scirpus lacustris sensu lato* | ?bulrush | nutlets |
| *S. setaceus* L. | bristle club-rush | charred and uncharred nutlets |
| *Eleocharis palustris sensu lato* | common spike-rush | nutlets |
| *Carex* sp(p) | sedges | charred and uncharred nutlets |

**Mosses** (all remains were leaves and/or shoot fragments unless otherwise indicated)

| | | |
|---|---|---|
| *Sphagnum* sp(p) | | leaves |
| *Polytrichum* sp(p) | | charred shoot fragments |
| *Fissidens* sp(p) | | |
| *Bryum* sp(p) | | |
| *Ulota* sp(p) | | |
| *Neckera complanata* (Hedw.) Hüb. | | |
| *Thuidium tamariscinum* (Hedw.) Br. Eur. | | |
| *Cratoneuron filicinum* (Hedw.) Spruce | | |
| cf *C. commutatum* (Hedw.) Roth | | |
| cf *Campylium* sp(p) | | |
| *Drepanocladus* sp(p) | | |
| *Calliergon giganteum* (Schimp.) Kindb. | | |
| *C. cuspidatum* (Hedw.) Kindb. | | |
| *Isothecium myurum* Brid. | | |
| *I. myosuroides* Brid. | | |

| Taxon | Vernacular | Parts |
|---|---|---|
| *Homalothecium sericeum* (Hedw.) Br. Eur./*H. lutescens* (Hedw.) Robins. | | |
| *Eurhynchium* cf *striatum* (Hedw.) Schimp. | | |
| *E. praelongum* (Hedw.) Br. Eur. | | |
| *Eurhynchium* sp(p) | | |
| *Hypnum* cf *cupressiforme* Hedw. | | |
| *Rhytidiadelphus* sp(p) | | |

## Fungi

| Taxon | Vernacular | Parts |
|---|---|---|
| *Rosellinia* cf *mammiformis* (Persoon ex Fries) Cesati & de Notaris | | perithecia |
| *Rosellinia* sp(p) | | perithecia |

## Algae

| Taxon | Vernacular | Parts |
|---|---|---|
| Characeae | | oogonia |

## Invertebrates

| Taxon | Ecological code | Taxon | Ecological code |
|---|---|---|---|
| *Oligochaeta sp. (egg capsule) | u | *Trechus micros* (Herbst) | u |
| *Trichoptera sp (case) | oa-w | *Bembidion lampros* (Herbst) | oa |
| *Trichoptera sp (larva) | oa-w | *Bembidion doris* (Panzer) | oa-d |
| *Daphnia* sp (ephippium) | oa-w | *Bembidion obtusum* Serville | oa |
| *Cladocera sp (ephippium) | oa-w | *Bembidion guttula* or *mannerheimi* | oa |
| *Ostracoda sp | u | *Bembidion* (*Philochthus*) sp indet | oa |
| *Dermaptera sp | u | *Bembidion* sp | oa |
| *Drymus brunneus* (Sahlberg) | oa-p | *Pterostichus nigrita* (Paykull) | oa-d |
| *Derephysia foliacea* (Fallen) | oa-p | *Pterostichus ?strenuus* (Panzer) | oa |
| Corixidae sp | oa-w | *Pterostichus* sp | ob |
| *Megophthalmus* sp | oa-p | *Calathus fuscipes* (Goeze) | oa |
| *Aphrodes bicinctus* (Schrank) | oa-p | *Agonum obscurum* (Herbst) | oa-d |
| Cicadellidae spp | oa-p | ?*Agonum* sp | oa |
| Delphacidae spp | oa-p | *Amara* sp | oa |
| *Aphidoidea sp | u | ?*Harpalus* sp | oa |
| *Lepidoptera sp (pupa) | u | ?*Bradycellus* sp | oa |
| *Chironomidae sp (larva) | w | *Metabletus* sp | oa |
| *Bibionidae sp | u | Carabidae spp and spp indet | ob |
| *Diptera sp (adult) | u | *Haliplus* sp | oa-w |
| *Diptera sp (puparium) | u | *Hygrotus inaequalis* (Fabricius) | oa-w |
| *Dyschirius globosus* (Herbst) | oa | *Hydroporus* spp | oa-w |
| *Clivina fossor* (Linnaeus) | oa | Hydroporinae sp | oa-w |
| *Trechus obtusus* Erichson | oa | *Agabus* sp | oa-w |
| *Trechus quadristriatus* (Schrank) | oa | *Ilybius fuliginosus* (Fabricius) | oa-w |
| *Trechus secalis* (Paykull) | oa-d | *Agabus* or *Ilybius* sp | oa-w |

| | | | |
|---|---|---|---|
| *Colymbetes fuscus* (Linnaeus) | oa-w | *Anthobium atrocephalum* (Gyllenhal) | oa |
| *Dytiscus* sp | oa-w | *Anthobium* sp indet | oa |
| Dytiscidae sp indet | oa-w | *?Olophrum assimile* (Paykull) | oa |
| *Gyrinus* sp | oa-w | *Olophrum piceum* (Gyllenhal) | oa |
| *Hydrochus elongatus* (Schaller) | oa-w | *Acidota crenata* (Fabricius) | oa |
| *Hydrochus* sp indet | oa-w | *Lesteva heeri* Fauvel | oa-d |
| *Helophorus aquaticus* (Linnaeus) | oa-w | *Lesteva longoelytrata* (Goeze) | oa-d |
| *Helophorus grandis* Illiger | oa-w | *Omalium* sp | rt |
| *Helophorus* spp | oa-w | Omaliinae spp | rt |
| *Coelostoma orbiculare* (Fabricius) | oa-w | *Carpelimus bilineatus* Stephens | rt-sf |
| *Sphaeridium lunatum* or *scarabaeoides* | rf | *Carpelimus ?corticinus* (Gravenhorst) | oa-d |
| *Cercyon ?pygmaeus* (Illiger) | rf-st | *Carpelimus elongatulus* (Erichson) | oa-d |
| *Cercyon tristis* (Illiger) | oa-d | *Carpelimus ?rivularis* (Motschulsky) | ob-d |
| *Cercyon ustulatus* (Preyssler) | oa-d | Carpelimus spp indet | u |
| *Cercyon* sp | u | *Platystethus alutaceus* Thomson | oa-d |
| *Megasternum obscurum* (Marsham) | rt | *Platystethus arenarius* (Fourcroy) | rf |
| *Hydrobius fuscipes* (Linnaeus) | oa-w | *Platystethus ?nitens* (Sahlberg) | oa-d |
| *Anacaena* sp | oa-w | *Platystethus nodifrons* (Mannerheim) | oa-d |
| *Laccobius* sp | oa-w | *Anotylus ?nitidulus* (Gravenhorst) | rt |
| Hydrophilinae spp and spp indet | oa-w | *Anotylus rugosus* (Fabricius) | rt |
| *Abraeus* sp | l | *Anotylus sculpturatus* group | rt |
| *Acritus homoeopathicus* Wollaston | u | *Stenus* spp | u |
| *Acritus nigricornis* (Hoffmann) | rt-st | *Euaesthetus* sp | oa |
| *Onthophilus striatus* (Forster) | rt-sf | *Lathrobium* spp | u |
| *Ochthebius bicolon* Germar | oa-w | *Rugilus orbiculatus* (Paykull) | rt-sf |
| *Ochthebius minimus* (Fabricius) | oa-w | *Rugilus rufipes* Germar | rt-st |
| *Ochthebius* sp | oa-w | *Rugilus* sp indet | rt |
| *Hydraena ?nigrita* Germar | oa-w | Paederinae sp | u |
| *Hydraena testacea* Curtis | oa-w | *Othius myrmecophilus* Kiesenwetter | rt |
| *Hydraena* sp indet | oa-w | *Othius* sp | rt |
| *Limnebius aluta* (Bedel) | oa-w | *Gyrohypnus ?angustatus* Stephens | rt-st |
| *Limnebius ?papposus* Mulsant | oa-w | *Xantholinus gallicus* or *linearis* | rt-sf |
| *Limnebius truncatellus* (Thunberg) | oa-w | *Xantholinus longiventris* Heer | rt-sf |
| *Limnebius* sp indet | oa-w | Xantholininae sp indet | u |
| *Ptenidium* sp | rt | *Erichsonius cinerascens* (Gravenhorst) | oa-d |
| *Acrotrichis* spp | rt | *Philonthus* sp | u |
| Leiodidae sp | u | *Gabrius* sp | rt |
| *Agathidium* spp | u | *Quedius* sp | u |
| *Nargus velox* (Spence) | u | Staphylininae spp indet | u |
| *Catops* spp | u | *Tachyporus* sp | u |
| *Silpha atrata* Linnaeus | u | *Tachinus ?signatus* Gravenhorst | u |
| Scydmaenidae sp | u | *Hygronoma dimidiata* (Gravenhorst) | rtd |
| *Micropeplus fulvus* Erichson | rt | *Falagria caesa* or *sulcatula* | rt-sf |
| *Micropeplus staphylinoides* (Marsham) | rt | *Falagria* or *Cordalia* sp indet | rt-sf |
| *Megarthrus* sp | rt | *Aleochara* sp | u |

| | | | |
|---|---|---|---|
| Aleocharinae spp | u | *Lathridius minutus* group | rd-st |
| *Pselaphus heisei* (Herbst) | u | *Enicmus* sp | rt-sf |
| Pselaphidae spp | u | *Dienerella* sp | rd-sf |
| *Geotrupes* spp | oa-rf | *Corticaria* sp | rt-sf |
| *Colobopterus fossor* (Linnaeus) | oa-rf | *Corticarina* or *Cortinicara* sp | rt |
| *Aphodius ater* (Degeer) | oa-rf | *Alosterna tabacicolor* (Degeer) | l |
| *Aphodius contaminatus* (Herbst) | oa-rf | ?Cerambycidae sp | l |
| *Aphodius ?prodromus* (Brahm) | ob-rf | *Plateumaris* sp | oa-d-p |
| *Aphodius rufipes* (Linnaeus) | oa-rf | *Hydrothassa* sp | oa-d-p |
| *Aphodius ?sphacelatus* (Panzer) | oa-rf | *Prasocuris phellandrii* (Linnaeus) | oa-p-d |
| *Aphodius* sp and spp indet | ob-rf | Chrysomelinae sp | oa-p |
| *Serica brunnea* (Linnaeus) | oa-p | ?*Galerucella* sp | oa-p |
| *Phyllopertha horticola* (Linnaeus) | oa-p | *Phyllotreta* sp | oa-p |
| *Clambus* sp | rt-sf | *Chaetocnema ?concinna* (Marsham) | oa-p |
| *Microcara testacea* (Linnaeus) | oa-p-d | Halticinae sp | oa-p |
| *Cyphon* spp | oa-d | *Deporaus betulae* (Linnaeus) | oa-p |
| *Dryops* sp?p | oa-d | *Apion* sp | oa-p |
| *Esolus parallelepipedus* (Müller) | oa-w | *Phyllobius argentatus* (Linnaeus) | oa-p |
| *Ampedus ?balteatus* (Linnaeus) | u | *Barypeithes* sp | oa-p |
| *Melanotus erythropus* (Gmelin) | l | *Strophosomus* sp | oa-p |
| *\*Melanotus erythropus* (Gmelin) (larva) | l | *Sitona* sp | oa-p |
| *Athous haemorrhoidalis* (Fabricius) | oa-p | *Acalles* sp | u |
| *Ctenicera cuprea* (Fabricius) | oa-p | *Notaris acridulus* (Linnaeus) | oa-d-p |
| *\*?Actenicerus sjaelandicus* (Müller) (larva) | oa | *Orthochaetes* sp | oa-p |
| *\*Denticollis linearis* (Linnaeus) (larva) | u | *Ceutorhynchus* spp | oa-p |
| Elateridae sp | ob | Ceuthorhynchinae sp | oa-p |
| *\*Elateridae sp indet (larva) | ob | *Gymnetron ?pascuorum* (Gyllenhal) | oa-p |
| *Grynobius planus* (Fabricius) | l | *Rhynchaenus* sp | oa-p |
| *Anobium* sp | l | Curculionidae spp and spp indet | oa |
| *Lyctus linearis* (Goeze) | l-sf | *Scolytus* sp | l |
| *Brachypterus* sp | oa-p | *Hylesinus oleiperda* (Fabricius) | u |
| *Rhizophagus dispar* (Paykull) | l | *Dryocoetinus villosus* (Fabricius) | l |
| *Monotoma bicolor* Villa | rt-st | ?*Taphrorychus bicolor* (Herbst) | l |
| *Monotoma longicollis* (Gyllenhall) | rt-st | Scolytidae sp | l |
| *Monotoma* sp indet | rt-sf | Coleoptera spp | u |
| *Cryptophagus* spp | rd-sf | *\*Coleoptera spp indet (larva) | u |
| *Atomaria* sp | rd | *\*Proctotrupoidea sp | u |
| *Phalacrus caricis* Sturm | oa-p | *\*Hymenoptera sp | u |
| *Cerylon ferrugineum* Stephens | l | *\*Formicidae sp | u |
| *Orthoperus* sp | rt | *\*Insecta sp (pupa) | u |
| Corylophidae sp | rt | *\*Pseudoscorpiones sp | u |
| *Coccidula rufa* (Herbst) | oa-p-d | *\*Aranae sp | u |
| Coccinellidae sp | oa-p | *\*Acarina sp | u |
| *Stephostethus lardarius* (Degeer) | rt-st | *\*Lophopus crystallinus* (Pallas) | oa-w |

194  Sutton Common

Tables 2a–b  Data concerning assemblages of charred plant remains from Sutton Common

Table 2a  Quantification of charred material from those assemblages containing moderate or large quantities of remains other than wood charcoal (actual or estimated total number of cereal grains per kg >49, where this could be calculated; records in cases where very few remains were found are given in Table 2b)

NB Table 2a is divided into two parts

*Numbers estimated from, or including an estimated component from, a subsample of the one or more of the sieved fractions are shown in italics. '+' in the row for emmer grains indicates that a few grains within a much larger component of '?spelt may be referable to this species. '+' or '++' in the row for Cerealia indicates some/many unidentified cereal grain fragments also present. Scores on a four-point scale are given for charcoal, along with the size of the largest fragment (in millimetres)*

Key to abbreviations: Plant parts: f—one or a few fragments; fca—female cone axes; frtst—fruitstones; gl—glume; glb—glume-bases; lem—lemma fragments; nsf—nutshell fragments; rac—rachis fragments; scl—sclerotia; spf—spikelet forks. Context types: Po—posthole fill (Po4—from four-post structure); Pi—Pit fill; crem—'cremation'; dep—'deposit'

Table 2a (pt 1)

| Context | | 1093 | 1099 | 3004 | 3008 | 3016 | 3032 | 5408/5409 | 5431 | 5433 | 5635 | 7246 | 7246 | 7246 |
|---|---|---|---|---|---|---|---|---|---|---|---|---|---|---|
| Context type | | Po4 | Po4 | Po4 | Po4 | Po4 | Po4 | Po?4 | Po4 | Po4 | Po | Po4c | Po4c | Po4c |
| Four-poster group | | A | A | B | B | C | D | PP | N | N | - | T | T | T |
| Sample | | 1 | 1 | 8 | 10 | 12 | 46 | 1 | 1 | 1 | 2 | 1 | 2 | 5 |
| Wt (kg) | | 2.4 | 2.47 | 3 | 3 | 3 | 3 | 3 | 3 | 3 | 3 | ? | ? | ? |
| Approx proportion (% by weight) of 2–4mm fraction examined) | | 25 | 12 | 33 | 33 | 100 | 100 | 17 | 25 | 13 | 25 | 100 | 100 | 100 |
| Taxon | Parts | | | | | | | | | | | | | |
| Grains | | | | | | | | | | | | | | |
| *Triticum* cf *dicoccon*[1] | | + | + | | | | | | | | | | + | + |
| *T.* cf *spelta* | | *406*[1] | *392*[2] | *17* | *86* | *104*[2] | *25* | *827* | *178* | *135* | *197* | *45*[3] | *162*[3] | *120*[3] |
| *Triticum* sp(p) | | | | | | 3 | | | | | | | | |
| *Hordeum* sp(p) | | | *8* | *87* | *145* | *19* | *14* | *152* | *12* | *83* | *75* | *73*[4] | *170*[4] | *79*[4] |
| *Avena* sp(p) | | | | | | | | | | | | *1* | *(1)* | |
| Cerealia | | *174+* | *2085 ++* | *220+* | *83+* | *130+* | *111+* | *937 ++* | *130+* | *339+* | *1289+* | *35+* | *136+* | *37+* |
| Total grain | | *580* | *2485* | *324* | *314* | *256* | *150* | *1916* | *320* | *557* | *1561* | *154* | *469* | *236* |

|  |  | 242 | 1006 | 108 | 105 | 82 | 50 | 639 | 107 | 186 | 520 | ? | ? | ? |
|---|---|---|---|---|---|---|---|---|---|---|---|---|---|---|
| Nos grain/kg |  | 242 | 1006 | 108 | 105 | 82 | 50 | 639 | 107 | 186 | 520 | ? | ? | ? |
| **Wheat:Barley** |  | ∞ | 49 | 0.2 | 0.6 | 5.6 | 1.8 | 5.4 | 14.8 | 1.6 | 2.6 | 0.6 | 0.9 | 1.5 |
| **Chaff** |  |  |  |  |  |  |  |  |  |  |  |  |  |  |
| *Triticum dicoccum* | glb | 12 |  |  | 6 |  |  |  |  |  |  |  |  |  |
|  | spf |  |  | ?2 | ?6 |  | ?7 | ?1 |  |  |  |  | (11) |  |
| *T. spelta* | glb | 12+ | 33+ | 17 | 17 |  |  | 35 |  | 6 | 6 | 2 |  |  |
|  |  | ?29 | ?30 |  |  |  |  |  |  |  |  |  |  |  |
|  | spf | 8+ | 45+ | 3 | 5 | 2 | ?5 | 28 | ?2 |  |  | ?3 | ?5 | ?7 |
|  |  | ?25 | ?60 |  |  |  |  |  |  |  |  |  |  |  |
| *Triticum* sp | glb |  |  | 9 | 15 | 2 | 1 | 30 |  |  | 2 |  |  | 1 |
| (probably dicoccon/spelta) | spf |  |  | 4 | 12 |  | 2 | 66 | 3 |  | 3 | 1 |  |  |
| *Hordeum* sp(p) | lem |  |  |  |  |  |  | 4 |  |  |  |  |  |  |
|  | rac |  |  | 2 | 3 |  |  |  |  |  |  |  |  |  |
| Cerealia (glume/lemma fragments) |  |  |  |  |  |  |  | ++ |  |  |  |  |  |  |
| Total chaff |  | 86 | 168 | 37 | 64 | 4 | 15 | 160++ | 5 | 6 | 11 | 6 | 16 | 8 |
| **Grain:Chaff** |  | 6.7 | 14.8 | 8.8 | 4.9 | 64 | 10 | 12 | 64 | 93 | 142 | 25.7 | 29.3 | 29.5 |
| **Other propagules** |  |  |  |  |  |  |  |  |  |  |  |  |  |  |
| *Polygonum aviculare* agg. |  |  |  |  | 1 |  |  |  |  |  |  |  |  |  |
| *P. persicaria/lapathifolium* |  |  |  |  | 1 |  |  |  |  |  |  |  |  |  |
| *Rumex* sp(p) |  | 1 |  | 1 | 1 |  |  |  |  |  |  |  |  |  |
| *Bilderdykia convolvulus* |  |  | 10 | 1 | 1 |  |  | 3 | 2 |  | 10[6] |  | 1 |  |
| Polygonaceae |  |  |  |  |  |  |  | 1 | 1 |  |  |  |  |  |
| *Chenopodium ficifolium* |  |  |  |  |  |  |  | 2 |  |  |  |  |  |  |
| *C. album* |  | 3 |  | 3 | 1 |  | 1 | 7 | 1 |  |  |  |  |  |

(continued)

Table 2a (pt 1) Continued

| Context | 1093 | 1099 | 3004 | 3008 | 3016 | 3032 | 5408/5409 | 5431 | 5433 | 5635 | 7246 | 7246 | 7246 |
|---|---|---|---|---|---|---|---|---|---|---|---|---|---|
| Context type | Po4 | Po4 | Po4 | Po4 | Po4 | Po4 | Po?4 | Po4 | Po4 | Po | Po4c | Po4c | Po4c |
| Four-poster group | A | A | B | B | C | D | PP | N | N | - | T | T | T |
| Sample | 1 | 1 | 8 | 10 | 12 | 46 | 1 | 1 | 1 | 2 | 1 | 2 | 5 |
| *Atriplex* sp(p) | 1 | | 2 | | | | | | | 2 | | | |
| Chenopodiaceae | | | | | | | | 2 | | | | | |
| *Montia fontana* ssp *chondrosperma* | | | | | | | | | | | | | |
| *Brassica rapa* | | | | | | | | | | | | | |
| Leguminosae (<2 mm) | | 6 | | | | | 1 | | | 1 | | | |
| *Galium aparine* | | | | | | | | 1 | | | | | |
| *Galium* sp(p) | | | | 1 | | | | | | | | | (1) |
| *Plantago* cf *media* | | | | | | | 1 | | | | | | |
| *Matricaria maritima/perforata* | | | | | | | 1 | | | | | | |
| *Lapsana communis* | | 2 | | | | | | | | | | | |
| *Bromus* sp(p) | 2 | 89 | | | 1 | 1 | 4 | | 2 | 5 | 2 | 6 | 5 |
| Gramineae (large-seeded) | 16 | | | | | | | | | | | 4 | |
| Gramineae (medium-sized) | | | | | | | | | | | | | |
| Gramineae (small) | 3 | | | | | | | | 2 | | | | 1 |
| *Sparganium* sp(p) | | | | | | | 1 | | | | | | |
| *Scirpus setaceus* | | | | | | | | | | | | | |
| *Carex* sp(p) | 1 | | | | | | | | | 1 | | | |
| Indet | | | | | | | | | | | | | |

**Other plant material**

| | | | | | | | | | | | | | |
|---|---|---|---|---|---|---|---|---|---|---|---|---|---|
| Gramineae culm nodes | | | | | | + | | | | | | | |
| herbaceous detritus | + | | | | | | | | | | | | |
| root/rhizome fragments | | | | | | | | | | | | | |
| charcoal | ++25 | +15 | +15 | +15 | +15 | +10 | +10 | +10 | +10 | +10 | ++5 | ++5 | +5 |

**Notes**

[1] Counted amongst ?spelt grains; + indicates the likely presence of one or more tentatively identified emmer grains
[2] Probably includes at least some grains which were definitely spelt, on the basis of remnants of chaff adhering to them
[3] Includes some 'withered' or 'shrunken' grains
[4] Includes one or two specimens showing evidence of germination
[5] Including a small proportion of very small specimens
[6] All rather small specimens

Table 2a (pt 2)

| Taxon | Parts | 7257 | 7264 | 7265 | 31270 | 31351 | 31375 | 31381/31382 | 31434 |
|---|---|---|---|---|---|---|---|---|---|
| Context type | | Pi | Po4 | Po4 | Po4 | Po4 | Po4 | Po4 | Po4 |
| Four-poster group | | – | T | T | P | P | K | K | J |
| Sample | | 1 | 1 | 1 | 154 | 153 | 144 | 142 | 148 |
| Wt (kg) | | 3 | 3 | 3 | 3 | 3 | 3 | 3 | 3 |
| Approx proportion (% by weight) of 2–4 mm fraction examined | | 25 | 100 | 14 | 14 | 33 | 33 | 14 | 20 |
| **Grains** | | | | | | | | | |
| *Triticum* cf *dicoccon*[1] | | | | | | | | | |
| *T.* cf *spelta* | | 248[5] | 40 | 637 | 502 | 124[3] | 75[2] | 82[2] | 60 |
| *Triticum* sp(p) | | 353[5] | 80 | 28 | 31 | 25 | 49 | 37 | 5 |
| *Hordeum* sp(p) | | | | | | | | | |
| *Avena* sp(p) | | | | | | | | | |
| Cerealia | | 133+ | 80+ | 337+ | 432+ | 222+ | 248+ | 476+ | 115+ |
| Total grain | | 734 | 200 | 1002 | 965 | 371 | 372 | 595 | 180 |
| Nos grain/kg | | 245 | 66 | 334 | 321 | 123 | 124 | 198 | 60 |
| **Wheat:Barley** | | 0.7 | 0.5 | 22.8 | 16.2 | 4.9 | 1.5 | 2.2 | 12 |
| **Chaff** | | | | | | | | | |
| *Triticum dicoccum* | glb | | | | | | ?1 | | ?3 |
| | spf | | | | ?2 | | 1 | | ?2 |
| *T. spelta* | glb | | 1 | 37 | ?2 | 11 | 4 | 2 | 8 |
| | spf | | | 3 | 8 | 7 | | | |
| *Triticum* sp (probably *dicoccon/spelta*) | glb | | | 18 | 10 | 9 | | 2 | |
| | spf | | 1 | 30 | 21 | 11 | 2 | 14 | |

| | | | | | | | | |
|---|---|---|---|---|---|---|---|---|
| Hordeum sp(p) | lem | + | | | | | | |
| | rac | 1 | | | | | | |
| Cerealia (glume/lemma fragments) | | | | | | 1 | | |
| Total chaff | | 1+ | 2 | 88 | 43 | 39 | 8 | 18 | 13 |
| **Grain:Chaff** | | 734 | 100 | 11.4 | 22.4 | 9.5 | 46.5 | 33 | 13.8 |
| **Other propagules** | | | | | | | | | |
| Polygonum aviculare agg. | | | | | | | | | |
| P. persicaria/lapathifolium | | | | | | | | | |
| Rumex sp(p) | | | | | | | | | |
| Bilderdykia convolvulus | | f | | 2 | | | 2 | 1 | |
| Polygonaceae | | | | | | | | | |
| Chenopodium ficifolium | | | | | | | | | |
| C. album | | 1 | | 1 | | | | | |
| Atriplex sp(p) | | | | | | | 1 | | |
| Chenopodiaceae | | | | | | | | | |
| Montia fontana ssp chondrosperma | | | | | | | | | |
| Brassica rapa | | | | 1 | | | | | |
| Leguminosae (<2 mm) | | | | | | 2 | | | |
| Galium aparine | | | | 1 | | | | | |
| Galium sp(p) | | | | | | | | | |
| Plantago cf media | | | | | | | | | |
| Matricaria maritima/perforata | | | | | | | | | |
| Lapsana communis | | | | 89 | | | | | |
| Bromus sp(p) | | 1 | | | | | | | |

(continued)

Table 2a (pt 2)  Continued

| Context | 7257 | 7264 | 7265 | 31270 | 31351 | 31375 | 31381/31382 | 31434 |
|---|---|---|---|---|---|---|---|---|
| **Context type** | Pi | Po4 | Po4 | Po4 | Po4 | Po4 | Po4 | Po4 |
| **Four-poster group** | – | T | T | P | P | K | K | J |
| **Sample** | 1 | 1 | 1 | 154 | 153 | 144 | 142 | 148 |
| Gramineae (large-seeded) | | | | | | | | |
| Gramineae (medium-sized) | | | 12 | | | 2 | | 2 |
| Gramineae (small) | | | | | | | 5 | |
| *Sparganium* sp(p) | | | | | | | | |
| *Scirpus setaceus* | | | | | | | | |
| *Carex* sp(p) | | | | | | | | |
| indet | | | | | | | | |
| **Other plant material** | | | | | | | | |
| Gramineae culm nodes | | | | | | | | |
| herbaceous detritus | | | | | | | | |
| root/rhizome fragments | | | | | | | | |
| charcoal | +25 | ++20 | ++25 | +10 | +10 | +15 | ++30 | +10 |

Appendix 1   201

**Table 2b (pt 1)** Records of charred remains for assemblages consisting of very few individuals

Key as in Table 2a. Where no counts were made the data are present as '+' = present

*Context types (in addition to abbreviations used in Table 2a): IDN—inner ditch fill to N of E entrance; IDS—ditto, to S of E entrance; IDT, ditto, close to terminal; ODS—outer ditch fill to S of E entrance*

NB The table is divided into three parts

| Context | | 1079 | 1174 | 3002 | 3010 | 3012 | 3018 | 3020 | 3022 | 3150 | 3454 | 3492 | 3535[1] |
|---|---|---|---|---|---|---|---|---|---|---|---|---|---|
| Context type | | PoBR | Po | Po4 | Po4 | Po4 | Po4 | Po4 | Po4 | IDT | ODS | IDS | IDN |
| Four-poster group | | – | – | B | B | C | D | D | C | – | – | – | – |
| Sample | | 1 | 1 | 1 | 9 | 44 | 37 | 36 | 11 | 31 | 1 | 77 | 51+96 |
| Wt (kg) | | 0.44 | 3 | 3 | 3 | 3 | 3 | 3 | 3 | 3 | 3 | 3 | 6 |
| **Taxon** | Parts | | | | | | | | | | | | |
| **Grains** | | | | | | | | | | | | | |
| *Triticum* cf *dicoccon* | | | | | | | | | | | | | |
| *T.* cf *spelta* | | 1 | | 1 | + | 6 | 12 | 9 | 2 | 1 | | 3 | 17 |
| *Triticum* sp(p) | | | | | | | | | | | | | |
| *Hordeum* sp(p) | | | | | + | 13 | 5 | 27 | 1 | | | | |
| Cerealia | | | | 7+ | | 58+ | 37 | 92 | 1 | | | | |
| Total grain | | 1 | | 8 | + | 77 | 54 | 128 | 4 | 1 | | 3 | 17 |
| Wheat:Barley | | – | – | – | – | (0.5) | (2.4) | 0.3 | – | – | – | – | – |
| **Chaff** | | | | | | | | | | | | | |
| *Triticum dicoccum* | glb | | | | ?+ | | | | | | | | |
| | spf | | | | | | | | | | | | |
| *T. spelta* | glb | | 1 | | + | | 1 | | | | ?1 | | |
| | spf | | | | | | | | | | ?1 | | |

(continued)

202 *Sutton Common*

Table 2b (pt 1)  Continued

| Context | | 1079 | 1174 | 3002 | 3010 | 3012 | 3018 | 3020 | 3022 | 3150 | 3454 | 3492 | 3535[1] |
|---|---|---|---|---|---|---|---|---|---|---|---|---|---|
| Context type | | PoBR | Po | Po4 | Po4 | Po4 | Po4 | Po4 | Po4 | IDT | ODS | IDS | IDN |
| Four-poster group | | – | – | B | B | C | D | D | C | – | – | – | – |
| Sample | | 1 | 1 | 1 | 9 | 44 | 37 | 36 | 11 | 31 | 1 | 77 | 51+96 |
| *Triticum dicoccon/spelta* | glb | | | | | | | | | | 2 | | |
| | spf | | | | | | | | | | 2 | | |
| | gl fgts | | | | | | | | | | + | | |
| *Hordeum* sp(p) | rac | | | 5 | | | | | | | 3 | | |
| **Other propagules** | | | | | | | | | | | | | |
| *Alnus glutinosa* | fca | | | | | | | | | | | + | |
| *Corylus avellana* | nsf | | | | | | | | | | | | |
| *Polygonum aviculare* agg. | | | | | | | | | | | | | |
| *P. hydropiper* | | | | | | | | | | | | | |
| *P. persicaria* | | | | | | | | | | | | | |
| *P. lapathifolium* | | | | | | | | | | | | | |
| *Rumex* sp(p) | | | | | | | | | | | | | |
| *Bilderdykia convolvulus* | | | | | | | | | | | | | |
| *Chenopodium album* | | | | | | | | | | | | | |
| *Atriplex* sp(p) | | | | | | | | | | | | + | |
| *Montia fontana* ssp *chondrosperma* | | | | | | | | | | | | | |
| *Ranunculus* Section *Ranunuclus* | | | | | | | | | | | | | |
| *R. flammula* | | | | | | | | | | | | + | |
| *R.* cf *lingua* | | | | | | | | | | | | | |
| *Raphanus raphanistrum* | pod segs | | | | | 2 | | | | | | | |

| Taxon | | | | | |
|---|---|---|---|---|---|
| *Potentilla anserina* | | | | 1 | |
| *P.* cf *erecta* | | | | | |
| *Prunus spinosa* | frtst | | | 1 | 0.5 |
| Leguminosae (<2 mm) | | | | 1 | |
| *Rhinanthus* sp(p) | | | | | |
| *Plantago* cf *media* | | | | | |
| *Lapsana communis* | | | | | |
| *Iris pseudacorus* | | | | + | |
| cf *Glyceria* sp(p) | | | + | | |
| *Danthonia decumbens* | | | | | |
| *Bromus* sp(p) | 1 | | | | |
| Gramineae (medium-sized) | caryo | | | | |
| Gramineae (small) | | | | | |
| *Sparganium* sp(p) | | | | | |
| *Scirpus setaceus* | | | | | |
| *Carex* sp(p) | | + | + | + | |

**Other material**

| | | | | | |
|---|---|---|---|---|---|
| herbaceous detritus | | | + | + | |
| root/rhizome fragments | | + | + | + | |
| other organic material | + | | | | |
| ?burnt soil | | | + | + | + |
| ?burnt peat/organic soil | | | | + | + |

*(continued)*

204  Sutton Common

Table 2b (pt 1)  Continued

| Context | 1079 | 1174 | 3002 | 3010 | 3012 | 3018 | 3020 | 3022 | 3150 | 3454 | 3492 | 3535[1] |
|---|---|---|---|---|---|---|---|---|---|---|---|---|
| Context type | PoBR | Po | Po4 | Po4 | Po4 | Po4 | Po4 | Po4 | IDT | ODS | IDS | IDN |
| Four-poster group | – | – | B | B | C | D | D | C | – | – | – | – |
| Sample | 1 | 1 | 1 | 9 | 44 | 37 | 36 | 11 | 31 | 1 | 77 | 51+96 |
| burnt peat | | | | | | | | | | | | |
| charred moss stems | | | | | | | | | | | | |
| *Cenococcum* scl | | | | | | | | | | + | | |
| twig fragments | | | | | | | | | | | | |
| charcoal | +5 | +10 | +10 | +10 | +20 | +10 | +15 | +30 | +++ | +25 | ++25 | +++ |
| | | | | | | | | | 50 | | | 70 |

**Notes**
[1] The data for the two samples for this context were combined, although the residue for one of them was *not* examined during this work.

Table 2b (pt 2)

| Context | | 3536 | 3540 | 3559 | 3582 | 3589 | 3590 | 3609 | 5007 | 5220 | 7050 | 7143 |
|---|---|---|---|---|---|---|---|---|---|---|---|---|
| Context type | | IDN | IDN | IDN | IDS | IDS | IDS | IDN | Po | Po4 | Po?4 | Po4 |
| Four-poster group | | – | – | – | – | – | – | – | – | M | LL | S |
| Sample | | 97 | 99 | 101 | 102 | 103 | 104 | 98 | 1 | 1 | 6 | 1 |
| Wt (kg) | | 3 | 3 | 2.7 | 3 | 3 | 3 | 3 | 3 | 3 | 3 | 3 |
| **Taxon** | Parts | | | | | | | | | | | |
| **Grains** | | | | | | | | | | | | |
| Triticum cf dicoccon | | | | | | | | | | | | |
| T. cf spelta | | 2 | | | 1 | | 1 | 2 | 4 | 84 | 1 | 1 |
| Triticum sp(p) | | | | | | | | | | | | |
| Hordeum sp(p) | | 1 | | | | | | 1 | 9 | 3 | 14 | |
| Cerealia | | 2 | | | 1 | | | | 16 | 48+ | 10 | |
| Total grain | | 5 | | | 2 | | 1 | 3 | 29 | 135 | 25 | 1 |
| Wheat:Barley | | – | – | – | – | – | – | – | (0.4) | 28 | (0.07) | – |
| **Chaff** | | | | | | | | | | | | |
| Triticum dicoccum | glb | | | | | | | | | | | |
| | spf | | | | | | | | | ?1 | | |
| T. spelta | glb | | | | | | | | | 2 | | |
| | spf | | | | | | | | | | | ?2 |
| Triticum dicoccon / spelta | glb | | | 1 | | | | | | | | |
| | spf | | | | | | | | | 1 | | |
| | gl | | | | | | | | | | | |
| | fgts | | | | | | | | | | | |
| Hordeum sp(p) | rac | | | | | | | | | | | |

(continued)

Table 2b (pt 2) Continued

| Context | | 3536 | 3540 | 3559 | 3582 | 3589 | 3590 | 3609 | 5007 | 5220 | 7050 | 7143 |
|---|---|---|---|---|---|---|---|---|---|---|---|---|
| Context type | | IDN | IDN | IDN | IDS | IDS | IDS | IDN | Po | Po4 | Po?4 | Po4 |
| Four-poster group | | – | – | – | – | – | – | – | – | M | LL | S |
| Sample | | 97 | 99 | 101 | 102 | 103 | 104 | 98 | 1 | 1 | 6 | 1 |
| **Other propagules** | | | | | | | | | | | | |
| *Alnus glutinosa* | fca | | | | | | + | | | | | |
| *Corylus avellana* | nsf | | | | | | | | | | | |
| *Polygonum aviculare* agg. | | | | | | | + | | | | | |
| *P. hydropiper* | | + | | | | | | + | | | | |
| *P. persicaria* | | | | | | | | | 1 | | | |
| *P. lapathifolium* | | | | | | + | | | | | | |
| *Rumex* sp(p) | | | | | | + | | | | | | |
| *Bilderdykia convolvulus* | | | | | 2 | + | | | | | | |
| *Chenopodium album* | | | | | 3 | ++ | + | + | | | | |
| *Atriplex* sp(p) | | | | | | + | + | | | 1 | | |
| *Montia fontana* ssp *chondrosperma* | | + | | | | | | | | | | |
| *Ranunculus* Section *Ranunuclus* | | + | | | | + | + | | | | | |
| *R. flammula* | | | | | | | + | + | | | | |
| *R.* cf *lingua* | | | | | | | + | | | | | |
| *Raphanus raphanistrum* | pod | | | | | | | | | | | |
| | segs | | | | | | | | | | | |
| *Potentilla anserina* | | | | | | | + | + | | | | |
| *P.* cf *erecta* | | | | | | | | | 1f | | | |
| *Prunus spinosa* | frtst | 1 | | | | | | | | | | |
| Leguminosae (<2 mm) | | | | | | | | + | | | | |
| *Rhinanthus* sp(p) | | | | | | | | + | | | | |

206 *Sutton Common*

Appendix 1    207

| Taxon | | | | | | | | | | | | |
|---|---|---|---|---|---|---|---|---|---|---|---|---|
| *Plantago* cf *media* | | | | | 1 | | | | | | | |
| *Lapsana communis* | | | | | | | | | | | | |
| *Iris pseudacorus* | | | | | | | | | | | | |
| cf *Glyceria* sp(p) | | | | | | | + | | | | | |
| *Danthonia decumbens* | caryo | | | | 9 | ++ | ?+ | | | | | |
| *Bromus* sp(p) | | | | | 1 | | | | 1 | | | |
| Gramineae (medium-sized) | | | | | | | + | | | | | |
| Gramineae (small) | | | | | 2 | | | | | | | |
| *Sparganium* sp(p) | | | | | | | + | | | | | |
| *Scirpus setaceus* | | | | | 1 | ++ | + | | | | | |
| *Carex* sp(p) | | + | | | ++ | ++ | ++ | ++ | | | | |
| **Other material** | | | | | | | | | | | | |
| herbaceous detritus | | + | | | | + | + | | | | | |
| root/rhizome fragments | | + | | | + | ++ | ++ | + | | | | |
| other organic material | | | | | | | | | | | | |
| ?burnt soil | | + | | | + | + | | +++ | | | | |
| ?burnt peat/organic soil | | | | | | + | | | | | | |
| burnt peat | | | + | | | | | | | | | |
| charred moss stems | | | | | | + | | | | | | |
| *Cenococcum* | scl | + | + | ++ | | | ++ | + | | | | |
| twig fragments | | | | | | | +10 | | | | | |
| charcoal | | +++ | +10 | +5 | +++ | ++35 | ++70 | ++++ | +10 | +15 | +5 | +30 |
| | | 40 | | | 40 | | | 70 | | | | |

Table 2b (pt 3)

| | 7204 | 7243 | 7244 | 7244 | 7246 | 7269 | 7429 | 7430 | 7433 | 31088 | 31454 |
|---|---|---|---|---|---|---|---|---|---|---|---|
| Context | | | | | | | | | | | |
| Context type | Po?4 | Po4 | Po4c | Po4c | Po4c | Po4 | Po4 | Po4 | Po4 | Po4 | Po?4 |
| Four-poster group | NN | S | S | S | T | T | W | W | X | Y | RR |
| Sample | 1 | 2 | 1 | 2 | 4 | 1 | 1 | 1 | 1 | 88 | 170 |
| Wt (kg) | 3 | 3 | ? | ? | ? | 3 | 3 | 3 | 3 | 3 | 3 |
| **Taxon** / Parts | | | | | | | | | | | |
| **Grains** | | | | | | | | | | | |
| *Triticum* cf *dicoccon* | 1 | 2 | | | + | ?+ | | + | | | |
| *T*. cf *spelta* | 1 | 2 | 14 | 5 | 13 | 89³ | 22 | 38 | 22 | ++ | 42 |
| *Triticum* sp(p) | | | 2 | | | | | | | | |
| *Hordeum* sp(p) | 1 | 2 | 5+?5 | 6 | 20 | 8 | 14 | 14 | 36 | + | 4 |
| Cerealia | 1 | 1 | 9+?1 | 11 | 25 | 45 | 32+ | 38 | 69+ | + | 51 |
| Total grain | 3 | 5 | 36 | 22 | 68 | 142 | 88 | 93 | 127 | (>>1) | 97 |
| Wheat:Barley | - | - | (1.6) | (0.8) | 0.7 | 11.1 | 1.6 | 2.7 | 0.6 | | 10.5 |
| **Chaff** | | | | | | | | | | | |
| *Triticum dicoccum*  glb | | | | | | | | | | | ?1 |
| spf | | | | | | | | ?1 | | | |
| *T. spelta*  glb | | | 7 | | | 2 | 3 | ?1 | | + | 1 |
| spf | | | ?3 | | | 1 | 2 | | | + | |
| *Triticum dicoccon/spelta*  glb | | | | | | 4 | | 1 | | | |
| spf | | | | | | | | | 1 | | |
| gl | | | | | | | | | | | |
| fgts | | | | | | | | | | | |
| *Hordeum* sp(p)  rac | | | | | | | | | | | 1 |

Appendix 1    209

**Other propagules**

| Taxon | | | | | | |
|---|---|---|---|---|---|---|
| *Alnus glutinosa* | fca | | | | | |
| *Corylus avellana* | nsfl | 1 | | | | |
| *Polygonum aviculare* agg. | | | + | | | |
| *P. hydropiper* | | | | | | |
| *P. persicaria* | | | | | | |
| *P. lapathifolium* | | | | | | |
| *Rumex* sp(p) | | | | | f | |
| *Bilderdykia convolvulus* | | 2 | 1 | 1 | 1 | + |
| *Chenopodium album* | | 1 | | | | |
| *Atriplex* sp(p) | | | | | | |
| *Montia fontana* ssp *chondrosperma* | | | | | | |
| *Ranunculus* Section *Ranunculus* | | | | | | |
| *R. flammula* | | | | | | |
| *R.* cf *lingua* | | | | | | |
| *Raphanus raphanistrum* | pod | | | | | |
| | segs | | | | | |
| *Potentilla anserina* | | | | | | |
| *P.* cf *erecta* | | | | | | |
| *Prunus spinosa* | frtst | | | | | |
| Leguminosae (<2 mm) | | | | | + | |
| *Rhinanthus* sp(p) | | | | | | |
| *Plantago* cf *media* | | | | | | |
| *Lapsana communis* | | | | | | |
| *Iris pseudacorus* | | | | | | |
| cf *Glyceria* sp(p) | | | | | | |
| *Danthonia decumbens* | | | | | | |

*(continued)*

210  *Sutton Common*

Table 2b (pt 3)  Continued

| Context | | 7204 | 7243 | 7244 | 7244 | 7246 | 7269 | 7429 | 7430 | 7433 | 31088 | 31454 |
|---|---|---|---|---|---|---|---|---|---|---|---|---|
| Context type | | Po?4 | Po4 | Po4c | Po4c | Po4c | Po4 | Po4 | Po4 | Po4 | Po4 | Po?4 |
| Four-poster group | | NN | S | S | S | T | T | W | W | X | Y | RR |
| Sample | | 1 | 2 | 1 | 2 | 4 | 1 | 1 | 1 | 1 | 88 | 170 |
| *Bromus* sp(p) | | | | | | 1 | 2 | | 1 | | | |
| Gramineae (medium-sized) | caryo | | | | | | | | | | | |
| Gramineae (small) | | | | | | | | | | | | |
| *Sparganium* sp(p) | | | | | | | 2 | | | | | |
| *Scirpus setaceus* | | | | | | | | | | | | |
| *Carex* sp(p) | | | | | | | | | | | | |
| **Other material** | | | | | | | | | | | | |
| herbaceous detritus | | | | | | | | | | | | |
| root/rhizome fragments | | | | | | | | | | | | |
| other organic material | | | | | | | | | | | | |
| ?burnt soil | | | | | | | | | | | | |
| ?burnt peat/organic soil | | | | | | | | | | | | |
| burnt peat | | | | | | | | | | | | |
| charred moss stems | | | | | | | | | | | | |
| *Cenococcum* | scl | | | | | | | | | | | |
| twig fragments | | | | | | | | | | | | |
| charcoal | | +10 | +15 | ++5 | +5 | +10 | ++25 | +10 | +20 | +15 | ++25 | ++25 |

# Appendix 2 Characterisation studies of pottery
*by A Vince*

Samples of three Iron Age vessels excavated at Sutton Common, South Yorkshire, were submitted for study by Chris Cumberpatch. The vessels were found with other artefacts in what are interpreted as examples of structured deposition. Elsewhere on the site, as is typical of this part of Yorkshire, pottery was rare or absent.

## Petrological analysis

All three samples have a very similar appearance in thin section and were clearly made from the same raw materials. Therefore, a group description of the fabric is given here, with individual sections only being mentioned where the features are not shared by all samples. The samples show signs of post-depositional alteration:

a) There are moderate large angular voids which originally contained calcite.
b) These voids and other pores in the fabric are filled with phosphate (varying in colour from almost colourless to a dark red/brown) and unburnt clay minerals (soil matrix).

The amount of phosphate deposited on the sherds may be significant given their suggested structured deposition.

The following inclusion types were noted:

- Moderate angular voids ranging from c 0.1mm up to 2.0mm across. These have a roughly euhedral outline with faces at angles suggestive of calcite or dolomite crystals.
- Moderate subangular and rounded quartz grains up to 0.3mm across. Most of these grains are monocrystalline and some are well-rounded, suggesting a Permo-Triassic desert sand.
- Moderate angular mudstone fragments up to 2.0mm across. These show signs of stratification and contain abundant angular voids.
- Sparse euhedral quartz grains up to 0.5mm across. These are probably derived from the Lower Carboniferous Millstone Grit
- Sparse angular flint up 2.0mm across. These grains are too fine-textured and regular to be Carboniferous chert but might be rhyolite. Single fragments are present, in V2373 and V2371.
- Moderate subangular fragments of basic igneous rock, consisting of laths of plagioclase feldspar and pyroxene in a dark brown cryptocrystalline matrix, up to 2.0mm across (only present in V2373).

The groundmass consists of dark baked clay minerals (probably dark through unburnt carbon), sparse to moderate voids, sparse angular quartz, and sparse muscovite laths.

## Chemical analysis

Sub-samples of each sample were analysed using Inductively-Coupled Plasma Spectroscopy. The samples were obtained by mechanical removal of the original surfaces of the sherd and any broken edges for a fragment sufficiently large to produce a lump c 1.0g in weight. This lump was then crushed to a fine powder which was submitted to the Department of Geology at Royal Holloway College, London, where the analysis was carried out under the supervision of Dr J N Walsh.

A range of major, minor, and trace elements were measured. The major elements were measured as percent oxides and the remainder as parts per million (Tables 1 and 2).

Silica is not measured in this procedure, but can be estimated by subtraction of the measured oxides from 100%. This indicates a silica content ranging from 64.4% to 67.6%.

To take account of the dilution effect of variations in silica content, a lot of which could be due to variations in tempering, the data were normalised to $Al_2O_3$, which is mainly present in clay minerals (but also feldspars, which in this case form a significant proportion of the rock temper).

The most variable elements were phosphorus, barium, strontium, and lead. The first three of these, at least, are probably enhanced through post-depositional concretion of phosphates, as observed in the thin sections.

No samples of local clays of Permian age or clays developed on such strata were available for comparison but there are a few chemical analyses of vessels made from weathered Mercian Mudstone from sites in the Trent Valley, plus (to test the possibility of the voids being calcite from the Vale of Pickering) a series of samples from Romano-British and early Anglo-Saxon calcite-tempered wares and a few vessels tempered with basic igneous rock which may be comparable with V2373.

The Trent Valley samples have a very different composition from the Sutton Common sherds, as do samples from Easington, East Yorkshire, which contain erratic basic igneous rocks, but those fragments include rounded grains. The Sutton Common samples cannot be clearly distinguished from the remaining basic igneous rock-tempered samples, nor from the calcite-tempered samples

Table 1 Chemical analysis of pottery: major elements as percent oxides

| TSNO | $Al_2O_3$ | $Fe_2O_3$ | MgO | CaO | $Na_2O$ | $K_2O$ | $TiO_2$ | $P_2O_5$ | MnO |
|---|---|---|---|---|---|---|---|---|---|
| V2371 | 17.03 | 7.22 | 0.78 | 1.86 | 0.171 | 1.53 | 0.76 | 3.01 | 0.052 |
| V2372 | 18.82 | 10.47 | 1.01 | 1.52 | 0.1995 | 2.11 | 0.84 | 0.45 | 0.16 |
| V2373 | 19.64 | 7.89 | 0.86 | 1.79 | 0.2185 | 1.96 | 0.93 | 0.46 | 0.045 |
| Mean | 18.50 | 8.53 | 0.88 | 1.72 | 0.20 | 1.87 | 0.84 | 1.31 | 0.09 |
| StDev | 1.33 | 1.72 | 0.12 | 0.18 | 0.02 | 0.30 | 0.09 | 1.48 | 0.06 |

Table 2 Chemical analysis of pottery: minor elements as parts per million

| TSNO | Ba | Cr | Cu | Li | Ni | Sc | Sr | V | Y | Zr* | La | Ce | Nd | Sm | Eu | Dy | Yb | Pb | Zn | Co |
|---|---|---|---|---|---|---|---|---|---|---|---|---|---|---|---|---|---|---|---|---|
| V2371 | 622 | 109 | 31 | 34 | 38 | 17 | 299 | 101 | 25 | 75 | 37 | 92.00 | 49.00 | 3.73 | 1.38 | 5.10 | 2.60 | 513.43 | 73.00 | 13.00 |
| V2372 | 787 | 125 | 129 | 51 | 61 | 16 | 116 | 177 | 18 | 94 | 32 | 81.00 | 34.00 | 3.26 | 1.35 | 4.50 | 2.40 | 157.95 | 89.00 | 18.00 |
| V2373 | 549 | 130 | 79 | 39 | 55 | 19 | 152 | 181 | 20 | 89 | 40 | 95.00 | 48.00 | 3.73 | 1.41 | 4.60 | 2.30 | 140.90 | 94.00 | 16.00 |
| Mean | 652.67 | 121.33 | 79.67 | 41.33 | 51.33 | 17.33 | 189.00 | 153.00 | 21.00 | 86.00 | 36.33 | 89.33 | 43.67 | 3.58 | 1.38 | 4.73 | 2.43 | 270.76 | 85.33 | 15.67 |
| StDev | 121.93 | 10.97 | 49.00 | 8.74 | 11.93 | 1.53 | 96.95 | 45.08 | 3.61 | 9.85 | 4.04 | 7.37 | 8.39 | 0.27 | 0.03 | 0.32 | 0.15 | 210.33 | 10.97 | 2.52 |

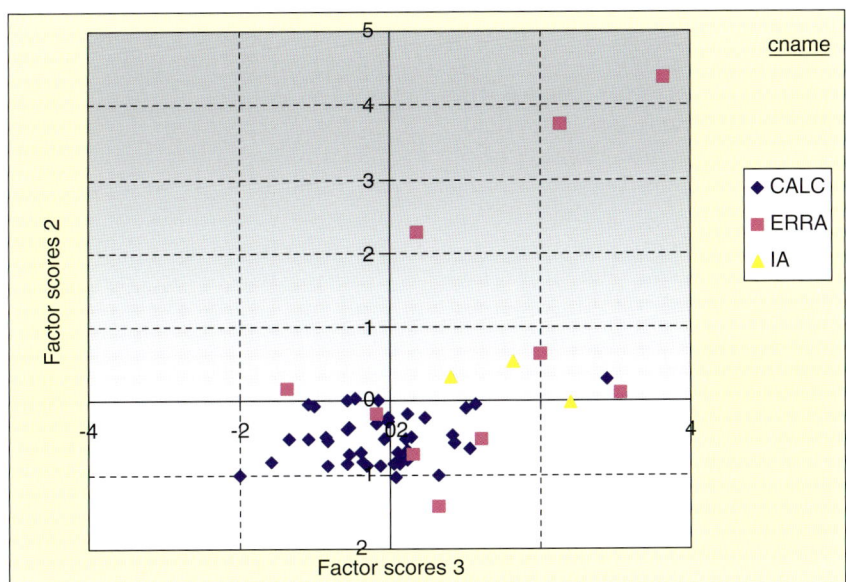

*Figure 2.1 Chemical analysis of the pottery: plot of two factors (F2 and F3) calculated in a factor analysis. CALC = calcite-tempered wares; ERRA = pottery from erratic basic igneous rocks from the Trent Valley; IA = Iron Age pottery from Sutton Common*

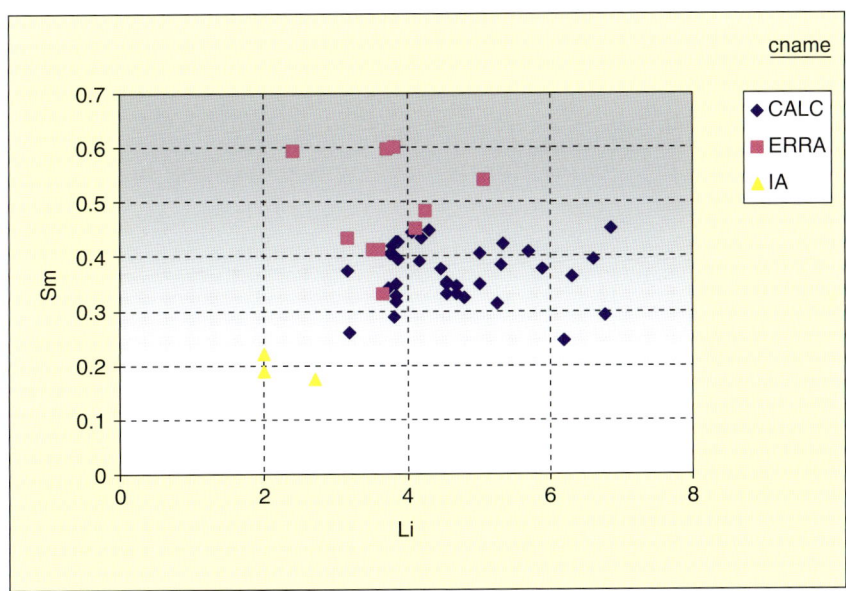

*Figure 2.2 Chemical analysis of pottery: Li and Sm in Sutton Common fragments against comparative groups. CALC = calcite-tempered wares; ERRA = pottery from erratic basic igneous rocks from the Trent Valley; IA = Iron Age pottery from Sutton Common*

(if those elements which occur in unleached limestone-temper, $CaCO_3$ and Sr, are omitted). Figure 2.1 is a plot of two factors (F2 and F3) calculated in a factor analysis of this dataset (the Sutton Common samples are labelled 'IA'). They show a wide range of compositions for the erratic-tempered samples and a tighter composition for the calcite-tempered wares but in neither case is there a complete separation of the Sutton Common samples.

In fact, only two elements in the Sutton Common analyses are distinctly different: Li and Sm, both of which are lower in concentration in the Sutton Common samples than in the comparanda. A plot of the values for these elements (Fig 2.2) shows that they distinguish both the calcite-tempered from the erratic-tempered samples, and both of these from the Sutton Common pieces.

## Discussion

The site lies close to the junction of the Permian Upper Magnesian Limestone and the Triassic Sherwood Sandstone but these deposits are masked to a great extent by boulder clay, fluvioglacial sands and gravels, and post-glacial alluvial sediments.

The angular voids might have been filled with sparry calcite, but lack the clear-cut euhedral outlines of the calcite found in late Roman and early Anglo-Saxon calcite-tempered wares from the Vale of Pickering. Furthermore, glauconite is common in that ware and is completely absent from the Sutton Common sherds. Perhaps the obvious identity of the voids is the Magnesian Limestone, which remains a strong possibility. However, the mudstone fragments, which are probably relict clay, are reminiscent of the marly facies of the Mercian Mudstone, in which case the voids might have been marl lumps. The Mercian Mudstone marls outcrop in the Trent Valley and on the eastern side of the Vale of York, but are mainly masked by Quaternary deposits and the Trent Valley option can probably be discounted through the difference in chemical composition and because the quartz sand grains do not include the fine-grained siltstone and rounded cherts which characterise the Trent Valley sands. A potentially much closer source is the Upper Permian Marl which outcrops above the Upper Magnesian Limestone and is therefore likely to occur close to Sutton Common (Edwards and Trotter 1954, 61).

The remaining inclusions can be considered in two groups. Firstly, the rounded quartz, flint/rhyolite, and the Millstone Grit sandstone may have been deliberately added, probably as detrital gravel. All the inclusions occur in fluvio-glacial sands in the Vale of York, South Yorkshire, and Nottinghamshire and these deposits are too variable to narrow down the source. The basic igneous rock is likely to have been added as a crushed rock, as suggested by Ian Freestone and Andrew Middleton for examples in East Yorkshire and the Vale of Pickering, or it may indicate the use of a boulder clay in which local and exotic materials were mixed. Numerous dolerite sills outcrop north of the region, and one might expect boulder clays in the valley to include fragments of them. However, most of the documented basic igneous erratics in Yorkshire boulder clays occur to the east of the Wolds and in the eastern part of the Vale of Pickering whereas erratics in the Vale of York consist mainly of Shap Granite and, possibly, rhyolite from the Lake District volcanics.

The thin section evidence therefore suggests that the pots may have been made from weathered Upper Permian Marl, or Mercian Mudstone, either directly or from material redeposited in boulder clay. Without local fieldwork and the consequent identification and sampling of potential clay sources, no clearer idea of the source can be determined although, it should be relatively simple to test the suggestion.

# Bibliography

Adams, M, Merrony, C & Sydes, R E, 1988 *Excavations at Sutton Common, South Yorkshire 1988*. Sheffield: South Yorkshire Archaeology Unit

Ainsworth, A M & Goulder, R, 2000a The effects of sewage-works effluent on riverine extracellular aminopeptidase activity and microbial leucine assimilation, *Water Research*, **34**, 2551–7

Ainsworth, A M & Goulder, R, 2000b Epilithic and planktonic leucine aminopeptidase activity and leucine assimilation along the River Tweed, Scottish Borders, *Sci Total Environ*, **251**, 83–93

Allcroft, A H, 1908 *Earthworks of England*. London: Macmillan

Andersen, S T, 1973 The differential pollen productivity of trees and its significance for the interpretation of a pollen diagram from a forested region, in H J B Birks & R G West (eds) *Quaternary Plant Ecology*. Oxford: Blackwell, 109–16

Armstrong, A L & Jackson, J W, 1923 Explorations of Harborough Cave, Brassington, *J Roy Anthropol Instit Great Britain and Ireland*, **53**, 402–16

Atkinson, S, 1994 An archaeological evaluation at Far Field Road, Edenthorpe, *Archaeology in South Yorkshire 1993–1994*. Sheffield: South Yorkshire Archaeology Service, 19–21

Avery, B W, 1990 *Soils of the British Isles*. Wallingford: CAB International

Avery, M, Sutton, J E G & Banks, J W, 1967 Rainsborough, Northants, England: Excavations, 1961–65, *Proc Prehist Soc*, **32**, 207–306

Baillie, M G L & Pilcher, J R, 1973 A simple crossdating program for tree-ring research, *Tree Ring Bulletin*, **33**, 7–14

Bass, W M, 1987 *Human Osteology: A Laboratory and Field Manual*. Columbia: Missouri Archaeology Society

Bateman, M D, Murton, J B & Crowe, W, 2000 Late Devensian and Holocene depositional environments associated with the coversands around Caistor, North Lincolnshire, UK, *Boreas*, **29**, 1–15

Bedwin, O, 1991 Asheldam Camp – an early Iron Age hill fort: the 1985 excavations, *Essex Archaeol Hist*, **22**, 13–37

Behre, K E, 1981 The interpretation of anthropogenic indicators in pollen diagrams, *Pollen et Spores*, **23**, 225–45

Bell, M, Fowler, P J & Wilson, S W, 1996 *The Experimental Earthwork Project 1960–1992*. York: CBA Res Rep **100**

Bennett, K D & Birks, H J, 1990 Post-glacial history of alder (*Alnus glutinosa* L.) in the British Isles, *J Quat Sci*, **5**, 123–33

Bennett, K D, Whittington, G & Edwards, K J, 1994 Recent plant nomenclature changes and pollen morphology in the British Isles, *Quat Newslett*, **73**, 1–6

Bersu, G, 1940 Excavations at Little Woodbury, part 1, *Proc Prehist Soc*, **6**, 30–111

Bevan, B (ed), 1999 *Northern Exposure: Interpretative Devolution and the Iron Ages in Britain*. Leicester: Leicester Archaeology Monograph **4**

Bevan, B, 2000 Peak practice: whatever happened to the Iron Age in the southern Pennines?, in J Harding & R Johnston (eds), *Northern Pasts: Interpretations of the later prehistory of northern England and Scotland*. BAR Brit Ser **302**. Oxford: British Archaeological Reports

Bewley, R H (ed), 1998 *Lincolnshire's archaeology from the air*. Lincoln: Soc Lincolnshire Hist Archaeol & Roy Comm Hist Monuments Engl

Binney, H A, Waller, M P, Bunting, M J & Armitage, R, 2005 The interpretation of fen carr pollen diagrams: the representation of the dryland vegetation, *Rev Palaeobot Palynol*, **134**, 197–218

Björdal, C G & Nilsson, T, 2002 Decomposition of waterlogged archaeological wood, in P Hoffmann, J A Spriggs, T Grant, C Cook & A Recht (eds), *Proc 8th ICOM Group on Wet Organic Archaeological Materials Conference*

Blaauw, M, Van der Plicht, J, & Van Geel, B, 2004 Radiocarbon dating of bulk peat samples from raised bogs: non-existence of a previously reported 'reservoir effect'?, *Quat Sci Rev*, **23**, 1537–42

Blockley, S P E, Lowe, J J, Walker, M J C, Asioli, A, Trincardi, F, Coope, G R, Donahue, R E, & Pollard, A M, 2004 Bayesian analysis of radiocarbon chronologies: examples from the European Late-glacial, *J Quat Sci*, **19**, 159–75

Boardman, S & Jones, G, 1990 Experiments on the effects of charring on cereal plant components, *J Archaeol Sci*, **17**, 1–11

Boessneck, J, 1969 Osteological differences between sheep (*Ovis aries* Linné) and goat (*Capra hircus* Linné), in D Brothwell & E Higgs (eds) *Science in Archaeology*. London: Thames and Hudson, 331–58

Bond, D, 1991 An Excavation at Wall Camp, Kynnersley, in Carver (ed) 1991, pp 98–105

Bonnor, L & Allen, M, 2000 A possible Iron Age barrow monument and Anglo-Saxon cemetery site at Kirkby la Thorpe, *Lincolnshire Hist Archaeol*, **35**, 21–34

Bowden, M & McOmish, D, 1989 The required barrier, *Scott Archaeol Rev*, **4**, 12–16

Bradley, R, 1978 *The Prehistoric Settlement of Britain*. London: Routledge

Bradley, R, 1990 *The Passage of Arms*. Cambridge: Cambridge University Press

Bradley, R, 2002 *The Past in Prehistoric Societies*. London & New York: Routledge

Bradley, R, 2005 *Ritual and Domestic Life in Prehistoric Europe*. Abingdon & New York: Routledge

Bradley, R, Entwistle, R & Raymond, F, 1994 *Prehistoric Land Divisions on Salisbury Plain. The Work of the Wessex Linear Ditches Project*. London: English Heritage

Branigan, R, 1989 An early landscape revisited, in D Kennedy (ed) *Into the sun. Essays in air photography in archaeology in honour of Derrick Riley*. Sheffield: Dept of Prehistory and Archaeology, University of Sheffield, 161–6

Braudel, F, 1949 *La Méditerranée et le monde méditerranéen à l'époque de Phillipe II*. Paris: Librairie Armand Colin

Brayshay, B A, & Dinnin, M H, 1999 Integrated palaeoecological evidence for biodiversity at the floodplain-forest margin, *J Biogeography*, **26**, 115–31

Brennand, M & Taylor, M, 2003 The survey and excavation of a Bronze Age timber circle at Holme-next-the-sea, Norfolk, 1998–99, *Proc Prehist Soc*, **69**, 1–84

Bronk Ramsey, C, 1995 Radiocarbon Calibration and Analysis of Stratigraphy: The OxCal Program, *Radiocarbon,* **37,** 425–30

Bronk Ramsey, C, 1998 Probability and dating, *Radiocarbon*, **40**, 461–74

Bronk Ramsey, C, 2000 *Oxcal 3.5*, http://www.rlaha.ox.ac.uk/calib.html

Bronk Ramsey, C, 2001 Development of the radiocarbon calibration program OxCal, *Radiocarbon*, **43**, 355–63

Bronk Ramsey, C, Ditchfield, P & Humm, M, 2004 Using a gas ion source for radiocarbon AMS and GC-AMS, *Radiocarbon,* **46**, 25–32

Brothwell, D R, 1972 *Digging Up Bones*. London: British Museum Press

Brothwell, D R, 1981 *Digging Up Bones*. 3rd edition. Oxford: Oxford University Press

Brück, J, 1995 A place for the dead: the role of human remains in the Late Bronze Age. *Proc Prehist Soc*, **61**, 245–77

Brück, J, 1999 Houses, lifecycles and deposition on Middle Bronze Age settlements in southern England, *Proc Prehist Soc*, **65**, 145–66

Brück, J, 2001 Body methaphors and technologies of transformation in the English Middle and Late Bronze Age, in J Brück (ed) *Bronze Age Landscape. Tradition and Transformation*. Oxford: Oxbow Books, 149–60

Brunaux, J-L, 1988 *The Celtic Gauls: gods, rites and sanctuaries.* London: Seaby

Brunaux, J-L (ed), 1991 *Les Sanctuaries Celtiques et le Monde Méditerranéen*. Paris: Editions Errance, Dossiers de Protohistoire **3**

Brunaux, J-L, Meniel, P & Poplin, F, 1985 *Gournay I: les fouilles sur le sanctuaire et l'oppidum*. Revue Archéologique de Picardie, Numéro spécial

Brunning, R, Hogan, D, Jones, J, Jones, M, Maltby, E, Robinson, M & Straker, V, 2000 Saving the Sweet Track. The in situ preservation of a Neolithic wooden trackway, Somerset, UK, *Conservation and Management of Archaeological Sites*, **4**, 3–20

Buck, C E, Cavanagh, W G & Litton, C D, 1996 *Bayesian Approach to Interpreting Archaeological Data*. Chichester

Buckland, P C, 1986 *Roman South Yorkshire: a source book*. Sheffield: Dept of Archaeology and Prehistory, Sheffield University

Buikstra, J E & Ubelaker, D H, 1994 *Standards for data collection from human skeletal remains*. Fayetterville: Arkansas Archaeol Surv Res Ser, **44**

Bullock, P, Fedoroff, N, Jongerius, A, Stoops, G, Tursina, T & Babel, U, 1985 *Handbook for soil thin section description*. Wolverhampton: Waine Research Publications

Bunting, M J, Armitage, R, Binney, H A & Waller, M P, 2005 Estimates of relevant source area of pollen assemblages from moss polsters in two Norfolk (UK) wet woodlands, *The Holocene*, **15**, 459–65

Burgess, A, 2001 The Iron Age, in Roberts *et al* 2001, 260–9

Caple, C, 1996 Parameters for monitoring anoxic environments, in M Corfield, P Hinton, T Nixon & M Pollard (eds), *Preserving archaeological remains in situ*. London: MoLAS

Caple, C & Dungworth, D, 1997 Investigations into waterlogged burial environments, in A Sinclair, E Slater & J Gowlett (eds), *Archaeological sciences: 1995*. Oxford: Oxbow Monogr **64**

Caple, C & Dungworth, D, 1998 *Waterlogged anoxic archaeological burial environments*. London: English Heritage. Ancient Monuments Laboratory Report 22/98

Carr, G & Knüsel, C, 1997 The ritual framework of excarnation by exposure as the mortuary practice of the early and middle Iron Ages of central southern Britain, in Gwilt & Haselgrove (eds) 1997a, 167–73

Carstairs, I, 2004 Raising the Levels, in Smith (ed) 2004, 79–84

Carver, M O H (ed), 1991, *Prehistory in Lowland Shropshire*. Trans Shropshire Archaeol & Hist Soc **67**

Catt, J A, 1990 Geology and relief, in S Ellis and D R Crowther (eds) *Humber Perspectives: a Region through the Ages*. Hull: Hull University Press, 13–28

Chadwick, A M, 1997 Towards a social archaeology of later prehistoric and Romano-British field systems in South Yorkshire, West Yorkshire and Nottinghamshire, *Assemblage*, **2**, http://www.shef.ac.uk/assem/2/

Chadwick, A M, 1999 Digging ditches but missing riches? Ways into the Iron Age and Romano-British landscapes of the north midlands, in Bevan (ed) 1999, 149–72

Chadwick, A M, 2004 'Heavier burdens for willing shoulders?' Writing different histories, humanities and social practices for the Romano-British countryside, in B Croxford, H Eckhardt, J Meade & J Weekes (eds), *Proc 13th Ann Theoretical Roman Archaeology Symposium, Leicester 2003*. Oxford: Oxbow Books, 90–110

Chadwick, A M & Cumberpatch, C G, 1995 Further work on the Iron Age and Romano-British landscape at Edenthorpe. *Archaeology in South Yorkshire 1994–1995*. Sheffield: South Yorkshire Archaeology Service, 41–9

Challis, A J & Harding, D W, 1975 *Later Prehistory from the Trent to the Tyne*. BAR Brit Ser **20** (2 parts). Oxford: British Archaeological Reports

Chambers, F M & Elliot, L, 1989 Spread and expansion of *Alnus* Mill. in the British Isles: timing, agencies and possible vectors, *J Biogeogr*, **16**, 541–50

Champion, T, 1987 The European Iron Age: assessing the state of the art, *Scott Archaeol Rev*, **4**, 98–107

Champion, T C & Collis, J R (eds), 1996 *The Iron Age in Britain and Ireland: Recent Trends*. Sheffield: J R Collis Publications

Chapman, H P, 1997 The Humberhead Levels from the air: a landscape in context, in Van de Noort & Ellis (eds) 1997, 397–407

Chapman, H P, 2000 Understanding wetland archaeological landscapes: GIS, environmental analysis and landscape reconstruction; pathways and narratives, in G Lock (ed) *Beyond the Map. Archaeology and the Spatial Technologies*. Amsterdam: IOS press & Nato Scientific Affairs Division, 49–59

Chapman, H P, 2001 Understanding and using archaeological surveys – the 'error conspiracy', in Z Stancic & T Veljanovski (eds) *Computing archaeology for understanding the past – CAA2000. Computer applications and quantitative methods in archaeology. Proc 28th conference, Ljubljana, April 2000*, BAR Int Ser **931**. Oxford: British Archaeological Reports, 19–23

Chapman, H P & Cheetham, J L, 2002 Monitoring and modelling saturation as a proxy indicator for *in situ* preservation in wetlands: a GIS-based approach, *J Archaeol Sci*, **29**, 277–89

Chapman, H P & Van de Noort, R, 2001 High-resolution wetland prospecting, using GPS and GIS: landscape studies at Sutton Common (South Yorkshire), and Meare Village East (Somerset) *J Archaeol Sci*, **28**, 365–75

Chatters, R M & Olson, E A (eds), 1965 *Radiocarbon and tritium dating: proceedings of the sixth international conference on radiocarbon and tritium dating*. Washington DC

Chowne, P, Girling, M & Grieg, J, 1986 Excavations at an Iron Age defended enclosure at Tattershall Thorpe, Lincolnshire, *Proc Prehist Soc*, **52**, 159–88

Clarke, R R, 1940 The Iron Age in Norfolk and Suffolk, *Archaeol J*, **46**, 1–113

Coles, B J, 1995 *Wetland Management. A survey for English Heritage*. Exeter: WARP

Coles, J M, 2001 Energetic Activities of Commoners, *Proc Prehist Soc*, **67**, 19–48

Coles, J M & Coles, B J, 1996 *Enlarging the Past. The Contribution to Wetland Archaeology*. Edinburgh/Exeter: Soc Antiq Scotland/WARP

Coles, J M & Minnett, S, 1995 *Industrious and Fairly Civilized: the Glastonbury Lake Village*. Taunton: Somerset County Council

Collis, J R, 1981 A theoretical study of hillforts, in G Guilbert (ed) *Hill-fort Studies: Papers presented to Dr A H A Hogg*. Leicester: Leicester University Press, 66–76

Collis, J R, 1994 An Iron Age and Roman Settlement at Owslebury, Hants, in Fitzpatrick & Morris (eds) 1994, 106–08

Collis, J R, 1995 States without centers? The Middle La Tène period in temperate Europe, in B Arnold & B B Gibson (eds) *Celtic Chiefdom, Celtic State*. Cambridge: Cambridge University Press, 75–80

Collis, J R, 1997 Celtic myths, *Antiquity*, **71**, 195–201

Collis, J R, 2000 Storage pits in southern and eastern Britain, in F Buxó & E Pons (eds) *Els Productes alimentaris d'Origen vegetal a l'edat del Ferro de l'Europea Occidental*. Actes du XXI$^e$ Colloque de l'AFEAF, Girona, mai 1998. Girona: Museu d'Arqeologia de Catalunya, Sèrie Monogràfica **18**, 351–8

Collis, J R, 2003 *The Celts. Origins, Myths and Inventions*. Stroud: Tempus

Cotton, M A & Frere, S S, 1968 Ivinghoe Beacon excavations, 1963–65, *Records of Buckinghamshire*, **18**, 187–260

Cumberpatch, C G, 1991 The production and circulation of Late Iron Age slip decorated pottery in Central Europe. University of Sheffield unpubl PhD thesis

Cumberpatch, C G, 1993 Excavations at Pickburn Leys, Adwick-le-Street, Doncaster (SE 534 067). *Archaeology in South Yorkshire 1992–1993*. Sheffield: South Yorkshire Archaeology Service, 36–42

Cumberpatch, C G, in prep *Later prehistoric pottery from Redhouse Farm, Adwick-le-Street, South Yorkshire*. Report for Northamptonshire Archaeology

Cumberpatch, C G, nd Prehistoric, Roman and later pottery from Doncaster Road, South Elmshall. Leeds: Archaeological Services (WYAS) unpubl report

Cumberpatch, C G & Chadwick A M, 1995 Further work on the Iron Age and Romano-British landscape at Edenthorpe, in C G Cumberpatch, J McNeil & S P Whiteley (eds) *Archaeology in South Yorkshire 1994–1995*. Sheffield: South Yorkshire Archaeology Service, 41–9

Cumberpatch, C G, Ixer, R, Leary, R, Morris, E & Walster, A, 2003 Pottery from excavations at Mellor, Stockport: A review. The Mellor Archaeological Trust unpubl report

Cumberpatch, C G, Walster, A & Vince, A, in prep *Later prehistoric pottery from excavations on the line of the A1 (M)*. Lancaster: Oxford Archaeology (North)

Cunliffe, B, 1974 (1st edition), 1978 (2nd edition), 1991 (3rd edition), 2005 (4th edition) *Iron Age communities in Britain. An account of England, Scotland and Wales from the seventh century BC until the Roman Conquest*. London & New York: Routledge [Note: the 4th edition has been used in preference to earlier editions where the same information has been presented]

Cunliffe, B, 1984 *Danebury: an Iron Age Hillfort in Hampshire: The Excavations, 1969–1978: Vol 1: the site & Vol 2: the finds*. London: CBA Res Rep **52**

Cunliffe, B, 1993 *Danebury*. London: Batsford/English Heritage

Cunliffe, B, 1995 *Danebury: an Iron Age hillfort in Hampshire, Vol 6. A Hillfort Community in Perspective*. York: CBA Res Rep **102**

Cunliffe, B & Poole, C, 1991 *Danebury: an Iron Age Hillfort in Hampshire: The Excavations, 1979–1988: Vol 4: the site & Vol 5: the finds*. London: CBA Res Rep **73**

Dark, P, 2000 *The Environment of Britain in the First Millennium AD*. London: Duckworth

Darvill, T & Fulton, A, 1998 *The Monuments at Risk Survey of England. Main Report*. Bournemouth: Bournemouth University & London: English Heritage

Davidson, A, 2002 *The coastal archaeology of Wales*. York: CBA & CADW, CBA Res Rep **131**

Davies, J A, Gregory, T, Lawson, A J, Rickett, R & Rogerson, A, 1991, *The Iron Age Forts of Norfolk*. East Anglian Archaeology **54**

Deberge, Y, Collis J R & Dunkley, J, (in press) *Clermont-Ferrand – Le Pâtural (Puy-de-Dôme). Evolution d'un établissement agricole gaulois (IIIe–IIe s avant J-C) en Limagne d'Auvergne*. Association Française d'Etude de l'Age du Fer

Dent, J S, 1982 Cemeteries and settlement patterns in the Iron Age on the Yorkshire Worlds, *Proc Prehist Soc*, **48**, 437–58

Dent, J S, 1985 Three cart burials from Wetwang, Yorkshire, *Antiquity*, **59**, 85–92

Dent, J S, 1995 Aspects of Iron Age Settlement in East Yorkshire. Sheffield University, unpubl doctoral thesis

Dickson, J A D, 1965 A modified staining technique for carbonates in thin section, *Nature*, **205**, 587

Dinnin, M H, 1997 The palaeoenvironmental survey of the Rivers Idle, Thorne and Old River Don, in Van de Noort & Ellis (eds) 1997, 81–155

Dixon, P, 1994 *Crickley Hill Vol 1: The Hillfort Defences*. Nottingham: Crickley Hill Trust and Dept of Archaeology, University of Nottingham

Edwards, W & Trotter, F M, 1954 *The Pennines and adjacent areas*. London: HMSO

Ellis, S, 1997 Physical background to the Humberhead Levels, in Van de Noort & Ellis (eds) 1997, 7–12

Ellison, A & Drewett, P, 1971 Pits and post-holes in the British Early Iron Age: some alternative explanations, *Proc Prehist Soc*, **37**, 183–94

Elsdon, S & Knight, D, 2003 *The Iron Age pottery*, in Field & Parker Pearson 2003, 87–92

English Heritage, 1998 *Dendrochronology: guidelines on producing and interpreting dendrochronological dates*. London: English Heritage

English Heritage, 1999 *Management for Archaeological Projects ($2^{nd}$ edition)*. London: English Heritage

Evans, C, 1990 Review of B A Purdy (ed), 1988 *Wet Site Archaeology*. Caldwell, New Jersey: The Telford Press, *Proc Prehist Soc*, **56**, 339–40

Evans, C, 1992 Wetland Central? Iron Age Centres in the Cambridgeshire Fenlands, in C Evans (ed), *Fenland Research* **7**. Cambridge: Fenland Project

Evans, C, 1997 Hydraulic communities: Iron Age enclosures in the East Anglian fenlands, in Gwilt & Haselgrove (eds) 1997a, 216–27

Evans, C, 2000 Cambridgeshire: Excavations Results, in A Crowson, T Lane & J Reeve (eds), *Fenland Management Project Excavations 1991–1995*. Sleaford: Lincolnshire Archaeol & Heritage Rep Ser **3**

Evans, C 2003 *Power and island communities: excavations at the Wardy Hill Ringwork, Coveney, Ely*. East Anglian Archaeology **103**

Faulkner, S P, Patrick, W H & Gambrell, R P, 1989 Field Techniques for Measuring Wetland Soil Parameters, *Soil Science Soc America J*, **53**, 883–90

Field, N & Parker Pearson, M, 2003 *Fiskerton: The 1981 excavations. An Iron Age timber causeway with Iron Age and Roman votive offerings*. Oxford: Oxbow Books

Finney, A, 1994 Presentation Survey: Skipwith Common. Malton: MAP Archaeological Consultancy Ltd unpubl report

Fisher, R A, Corbet, A S & Williams, C B, 1943 The relation between the number of species and the number of individuals in a random sample of an animal population, *J Animal Ecol*, **12**, 42–58

Fitzpatrick, A P, 1991 'Celtic (Iron Age) Religion' – traditional and timeless?, *Scott Archaeol Rev*, **8**, 123–9

Fitzpatrick, A P, 1994 Outside in: the structure of an Early Iron Age house at Dunston Park, Thatcham, Berkshire, in Fitzpatrick & Morris (eds) 1994, pp 68–72

Fitzpatrick, A P, 1997a Everyday life in Iron Age Wessex, in Gwilt & Haselgrove (eds) 1997a, 73–86

Fitzpatrick, A P, 1997b *Archaeological Excavations on the Route of the A27 Westhampnett Bypass, West Sussex, 1992 Vol 2*. Salisbury: Wessex Archaeology Rep 12

Fitzpatrick, A P & Morris, E L (eds), 1994 *The Iron Age in Wessex: recent work*. Salisbury: Trust for Wessex Archaeology & Association Française d'Etude de l'Age du Fer

Fleming, A, 1988 *The Dartmoor Reaves: Investigating Prehistoric Land Divisions*. London: Batsford

Fletcher, M & Spicer, D, 1988 Clonehenge: an experiment with gridded and non-gridded survey of data, in S P Q Rahtz (ed), *Computer Applications in Archaeology 1988*, BAR Int Ser **446**. Oxford: British Archaeological Reports, 309–24

Fletcher, W & Thomas, G, 2001 Introduction to the identification and categorisation of archaeological wood and woodworking techniques, in S Ellis, H Fenwick, M Lillie & R Van de Noort (eds), *Wetland Heritage of the Lincolnshire March; an Archaeological Survey*. Hull: Humber Wetlands Project, University of Hull, 279–81

Forde-Johnston, J, 1976 *Hillforts of the Iron Age in England and Wales, A Survey of the Surface Evidence*. Liverpool: Liverpool University Press

Fowler, C, 2004 *The Archaeology of Personhood*. London & New York: Routledge

French, C, 2004 Evaluation survey and excavation at Wandlebury Ringwork, Cambridgeshire, 1994–97, *Proc Cambridge Antiq Soc* **93**, 15–65

French, C & Pryor, F, 1993 *The South-West Fen Dyke Survey Project 1982–86*. East Anglian Archaeology **59**

Gaunt, G D, 1994 *Geology of the Country around Goole, Doncaster and the Isle of Axholme. Memoir for one-inch sheets 79 and 88 (England and Wales)*. London: HMSO

Gearey, B R, 2005 Palaeoenvironmental Investigations at Thorne and Hatfield Moors: Research in Mitigation of Continued Peat Extraction. Hull: WAERC unpubl Report

Gearey, B R & Lillie, M C, 1999 Aspects of Holocene vegetational change in the Vale of York, in R Van de Noort & S Ellis (eds), *Wetland Heritage of the Vale of York. An Archaeological Survey*. Hull: Humber Wetlands Project, University of Hull, 109–25

Gebhard, R, 1989 *Der Glasschmuck aus dem Oppidum von Manching*. Stuttgart: Die Ausgrabungen in Manching **11**

Gelfand, A E & Smith, A F M, 1990 Sampling approaches to calculating marginal densities, *J American Statistics Assoc*, **85**, 398–409

Gent, H, 1983 Centralised storage in later prehistoric Britain, *Proc Prehist Soc*, **49**, 243–67

Geomorphological Services Ltd, 1990 Hydrological appraisal of Sutton Common, Askern, South Yorkshire. Geomorphological Services Ltd unpubl report

Giles, M & Parker Pearson, M, 1999 Learning to live in the Iron Age: dwelling and praxis, in Bevan (ed) 1999, 271–31

Gilks, W R, Richardson, S & Spiegelhalter, D J, 1996 *Markov Chain Monte Carlo in Practice*. London: Chapman and Hall

Gillings, M & Wise, A (eds), 1999 *GIS guide to good practice*. York: Archaeology Data Service

Girling, M A, 1988 The bark beetle *Scolytus scolytus* (Fabricius) and the possible role of elm disease in the early Neolithic, in M Jones (ed) *Archaeology and the Flora of the British Isles*. Oxford Univ Comm Archaeol Monogr **14**, 34–8

Göransson, H, 1986 Man and forests of nemoral broad-leaved trees during the Stone Age, *Striae*, **24**, 143–52

Gosden, C, 1997 Iron Age landscapes and cultural biographies, in Gwilt & Haselgrove (eds) 1997a, 202–07

Gouzel, C, 1996 *Le Cimitière rural gallo-romain du Pâtural (Commune de Clermont-Ferrand). Mémoire de Maîtrise d'Histoire de l'Art. Université de Blaise Pascal*, Clermont-Ferrand

Gransar, F, 2002 La batterie des silos de Soupir 'Le Champ Grand Jacques' (Aisne): contribution à l'identification d'une centralisation du stockage à La Tène B dans le nord de la France, in B Méniel & B Lambot (eds)

Découvertes récentes de l'Âge du Fer dans le Massif des Ardennes et ses Marges. Repas des Vivants et Nourriture pour les Morts en Gaule. Actes du XXV$^e$ Colloque international de l'Association Française pour l'Étude de la Âge du Fer, Charleville-Mézières 2001. Reims: Société Archéologique Champenoise, 67–80

Grant, A, 1982 The use of tooth wear as a guide to the age of domestic ungulates, in B Wilson, C Grigson & S Payne (eds), *Ageing and Sexing Animal Bones from Archaeological Sites*, BAR Brit Ser **109**. Oxford: British Archaeological Reports, 7–23

Green, B, 1993 The Iron Age, in P Wade-Martins (ed) *An Historical Atlas of Norfolk*. Chichester: Phillimore & Company, 32

Green, M J, 2001 *Dying for the Gods: Human Sacrifice in Iron Age and Roman Europe*. Stroud: Tempus

Grieg, J R, 1982 Past and present lime woods of Europe, in M Bell & S Limbey (eds), *Archaeological Aspects of Woodland Ecology*, BAR Brit Ser **146**. Oxford: British Archaeological Reports, 23–55

Griffiths, W E, 1949 Roman Coins from Dinas Dinlle, *Trans Caernarvonshire Hist Soc*, **10**

Grime, J P, Hodgson, J G & Hunt, R, 1991 *Comparative Plant Ecology*. London, Unwin Hyman

Grimm, E, 1991 *TILIA and TILIA.GRAPH*. Springfield: Illinois State Museum

Guichard, V & Orengo, L, 1999 Ensembles funéraires du I$^{er}$ s avant J-C à Chaniat, Malintrat, (Puy-de Dôme), in C Mennessier-Jouannet (ed) *Project collectif de Recherche sur les Mobiliers du second Age du Fer en Auvergne. Rapport Annuel 1999*. Mireflleurs: Assoc pour la Recherche sur l'Âge du Fer en Auvergne

Guido, M, 1978 *The Glass Beads of the Prehistoric and Roman Periods in Britain and Ireland*. London: Rep Res Comm Soc Antiq London **35**

Guilbert, G, 1975 Planned hillfort interiors, *Proc Prehist Soc*, **41**, 203–21

Guilbert, G & Garton, D, 2001 Some fieldwork in Derbyshire by Trent & Peak Archaeological Unit in 1998–99, *Derbyshire Archaeol J*, **121**, 196–231

Gwilt, A & Haselgrove, C C (eds), 1997a *Reconstructing the Iron Age. New Approaches to the British Iron Age*. Oxford: Oxbow Monograph **71**

Gwilt, A & Haselgrove, C C, 1997b Approaching the Iron Age, in Gwilt & Haselgrove (eds) 1997a, 1–8

Haevernick, T E, 1960 *Die Glasarminge und Ringperlen der Mittel- und Spätlatènezeit auf dem Europäischen Festland*. Bonn: Rudolf Habelt

Hahn-Weinheimer, P, 1955 Spektrochemische und Physikalische Untersuchungen an latènezeitlichen Glasfunden aus dem Oppidum von Manching. Frankfurt-am-Main: Beilage zum Sammelblatt des Historischen Vereins Ingolstadt **65**

Hall, A, 2003 Recognition and characterisation of turves in archaeological occupation deposits by means of macrofossil plant remains. Portsmouth: EH Centre for Archaeology Report **16/2003**

Hall, D, 1987 *Cambridgeshire Survey, Peterborough to March, The Fenland Project No 2*. East Anglian Archaeology **35**

Hall, D & Coles, J, 1994 *Fenland Survey. An Essay in Landscape and Persistence*. London: English Heritage Archaeological Report **1**

Hall, A R & Kenward, H K, 1990 Environmental evidence from the Colonia: General Accident and Rougier Street. *The Archaeology of York* **14**(6), 289–434 + Plates II–IX + Fiche 2–11. London: CBA

Halstead, P, 1985 A study of mandibular teeth from the Romano-British contexts at Maxey, in F Pryor & C French *The Fenland Project No 1: Archaeology and Environment in the Lower Welland Valley*. East Anglian Archaeology **27**, 209–14

Hambledon, E, 1999 *Animal Husbandry Regimes in Iron Age Britain*, BAR Brit Ser **282**. Oxford: British Archaeological Reports

Harding, D W, 2004 *The Iron Age in Northern Britain. Celts and Romans, Natives and Invaders*. London & New York: Routledge

Haselgrove, C C, 1992 Warfare, ritual and society in Iron Age Wessex, *Archaeol J*, **149**, 407–15

Haselgrove, C C, 1999 Iron Age societies in central Britain: retrospect and prospect, in Bevan (ed) 1999, 253–78

Haselgrove, C C, Armit, I, Champion, T, Creighton, J, Gwilt, A, Hill, J D, Hunter, F & Woodward, A, 2001 *Understanding the British Iron Age: an agenda for action*. Salisbury: Iron Age Research Seminar & the Prehistoric Society

Havis, R & Brooks, H, 2004 *Excavations at Stansted Airport, 1986–91. Vol 1: Prehistoric and Romano-British*. East Anglian Archaeology **107**

Head, R, Chapman, H, Fenwick, H & Van de Noort, R, 1997 The archaeological survey of the Rivers Aire, Went, former Turnbridge Dike (Don North Branch) and the Hampole Beck, in Van de Noort & Ellis (eds) 1997, 229–64

Henderson, J, 1982 X-ray Fluorescence Analysis of Iron Age Glass. University of Bradford: unpubl doctoral thesis

Henderson, J, 1988 Electron probe microanalyses of mixed alkali glasses, *Archaeometry*, **30**, 77–91

Henderson, J, 1991 Industrial specialisation in Late Iron Age Britain and Europe, *Archaeol J*, **148**, 104–48

Henderson, J, 2000 *The Science and Archaeology of Materials*. London & New York: Routledge

Hessing, W & Kooi, P, 2005 Urnenvelden and brandheuvels. Begraving and grafritueel in late bronstijd en ijzertijd, in L Louwe Kooijmans, P van den Broeke, H Fokkens & A van Gijn (eds) *Nederland in de Prehistorie*. Amsterdam: Bert Bakker, 631–54

Hey, G, Bayliss, A & Boyle, A, 1999 Iron Age inhumation burials at Yarnton, Oxfordshire, *Antiquity*, **73**, 551–62

Hill, J D, 1989 Re-thinking the Iron Age, *Scott Archaeol Rev*, **6**, 16–24

Hill, J D, 1994 Why we should not take the data from Iron Age settlement for granted: recent studies of intra-settlement patterning, in Fitzpatrick & Morris (eds) 1994, 4–8

Hill, J D, 1995a *Ritual and rubbish in the Iron Age of Wessex*, BAR Brit Ser **242**. Oxford: British Archaeological Reports

Hill J D, 1995b How should we understand Iron Age societies and hillforts? A contextual study from southern Britain, in Hill & Cumberpatch (eds) 1995, 45–66

Hill, J D, 1996 The identification of ritual deposits of animal bones. A general perspective from a specific study of 'special animal deposits' from the southern English Iron Age, in S Anderson & K Boyle (eds), *Ritual Treatment of Human and Animal Remains*. Proc 1st meeting of the Osteoarchaeological Research Group held in Cambridge on 8 October 1994. Oxford: Oxbow, 17–32

Hill, J D & Cumberpatch, C G (eds), 1995 *Different Iron Ages: studies on the Iron Age of temporal Europe*. BAR Int Ser **S602**. Oxford: British Archaeological Reports

Hill, J D, Evans, C & Alexander, M, 1999 The Hinxton Rings – a late Iron Age cemetery at Hinxton, Cambridgeshire, with a reconsideration of Northern Aylesford-Swarling distributions, *Proc Prehist Soc*, **65**, 243–73

Hingley, R, 1990 Boundaries surrounding Iron Age and Romano-British settlements, *Scott Archaeol Rev* **7**, 96–113

Hingley, R, 1997 Iron, ironworking and regeneration: a study of the symbolic meaning of metalworking in Iron Age Britain, in Gwilt & Haselgrove (eds) 1997a, 9–18

Hingley, R, 1999 The creation of later prehistoric landscapes and the context of the reuse of Neolithic and Earlier Bronze Age Monuments in Britain and Ireland, in Bevan (ed) 1999, 233–51

Hodder, I & Hedges, J W, 1977 'Weaving combs': their typology and distribution with some introductory remarks on date and function, in J R Collis (ed) *The Iron Age in Britain – a review*. Sheffield: Dept of Prehistory and Archaeology, University of Sheffield, 17–28

Hogan, D V, Simpson, P, Jones, A M & Maltby, E, 2002 Development of a protocol for the reburial of organic archaeological remains, in P Hoffmann, J A Spriggs, T Grant, C Cook & A Recht (eds), *Proc 8th ICOM Group on Wet Organic Archaeological Materials Conference*, 187–212

Holden, J L, Phakley, P P & Clement, J G, 1995a Scanning electron microscope observations of incinerated human femoral bone: a case study, *Forensic Sci Int*, **74**, 17–28

Holden, J L, Phakley, P P & Clement, J G, 1995b Scanning electron microscope observations of heat-treated human bone, *Forensic Sci Int*, **74**, 29–45

Horne, P & Kershaw, A (eds), forthcoming 'A perfect flat ... broken by several bold swells' – day school on the archaeology of the Vale of York. York: English Heritage

Howell, J K, 2001 *Swillington Common*, in I Roberts, A Burgess & D Berg 2001 *A New Link to the Past. The Archaeological Landscape of the M1–A1 Link Road*. Leeds: West Yorkshire Archaeology Service; Yorkshire Archaeology **7** 47–67

Humphrey, J, 2003 *Re-searching the Iron Age. Selected papers from the proceedings of the Iron Age Research Student Seminars, 1999 and 2000*. Leicester: Leicester Archaeology Monographs **11**

Huntley, B & Birks, H J B, 1983 *An atlas of past and present pollen maps for Europe 0–13000 years ago*. Cambridge: Cambridge University Press

Ingold, T, 1993 The Temporality of the Landscape, *World Archaeology*, **25**, 152–74

Ingold, T, 2000 *The Perception of the Environment. Essays in Livelihood, Dwelling and Skill*. London & New York: Routledge

Jackson, R P J & Potter, T W, 1996 *Excavations at Stonea, Cambridgeshire 1980–85*. London: British Museum Press

Jacobson, G L & Bradshaw, R H W, 1981 The selection of sites for palaeovegetational research, *Quat Res*, **16**, 80–96

James, S, 1999 *The Atlantic Celts: Ancient People or Modern Invention?* London: British Museum Press

Johnson, E, 1985 Current developments in bone technology, in M B Schiffer (ed), *Advances in Archaeological Method and Theory Vol 8*. New York: Academic Press, 157–235

Johnson, M, 1999 *Archaeological theory: an introduction*. London: Blackwell

Jones, B & Mattingley, D, 1990 *An Atlas of Roman Britain*. Oxford: Blackwell

Jones, G & Halstead, P, 1995 Maslins, Mixtures and Monocrops: the Interpretation of Archaeobotanical Crop Samples of Heterogeneous Composition, *J Archaeol Sci*, **22**, 103–14

Jones, L, 2002 Land at Catesby Business Park, Balby Carr, Doncaster, South Yorkshire: an archaeological excavation 2002. Post-excavation assessment and research design. Birmimgham: Birmingham University Field Unit unpubl report

Jones, M, 1999 Plant exploitation, in Champion & Collis (eds) 1999, 29–40

Jones, R J A & Evans R, 1975 Soil and crop marks in the recognition of archaeological sites by air photography, in D R Wilson (ed), *Aerial reconnaissance for archaeology*. London: CBA Res Rep **12**, 1–11

Jones, S, Macsween, A, Jeffrey, S, Morris, R & Heyworth, M, 2003 *From the Ground Up. The Publication of Archaeological Projects: a User Needs Survey*. York: CBA

Jope, E M, 2000 *Early Celtic Art in the British Isles*. Oxford: Oxford University Press

Kenward, H K, 1978 The analysis of archaeological insect assemblages: a new approach. *The Archaeology of York* **19**. London: CBA, 1–68 + plates I–IV

Kenward, H K, 1982 Insect communities and death assemblages, past and present, in A R Hall & H Kenward (eds) *Environmental archaeology in the urban context*. London: CBA Res Rep **43**, 71–8

Kenward, H K, 1988 Insect remains, in E Schia (ed), *De arkeologiske utgravninger i Gamlebyen, Oslo. Vol 5 Mindets Tomt – Söndrefelt*. Öure Ervik: Alvheim & Eide, 115–40

Kenward, H K, 1992 Rapid recording of archaeological insect remains – a reconsideration, *Circaea, J Assoc Environ Archaeol*, **9**, 81–8

Kenward, H, K, 1997 Synanthropic decomposer insects and the size, remoteness and longevity of archaeological occupation sites: applying concepts from biogeography to past 'islands' of human occupation, *Quat Proc*, **5**, 135–51

Kenward, H K, Engleman, C, Robertson, A, & Large, F, 1986 Rapid scanning of urban archaeological deposits for insect remains, *Circaea, J Assoc Environ Archaeol*, **3**, 163–72

Kenward, H K & Hall, A R, 1995 Biological evidence from AngloScandinavian deposits at 16–22 Coppergate. *The Archaeology of York* **14**. York: CBA, 435–797 + xxii + loose figures

Kenward, H K & Hall, A R, 1997 Enhancing bioarchaeological interpretation using indicator groups: stable manure as a paradigm, *J Archaeol Sci*, **24**, 663–73

Kenward, H K, Hall, A R & Jones, A K G, 1980 A tested set of techniques for the extraction of plant and animal macrofossils from waterlogged archaeological deposits, *Sci & Archaeol*, **22**, 3–15

Kenward, H K & Large, F, 1998 Recording the preservational condition of archaeological insect fossils, *Environ Archaeol*, **2**, 49–60

Kilian, M R, Van der Plicht, J & Van Geel, B, 1995 Dating raised bogs: new aspects of AMS $^{14}$C wiggle matching, a reservoir effect and climatic change, *Quat Sci Rev*, **14**, 959–66

Kilian, M R, Van der Plicht, J & Van Geel, B, 2000 $^{14}$C wiggle matching of raised bog deposits and models of peat accumulation, *Quat Sci Rev*, **19**, 1011–33

Kirby, J R & Gearey, B R, 2001 Wetland and Dryland Vegetation Dynamics in the Humber Lowlands, in M A Atherden (ed), *Wetlands In the Landscape: Archaeology, Conservation and Heritage*. York: PLACE Research Centre, 41–68

Klein, R G & Cruz-Uribe, K, 1984 *The Analysis of Animal Bones from Archaeological Sites*. Chicago: University of Chicago Press

Kloet, G S & Hincks, W D, 1964–77 *A check list of British Insects* (2nd edn). London: Royal Entomological Soc

Knight, D, 1984 *Late Bronze Age and Iron Age Settlement in the Nene and Great Ouse Basins,* BAR Brit Ser **130**. Oxford: British Archaeological Reports

Knight, D, 1992 Excavations of an Iron Age settlement at Gamston, Nottinghamshire, *Trans Thoroton Soc Nottinghamshire*, **96**, 16–90

Knight, D, 2002 A regional ceramic sequence: pottery of the first millennium BC between the Humber and the Nene, in J D Hill and A Woodward (eds) *Prehistoric Britain: the ceramic basis*. Oxford: Oxbow, 119–42

Knight, D & Howard, A J, 2004 *Trent Valley Landscapes. The Archaeology of 500,000 Years of Change*. King's Lynn: Heritage Marketing and Publications

Knüsel, C J, 2005 The physical evidence of warfare – subtle stigmata?, in M Parker Pearson & I J N Thorpe (eds) *Violence, Warfare, and Slavery*, BAR Int Ser **S1374**, 49–65. Oxford: British Archaeological Reports

Kohler, T, 2004 Feeding the fen, in Smith (ed) 2004, 85–92

Kunkel, O, 1961 Zur Frage keltischer Glasindustrie nach einer Manchinger Fundgruppe. *Germania*, **39**, 322–9

Lambrick, G, 1990 Farmers and shepherds in the Bronze Age and Iron Age, *Current Archaeology*, **121**, 14–18

Lanting, J N, Aerts-Bijma, A T & Van der Plicht, J, 2001 Dating of cremated bones, *Radiocarbon*, **43(2A)**, 249–54

Leah, M D, Wells, C E, Stamper, P, Huckerby, E & Welch, C, 1998 *The Wetlands of Shropshire and Staffordshire*. Lancaster: North West Wetlands Survey **5,** Lancaster Imprints **7**

Lillie, M C, 1997 The palaeoenvironmental survey of the Rivers Aire, Went, former Turnbridge Dike (Don north branch), and the Hampole Beck, in Van de Noort & Ellis (eds) 1997, 47–78

Lillie, M & Gearey, B, 2000 The palaeoenvironmental survey of the Hull valley, and research at Routh Quarry, in Van de Noort & Ellis (eds) 2000, 31–82

Lillie, M C & Schofield, J E, 2002 Sutton Common, Askern Borehole Survey. Hull: WAERC Report, SCOM/02–01

Lowe J J & Walker M J C, 2000 Radiocarbon dating the last glacial-interglacial transition (14C ka BP) in terrestrial and marine records: the need for new quality assurance protocols, *Radiocarbon*, **42**, 53–68

Magilton, J R, 1978 Excavations at Ling Farm, Dunsville, Hatfield, *Yorkshire Archaeol J*, **50**, 57–63

Malim, T, 1992 Excavations and Site Management at Stonea Camp, Wimblington 1990–1992, in C Evans (ed) *Fenland Research* **7**. Cambridge: Fenland Project

Malim, T, 2005 *Stonea and the Roman Fens*. Stroud: Tempus

Malim, T & McKenna, R, 1993 Borough Fen: Iron Age Fort, Newborough, Cambridgeshire, in C Evans & J Pollard (eds) *Fenland Research* **8**. Cambridge: Fenland Project

Manby, T G, 1988 Multiple ditched enclosures: Little Smeaton, West Yorkshire, in D N Riley (ed) *Yorkshire's Past from the Air*. Sheffield: Dept of Archaeology and Prehistory, University of Sheffield, 26–7

Manby, T G, 2003a The Neolithic and Bronze Ages: a time of early agriculture, in Manby *et al* 2003, 35–116

Manby, T G 2003b The Iron Age of central and Pennine Yorkshire, in Manby *et al* 2003, 121–4

Manby, T G, Moorhouse, S & Ottaway, P, 2003 (eds), *The Archaeology of Yorkshire. An Assessment at the beginning of the 21st Century*. Leeds: Yorkshire Archaeol Soc Occas Paper **3**

Margary, I D, 1957 *Roman Roads in Britain (Vol II) North of the Foss Way–Bristol Channel*. London: Phoenix House

Martin, E, 1988 *Burgh: The Iron Age and Roman Enclosure*. East Anglian Archaeology **40**

Martin, E, 1999 The Iron Age, in D Dymond & E Martin (eds), *An Historical Atlas of Suffolk*. Sudbury: Suffolk County Council

Matthews, K J, 1997 Immaterial culture; Invisible peasants and consumer subcultures in north-west Britannia, in K Meadows, C Lemke & J Heron (eds), *TRAC96: Proc 6th Ann Theoretical Roman Archaeology Conference*. Oxford: Oxbow Books, 120–32

Matthews, K J, 1999 The Iron Age of north-west England and Irish Sea trade, in Bevan (ed) 1999, 173–96

Mayer, L M, 1989 Extracellular Proteolytic-Enzyme Activity in Sediments of an Intertidal Mudflat, *Limnology and Oceanography*, **34**, 973–81

McInnes, I, 1968 The excavation of a Bronze Age cemetery at Catfoss, East Yorkshire, *East Riding Archaeologist*, **1**, 2–10

McKinley, J I, 1990 Cremated bone from Iron Age burials at Icknield Way, Baldock. Salisbury: Wessex Archaeology unpubl report for Letchworth Museum

McKinley, J I, 1993 Bone fragment size and weights of bone from modern British cremations and its implications for the interpretation of archaeological cremations, *Int J Osteoarchaeol*, **3**, 283–7

McKinley, J I, 1994a *The Anglo-Saxon cemetery at Spong Hill, North Elmham Part VIII: The Cremations*. East Anglian Archaeology **69**

McKinley, J I, 1994b Bone fragment size in British cremation burials and its implications for pyre technology and ritual, *J Archaeol Sci*, **21**, 339–42

McKinley, J I, 1997a The cremated human bone from burial and cremation-related contexts, in Fitzpatrick (ed) 1997b, 55–72

McKinley, J I, 1997b Bronze Age 'Barrows' and the Funerary Rites and Rituals of Cremation, *Proc Prehist Soc*, **63**, 129–45

McKinley, J I, 2000 Phoenix rising; aspects of cremation in Roman Britain, in M Millett, J Pearce & M Struck (eds) *Burial, Society and Context in the Roman World*. Oxford: Oxbow Books, 38–44

McKinley, J I, 2004 Compiling a skeletal inventory: cremated human bone, in M Brickley & J I McKinley (eds) *Guidelines to the Standards for Recording Human Remains*. Brit Assoc Biolog Anthropol & Osteoarchaeol and Institute of Field Archaeologists, 9–12

Merrony, C J N, 1993 The archaeological assessment in advance of the Dearne Towns Link Road (stage 4) development at Goldthorpe. *Archaeology in South Yorkshire 1992–1993*. Sheffield: South Yorkshire Archaeology Service, 43–52

Miller, K, 2004 From first farmers to flagship, in Smith (ed) 2004, 31–42

Monckton, A, 1999 *Charred plant remains from Concerto Camp, Iron Age hillfort, Worcestershire*. London: English Heritage (Ancient Monuments Lab Rep **23/1999**)

Mook, W G, 1986 Business meeting: recommendations/resolutions adopted by the Twelfth International Radiocarbon Conference, *Radiocarbon*, **28**, 799

Moore, P D, Webb, J A & Collinson, M E, 1991 *Pollen Analysis*. Oxford: Blackwell

Morlan, R E, 1984 Toward the definition of criteria for the recognition of artificial bone alterations, *Quat Res*, **22**, 160–71

Morris, E L, 1991 Report on the Prehistoric Ceramics Found at Wall Camp, Kynnersley, in Carver (ed) 1991, 55–8

Morse, M, 2005 *How the Celts came to Britain. Ancient Skulls and the Birth of Archaeology.* Stroud: Tempus

Munro, M A R, 1984 An improved algorithm for crossdating tree-ring series, *Tree Ring Bulletin*, **44**, 17–27

Murphy, P, 1992 *Stanway, Essex: plant remains from Late Neolithic/Early Bronze and Middle Iron Age pits and Late Iron Age burials.* London: English Heritage (Ancient Monuments Laboratory Report **29/92**)

Musson, C R, 1991 *The Breiddin Hillfort, a later prehistoric settlement in the Welsh Marches.* London: CBA Res Rep **76**

Nayling, N, 2001 *Tree-ring analysis of timbers from Sutton Common, Askern, South Yorkshire.* London: English Heritage (Centre for Archaeology Report **24/2001**)

Needham, S P, 1996 Chronology and periodisation in the British Bronze Age, *Acta Archaeologica*, **67**, 121–40

Needham, S P & Ambers, J, 1994 Redating Rams Hill and reconsidering Bronze Age enclosure, *Proc Prehist Soc*, **60**, 225–44

Nielsen-Marsh, C, Gernaey, A, Turner-Walker, G, Hedges, R, Pike, A & Collins, M, 2000 The chemical degradation of bone, in M Cox & S Mays (eds) *Human Osteology in Archaeology and Forensic Science.* London: GMM, 439–54

Noakes, J E, Kim, S M & Stipp, J J, 1965 Chemical and counting advances in Liquid Scintillation Age dating, in Olsson and Chatters (eds) 1965, 68–92

Olivier, A, 1996 *Frameworks for Our Past.* London: English Heritage

Olivier, A, 2004 Great expectations: the English Heritage approach to the management of the historic environment in England's wetlands, *J Wetland Archaeol*, **4**, 155–68

Olivier, A & Van de Noort, R, 2002 *English Heritage Strategy for Wetlands.* Exeter: University of Exeter

Oswald, A, 1997 A doorway on the past: practical and mystical concerns in the orientation of roundhouse doorways, in Gwilt & Haselgrove (eds) 1997, 87–95

Otlet, R L, 1977 Harwell radiocarbon measurements II, *Radiocarbon*, **19**, 400–23

Otlet, R L, 1979 An assessment of laboratory errors in liquid scintillation methods of $^{14}$C dating, in R Berger and H E Suess (eds) *Proc 9th International Radiocarbon Conference.* PLACE: University of California Press, 256–67

Otlet, R L, Huxtable, G, Evans, G V, Humphreys, D G, Short, T D & Conchie, S J, 1983 Development and operation of the Harwell small counter facility for the measurement of $^{14}$C in very small samples, *Radiocarbon*, **25**, 565–75

Otlet, R L & Warchal, R M, 1978 Liquid scintillation counting of low-level $^{14}$C dating, *Liquid Scintillation Counting*, **5**, 210–18

Outram, A K, 2001 A new approach to identifying bone marrow and grease exploitation: why the 'indeterminate' fragments should not be ignored, *J Archaeol Sci*, **28**, 401–10

Outram, A K, 2002 Bone fracture and within-bone nutrients: an experimentally based method for investigating levels of marrow extraction, in P Miracle & N Milner (eds) *Consuming Passions and Patterns of Consumption.* Cambridge: McDonald Institute for Archaeological Research, 51–64

Outram, A K, 2005 Applied Models and Indices vs High-Resolution, Observed Data: Detailed Fracture and Fragmentation Analyses for the Investigation of Skeletal Part Abundance Patterns, *J Taphonomy*, **2:3** (for 2004), 167–84

Parker Pearson, M, 1996 Food, fertility and front doors in the first millennium BC, in Champion & Collis (eds) 1996, 117–32

Parker Pearson, M, 1999 *The Archaeology of Death and Burial.* Stroud: Sutton

Parker Pearson, M & Field, N, 2003 (eds), *Fiskerton: An Iron Age timber causeway with Iron Age and Roman votive offerings.* Oxford: Oxbow Books

Parker Pearson, M & Merrony, C, 1993 Sutton Common Desiccation Assessment 1993: interim report. Sheffield: Dept of Prehistory and Archaeology, University of Sheffield & South Yorkshire Archaeology Unit; Doncaster: Doncaster Museum unpubl report

Parker Pearson, M & Richards, C, 1994 Architecture and order: spatial representation and archaeology, in M Parker Pearson & C Richards (eds) *Architecture and Order: Approaches to Social Space.* London: Routledge, 38–72

Parker Pearson, M & Sydes, R, 1997 The Iron Age enclosures and prehistoric landscape at Sutton Common, South Yorkshire, *Proc Prehist Soc*, **63**, 221–59

Parker, A G, Goudie, A S, Andersen, D E, Robinson, M A & Bonsall, C, 2002 A review of the mid-Holocene elm decline in the British Isles, *Progress in Physical Geography*, **26**(1), 1–45

Pasley, S & Cheetham, V, 2004 Value in wetness, in Smith (ed) 2004, 93–102

Payne, S, 1973 Kill-off patterns in sheep and goat: the mandibles from Asvan Kale, *Anatolian Studies*, **23**, 281–303

Payne, S, 1985 Morphological distinctions between the mandibular teeth of young sheep, *Ovis*, and goats, *Capra*, *J Archaeol Sci*, **12**, 139–47

Pennant, T, 1773–76 (reprint 1991) *A Tour in Wales (Vol 2).* Wrexham: Bridge Books

Pitt-Rivers, A, 1888 *Excavations in Cranborne Chase, Vol II*. London: private publication

Ponnamperuma, F N, 1972 The chemistry of submerged soils, *Advances in Agronomy*, **24**, 29–96

Poremba, K, 1995 Hydrolytic Enzymatic-Activity in Deep-Sea Sediments, *Fems Microbiology Ecology*, **16**, 213–21

Powell, K L, Pedley, S, Daniel, G & Corfield, M, 2001 Ultrastructural observations of microbial succession and decay of wood buried at a Bronze Age archaeological site, *Int Biodeterioration & Biodegradation*, **47**, 165–73

Powlesland, D, 2005 Excavations in Heslerton. DigIT Experiments in Digital Recording. Yedingham: The Landscape Research Centre unpubl report

Proctor, J, 2002 Late Bronze Age/Early Iron Age placed deposits from Westcroft Road, Carshalton: their meaning and interpretation, *Surrey Archaeol Coll* **89**, 65–103

Pryor, F, 2001 *The Flag Fen Basin: archaeology and environment of a fenland landscape*. English Heritage, Swindon

Purdy, B A (ed), 2002 *Enduring Record. The Environmental and Cultural Heritage of Wetlands*. Oxford: Oxbow Books

Rackham, O, 1980 *Ancient woodland: its history, vegetation and uses in England*. London: Edward Arnold

Reimer, P J, Baillie, M G L, Bard, E, Bayliss, A, Beck, J W, Bertrand, C J H, Blackwell, P G, Buck, C E, Burr, G S, Cutler, K B, Damon, P E, Edwards, R L, Fairbanks, R G, Friedrich, M, Guilderson, T P, Hogg, A G, Hughen, K A, Kromer, B, McCormac, G, Manning, S, Bronk Ramsey, C, Reimer, R W, Remmele, S, Southon, J R, Stuiver, M, Talamo, S, Taylor, F W, Van der Plicht, J & Weyhenmeyer, C E, 2004 IntCal04 Terrestrial radiocarbon age calibration, 0–26 Cal Kyr BP, *Radiocarbon*, **46**, 1029–58

Riley, D N, 1973 Aerial reconnaissance of the West Riding magnesian limestone country, *Yorkshire Archaeol J,* **45**, 14–17

Riley, D N, 1980 *Early Landscapes from the Air. Studies of crop marks in South Yorkshire and north Nottinghamshire*. Sheffield: Dept of Prehistory and Archaeology, University of Sheffield

Riley, D N, 1982 *Aerial Archaeology in Britain*. Aylesbury: Shire Archaeology

Riley, D N, 1983 The frequency of occurrence of cropmarks in relation to soils, in G S Maxwell (ed), *The impact of aerial reconnaissance on archaeology*. London: CBA Res Rep **49**, 59–73

Robbins, G, 1999 Research and regionality: South Yorkshire as an example, in Bevan (ed) 1999, 43–9

Roberts, I, 2003 *Excavations at Topham Farm, Sykehouse, South Yorkshire*. Leeds: Archaeological Services (WYAS) Publication **5**

Roberts, I, in prep Late prehistoric and Romano-British land division in South and West Yorkshire: an overview of the evidence

Roberts, I, Burgess, A & Berg, D, 2001 *A New Link to the Past. The Archaeological Landscape of the M1–A1 Link Road*. Leeds: Archaeological Services (WYAS) Publication **7**

Roberts, I & Richardson, J, 2002 *Iron Age and Romano-British settlement enclosures at Moss Carr, Methley, West Yorkshire*. Leeds: Archaeological Services (WYAS) Publication **2**

Rogers, J & Waldron, T, 1995 *A Field Guide to Joint Disease in Archaeology*. Chichester: Wiley

Roy Comm Ancient Hist Monuments Wales Inventories, 1960 *Caernarvonshire, Vol II Central, The Cantref of Arfon and the Commote of Eifionydd*. London: HMSO

Rozanski, K, Stichler, W, Gonfiantini, R, Scott, E M, Beukens, R P, Kromer, B & Van der Plicht, J, 1992 The IAEA $^{14}$C intercomparison exercise 1990, *Radiocarbon*, **34**, 506–19

Samuels, J & May, J, 1980 The excavations, in D N Riley (ed) 1980, 73–81

Sands, R, 1997 *Prehistoric Woodworking. The Analysis and Interpretation of Bronze and Iron Age Toolmarks*. London: Institute of Archaeology, UCL

Scarre, C, 1989 Review of J M Coles & A J Lawson (eds), 1987 *European Wetlands in Prehistory*, Clarendon Press, Oxford, *Proc Prehist Soc*, **55**, 274–5

Scheuer, L & Black, S, 2000 *Developmental Juvenile Osteology*. London: Academic Press

Schmid, E, 1972 *Atlas of Animal Bones*. London: Elsevier

Schwartz, J H, 1995 *Skeleton Keys: an introduction to human skeletal morphology, development and analysis*. Oxford: Oxford University Press

Scott, E M, 2003 The 3rd international radiocarbon intercomparison (TIRI) and the fourth international radiocarbon intercomparison (FIRI) 1990 – 2002: results, analyses, and conclusions, *Radiocarbon*, **45**, 135–408

Scott, E M, Harkness, D D & Cook, G T, 1998 Inter-laboratory comparisons: lessons learned, *Radiocarbon*, **40**, 331–40

Seager-Smith, R H, 1998 Further Excavations at the Iron Age Enclosure at Tattershall Thorpe, Lincolnshire by Peter Chowne, 1986, *Lincolnshire Hist Archaeol*, **33**, 7–19

Sharples, N M, 1991 *Maiden Castle: Excavations and Field Survey 1985–86*. London: English Heritage

Shore, J S, Bartley, D D, & Harkness, D D, 1995 Problems encountered with the $^{14}$C dating of peat, *Quat Sci Rev*, **14**, 373–83

Silver, I, 1969 The ageing and sexing of domestic animals, in D Brothwell & E Higgs (eds) *Science in Archaeology*. London: Thames and Hudson, 283–302

Simpson, W G, 1966 Romano-British settlement on the Welland Gravels, in A C Thomas (ed) *Rural Settlement in Roman Britain*. London: CBA Res Rep **8**, 15–25

Slota, Jr P J, Jull, A J T, Linick, T W & Toolin, L J, 1987 Preparation of small samples for $^{14}$C accelerator targets by catalytic reduction of CO, *Radiocarbon*, **29**, 303–06

Smith, G, 1991 Excavations at Ham Hill, 1983, *Somerset Archaeol Natur Hist*, **134**, 27–45

Smith, G, 1993 *Coastal Erosion Survey: Aberdaron Bay to Great Orme*. Gwynedd Archaeological Trust Rep **79**

Smith, R (ed), 2004 *The Marsh of Time. Saving Sutton Common*. Tiverton: Halsgrove

Stanford, S C, 1971 Invention, adoption and imposition – the evidence of the hill-forts, in M Jesson & D Hill (eds) *The Iron Age and its Hill-Forts*. Southampton: Southampton University Archaeological Society, 41–52

Stanford, S C, 1974 *Croft Ambrey*. Hereford

Stanford, S C, 1981 *Midsummer Hill: an Iron Age hillfort on the Malverns*. Leominster: S C Stanford

Stanford, S C, 1984 The Wrekin Hillfort Excavations 1973, *Archaeol J* **141**, 61–90

Stead, I M, 1961 A distinctive form of La Tène barrow in Eastern Yorkshire and on the Continent, *Antiquarian J*, **41**, 44–62

Stead, I M, 1968 An Iron Age Hill-fort at Grimthorpe, Yorkshire, England, *Proc Prehist Soc*, **34**, 148–90

Stead, I M, 1979 *The Arras Culture*. York: Yorkshire Philosophical Society

Stead, I M, 1985 *Celtic Art*. London: British Museum Press

Stead, I M, 1991a *Iron Age Cemeteries in East Yorkshire. Excavations at Burton Fleming, Rudston, Garton-on-the-Wolds, and Kirkburn*. London: English Heritage

Stead, I M, 1991b The Snettisham treasure: excavations in 1990, *Antiquity*, **65**, 447–65

Stenhouse, M J & Baxter, M S, 1983 $^{14}$C dating reproducibility: evidence from routine dating of archaeological samples, *PACT*, **8**, 147–61

Stockmarr, J, 1971 Tablets with spores used in absolute pollen analysis. *Pollen et Spores*, **13**, 615–21

Stoertz, C, 1997 *Ancient landscapes of the Yorkshire Wolds: aerial photographic transcription and analysis*. Swindon: RCHME

Stopford, J, 1987 Danebury: an alternative view. *Scott Archaeol Rev*, **4**, 70–5

Stuiver, M & Kra, R S, 1986 Editorial comment, *Radiocarbon*, **28**(2B), ii

Stuiver, M & Polach, H A, 1977 Reporting of $^{14}$C data, *Radiocarbon*, **19**, 355–63

Stuiver, M & Reimer, P J, 1986 A computer program for radiocarbon age calculations, *Radiocarbon*, **28**, 1022–30

Stuiver, M & Reimer, P J 1993 Extended $^{14}$C data base and revised CALIB 3.0 $^{14}$C age calibration program, *Radiocarbon*, **35**, 215–30

Stuiver, M, Reimer, P J, Bard, E, Beck, J W, Burr, G S, Hughen, K A, Kromer, B, McCormac, G, van der Plicht, J & Spurk, M, 1998 INTCAL98 Radiocarbon Age Calibration, 24000–0 cal BP, *Radiocarbon*, **40,** 1041–83

Surtees, S F, 1868 *Footprints of Roman Occupation in the Southern Parts of North Humber Land*. Leeds: Baines

Sydes, R E, 1992 Report on the re-excavation of Trench A/C, Sutton Common, South Yorkshire. Sheffield: Dept of Archaeology and Prehistory, University of Sheffield unpubl report

Sydes, R E, 1993 Excavations at Pickburn Leys, Adwick-le-Street, Doncaster, *Archaeology in South Yorkshire 1992–1993*. Sheffield: South Yorkshire Archaeology Service, 36–42

Sydes, R E & Symonds, J, 1987 Sutton Common 1987, Excavation Report. Sheffield: South Yorkshire Archaeology Unit unpubl report

Tamers, M A, 1965 Routine carbon-14 dating using liquid scintillation techniques, in Chatters & Olson (eds) 1965, 53–67

Taylor, M, 2003 The wooden remains, in Field & Parker Pearson 2003, 25–48

Thomas, R, 1997 Land, kinship relations and the rise of enclosed settlement in first millennium BC Britain, *Oxford J Archaeol*, **16**, 211–18

Tilley, C, 1994 *A phenomenology of landscape – places, paths and monuments*. Oxford: Berg

Tiquia, S M, 2002 Evolution of extracellular enzyme activities during manure composting, *J Applied Microbiol*, **92**, 764–75

Tiquia, S M, Wan, J H C, & Tam, N F Y, 2001 Extracellular enzyme profiles during co-composting of poultry manure and yard trimmings, *Process Biochemistry*, **36**, 813–20

Trigger, B, 1990 *A History of Archaeological Thought*. Cambridge: Cambridge University Press

Tuohy T, 1999 *Prehistoric Combs of Antler and Bone, Vols I and II*, BAR Brit Ser **285**. Oxford: British Archaeological Reports

Tutin, T G, Heywood, V H, Burges, N A, Moore, D M, Valentine, D H, Walters, S M & Webb, D A (eds), 1964–80 *Flora Europaea*, **1–5**. Cambridge: Cambridge University Press

Tweddle, J, 2001 Regional vegetational history, in M D Bateman, P C Buckland, C D Frederick & N J Whitehouse (eds), *The Quaternary of East*

Yorkshire and North Lincolnshire. London: QRA, 35–47

Tyers, I, 1998 *Tree-ring analysis and wood identification of timbers excavated on the Magistrates Court Site, Kingston upon Hull, East Yorkshire.* Sheffield: ARCUS Report **410**

Tyers, I, 1999 *Dendro for Windows program guide 2nd edn.* Sheffield: ARCUS Report **500**

Van Beek, G C, 1983 *Dental Morphology: an illustrated guide.* Bristol: Wright PSG

Van de Noort, R, 2004a *The Humber Wetlands. The Archaeology of a Dynamic Landscape.* Bollington: Windgather Press

Van de Noort, R, 2004b Sutton Common: Updated project design. Exeter: University of Exeter unpubl report

Van de Noort, R & Chapman, H P, 1999 *An archaeological assessment in preparation of a management plan at Sutton Common, Sutton, South Yorkshire.* Hull: Centre for Wetland Archaeology, University of Hull

Van de Noort, R & Chapman, H P, 2001 Sutton Common, Sutton, South Yorkshire. Project Design SCOM001–03 (v2). Exeter: University of Exeter unpubl report

Van de Noort, R, Chapman, H P & Cheetham, J L, 2001a In situ preservation as a dynamic process: the example of Sutton Common, UK, *Antiquity*, **75**, 94–100

Van de Noort, R, Chapman, H P & Cheetham, J L, 2001b Science-based conservation and management in wetland archaeology, in Purdy (ed) 2002, 277–86

Van de Noort, R & Davies, P, 1993 *Wetland Heritage. An Archaeological Assessment of the Humber Wetlands.* Hull: University of Hull

Van de Noort, R & Ellis, S (eds), 1997 *Wetland Heritage of the Humberhead Levels, an archaeological survey.* Hull: Humber Wetlands Project, University of Hull

Van de Noort, R, Fletcher, W, Thomas, G, Carstairs, I & Patrick, D, 2002 *Monuments at Risk in England's Wetlands – Final Report.* Exeter: University of Exeter

Van de Noort, R & O'Sullivan, A, 2006 *Rethinking Wetland Archaeology.* London: Duckworth

Van de Noort, R & Panter, I, 2000 Rubbish and Archaeology, *Past*, **34**, 2

Van der Sanden, W, 1996 *Through Nature to Eternity. The Bog Bodies of northwest Europe.* Amsterdam: Batavian Lion International

Van der Veen, M, 1992 *Crop Husbandry Regimes. An Archaeobotanical Study of Farming in northern England 1000 BC – AD 500.* Sheffield: J R Collis Publications

Van Heeringen, R & Theunissen, L, 2002 Repeated water table lowering in the Dutch Delta: a major challenge to the archaeological heritage management of pre- and protohistoric wetlands, in Purdy (ed) 2002, 271–6

von den Driesch, A, 1976 *A Guide to the Measurement of Animal Bones from Archaeological Sites.* Harvard: Harvard University Press

Wainwright, G J, 1968 The excavation of a Durotrigian Farmstead near Tollard Royal in Cranborne Chase, Southern England, *Proc Prehist Soc*, **34**, 102–47

Wainwright, G J, 1969 The excavation of Balksbury Camp, Andover, Hants, *Proc Hampshire Field Club*, **26**, 21–55

Wainwright, G J, 1979 *Gussage All Saints. An Iron Age Settlement in Dorset.* London: Dept of the Environment Archaeological Rep **10**

Walker M J C, Bryant, C, Coope, G R, Harkness, D D, Lowe, J J & Scott, E M, 2001 Towards a radiocarbon chronology of the Late-Glacial: sample selection strategies, *Radiocarbon*, **43**, 1007–21

Waller, M P, Binney, H A, Bunting, M J & Armitage, R, 2005 The interpretation of fen carr pollen diagrams: pollen-vegetation relationships within the fen carr, *Rev Palaeobot & Palynol*, **133**, 179–202

Ward, G K & Wilson, S R, 1978 Procedures for comparing and combining radiocarbon age determinations: a critique, *Archaeometry*, **20**(1), 19–31

Waterbolk, H T, 1977 Walled enclosures of the Iron Age in the north of the Netherlands. *Palaeohistoria*, **19**, 97–172

Watson, M, 2002 *Shropshire an Archaeological Guide.* Shrewsbury: Shropshire Books & Shropshire County Council

Webster, J, 1995 Translation and subjection: translation and the Celtic Gods, in Hill & Cumberpatch (eds) 1995, 170–83

Webster, J, 1999 Here be dragons! The continuing influence of Roman attitudes to northern Britain, in Bevan (ed) 1999, 21–31

Wheeler, R E M, 1943 *Maiden Castle, Dorset.* London: Rep Res Comm Soc Antiq London **12**

Whimster, R, 1981 *Burial Practices in Iron Age Briain. A Discussion and Gazetteer of the Evidence c 700 BC – AD 43*, BAR Brit Ser **90**. Oxford: British Archaeological Reports

White, T D, 1991 *Human Osteology.* London: Academic Press

Whiting, C E, 1936 Excavations on Sutton Common, 1933, 1934 and 1935, *Yorkshire Archaeol J*, **33**, 57–80

Williams, H, 2003 The Archaeology of Death, Memory and Material Culture, in H Williams (ed) *Archaeologies of Remembrance – death and memory in past societies.* Amsterdam: Kluwer, 1–24

Williams, J & Brown, N, 1999 *An Archaeological Research Framework for the Greater Thames Estuary.* Chelmsford: Essex County Council.

Woodward, A & Leach, P, 1993 *The Uley Shrines: Excavations of a Ritual Complex on West Hill, Uley, Gloucestershire 1977–79.* London: English Heritage

Xu, S, Anderson, R, Bryant, C, Cook, G T, Dougans, A, Freeman, S, Naysmith, P, Schnabel, C & Scott, E M, 2004 Capabilities of the new SUERC 5MV AMS facility for $^{14}$C dating, *Radiocarbon*, **46**, 59–64

# Index

Page numbers in *italics* denote illustrations.

aerial photography  *40*
agriculture
   Neolithic–Bronze Age  63, 66–7
   Iron Age  101, 135, 170
Alfred, King  174
Allcroft, A Hadrian  4
Almondbury (W Yorks), hillfort  111
animal bone
   marsh-fort
      age  141–2
      assemblage  139
      bone fracture and taphonomic history  142
      deposition  15, 149–50
      human inhumations, associated with  139, 142
      species and element abundance  139, *140*, 141
   methodology  49–50
   mortuary rings  157, 162, 164, 176
Anne, Major Crathorne  4
antler *see* weaving comb
APS UK  33
Arbury Camp (Cambs), enclosure  *171*, 172
ARCUS  169
arrowheads  4, *65*, 66
Asheldam Camp (Essex), pits  134, 182
Askern (S Yorks)
   Campsmount School  *32*, *33*
   Junior School  32, 33
   limestone  52
   Miners' Welfare  33, 34
   Town Council  33
Askham Bog (N Yorks), pollen  61
Aslockton (Notts), enclosure  111
Athelney (Som), enclosure  174
Aulnat (France), glass-working  160
Austerfield (S Yorks), field system  168
axes
   copper alloy  54–6
   stone  54, 64, *65*, 66

Balby Carr (S Yorks), field system  169
Balksbury (Hants), granaries  134
ball, baked clay  5, 136
bangle, copper alloy  119; *see also* bracelet, gold
banks
   far outer
      dating  95
      discussion  111, 113
      excavation evidence  78, 85, 88, 89
   palisade bank
      dating  95
      discussion  111, 113
      excavation evidence  78–9, *81–2*, 83, 85
      excavation methodology  37

   geoarchaeology  109, *110*
   reconstruction  *111*
   wood technology  97, *98*, 99
   smaller enclosure  72–3
   *see also* box rampart
barrows, Iron Age  151, 162, 163–4
Barwick-in-Elmet (W Yorks), hillfort  111
baskets, preservation experiment  *32*, 33
beads
   amber  136
   glass  136, 176
      analysis  49, 158, 159
      dating  160
      description  158
      discussion  160, 162
      production  157–8
      stratigraphic location  153, 158
      technology  158–60
   shale  136
beam slots  76–7
Bennett, W T, plan by  4, *6*, 72
Bersu, Gerhard  131
The Berth (Shrops), enclosure  172, *173*, 174
Blackbury Camp (Devon), defences  72
Bole Ings (Notts), pollen  61
bone *see* animal bone; antler; human bone
Boney's Island (Suffolk), enclosure  173
Booth, Andrew  20, 33
Borough Fen (Cambs), earthwork  170, *171*, 172, 174
box rampart
   dating  91, 95
   discussion  111, 113, 175
   excavation evidence  83, *84–5*, 89–90, 91
   reconstruction  *111*
   wood technology  99
bracelet, gold
   analysis  49, 161, 162
   description  160, *161*
   discussion  161, 176
   findspot  160
   *see also* bangle, copper alloy
Breiddin (Shrops), quern  148
Burgh (Suffolk), enclosure  *171*, 172
burials *see* cremations; inhumations; mortuary rites
Burton Agnes (E Yorks), pits  182

Carshalton (Surrey), querns  147
Carstairs Countryside Trust  1, 8, 20, 33, 184
Castle Henllys (Pembs), granaries  181
Castleford (W Yorks), Roman fort  169
Castleheads (N Yorks), defences  111
Catfoss (E Yorks), mortuary enclosures  58

229

causeway
    discussion   111, 112, 113, 180
    excavation evidence   74–5, 76
    formation processes   35
Celts   10–11
centralisation   11, 182
charcoal   106, 107, 108
Charlton, G V   4
Chauniat (France), cremation   183
Cheetham, James   17
Clare Camp (Suffolk), enclosure   *171*, 172
Claremont-Ferrand (France), Pâtural   160, 183
Concerto Camp (Worcs), pits   134, 182
Corbett, Dr   4
Countryside Agency   20, 25, 33
Cranborne Chase (Dorset), four-post structure   131
Credenhill (Herefs), granaries   134
cremations
    Bronze Age   44, 46–7, 49, 56–8, 66
    Iron Age
        bone analysis   49
        dating   156
        discussion   162–3, 164–5, 176, 183–4
Crickley Hill (Glos), granaries   134, 181
Croft Ambrey (Herefs), granaries   132, 134
Crook Hills   4
crop processing   126
Cunliffe, Barry   13

Danebury (Hants)
    four-post structures   114, 134, 181, 182
    pits   129, 134, 179, 180, 182
    roads   120
    wood technology   101
Dane's Graves (E Yorks), pottery   179
dating
    glass beads   160
    marsh-fort   177–9
    *see also* dendrochronology; radiocarbon dating
Day, Mr   4
defences
    dating evidence   94–5
        dendrochronology   91–3, 94
        radiocarbon dating   44, 47, 93–4
        stratigraphy   91
    discussion   109–13, 175, 177, 180
    excavation evidence   68, *71*, 72
        causeway   74–5, 76
        eastern entrance   85, *86–90*, 91
        larger enclosure   77–8, *79–85*
        previous excavations   5–6
        smaller enclosure   72, *73*
        western entrance and approach   75, *76–7*
    excavation methodology   37, *39*
    formation processes   35
    geophysical survey   68, *69–70*, 71
    palaeoenvironmental evidence
        geoarchaeology   109, *110*
        insect and plant remains   104–9, 133
        pollen analysis   101–4, 105

    reconstruction   *111, 112*
    wood technology
        box rampart   99
        eastern entrance   99, *100–1, 102–3*
        palisade bank   97, *98*, 99
        western entrance   95, *96–7*
    *see also* structured deposition
DEFRA   33
dendrochronology
    defences   91–3, 94
    interior structures   123
    methodology   48–9
designation   24
Devil's Hill (N Yorks), defences   111
Digital Elevation Model   8, *9, 10*
Dinas Dinlle (Gwynedd), enclosure   *173*, 174
dirk blade, copper alloy   136
ditches
    excavation methodology   37, *39*, 40, *41*
    inner ditch
        discussion   111, 112, 180
        excavation evidence   *82–3*, 85, 90–1, 95
        insect and plant remains   106–7, 107–9
        pollen analysis   101–4, 105
    mortuary enclosure   55, 56
    mortuary rings
        discussion   162, 163
        excavation evidence   151, 152, 153, 154, 155, 156
    outer ditch
        discussion   111
        excavation evidence   78, *79–80*, 85, 86–8, 95
        insect and plant remains   107, 108–9
    smaller enclosure   72–3, 133–4
    structured deposition   15, 113, 133–4, 148–50, 176, 182–3
Dolby, Malcolm   6
Doncaster (S Yorks)
    Archaeological Society   37
    Community Arts   33
    Grammar School   4
    Museum   3, 6, 7, 33, 72
    Naturalists' Society   33
    Scout Association   33
Downholme (N Yorks), hillfort   111
drainage *see* wetland management
druids   10
dug-out vessel   5, 136
Dun Drainage Commissioners   33

East Leicestershire hoard   161
Eastwood, Stuart   6
Edenthorpe (S Yorks)
    field system   169
    pottery   167
Elm Decline   62
enclosure, concept of   179–82; *see also* mortuary enclosure; mortuary rings; smaller enclosure
English Heritage
    National Mapping Programme   168

*Strategy for Wetlands* 23–5
Sutton Common Project, role in   1, 7, 17, 19, 20, 33, 68
English Nature   20, 25, 33
entrances
  dating evidence   91–3, 94–5
  discussion   111, *112*, 113, 175, 180
  excavation evidence
    eastern   85, *86–90*, 91
    western   *16*, *75*, *76*–7
  geophysical survey   68, *69–70*, 71
  wood technology
    eastern   99, *100–1*, *102*–3
    western   95, *96*–7
Essendon (Herts), gold   161
European Union Water Framework Directive   25
excarnation   183
Exeter University   17, 33, 42–3

feasting   164, 182
Fenwick, Helen   17
Ferrybridge (W Yorks)
  field system   169
  four-post structure   134
Field, Naomi   13
field systems   67, 166–8, 169–70
fire, used to clear vegetation   35
Fiskerton (Lincs)
  causeway   13, 76, 176, 179
  gold   161
  pottery   143
  wood technology   97, 99
Flag Fen (Cambs) 24
Fletcher, William   17
flints
  previous fieldwork   4, 5, 7–8, 54
  1999–2003 fieldwork   64, *65*, 66
Foot and Mouth Disease   16, 32
four-post structures *see* granaries

Garton Slack (E Yorks), cemetery   164
Garton Station (E Yorks), cemetery   163
gate, evidence for   77; *see also* entrances
geoarchaeology
  defences   109, *110*
  interior structures   130, *131*, *132*
  methodology   51
  mortuary rings   *157*, 158
geology   40, 51–2, *53*
geophysical surveys   7, 17, 41–2, 68, *69–70*, 71
Glascote (Staffs), torc   161
glass *see* beads
Glastonbury (Som)
  dating   179
  granaries   132
  weaving combs   147
gold *see* bracelet
Goldcliff (Mon), wood   176
Gournay-sur-Aronde (France), ritual site   182
granaries
  discussion   131–2, *133*, 134–5, 175, 177, 180–1

  distribution   *115*, 120
  distribution in northern Europe   *181*
  excavation evidence   114, *115–16*, 117, 120, *121*
  geoarchaeology   130, *131*, *132*
  mortuary rings, association with   164–5
  plant remains   126–9; *see also* structured deposition
  previous excavations   7
  wood technology   123, *124*
Grantham, Brundell and Farran   33
Gravelly Guy (Oxon), pits   182
Greatford (Lincs), enclosures   183
Grim's Ditch (W Yorks) 170
Grimthorpe hillfort (E Yorks)
  burials   164
  defences   111, 175
  function   13
  granaries   181
  interior   134
'guard chambers' 89
Gussage All Saints (Dorset), four-post structures   131

Ham Hill (Som), pits   134, 182
Hampole Beck palaeochannel   1, *3*
  Digital Elevation Model   8, *9*
  landscape context   53, *54*, 112
  pollen analysis   50–1, 54, 58, *59*, 60–1, 62–4
  project design   16, 17
  radiocarbon dating   44, 45, 46, 60, *61*
  sediment accumulation   61–2
  soil redox monitoring   *29*
Harborough Cave (Derbys), weaving comb   147
Harding, Dennis   13
Hatfield Chase (S Yorks) 21
Hatfield Moors (S Yorks) 53, 168, 170
Hecataeus   11
Hengistbury Head (Hants), glass   160
Heritage Lottery Fund   20, 25, 33
Heslerton (N Yorks), mortuary rings   162, 163
Heuneburg (Germany), settlement   182
Hill, S, plan by   4, *6*, 72
hillforts
  and marsh-forts   177, 179–82
  research contexts   10, 11, 12–13, 112
  research objectives   14
Hinxton Rings (Cambs), barrows   163, 164
Holkham (Norfolk), enclosure   *171*, 172, 174
Holme-next-the-Sea (Norfolk), timber   99
Hull University   7, 17, 33, 42
human bone
  Bronze Age   56–7
  marsh-fort
    age   137–9
    associated with animal bone deposits   142
    discussion   139
    findspot   137, *138*
    number of individuals and skeletal elements present   137
    sex   139

methodology  49
mortuary rings  156–7, 162
previous fieldwork  4
Humber Wetlands Project  7–8, 12
hunting, evidence for  66
hurdling  7, 117
Husdon, Mike  33
huts, identified by Whiting  7

Iceni  172
Ingleborough (N Yorks), hillfort  111
ingot, gold *see* bracelet, gold
inhumations
   bone  137–9, 142
   discussion  15, 149–50, 177, 182–3
   excavation evidence  88, 137, *138*
insect remains
   discussion
     defences  104–9
     well  130
   listed  191–3
   methodology  40, *41*, 51
Ipswich (Suffolk), torc  161
Irish Annals  10
Iron Age studies  10–11
iron-working  169
Isidore of Seville  11
Isle of Axholme (Lincs), Iron Age sites  166
Issitt, Frances and Michael  17
Ivinghoe Beacon (Bucks), granaries  134

Kilham (E Yorks), pits  182
Kirkburn (E Yorks), cemetery  163, 164
Kirkby la Thorpe (Lincs), barrows  163–4
Kirkstead (Lincs), enclosure  170
Kynnersley (Shrops), village  172

ladder (raft) 7, 72, 117, 136, 184
Lake Humber  35, 53
land division  169, 170
landscape  66–7
   geology  *53*
   human activity, early  54, *55*, 56–8
   landscape context  53, *54*
   palaeoenvironment  58–64
Lent-Laauwiksstraat (Neths), cemetery  165
Lillie, Malcolm  17
Little Smeaton (N Yorks), enclosure  13
Little Woodbury (Wilts), four-post structures  131, 134
Longley, Stan  33

M1–A1 Link Road excavations  13, 144, 168, 169
Magnesian Limestone Project  169
Maiden Castle (Dorset)
   defences  72
   granaries  134, 182
Manching (Germany), glass-working  160
marsh-fort
   artist's impressions  *14, 178*
   defences *see* defences
   defined  1–3

discussion
   chronology  177–9
   contexts  166; local  166, *167*, 168;
     national  170, *171*, 172, *173*, 174;
     regional  168–70
   enclosed settlement debate  179–82
   function  175–7
   site preservation  184–5
finds  136
   descriptions *see* pottery; querns; weaving comb; yew wood fragments
   discussion  147–50
   structured deposition  136–7
interior structures
   general plan  120
   overview and discussion  114, 131–5
   *see also* granaries; mortuary rings; pits; six-post structures; well
Meare (Som)
   glass beads  157, 160
   granaries  132
   weaving combs  147
Mellor (Ches), pottery  144
metal detector survey  37, 160
metalwork, Bronze Age  54–6, 66
Midsummer Hill (Herefs), granaries  132, 134
Miles, David  25
Mitchell, Neil  17, 33, *40*
Moel y Gaer (Clwyd), granaries  134, 181
Mont Lassois (France), settlement  182
mortuary enclosure, Bronze Age  *55*, 56, 57–8, 66, 175
mortuary rings
   animal bone  157
   dating  156
   defined  1–3
   discussion  161–2, *163*, 164–5, 175, 176, 177, 183–4
   excavation evidence  151, *152–5*, 156
   finds  157–60, *161*, 162
   geoarchaeology  *157*, 158
   human bone  156–7
mortuary rites  15, 162, *163*, 164–5, 176, 182–4
Moss Carr (W Yorks), pottery  144

Narborough Camp (Norfolk), enclosure  *171*, 172
National Monuments Record  3
National Nature Reserves  24
National Trust  25
Natural England  24
net sinker  5, 136
North Doncaster Rural Trust  33
Norton Junior School  32, 33
Norton Parish Council  33

Open Days  24, 34
outreach programme  24, 32–4
Owslebury (Hants), cremation  183

palaeoenvironmental evidence
   defences
     geoarchaeology  109, *110*

insect and plant remains 104–9
  pollen 101–4
 interior structures
  geoarchaeology 130, *131*, *132*
  plant and insect remains 126–30
 landscape context 58–64, 175–6
 mortuary rings *157*, 158
 sampling and analyses methodologies 40–1, 50–2
palisade, Bronze Age 5, 6, 175; *see also* banks, palisade bank
Parker Pearson, Michael 1, 7, 13, 175
pathways 4, 120, 134
pavement 35, 77
peat 44, 45–8, 107, 108
Peat Moors Centre (Som) 24
Pennant, Thomas 173
Pickburn Leys (S Yorks), pottery 144, 167, 169
Pilgrim Trust 33
pine, use of *124*, 125, 134
pits
 discussion 133, 134, 175, 181–2
 excavation evidence 120, *122*
 plant remains 129–30
 sampling 40, 41
 *see also* well
Pitt-Rivers, Augustus 131
planks 5, *96*–7
plant remains
 discussion by context
  defences 104–9, 133–4, 150
  four-post structures 126–9, 132, *133*, 134, 148
  pits 129–30, 133
  postholes 129
  well 130
 listed
  charred 194–200, 201–10
  complete 186–91
 methodology
  analysis 50–1
  sampling 40, *41*
 radiocarbon dating 44, 45
 *see also* structured deposition, granaries
Pliny 10
ploughing 21, 35
pollen analysis
 defences 101–4, 105
 Hampole Beck 58, *59*, 60, 62–4
 methodology 40, 50
postholes/posts
 dendrochronology
  defences 91–3, 94
  interior structures 123
 excavation evidence
  alignments 120, *121*
  box rampart 83, *84*, 85
  causeway 74
  eastern entrance 86, *87*, 88, 89, *90*
  four-post structures 114, *115–16*, 117
  other structures 119–20, *121*
  western entrance 76, *77*

formation processes 35, *36*
 sampling 40, 41
 wood technology
  eastern entrance 99, *100–1*, *102*
  interior structures 123–4
  western entrance 95–6
 *see also* granaries; six-post structures; stakeholes/stakes
Potteric Carr (S Yorks), enclosure 166, 170
pottery
 analysis 49
 characterisation studies 211–14
 deposition 15, 144
 description 142, *143*, 144–5, 150
public access 24, 34
pyre debris, Bronze Age *55*, 56–8, 66; *see also* mortuary rings

Queen's Barrow (E Yorks), gold ring 161
querns
 deposition 15, 148, 150, 176
 description 145–7
 distribution *146*
 excavation evidence 91, 133, 136

radiocarbon dating
 cremation, Bronze Age 57
 defences 93–4, 95
 Hampole Beck palaeochannel 60, *61*
 methodology 44–8
raft *see* ladder
rails, wooden 117, *118–19*, 124
Rainsborough (Northants), granaries 134
raised platforms 117, 132
Ramsar sites 24, 25
rectangular structures 117
Red House Farm (S Yorks), pottery 144
Ribemont-sur-Ancre (France), ritual site 182
Riggs Farm (E Yorks), cremations 164
Riley, Derrick 6, 67, 168
Robinson, Peter 166
Rotherley Group III (Dorset), four-post structures 134
Royal Society for the Protection of Birds 24, 25
Rubbish and Archaeology Project *32–3*, 34
Rudston (E Yorks), cemetery 163
Rushy Moor 20, 33, 54

sacrifice 164, 182–3
sampling 40, *41*
E Sheard Family Trust 33
Sheffield University 7, 42
Shirley Pool
 management 20, 23, 33, 184
 marsh-fort entrance, as barrier to 85
 palaeoenvironment 101
 peat 54, 68
Shirley Wood 7, 54
Sites of Special Scientific Interest 24
six-post structures 117, 120, 134

Skipwith Common (S Yorks)
cemetery   163, 164
defences   111
enclosure   *171*
slot trench   88–9
smaller enclosure
conservation   184
defences   72, *73*, 109–11, 113
geophysical survey   68, *69–70*
plant remains   133
Smith, Robert   17
Snettisham (Norfolk), torcs   161
social structure   11, 176–7, 182
soils
geoarchaeology
defences   109, *110*
interior structures   130, *131*, *132*
methodology   51
mortuary rings   *157*, 158
microbiological assessment   30–1
sampling   40
soil redox monitoring   28, *29*, 30
Someren-Waterdael (Neths), cemetery   165
Soupir (France), pits   182
South Kirby (S Yorks), hillfort   111
South Yorkshire Archaeology Unit/Service   7, 72, 169
Special Protection Areas   24
stake-built structure   120, *121*, 134, 175
stakeholes/stakes
box rampart   83, 99
causeway   4, 74, 75, 76
eastern entrance   *86–7*, 88, *89*, 91, 99
palisade bank   *81–2*, 83, 97, *98*, 99
sampling   40
well   117, 119, 124
western entrance   76
*see also* postholes/posts
Stanway (Essex), pits   182
Stanwick (N Yorks), oppidum   111
Staple How (N Yorks), hillfort   111, 179
Starr Inn   33
Staxton (N Yorks), pottery   179
Stead, Ian   37, 160
Stonea Camp (Cambs), enclosure   *171*, 172, 174
Strabo   11
structured deposition
concept of   15, 136–7, 144
defences   113, 133–4, 148–50, 176, 182–3
granaries   132, *133*, 134, 145–7, 148, 175, 177, 180–1
pits   133, 181–2
*see also* votive deposits, Bronze Age
Surtees, Scott F   4, 21
Sutton Common
early fieldwork
enclosure, mapping and early descriptions   4, *5*
excavations, earliest   4
excavations by Whiting   4–5, *6*
excavations 1980s–early 1990s   6–7, *8*
Humber Wetlands Project   7–8
micro-topographical survey   8, *9*, *10*
fieldwork 1997–2003
archive   3
background   20
methodologies   35; analyses   42–52; excavation   36, *37–8*, *39*; formation processes   35, *36*; geophysical survey   41–2; recording   *38–40*; sampling   40, *41*
project design and organisation   15–16, *17–18*, 19
research contexts and aims   9–15, 20–1
results   33–4, 184–5
location   *2*
Rubbish and Archaeology Project   *32–3*
wetland management *see* wetland management
*see also* landscape; marsh-fort; mortuary enclosure; mortuary rings
Swarkestone Lowes (Derbys), enclosure   111
Swillington Common (N Yorks), enclosure   13, 144
Sydes, Robert   1, 7, 175

Tacitus   172
Tallington (Lincs), four-post structures   134
Tattershall Thorpe (Lincs), enclosure   111, 170, *171*
Thomas, Gavin   17
Thorganby (N Yorks), cremations   164
Thorne Moor (S Yorks)   53
Thorpe Thewles (Cleveland), grain deposits   134
Thwing (E Yorks), enclosure   111
Tollard Royal (Dorset), four-post structures   134
Topham Farm (S Yorks), pottery   144
torcs   161
trackways   169
Turton, Neville   33
turves, burnt   106, 107, 108

Uley (Glos), shrine   164

Value in Wetness Initiative   25
vegetation
early Holocene   62
Neolithic and Bronze Age   62–4
Iron Age   64
Vermuyden, Cornelius   21
vessel fragment, wooden   7
votive deposits, Bronze Age   56, 66

Wainwright, Geoffrey   131
Wall Camp (Shrops), enclosure   172, *173*, 174
walling
discussion   111
excavation evidence   77–8, 83, 85
insect and plant remains associated with   104
stone analysis   51–2, 175

Wandlebury (Cambs), enclosure 172
Wardy Hill (Cambs), enclosure 134, *171*, 172, 174, 182
warfare 180
Warham (Norfolk), enclosure *171*, 172
Watson, Richard 33
weaving comb 15, 91, 136, *147*, 150, 176
wedge, timber 101, *103*
well
 discussion 134, 175
 excavation evidence 117, *118–19*, 120
 plant and insect remains 41, 130
 wood technology 124
Wentbridge (W Yorks), flints 66
West Moor Park (S Yorks), enclosures 169
West Yorkshire Archaeology Service 168, 169
Westhampnett (W Sussex), cremations 57, 163, 183
wetland management
 drainage and rewetting 21, *22–3*
 English Heritage strategy 23–5
 hydrological studies and monitoring 25
  conclusions 31–2
  hydrological monitoring *26–8*
  microbiological assessment 30–1
  soil redox monitoring 28, *29*, 30
  Sutton Common as beacon site 25
Wetwang Slack (E Yorks), cemetery 158, 160, 161
wheel 5, *73*, 117, 136
Whimster, Rowan 183

Whiting, C E 4–6, 72, 77–8, 79, 83, 85, 88
Wiegel, Bev 33
Winchester hoard 161
Wincobank (S Yorks), hillfort 111
Witham Valley (Lincs) 170
wood remains
 analysis 42–4
 dendrochronology 48–9
 hydrological monitoring *28*
 sampling 40
 *see also* ladder; planks; postholes/posts; radiocarbon dating; stakeholes/stakes; vessel fragment; wheel; wood technology
wood technology 176
 box rampart 99
 eastern entrance 99, *100–1*, *102–3*
 interior structures 123, *124*, *125*
 palisade bank 97, *98*, 99
 research objective 15
 western entrance 95, *96–7*
woodland clearance
 Neolithic–Bronze Age 54, 62–4, 66–7, 168
 Iron Age 64, 67, 135, 168, 170
woodland management 15, 176
woodworking *see* wood technology
WREN Environmental 20, 33

Yarnton (Oxon), burials 183
yew wood fragments 15, 147, 149, 176

Zeijen (Neths), granaries 181